PSYCHOLOGY OF LANGUAGE

PSYCHOLOGY OF LANGUAGE

THEORY AND APPLICATIONS

SHELIA KENNISON

 macmillan international HIGHER EDUCATION

 RED GLOBE PRESS

First published 2019 by
RED GLOBE PRESS

Red Globe Press in the UK is an imprint of Springer Nature Limited, registered in England, company number 785998, of 4 Crinan Street, London, N1 9XW.

Red Globe Press® is a registered trademark in the United States, the United Kingdom, Europe and other countries.

ISBN 978–1–137–54526–8 paperback

This book is printed on paper suitable for recycling and made from fully managed and sustained forest sources. Logging, pulping and manufacturing processes are expected to conform to the environmental regulations of the country of origin.

A catalogue record for this book is available from the British Library.

A catalog record for this book is available from the Library of Congress.

CONTENTS

LIST OF FIGURES

LIST OF TABLES

LIST OF LANGUAGE SPOTLIGHT BOXES

LIST OF CLASSIC RESEARCH BOXES

LIST OF RESEARCH DIY BOXES

PREFACE

When people ask what I do, I tell them that I am a psychologist who studies language. The common response is "How do you do that?" This book aims to answer that question. In writing it, I have had the opportunity to revisit some of my favorite topics in language research. The book is intended for a college course in linguistics, psychology or related disciplines. Above all, I have tried to make the prose accessible to all students, regardless of background.

The book contains 14 chapters, each focusing on a different aspect of the psychology of language. The process of selecting the topics for the chapters involved examining numerous syllabi and other similar books. Chapter 1 discusses the reasons that language research can be valuable to society, as well as the history of psycholinguistics, and contemporary controversies in the field. Chapter 2 examines how language (human communication) differs from the communication systems of other animals and the theories about how it might or might not have evolved. Chapters 3, 4, and 5 provide in-depth reviews of speech perception, speech production, and visual word recognition, respectively. The comprehension of sentences is covered in Chapter 6, and the comprehension of discourses in Chapter 7. Chapter 8 surveys the theories of language development and the research that documents how children acquire their first language. Chapter 9 focuses on the social aspects of language, with an emphasis on speech production. Chapter 10 discusses the research with individuals who know two or more languages. Chapter 11 reviews the perceptual and cognitive processes involved in learning to read across languages. Chapter 12 focuses on the neural basis of language. Chapter 13 examines the history of signed languages, their acquisition, production, and comprehension, and Chapter 14 examines language disorders across the lifespan.

Each chapter contains three special features. First, Language Spotlight highlights a language with a particularly interesting characteristic relevant to the topic of the chapter. Second, Classic Research provides an in-depth examination of an early study in psycholinguistics that had a large impact. Lastly, Research DIY describes a research project you can conduct yourself. Each one is designed to connect to the research described in the chapter. Other pedagogical features include lists of key terms and review questions within each chapter, and a comprehensive Glossary at the end of the book. At the end of each chapter, there is a list of recommended books, films, and websites that readers can use to explore each topic further.

There are so many questions yet to be asked in language research. My greatest hope is that this book will find its way into the hands of those who will choose to conduct future research in psycholinguistics. The field of psycholinguistics is relatively small. There is room for it to grow.

ACKNOWLEDGMENTS

This book would not have been possible if not for the help I received from collaborators, former teachers, and family. I thank my Red Globe Press editors, Paul Stevens and Luke Block, Kerry Squires, Amy Brownbridge, Cathy Scott, and Stephanie Farano. I felt in very capable hands at every stage of the process. I am deeply appreciative and thank Maggie Lythgoe for her meticulous copyediting. Her work was important in making sure that the text is as clear and concise as possible. I would like to thank my teachers and colleagues from the Amherst Department of Psychology at the University of Massachusetts who shared with me their fascination with language. Of these individuals, I would like to thank Charles Clifton, Jr., my dissertation advisor, the late Keith Rayner, Lyn Frazier, Sandy Pollatsek, Judith Kroll, James Royer, and Geert de Vries. I also would like to thank current and former students with whom I shared early drafts of chapters: Rachel Messer and J. Michael Bowers. Both are now faculty members at the university level themselves. They gave me valuable feedback and encouragement along the way. Lastly, I sincerely thank my husband Lawrence Liggett for support throughout the long process, multiple drafts, and recurring conversations about whether a particular topic may or may not be of interest to readers. Among our many common interests, we share a love of language, grammar, proper spelling, uncommon words, and unusual names.

1

WHAT IS PSYCHOLINGUISTICS?

Chapter Content

Photo 1.1 Many spiritual practices involve experiencing long periods of silence, which can be difficult to sustain. What is the longest you have gone without talking?

Consider your typical day. How many of your activities involve language? During our waking hours, it is rare for an hour to go by without our hearing or producing some form of language. We listen to conversations, television programs or songs. We send emails and text messages. We read websites and textbooks. When we are reading silently or thinking about a problem, we sometimes experience **inner speech**, which is the voice in our mind that articulates the words on the page or our thoughts. For most of us, we are completely without language for only brief periods in our daily lives. The aim of this book is to introduce you to the academic discipline of **psycholinguistics**, which focuses on the study of human language with an emphasis on how it is acquired, produced, and comprehended. The related field of **linguistics** is the scientific study of language as a formal system of rules just as mathematicians study mathematics as a formal system. Psycholinguistics is considered a subspecialization within **cognitive psychology**, which focuses on understanding human cognition and decision-making. Cognitive psychology and psycholinguistics are included in the broad interdisciplinary field of **cognitive science**, which aims to understand the nature of intelligence, both artificial intelligence and intelligence in humans and other animals (Sobel & Li, 2013). The disciplines that are included under the interdisciplinary umbrella of cognitive science include psychology, linguistics, anthropology, philosophy, computer science, and neuroscience. Because one of the challenges for those creating examples of artificial intelligence is achieving naturalistic communication with humans, research in psycholinguistics will be increasingly important as the field of artificial intelligence expands.

Throughout this book, we will examine how language works and what cutting-edge scientific research is revealing about how we process language. In this chapter, we will begin by asking "why study language?" As you will see, the answer is that understanding how language works can solve real-world problems and improve the daily lives of large numbers of people. In the second section, we will review the historical roots of psycholinguistics and how 20th-century events played a central role in launching psycholinguistics as its own discipline.

By understanding how perspectives on psycholinguistics became of interest in the past and how those perspectives evolved over time, we can understand better contemporary research. In the last section, we will explore five hot topics in psycholinguistic research, which have intrigued scholars in the past and continue to motivate new research projects. As you progress through the textbook, you will find that these themes will be revisited numerous times.

Why Study Language?

Only through a detailed understanding of human language can important real-world problems be solved. In this section, we will consider three areas in which psycholinguistic research has already led to important conclusions and promises to make future major advances: the diagnosis and treatment of language delays and disorders; improving how people communicate with one another; and developing procedures that reduce miscommunication and other human errors in critical communications in workplaces.

Diagnosing and Treating Language Disorders

There are numerous language and speech-related disorders, many of which currently have no cure. Those experiencing a language disorder, including children whose language development is delayed, should seek an assessment by a **speech-language pathologist**, who is trained in assessing speech disorders and providing treatment. Because speech-language pathologists are specialists, patients and their families are typically referred to them by others, such as school personnel when the patient is a child or by a doctor. Speech-language pathologists receive specialized training in graduate programs in the science of disorders and the clinical practice involved in the treatment of disorders. In many countries, speech-language pathologists are licensed professionals who are required to obtain continuing education, which allows them to stay up to date on new developments in the field. The number of career opportunities related to assessing and treating speech and language disorders is expected to grow in the coming decades (Bureau of Labor Statistics, 2015). One reason for the growth is due to the aging of the global population. As the average age of the population increases, more people will be living with language impairments caused by accidents, brain injury resulting from strokes, and other age-related diseases (e.g., Parkinson's disease and Alzheimer's dementia). With future research, there is the promise that effective treatments and/or cures may be discovered. Language disorders are explored in depth in Chapter 14. Chapter 8 discusses how children develop language skills. Some children experience delays in language development and are routinely referred for an assessment by a speech-language pathologist.

Before we move on, Table 1.1 lists some Latin abbreviations you will encounter in this textbook and other academic publications.

Facilitating Communication

Many people experience difficulties communicating due to injuries, diseases, and/or disorders. Increasingly, technology is being developed to make communicating possible for some and easier for others. Such technologies are referred to as

Table 1.1 Frequently Used Latin Abbreviations and Their Meanings

Abbreviation	Unabbreviated Latin	Meaning	Example
AD	*Anno Domini*	in the year of our Lord	
BC	before Christ	before Christ	
c.	*circa*	around	
cf.	*confer*	for comparison	
e.g.	*exempli gratia*	for example	I love candy (e.g.,
et al.	*et alii*	and others	
etc.	etcetera	and so on	
i.e.	*id est*	that is or in other words	
ibid.	*ibidem*	in the same place (source)	
vs.	*versus*	against	
viz.	*videlicet*	that is to say	

Source: U.S. Government Printing Office (2008)

Photo 1.2 Professor Stephen Hawking relied on augmentative communication. Have you heard him speak with the help of the computer?

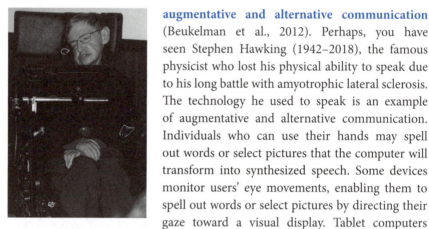

augmentative and alternative communication (Beukelman et al., 2012). Perhaps, you have seen Stephen Hawking (1942–2018), the famous physicist who lost his physical ability to speak due to his long battle with amyotrophic lateral sclerosis. The technology he used to speak is an example of augmentative and alternative communication. Individuals who can use their hands may spell out words or select pictures that the computer will transform into synthesized speech. Some devices monitor users' eye movements, enabling them to spell out words or select pictures by directing their gaze toward a visual display. Tablet computers equipped with voice synthesizing software have enabled more people to increase their ability to communicate with other. Some individuals with autism spectrum disorder experience great difficulty in producing speech; consequently, some rarely speak at all. Tablet computers have provided them with the ability to express their thoughts to others more easily than ever before (CBS News, 2014).

Communication is also facilitated by technology that can translate one language into another. When we travel to other countries or host visitors to our country, we may need a translator to facilitate communication. Increasingly, there are software applications on websites and available for cell phones that can translate text or spoken sentences into another language. The translations are most accurate for single words and relatively simple phrases, especially those used most frequently (e.g., *Where is the restroom?*). If you have used such products, you might have concluded that the technology still has a lot of room for improvement, as the translations for full sentences often do not match the translation that would be provided by a native speaker of the language.

Communication is also facilitated through the teaching of foreign languages. Research is needed to find rapid and effective methods to teach foreign languages. Imagine that you received a dream job offer. The job has a great salary and excellent opportunities for future promotions. Your background and skill set fit perfectly with the job description. There's only one problem. The job requires you to be bilingual in a language you have never studied. You'd be willing to learn the language. But how long would that take? Unfortunately, research suggests that the time needed to become fluent in a second language varies widely, depending on the individual, as well as the language being learned and the person's first language. Chapter 10 explores the various methods of teaching second languages and discusses what the research says about which methods produce the most desirable outcomes.

Language in the Workplace

Because language is an ever-present part of our lives, numerous products that people use every day are designed with careful consideration of how they will be used. The particular size of text displayed on the screen is carefully tested. The color of the background screen and the color of the letters of text are also important. The field of **human factors** aims to design optimal products through understanding how people use the products and analyzing any errors or problems they may have when using the products. Consider the amount of planning and testing that has gone into the design of highway signs to ensure that the letters can be easily comprehended at varying rates of speed in time for drivers to use the information and make any needed lane changes. Research in human factors has focused on areas in which human error may lead to the loss of life; for example, the work of pilots and air traffic controllers, not only regarding how information is displayed to them, but also in how they communicate (Wickens, 2002). Optimal communication is needed to avoid errors of the type that lead to accidents, including plane crashes (Estival et al., 2016).

Hospitals are a second type of workplace in which human factors research can lead to improvements in comprehension and communication (Mitchell et al., 2014). Healthcare providers (e.g., doctors and nurses) pass on medical information about patients to one another. Some of the information may be in hardcopy form and other information may be in an electronic format or orally transmitted. Other examples of healthcare communication include that which occurs between healthcare providers and patients. Healthcare providers provide critical information to patients about how they should care for their health by taking medicines, avoiding specific activities, foods, or over the counter medicines. How well do patients understand and remember the information they are told when they are with their doctor or nurse? When healthcare providers ask questions of patients, do patients understand the purpose of the questions and provide complete and accurate answers? Some questions may involve areas that are so personal that patients may be too embarrassed to answer honestly. Research may be able to help healthcare providers to find ways of asking personal questions that lead patients to feeling less embarrassed, which would lead to more informative and more accurate responses.

Communication is also critically important for **first responders** (e.g., firefighters, police officers, and emergency medical personnel), as well as the individuals whose job it is to handle the emergency calls from individuals in distress. Under conditions of high stress and/or high emotion, miscommunication may increase, which may have dire consequences (Pun et al., 2017; Ulmer et al., 2011). Emergency vehicles may be dispatched to incorrect locations (Cloherty, 2017). Callers and dispatchers may fail to convey critical information to one another. Responding personnel may fail to communicate with one another, such as regarding the planned course of action at the scene of the emergency. As communication technology advances, more research will be needed to identify common pitfalls and best practices and develop effective training techniques to reduce miscommunication.

In this section, we reviewed three areas where research on language can solve real-world problems. There are many more. In the coming week, as you go about your weekly routine, see if you can think of ways in which research on language could solve problems you encounter.

 **Time out for Review**

Key Terms

Augmentative and alternative communication
Cognitive psychology
Cognitive science

First responders
Human factors
Inner speech
Linguistics

Psycholinguistics
Speech-language pathologist

Review Questions

1 What is cognitive science? How is it related to the fields of psycholinguistics and linguistics?
2 What are some of the real-world problems that research on language may help solve?

The Historical Roots of Psycholinguistics

As a formal field of study, psycholinguistics is a young discipline. In fact, the term "psycholinguistics" is not yet 100 years old. It was first used in 1936 by Kantor ([1936] 1952) in his book *An Objective Psychology of Grammar*. Later, in 1946, a student of Kantor's used the term in an article in a prominent psychology journal (Pronko, 1946). In 1951, the term was used at Cornell University, at the first conference on the psychology of language (Osgood & Sebeok, 1954). Yet, despite the relatively short history of the term, an interest in language and some understanding about the nature of language can be found throughout the historical record. Table 1.2 lists a few important firsts in human communication. With innovations in communications technology occurring rapidly this century, we can likely look forward to even more changes in how people communicate with one another in daily life. How many of the social networking platforms and search engines listed in Table 1.2 do you use?

In this section, we will review how scholars through the ages approached the study of language. These scholars include those who lived thousands of years ago and those whose work occurred in the 19th and 20th centuries. Some of the earliest insights into language are still relevant today. We start our discussion with contributions from the ancient world and the proliferation of

Table 1.2 Important Firsts in Human Communication

193000 BC	Earliest (estimated) human language
3000 BC	Earliest example of writing
1450	First printing press
1590	First play written by Shakespeare
1829	First patent for a typewriter
1832	First telegraph transmission
1876	First telephone call
1897	First radio transmissions
1913	First television transmissions
1971	First email sent
1975	First personal computer sold
1990	First PowerPoint software
1997	First Google searches
2005	First YouTube video
2006	First Tweet
2010	First Instagram post
2011	First Snapchat post

the printing of documents in the 1400s. We continue our discussion with the work of the scholars from the 19th century who aimed to understand language and human behavior in terms of its structure. The term **structuralism** describes this approach to language and the mind (Benjamin, 2007). We end in the 20th century with discussions of how language was studied by psychologists and events leading up to the cognitive revolution, which set in motion the events leading up to psycholinguistics becoming its own field of study.

Language and the Mind in the Ancient World

The historical record is, by definition, those events for which there is a written record, preserved in a book, piece of paper, or, in some cases, stone walls or tablets. Historians are able to understand the past because so many cultures have long traditions of producing and preserving written documents. The use of writing has been estimated to date back 5,400 years (Powell, 2009). For cultures with a long history of writing, there is a more complete historical record. Even today, there are many cultures with no written form of their spoken language (Simons & Fennig, 2017). The oldest known samples of writing are from Mesopotamia around 3500 BC (Bottéro, 1992). The modern countries that correspond to this region include Iraq, Iran, Syria, and Turkey. Writing appears to have been developed in different regions of the world independently. In China, the oldest known writing dates back to 1200 BC (Boltz, 1986). In Mexico, excavations have yielded samples dating back to 650 BC (Pohl et al., 2002). The invention of writing appears to have grown out of a need to record the exchange of goods (i.e., commercial transactions) (Bottéro, 1992). When the exchanges people were making became larger and impossible to remember accurately, written documentation was the solution to the problem of forgetting.

The English language has a long history as a written language. A recent discovery at the ruins of a church in England revealed the oldest example of

English writing, dated around 600 BC (*The Telegraph*, 2010). Chapter 11 explains how English's long history as a written language may have contributed to its confusing system of spelling. Because of contact with other languages through the centuries, many words in English have been borrowed. Most dictionaries will provide information about the **etymology** (history of the word) in the entry for the word. For example, the word *zombie* has its origins in West Africa. The words *lemon* and *candy* were borrowed from Arabic. The words *moose, opossum*, and *raccoon* were borrowed from Native American languages. In one analysis of English words in the Merriam Webster Dictionary, approximately 75 percent of words originated in other languages (Tilque, 2000).

When scholars examine the historical record, there is clear evidence that people in ancient societies were taking note of the mysteries of language, particularly those related to medical conditions. Some of the oldest written documents recorded information that would be beneficial for doctors to know. One such document is the Edwin Smith Papyrus, an Egyptian document from the 16th century BC containing descriptions relevant to a wide variety of medical conditions and treatments (Minagar et al., 2003). The papyrus describes a person with an injury that could correspond to aphasia, which is any disruption of language due to a brain injury:

> One having a wound in his temple, penetrating to the bone, (and) perforating his temporal bone; while he discharges blood from both his nostrils, he suffers with stiffness in his neck, (and) he is speechless. An ailment not to be treated. (Minagar et al., 2003)

The papyrus provides clear evidence that even so long ago, there was an understanding that brain injury could lead to a problem using language. Today, the term **aphasia** refers to any disruption of language due to an injury to the brain. It is quite likely that as long as there have been people talking to other people, there have been individuals interested in thinking about how people use language and how language works.

The scholars of Ancient Greece are widely recognized as having made major contributions in advancing thinking on a variety of topics, including philosophy and the mind. Language was also a topic that intrigued the Greek philosophers, including Plato, the most famous, who is believed to have lived around 400 BC (Nails, 2006). Although none of Plato's writings have survived, his teachings have survived in the writing of his student Socrates. Plato's theory of language is found in Socrates' *Cratylus* (Partee, 1972). Plato viewed language as not only distinct from knowledge, but also thought. Words were viewed as imprecisely representing reality. Plato's description of abstract symbolism is best illustrated by his allegory of the cave. With the allegory, Plato explains that words are not names for the physical objects that are visible in the world; rather, they are names for our understanding of the object in the world, which is invisible. In the allegory, a group of people have been held captive in a cave since childhood. They have been chained so that they cannot move. Even their necks are chained so that they cannot move their heads from side to side. Behind them a fire burns, creating light in the cave. On the wall in front of them, they can see shadows created by the firelight and the movement of people carrying objects walking in the space behind them, between where they are chained and the fire. Because the captives cannot see anything behind them, they can only conclude that the shadows on the wall are actual things rather than merely the reflection of physical objects. The entire allegory of the cave is quite long with numerous insights about subjects other than language. The introduction of the cave, the captives, the fire and the shadows provides a useful illustration of how words, like the shadows on the cave wall, can be viewed as things, but they are distinct from the physical objects in the world to which they refer. Psycholinguists agree that for this reason, a word is a symbol or something that represents an entity and refers to it, but is distinct from the entity.

The use of the written word to refer to objects in the real world and states of mind saw a huge increase following the invention of the printing press in the 1400s. The first printing press was invented by German blacksmith Johannes Gutenberg around 1440, and for the first time ever, copies of one-of-a-kind ancient documents could be produced. The printing press had a profound effect on human history. The number of historical documents surviving to the modern day was vastly increased by the invention of the printing press. Furthermore, for the first time in human history, people outside the wealthy ruling class had access to the written word, and learning to read became a goal for more than just the few (Eisenstein, 2005). Over the next century, classical works that had previously only been available to a few highly educated individuals were available throughout Europe. The classical works were written in a variety of different languages, many of which had ceased to be spoken centuries before (e.g., Ancient Greek, Sumerian, Egyptian, Sanskrit, Aramaic). Accomplished scholars were able to read the ancient works in the language in which the documents were written. Scholars needed to be able to learn to read languages they did not speak and some languages that were no longer spoken by anyone (e.g., Latin, Sanskrit). Two of the most famous 19th-century language scholars were the Brothers Grimm who became well known for documenting folk stories, which have become some of Western culture's favorite children's tales, such as Snow White, Sleeping Beauty, and Cinderella (Zipes, 2002). Through their study of folk stories, they examined the historical changes in the German language and spread their understanding in a German dictionary entitled *Deutsches Wörterbuch*.

Following the invention of the printing press, major advances in understanding of how languages differed from one another occurred. Through the study of the ancient texts, scholars could begin to theorize why some languages had more in common than others. Scholars could also study documents from a single language over long periods of time, in some cases centuries, and document how the language changed over time. As the number of studies increased, researchers began to theorize about why some languages were more similar than others. They proposed the existence of a **language family**, which is a group of languages that share the same ancestor language from which the languages in the language family evolved over time through migration, separation of populations, and language change. For example, the modern Romance languages (i.e., Italian, French, Spanish, Portuguese, and Romanian) share the same ancestor language Latin. Using the written documents that have survived, linguists have been able to propose the changes that occurred over time to result in each of the Romance languages. Figure 1.1 shows a portion of the Indo-European language family, which includes English, German, and Dutch, but also some languages that may surprise you – Greek, Hindi, and Persian. Indo-European is a large language family (Beekes, 1995). Have you heard of any other language families?

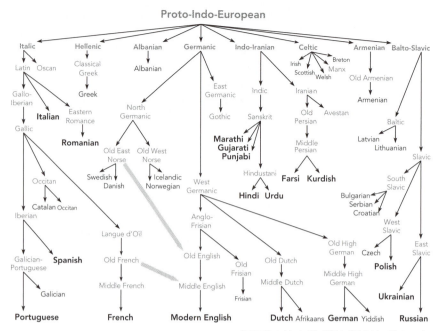

Figure 1.1 Portion of the Indo-European Language Family
Credit: Professor Jack Lynch

Prepared by Jack Lynch. Edited 22 Feb. 2014. Jack.Lynch@rutgers.edu

Structuralist Approaches to Language and the Mind

In the 19th century, scholars from a variety of disciplines began to approach the topics of those disciplines by attempting to identify the relevant structures. In linguistics, a prominent structuralist was Ferdinand de Saussure (1857–1913), a Swiss philosopher. He studied Hittite, an extinct language last spoken around 1100 BC (Bryce, 1999), and the historical changes in the Indo-European language family (Beekes, 1995). Saussure's observations and theories about language were published in 1916 in *Course in General Linguistics*, which was compiled by students Charles Bally and Albert Sechehaye from notes from his lectures. In this book, he compared language to chess. Language has words whose order in sentences is determined by a set of grammatical rules (Saussure, [1916] 1977). The words are similar to the pieces on a chess board. The grammatical rules of language are similar to the rules of chess, which constrain how each chess piece can be moved. The term **grammar** refers to the entire set of rules that describe how a language can be used. De Saussure pointed out that all human languages, regardless of how developed the society in which the language was spoken, are complex and rule-governed. His claim that there was no such thing as a *primitive language* contrasted sharply with the prevailing prejudices of the time, which targeted populations around the globe as being savages and subhuman.

In psychology, structuralism was the focus of the first experimental laboratory for the study of the human mind. Wilhelm Wundt (1832–1920) established the first psychology laboratory in 1879 in Leipzig, Germany. Wundt was a German researcher who studied medicine in college and later physiology, studying with Hermann von Helmholtz (1821–1894), an expert in physiology and physics. Under Helmholtz's guidance, Wundt studied sensation and perception. Wundt aimed to identify the structures of the mind, which he identified as images, feelings, and thoughts. The primary methodology Wundt and his students used to study sensation and perception was **introspection**.

Participants in the experiments were trained to report verbally their experience of a particular sensation or perception. Wundt envisioned the process of introspection as including two parts: internal perception, which would likely correspond to registering the experience with the senses; and self-observation, which would likely correspond to the process of consciously trying to reflect on the internal perception (Danziger, 1980).

In his writings, Wundt ([1897] 1999) demonstrated an interest in language. He discussed multiple aspects of language, including the fact that language varies across cultures and that language is the primary means by which we can label our sensory and perceptual experiences. He noted the *poverty of language*, because, at times, there are not words to describe one's subjective feelings (Wundt, [1897] 1999, p. 7). He believed that understanding the nature of language could reveal the workings of the human mind (Blumenthal, 1970). He also proposed a theory of language production, in which he expressed his view that the sentence, rather than the word, is the fundamental unit of speech production:

> *The sentence ... is not an image running with precision through consciousness where each single word or single sound appears only momentarily while the preceding and following elements are lost from consciousness. Rather, it stands as a whole at the cognitive level while it is being spoken. (Wundt, 1912, cited in Blumenthal, 1970, p. 21)*

Wundt trained dozens of the future leaders of psychology, many of whom went on to train dozens more future leaders. Many of those students of students also trained more students. This explains why psychology flourished in the early part of the 20th century. Thus, Wundt can be seen as one of the founding figures of modern psychology. His work is a testament to the impact that a single individual can have in the course of history. A small number of researchers trained by Wundt or Wundt's students ended up studying psycholinguistics and training their students to carry on similar work. Even today, many psycholinguists take pride in the fact that they can trace their academic family tree back to Wundt. They do this by identifying their own research advisor's advisor and that advisor's advisor, and so on. A great many academic family trees lead directly back to Wundt.

Behaviorism and Verbal Behavior

In the early part of the 20th century, the study of human behavior, including behavior related to language, moved away from the examination of mental experiences through introspection in favor of the examination of observable actions. In 1913, psychologist John B. Watson (1878–1958) published his article "Psychology as the behaviorist views it," also known as the "behaviorist manifesto," in which he argued that research should focus on observable behavior and its causes (Watson, 1913). Watson's focus on observable behavior contrasted sharply with Wundt and his students' methodology, which relied on subjective reports of sensations and perceptions (Benjamin, 2007). In what is now referred to as **behaviorism**, Watson argued that behaviors could be learned through a process called **classical conditioning**, which was the same process at work in the popular example of Pavlov's studies, in which a dog would salivate to the ringing of a bell alone, after having experienced several mealtimes in which a bowl of food was presented at the same time as the bell. The salivating is the **conditioned response** that dogs *learned* to produce in the presence of the **conditioned stimulus** – the bell. Watson and others showed that learning through classical conditioning is powerful because the conditioned stimulus need not have any relationship with the conditioned response prior to the learning experience.

Watson's approach to language was similar to his approach to any other human behavior. The focus was on the observable and what was internal was of little interest. In describing the emergence of language in the infant, Watson (1931, p. 225) states that "in the beginning [it is] a very simple type of behavior. It is really a manipulative habit." Watson later came to be seen as one of the leading experts on child psychology due, in part, to his book *The Psychological Care of the Infant and the Child* (1928). However, due to the controversy surrounding one of his most famous studies with the infant Little Albert, history is not likely to remember him as the ideal scholar to provide advice on childrearing. Watson and his then graduate student Rosalie Raynor showed that an infant having no fear of a rat could learn to fear a rat through several trials in which a hammer was used to strike a pipe located behind the child's head each time the rat was presented (Watson & Raynor, 1920). The rat starts out just like the bell in Pavlov's studies, becoming the conditioned stimulus, causing a large fear response, including crying. The study is rightly criticized on ethical grounds, as Little Albert experienced psychological distress without experiencing any benefit from the study. Also, there were no recorded efforts to undo the conditioning experienced in the study, which could have ensured that Little Albert left the study as he entered it, showing no fear of rats. The study of Little Albert has led to a great deal of myth and mistakes in the recounting of the study (Harris, 2011). In recent years, attempts have been made to track down the identity of the infant who was so famously called Little Albert (Beck et al., 2009; Powell et al., 2014).

The behaviorist view of language is most closely associated with psychologist B. F. Skinner (1904–90), who published his book *Verbal Behavior* in 1957. He viewed language, as all other human behavior, as explainable through learning principles. Skinner was responsible for identifying and studying a new type of learning that he called **operant conditioning**. He proposed that the frequency of naturally occurring behaviors could be increased or decreased through actions that produced either positive or negative experiences for the organism. Any action that served to increase the frequency of a behavior was called a **reinforcement**. Any action that served to decrease the frequency of a behavior was called a **punishment**. For example, a parent whose toddler throws a tantrum in the toy store may be able to decrease the frequency of tantrums during shopping by scolding the toddler. The same parent may work to increase the frequency of good behavior during shopping by giving the toddler a small reward (i.e., stickers or candy) when the toddler has been well behaved throughout the shopping trip.

In *Verbal Behavior*, Skinner laid out a complex account of how a range of language behaviors come to be reinforced in the course of daily life. In the quote below, Skinner (1957, pp. 29–30) explains how, in his view, parents' interactions with children reinforce verbal behavior:

> *In teaching the young child to talk, the formal specifications upon which the reinforcement is contingent are at first greatly relaxed. Any response which vaguely resembles the standard behavior of the community is reinforced.*

When these begin to appear more frequently, a closer approximation is insisted upon. In this manner, very complex verbal behaviors may be reached.

For a small number of utterances, his account works well. A mom shows her child a banana and carefully pronounces the word, and then waits for the child to say the word. Mom repeats the action, encouraging the child to pronounce the word. Mom's smiling and body language serve as a positive reinforcement each time the child produces sounds similar to the target. Soon, the child is on her way to saying the word when shown the fruit. Even in the workplace, adults may find themselves saying specific words or expressions in the context of specific triggers. You see your classmate or co-worker in the corridor in the morning. You say "Hi" and the person smiles, which is a nice experience for you. You are reinforced, and then you are more likely to say "Hi" again the next time you see the person. In fact, each morning you see the person, you find yourself saying "Hi" almost automatically. It is that ingrained. However, the bulk of human language use on a daily basis cannot be explained as easily as these examples.

Skinner's approach to language focused only on the observable behaviors related to language. In fact, within behaviorism, there were those who rejected the existence of mental processes (Carlson & Buskist, 1997). Skinner was one. In 1990, at a lecture at Harvard University shortly before his death, Skinner was asked by a student who had listened to his hour-long speech, as I did, whether he had changed his opinion about the nonexistence of mental processes. He asserted that he had not, that there was no need to appeal to mental processes to explain any behavior. The student seemed surprised by the answer. The room was silent for a minute, then the host informed us all that the question was the last of the day and we should all thank Professor Skinner, which we did with applause.

The Cognitive Revolution

Historians of science often report 1960 as the beginning of the cognitive revolution, although individuals who were alive during the middle of the 20th century would likely view the transition from behaviorism to the cognitive approach as more gradual (Benjamin, 2007). One of the events that many point to as a contributing factor in the shift away from behaviorism toward cognitive psychology was the 1959 review of Skinner's book that appeared in the journal *Language.* The now-famous book review was written by Noam Chomsky (1928–), a linguistics professor at MIT. In his review, Chomsky (1959) provided a description of language that enabled even those without much knowledge about language to understand that Skinner's approach was insufficient. Chomsky (1959, p. 57) pointed out that knowing a language involves knowing the rules of the language (the grammar) and the knowledge brings with it the ability to make fine-grained judgments about samples of the language: "One who has mastered the language [can] distinguish sentences from non-sentences … understand new sentences (in part), [and] … note certain ambiguities." He also pointed out that any sentence more than 10 words long is likely to be a sentence that has not been produced before and will not be produced in its exact form again. Knowing a language means that one can understand novel forms of the language (e.g., words and sentences).

Chomsky proposed the **nativist view of language,** claiming that people come into the world equipped biologically to learn language. He coined the term **language acquisition device** (LAD) to describe the organ of the mind that enables infants to learn language so rapidly. The LAD was never intended to refer to a single location in the brain. In later writing, Chomsky used the term **universal grammar** to refer to the knowledge of language that is needed for children to be able to learn any human language to which they are exposed within the first few years of life (Chomsky, 1965, 1968, 1986). Chomsky's approach to language is referred to as the **generative approach**, because of the emphasis on the fact that knowing a language involves knowing the rules of the language and with the rules one can generate new forms. Table 1.3 lists the types of rules contained in any language's grammar. When learning a second language in a classroom, individuals must become consciously aware of the rules and how they apply. When learning a first language from birth, the acquisition of the rules occurs unconsciously. These rules will be discussed in later chapters.

Table 1.3 Types of Rules Contained in a Language's Grammar

Type of rule	Relevant domain
Syntactic rules	Word order
Phonological rules	Sound of words and phrases
Morphological rules	Word formation
Semantic rules	Meaning of words and sentences
Pragmatic rules	Social norms involved in language use

As you will find, for each type of rule, there is much to be discovered about how the rule is learned and also how the rule is applied during the various examples of language use. For now, we can get started understanding each of the categories of rules. **Syntactic rules** involve the basic ordering of major elements in sentences, such as the subject (S), verb (V), and object (O). In English, Spanish, French, Italian, and many other languages, the basic word order is SVO, because in the typical sentence, the subject precedes the verb, which precedes the object. Japanese and Hindi are examples of languages with SOV word order, because in the typical sentence, the verb follows the object, which follows the subject. Across languages, all possible word orders are observed (Greenberg, 1966). Table 1.4 gives an example of each of the six possible word orders with a sample language and sample sentence.

Table 1.4 Six Possible Word Orders with Example Language and Sentence

Basic word order	Language	English equivalent
SVO	English	Kids love puppies.
SOV	Japanese	Kids puppies love.
VOS	Tzotzil	Love puppies kids.
VSO	Irish	Love kids puppies.
OSV	Xavante	Puppies kids love.
OVS	Huarijio	Puppies love kids.

Source: Adapted from Tomlin (1986)

Phonological rules are involved in the sounds of the language. The smallest unit of sound in language is a **phoneme**. There are two categories of phonemes: **vowels** (a, e, i, o, and u) and **consonants** (/b/, /k/, /d/, /g/, and /k/). For vowels, the airflow during the production of the sound is not obstructed. For consonants, the airflow may be completely stopped (e.g., /b/, /p/, /d/, /t/, /k/ or /g/) or partially obstructed (e.g., /f/, /v/, /s/, and /z/). Languages vary in the number of phonemes they contain. Across all languages, there are 107 phonemes (International Phonetic Association, 1999). English has only 40 different phonemes (Roach, 2000). Some languages have far fewer phonemes than English. For example, Rotakas, a language spoken on the island of Bougainville near Australia, has 11 phonemes (Robinson, 2006). Phonological rules dictate how the phonemes in a language are arranged to form the words and how sounds should be realized within words and sentences. Because phonological rules for one's first language are learned unconsciously during childhood, you may find it difficult to identify the phonological rules you are using when you speak.

In American English, the flap rule is an example. The pronunciation of the phoneme /t/ depends on what other sounds in the word surround it. When /t/ is surrounded by vowels, as in *water,* the /t/ is produced with a flap of the tongue against the ridge just behind the front upper teeth. The result is more of a /d/ sound rather than a /t/ sound. In contrast, when a consonant occurs before the /t/, then the /t/ is pronounced as a /t/, as in *renter* or *wilted*. The /t/ in *renter* and *wilted* is produced with front teeth closed. When the word *water* is produced, the flap sound is produced when the tongue lightly touches the alveolar ridge, which is a part of the mouth located just behind the upper teeth. In Figure 1.2, the regions of the mouth are labeled.

Figure 1.2 Locations in the Mouth
During speaking, the parts of the mouth and throat work together to produce speech. Can you name the speech sounds in English that are produced with the lips closed?

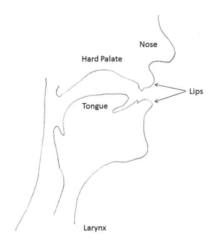

Morphological rules specify how new words can be formed through the combination of **root words** (also called stems), prefixes, and suffixes. The smallest unit of meaning in a language is referred to as a **morpheme**. In English, many words consist of a single morpheme, such as *chair, berry, and camel*. Some words do contain more than one morpheme when prefixes or suffixes are added to other morphemes, such as *antisocial* and *hopeful*. Table 1.5 lists some common prefixes and suffixes in English and some sample words in which they appear. As you will learn in Chapter 8, between the second and fourth years of life, English-speaking children learn how to use many of the most common prefixes and suffixes in the language. The Classic Research box reviews the research demonstrating that young children learn to apply morphological rules by age three.

Semantic rules are those involved in the meaning of words and sentences. One of Chomsky's most famous example sentences is *Green ideas sleep furiously* (Chomsky, 1957). With this example, Chomsky pointed out the separateness of syntax and meaning. The sentence is certainly nonsensical in meaning but well

Table 1.5 Common English Prefixes and Suffixes with Example Words

Prefixes	Example words
Mis-	misunderstand, misinterpret, misstep, misspell
Un-	undo, uncover, unfold, unroll
Re-	reapply, rewrite, repossess, reword, resend
Anti-	antisocial, antihero, antimatter, antivenom
Inter-	interaction, intermediate, interracial, interdental
Suffixes	
-ish	childish, selfish, sheepish, devilish, clownish
-ness	happiness, closeness, kindness, promptness
-ly	slowly, sweetly, angrily, patiently, wildly
-er	lover, writer, fighter, dancer, caller
-ful	tearful, helpful, mindful, cheerful

formed when it comes to syntactic structure. When speakers of the same language interpret the meanings of sentences, they end up with similar interpretations. The consistency in interpretation is amazing considering all the possibilities for individual variation. For example, when confronted with a sentence such as: "Tanya had already eaten lunch," listeners will understand that Tanya had eaten something edible (e.g., salad, burger, etc.), rather than something inedible (e.g., shoe, hat, etc.) (Searchinger et al., 2005). Speakers of the same language can also determine that sentences with different structures have the same meaning. For example, the sentences *The cow kicked the horse* and *The horse was kicked by the cow* mean the same thing, although the arrangement of the words in the sentences differ. The first sentence is an **active sentence**, where, by definition, the subject of the sentence is the agent or doer of the action. The second sentence is

Classic Research | The Wug Test

Imagine that you are shown a picture of a small bird and are told that it is called a *wug*, and then you are shown a picture with two birds with the statement: "Now there are two of them. There are two _____." What would you say? Jean Berko (1958) carried out this task with children around the age of three years and found that they came up with the correct answer – *wugs*. In a second condition, children saw a picture of a person performing an action with an object and then were asked to fill in the blank: *This man is ricking. Yesterday, he _____.* The study elegantly showed that children can produce grammatically well-formed words they had never experienced before. The children were demonstrating the principle of productivity (see Chapter 2). They used the rules of grammar they had already acquired to create new words. By using non-words in the conditions (i.e., wug and rick), Berko (1958) ensured that children could not rely on past experiences when interpreting the words or in producing the plural noun form or past tense verb form. A strict behaviorist account of language development, such as Skinner's (1957), cannot easily explain these results. It is interesting to note that the results were published one year before the publication of Chomsky's review of Skinner's (1957) *Verbal Behavior*.

a **passive sentence**, where, by definition, the subject of the sentence is the patient or the entity that is changed during the action.

Pragmatic rules pertain to the social rules of language. For languages, such as English, some may argue that knowledge about the social rules of language are not part of the grammar at all. However, there are other languages in which social aspects of the language involve syntactical, morphological, and/or phonological variations depending on the social status of a person with whom one is speaking. For example, in Japanese, when speaking with an elder, different forms of verbs and sometimes different vocabulary are used (Matsumoto, 1997). The highest level of polite language in Japanese is called *teineigo*. When speaking using teineigo, the suffix -desu is added to most nouns and -masu to most verbs. Other suffixes are added to objects in sentences. A second example comes from an indigenous language in Australia, Yanyuwa, in which separate dialects are spoken by men and women in the community (Kirton, 1988). In the two dialects, the root words are the same, but men and women produce the root words with different suffixes (Bradley, 1988). All children initially learn the dialect of the mother, but when boys enter puberty, they begin speaking the men's dialect. The rite of passage from boyhood to manhood involves a change in how one speaks to others.

Chomsky's insights about language include the distinction between the knowledge of language, which he called **language competence**, and the use of language, which he called **language performance** (Chomsky, 1986). He argued that errors may occur during the use of language that do not stem from inaccurate information in the knowledge of language. One common type of error is a tip-of-the-tongue (ToT) state. When we speak, we want to produce a word that is well known to us, but we temporarily cannot think of the word. We might even say, "Oh, it's on the tip of my tongue." Later on, the word we were searching for may come to mind. When we experience ToT, our knowledge of the particular word or our language competence is fine. The problem is with our language performance. Chapter 4 explores the types of errors that occur during speaking and what they tell us about how speech is planned.

Over the past 75 years or so, the field of psycholinguistics has grown, attracting researchers with a wide array of interests. Researchers who have chosen the study of language for their educational projects or for their career typically focus on a relatively narrow topic. Some researchers investigate the psychological processes involved in written language comprehension (reading), specifically whether readers can generate expectations about the words or types of phrases that may occur later in a sentence. Other researchers focus on auditory language comprehension (listening). Still others study issues in language production (speaking, writing, signing when using a signed language), language acquisition (child language development or second language acquisition), or language disorders. While researchers in these subfields may use different methodologies, there is an emphasis on measurement: how quickly tasks involving language stimuli can be carried out and the accuracy of judgments. For example, for those who study reading comprehension, experiments typically involve the measurement of reading time and accuracy in comprehension questions. For those who study language production, experiments often involve measuring the time taken to begin speaking following the presentation of a word or signal and the percentage of the time that the participant pronounced the stimulus correctly.

One of the biggest challenges in studying language scientifically is time, specifically because our production and comprehension of language occurs rapidly. Most of the time, it occurs so rapidly that when we try to reflect on how we do it, we have little to report. Have you ever tried to record how much time passes between your feeling that you have something to say and the exact moment when you are saying the words? For the next sentence on this page, take note of how much time seems to pass between your reading the line and your sense that you understand what the line means. The cognitive processes involved in language production and comprehension occur exceedingly fast, so fast that they seem to take no time at all. These difficulties in studying the cognitive processes involved in language are one of the reasons psycholinguistics is so fascinating. The Research DIY box outlines an experiment you can carry out with your friends and family. The topic is the Stroop effect (Stroop, 1935), which provides an excellent illustration of how rapidly occurring mental processes can affect our ability to carry out a relatively simple task (i.e., simply name the color of the letters making up a word). Just as a researcher would prepare to conduct a study, first obtain and construct the necessary materials and practice following the instructions without participants, taking note of how long the task takes. When you are ready to test your first real participant, contact those who may be willing to help you out, and schedule each for a session.

Research DIY

The Stroop Effect

The Stroop effect acquired its name from John Ridley Stroop, an American psychologist who described the effect in an article published in 1935 (Stroop, 1935). Stroop wasn't the first person to discuss the effect though. The German researcher Erich Rudolf Jaensch had published a description of the effect in 1929 (Jaensch, 1929), and the earliest work to describe the effect was James McKeen Cattell's (1886) dissertation. Cattell, an American, studied under Wilhelm Wundt in Leipzig.

Experiment

You will need 40 blank, unlined index cards and markers or pencils in the following colors: blue, red, green, black, and purple. Separate the cards into two groups of 20. Think of the groups as Set 1 and Set 2. For Set 1, create four cards for each of the color words, writing the word on the card using a marker of the same color (i.e., four cards on which the letters B L U E are written in blue). After all the cards are created, put the cards in quasi-random order. An easy way to do this is to put all the cards in a bag, close your eyes, and draw out the cards one by one, placing them in that order on a desk. This ordering of cards can be used for all participants. To preserve the order, secure the stack with a rubber band or clip. For Set 2, create four cards for each of the color words, but this time, write each color word in a color that is different from the color referred to by the color word (i.e., B L U E is written in red, green, black, and purple ink only). Create a random ordering of the cards as you did for Set 1 and secure the order. The instructions for the task are as follows:

> In the following task, you will see a series of cards on which words have been written in different colors. I will show you the cards one at a time. When I turn over each card, name the color in which the word is written as quickly as you can. The word itself is not important for

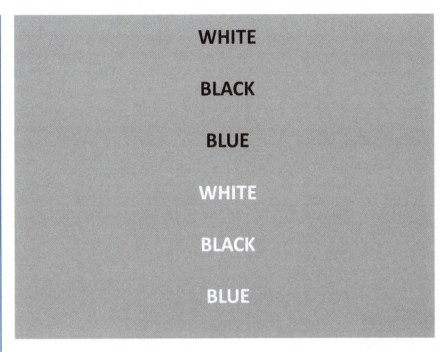

Figure 1.3 The Stroop Effect
The classic Stroop task requires the participant to name the color in which each word is printed. Try naming the colors for the letter sequences opposite. Do two items seem easier to name?

the task, so you can ignore it. There are two sets of cards. After you complete both sets, I will ask you to comment on any differences you noticed in how you performed on the two sets.

During the task, show the participant the cards from Set 1 first followed by the cards from Set 2. After they complete Set 2, ask them: "Were you able to respond faster to the cards from Set 1 or the cards from Set 2?" If they indicate that they noticed a difference in how they responded to the two sets of cards, ask: "Why do you think this difference occurred?"

Participants may speculate that Set 2 seemed easier to respond to because it occurred after Set 1, and they would be correct. Practice effects are commonly observed in all behavioral studies. The more one carries out a task, the faster and more accurate one becomes. If your participants do not mention the possibility of the ordering of the two sets of cards, you can mention it. Then, have the volunteers perform the task again, and this time, have them complete the cards in Set 2 first followed by the cards in Set 1. In my experience, the effect is so strong that it does not disappear with this amount of practice. Your participants will likely report that the cards from Set 2 are harder than the cards from Set 1 (i.e., it takes longer to name the color of the ink and, sometimes, the participant may make errors, naming the word written on the card instead of the color of the ink).

Explanation

The popular explanation for the Stroop effect is that reading the word occurs so rapidly that even when the instructions of the task do not require participants to read the word, they cannot avoid it (MacLeod, 1991). The topic of visual word processing is examined in Chapter 5. Once the word is read, it is in their mind and when the word is different from the word they get ready to name as the color of the ink, there is confusion. This leads to more time being taken to name the color and sometimes to the wrong color being named. For more information about the Stroop effect, reviews of numerous Stroop studies can be found in Jensen & Rohwer (1966) and MacLeod (1991, 1992).

In this section, we reviewed thousands of years of history related to the study of language and the mind. Table 1.6 provides a timeline of the major approaches to language, the relevant historical figures, and the years they lived. Since the 1960s, research in psycholinguistics has been strongly influenced by Noam Chomsky's view that humans are born with innate knowledge of language, which enables children to acquire language quickly with little or no direct instruction by parents. In the rest of this chapter, we will review current hot topics in psycholinguistics, and the reasons researchers conduct research on language.

Table 1.6 Timeline of the Study of Language from the 19th Century to the Present

Approach to language	Contributor	Years
Structuralism (linguistics)	De Saussure	1857–1913
Structuralism (psychology)	Wundt	1832–1920
Behaviorism (classical conditioning)	Watson	1878–1958
Behaviorism (operant conditioning)	Skinner	1904–1990
Generative approach	Chomsky	1928–present

 Time out for Review

Key Terms

Active sentence
Aphasia
Behaviorism
Classical conditioning
Conditioned response
Conditioned stimulus
Consonant
Etymology
Generative approach
Grammar
Introspection

Language acquisition device
Language competence
Language family
Language performance
Morpheme
Morphological rules
Nativist view of language
Operant conditioning
Passive sentence
Phoneme
Phonological rules

Pragmatic rules
Punishment
Reinforcement
Semantic rules
Structuralism
Root words
Syntactic rules
Universal grammar
Vowel

Review Questions

1 What was Plato's theory of language, specifically regarding words and their meaning?
2 Who was Ferdinand de Saussure? What did he mean when he said that language was similar to a game of chess?
3 Describe Wilhelm Wundt's role in the history of psychology and the study of language processing.
4 What was the behaviorist approach to language? In what way did B. F. Skinner attempt to use behaviorism to explain language?
5 What was the cognitive revolution? When did it occur? How did the study of psychology differ before and after the cognitive revolution?
6 Describe Noam Chomsky's view of how language is learned and used in daily life.
7 How do psycholinguists define grammar? Identify five types of rules that would be included in a language's grammar.

Hot Topics in Psycholinguistics

Some of the topics that researchers in psycholinguistics investigated in the 20th century continue to intrigue researchers today and motivate new studies. Some of these topics involve theoretical controversies, for which there are competing points of view, and the research findings that have been obtained so far are inconsistent and/or inconclusive. No single theoretical perspective provides a complete explanation. In subsequent chapters of this book, you will learn about five major areas of controversy. Is language special? How does the brain process language? What role do genes play in language? What roles do nature and nurture play in language and language processing? Does language influence thought? Areas of controversy present opportunities for future research. Will you be someone who conducts the study that settles one of the debates?

Is Language Special?

Noam Chomsky's view that language is innate to humans is a view that distinguishes language ability from other types of human abilities (Chomsky, 1965, 1968, 1986). In Chapter 2, we discuss how language differs from forms of communication by other species and also the attempts to teach a variety of other species language. Chomsky's view that language is part of the human biological endowment suggests that other species would not be able to acquire language, because those species' biology is different. On the other hand, the view of the behaviorists is that humans and animals can learn just about anything that a researcher would aim to train them to do. B. F. Skinner was famous for teaching pigeons to perform a wide variety of human behaviors, such as playing ping pong (Koren, 2013). Some researchers have argued that learning language is no different from learning any other human skill, such as learning algebra or learning to knit (Saffran, 2003; Saffran et al., 1996; Seidenberg & McClelland, 1989). They believe that the general neural mechanisms involved in learning all cognitive skills are also involved in

Photo 1.3 The principles of behaviorism provide the basis for modern animal training. Have you tried teaching a pet to perform a trick using positive reinforcement?
Credit: The Torch

learning language. Neural mechanisms, in their view, are able to capitalize on information about statistical co-occurrences in the language input, which can lead to knowledge structures and emergent processing routines, known as the **statistical learning approach**.

The notion that language is special and may be handled differently by the brain than other types of processing is consistent with Jerry Fodor's view that the brain contains *genetically determined modules* having specific *neural structures*, which he referred to as "modules" (Fodor, 1983). Modules were viewed as *autonomous* (independent) from other modules. The term **modularity** describes this view of the brain. Fodor described the characteristics of modules of the mind. Each module was *domain-specific*, handling information of one type. For example, a module for visual processing would be located in a specific location of the brain, handle only information related to vision, and operate independently from modules handling other types of information (e.g., hearing, sense of touch, taste, smell, etc.). Although tremendous advances have been made in understanding what areas of the brain are involved in a variety of types of processing, there is a long way to go before researchers can track, millisecond by millisecond, how the flow of information occurs within and between regions of the brain. If such fine-grained detailed information can be obtained about how the brain processes information, it may then be possible to determine the extent to which regions of the brain function as modules in the sense Fodor (1983) suggested. In psycholinguistics, those researchers who view the brain as modular envision separate modules, each involved in a specialized type of language function (Frazier, 1990). The issue of modularity figures prominently in models of visual word recognition (Chapters 5 and 11), speech production (Chapter 4), sentence processing (Chapter 6), and discourse processing (Chapter 7).

How Does the Brain Process Language?

Since the mid-1800s, there has been clear evidence that specific locations in the brain play central roles in language. The studies of Pierre Paul Broca (1824–80) and Carl Wernicke (1848–1905) resulted in the identification of two areas of the brain carrying their names to this very day (Kolb & Wishaw, 2009). Broca and Wernicke, working separately, identified individuals with acquired language problems. After keeping careful notes about patients' problems with language and carrying out examinations of patients' brains following their deaths, they were able to link specific language deficits to damage found in a specific area of the brain. Broca identified an area located in the frontal region of the left hemisphere, which was linked to great difficulties in producing speech. Wernicke identified an area located in the left hemisphere in the back or posterior part of the hemisphere roughly behind the ear, which was linked to great difficulties in comprehending speech.

Over the past 130 years, a great deal has been learned about how the brain is involved in language processing. Researchers continue to search for additional locations in the brain that are involved in specific types of language processing. Major steps forward have been gained since the innovation of brain imaging technologies, which enable researchers to obtain information about which brain regions are most active as participants perform tasks involving language as well as other cognitive processing. Functional magnetic resonance imaging (fMRI) is an important brain imaging technology (Benjamin et al., 2017).

Photo 1.4 An EEG experiment may involve as many as 256 electrodes. Would you be willing to participate in an EEG study?

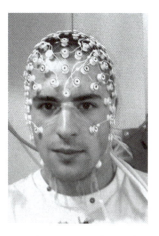

FMRI provides excellent information about the locations of the brain; however, an important limitation is that it does not provide fine-grained resolution regarding how the cognitive processing occurs in real time, millisecond by millisecond. Electroencephalography (EEG), another brain imaging technology, provides excellent information about the time course of processing, but poorer information about the location of processing within the brain. In an EEG study, electrical activity is recorded from electrodes placed on a participant's scalp. The recording of activity is usually linked to the presentation of a stimulus (i.e., a sound or visually presented word or picture). Research has shown that there are bursts of electrical activity produced by the brain during perceptual and cognitive processing, occurring as early as 100 milliseconds following the presentation of the stimulus (Toga & Mazziotta, 2000). In Chapter 12, we will discuss additional methods for investigating which areas of the brain are involved in language processing. Several of these methods are relatively new and enable researchers to investigate brain processing more easily than ever before. Research related to the brain and language will also be discussed in Chapters 13 and 14.

What Roles do Nature and Nurture Play in Language?

The terms "nature" and "nurture" have long been used to refer to the biological and environmental influences on development, respectively. Few, if any, scholars today believe that human behavior can be fully explained through explanations that are purely nature (biological) or purely nurture (environmental influences). Matt Ridley (2003, p. 6) makes this point in his book *Nature via Nurture*:

> It is genes that allow the human mind to learn, to remember, to imitate, to imprint, to absorb culture and to express instincts. Genes are not puppet masters, nor blueprints. Nor are they just the carriers of heredity. They are active during life; they switch each other on and off; they respond to the environment.

The biological and environmental influences involved in language will be discussed in multiple chapters in this book. For example, in Chapter 8, you will learn more about the views of language development. On one hand, there is the behaviorist view of language promoted by Skinner, which emphasized nurture. On the other hand, there is the nativist view that you have learned about in this chapter, popularized by Chomsky, which emphasized the role of nature in language. Similar views about the innateness of language knowledge have been described by Stephen Pinker in his book *The Language Instinct* ([1994] 2007). Both Chomsky and Pinker point out the ease at which children acquire language and do so at relatively similar rates regardless of where they are born in the world and what language(s) they are learning. They also emphasize the fact that children learn language with little or no direct instruction from their caregivers.

Additional support for the view that language is an instinct rather than a skill acquired through conditioning came from the neuropsychologist Eric Lenneberg (1964, 1967), who argued that there is a period in development in which language is learned best – the **critical period hypothesis**. Lenneberg was not the first to suggest that humans had a critical period for language acquisition, as other animals had critical periods for learning species-typical behaviors; Penfield and Roberts ([1959] 2014) first proposed that humans have a critical period for learning language. The observation that there were critical periods in birds' development dates back to the 1870s when **imprinting** was first described (Spalding, 1873). Soon after hatching, a bird tends to follow whatever individual is present, even if that individual belongs to another species. Others have noted that there is a critical period for songbirds to acquire their species' tune (Nottebohm, 1969). If a songbird is not exposed to the song during the critical period, the song will not be fully mastered. In humans, cases of severely neglected children have been cited as examples of children failing to acquire a first language fully due to missing the critical period (Curtiss, 1977). Acquiring a second language is particularly difficult in adulthood, because the critical period for language learning has passed. Have you tried learning a second language? Was your experience of learning a second language evidence for or against the critical period hypothesis?

Among the evidence that supports the existence of a critical period for learning language are cases of children – known as **feral children** – who have experienced severe neglect, which prevented them from receiving regular language input from adults in their environment . A famous case from the 1970s was described in the documentary *Genie: The Secret of the Wild Child.* Genie (not her actual name) had been kept isolated in a room at her home and bound to a portable toilet most of the time. She was rescued when she was 13 years old and was unable to speak. She was examined by a variety of experts (e.g., doctors, psychologists, linguists, social workers). She became the focus of a multi-year study funded by the National Science Foundation, which aimed to determine whether Genie could learn language. Ultimately, the results showed that Genie's spoken language ability was extremely limited; however, she showed an aptitude for learning the signs of American Sign Language (ASL). She learned numerous signs, but was unable to fully master sentence structure (i.e., syntax) (Curtiss, 1977). The sequences of signs she produced did not conform to ASL grammar.

Previous cases of feral children discovered with little or no language ability seem to have fared similarly to Genie. For example, a boy who came to be called Victor was discovered in 1800 in Aveyron, France (Lane, 1975). He was estimated to be between 9 and 12 years when he was captured. He was taken in by a local doctor named Jean Marc Gaspard Itard, who attempted to teach him to communicate and to carry out the basic tasks of living and socializing with others (Lane, 1975). Victor made moderate progress learning household tasks (e.g., setting a table), but made little progress in learning to speak. He died in 1828. The story of Victor and his teacher Itard was dramatized in Truffaut's 1970 film *L'Enfant Sauvage* (*The Wild Child*). In an unusual coincidence, the film was released the same year that Genie was found and became the focus of a research study on language development. The researchers who came together to study Genie's progress were aware of the film and the similarity between Genie's and Victor's stories (Garmon, 2007).

Unfortunately, there are new cases of severely neglected children described in newspaper articles around the world each year. None of the cases, alone, can definitely prove the critical period hypothesis true or false, because individual case studies involve too many uncontrolled variables to enable researchers to conclude that the lack of progress in language acquisition was due to the age at which language input was consistently available. For example, in the case of Genie, researchers debated the possibility that Genie suffered from some form of cognitive impairment from birth, which may have contributed to her language learning difficulty (Garmon, 2007). Researchers interested in testing the critical period hypothesis have looked beyond cases of feral children. In Chapter 10, you will learn about some of this research, which tests the prediction of the critical period hypothesis using information collected from adults who have learned second languages.

What Role do Genes Play in Language?

With each passing week, we learn more about the science of genetics and the mysteries that are coded in DNA, which provides the blueprint for all lifeforms on earth, plant and animal (Kolb & Wishaw, 2009). The genetic material of humans is composed of 23 chromosomes, which involve approximately 25,000 genes. Between 1990 and 2003, the human genome project has aimed to understand what the genes do (Human Genome Project, n.d.).

Language researchers have demonstrated that specific genes play a role in some language disorders. For example, a mutation on chromosome 7 that regulates FoxP2, a protein, has been implicated as the cause of an inherited language disorder in which an individual has difficulty producing speech (Estruch et al., 2016; Fisher, 2006; Marcus & Fisher, 2003; Vargha-Khadem et al., 2005). Genes have also been identified as possible causes of inherited forms of reading disability or dyslexia (Gibson & Gruen, 2008) and stuttering (Kraft & Yairi, 2011).

Does Language Influence Thought?

The Greek historian Herodotus (484–425 BC) is credited as being the first to suggest that people who speak different languages may differ in other ways, such as their personality. He suggested that Greeks and Egyptians differed so much in personality because the languages used by the two groups were written in different directions (Fishman, 1980; Hunt & Agnoli, 1991). At that time, as now, Egyptian was written right to left and Greek was written left to right. Today, while no one believes that personality traits are shaped by the language one speaks, there is still debate regarding how one's language affects memory processing and perception.

Benjamin Whorf (1956) proposed that the language one speaks affects one's thinking. He and his mentor Edward Sapir promoted this view, referred to as the **Sapir-Whorf hypothesis**. Over the years, many versions of the view have been proposed. An extreme version of the view claimed that speakers of languages without specific words to describe certain objects in the world may not perceive those objects. For example, there are languages without a word for the color red. The extreme view of the Sapir-Whorf hypothesis would predict that such individuals may not be able to perceive the color red. This version of the view is called **linguistic determinism**. Other discussions of the extreme view pertained to the Hopi language, which is spoken in Arizona and New Mexico. Whorf (1956) claimed that because Hopi had no formal way to represent time, speakers of the language are likely to perceive time differently than speakers of other languages in which time is formally represented in the tense system of verbs, such as in English. Whorf's experience with the languages he studied was primarily through written documents; consequently, he has been criticized for making bold claims about languages whose speakers he had little direct contact with (Deutscher, 2010; Pinker, [1994] 2007). Researchers continue to investigate the extent to which language affects thinking. The Language Spotlight box takes an in-depth look at the language Pirahã and recent work supporting the notion that speakers' cognitive processing may be influenced by the characteristics of the language they speak. The less extreme view claimed that the language spoken can influence the cognitive processing of the speaker, leading to some concepts being easier to process or remember. This version of the view is called **linguistic relativity** (Rollins, 1980). Scholars who have examined Whorf's writings have suggested that sometimes Whorf himself appeared to embrace this less extreme view.

Language Spotlight

Pirahã

If a language does not have many number words, will speakers of that language have difficulty solving problems involving numbers? One such language exists in a remote corner of the Amazon rainforest and provides us with the answer to this question. Pirahã is a language spoken by the Pirahã people, a hunter-gatherer tribe living along the Maici River in northwestern Brazil. Daniel Everett (2005, 2007), a Christian missionary from the USA, spent over 30 years living with the tribe, learning their language and cultural norms. The language has only 11 phonemes (8 consonants and 3 vowels), which allows it to be qualified as one of three known languages with the fewest number of phonemes (Everett, 2008). The other languages with only 11 phonemes are Hawaiian and Rotokas, a language spoken in Papua New Guinea.

Pirahã has a complex verb marking system with ways of adding morphemes to a verb stem to communicate whether an event was observed by the speaker (Gordon, 2004). In English, verbs take on suffixes to indicate past tense (i.e., -ed) or the present progression (i.e., -ing). In Pirahã, one suffix would be added to a verb to indicate that the event was not observed by the speaker and a different suffix would be added to the verb to indicate that the event had been observed by the speaker. One of the most researched features of the language is the fact that it contains very few words for numbers (Everett, 2005; Gordon, 2004). There is a word for *one*, which is *hoi* pronounced with a falling tone. To say *two*, one would say *hoi* with a rising tone. If one would like to say *many*, one would use the words *baagi* or *aibai*. There are no other words in the language to express quantity (i.e., number or amount). The lack of number words is not

continued

continued

problematic in daily life as there is only limited trading with other groups. The tribe trades nuts, which they harvest from plants they grow (Colapinto, 2007). The culture is one in which individuals do not engage in the accumulation or storage of food (Colapinto, 2007). They go through periods of not eating as a cultural practice (Everett, 2008). When they want to eat, they find food in the forest where they live, such as fish and small game.

Many research studies have examined how speakers of Pirahã can perform memory tasks in which keeping track of quantity is necessary (Frank et al., 2008; Gordon, 2004). In Gordon's (2004) study, participants were shown an arrangement of objects, such as small batteries. After the objects were removed, the experimenter asked the participants to re-create the arrangement of objects. The results showed that participants performed well when there were a small number of objects, but inaccuracy increased as the number of objects increased. Gordon (2004) concluded that speakers of Pirahã used a strategy of estimating quantities rather than tracking the exact number of objects. In a more recent study, Frank et al. (2008) showed that when tasks required participants to remember large numbers of objects, performance was poor; however, when participants were asked to judge whether two arrangements contained the same number of objects while the arrangements remained in view, they performed better. In sum, the memory processing of speakers of Pirahã supports the weak version of the Whorfian hypothesis, referred to as linguistic relativity.

 Time out for Review

Key Terms

Critical period hypothesis	Linguistic determinism	Sapir-Whorf hypothesis
Feral children	Linguistic relativity	Statistical learning
Imprinting	Modularity	approach

Review Questions

1 What is meant by the view *human language is special*? What is the opposing perspective about language?
2 What is the nature–nurture debate as it pertains to the psychology of language?
3 What is the critical period hypothesis? Provide an example of evidence that supports the existence of a critical period for language acquisition.
4 To what extent has the study of genetics produced findings relevant to psycholinguistics?
5 How do linguistic determinism and linguistic relativity differ?

Summary

Many aspects of daily life can be improved through the scientific studies of psycholinguistics, including the diagnosis and treatment of language disorders, facilitating communication between those with communication problems, and ensuring that critical communications in the workplace achieve desired outcomes. In contemporary research, there are points of particular interest that generate new research. These include: whether language is special, requiring explanations that are distinct from other abilities; how specific brain regions are involved in different types of language processing; the roles of nature and nurture in language acquisition and language processing; the relationship between language acquisition and processing to individual's genetic makeup; and the role of language on thought. The way in which these topics are approached by researchers is influenced by how the field has developed historically. Informal studies of psycholinguistics are likely to date back to the earliest period of human history, but the study of language began formally as a topic of interest to philosophers. In the 19th century, contributions by linguist Ferdinand de Saussure and psychologist Wilhelm Wundt set the stage for 20th-century advances in the field. In the late 1950s, the contrasting views of behaviorist B. F. Skinner and linguist Noam Chomsky gained international attention, highlighting nurture versus nature perspectives that continue to divide the field today. Skinner's extreme *nurture* position claims that all language behavior arises from prior learning experienced, and Chomsky's extreme *nature* position claims that the knowledge that enables rapid language acquisition is innate.

Recommended Books, Films, and Websites

Curtiss, S. (1977). *Genie: A Psycholinguistic Study of a Modern-day "Wild Child."* New York: Academic Press.

Garmon, L. (Producer) (2007). *Secret of the Wild Child* [DVD]. NOVA. Boston: WGBH Educational Foundation. Available from www.pbs.org.

Labov, W., Ash, S. & Boberg, C. (2006). *The Atlas of North American English.* Berlin: Mouton de Gruyter.

Lebrun, D. (Writer/Director/Producer) & Guthrie, R. (Producer) (2008). *Cracking the Maya Code* [Television series]. NOVA. Boston: WGBH Educational Foundation. Available from www.pbs.org.

Levelt, W. (2013). *A History of Psycholinguistics.* Oxford: Oxford University Press.

Pullum, G. K. (1991). *The Great Eskimo Vocabulary Hoax and Other Irreverent Essays on the Study of Language.* Chicago: University of Chicago Press.

Searchinger, G., Male, M. & Wright, M. (Writers) (2005). *Human Language Series* [DVD]. United States: Equinox Films/Ways of Knowing Inc.

Simons, G. F. & Fennig, C. D. (eds) (2017). *Ethnologue: Languages of the World* (18th edn). Dallas, TX: SIL International. Online version: www.ethnologue.com.

2 HOW DOES LANGUAGE DIFFER FROM COMMUNICATION IN OTHER SPECIES?

Chapter Content

Photo 2.1 Honey bees communicate to each other using the waggle dance. Have you heard about the recent decline in the world bee population?
Credit: Bartosz Kosiorek

In this chapter, we examine how the communication system of humans (i.e., language) differs from communication systems in other species and what the comparison suggests about how language might have evolved. In the first section, we examine the attempts to teach language to animals. The second section describes the features of communication systems that distinguish language from communication systems in other species. In the third section, we discuss the states of mind that researchers view as important in human communication and the extent to which these can be found in non-human species. In the last section, we examine various perspectives on the evolution of language.

Can Animals Acquire Language?

As you recall from Chapter 1, among the theoretical approaches to language, there is a disagreement about the extent to which the roles of *nature versus nurture* are responsible for language. Behaviorists, such as B. F. Skinner (1957), view language as learnable in the same way that other behaviors are learnable, through experiences in which behaviors are modified using reinforcements and/or punishments. This view of language predicts that with appropriate learning experiences, language could be acquired by non-human animal species. In contrast, Chomsky's (1986) nativist view of language emphasizes the role of innate knowledge in the acquisition of language by infants. Consequently, the nativist view predicts that language is learnable in humans, but would not be fully learnable by other species.

Beginning in the 20th century, researchers aimed to determine whether non-human animal species could acquire language. The numerous attempts have failed to produce an animal that can hold its own in a conversation with a person. The only true examples of talking animals are in animated films and television shows. However, the long-term efforts of some of these investigations have produced impressive results, suggesting that while the syntactic nature of language is the most difficult to master, the acquisition of vocabulary and the ability to convey meaning to another can be achieved. In this section, we review the studies involving chimpanzees from the 1930s to the 1970s – **Gua**, **Viki**, and **Washoe**, and more recent studies with **Koko**, a gorilla, and **Kanzi**, the **bonobo**. We also discuss studies involving **Chaser**, a domesticated dog, **Alex**, an African gray parrot, and numerous bottlenose dolphins. The Classic Research box explores one of the most famous studies of animal–human communication, the case of Clever Hans.

Classic Research

The Case of Clever Hans

Clever Hans was a horse owned by William von Osten, a German school teacher with an interest in animal training (Pfungst, [1911] 1965). Von Osten claimed to have taught Hans to do a variety of amazing feats, including solving mathematical problems presented to him in spoken or written questions. For example, von Osten would ask Hans, "What is two plus three?" Hans would stomp five times with one hoof. He was able to respond to questions involving addition, subtraction, multiplication, division, and fractions. He answered questions involving the calendar as in *if the 6th of the month is a Monday, what date is Friday*? (Pfungst, [1911] 1965). When the German Board of Education investigated, it was unable to find any evidence of deceit on the part of von Osten (Pfungst, [1911] 1965). Subsequently, the psychologist Oscar Pfungst carried out further testing. He found that Hans could even answer correctly when questions were asked by someone other than von Osten. He observed a curious outcome. Hans' accuracy was high when the answer to the question was known by von Osten (i.e., 89 percent), but low when von Osten did not know the answer (i.e., 6 percent). Ultimately, Pfungst was able to show that Hans was able to pick up on subtle cues in the body language of von Osten, which enabled him to infer the correct answer. For example, von Osten's posture and facial expression subtly changed when Hans initiated the correct response. Hans was able to use those cues to know when to stop. Von Osten was likely not aware that he was providing such cues to Hans. Although von Osten never accepted Pfungst's explanation for Hans' performance, the field of psychology became convinced.

The story of Clever Hans appears in many psychology textbooks as a cautionary tale. Later cases of language learning by non-human animals had to demonstrate the animal's ability to perform tasks with different trainers and without relying on a trainer's nonverbal cues. Further, demonstrations would be subjected to careful scrutiny. As you read on about some of the early studies involving chimpanzees, the methodological rigor may have been lacking. However, studies with gorillas, bonobos, parrots, dolphins, and dogs are being carried out with the highest level of methodological control.

Chimpanzees, Gorillas, and Bonobos

In the 20th century, there were multiple attempts to find out whether chimpanzees could learn language. The first of the chimpanzee projects started in the 1930s (Kellogg & Kellogg, 1933). The chimpanzee's name was Gua. She was a young female. Professor Winthrop Kellogg and his wife Luella lived in Bloomington, Indiana near the University of Indiana where Professor Kellogg worked. They welcomed Gua into their home to raise her along with their infant son Donald. The somewhat weird experiment lasted only nine months. In that time, Gua learned to use a spoon and drink from a cup, and she could also shake hands. The Kelloggs considered the experiment a failure because Gua never learned to speak.

In 1951, a second married couple followed in the Kellogg's footsteps, taking into their home another chimpanzee called Viki (Hayes, 1951; Hayes & Nissen, 1971). Keith Hayes and his wife Catherine tried to teach Viki language while they cared for her in their home as they would a child. When they observed that Viki had particular trouble producing speech, they enlisted the help of a speech therapist. Of course, the speech therapist likely had no experience with chimpanzee patients. It may not be surprising that the introduction of a speech therapist resulted in little improvement. After two years, Viki's vocabulary contained only two words, and the project ended, also a failure.

In the late 1960s, the most famous of all the language-learning chimpanzees started her training. The chimpanzee's name was Washoe (1965–2007). Washoe was female, born in West Africa, and originally taken from the wild for possible use in the US space program. Allen and Beatrix Gardner, then professors at the University of Nevada, Las Vegas, acquired Washoe in the late 1960s. They aimed to teach Washoe language, but realized that chimpanzees may not be well suited to master human speech, as shown in the previous attempts with Gua and Viki. They also noted that the physical characteristics of the chimpanzee's vocal tract were not compatible with making human speech sounds. The Gardners began teaching Washoe American Sign Language (ASL) and the training sessions were modeled on how ASL was taught to children (Gardner & Gardner, 1975). Other aspects of Washoe's daily life were similar to that of a human child. Washoe wore clothes, took meals at the table with the Gardners, and had a trailer in which there was furniture (e.g., a bed, sofa, refrigerator, etc.). In learning ASL signs, Washoe made great progress, mastering around 350 signs. One of Washoe's most impressive accomplishments was the production of a completely novel combination of signs. Washoe saw a swan. She had been taught the sign for swan. However, she produced a combination of two signs that she did know, "water + bird." It has also been reported that Washoe taught her adopted son to use signs (Fouts et al., 1989). Ultimately, there was no evidence that Washoe mastered word order rules when she produced sequences of signs. However, Washoe had an adopted son Louis who she taught to sign (Fouts et al., 1989). Washoe was one of the most famous of the chimpanzees to learn ASL.

Also in the 1960s, David and Ann Premack began teaching chimpanzees a language-like system at the University of Pennsylvania (Premack & Premack, 1983). One of the chimpanzees showed noteworthy performance. Sarah was one of nine chimpanzees that were trained to use plastic objects of various sizes, textures, and shapes. The animals were taught rules about how the objects were to be ordered, to simulate language. This laboratory language was referred to as *Premackese*. Sarah performed simple tasks with success, coming up with novel sequences that involved exchanging a symbol from a previous trial with a new symbol (e.g., *Lisa show banana Sarah* from *Lisa show apple Sarah*). Ultimately, the research produced no evidence that Sarah's manipulations of the symbols involved systematic ordering that would approximate syntactic relations in language.

About a decade later, Professor Herbert Terrace began his project to teach ASL to Nim Chimpsky (Terrace et al., 1979). You may have heard about or seen the 2008 documentary film about the case of Nim Chimpsky called *Project Nim* (Hess, 2008). It describes the work of Professor Herbert Terrace whose personal mission was to prove Noam Chomsky wrong about human language being learnable only by humans. As a professor at Columbia University, he gained some publicity for his project in which he and his students aimed to teach a chimpanzee he named Nim Chimpsky to use a human language. The name he picked for the chimpanzee was an obvious reference to Chomsky. Terrace believed that he could improve on the prior attempts to teach chimpanzees language. Ultimately, Nim's mastery of ASL was relatively modest. Only about 125 signs were acquired. Terrace concluded that Nim never achieved the ability to produce signs in a way that followed word order rules of ASL. As an illustration of Nim's lack of appreciation for word order, Terrace (1979) pointed out that Nim once produced the following sequence of signs: "Give orange me give eat orange me eat orange give me eat orange give me you." It is pretty obvious what Nim was trying to communicate; however, the sequence is a random ordering of signs, rather than a sentence with a grammatical order.

Chimpanzees and humans belong to the family *Hominidae*, which includes all the great apes. Figure 2.1 displays the family *Hominidae*. The family includes gorillas, orangutans, gibbons, and bonobos, our closest genetic relative (Bradbury & Vehrencamp, 2011). Recent genetic analyses indicate that humans share

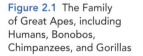

Figure 2.1 The Family of Great Apes, including Humans, Bonobos, Chimpanzees, and Gorillas

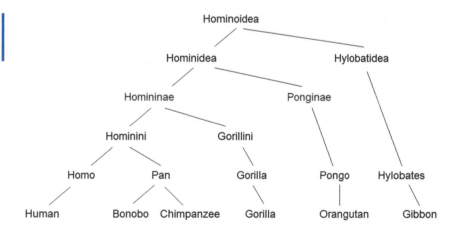

98.7 percent of their DNA with chimpanzees and bonobos (Prufer et al., 2012) and 98.4 percent with gorillas (Marks, 2002). Despite the genetic similarity between humans and the other great apes, the estimates for when the last common ancestor lived are 25 million years. Our discussion of the remaining attempts to teach non-human primates language includes the case of Koko, a western lowlands gorilla, and Kanzi, one incredibly impressive bonobo.

Koko (1971–2018) was taught to understand spoken English and ASL for more than 30 years (www.koko.org). Over the years, you may have seen news reports about Koko and Francine "Penny" Patterson, her primary trainer. During her life, Koko became a celebrity. She gained a lot of attention when it became known that she had a pet kitten of her own. In terms of her language development, she learned to understand around 2,000 spoken English words and was able to produce about 1,000 ASL signs. There are one or two occurrences where Koko is believed to sign a completely novel sign combination, which would demonstrate that Koko is using her ASL productively. For example, on one occasion when she was unhappy with one of the workers interacting with her, she signed "dirty toilet devil" (Gorney, 1985). Koko had never experienced this sequence of signs before as a listener, but it seems reasonable to assume that she was getting her displeasure across with the new combination.

Let's end our discussion with the most impressive example from the family of great apes. Kanzi is a bonobo that has been learning to use a communication system based on human language since the early 1980s (Greenfield & Savage-Rumbaugh, 1991; Savage-Rumbaugh & Lewin, 1994; Savage-Rumbaugh et al., 1998). Kanzi was born in 1980 and is housed at the Great Ape Trust in Des Moines, Iowa. In 2006, it was reported that Kanzi demonstrated comprehension of 3,000 spoken English words (Raffaele, 2006). When an interviewer tests Kanzi's comprehension, the interviewer says a word out loud and Kanzi points to the appropriate picture on a board called a lexigram that is positioned between the interviewer and Kanzi. Soon after being born at a facility at Emory University, Kanzi was snatched from his birth mother by a dominant female. It was Matata, the dominant female that was originally enrolled in the communication study. Kanzi tagged along for the lessons. Although Kanzi spent the time off to the side appearing not to engage in the activities of Matata, eventually it became clear that Kanzi's understanding of spoken language was good, with individual words as well as simple sentences, such as *put the bowl in the backpack* or *carry balloon to bedroom* (Greenfield & Savage-Rumbaugh, 1991; Savage-Rumbaugh et al., 1990).

In summary, there have been numerous studies involving non-human primates being taught either spoken English or ASL. Teaching non-human primates to speak has been a complete failure; however, teaching them to use ASL has been a success. Learning individual signs appears to be something that non-human primates can do quite well. The number of signs that are acquired does not come anywhere close to the number of words that people know. Acquiring the intricacies of word order appears to be much more challenging.

Alex, the African Gray Parrot

In popular culture, talking parrots are quite familiar. Parrots demonstrate a remarkable ability to imitate the sounds they hear. African gray parrots can live between 50 and 70 years (Wright, 2012). Language research with African gray parrots has led to one particular member of the species becoming quite the celebrity. His name was Alex (1976–2007). Dr. Irene Pepperberg (1981, 1983, 1987, 1998, 2009), his trainer, conducted studies with him for over three decades. To train him, she used the model/rival technique, which involved two trainers. Alex would be allowed to observe the trainers interacting and performing a task. In the observed interaction, Alex would see one trainer ask the other to do something (e.g., pick up the red block). The second trainer would do the task correctly, and then the first trainer would give the second trainer a reward, such as a treat or lots of positive attention. Alex would also observe the second trainer performing the task incorrectly, and the first trainer giving no reward. Then, it was Alex's turn to perform tasks. After years of experimenting with different combinations of objects and object characteristics (e.g., color, size, etc.), it became clear that Alex was able to comprehend the spoken commands (e.g., show me the yellow circle). Alex and Irene were frequently interviewed and asked to demonstrate Alex's remarkable ability to understand spoken English. Before he died in 2007, Alex's vocabulary was assessed at 150 words and he could identify at least 50 objects (*Economist*, 2007). He was also able to distinguish the number of objects shown to him up to six. For example, he might be shown a set of four blocks and asked "How many blocks, Alex?" He would accurately respond, "four." Pepperberg has continued her research since Alex's death and has been training other African gray parrots, Griffin and Arthur.

The vocalizations of birds are often described as "whistles." Whistling is also something that humans produce to signal others with a brief, loud alert or to produce a melody of a favorite song. You may be surprised to learn that whistles can also be found in human languages. Some languages, such as Shona in the Bantu language family, have individual whistled phonemes (Fivaz, 1970; Myers, 1987). There are also entire communication systems used by people that are produced entirely through whistling. In the Language Spotlight box, we examine an example of a whistled language used in the Canary Islands, a chain of islands northwest of Africa.

Silbo Gomero: A Whistled Language

Photo 2.2 A man whistles across the highlands. How far do you think the sound of whistling would travel?
Credit: Akalvin

Whistling in humans is a behavior reminiscent of the behavior of birds as well as some other animals (e.g., rodents, walruses, dolphins, and whales). Linguists have found that human languages are produced in whistled form in some places in the world, where people have the need to communicate over long distances, such as in forests or over mountain ranges (Busnel & Classe, 1976). In the Canary Islands, one of the most well-researched whistled languages is used

continued

continued

by some of the residents of the small island of La Gomera. The mountainous terrain of La Gomera presented residents with a need to communicate across deep ravines and narrow valleys. The area is believed to have been inhabited since the late 1400s by those who spoke a language called Gaunches, which may have been a Berber language (Hayward, 2000). When the area was settled in the following century by Spain, Spanish became the dominant language. In Silbo Gomero, the whistle sounds reflect a transformation of Spanish, the primary language spoken throughout the region.

Mastery of the whistled language is challenging, as whistles are produced not only with the lips and tongue, but also with the hands. Whistlers must be able to precisely change the shape of the interior of the throat and mouth. Careful analysis of the physical properties of the whistled phonemes has been conducted (Meyer, 2008; Rialland, 2005). Whistled sounds can vary in tone and in manner of production (e.g., continuous and partial or complete stoppage of airflow). In 2009, UNESCO named Silbo Gomero as a Masterpiece of the Oral and Intangible History of Humanity (UNESCO, 2009). The official documents describing the language report that Silbo Gomero contains six whistle sounds, four corresponding to consonants and two corresponding to vowels. Linguistic analyses suggest that the six core whistles can produce ten distinct consonants (Rialland, 2005) and five distinct vowels (Meyer, 2008). Although the number of speakers of Silbo Gomero are declining, the remaining speakers are part of what draws tourists to the region each year (Phillips, 2009). In 2009, a documentary about Silbo Gomero was made with financial support from UNESCO. Historical documentation shows that Silbo Gomero was used by indigenous inhabitants of the region before the 1400s. Silbo Gomero continues to be used in a wide range of social gatherings and festivals in the area, including religious ceremonies. With the reduction in the number of people earning a living through the raising of livestock and agriculture since the 1960s, the numbers of people learning and using it regularly have declined. There are efforts underway to preserve it and prevent it from becoming extinct. In 1999, a law mandated that Silbo Gomero be a required course of study for all primary and secondary school children. In a brain imaging study by Carreiras et al. (2005), the results showed that the language areas in the left hemisphere were activated as Silbo Gomero was used.

Dolphins

The communications of dolphins in their natural habitat has received a great deal of attention (Janik, 2009, 2013, 2014). Dolphins produce a variety of sounds to communicate, including whistles, pulsed calls, and clicks. They also use echolocation. One of the more surprising findings of this research is that dolphins can learn vocalizations that refer to other dolphins, similar to how humans refer to each other with names (King & Janik, 2013). Since the 1980s, Louis Herman (1930–2016) and colleagues (Herman, 1980, 2010, 2012; Herman et al., 1984) have been conducting studies with bottlenose dolphins (specifically *Tursiops truncatus*) at the Kewalo Basin Marine Mammal Laboratory in Honolulu, Hawaii. In 34 years, researchers have trained dolphins using commands delivered in an artificial language having word order rules like human language. The studies have concentrated on the ability of dolphins to understand an artificial language (versus producing meaningful vocalizations). When communicating to the dolphins, trainers will either play sounds from a computer or use gestures involving arm and hand movements. The dolphin then attempts to carry out the action described in the communication. The dolphins have demonstrated an impressive ability to respond accurately, even when commands are sentences they are experiencing for the first time (i.e., novel instances of the artificial language) or are simple sentences requiring the appreciation of word order rules. Demonstrations of dolphins comprehending simple sentences are impressive, with dolphins distinguishing the commands *put human in basket* and *put basket on human* (Herman & Uyeyama, 1999).

Dogs

Research on the ability of domesticated dogs to understand human language as well as other communications dates back to the middle of the 20th century (Eckstein, 1949). Over the past decade, there has been increased interest in the comprehension abilities of dogs (see Bensky et al., 2013 for review). John Pilley, a professor at Wofford College, Spartanburg, South Carolina, has spent years teaching his Border collie Chaser to understand words (Pilley, 2013; Pilley & Reid, 2011). To date, Chaser understands over 1,000 spoken words. He demonstrates his ability to understand the words by selecting the appropriate object from many objects present in the ground. During the training phase, an object was presented to Chaser and Professor Pilley said to Chaser, "This is X. This is X." Recent work demonstrates Chaser's ability to comprehend simple sentences, such as *Ball take frisbee* (Pilley, 2013). Careful testing demonstrated that Chaser was able to comprehend the simple sentences even when novel objects were introduced into sentences.

In summary, non-human animals demonstrate the ability to learn the vocabulary of human languages, either in the form of manual signs, the use of a symbol board or the comprehension of gestures. The ability to follow the grammatical rules of languages has proven to be more challenging to master. Thus far, the comprehension of simple sentences (under rigorous laboratory conditions) has been observed only in Kanzi, the bonobo, bottlenose dolphins, and domesticated dogs. As the research into the minds of non-human animals continues to grow, there is the likelihood that future studies will reveal additional relevant findings. This work is likely to involve species with a long history of interaction with humans, such as elephants (Sukumar, 2003) and horses (Dorey et al., 2014; Leblanc, 2013; Yeon, 2012).

Key Terms

Alex	Clever Hans	Koko
Bonobo	Gua	Viki
Chaser	Kanzi	Washoe

Review Questions

1 Describe the case of Clever Hans. How did the case lead to improvements in the study of animals learning to understand language?
2 Describe the efforts that have been made to teach chimpanzees to talk and use ASL. How successful have those efforts been in terms of learning vocabulary and mastering sentence structure?
3 Describe the project that has been conducted with Koko. What aspects of language has Koko been able/unable to master?
4 Describe the project that has been conducted with Kanzi. What aspects of language has Kanzi been able/unable to master?
5 Describe the research that has been done teaching an African gray parrot to comprehend language.
6 What is Silbo Gomero? When compared to other languages, what makes it stand out?
7 Describe the research teaching bottlenose dolphins to understand a human-like communication system. What have the dolphins been able to learn to do?
8 Describe the research that has investigated the abilities of domesticated dogs to learn to understand spoken words and sentences.

What are the Distinctive Characteristics of Human Language?

The question of how language differs from communication in other species has likely been pondered since there have been people on the earth. In the 1960s, the linguist Charles Hockett Jr. carried out an in-depth examination of communications systems across species and identified the design features that distinguish language from the forms of communication used by a wide range of other species (Hockett, 1960). He argued that 13 of these design features were present in language. These 13 design features are listed in Table 2.1. Our understanding of human language has advanced since Hockett's work. For example, the first design feature in the table seems odd, as there are languages that do not use the vocal-auditory channel. Sign languages, such as American Sign Language (ASL) and British Sign Language (BSL), utilize the manual-visual channel. Nevertheless, Hockett's observations provide a useful way of comparing communications systems. For our discussion, we will focus on five design features: semanticity, which refers to the fact that a specific communication has a unique meaning; displacement, which means that a communicator can refer to events in the past and future, as well as the present; arbitrariness, which refers to the fact that there is no inherent relationship between the form (sound or written) a communication takes and the meaning of the communication; discreteness, which refers to the communication being composed of smaller parts, such as words and phonemes in language; and productivity, which refers to the ability of the communicator to create new forms that listeners have never experienced, yet are able to understand.

Table 2.1 Thirteen Design Features of Human Communication

Design feature	Description
Vocal-auditory channel	Communication involves vocalization and hearing
Broadcast transmission and directional reception	Vocalizations are multidirectional; hearing is unidirectional
Transitoriness (rapid fading)	Vocalizations last a finite amount of time
Interchangeability	The communications one makes, one can also interpret
Total feedback	Communications can be perceived and modified during production
Specialization	The signal is for communication versus another function
Semanticity	Specific sounds have specific meanings
Arbitrariness	The meaning of the communication is not related to the physical form that the communication takes
Discreteness	The communication can be decomposed into smaller units, which can be perceived individually
Displacement	Communications can refer to entities not present, from the past, future or one's imagination
Productivity	Novel communications can be created and understood
Traditional transmission	Language is transmitted from person to person through social interaction
Duality of patterning	Communications are composed of units, which individually are meaningless (i.e., sounds)
Prevarication	Communications can be false (i.e., deceptive)
Reflexiveness	Language can be used to communicate about language
Learnability	Language can be taught and learned

Source: Adapted from Hockett (1960)

Semanticity

The design feature **semanticity** is observed in many communication systems. The one-to-one correspondence between a vocalization and a meaning has been well documented in the calls of vervet monkeys, a species that lives in Africa. They have 36 different calls, each associated with a unique meaning (Estes, 1992; Seyfarth & Cheney, 1992). Some of the calls are social in nature, only used with others during social interaction (Tomasello & Call, 1997; Seyfarth & Cheney, 1992). Some of the calls are **alarm calls,** which signal the presence of a specific predator (e.g., leopard or snake). Alarm calls are observed in numerous species (Bradbury & Vehrencamp, 2011;

Gill & Bierema, 2013). Animals signal the presence of a threat, such as a predator, with a specific vocalization. Many animals have distinct vocalizations for different types of predators. For example, in non-human primates, there may be a distinct vocalization to signal the presence of a leopard and a different one to signal the presence of a snake (Seyfarth et al., 1980a, 1980b). Across a wide variety of species, there are predators from the ground (i.e., terrestrial), such as leopards and snakes, and predators from the sky (i.e., aerial), such as hawks and bees. The acoustic characteristics of calls signaling aerial predators appear to differ from the acoustic characteristics of calls signaling terrestrial predators (Bradbury & Vehrencamp, 2011). Elephants have an alarm call specifically for bees. When elephants move or fell trees containing bee nests, they may produce the low rumble alarm call signaling the presence of bees.

Human language involves semanticity in a much larger scale than in other species. When we try to figure out the number of words the average person knows, the number is so large that it is not feasible to count them one by one. A commonly cited estimate is that the typical 18-year-old in the USA going to college may know as many as 100,000 word families (Nation & Waring, 1997). A word family includes words that share the same root, as in *construct*, *construction*, *constructing*, *constructed*, etc. Individuals may differ a great deal in the numbers of words that they know.

The complexity in human vocabulary far exceeds the complexity observed in the calls of vervet monkeys and other animals. Across languages, there are differences in what words are represented in the vocabulary. Languages vary in the number of color words they have. Some languages have only two, one to refer to dark things and one to refer to light things (Berlin & Kay, 1969). Russian has two words to refer to the color blue, one to refer to the color that English speakers would call sky blue and another one to refer to dark blue. Because humans have the capacity to learn and remember so many vocabulary items, it is not surprising that different languages would develop differences. For example, English does not have a word that means *to travel to the countryside to clear the mind,* as Dutch has in the word *uitwaaien*. German lacks a translation equivalent for the English word *to wonder,* which can be described as meaning to think for a long, but unspecified time about some specific topic. It remains to be determined whether there is an upper limit on the number of vocabulary items that a language can have and that the average speaker knows.

Arbitrariness

Hockett's (1960) design feature **arbitrariness** describes the fact that the relationship between the meaning of a word and the form (sound or written) typically has no inherent relationship. A key example of this principle is that different human languages use different words to refer to the same objects. Those who speak English referred to beds as *beds*. Speakers of French refer to them as *lits*. Speakers of Spanish refer to them as *camas*. Speakers of German refer to them as *Betten*.

There are notable exceptions to the typical arbitrariness observed in language. For example, in manually signed languages, such as American Sign Language, some signs take the shape of the objects to which they refer (e.g., the sign for tree has some resemblance to a tree) (Valli & Lucas, 2000). In spoken language, exceptions to arbitrariness can also be found in the small number of words that sound like the thing to which they refer (e.g., *zip, buzz,* and *pow*). Such words are examples of **onomatopoeia**. Other words also appear to involve a relationship between the sounds of the word and the meaning in the language. For example, in English, words with meaning related to *nose* often contain the sound /sn/, as in *sneeze, snore, snooze, snout, snicker, sneer, snot,* and so on. Also, words related to shining or being shiny often start with /gl/, as in *glisten, glimmer, glitter, glare, glossy, glint,* and so on. The notion that sounds can be associated with meaning has been called **sound symbolism** (Hinton et al., 1994).

The presence of arbitrariness in the communication of other species is unlikely, although Hockett (1960) suggested that gibbon communication may provide an example. Recent studies by experts in gibbon communication refute the claim (Jolly, 1972). You may be wondering whether the honey bee's **waggle dance** has the design feature arbitrariness. Bee communication does not have the design feature of arbitrariness, since the waggle dance has a direct relationship with the meaning of the message, specifically the distance to the location of the food source in terms of the angle of the sun. The meaning of the message, specifically the location of food relative to the position of the sun, is reflected in the movements made during the waggle dance. If arbitrariness can be found in any communication system of non-human animals, it is likely to be less impressive than the arbitrariness observed in language.

Displacement

Hockett (1960) pointed out that language enables people to describe events that are not in the here and now (i.e., either from the past or events anticipated in the future). Communication systems that have this characteristic are described as having the design feature **displacement**. The event does not have to occur when the communication occurs (i.e., out of sight). When one considers the communications of other animals, the communication typically occurs around the time of the event. For example, your dog barks because the food dish is empty at that time. We would not presume that a dog's barking reflects its concern about the food dish's condition yesterday. A vervet monkey's alarm call signaling the presence of a snake would only be produced when the snake had been detected. It would not signal having seen a snake four hours earlier.

There is one communication system in non-human species that appears to have the design feature displacement. Honey bees communicate to one another about the location of food sources with their waggle dance. Bees leave the hive to find food. When they are successful, they come back to the hive to tell the others. The waggle dance has been shown to contain information about the location of the food (Riley et al., 2005; von Frisch, 1950, 1967, 1974). Hockett (1960) described bee communication as having the design feature of displacement, because the bee communicates the location of a food source once it is back at the hive and the food source is no longer present.

Across languages, one finds a great flexibility in how people can refer to events that are not happening in the here and now (Bybee et al., 1994). In English, one can say *he is singing,* and the listener infers that the event is occurring now. One can say *he sang,* and the listener infers that the event occurred in the past and is not occurring now. For *he will sing,* the listener infers that the event has not yet started, but will begin at some time in the future. Languages also vary in how they express the attitude or mood of the speaker. An utterance may be a statement of fact or hypothetical (i.e., something that might be true, but it is not certain). Some languages, such as Turkish, have different ways to express an event that occurred in the past and was witnessed directly by the speaker, and an event that occurred in the past but was not witnessed by the speaker. As we will discuss later in this chapter, the states of mind of humans and animals differ; thus, it may not be surprising that human communication is enriched with complex ways to express states of mind, but animal communication systems appear not to be.

Discreteness

The design feature **discreteness** refers to the ability for communications to be broken down into smaller units. Utterances can be broken down into words, words can sometimes be broken down into morphemes, and morphemes can be broken down into individual phonemes. All words are composed from the same set of basic units, arranged in different ways. Research on the acoustic characteristics of alarm calls in meerkats suggests that alarm calls contain two types of information: the type of predator and **urgency**, which reflects the level of fear from the animal producing the call (Manser, 2001; Manser et al., 2001, 2002). Three levels of urgency have been identified in the alarm calls of meerkats: low, medium, and high.

In animal communication systems, an amazing example of discreteness has recently been discovered in the communications of prairie dogs (Slobodchikoff et al., 2009b). Recent work by Slobodchikoff and colleagues not only provides evidence for a surprising fact about prairie dog communication, but also illustrates the challenges of carrying out such work (Slobodchikoff, 2002; Slobodchikoff et al., 2009a, 2009b). Prairie dogs live in colonies in relatively large areas of land in southwestern USA. The research team carried out studies on prairie dogs in their colonies and in a controlled laboratory environment. The starting point of their research was to understand the communications of prairie dogs, which included alarm calls. Gunnison's prairie dogs, the specific species that Slobodchikoff and his team studies, have distinct calls for different predators: coyotes, dogs, red-tailed hawks, and humans. When an alarm call is produced in a colony, the response depends on the alarm call. When the predator is a hawk, prairie dogs that are directly below the hawk and in the direction of its flight path dive into their burrows. Other prairie dogs stand and watch the hawk. When the predator is a human, all prairie dogs hearing the alarm call dive into their burrows and stay out of sight. When the predator is a coyote, all above ground prairie dogs run to their burrows and remain at the entrance, and below ground prairie dogs emerge from below ground, but remain watchful at their burrows' entrances. For calls signaling a dog, the prairie dogs stand watchful and only run to take cover in their burrows if the dog comes too close.

In order to determine that different alarm calls led prairie dogs to adopt the specific escape behavior, Kiriazis and Slobodchikoff (2006) carried out an experiment in a prairie dog colony in which they recorded different alarm calls and later played one of them when no predator was present. After playing the alarm call, the effect of the alarm call on the behavior of the prairie dogs in the colony was

Photo 2.3 Prairie dogs living in a colony. Have you ever heard the calls produced by a prairie dog?
Credit: Mathae

videotaped. They also played nonsense sounds and recorded the colony's behavior. The researchers then analyzed the behavior they had captured. They found that the escape behavior exhibited depended on the alarm call, and concluded that the alarm call contained information about the type of predator. Subsequent studies have shown that prairie dogs have alarm calls for other predators, such as badgers, grey foxes, and cats, and for animals that are not predators, such as antelope, elk, and cows (Slobodchikoff et al., 2009b).

In some of the studies, researchers have created artificial predator and non-predator animal silhouettes that can be moved into the colony through the use of ropes and pulleys. When they bring one of the artificial intruders into the colony, they record the calls that individual prairie dogs produce. These studies have demonstrated the one-to-one correspondence between the prairie dog call and the type of intruder. In a series of studies in which a human intruder walked through a colony and the clothing of the intruder was manipulated and the alarm calls of the prairie dogs were recorded, prairie dogs' calls appeared to vary as a function of the color of the intruder's T-shirt (Slobodchikoff et al., 1991). Slobodchikoff et al. (2009a, 2009b) suggest that prairie dog communication has the design feature of discreteness, because prairie dogs' alarm calls appear to be composed of parts that communicate information about the species of the predator, the size of the predator, as well as the color of the predator.

Productivity

The design feature **productivity** refers to the fact that new messages can be created. In language, the new messages may be new words that are the result of using morphological rules to form new words. For example, a person tells you about an object, called a *klug*, they picked up during their travels. The person could point out that she has a *klug*, but you are *klug*less. You have never heard that word before, but using your knowledge of morphology and your knowledge of the new word *klug*, you can understand what was meant. More importantly, all speakers of English would interpret *klugless* similarly. Productivity is particularly relevant to the fact that most sentences that people produce and comprehend have never been experienced before. As you recall from Chapter 1, Noam Chomsky pointed to the productivity of language as a reason why behaviorism could not provide an adequate explanation of how language is learned. Sentences over 10 words are highly likely to be unique, not having been experienced by a listener before and unlikely to be produced exactly in that order again (Searchinger et al., 2005). The vast majority of human language communication involves producing and comprehending completely novel utterances. Productivity is observed in at least one other species. The honey bee's waggle dance is described as having productivity, because it can communicate all possible locations, which would result in an infinite number of dance configurations (Hockett, 1960).

An important aspect of the productivity in language is the existence of **syntactic recursion** (Hauser et al., 2002; Fitch et al., 2005). The grammatical rules for constructing a sentence allow for infinitely long sequences. Examples of the long sentences permitted by recursion are found in the classic children's rhyme "The House that Jack Built" (Halliwell, 1846):

This is the house that Jack built.

This is the malt
That lay in the house that Jack built.

This is the rat,
That ate the malt
That lay in the house that Jack built.

This is the cat,
That kill'd the rat,
That ate the malt
That lay in the house that Jack built.

This is the dog,
That worried the cat,
That kill'd the rat,
That ate the malt
That lay in the house that Jack built.

The rhyme continues on for six more stanzas and could go on forever. In everyday language use, we do not observe infinitely long sentences because there are limits to memory, which make complex sentences hard to comprehend. The power of recursion in language is not only demonstrated in our ability to produce long sentences, but also in the ability of any speaker of our language to understand the sentences that we produce. Chapter 6 examines the experimental evidence that demonstrates the role of memory in comprehension failures for complex sentence structures.

In this section, we reviewed five important design features of language: semanticity, displacement, arbitrariness, discreteness, and productivity. For each, we learned about individual cases where communication systems of non-human species share the design feature with human language. However, there are no communication systems of non-human animals that have all design features. In the next section, we examine how the states of mind differ in humans and animals, as these differences may provide insight into how human communication differs from communication in other species.

 Time out for Review

Key Terms

Alarm call	Onomatopoeia	Syntactic recursion
Arbitrariness	Productivity	Urgency
Discreteness	Semanticity	Waggle dance
Displacement	Sound symbolism	

Review Questions

1 What is meant by the design feature discreteness? Why is language viewed as having this feature, but the communication systems of non-human primates in the wild do not? Discuss the research on prairie dog communication and explain why it provides evidence for discreteness.
2 In your own words, explain what is meant by the principal of arbitrariness in communication. To what extent do non-human animal forms of communication and language demonstrate exceptions to the principle of arbitrariness?
3 What is semanticity? Describe how the alarm calls of many animal species involve this design feature.
4 Explain the design feature displacement. To what extent do communication systems of non-human animals include displacement?
5 What is meant by the principle of productivity? How is human language productive? To what extent are non-human animal forms of communication productive?

How do Human and Non-human Minds Differ?

Our understanding of the differences between language and the communication systems of non-human species can be deepened by understanding how human minds differ from the minds of other animals. The notion that non-human animals have states of mind is a relatively new one and may still be controversial. In this section, we examine recent research suggesting that some, but not all, non-human animals have states of mind that are believed to be involved in human interaction and communication. First, we discuss theory of mind, which is the appreciation that other individuals can possess different knowledge. Second, we investigate the various types of deceptive communications that occur in non-human species. Lastly, we examine the extent to which non-human animals have self-awareness.

Theory of Mind

For humans, being an effective communicator involves having an understanding not only of what one plans to communicate, but also what the intended audience members know about the topic as well as their current states of mind. The term **theory of mind** refers to the basic understanding that others may have different knowledge (Coolin et al., 2017). For most children, theory of mind develops between the third and fourth year of life. Psychologists have used a variety of tasks to determine whether theory of mind is present, such as the **false belief test** (Baron-Cohen et al., 1985; Wimmer & Perner, 1983). In one such test, a child is shown a matchbox and asked "What do you think is in the box?" Usually, the child says "Matches." The box is opened to show that there are not matches inside, but something else, such as M&Ms. On cue, another person enters the room and the child is asked, "What do you think he will think is in the box?" If the child has developed theory of mind, the child will appreciate that the new person will not know there are M&Ms inside the matchbox and is likely to assume that matches are inside the matchbox. In this case, the child will respond "Matches." The child who has not yet developed theory of mind will respond "M&Ms." This type of responding has been described as reflecting a "curse of knowledge" (Camerer et al., 1989), because each person assumes that their own knowledge is the same as that in others' minds.

Recent research has suggested that individuals with autism may be delayed in developing theory of mind or may not develop it at all (Baron-Cohen, 2009). Autism is a developmental disorder characterized by varying degrees of social impairment. In Chapter 14, you will learn more about the language deficits commonly observed in individuals with autism. The inability of individuals with autism to understand the minds of others has been noted as a core aspect of the disorder. Simon Baron-Cohen (1990, 2009) introduced the term **mind blindness** to describe autism. Individuals with autism who do not develop theory of mind are locked into a state in which their view of others' minds is that they only contain the knowledge that their own mind contains. If one has an erroneous assumption that others know what one knows, then why is there a need to communicate?

The presence versus absence of theory of mind in non-human primates has been debated since the 1970s (Premack & Woodruff, 1978). Support for the view that non-human primates may possess some appreciation for the minds of others came from Jane Goodall's (1986) observations of chimpanzees interacting with one another sharing food or being aggressive. Laboratory experiments conducted by Tomasello and colleagues (Call & Tomasello, 1999; Schmelz et al., 2011) investigated chimpanzees' and orangutans' ability to perform a nonverbal version of a false belief test, comparing it with the performance of five-year-old children. In Call and Tomasello's (1999) study, there were two researchers and two boxes in view of the test subjects. The first researcher would place food under one of the boxes. Half the time, the second researcher was present, watching the actions of the first researcher. Then, the second researcher would point to the box containing the food, as a way of communicating to the subject where the food was located. In other conditions, subjects were able to observe that the second researcher had not watched the first researcher place the food in one of the boxes. The important question was whether the subjects would rely on the second experimenters' pointing as a function of whether they had seen the second experimenter watch where the food was placed. Chimpanzees and orangutans did not respond differently based on the second researcher's knowledge; however, the children did.

In Schmelz et al.'s (2011) study, there was a table, two opaque boards, some food that appealed to chimpanzees, and two chimpanzees. The boards were positioned such that one was flat and one was slanted, suggesting that there might be food beneath it. Each chimpanzee was permitted to explore the table when alone. When they did, each would examine the slanted board, presumably searching for something that might be good to eat. When pairs of chimpanzees were allowed to explore the table by taking turns, the researchers found that they avoided exploring under the slanted board if the other chimpanzee had searched on the previous turn, suggesting that they might have presumed that the other chimpanzee would have searched the most obvious location and would have removed any food that might have been there.

Deceptive Communication

In discussions of whether non-human species possess theory of mind, an important type of evidence for theory of mind is the use of deceptive communication, which refers to communications whose intent is to cause others to form an inaccurate understanding of a specific circumstance. Humans produce deceptive communications or lie regularly. In a laboratory study conducted by Feldman et al. (2002), each participant was asked to meet a stranger and to talk with that person for 10 minutes. Half the participants were told that they would meet the stranger again three more times. The other half were told that they would not meet the stranger again. The participants were later asked to review the recordings and to label their statements as true or not true. A whopping 78 percent of the statements made to the stranger whom they would not meet again were later coded by the speaker as not truthful (e.g., little lies, exaggerations, big whoppers). Although we may not like to acknowledge it, we all use deception in our daily lives. When we use deception with another person, we rely on our theory of mind to appreciate the other person's state of mind so that we may choose our words carefully to craft the most believable falsehood. That is a pretty complex endeavor. An important question is whether it is possible to find deceptive communication in other species. Finding human-like levels of deception in other species may indicate that those species also have theory of mind.

In non-human communication systems, three of the most commonly discussed types of deceptive communications are: distraction displays; lying, which refers to making a communication that is not accurate in the context; and withholding information, which refers to failing to make a communication in an appropriate context for the purposes of misleading others. **Distraction displays** are most commonly observed when a predator is threatening offspring. Doves and other birds may exhibit what has been called "broken-wing displays" to distract a predator from a nest of offspring (Bradbury & Vehrencamp, 2011). The adult will hold a wing low to the ground as it walks away from the nest. Similar displays to distract predators have been observed in fish. In the 20th century, those trying to understand animal behavior are frequently cautioned by leading scientists not to engage in **anthropomorphism**, which involves attributing human-like thoughts, emotions, and empathy to animals (Eacker, 1975). To some extent, researchers may have neglected studying the minds of animals for fear of being accused of anthropomorphism. Frans de Waal's (1997) essay begins with the following quote: "To endow animals with human emotions has long been a scientific taboo. But if we do not, we risk missing something fundamental, about both animals and us."

Lying has been observed in several animal species. Examples of lying occur commonly in many species of birds. A bird that has found a rich food source may make an alarm call, presumably to keep other birds from the area (Bradbury & Vehrencamp, 2011). False alarm calls occur in an effort to obtain better mating prospects. Male birds and male squirrels have been observed making false alarm calls to disrupt the mating of a male–female pair. When the members of the pair stop their mating following the alarm call, the male that made the false alarm call has an opportunity to mate.

Animals have been observed **withholding information** about food sources. For example, male roosters produce a unique call to signal the presence of food. When there are competing males in the environment and food is found, male roosters never give this food call (Bradbury & Vehrencamp, 2011). In non-human primates, similar food calls exist. When food is discovered by an individual that is alone, typically no food call is given. The individual later returns to the location of the food to have the feast all to itself. Chimpanzees, in particular, have been observed noticing a food source or object, not responding to it, leaving the area, waiting and watching in the distance for others to leave, so that it might go back and retrieve the item for itself. This behavior may seem to be strangely human-like, something children might do when in a competitive scavenger hunt. Research suggests that humans engage in deception regularly (Feldman et al., 2002; Zimbler & Feldman, 2011). The Research DIY box invites you to conduct a survey to investigate how frequently people believe deception is used by others and by themselves.

Research DIY

Human Deception

Research on human deception has grown over the past few decades, particularly among researchers interested in detecting lies that might occur when someone is interviewed by law enforcement personnel (Vrij, 2015). Estimates for the frequency of lying in daily life have come from diary studies in which individuals are asked to keep a record of their own deception over time. Using this technique, DePaulo et al. (1996) estimated that people lie about once or twice daily and in approximately 20 percent of their interactions with others. Higher estimates of lying frequency have been obtained in laboratory studies in which individuals are asked to interact with someone they do not know well. Later, they are asked to view a video of the interaction and judge their statements as truths or lies. Feldman et al. (2002) found that people told more lies when trying to appear more likeable or more competent to their conversational partner. On average, participants told 1.75 lies in the 10-minute interaction. They did observe individual differences in lying, as 60 percent of participants told at least one lie, but 40 percent of participants told no lies. In a correlational study, Fischer & Kennison (2007) found that those who believed that others lied frequently reported lying more often themselves.

For your survey, use the questions below to compare people's estimations about their own lying frequency and that of others. For each statement, instruct your volunteer to indicate frequency on the following scale:

1 = Never

2 = 1 or 2 times per month

3 = 1 or 2 times per week

4 = more than 1 to 2 times per week, but less than once a day

5 = 1 or 2 times a day

6 = a few times more than 1 or 2 times day

7 = many times per day

Questions

For the following questions, select the frequency rating that is most true for you.

_____ 1. How frequently do you lie to close friends?

_____ 2. How frequently do you lie to parents/guardians?

_____ 3. How frequently do you lie to romantic partners?

_____ 4. How frequently do you lie to those you do not know well?

For the following questions, select the frequency rating you believe is true for other people.

_____ 5. How frequently do other people lie to close friends?

_____ 6. How frequently do other people lie to parents/guardians?

_____ 7. How frequently do other people lie to romantic partners?

_____ 8. How frequently do other people lie to those they do not know well?

Recruit at least 10 people for the survey. For each respondent, sum the responses for questions 1–4 and questions 5–8. Higher sums reflect more frequent lying. How similar are the sums for the two sets of questions when you compare the sums for each participant?

Self-awareness

Over the past few decades, the number of studies investigating animal minds has increased. Ultimately, this research will be able to determine whether self-awareness exists in non-human animals. One of the tests that has been used to explore states of mind in animals is the **mirror self-recognition test**, which was introduced by Gallup (1970). In the original studies, Gallup observed the behavior of chimpanzees that were kept alone in a room with a full-length mirror. Over the course of two days, the chimpanzees appeared to recognize that the mirror contained a reflection of themselves, as they used the mirror to help them groom parts of their bodies they previously could not see without the mirror. Gallup later anesthetized the chimpanzees and placed a red mark on their brow. They were returned to the room without the mirror in order to determine whether they showed any awareness of the mark on their brow. After 30 minutes, the mirror was put back in the room with the animals. When observing their reflections in the mirror, chimpanzees touched their brow more often than they had before the mirror was placed in the room.

Since Gallup's (1970) studies, the mirror self-recognition test has been used with a variety of animal species. Those species that demonstrate mirror self-recognition include bonobos (Walraven et al., 1995; Westergaard & Hyatt, 1994),

Photo 2.4 A dog looks in a mirror. Do you think dogs can pass the mirror self-recognition test?

dolphins (Marten & Psarakos, 1995; Reiss & Marino, 2001), whales (Delfour & Marten, 2001), and magpies (Prior et al., 2008). Species that have failed to demonstrate mirror self-recognition include gibbons (Ujhelyi et al., 2000), Asian elephants (Plotnik et al., 2006), pandas (Ma et al., 2015), sea lions (Hill et al., 2015), and pigeons (Uchino & Watanabe, 2014).

In the future, new research promises to deliver new insights into differences between human and animal minds. There are numerous species whose cognition has yet to be studied in depth. One day, it will be possible to determine how self-awareness across species is related to the design features in each species' system of communication. This knowledge will inform discussions about how communication behaviors may have evolved. The topic of how language may have evolved is the last section in this chapter. As you will see, there are many more questions than answers.

 Time out for Review

Key Terms

Anthropomorphism	False belief test	Mirror self-recognition test
Consciousness	Lying	Theory of mind
Distraction displays	Mind blindness	Withholding information

Review Questions

1 What is theory of mind? What evidence is there for the existence of theory of mind in humans and other animal species?
2 What has research with non-human species shown about the typical types of deceptive communication that have been observed?
3 What is the mirror self-recognition test? What animals have been shown to pass the test?

How Did Language Evolve?

There has been a great deal of speculation about how language began (Fitch et al., 2005; Fitch et al., 2010; Hauser et al., 2002). Many evolutionary biologists working today likely share Charles Darwin's (1809–82) view about the origins of language. Darwin (1871, p. 56) proposed: "I cannot doubt that language owes its origin to the imitation and modification, aided by signs and gestures, of various natural sounds, the voices of other animals, and man's own instinctive cries." The question remains whether language is the result of slow and gradual evolution, beginning with a relatively simple state and changing into the complex grammatical system of modern language, or whether the modern complex grammatical system we have today first emerged on the planet when modern humans began and remains relatively unchanged since then. In this section, we begin our discussion with a review of some theories of language evolution. We then discuss the relationship between the anatomy of primates and the features present in humans that enable speech. We end our discussion with evidence obtained from fossils and what it suggests about how our prehistoric relatives communicated.

Theories of How Language Evolved

Some early theories of how language might have evolved slowly were first proposed in the 1800s (Müller, [1861] 1996). Let's review three of these theories. First, the advocates of the **bow-wow theory** claim that the first human utterances were imitations of the sounds made by objects and other forms of onomatopoeia (Aitchison, 1998). The bow-wow theory suggests that the first human utterances were examples of onomatopoeia. A second theory is the **pooh-pooh theory**, whose proponents claim that the first utterances of humans were exclamations (e.g., oh, mmm, ouch, etc.). Last, the **yo-he-ho theory** claims that humans' first utterances were noises made during hard work. Unfortunately, none of these theories has been developed enough to explain how human utterances ultimately became as complex as they are today.

More recent theories focus on different aspects of daily life that are important in the origin of language. One view suggests that language served to maintain social relationships, which became increasingly challenging as the groups in which humans lived grew larger (Dunbar, 1996). Language enabled members of a group to learn about one another through gossiping during close interactions. Other primates spend time grooming one another (i.e., examining and cleaning body areas), which promotes hygiene, social bonding, and may reduce stress (Pellis & Pellis, 2010). Dunbar (1996) proposes that language began as a form of vocal grooming. Talking may have served to bind members of a community together, with gossiping about other members of the group serving as the conversational content. Recent research provides preliminary support for the view (Lyons & Hughes, 2015).

The alternative to the view that language slowly evolved requires modern human language to have emerged suddenly on the planet, most likely due to one or more genetic mutations occurring in a relatively short period of time (Crow, 2002; Klein & Edgar, 2002). Some have linked the likely emergence of modern human language to the relative explosion in symbolic art that started around 50,000 years ago (Klein & Edgar, 2002). The same type of mind that created the symbolic art found among the cave paintings may have been the same type of mind to produce the complex form of communication we have today. Other scholars have suggested that the genetic variation that resulted in some humans having a modern language ability may have become particularly attractive to those who did not have it, so such individuals became desirable mating partners (Desalles, 2007).

Anatomy and Speech

The 20th-century attempts to teach chimpanzees to learn to produce spoken language failed. The reason that speaking is so difficult for chimpanzees lies in their anatomy. Chimpanzees are limited in the sounds they can produce because of the shape of their skulls and the location of the **larynx** (voice box) in the throat (Lieberman, 2007). In modern adult humans, the larynx is positioned in the throat in such a way that it is possible to produce speech sounds relatively rapidly, which is required if one is to produce syllables containing combinations of consonants and vowels. At birth, the larynx in modern humans is positioned relatively high. Around the fourth month, it descends (Lieberman et al., 2001). Having a lowered larynx poses a danger, because the larynx is then close to the opening of the windpipe. There is an increased danger of choking on food when the larynx is in this low position. Lieberman has commented that the evolutionary advantage for having a low larynx must have been so great that it outweighed the disadvantage of increasing the risk of death due to choking (Searchinger et al., 2005).

The Fossil Record

Those who advocate for theories suggesting a slow evolution in human communication that culminates with modern human language believe that the fossil record provides clues to how human communication began and changed. Physical differences in the vocal tract and brain of modern humans and other members of the family tree of primates can be studied to identify times in human history where physical changes may have influenced human communication. For example, the positioning of the larynx in humans differs from that found in fossils of **Neanderthals** (*Homo neanderthalensis*) as well as modern apes, which includes chimpanzees (Lieberman, 2007). In contrast, **Early European Modern Humans** (EEMH), referred to in the past as Cro-Magnons, may have been able to speak in a way similar to modern humans (Lieberman, 2007).

In recent years, new fossil discoveries have led to changes in the timeline of modern humans and the prehistory family tree. The common ancestor for Neanderthals and EEMHs lived around 660,000 years ago. Neanderthals are believed to have existed from 400,000 years ago till about 30,000 years ago. EEMHs existed as far back as 45,000 years ago and coexisted for about 15,000 years with Neanderthals. EEMHs were more similar to modern humans than Neanderthals. The faces of EEMHs were wider than modern humans. They had a larger skull and stockier frame and stood around 5'5" (McHenry, 2009). They were hunters and used flint tools that they made. They used flax to make textiles. The cave paintings referred to above have been found in caves where EEMH fossils have been found. The implication is that the cave painters were EEMHs (Wild et al., 2005). In contrast, Neanderthals were much stronger than modern humans. However, they were also about 5'5" tall, with a skull that was about the same size. The back of the skull did not contain the arch that is present in the skulls of modern humans (Lieberman, 2007). They were also hunters and makers of stone tools. It used to be thought that they did not produce symbolic art; however, this claim has recently been disputed (Mithen, 2006). Because some Neanderthal fossils have been found with musical instruments (e.g., flutes) made from tiny bird bones, Mithen's (2006) view is that Neanderthals may have had a well-developed musical culture.

 Time out for Review

Key Terms

Bow-wow theory

European Early Modern Human (EEMH)

Larynx

Neanderthal

Pooh-pooh theory

Yo-he-ho theory

Review Questions

1   Describe the various theories about how human language evolved. Is there a consensus about which of the theories is the best?
2   How did Neanderthals and European Early Modern Humans likely differ? How did their communication abilities likely differ from modern humans?

Summary

There have been many attempts to teach non-human animals language. These include chimpanzees, gorillas, bonobos, parrots, dolphins, and dogs. Many species have been able to learn to acquire vocabulary. Few species have demonstrated the ability to understand novel sentences. Those that have displayed promise in this area are Kanzi, the bonobo, bottlenose dolphins, and Chaser, the dog. When we compare the ways in which humans and animals typically communicate, we focused on 5 of the 13 design features identified by Hockett: semanticity, arbitrariness, productivity, displacement, and discreteness. Although researchers have competing views about how language may have evolved, there is no consensus about whether language resulted as a slow evolutionary process from a simple communication system to the complex grammatical system that exists today. An alternative view is that language appeared on the planet along with the first modern humans who because of their biology, including a larger brain, had this new way of communicating with one another (i.e., with syntax). Facts from the fossil record can be used to theorize about how language evolved, specifically how the anatomy of the vocal tract and skull changed over time.

Recommended Books, Films, and Websites

Bradbury, J. W. & Vehrencamp, S. L. (2011). *Principles of Animal Communication* (2nd edn). Sunderland, MA: Sinaur.

Corballis, M. C. (2011). *The Recursive Mind: The Origins of Human Language, Thought, and Civilization*. Princeton, NJ: Princeton University Press.

De Waal, F. (2005). *Our Inner Ape: A Leading Primatologist Explains Why We Are Who We Are*. New York: Riverhead/Penguin.

Friends of Washoe. www.friendsofwashoe.org.

Hess, E. (2008). *Nim Chimpsky: The Chimp Who Would Be Human*. New York: Bantam.

Ottenhiemer, H. J. (2009). *The Anthropology of Language* (3rd edn). Belmont, CA: Wadsworth Cengage Learning.

Pepperberg, I. (2009). *Alex and Me: How a Scientist and a Parrot Discovered a Hidden World of Animal Intelligence – and Formed a Deep Bond in the Process*. New York: Harper Paperbacks.

Phillips, F. (Director/Writer/Producer) (2009). *Written in the Wind*. Available from www.francescaphillips. com/whistling-language.

Rubin, J. (Director/Writer/Producer) (2008). *Ape Genius* [Television series]. NOVA. Boston: WGBH Foundation. Available from www.pbs.org.

Savage-Rumbaugh, S. & Lewin, R. (1994). *Kanzi: The Ape at the Brink of the Human Mind*. Hoboken, NJ: Wiley.

Schroeder, B. (Director) (2007). *Koko: The Talking Gorilla*. United States: Criterion.

Sebeok, T. A. & Umiker-Sebeok, J. (1980). *Speaking of Apes: A Critical Anthology of Two-way Communication with Man*. New York: Plenum Press.

Terrace, H. S. (1979). *Nim*. New York: Knopf.

White, J. B. (Producer) (2009). *Becoming Human*. [Television series]. NOVA. Boston: WGBH Foundation. Available from www.pbs.org.

3 HOW IS SPEECH PERCEIVED?

Photo 3.1 We are able to hear what people are saying even when they whisper and when the surrounding environment is noisy. Have you ever had a slip of the ear?

When you call the customer service number of most major companies, you are likely to be asked to use spoken responses. You may hear an automated message say "Please press 1 for English" or "Why are you calling today?" Over the past 30 years, there have been great advances in speech recognition software; however, as you may have noticed, the programs are far from being able to understand speech as well as people can. The failures of software programs are because it is incredibly difficult to program a computer to recognize speech. If researchers could completely describe how humans perceive speech, it would be possible to develop software programs to use human speech as input flawlessly. The fact that we still do not understand fully how this fundamental human ability is possible underscores just how remarkable this basic human ability is.

In this chapter, we will learn about why our ability to recognize speech accurately across so many different speakers and so many different situations is truly amazing. Research in speech perception began in the 20th century, first focusing on how the physical properties of speech correspond to phonemes, syllables, and words. This research documented how remarkably flexible the human listener is in accurately perceiving speech across speakers and contexts (Goldstone et al., 1997). In the first section, we discuss the nature of speech and some of the challenges for the listener when trying to identify individual words and phonemes from the speech signal. This section also describes the building blocks of speech. The next section examines the classic and most prominent theoretical models of speech perception and the empirical evidence supporting them. Lastly, we examine the popular question of how speech perception and music perception are related. Recent research has yielded some surprising findings regarding how a person's native language might be related to their ability to perceive musical tones.

Speech Perception is Easy, but Hard to Understand

The seemingly effortless way in which we comprehend speech most of the time is surprising considering the complexity of the process. For the typical listener, understanding speech usually takes little effort. Researchers distinguish the process of **sensation** or registering a stimulus with our senses (e.g., hearing, vision, touch, smell or taste) from the process of **perception** or recognizing the identity of the stimulus (Goldstein, 2015). Auditory perception occurs so rapidly that it is unlikely that we become consciously aware of this early stage of processing, when we are registering sound waves. During the perception of speech, sensation occurs when sound waves are registered first by the ear, which transfers the information to the auditory nerve, which sends the information to the brain. Only when we hear an unfamiliar sound, when perception takes longer than usual, do we become consciously aware of the sensory input before it has been interpreted. Even then, we are likely reflecting on our memory of the sensory input, rather than the sensation itself. Registering the sensation occurs so quickly that we are not consciously aware of it. Our memory for the sounds we hear is called **echoic memory** and can last up three to four seconds (Hicks, 1974). Everything we hear is stored briefly in **sensory memory**, in a representation that preserves the detail contained in the incoming stimulus. This is beneficial because, as listeners, we are dependent on the speaker in terms of how quickly the speech is produced. If a speaker talks rapidly, we might fall behind as we are listening. In such circumstances, we may be able to use the information from memory to figure out what the speaker has said. In other cases, because we are listening when the perception of speech is compromised (e.g., noisy contexts), we may rely on echoic memory.

Perceiving Speech

Those who study speech perception aim to understand how the acoustic characteristics of speech are decoded by the listener so that they arrive at the perception of what has been said. A useful approach to explaining the perception of sounds is referred to as **pattern recognition** by psychologists (Fahle, 1994). The process of perception can be thought of as one in which the listener compares an incoming sound to the sounds stored in memory, which has been built up through a lifetime of experience hearing speech. The process of searching may end when there is a close match between one of the sound memories and the incoming sound. For example, imagine the incoming sound is a whistle, the type used by an athletic coach. The sound waves are registered by the auditory system, transferred into a pattern of sound energy that can be interpreted by the brain. As soon as the sound wave is detected by the listener, the listener's memory system becomes involved, with all the memories of similar sounds becoming activated and compared with the incoming sound pattern. In this example, if one has heard the sound of a whistle before, then the memories of the prior times in which a whistle was heard are the closest matches to the incoming sound. The listener perceives the incoming sound as a whistle.

One can easily imagine how pattern recognition might work to explain the perception of speech. However, as we will see, there are challenges because of the highly variable nature of sound wave patterns in speech. The acoustic characteristics of speech can be understood in visual displays called **speech spectrograms** (Flanagan, 1972). Speech spectrograms display the frequency of sound produced over time. Time in milliseconds is plotted on the horizontal or x-axis and the amount of energy in the sound waves or hertz (Hz – cycles per second) is plotted on the vertical or y-axis. The spectrogram shows how the energy in speech changes throughout the production of an utterance. Figure 3.1 displays a speech spectrogram of a speaker saying *I owe you.* The complete absence of sound would result in a vertical strip of white space in the graph. As you can see, the graph contains no white space; thus, sound is continuously present. The darker bands in the graph reflect the fact that there are many more wave forms (i.e., up and down cycles) being produced per unit of time. Such bands can be indicative of complex sound patterns occurring during the production of vowels. The term **formant** describes the distinctive bands of complex sound patterns that are associated with the production of vowels.

A first step in understanding how speech perception occurs is careful analysis of the acoustic characteristics of speech. The central question is whether it is possible to determine what parts of the speech stream correspond to words, syllables, and phonemes. When researchers have analyzed the acoustic characteristics of speech, they first observe that it is unclear how the listener is able to determine where one word ends and the next word begins. As you can see in Figure 3.1, the speaker of the phrase *I owe you* has not produced a period of silence between the words; so, for the listener of this utterance, it would not be easy to determine when one word ended and the next word began. Can you guess where the word *you* begins? The **segmentation problem** describes the fact that the boundaries between words are not easy to perceive by listeners (Cutler, 1994). Typically, the sound we produce at the end of one word does not end before we begin producing the sound for the beginning of the next word.

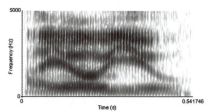

Figure 3.1 Speech Spectrogram of the Sentence *I owe you*
Credit: Jonas Kluk

Researchers in the 1950s approached the segmentation problem by examining the contents of numerous speech spectrographs and trying to find a characteristic of words or phonemes that might be among the easiest to identify by a listener. For example, it is a reasonable assumption that it would be possible to distinguish when the vocal cords are vibrating during the production of a sound versus when the vocal cords are not vibrating. The term **voicing** has been used to refer to the feature of phonemes when they are produced when the vocal cords are vibrating, as occurs for all vowels and some consonants (e.g., /b/, /g/, and /d/) (Ladefoged, 2006). In English, there no vowels that are produced without voicing (i.e., voiceless), but there are several voiceless consonants (e.g., /p/, /t/, /k/).

As speech research progressed, it was found that the segmentation problem was not the only challenge in understanding how words and phonemes are identified by listeners. Perhaps a more challenging problem is the fact that the acoustic properties of speech are highly variable, not only across speakers, but also for the same speaker producing a word or phoneme in a different sentence context. Each time a speaker says a word, the physical properties of the sound waves differ substantially. Researchers have referred to this problem in understanding speech perception as the **problem of invariance** (Pisoni, 1993). It is not the case that there is a pattern of sound energy that is the same or invariant each time a specific phoneme, syllable or word is produced. Some of the variation occurs because the production of phonemes, syllables, and words is influenced by the sounds that are produced before or after it. Other variation can occur because of the speaker's physical state (e.g., well vs. ill), level of energy (e.g., alert vs. fatigued), and so on. Remember the last time you had a sore throat or congestion due to a head cold. There were likely changes in how your voice sounded to others.

The problem of invariance also stems from the fact that speakers' production of words and syllables involves the production of multiple phonemes simultaneously, a phenomenon referred to as **co-articulation** (Hardcastle & Hewlett, 2006). During the production of syllables, the way in which a phoneme is produced is influenced by the immediately preceding phoneme and can be influenced by the immediately following phoneme. When speakers produce a phoneme, the phoneme's physical properties vary as a function of the phonemes produced before and after it. Consider the differences in how you would produce the syllables, *bee, boo,* and *buh*. Try pronouncing those syllables now. How does the production of the /b/ change? When you produce *bee* and *buh*, the lips open and close more horizontally than when you produce *boo*. When you produce *boo*, the lips have a more rounded shape. When you say *buh,* the mouth is open and more relaxed than for *boo*.

Differences in the physical properties of speech vary tremendously across speakers. Even when many speech samples are taken from the same speaker and analyzed, researchers find incredible variability for the same phonemes, syllables, and words. No two utterances of the same word by the same speaker are the same. Computer programs, such as Siri on Apple's iPhone, frequently make mistakes in understanding our speech when our friends do not. Technology often fails when one's voice characteristics are affected by having a head cold or congestion due to allergies. People are able to handle the variability in the speech stream through a process of **normalization** (Pisoni, 1993). You may experience normalization when you watch films featuring an actor whose accent may be unfamiliar to you. You might experience difficulty understanding the actor as the film begins, but gradually you come to understand the actor with little problem. Understanding the actor gets easier and easier as you experience more of the speech. You can thank your perceptual system, which makes the adjustments needed to overcome the speaker's unusual speech patterns. Normalization is always occurring. Most of the time, we are not consciously aware that the perception of speech starts out more slowly and gets easier the more we listen to the speaker.

The sounds we can perceive are limited to the estimated range of 20–20,000 Hz (Moller, 2006). Higher frequency sounds have more cycles per second. Examples of low frequency sounds include the rumbling of thunder, a bass drum, or a deep masculine voice. Examples of high frequency sounds include a whistle, birds tweeting, or children's voices and shrieks. Across animals, the range of hearing varies, with elephants typically able to perceive sounds lower in frequency than humans can hear and dogs typically able to perceive sounds higher in frequency than humans can hear (Fay & Popper, 1994). Across individuals, the actual range of perception may vary.

Age-related Changes in Hearing

As we age, our ability to adapt to the variation in speech changes (Yonan & Sommers, 2000). There is a general decline in hearing as we age. The medical term for the phenomenon is **presbycusis**, which comes from the Greek *presbys* for elder and *akousis* for hearing. Approximately 30 percent of those 65 years of age and older have hearing loss, and for those 75 years and older, the percentage can be as high as 50 percent (National Institutes of Health, 2017). Typically, aging adults find it increasingly difficult to hear high frequency sounds, such as the telephone ringing or children's voices, while they continue to be able to hear low-pitch sounds, the rumbling sounds of heavy vehicles, and deep masculine voices. Changes in hearing ability (i.e., the sensation level of processing) across the lifespan lead to changes in auditory perception that can affect speech comprehension (Jerger et al., 1989; Morrell et al., 1996; Schneider & Pichora-Fuller, 2001). Because older adults' ability to perceive high frequency sounds decreases with age, there is an increasing difficulty in perceiving the phonemes involved in the production of high frequencies. For example, older adults may have trouble distinguishing /s/ and /th/ as well as other consonants that differ only in voicing (e.g., /b/ vs. /p/, /d/ vs. /t/, and /g/ vs. /k/) (Tremblay et al., 2002). Known as **slips of the ear**, they can become more and more common. For example, an older adult is much more likely to mishear the expression *the great legs* as *the Great Lakes* than a younger adult. Slips of the ear that occur frequently can be an indication of more serious types of hearing loss and should be discussed with an **audiologist**, a healthcare professional trained and licensed in diagnosing and managing hearing loss.

Photo 3.2 As we age, we experience changes in our hearing that lead to an increase in the misperception of phonemes. Have you observed older adults in your family mishearing words?
Credit: I Craig

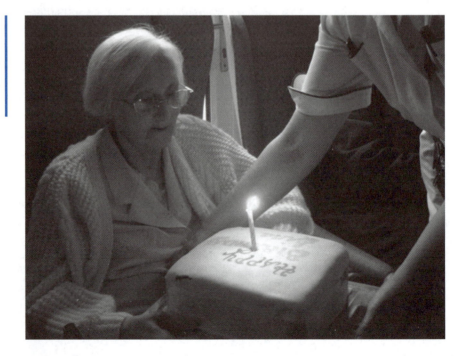

In recent years, the fact that younger and older people perceive some frequencies of sounds differently has been used to create ringtones that young people can easily hear, but older people have trouble hearing or may not hear at all. The high frequency ringtone invented by Howard Stapleton in 2005, the Mosquito, has been dubbed the "Teen Buzz" (Block, 2006). Few people over 30 years of age can hear it. Young people use it as a text message ringtone. Because teachers, parents, and bosses usually cannot hear it, the ringtone is useful when cell phones are not allowed; the use of the cell phone to receive can go undetected. The experiment in the Research DIY box will enable you to determine whether the perception of different sound frequencies varies across people of different ages.

In this section, we examined the characteristics of speech that make the process of speech perception difficult to explain. The time taken between sensing a sound to perceiving it includes a process called pattern recognition. The incoming sound is compared with prior memories of sounds. When the incoming sound is highly similar to a previously experienced sound, the listener infers that the identity of the old sound is also the identity of the incoming sound. However, the physical characteristics of speech are highly variable, suggesting that perfect matches between incoming sounds and memory would be quite rare. In addition, our ability to hear different frequencies of sound changes across the lifespan. Nevertheless, we still manage to perceive what people around us are saying. That means that our understanding of how speech perception is handled by the mind is not complete. In the next section, we go into more detail about the nuts and bolts of the sounds of speech, which will help us understand more about how the amazing feat of speech perception likely occurs.

The Building Blocks of Speech

The sound waves that carry speech to our ears contain sentences, words, and phonemes. The job of the listener is to find them. As we learned in Chapter 1, in each language, the combinations of sounds to form words and sentences follow phonological rules. For example, in English, all the words and sentences result from the combination of 44 phonemes (Ladefoged, 2006). Of these, 25 are consonants, which are sounds produced with either partial or complete interruption of the airflow. Table 3.1 lists the phonemes in English with examples. For example, the words *mom* and *dad* begin with sounds produced with consonants that involve a complete obstruction of airflow. Such consonants are referred to as **stop consonants**, as the airflow is completed stopped. There are 15 English vowels. Vowels are sounds that are produced without any interruption of the airflow. For example, the exclamations *Oh!* and *Ah!* are vowels. We write the exclamations with the letter *h,* but there is only one phoneme in each exclamation. In English, the relationship between how words sound and how they are spelled is particularly loose.

For the rest of this chapter, we must focus our attention specifically on the sounds in words rather than the letters used to spell the sound. Chapters 5 and 11 discuss the relationship between how words sound and how they appear in written form, either in terms of spelling as in English or in terms of complex symbols as in Chinese.

Can You Hear Teen Buzz?

As we age, we become less able to perceive sounds produced at high frequencies. In this experiment, you can test this phenomenon for yourself. For stimuli, you can use four sounds, each produced at a different frequency. The following sound frequencies can serve as stimuli: 8000 Hz, 12000 Hz, 15000 Hz, and 17400 Hz. The first sound is usually perceivable by all ages, the second by people younger than 50, the third by people younger than 40, and the last sound is generally perceived only by people under 18. It is used in the electronic device called the Mosquito, which is used in the UK by store owners to prevent teenagers from loitering in the stores (Campbell, 2008). This tone can be found and downloaded from Wikipedia (2017). The sounds can be played from a computer or downloaded from the following website: www.macmillanihe.com/kennison-psychology-of-language.

For your test, recruit five people for each of the four age groups: 15–24, 30–39, 40–49, and over 50. Play each participant each of the sounds. Using the worksheet below, you can note whether the person reported hearing the sound by circling "Y" if the sound was heard and "N" if it was not heard.

Participant age	8000 Hz	12000 Hz	15000 Hz	17400 Hz
_____	Y N	Y N	Y N	Y N
_____	Y N	Y N	Y N	Y N
_____	Y N	Y N	Y N	Y N
_____	Y N	Y N	Y N	Y N
_____	Y N	Y N	Y N	Y N

As in empirical research conducted in laboratories, it would be useful to present each participant with multiple examples of each of the sounds. In the present study, you can have each participant hear each sound five times. In such studies, stimuli are arranged in blocks of trials. In the present study, you can create five blocks of stimuli. In each block, the participant will hear each one of the sounds once. The ordering of the sounds within each block can be randomized. In order to carry out this complicated design, you should plan out the entire sequence of sounds before you meet the first participant. A sample sequence would be as follows:

	Trial 1	Trial 2	Trial 3	Trial 4
Block 1	15000 Hz	8000 Hz	12000 Hz	17400 Hz
Block 2	12000 Hz	15000 Hz	17400 Hz	8000 Hz
Block 3	8000 Hz	17400 Hz	15000 Hz	12400 Hz
Block 4	17400 Hz	12000 Hz	8000 Hz	15000 Hz
Block 5	15000 Hz	17400 Hz	8000 Hz	12000 Hz

Table 3.1 Phonetic Symbols for Consonants and Vowels in English

Consonants				Vowels			
Symbol	Example	Symbol	Example	Symbol	Example	Symbol	Example
/t/	tap	/r/	rest	/ɪ/	it	/aʊ/	vow
/d/	deep	/l/	list	/e/	red	/ɪə/	ear
/p/	pot	/w/	wolf	/æ/	sad	/eə/	hair
/b/	bell	/j/	yell	/ɒ/	hot	/ɑː/	art
/k/	kid	/θ/	thirst	/ʌ/	gut	/ɔː/	thought
/g/	gum	/ð/	them	/ʊ/	hood	/ʊə/	sure
/m/	mill	/ʃ/	sheep	/iː/	geese	/ɜː/	fur
/n/	numb	/ʒ/	pleasure	/eɪ/	ace	/u/	you
/s/	sit	/h/	her	/aɪ/	eye	/i/	tee
/z/	zinc	/tʃ/	chain	/ɔɪ/	voice	/ə/	uh
/f/	frog	/dʒ/	jump	/uː/	loop		
/v/	vat	/ʔ/	football	/əʊ/	so		

As you recall from Chapter 2, the larynx produces the voice. Air is passed through the folds of the larynx, creating the complete range of complex sounds we use for speaking and singing. When the vocal cords vibrate during the production of a sound, the phoneme is described as having the feature voicing. All vowels in English involve voicing, but only some of the consonants do. There are pairs of consonants that differ only in the feature voicing (e.g., /b/ and /p/, /d/ and /t/, and /g/ and /k/). These pairs of consonants have received a great deal of attention by speech perception researchers. When listeners perceive these phonemes, they appear to be sensitive to the amount of silence between the beginning of the sound and when voicing begins. This period of time is referred to as **voice onset time** (VOT). Research in the 1970s showed that the VOT of a /p/ is 25 milliseconds or more (Wood, 1976); with a VOT of less than 25 milliseconds, listeners always perceive a /b/.

Consonant pairs also vary in terms of other features, including place of articulation and manner of articulation. **Place of articulation** indicates the place in the vocal tract where the airflow is partially obstructed or completely stopped. The **manner of articulation** refers to the extent to which the airflow is stopped completely or partially. For some phonemes (e.g., /b/ and /p/), the airflow is completely stopped at the lips. These consonants are described in terms of place of articulation as **labials** and in terms of manner of articulation as stop consonants. When the airflow is stopped at the teeth, as with /t/, /th/, and /th-voiceless/, the place of articulation is described as dental. While /t/ is a dental stop consonant, /th/ and /th-voiceless/ involve only a partial interruption of airflow and are referred to as **fricatives**. Table 3.2 lists the place and manner of articulation for the English consonants. Figure 3.2 provides an illustration of the vocal tract.

Table 3.2 English Consonants Categorized by Place and Manner of Articulation

Consonant	Place of articulation	Manner of articulation
/b/ /p/	bilabial	stop
/m/	bilabial	nasal
/w/	bilabial	glide
/f/ /v/	labial-dental	fricative
/th/ /th-voiceless/	dental	fricative
/d/ /t/	alveolar	stop
/s/ /z/	alveolar	fricative
/n/	alveolar	nasal
/l/ /r/	alveolar	liquid
/judge/ /azure/	palatal	fricative
/x/ /d/	palatal	affricate
/j/	palatal	glide
/g/ /k/	velar	stop
/ŋ/	velar	nasal
/h/	glottal	fricative

Source: based on Ladefoged (2006)

Figure 3.2 Vocal Tract
Speech involves the precise coordination of the many parts of the human vocal tract. When you are talking with your friends, do you ever become aware of how many times your tongue touches the roof of your mouth?
Credit: Tavin

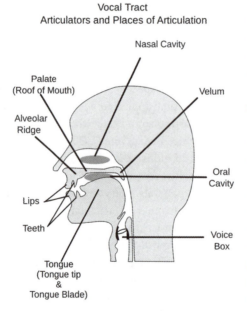

Vocal Tract
Articulators and Places of Articulation

Phonemes are combined to form words, which may be one or more syllables. In English, **syllables** contain at least a vowel, but may contain one or more consonants. The beginning of a syllable is the **onset** and the remainder of the syllable is the **rime**. For example, in the words *sprint, throw,* and *bland*, the onsets are *spr*, *thr*, and *bl* and the rimes are *int*, *ow*, and *and*. Syllables are produced with varying amounts of accent or **stress**. Words with multiple syllables can vary in their stress pattern. In English, stress is often placed on the first syllable, as in *table, window,* and *zebra.* English words that have been borrowed from other languages often do not have heavy stress on the first syllable. For example, *facetious* is produced with a heavier stress on the second syllable rather than on the first syllable. The stress pattern of English is described as "variable," possibly because numerous words have been borrowed from other languages (Tilque, 2000). In other languages, the stress pattern is highly predictable. For example, in Finnish, Hungarian, and Czech, first syllable stress is the norm. In Polish, the stress is typically on the penultimate syllable. In Macedonian, the stress regularly occurs on the syllable that is third from the end of the word. The overall stress pattern of a language can be a recognizable characteristic without even knowing the language (Mehler et al., 1988). In Chapter 8, you will learn about an experiment that shows that infants are able to distinguish the phonemes that were not experienced in their home environment (Werker & Tees, 1984).

When considering the production of full utterances, whether they be phrases or full sentences, we must also consider the rhythm of how the sequence is produced and the pattern of stress that may be used to produce the sequence. **Prosody** refers to the pattern of stress and rhythm of speech (Wells, 2007). In English, one of the most noticeable prosodic patterns is the difference in the production of statements versus questions. When speakers make statements, the pitch of the speech falls gradually throughout the production of the sentence. When speakers ask questions, pitch increases at the end of the question. The rising pitch pattern for questions in English can be used with a single word. When *lunch* is said with a rising pitch, the listener is likely to interpret it as a question "Do you want lunch?" or "Would you like to go to lunch together?" When *lunch* is produced with a falling pitch, it would not be interpreted as a question, but rather as a statement, pointing out that it is lunchtime or that the lunch food has arrived. Interestingly, in some English dialects, the falling pitch for statements has undergone a change (Ching, 1982; Lakoff, [1975] 2004). The phenomenon of **uptalk** has been studied in regions of the USA, Australia, and New Zealand (Hoffman, 2013). Some have noted that the use of uptalk, particularly by women, may be viewed as conveying tentativeness or a lack of competence and should be avoided in job interviews and the workplace (Dallet, 2014).

For the listener, a speaker with a varied intonational pattern is often preferred to one who speaks in monotone. Although we are able to detect the presence of the melodic quality in another's speech, identifying the physical properties of prosody in speech remains challenging. Prosodic variations in speech add another layer of variability, including changes in pitch and loudness of the voice, the duration of words, and the stress pattern across words (Collins & Mees, 2013). Listeners must be able to interpret the variations in meaning associated with prosodic changes, while extracting the information needed to identify phonemes. There are also contextual circumstances that lead to speakers producing words in sentences with added stress, such as when one word is intended to be contrasted with another. For example, a speaker would say "I wanted the *pretzels,* not the chips." Words are also stressed when they are the topic of the conversation, as in "I can't believe that *the car* has gone." Most of the time, listeners are able to navigate all these circumstances effortlessly, being able to interpret the changes in meaning associated with the many subtle changes in the sounds produced by the speaker.

The phonological rules involved in the production of speech and used during the perception of speech typically operate rapidly and below the level of conscious awareness. Across languages, these phonological rules differ. Languages can vary in their stress pattern and also the extent to which the beginnings of words coincide with a stressed or unstressed syllable. Across languages, how listeners solve the segmentation problem varies (McQueen, 1988; Tyler & Cutler, 2009). For learners of second languages, becoming a proficient listener in the second language involves becoming aware of the acoustic regularities in that language and using them to identify word boundaries during listening. In English, stress tends to be placed on the beginnings of words; thus, word boundaries often coincide with the onset of a stressed syllable (Cutler & Norris, 1988, Vroomen et al., 1998). However, in other languages, listeners cannot use syllable stress as a cue to signal a word boundary. The Language Spotlight box describes a phonological process in French by which word boundaries are further blurred through a process referred to as **phonological liaison**. If you are a native speaker of English or other languages in which stress tends to fall on the beginnings of words (e.g., Dutch or German), you may have found that becoming a proficient listener of French was particularly challenging (Tremblay & Spinelli, 2013, 2014).

Language Spotlight

Phonological Liaison in French

In English, word boundaries always correspond to syllable boundaries. The beginning of a word always corresponds to the beginning of a syllable. In French, word boundaries sometimes do not correspond to syllable boundaries. The phonological rules of French dictate that a word's final consonants are pronounced only in certain phonological environments. For example, in the noun phrase *mes frères* (my brothers), the final consonant /s/ in *mes* is not pronounced because the following word begins with a consonant – this is known as "without liaison." When the following word begins with a vowel or words beginning with a silent *h*, as in *mes amis* (my friends), the final consonant /s/ is pronounced – "with liaison." Often the combination is pronounced with the final consonant being realized as the beginning of the syllable that begins the following word. The result is that for such combinations the word boundary is made more ambiguous. Table 3.3 lists examples of word pairs in which liaison does and does not occur in French.

Table 3.3 Examples of French Word Pairs with and without Liaison

With liaison	Translation	Without liaison	Translation
les‿abricots	the apricots	les bananes	the bananas
vos‿enfants	your children	vos bébés	your babies
mon‿ami	my friend	mon chien	my dog
nous‿avons	we have	nous vivons	we live
un‿homme	a man	un chat	a cat
six‿oeuf	six eggs	six bonbons	six candies
grands‿animaux	large animals	grands jardins	big gardens
ces‿artistes	those artists	ces tourists	those tourists
leurs‿orchidées	their orchids	leurs tulipes	their tulips
son‿oisseau	her bird	son chien	her dog

Speakers of French must learn that there are cases of obligatory liaison, optional liaison, and impossible liaison. This knowledge is then used during speech perception to determine how the perceived phonemes correspond to individual words. In the circumstance without liaison, when listeners hear /le bonbon/, the word boundary corresponds to the onset of the second syllable at the /b/. In contrast, when listeners hear /le za mi/, the word boundary is just before /a/, which is after the onset of the second syllable. Consequently, in cases containing liaison, syllable boundaries do not correspond to word boundaries.

In summary, we reviewed the building blocks of speech. Consonants and vowels make up syllables. One or more syllables make up words. Syllables can be broken down into onsets and rimes. Syllables may or may not be produced with added force or accent. Across words, phrases and sentences, that pattern of accented and unaccented syllables is referred to as prosody. Individual words may be stressed to indicate that they are being contrasted with other words or that they have some importance in the conversation. In English, word boundaries typically occur at syllable boundaries, but in other languages, this is not always the case. In the next section, we examine the competing theories of human speech perception and review the extent to which each has been supported by research findings.

 Time out for Review

Key Terms

Audiologist	Perception	Slip of the ear
Co-articulation	Phonological liaison	Speech spectrogram
Echoic memory	Place of articulation	Stop consonant
Formant	Presbycusis	Stress
Fricatives	Problem of invariance	Syllable
Labials	Prosody	Uptalk
Manner of articulation	Rime	Voice onset time (VOT)
Normalization	Segmentation problem	Voicing
Onset	Sensation	
Pattern recognition	Sensory memory	

Review Questions

1 The physical characteristics of speech make it challenging to explain how speech is perceived so reliably. Two of these characteristics are addressed in the segmentation problem and the problem of invariance. What are these problems and why are they challenges for understanding how speech is perceived?
2 What is co-articulation? How does co-articulation make the task of speech perception more difficult to explain?
3 How does the process of normalization affect our ability to understand speech?
4 How does aging influence sound perception in humans? How do these changes affect the perception of phonemes?

Models of Attention and Speech Perception

Since the 1950s, researchers have theorized about how people comprehend speech. The earliest theories focused on attention and speech, specifically whether speech that is ignored is processed at all. We will review the major theories in chronological order, so that you can appreciate how researchers' thinking about speech perception has evolved over time. We begin our discussion with theories of selective attention followed by the motor theory of speech perception, the cohort model, the trace model, and several revisions of the cohort and trace models. Because of late 20th-century advances in computer technology, the most recent models of human speech perception rely heavily on assumptions inspired by insights obtained from computer models.

Theories of Selection Attention: Listening and Ignoring

When we listen to speech, we are rarely in an ideal setting for listening. Despite this, we usually have little trouble understanding what others are saying. Even when we are in a crowded restaurant surrounded by many conversations, without thinking too much about it, we are able to focus on the person with whom we are talking and ignore all the other conversations around us. The term **selective attention** refers to our ability to focus our attention on one stream of input among many streams of input (Lamy et al., 2013). We are able to do this without much effort. Early studies on selective attention investigated the extent to which information that was not selected or paid attention to was interpreted at all. These studies were conducted in a laboratory setting where researchers could carefully control what participants heard and when they heard it.

Studies of Attention during Listening

The processes involved in speech perception have been studied by researchers who have controlled the sounds participants hear in each ear. In laboratory studies, sounds are presented through special headphones to either both ears at once or only one ear, known as the **dichotic listening task** (Hugdahl, 1988). In early studies, participants listened to two streams of speech played simultaneously, one in each ear (Cherry, 1953). Participants were asked to repeat what they heard in one of the speech streams, while ignoring the other speech stream. After the task, participants were asked if they could remember anything from the speech they had ignored. Participants were unable to report any of the ignored speech. Participants did not notice when the speech in the unattended stream changed from English to German. In one study, they were able to recall whether the speaker was male or female or whether the unattended speech was non-speech sounds versus actual speech.

Cherry's (1953) results suggested that when one directs attention toward one source of speech and away from another, the unattended source is not processed at all. These results and others provided support for a model of selective attention

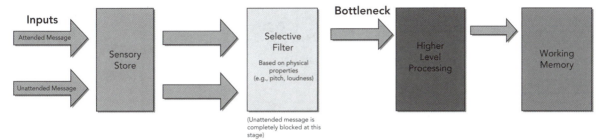

Broadbent's Filter Model

Inputs

Attended Message

Unattended Message

Sensory Store

Selective Filter

Based on physical properties (e.g., pitch, loudness)

(Unattended message is completely blocked at this stage)

Bottleneck

Higher Level Processing

Working Memory

Figure 3.3 Broadbent's (1958) Filter Model Information that is ignored by the listener is prevented from receiving higher level processing and entering working memory. Do you think that we ignore more speech than we pay attention to or vice versa?
Credit: Kyle Farr

proposed by Broadbent (1958). Figure 3.3 illustrates the stages of processing in this model. Information that is not attended (i.e., is ignored) is not analyzed at the level at which perception can occur and so is not entered into memory. Working memory is a type of short-term memory that can be described as our mental blackboard, which we use to carry out mental calculations, solve problems, and keep track of what is occurring in our immediate surroundings (Baddeley, 2012).

Later studies showed that unattended speech is not completely ignored; rather, listeners are aware of the meaning of the speech even though they may not believe that they are listening to it (Gray & Wedderburn, 1960; Moray, 1969; Wood & Cowan, 1995). Moray (1969) asked participants to listen to two streams of speech while repeating aloud what was heard in one of the streams. During the task, the participant's name was played in the unattended speech stream. The results showed that one out of three participants reported hearing their name. In a particularly creative study, Gray and Wedderburn (1960) asked participants to repeat what they heard in one of two streams. Participants heard "Dear 7 Jane" in one ear and "9 Aunt 6" in the other. Rather than repeat the nonsensical sequence, "Dear 7 Jane," participants produced "Dear Aunt Jane." The results showed that participants' attention switched from the attended stream to the unattended stream and back.

Gray and Wedderburn's (1960) study documents something most of us have experienced in our daily lives. We may be in a crowded room where many conversations are occurring, then, out of nowhere, we hear our name from across the room. Somehow, we are able to attend selectively to speech that is meaningful to us even when spoken in a noisy, distracting environment. The meaningful speech is captured by our attentional processing systems, referred to as the **cocktail party effect**. The cocktail party effect, like the Gray and Wedderburn's (1960) results, demonstrates that when we ignore sounds in the environment, we continue to process them. If the ignored information becomes important to us, we can rapidly bring it into the primary focus of our attention.

Although Broadbent's (1958) selective filter model of auditory attention ultimately proved to be incorrect, it was influential in providing a useful framework for understanding speech perception. The model was revised by Rebecca Treisman, a student of Broadbent. In the revised model, Treisman (1969) eliminated Broadbent's selective filter and replaced it with the attenuator, which analyzed speech in terms not only of its acoustical characteristics, but

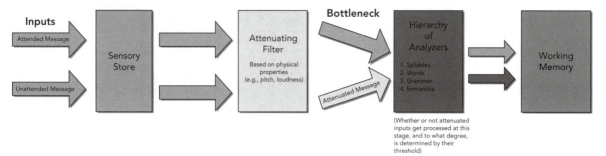

Treisman's Attenuation Model

Inputs → Attended Message, Unattended Message → Sensory Store → Attenuating Filter (Based on physical properties (e.g., pitch, loudness)) → Attenuated Message → **Bottleneck** → Hierarchy of Analyzers (1. Syllables 2. Words 3. Grammar 4. Semantics) → Working Memory

(Whether or not attenuated inputs get processed at this stage, and to what degree, is determined by their threshold)

Figure 3.4 Treisman's (1969) Attenuation Model
As you are reading now, are there any sounds in the environment that you are ignoring?
Credit: Kyle Farr

also its linguistic structure (phonemes, syllables, and words) and meaning. Figure 3.4 displays Treisman's attenuation model. Ignored speech would be processed by the attenuator just as speech receiving the listeners' full attention; however, after being processed by the attenuator, the ignored speech would be associated with lower activation levels than those of the attended speech. Both types of speech (ignored and attended) are analyzed by the dictionary unit, which contains information about all the words known by the listener and stored in long-term memory. Treisman (1969) further proposed that words in the dictionary unit vary in how strong a speech signal must be in order to cause the word to be perceived. Words that listeners experience frequently could be perceived even by weak input from an ignored source of speech. For words that listeners experience infrequently, stronger input would be required to perceive the word, such as input coming from an attended source of speech. The words activated by the dictionary unit are transferred into working memory for further processing.

Treisman's (1969) model represented a major step forward in thinking not only about how speech is perceived, but also how knowledge of words may be stored in memory and activated during processing. Nevertheless, the model was refuted by an experiment conducted by Donald Mackay (1973), which used the dichotic listening test. Participants heard an ambiguous sentence, such as *They were throwing stones at the bank,* in one ear. (The sentence is ambiguous because the word bank has two meanings: a place where money is stored, but also land alongside a river.) While participants repeated the sentence they heard, they were exposed to the words *river* or *money* in their other ear. After experiencing multiple trials of ambiguous sentences presented with related words in the unattended ear, participants were presented with pairs of sentences and asked to select the one that was closest in meaning to the previous sentence they heard. The results showed that the word presented in the unattended ear influenced participants' memory judgments. Mackay (1973) proposed a revision to Treisman's (1969) model, which has been described as a late selective attention model. Both Broadbent and Treisman's models could be classified as early selective attention models, as ignored information was prevented from receiving higher level processing relatively rapidly. In MacKay's (1973) model, ignored information is processed at the level of semantic meaning and was able to influence conscious processing of attended information.

Recent research has shown that people are better able to ignore unattended speech streams than others. Conway and colleagues have shown that individuals who differ in working memory capacity perform differently in dichotic listening tests (Colflesh & Conway, 2007; Conway et al., 2001). Individual differences in working memory have been measured in a variety of ways. One method is called **digit span** (Donolato et al., 2017). To measure digit span, a researcher reads aloud a series of digits (e.g., 4, 9, 2, 7, 5), and participants are asked to recall the digits. Over many trials, the number of digits in the sequence is varied. The participant's digit span is the number of digits that can be remembered in a given sequence. Individuals with high working memory capacity (i.e., have higher digit spans) are less likely to report information from the unattended channel than individuals with low working memory capacity (i.e., have lower digit spans), suggesting that higher working memory capacity enables participants to be more successful in ignoring the unattended speech stream as well as switching back and forth between the attended and unattended speech streams (Colflesh & Conway, 2007).

Dichotic listening tests have also been used to investigate the extent to which the two hemispheres of the brain are involved in processing speech and non-speech sounds. For example, studies have demonstrated that most participants respond more quickly to words presented to the right ear than the left ear (Kimura, 1961; Studdert-Kennedy et al., 1972) and respond more quickly to non-linguistic sounds when they are presented to the left ear than the right ear (Bryden, 1988). Later in Chapter 12, we will take a closer look at how the two hemispheres of the brain make different contributions to the processing of language.

In summary, theories of selective attention have undergone several revisions since their first proposal in the 1950s. The models have varied in terms of how much processing ignored information receives. Evidence from laboratory studies, such as MacKay (1973), demonstrated that ignored information is processed at high levels, including the level of meaning. Furthermore, the meaning of ignored information was shown to influence processing of information receiving listeners' full attention. Recent research has shown that there are individual differences in attentional processing during listening that are related to working memory. Individuals with high working memory capacity are better able to ignore unattended information.

Motor Theory of Speech Perception

One of the oldest theories of speech perception is the motor theory of speech perception, first proposed by Liberman and colleagues (Liberman et al., 1967; Liberman & Mattingly, 1985). Motor theory proposed that speech perception was closely tied to speech production, so closely tied that speech perception involved using the speech input to identify the physical movements that must be made by the vocal tract to produce the sounds. When the theory was first proposed, it appeared consistent with research showing that the perception of phonemes typically occurs in an all-or-none fashion, with the listener perceiving a sound as one phoneme or another. In reality, sounds can vary a great deal acoustically and be something in between the best example of one phoneme and the best example of another phoneme. Research in the 1980s showed that at birth, infants are able distinguish the phonemes in languages other than their mother tongue (Werker & Tees, 1984). Over the twelve months following birth,

Figure 3.5 Voice Onset Time

Credit: Graph from Wood, C. C. (1976). Discriminability, response bias, and phoneme categories in discrimination of voice onset time. *The Journal of the Acoustical Society of America*, 60, 1381–1389

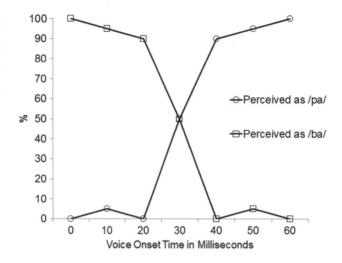

infants' perceptual abilities adapt as a result of their experiences. Gradually, they cease to be able to distinguish phonemes that are not found in the language(s) they are learning (Jusczyk, 1999; Kuhl et al., 2006; Kuhl, 2007; Werker & Tees, 1984). **Categorical perception** is the ability of organisms to distinguish between categories of sounds. Categorical perception is not unique to humans. Kuhl (1987) demonstrated that chinchillas also exhibit categorical perception. However, unlike children whose perceptual abilities are dramatically changed by their exposure to speech sounds, the perceptual abilities of other animals do not appear to change across their lifespan.

Studies of categorical perception often use pairs of stop consonants that differ only in voicing (e.g., /p/ and /b/, /t/ and /d/, and /k/ and /g/). For these consonants, the manner and place of articulation are the same, but /p/, /t/, and /k/ are voiceless, being produced without the vibration of the vocal cords. In contrast, /b/, /d/, and /g/ are produced with voicing. Speech research has found that listeners are sensitive to the amount of time between the onset of the phoneme and when voicing begins – voice onset time (VOT). For example, a determining factor in whether listeners perceive the voiced consonant /b/ versus the voiceless consonant /p/ turns out to be when voicing is perceived relative to when the beginning of the phoneme is perceived. When there are 25 or more milliseconds of silence at the beginning of the sound, listeners perceive a /p/; otherwise listeners perceive a /b/. Figure 3.5 displays the graph of the relationship between voice onset time and the perception of /p/ versus /b/ from Wood (1976).

The motor theory of speech perception is intuitively appealing, because it is the case that humans have the remarkable ability to produce sounds they hear even when they have not seen the speaker producing the sign. The listener needs only to hear the sound to be able to imitate it. Liberman and colleagues were familiar with the problem of invariance in the acoustics of speech. They reasoned that although the speech sounds vary a great deal across the contexts in which they are produced, the articulatory gestures used to produce the speech sounds would vary less. Consequently, if listeners were able to associate in memory specific speech sounds to their corresponding articulatory gestures, then it may be possible to explain how speech is deciphered. Liberman had a background in behaviorism, which may also explain why he focused on the gesture as a core element in the theory. Although there are some researchers who are still proponents of the theory (Galantucci et al., 2006), overall the theory has fallen out of favour, being supplanted by less abstract theories that make clearer predictions that can be tested in perceptual experiments.

The fact that it is possible to decode speech by watching the movements of a speakers' lips alone supports the notion that there is an important link between speech comprehension and the physical movements used to produce speech. Individuals who are deaf or have hearing impairments can rely on **lip-reading** to understand the speech of others (Woodhouse et al., 2009). Learning to lip-read may be easier for those who have had experience with sound than for those born deaf. In Chapter 13, we explore the language of the deaf when we discuss the acquisition and use of sign languages (e.g., American Sign Language). In the study of the psychology of language, the experiences of deaf and hearing-impaired individuals have revealed important insights into how the brain organizes information about the different parts of language and how the brain may store information about spoken and signed languages differently. Definitive evidence that listeners generally use information they see when watching speakers was discovered in the 1970s. The Classic Research box reviews an intriguing effect accidentally discovered by a research assistant.

Interest in the motor theory of speech perception was reinvigorated in the 1990s, after neuroscientists discovered neurons that fired anytime an organism viewed an action being performed or when the organism performed the action itself (di Pellegrino et al., 1992; Gallese et al., 1996). These intriguing cells in the brain are called **mirror neurons**. They were originally discovered in the brains of monkeys. For some, mirror neurons led to renewed interest in the motor theory of speech perception (Fogassi & Ferrari, 2007; Holt & Lotto, 2014) because they appeared to provide evidence of the link between perceptual and motor processes. Nevertheless, the existence of mirror neurons has not provided further understanding about how listeners rely on the link to achieve speech perception. The complexities involved in the communications that occur between the sensory and motor systems are not yet completely understood (Case et al., 2015). Future work from neurologists will likely be able to explain exactly why there are seemingly unnecessary links between visual perception and speech. For example, a recent experiment showed that participants who were shown silent videos of a person speaking were significantly less able to interpret the speech through lip-reading when their ability to mimic the actions was blocked than when it was not (Turner et al., 2015). In the former condition, they were required to hold a tongue depressor horizontally in their mouths while watching the video of the speaker, and in the latter condition, they were required to squeeze a ball in one hand.

In summary, the motor theory of speech perception was one of the earliest theories of speech perception, with several interesting ties to facts about the perception of speech. So far, it has not been successful in producing a complete understanding of how speech perception occurs. However, some researchers still embrace the model as a useful framework for investigating human speech perception. Interest in the theory has been increased since the discovery of

Classic Research — The McGurk Effect

A compelling piece of evidence supporting the motor theory of speech perception was discovered in the 1970s. Researchers stumbled on an auditory illusion that can occur during speech perception. The illusion demonstrated that listening can be influenced by more than one of our senses. In some cases, what we hear can be influenced by what we are seeing. The McGurk effect refers to an auditory illusion that was first demonstrated in the laboratory in which listeners perceived a phoneme different from the one presented. The illusion was first reported by McGurk and MacDonald (1976). While MacDonald was a research assistant in McGurk's laboratory, he discovered the illusion by accident, when he had been asked by McGurk to edit video and audio samples. He found that when a video of a face pronouncing one syllable (e.g., *ba ba ba*) was played together with an auditory recording of a different syllable (e.g., *ga ga ga*), he would hear a third syllable entirely (e.g., *da da da*). The illusion suggests that hearing speech sounds can be influenced by visual processing. The systematic pattern that has been observed by numerous studies that have investigated the McGurk effect is that listeners' perception of the syllable shows that visual information alters the listeners' interpretation of the initial phoneme's place of articulation. The place of articulation for the /b/ is the lips, which are closed in the video, and the place of articulation for the /g/ is in the throat, which can be heard on the audio recording. The phoneme that is perceived is a consonant that shares the feature of voicing with both the /b/ and /g/, but has the place of articulation in between the lips and throat. The illusion appears to be an averaging of the visual and auditory input.

Since its accidental discovery, the McGurk effect has been the subject of numerous investigations. For example, the effect is not limited to English-speaking participants. In a study that compared the frequency of perceiving the McGurk effect, similar frequencies were observed for a sample of native Mandarin speakers living in China and native English speakers living in the USA (Magnotti et al., 2015). These results suggest that cultural differences in how listeners attend to speakers' faces during conversations do not lead to differences in the extent to which listeners integrate visual information during speech perception. Somewhat surprisingly, the McGurk effect is also observed in deaf individuals who hear with the assistance of cochlear implants (Rouger et al., 2008), as well as hearing infants as young as four or five months of age (Bristow et al., 2009; Burnham & Dodd, 2004). Recent research has shown that there are significant individual differences among hearing participants (Mallick et al., 2015). For example, women tend to experience the McGurk effect more strongly than men (Irwin et al., 2006).

mirror neurons, which demonstrate that there is a neural link between visual perception and the systems involved in the production of movement.

Morton's Logogen Model

John Morton's (1969, 1979) **logogen model** was designed to explain word recognition. The word "logogen" was formed from two Greek words, *logos* meaning *word* and *genus* meaning *birth*. The **logogen** was viewed as the presentation of a morpheme or word in our mind, stored in memory. The logogen contains information about the morpheme's meaning, sound, and spelling. To recognize a word during reading, a person could hear or read a word and the sensory input triggers activation in our memory representations. For spoken words, the sensory input would be auditory. For written words, the sensory input would be visual. Morton (1969) stipulated that in order for a word to be recognized, there must be an adequate amount of activation triggered by the sensory input. He further argued that the reader could be influenced by expectations due to contextual information; thus, the model allowed top-down as well as bottom-up processing.

The Cohort Model

The most influential model of speech perception, thus far, is the cohort model (Marslen-Wilson, 1987, 1990; Marslen-Wilson & Tyler, 1980; Marslen-Wilson & Welsh, 1978). The word *cohort* refers to a *group*. In the model, during the perception of spoken words, listeners are described as activating in memory words that begin with similar phonemes and syllables as the incoming speech. Within the first 200 milliseconds of a word being spoken, the listener is believed to activate possible matches to the stimulus from memory. The memory matches of the similar sounding words that are initially activated form the cohort. For example, when listeners hear the phonemes /kandl/, they first activate in memory all the words they know beginning with */kand/, /kan/, /ka/, and /k/*. The words sharing similar onsets can be thought of as a cohort or grouping of similar items. As more of the word is perceived, listeners narrow down the possible matches, until finally the listener selects the best candidate among the alternatives. The **uniqueness point** is the point in processing at which a single remaining candidate is left and all other possible candidates are no longer considered (Marslen-Wilson & Welsh, 1978). For some words, the uniqueness point corresponds to the point at which they are recognized in speech. The point of recognition for a word is the **recognition point**. Once the best candidate is selected, then it is integrated into the preceding context. In many cases, the uniqueness point will be the recognition point, but it may not always be so. In the cohort model, there are three proposed stages of word perception during listening: access; selection; and integration (Marslen-Wilson & Welsh, 1978).

The notion that there is a recognition point during spoken word perception that occurs before the end of the word is consistent with research from the 1970s in which researchers demonstrated that word perception could be successful even when listeners heard only a fraction of the speech stimulus. This is referred to as the **gating paradigm** (Grosjean, 1980). In the field of electronics, the term "gating" is used to refer to selecting a portion of a waveform. Sound waves can be selected from a speech stream and played to a listener. Researchers investigating speech perception have gated speech waves and played portions of the speech signal to listeners in order to determine how much or how little of the speech had to be heard for the word to be perceived (Ellis et al., 1971; Grosjean, 1980; Nooteboom, 1981; Tyler, 1984). The isolation point is the duration of the stimulus that must be played for the word to be identified, based on its acoustic characteristics alone (Grosjean, 1996).

An important theoretical question was how listeners use information from the context to generate or access the cohort of candidates and then to select and integrate the recognized word (Taft & Hambly, 1986). In the early descriptions of the model, the processing to generate the cohort was envisioned as driven completely by the sensory input. In the case of listening, the input is the speech that is heard. **Bottom-up processing** involves using only information available in the stimulus. In contrast, **top-down processing** goes beyond the information in the stimulus to make a determination. Expectations generated from information in memory can influence how the stimulus is interpreted. A revised version of the cohort model (Marslen-Wilson, 1989; Marslen-Wilson & Warren, 1994) proposed that top-down processing may influence relatively late aspects of processing. The context would not prevent the activation of possible words in the cohort or be used to select one of the candidates from the cohort, but information about the context may be used to integrate the selected word. For example, a group of people are having lunch, and one person says, "Who made the salad? I really hate gar… ." If the word turns out to be *garlic,* it may be expected to a greater extent than the word *gardening* and be integrated into the context faster.

In a particularly intricate and compelling study to provide evidence for the cohort model of speech perception, Zwitserlood (1989) demonstrated how the activations of different members of the cohort change over time. More importantly, the experiment's results revealed that listeners do not use information from biasing sentence context to guide the activation of initial members of the cohort, but they can use contextual information to narrow down the cohort before encountering the recognition point of the target word. In the experiment, as participants listened to sentence fragments, they made a judgment about a visually presented word. **Cross modal tasks** are used in experiments in which participants process language in two sensory modalities – auditory and visual. The participant's task was to decide as quickly and as accurately as possible whether the visually presented word was a word versus not a word. Since the 1970s, this judgment has been known as a lexical decision and the task is the **lexical decision task** (Meyer & Schvaneveldt, 1971; Meyer et al., 1975; Schvaneveldt & Meyer, 1973).

Zwitserlood (1989) carefully selected target words for the lexical decision task and constructed sentence fragments. The experiment was conducted in Dutch with native Dutch speakers. In an example trial, the sentence fragment was presented up to a target syllable */kap/,* which would lead to the activation of the Dutch words *kapitein* (captain) and *kapitaal* (capital). In the experiment, Zwitserlood (1989) used four versions of each sentence fragment, which varied the amount of the syllable that participants heard before the word appeared on the screen for the lexical decision task. Sentence contexts were strongly biasing toward one of the possible words (e.g., *With dampened spirits the men stood around the grave. They mourned the loss of their captain vs. The next word is captain*). For each target word fragment (e.g., /kap/), prior testing using the gating paradigm was carried out with the word fragment in the biasing and the neutral contexts to determine the recognition point, when the word is unambiguously recognizable, and the isolation point, when the word is recognizable by the majority of people but instances of the alternative word also occur; and two earlier points, with the earliest point leading to the production of more alternative words versus target words. Participants made a lexical decision to Dutch words meaning *ship* or *money* (i.e., *schip* and *geld*)or to a non-word control. The results of the experiment showed that biasing context did not influence reaction times to the lexical decision words when they were presented quickly after the onset of the target word; thus, context did not prevent participants from activating the competitor word as part of the initial cohort. The effect of context was observed when the lexical decision word was presented later on with the word related to *captain* being responded to more quickly than the word related to the competing word *capital*. The results showed that listeners use information from the context during the process of integrating words into their mental representation of the overall meaning of the sentence.

Recent research utilizing a different methodology provides some of the most compelling studies supporting the cohort model. The research used the **visual world paradigm**, which involves recording eye movements as participants interact with a visual scene or a display of physical objects and listen to spoken instructions (Cooper, 1974; Allopenna et al., 1988; Tanenhaus et al., 1995). As the speech stream unfolds over time, the researchers measure eye movements. By analyzing what the listener looks at during the speech stream, the researchers can infer what words the speech stream has activated in the listener's mind. The visual world paradigm has been used to investigate numerous aspects of language processing. Because there is a necessary reliance on a predetermined array of objects that constrains what participants can see, some researchers have suggested that participants may not reflect typical language processing (Huettig et al., 2011).

In an early study, Allopenna et al. (1988) used the visual world paradigm to investigate speech perception. Participants were shown a set of objects situated in front of them. They were told that they would hear instructions played over speakers and they should carry out the activity specified in the instructions. In one trial, they viewed an array of objects, including a carriage, a speaker, a beetle, and a beaker. They heard "Pick up the beaker." Analysis of eye movements showed that, overall, participants looked most often at the beaker and least often at the carriage. Of particular interest was the fact that the beetle received as many looks as the beaker within 400 milliseconds following the onset of the word *beaker*. After that point, the number of looks to the beetle declined sharply, while the number of looks to the beaker increased. The results suggested that on hearing the first part of the word *beaker,* both words came to mind. After the 400 millisecond point, there was a slight increase in the number of looks to the word *speak*er, which had a similar ending as the word *beaker*. These results and others provide insight into how the perceptions of sounds lead to the activation of mental representations of words.

Characteristics of words themselves can predict how likely they are to be perceived. One of the most robust phenomena in listening and reading is the **word frequency effect** – there is a processing advantage for common (more frequent) words versus uncommon (less frequent) words (Brysbaert et al., 2011). Early research in speech perception showed that common words were more likely to be perceived than uncommon words (Savin, 1963; Tyler, 1984; Warren & Marslen-Wilson, 1987). For example, using a gating task, Tyler (1984) showed that high frequency words were significantly more likely to be perceived during the briefest presentations of spoken words when compared to medium and low frequency words. As participants heard longer segments of the words, the rate of responding with high frequency words declined. The word frequency effect has also been explored in numerous studies of visual word perception (Rayner et al., 2012). We examine the theories of the word frequency effect as well as other word-specific variables that affect word perception in Chapter 4.

In summary, the cohort model of speech perception has been an influential theory since its inception in the 1980s. Listeners hear the speech stream and activate in memory a cohort of words that contain the phonemes that are heard. As more of the speech stream is processed, the words in the cohort are gradually reduced to contain only those words having the phonemes that have been heard. Listeners may perceive the word by either determining that the cohort has been reduced to a single word with the characteristics matching the speech stream or selecting a target word from other contenders in the cohort.

The TRACE Model

The **TRACE model** of speech perception (Elman & McClelland, 1988; McClelland & Elman, 1986; McClelland et al., 1986) is a computer program created in 1986 to recognize individual words. It is designed to receive speech as input and the identity of the speech as output, thereby simulating human speech perception. Computer models of human cognitive processes became possible in the decades since the cognitive revolution in 1960 and became much easier to create since the mass availability of computers in the 1980s. The TRACE model utilized a type of computer architecture known as **connectionism** (Dawson, 2004). There are two central elements in a connectionist model: **nodes**, which can be thought of as representing in an abstract, metaphoric way neurons or groups of neurons in the brain; and **connections**, which correspond loosely to how neurons communicate. Researchers specify the number and organization of nodes and connections. The TRACE model is composed of three layers of nodes, representing the features (F), phonemes (P), and words (W). The input is used by the feature layer. The processing carried out in the feature layer can be used by the phoneme layer. The processing carried out in the word layer can be used by the word layer. Importantly, the processing in the word layer can also be used by the phoneme layer. The organization of the layers and how information passes between layers are illustrated in Figure 3.6.

As you learned in Chapter 1, an important theoretical debate in psycholinguistics involves the debate about whether there are specialized modules involved in carrying out different aspects of language processing. Researchers who reject the existence of language modules advocate interactive processing models, in which processing involves the use of multiple types

Figure 3.6 The TRACE Model

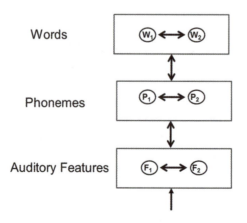

Words

Phonemes

Auditory Features

of information consulted simultaneously (i.e., in parallel versus serially, one process at a time). One of the most compelling aspects of connectionist models is that they are designed to also simulate human learning. Models are equipped with a learning rule to dictate how the numerical settings of the nodes are changed based on how different the model's output is from the input. A model that is able to *identify* a spoken word input would produce an output that is identical to the input. In the beginning of any model, perfect identification does not occur. So, a common learning rule involves making numeric changes to the nodes based on how far from the correct output the model is. Over numerous input-output tests, with nodes being adjusted based on how incorrect the output is, the model gets better at producing accurate responses.

In the 1980s and 90s, the TRACE model and the interactive processing that it allows promised to provide explanations for the apparent top-down processing effects in speech perception that researchers had discovered. Some of these examples involved listeners easily able to perceive incomplete or ambiguous speech. For example, experiments conducted in 1980 demonstrated what is now called the **Ganong effect** (Ganong, 1980). Listeners' perception of an ambiguous speech stimulus depended on the surrounding context. When one hears an ambiguous speech sound between a /g/ and a /k/, it was shown to be perceived as a /g/ when it precedes -ift and as a /k/ when it precedes -iss. The listener perceives *gift* and *kiss,* respectively. The results are consistent with listeners using information about the context during word recognition. Using contextual information in this way is an example of top-down processing. Within the TRACE model, these results can be viewed as arising from the flow of information between the phoneme and word level layers and the flow of information between the phoneme and feature information. Despite the fact that some feature-level information is missing from the input, the subsequent input involving two or three phonemes (i.e., /is/ and /ift/, respectively) leads to the words *gift* and *kiss* being highly active at the word level and that information can lead to activations of /g/ and /k/ at the phoneme level. That information leads to activation at the feature level of more g-like or more k-like features.

Another line of research from the 1970s provides an example of listeners using contextual information to comprehend speech, specifically when a phoneme is missing. The research conducted by Warren and colleagues (Obusek & Warren, 1973; Warren, 1970; Warren & Warren, 1970) demonstrated the **phonemic restoration effect**. Using software that could edit a recorded sample of speech, Warren and colleagues removed the band of energy corresponding to a single phoneme and replaced it with a recording of a cough. For example, in the sentence *The state governors met with their respective legislatures convening in the capital city*, the first /s/ in *legislatures* was removed and replaced with the sound of a cough. When the altered recording was played for listeners, a curious thing happened. No one noticed the missing phoneme. Everyone perceived the /s/ despite it not being present in the recording. If the /s/ were replaced with a tone or a buzz, listeners performed similarly, recognizing the word as *legislatures* and not noticing that anything was missing. However, they found that if the phoneme /s/ was replaced by silence, listeners noticed that the phoneme was missing and they had not perceptually restored it with the help of top-down processing.

Warren and Warren (1970) further showed that listeners can use information from a relatively distant part of the sentence context during word perception. They created a beginning sentence fragment in which the first phoneme of the target word was replaced with a cough. The sentence fragment was spliced together with four different sentence endings. The resulting sentences are shown here:

1   It was found that the *eel was on the orange.
2   It was found that the *eel was on the axle.
3   It was found that the *eel was on the shoe.
4   It was found that the *eel was on the table.

The results showed that, once again, listeners did not perceive that there was a phoneme missing from the sentence. Interestingly, the phoneme that was restored on the basis of top-down processing differed across the four sentences:

1   When the last word of the sentence was *orange*, listeners interpreted the target word as *peel*.
2   When the last word of the sentence was *axle*, listeners interpreted the target word as *wheel*.
3   When the last word of the sentence was *shoe*, listeners interpreted the target word as *heel*.
4   When the last word of the sentence was *table*, listeners interpreted the target word as *meal*.

The phonemic restoration effect continues to be researched. For example, children have been shown to experience it less often than adults (Newman, 2004, 2006). Liederman et al. (2011) investigated whether the likelihood of experiencing the effect differed for men and women. The results showed that while men and women experience the phonemic restoration effect frequently, women experience it more often than men. Woman appeared to use top-down processing more than men, although it is unclear why this is so. Research also showed that when listeners increased cognitive demands, as when one must carry out a visual search task during listening, the occurrence of phonemic restoration increases (Mattys et al., 2014).

In a series of studies, Arthur Samuel (1981a, 1981b, 1987, 1991, 1996; Samuel & Ressler, 1986) investigated the theoretical question of what exactly listeners were restoring in previous phonemic restoration tasks. Were listeners experiencing this auditory illusion by restoring actual phonemes associated with perceptual features, or by restoring more abstract, high-level information? Because listeners are not consciously aware of how the phonemic restoration effect occurs, the only way to answer the question was with cleverly designed experiments. Samuel (1981a) varied the type of sound used to replace the missing phoneme. Samuel aimed to determine the extent to which the phoneme restoration effect was due to top-down or bottom-up processing. He hypothesized that the effect stemmed from bottom-up, perceptual processing rather than top-down processing, which had been the prevailing view. He obtained support for the hypothesis by showing that the likelihood that a phoneme would be restored depended on the perceptual characteristics of the missing phoneme and the type of sound used to replace the phoneme. Missing vowels were more likely to be restored when replaced by a tone versus white noise (high energy sound often described as hissing). In contrast, missing fricatives (e.g., /f/ as in *fixture* and /θ/ as in *thin*) were more likely to be restored when replaced by white noise than a tone. Subsequent experiments showed that when the missing phoneme occurred in a word with lots of words with similar sounds (neighbors), listeners were more likely to experience phonemic restoration than when the missing phoneme occurred in a word with few similar sounding words. The **neighborhood effect** (Goldinger et al., 1989; Luce et al., 1990) refers to the fact that during visual word recognition, words sharing letters with other words are recognized faster than other words. In a lexical decision task, the neighborhood effect claims that words with larger neighborhood sizes will have quicker reaction times, suggesting that neighbors facilitate the activation of other neighborhood words.

Samuel (1996) carried out additional experiments in which he investigated whether the likelihood of phoneme restoration depended on whether the missing sound occurred in an actual word (e.g., *bent*) versus a pseudoword (a sequence of sounds that do not correspond to a known English word, e.g., *benk*). He pointed out that within the TRACE model, greater phonemic restoration would be expected in words rather than in pseudowords, as information from the word level of nodes could influence processing at the phoneme level for conditions involving actual words, but not for conditions involving pseudowords. In theories of speech perception that are strictly modular, performance in the word and pseudoword conditions would not be expected to differ. The results of five experiments provided evidence for the TRACE model prediction of a lexical effect (i.e., status as a word mattered). However, the lexical effect was remarkably small.

There is no consensus about which model provides the most complete account of how speech is perceived. A number of alternative models of speech perception have been proposed, including the race model (Cutler & Norris, 1979), the general auditory approach to speech perception (Diehl & Kluender, 1989; Diehl et al., 1991; Pardo & Remez, 2006) and the fuzzy logical model of speech perception (Massaro & Chen, 2008; Massaro & Oden, 1995; Oden & Massaro, 1978). Future research is needed to determine which model will emerge as the winner, generating predictions that are confirmed in research studies and being able to account for other perceptual phenomena that are discovered.

In this section, we reviewed models of speech perception and the research that has been conducted to test their assumptions. The oldest model is the motor theory of speech perception, which emphasizes the link between listening and speaking. We then reviewed the most impactful model thus far – the cohort model. Listening involves activating in memory similar sounding words and relying on the unfolding context to reduce the possibilities. The research suggests that listeners rely on information from the context relatively late in the process of word perception. The last model reviewed was the TRACE model, which provided a framework in which the use of top-down information during speech perception is possible. Despite the promise of connectionist models like the TRACE model to account for non-modular top-down processing effects, research consistently shows that the role of context in recognizing speech is limited.

 Time out for Review

Key Terms

Bottom-up processing
Categorical perception
Cocktail party effect
Connectionism
Connections
Cross modal task
Dichotic listening technique
Digit span
Ganong effect

Gating paradigm
Lexical decision task
Logogon
Logogen model
McGurk effect
Mirror neurons
Neighborhood effect
Nodes
Phonemic restoration effect

Recognition point
Selective attention
Top-down processing
TRACE model
Uniqueness point
Visual world paradigm
Word frequency effect

Review Questions

1 What is the dichotic listening task? What has the research using the technique shown about the nature of selective attention?
2 What is the McGurk effect? How is the effect evidence that we use our eyes to hear?
3 What is the motor theory of speech perception? What evidence provides support for the theory?
4 What is the cohort model of speech perception? What evidence provides support for the theory?
5 If one heard the syllable "can," list at least five words that would be activated in memory according to the cohort model of speech perception.
6 What is the visual world paradigm? How is it used to investigate speech perception?
7 What is the TRACE theory of speech perception? What evidence provides support for the theory?
8 What is the phonemic restoration effect? What factors have been shown to influence the likelihood that a listener will experience it?
9 How do researchers distinguish top-down and bottom-up processing in the context of speech perception?

The Link between Speech Perception and Music Processing

Researchers have explored possible links between language and music since the 1800s (Darwin, [1872] 2007). Recent research by Diana Deutsch (2013) has investigated individual differences in musical pitch perception. A series of studies has found that the acoustic characteristics of speakers' native language may predict the likelihood of speakers having **perfect pitch** – the ability to identify or reproduce a musical note without relying on a reference note (Bachem, 1955). Among native English speakers, perfect pitch is relatively rare, found in only 1 in 10,000 people (Profita & Bidder, 1988; Takeuchi & Hulse, 1993). Well-known musicians and composers have been reported as having perfect pitch, including Mozart and Beethoven (Deutsch, 2013). However, having perfect pitch does not necessarily predict overall musical ability in an individual.

Recent research suggests that among native speakers of tonal languages (e.g., Mandarin, Cantonese, Vietnamese, and Thai), perfect pitch is much more common than among speakers of non-tonal languages (e.g., English) (Deutsch, 2013). Tonal language words are associated with a distinguishing pitch. For example, in Mandarin, the word *ma* produced with a high pitch means *mother*, but means *hemp* when produced with a pitch that changes from low to high (also called a rising pitch). In Mandarin, the pitch pattern for a word can also be from high to low (also called falling pitch). The word *ma* can be produced with five pitch patterns yielding five distinct words (Yip, 2002). In multisyllabic words, each syllabic can have its own pitch pattern. Tonal languages are more common in some parts of the world (e.g., Asia, Africa, and Central America) than in others (e.g., Europe).

In a study with speakers of a non-tonal language, Burnham and Brooker (2002) presented participants with Thai tones under three different conditions: speech; filtered speech; and violin tones. They found that participants with perfect pitch were far more accurate in discriminating the tones than participants without perfect pitch. Research by Deutsch and colleagues (Deutsch, 2002; Deutsch et al., 2004; Deutsch et al., 2006; Deutsch et al., 2009) has shown that speakers of tonal languages are more likely to have perfect pitch than speakers of non-tonal languages. Deutsch et al. (2006) compared performance on pitch perception for two groups of music students, one in the USA and one in China. Information about the language background and the musical training of both groups was obtained. The results showed that performance on pitch perception was affected by both factors. For both groups, the earlier in life that musical training had been started, the more accurate participants were. Overall, students in China performed far more accurately on the pitch perception task than students in the USA.

The speech-to-song illusion occurs when a short excerpt of speech comes to sound as though it is being sung, when it is listened to over and over again (Deutsch et al., 2011). Deutsch discovered the illusion serendipitously while preparing an audio recording for publication. The exact sequence must be repeated in order for the illusion to occur. The illusion has been found to occur in other languages, such as German (Falk & Rathcke, 2010) and Mandarin (Zhang, 2011). The explanation for the illusion is that perceiving speech sequences repeatedly may come to activate the regions of the brain involved in processing music (Tierney et al., 2013). The specific manner in which the brain activation occurs is unknown. One suggestion is that the repeated activations of the interconnected representations of words in memory result in a reduction of detail of specific words being perceived (Castro, 2014).

Interestingly, there has been research investigating how melodies are recognized (Dalla Bella et al., 2003). The researchers' approach was to determine whether melodies might be activated in memory during listening in the same way that words are as described by the cohort model. They used the gating technique to create melody fragments of varying durations. Participants listened to melody fragments from familiar and unfamiliar melodies. The results showed that participants recognized melodies after listening to about three seconds, which typically corresponded to the melody's isolation point. Familiar melodies were recognized earlier than unfamiliar melodies. Performance across participants was not significantly related to prior training in music. Dalla Bella et al.'s (2003) view of how melodies are recognized within the cohort model framework is that after hearing the beginning notes of a melody, the access stage involves a cohort of similar sounding melodies being activated in the listener's mind. As listening continues, the selection stage involves pruning the cohort of melodies that do not match the input until a single melody remains in the cohort, which would be the melody that the listener recognizes as the melody being played.

Schulkind and colleagues have argued that melody recognition occurs in a fashion similar to how words are recognized during speech perception (Schulkind, 2004; Schulkind & Davis, 2013). In many studies, they investigated how critical the hearing of initial notes of a melody is to melody identification. In Schulkind and Davis (2013), melodies were edited using sound wave editing software to delete individual notes. The location of the deleted notes was varied. In Experiment 1, deleted notes occurred either early in the melody or later in the melody. In Experiment 2, participants heard the melody with the first, third, fifth, seventh, ninth, or eleventh note deleted. In both experiments, performance was significantly less accurate when initial notes were deleted. The authors point out that participants' errors appeared inconsistent with the cohort model. When participants could not identify the melody, they most often could not guess what it was. In accordance with the cohort model, all melodies should have led to the activation of a cohort of melodies during the access stage; thus, multiple competing melodies should always come to mind and be available to be used as a response when the correct melody was not chosen as the response. Schulkind and Davis (2013) concluded that melodies appear to be recognized in an "all or none" manner, which cannot be accounted for in the current cohort model.

This section reviewed some of the connections between speech perception and the perception of music. We learned that those who grow up speaking tonal languages may be more likely to develop perfect pitch than those who grow up speaking non-tonal languages. We also learned that language learning and acquisition of perfect pitch may have a critical period. Recent research has attempted to explain how melodies are recognized. The cohort model was used as a framework. The earliest study produced results consistent with the cohort model; however, subsequent studies suggest that melody recognition may occur differently than speech.

Time out for Review

Key Terms

Perfect pitch

Review Questions

1   What is perfect pitch? To what extent is having perfect pitch related to one's previous language experience?
2   To what extent are speech and melodies recognized similarly? Does the research suggest that one model can explain both types of perception?

Summary

Speech perception is an amazing human ability that computers have only recently been programmed to simulate. The nature of speech presents challenges for humans and computers. The phonemes, syllables, and words in speech are not cleanly separated, which is referred to as the segmentation problem, and some speech sounds are articulated together causing the sounds to overlap – co-articulation. The physical characteristics of speech vary widely across speakers and also for the same speaker, which is referred to as the problem of invariance. The human listener adapts quickly to different speakers, but as we age, we experience changes in our ability to perceive some frequencies of sound. These perceptual changes affect the perception of some phonemes more than others. Over the past 40 years, there have been several theories of speech perception proposed. Among the most important facts that the models must explain is our effortless ability to fill in missing information during speech perception, enabling us to perceive phonemes that are present in the speech stream. Of the models, contemporary researchers tend to prefer the cohort or TRACE models for their ability to explain a wide range of data; however, as you learned, the architecture and assumptions in the models are quite different. Lastly, you learned about a relatively new line of research showing a link between how we perceive speech and how we perceive musical melodies; however, more research is needed in order to determine if a single theory can account for both types of perceptual processing.

Recommended Books, Films, and Websites

Deutsch, D. (2013). *Psychology of Music* (3rd edn). New York: Academic Press.

Fowler, C. A., Shankweiler, D. & Studdert-Kennedy, M. (2016). Perception of the speech code revisited: Speech is alphabetic after all. *Psychological Review*, 123(2), 125–50.

Hugdahl, K. (1988). *Handbook of Dichotic Listening: Theory, Methods and Research*. New York: Wiley.

International Dialects of English Archive. www.dialectsarchive.com.

NOVA (1995). *Mystery of the Senses: Hearing*. [TV Series]. United States: Public Broadcasting System.

Pisoni, D. & Remez, R. (2011) *The Handbook of Speech Perception.* New York: Wiley-Blackwell.

Rossing, T. D., Moore, F. R. & Wheeler, P. A. (2001). *Science of Sound* (3rd edn). Boston, MA: Addison-Wesley.

4

HOW IS SPEECH PLANNED AND PRODUCED?

Chapter Content

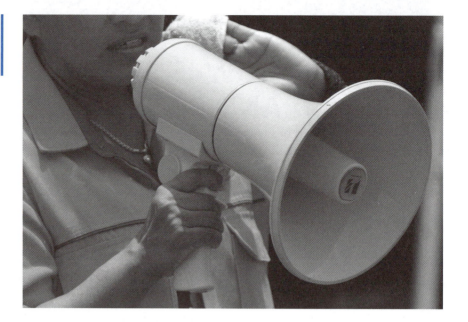

Talking is an activity that occupies a great deal of our time. On rare occasions, we intend to say one word, but say another instead. These are known as **speech errors** and also **slips of the tongue**. Most of the time, our speech is error-free and smooth. Speech professionals refer to the smoothness of speech as **speech fluency**. In contrast, **disfluencies** are utterances in which there is a reduction in the normal flow of speech, as when one pauses or stutters. It is important to note that speech-language pathologists may use the term "disfluency" to refer to speech problems more narrowly than psycholinguists, as the former are usually focused on getting clients to produce *normal* sounding speech. In contrast, psycholinguists are more likely to take into consideration how speakers are planning and implementing an utterance from the point of selecting the utterance's intention to evaluating whether the articulated utterance had the intended effect on the listener. Estimates suggest that disfluencies are quite rare, occurring in only about 6 percent of utterances (Bortfeld et al., 2001; Fox Tree, 1995).

In this chapter, we learn about the research on speech planning and production. In the first section, we examine how the study of speech errors yielded important insights into speech planning. The second section describes the laboratory experiments on speech production, which created situations in which participants produced speech errors at a higher rate than in everyday life. The section also highlights the critical findings that informed contemporary models of speech production. In the third section, we review the models of speech planning and speech production that researchers have proposed over the last four decades. Lastly, we discuss the relatively small literature on the planning of handwriting and typewriting.

Naturalistic Studies of Speech Production

A great deal of what is known about how speech is produced has been discovered through the collection and analysis of mistakes during speaking, known as speech errors or slips of the tongue. Researchers keep systematic and careful records of the errors they observe, using a methodology known as **naturalistic observation**. For most speakers, speech errors occur infrequently, affecting only about 2 percent of our utterances (Deese, 1978, 1984) or less (Bock & Miller, 1991); thus, researchers must devote a great deal of time to record enough examples for their analyses. As you will learn in this section, the study of speech using naturalistic observation has a relatively long history and has yielded numerous insights into how speech is planned.

Speech Errors

Speech errors can sometimes catch our attention during conversations. In the rare case, they may make the news. In an example from 2016, President Alexander Lukashenko of Belarus, an Eastern European country between Poland and Russia, addressed his nation in a live television broadcast (Towers, 2016). Most of the country's citizenry was watching closely. During his speech, he intended to deliver an encouraging bit of advice to people and said that citizens should *develop themselves*, but instead, he said that citizens should *undress themselves*. In the following hours and days, social media sites were filled with photos of citizens following the presidential command. People posted photos of themselves in various levels of undress doing everyday activities (e.g., sitting at a desk at work, doing household chores, chopping wood, playing in a garage band, etc.). Everyone understood that President Lukashenko did not actually want them to undress themselves, but the error provided an opportunity to have a little fun. Lukashenko explained that the error was due to his unfamiliarity with a new technology being used for the broadcast.

When you think about speech errors, you are likely to first think of the classic type first described by Sigmund Freud ([1901] 1971). Freud focused primarily on the type of error that can be perceived by listeners as reflecting the speaker's unconscious state of mind. For example, a speaker may find the listener attractive and produce an error that inadvertently makes a reference to something about romance, dating or sex. Freud wrote about a professor who said the following during one of his lectures: "In the case of female genitals, in spite of many temptations ... I beg your pardon, experiments." Such errors are referred to as **Freudian slips**. It is important to note that not all Freudian slips are related to sexual themes. Any error in which the listener could interpret the error as revealing the mind of the speaker without the speaker wanting it revealed could be categorized as a Freudian slip. Consider the case of the employee who intended to give his overweight supervisor a compliment by saying *He is a great leader,* but instead said *He is a great eater.* You are likely to be able to find many examples of Freudian slips using popular Internet search engines.

Freudian slips do occur; however, research suggests that they may be among the rarest types of speech error. More run-of-the-mill speech errors, called **spoonerisms**, are those in which the speaker transposes the initial sounds or letters of two or more words. Such errors are unlikely to be related to taboo themes. They are named after Reverend William Archibald Spooner (1844–1930), who was famous for the large number of errors he made. Spooner worked at the prestigious Oxford University (Hayter, 1977), lecturing on philosophy, divinity, and history. One of his well-known slips of the tongue was:

You have hissed all my mystery lectures, and were caught fighting a liar in the quad. Having tasted two worms, you will leave by the next town drain.

Can you figure out what he intended to say? Instead of *hissed,* he likely intended to say *missed.* Instead of *fighting a liar,* he likely intended to say *lighting a fire.* He was well liked by students and colleagues, perhaps due to his status at Oxford and/or his other personal characteristics. His errors were noticed and a source of amusement. Table 4.1 provides some additional examples of Spooner's errors.

Table 4.1 Examples of Spooner's Notable Speech Errors

Utterance	Intended utterance
It is kisstomary to cuss the bride.	It is customary to kiss the bride.
A well boiled icycle	A well-oiled bicycle
Go and shake a tower	Go and take a shower
Such Bulgarians should be vanished	Such vulgarians should be banished
Is the bean dizzy?	Is the dean busy?
Will nobody pat my hiccup?	Will nobody pick up my hat?

Source: Hayter (1977)

The contemporary science of speech errors begins with the work of Victoria "Vicki" Fromkin (1923–2000) (Fromkin, 1971). She received her PhD from the University of California, Los Angeles, where she spent her entire career as a professor and an administrator. She is best known for her textbook *An Introduction to Language* (Fromkin et al., 2013), first published in 1973 and now in its 10th edition. Over the years, co-authors have worked on keeping the book current. Her research on speech errors is but one of her many contributions to psycholinguistics. Fromkin (1988) pointed out that speech errors have been studied as far back as the 8th century: in *Errors of Populace,* al-Kisaa'i, an Arab linguist, described his efforts to collect and analyze speech errors. In the area of speech error research, she noted that her work followed in the tradition of researchers whose work began in the late 1800s (Meringer, 1908; Meringer & Mayer, [1895] 1978).

Fromkin's work was groundbreaking because not only did she collect the largest corpus of errors, but also information about the context and the likely intended utterance. Our understanding of how speech is planned and produced began with the collection of large samples of speech errors observed in everyday life. Her model of speech planning served as a starting point in the 20th century for understanding how speech is planned and produced, both our speech that contains an error and our speech that is error-free. We will review her model in detail later in this chapter. Table 4.2 provides examples of speech errors Fromkin categorized by type. As you review them, do you think that they are similar to the ones Spooner made?

On first glance, the examples in Table 4.2 of speech gone awry may appear chaotic. Phonemes are sometimes left out (omissions) and sometimes put in the wrong places (additions). A pair of phonemes may appear in switched positions (exchanges). Phonemes that should be produced later in an utterance appear earlier than they should (anticipations), and phonemes that were produced early in an utterance get produced again later (perseverations). When considering errors involving whole words, we find similar types of errors. An intended word may be omitted from the utterance or an unintended word inserted. Words

Table 4.2 Examples of Speech Errors Categorized by Type

Type of error	Example	Intended utterance
Omission	two hundred dugs	two hundred drugs
Addition	and by allowzing two separate cases	and by allowing two separate cases
Lexical substitution	it's at the bottom of the stacks	it's at the top of the stacks
Morpheme substitution	it was long underdue	it was long overdue
Phonological substitution	the bottle of the page	the bottom of the page
Lexical exchange	a fifty pound dog of bag food	a fifty pound bag of dog food
Phonological exchange	for mar fore	for far more
Anticipations	a reek long race	a week long race
Perseverations	alsho share	also share
Blends	Did you bring your clarinola?	Did you bring your clarinet/viola?
Morpheme shift	and Rachel come ins	and Rachel comes in
Morpheme stranding	He has already trunked two packs	He has already packed two trunks

Source: Fromkin (1971)

from the utterance may be involved in an exchange, appearing in switched positions. Word exchanges typically involve the switching of two words from the same syntactic category (noun, adjective, or verb) (Garrett, 1975; Stemberger, 1985). Occasionally, an utterance may contain an attempt to say a word, but it is a combining of two related words (a blend). In addition to phonemes and words, individual morphemes may be involved in speech errors. A morpheme may be omitted or inserted. An intended morpheme may be substituted for an unintended one. A morpheme may be produced earlier or later than intended (morpheme shifts). Some errors involve morphemes appearing in incorrect locations. Consider the error *They are Turking talkish*. The suffixes *-ing* and *-ish* are in the right place but attached to the wrong words, while the root words have switched places. These are called **morpheme stranding errors**, perhaps because the morphemes have been left stranded in their original positions by the root words that have moved.

Even more complex errors have been observed in languages with tones, which allow speakers to produce syllables with either different pitch contours. The same syllable can be produced with pitch rising or falling across the production of the syllable or with a mixed pattern in which pitch initially rises as the syllable is produced and then falls by the end of the production of the syllable. Numerous languages have tones: including the Bantu languages of Africa; dialects of Chinese, including Mandarin; Thai; and Norwegian (Yip, 2002). The Language Spotlight box discusses speech errors involving tones in Mandarin.

Some types of errors show up more frequently in speech error corpora than others. Anticipations have been found to be more frequent in Meringer's (1908) German corpus, in Cohen's (1966) corpus of Dutch (Nooteboom, 1973),

Speech Errors Involving Tones in Mandarin

Mandarin has 26 consonants, 12 vowels, 4 tones, and 1 tone that is characterized as neutral (Wan, 2006). The tone with which a syllable is produced often changes the meaning. For example, the word *ma* can be produced with four different tones, resulting in three distinct meanings. When *ma* is produced with a high and steady tone, the meaning is *mother*. When it is produced beginning with a high pitch that falls to the end, the meaning is *to scold*. When the pitch starts with a middling pitch and rises to the end, the meaning is *to bother*. *Ma* can also mean *horse*, if the speaker's pitch starts high, falls until the middle of the syllable, and then rises to the end. When produced with a neutral tone, *ma* functions as a particle that signals that the utterance is a question. When learning Mandarin, the tone must be learned word by word, just as the consonant-vowel sequence is learned.

Until recently, little was known about how tones are involved in speech errors in Mandarin (Wan, 2006, 2007; Wan & Jaeger, 2003). Of particular interest was whether the involvement of tone in errors differed from the involvement of consonants and vowels in errors. Wan (2006) analyzed a corpus of 2,515 speech errors produced by speakers of Taiwanese Mandarin and found that errors most often involved consonants and least often vowels (48 percent), with errors involving tone less often than consonants (7 percent), but more often than vowels (23 percent). The results are consistent with prior research by Gandour (1977) whose corpus of speech errors in Thai indicated that tone was independent of the consonants and vowels on which it occurred. Wan (2007) compared the tone errors with those involving consonants and vowels by type of error (perseverations, anticipations, and exchanges) and found that tone was involved as often in the different types of errors as consonants and vowels. Wan's (2007) data also replicated a second aspect of Gandour's (1977) work, showing that falling tones are more frequently involved in speech errors than other tones. More research is needed to investigate how the consonants, vowels, and tones of utterances are planned during normal speaking (see also Shen, 1992). In Chapter 12, you will learn about how speech is impaired following brain injury in speakers of Shona, a tonal language spoken in Africa.

and in Schelvis's (1985) corpus of Dutch (Nooteboom, 2005) (i.e., 61 percent, 78 percent, and 60 percent respectively). The next most frequent type of error was perseverations (28 percent, 15 percent, and 22 percent). Exchanges occurred only 11 percent, 7 percent, and 18 percent of the time. Some have argued that exchange errors occur more commonly than these data suggest (Shattuck-Hufnagel, 1979). Relying on corpora analyses to estimate the frequencies of different types of errors may be problematic. There are many factors that may lead to inaccuracy in speech error collection, such as mishearing what has been said (also referred to as a slip of the ear), individual inaccuracy-prone practices or bias on the part of observers, and differences in how easy some errors can be heard compared to others (Perez et al., 2007). For example, listeners may fail to notice lexical substitutions in which an error sounds similar to the intended word, known as **malapropisms**. For example, someone might say *Texas has a lot of electrical votes* rather than *electoral votes*. The listener is left to guess what the speaker aimed to say. **Observer bias** refers to any inaccuracies introduced into a dataset due to the observer. In the next section, we will see whether the frequency estimates obtained in laboratory studies of speech errors are different from those obtained in these corpora studies.

Since Fromkin's (1971) work on speech errors, there have been numerous studies of speech errors in different populations of participants. The research is important because it is valuable to know whether the types of errors that occur do so with the same frequencies across different types of speakers. In the Classic Research box, you will learn about Jeri Jaeger's (1992, 2005) research comparing children's speech errors to those made by adults. Other research has shown that speech errors are not the only type of language production errors that occur. In languages in which the hands, rather than the vocal tract, are used to communicate (e.g., American Sign Language), signers produce **slips of the hand** (Newkirk et al., 1980). In a corpus study, Newkirk et al. (1980) collected 131 examples of slips of the hand. Chapter 13 looks at the psycholinguistic processes involved in the acquisition and use of signed language. Later in this chapter, we will discuss language production errors, **slips of the finger**, which occur during handwriting and typewriting (Berg, 2002).

So far, we have reviewed the various types of speech errors that occur in everyday settings. Errors can involve phonemes, morphemes, and whole words that are omitted and inserted incorrectly into an utterance. Elements of the same type (phonemes, morphemes and whole words) may appear in switched locations. When words are exchanged, they are most often words of the same syntactic category (noun, verb, or adjective). The many examples of speech errors available have come from corpora of errors collected by researchers, such as Fromkin (1971), who have used naturalistic observation. This has its disadvantages, including observer bias. In the next section, we examine more ways in which speech disfluency can occur.

Speech Disfluencies

Most of the time, speakers' disfluencies occur without much notice on the part of listeners. The most prominent type of disfluency is one in which an error has been detected by the speaker and the speaker makes a correction. The term **repair** refers to speakers' spontaneous correction of errors during speech. Examples of repairs were recorded in Fromkin's (1971) corpus. Her careful recording also showed that speakers often notice they have made an error and rapidly correct it, as in *The exam will occur in class on Wednesday, I mean, Friday*. Studies of repairs have found that speakers tend to repair an error immediately following the error, rather than later in the conversation (Nooteboom, 1967, 1969, 1980). Nooteboom (1980) showed

Jaeger's Corpus of Children's Speech Errors

Prior to Jaeger's (1992, 2005) work, there had not been a compiled corpus of speech errors produced by children. Jeri Jaeger, a linguistics professor at the University of Buffalo, spent ten years collecting speech errors made by her own children and by children she observed in preschool settings. The final corpus contained 1,383 errors. Her corpus was the largest containing children's errors. Stemberger's (1989) corpus contained less than half the number of errors in Jaeger's corpus (2005). Errors recorded from Jaeger's children Anna, Alice, and Bobby occurred when they were between the ages of two and six. Her corpus also included errors submitted to her by colleagues from their observation of their own children. A particularly memorable error included in her corpus was one made by her daughter Anna, who at age four played the role of the Little Pig in the play *The Three Little Pigs*. In response to the Big Bad Wolf saying "Little Pig, Little Pig, let me come in," Anna said "No, not by the chair of my hinny hin hin." This error is an example of a phonological exchange. The /h/ of *hair* was exchanged with the /ch/ of *chinny, chin, chin*. Using data from the corpus, Jaeger (1992) analyzed children's errors in terms of phonological features (e.g., place of articulation, nasality, and voicing) and compared the analyses to a similar one carried out on speech errors made by adults (Broecke & Goldstein, 1980). The comparison showed that both the errors of children and adults most frequently involve place of articulation, and are least likely to involve nasality. Children's errors were found to involve voicing less often than adults' errors. In her book, Jaeger (2005) convincingly argues that children's errors can be classified in the same categories as the adult errors observed by Fromkin (1971).

Photo 4.2 Children produce speech errors just as adults do. Do you think children notice each other's speech errors when they occur?
Credit: Tup Wanders

that speakers do not generally initiate a repair in the middle of a word. Repairs tend to follow the completion of the word containing the error. His results also showed that speakers repaired errors more often than not (64 percent of the time). The sequence of processing involved in the typical repair includes: speakers noticing an error while speaking and initiating an interruption; planning and producing a **filled pause** (e.g., *uh* or *um*) and possibly other words to indicate an error was made; and planning and producing the intended utterance. Nooteboom's (1980) study suggested that the type of speech error in which the speaker does not make a repair, leaving the listener to hear an unintended message, does occur often enough (approximately 36 percent of the time) to lead to communication failures in conversations. Chapter 9 examines cognitive and social aspects of conversation. Repairs during speaking, particularly the filled pauses that occur during repairs, create a disruption in the flow or smoothness of speech. In the next section, we review what is known about the causes of disfluency and the implications for models of speech planning and production.

In addition to repairs, the other ways in which the flow of speech may be disrupted include filled pauses that occur without a repair, silences, hesitations caused when the speaker has difficulty producing the appropriate word, and stuttering. Typically, filled pauses do not convey linguistic meaning to the listener during our conversations, which explains why most of the time we do not even notice when we use them or when we hear them in others' speech. However, the studies of filled pauses suggest that they can tell us a lot about how speech is planned and produced. Across languages, filled pauses have different phonological characteristics. When speakers of English produce filled pauses, they say *um* or *uh*. Speakers of other languages have similar fillers. German speakers may say *ah*. French speakers may say *euh*. An early proposal was that filled pauses were used by speakers to indicate to others in the conversation that they wished to continue their turn versus being ready to allow another speaker to begin speaking (Maclay & Osgood, 1959). An alternative view suggested that the filler is generated automatically when speech planning hits a snag (Levelt, 1989). The latter view was supported by studies showing that filled pauses were more likely to occur before unpredictable and infrequently used words (Beattie & Butterworth, 1979; Levelt, 1983; Schnadt & Corley, 2006) and also before words having more than one interpretation (Schachter et al., 1991). In an analysis of a large sample of speech from naturalistic settings, Clark and Fox Tree (2002) found a difference between speakers' use of *uh* and *um*. The filler *um* was used before longer delays, and the filler *uh* was used before shorter delays. They proposed that the fillers *um* and *uh* were words, stored in the mental lexicon and retrieved during speech planning as are other words.

Silences during speaking are similar to filled pauses, as they provide more time for the speaker to complete the planning for the upcoming utterance. Having too many silences while speaking can interrupt the flow of speech; however, silences during speaking are common, sometimes accounting for up to half of the time taken by the speaker (Goldman-Eisler, 1968). Research has shown that silences during speaking can last between 250 milliseconds to over 2.5 seconds. A number of studies suggest that the periods of silence during speaking may be related to the speaker's speech planning. During the period of silence, the speaker may be planning the next word or phrase in the utterance (Goldman-Eisler, 1958a, 1958b; Kircher et al., 2004).

Occasionally, a speaker may pause during speaking because the word they would like to say has suddenly slipped their mind. It is a word the speaker knows, but cannot produce at that particular moment. Often the speaker will think of the word later. Such occurrences are referred to as **tip-of-the-tongue (ToT) states** (Schwartz & Brown, 2014). When ToT states occur, a speaker has trouble producing a familiar word. Research on ToT states suggests that speakers have partial awareness of the word that cannot be fully produced. They are often able to report similar sounding words, the number of syllables, or the beginning phoneme. Research starting in the 1990s showed that speakers experience ToT more often when trying to produce infrequent versus frequent words (Brown, 1991); when trying to produce words that are dissimilar versus similar to other words (Harley & Brown, 1998); and when trying to produce proper names versus non-names (Burke et al., 2000). ToT occurs in some speakers more than others. For example, the prevalence of ToT states increases with age (Burke et al., 1991; James & Burke, 2000; Dahlgren, 1998; White & Abrams, 2002). ToT states occur more often in bilinguals than monolingual speakers (Gollan & Acenas, 2004; Gollan & Silverberg, 2001). In the next section, we will be able to determine how the different models of speech planning account for the ToT evidence.

Lastly, the most noticeable and most disruptive of all speech disfluencies is **stuttering.** Stuttering involves difficulty articulating speech smoothly. For most of us, stuttering rarely happens, while for others, stuttering is a long-term problem. A common speech pattern for the individual for whom stuttering is a long-term problem is the repeating of speech sounds at the beginnings of words, such as *ki ki ki ki kick* or *buh buh buh buh ball*. Single speech sounds can also be elongated, as in *sssssssssssssick* and *nnnnnnnnnice*. Speech may contain numerous disfluencies in which there are periods of silence or filled pauses, as in *What is … your … um … um … um … name? Uh … uh … uh … where … um … um … um … do you … um … um … um … live?* Only about 5 percent of the population experiences long-term stuttering (Mansson, 2000). Across individuals, the severity of symptoms varies widely.

Historically, stuttering was seen to be caused by the speaker's psychological problems (Ward, 2006). The modern view of stuttering is that it happens because of glitches in cognitive and/or neural processing that occur during the planning and production of speech. Four types of stuttering exist:

1 The most familiar and most common type is the developmental form, which begins during childhood and typically disappears within two years (Yairi, 1993). It is believed to be related to the biological and cognitive changes that occur as the child ages.

2 The second type of stuttering is inherited, resulting from genetic mutations (Raza et al., 2015). Individuals are affected their entire lives.

3 The third type occurs due to a traumatic brain injury, such as a stroke or blow to the head. Someone who previously had no difficulty producing speech sustains damage to the brain and subsequently has trouble speaking fluently.

4 The fourth type of stuttering is caused by psychological rather than physical factors, such as the speaker's trauma history or underlying thought disorder (e.g., OCD or schizophrenia).

Research that has studied individual speakers affected by stuttering has shown that some types of phonemes and words are more likely to be produced with a stutter than others. Consonants are more likely to be stuttered than vowels (Bernstein, 2005; Quarrington et al., 1962). Nouns were more likely to be stuttered than other types of words (e.g., verbs, adjectives, adverbs) (Quarrington et al., 1962). Words that are infrequent in the language are more likely to be stuttered than common words (Danzger & Halpern, 1973; Hubbard & Prins, 1994; Prins et al., 1997). As you may recall from Chapter 3, "word frequency effect" could be used to describe this pattern of results.

Many people who stutter also produce rapid speech that has unusual speech rhythms. The term **cluttering** describes this relatively rare speaking disorder (Ward, 2006). There are individuals who have the cluttering type of speech patterns who do not stutter. Cluttering can also involve unusually high levels of co-articulation, especially in long words (Góral-Półrola et al., 2016; St. Louis et al., 2007). Speakers diagnosed with cluttering may not be fully aware how their speech sounds to others. The physical act of speaking is not difficult or effortful. To others, speakers with cluttering appear unorganized, poor listeners, and/or distracted. Unlike stuttering, cluttering may also involve thought patterns as well as speaking and writing patterns. An interview with a person with cluttering described her experience when speaking as: "It feels like … about twenty thoughts explode on my mind all at once, and I need to express them all" (Reyes-Alami, 2003). Van Zaalen et al. (2009) proposed that there are two distinct types of cluttering: syntactic cluttering and phonemic cluttering. Recent brain imaging research has shown that those who clutter exhibit abnormal brain activity in several areas involved in the control of speech. We will discuss more disorders related to language in Chapter 14.

In summary, you learned that there is a wide range of speech errors involving the omission, insertion, or exchange of phonemes, morphemes, and whole words. Occasionally, when speakers produce an error, they detect the error and clarify their utterance with a repair. We learned about other examples of speech disfluencies, including silences, pauses, and tip-of-the-tongue states. Severe disfluency can occur for people affected by stuttering and/or cluttering. Those with long-term symptoms of stuttering and cluttering typically seek treatment from a speech-language pathologist. As we will see in the next section, speech errors, the occurrences of filled pauses and ToT states during speaking provide important insights into how we plan and produce our speech.

 Time out for Review

Key Terms

Cluttering
Disfluencies
Filled pause
Freudian slip
Malapropism
Morpheme stranding error

Naturalistic observation
Observer bias
Repair
Slip of the finger
Slip of the hand
Slip of the tongue

Speech error
Speech fluency
Spoonerism
Stuttering
Tip-of-the-tongue
   (ToT) state

Review Questions

1   What was Sigmund Freud's view of the cause of slips of the tongue?
2   Who was Reverend William Archibald Spooner? What contribution did he make to the study of speech planning and production?
3   What was Victoria Fromkin's contribution to the study of speech planning and production?

4 To what extent are the speech errors produced by children similar to or different from speech errors produced by adults?

5 What is a filled pause? When do they occur in speech? What have research studies shown about what filled pauses reveal about how speech is planned and produced?

6 What is a ToT state? What types of words are most likely to lead to a ToT state?

7 What are the characteristics of stuttering and cluttering?

Laboratory Studies of Speech Production

Since the middle of the 20th century, researchers have used laboratory settings to study speech errors specifically and speech production more generally. Researchers invite speakers to the laboratory, where conditions can be controlled and speech can be recorded. Researchers devise tasks for speakers to perform. Each task focuses on a specific aspect of speech processing. Some of the earliest laboratory research on speech production documented how speech varies across individuals. As you recall from Chapter 3, the wide variation in the physical properties of speech contributed to the challenge of explaining how listeners perceive speech. Research starting in the 1950s showed that there are many ways in which speech can vary across individuals. Most of the variation that occurs in how quickly people speak, the loudness of voice, or the clarity of speech goes unnoticed and/or has little impact on the intelligibility of the speech. Studies conducted in the 1960s showed that speakers vary in their rate of speaking (Goldman-Eisler, 1958a, 1958b, 1968). Some people are fast talkers. Some people are slow talkers. Those studies calculated speaking rate in terms of the number of syllables produced per minute. Goldman-Eisler's work documented that individuals' speaking rate is remarkably stable. Those who are fast talkers or slow talkers typically talk quickly or slowly all the time. The research also revealed that our perception of others' speaking rate is strongly influenced by the pauses in our speech, rather than by speech itself. The pauses make up between 40 and 50 percent of our utterances. Fast talkers produce shorter pauses between words than slow talkers.

Research investigated differences in speaking rate due to age. Nip and Green (2013) found that in the young, speaking rate increased with age, as small children speak more slowly than older children. The pausing in the speech of younger participants was longer than in the speech of older participants. They also found that the speed of articulatory movements did not vary significantly with age. Among adults, speaking rate declines in middle age and beyond; however, the slowing in speech is not due to the amount of pausing in speech nor the speed of the lip or jaw movements (Mefferd & Corder, 2014). Older adults may experience more stiffness during speaking, affecting other areas of the vocal tract, such as the tongue, muscles in the throat, and larynx. Changes in these areas may contribute to the slowing of speech. It is also possible that a slowing in cognitive processing, such as those processes involved in formulating the morphological and phonological content of utterances, contributes to the trend (Burke & MacKay, 1997; Thornton & Light, 2006).

Some of the most compelling laboratory studies of speech production involved the manipulation of variables that researchers hypothesized would affect what is said or how quickly it is said. When researchers manipulated variables under laboratory conditions, it is possible to determine whether the manipulation caused an observed result. A **true experiment** is an investigation in which the researcher manipulates one or more variables in order to measure the influence on one or more outcome variables. Unlike studies using naturalistic observation, in laboratory settings, researchers can reduce and sometimes eliminate the effect of confounding variables on the study results. The true experiment is the only research methodology that can establish a causal link between variables (Smith & Davis, 2012). In this section, we will learn about two categories of experiments: those investigating the production of words or word pairs and those investigating the production of sentence or sentence fragments.

Word Production

Many of the laboratory speech experiments are designed to induce speakers to produce speech errors more frequently than they typically would. If relying only on naturally occurring (versus induced) speech errors, researchers would need to spend many hours to accumulate an adequate sample of speech errors. Baars and colleagues described a procedure they developed and refined to induce speech errors in the laboratory (Baars, 1980; Baars & Motley, 1976; Baars et al., 1975). Baars (1980) presented participants with carefully chosen pairs of words and asked them to say each pair as quickly as possible, while responses were recorded. Consider the word pairs in 1:

1 ball dip
    buzz door
    bean dump
    bat deck
    darn bore

The sequence of the word pairs created phonological bias. Baars (1980) found that participants made errors producing the last pair around 30 percent of the time, saying *barn door* rather than darn bore. By presenting the words in the order he did, he was biasing participants to produce a particular phonological pattern. The procedure is known as the Spoonerisms of Laboratory Induced Predisposition or **SLIP technique** (Baars et al., 1975). The explanation was that participants' previous productions of a word beginning with /b/ followed by a word beginning with /d/ lead them to find it easier and easier to produce such a sequence. The experimenter creates phonological bias by presenting participants with the pairs of words having the same initial phonemes. The technique was instrumental in providing conclusive evidence that when speakers make errors during word production, their errors are significantly more likely to be a word (albeit, the incorrect word, e.g., *deed cop*) rather than a sequence of phonemes that does not make up an actual word (e.g., *keed dop*). Researchers refer to this pattern of results as the **lexical bias effect**. Subsequent studies have also observed results consistent with the lexical bias effect in English (Dell & Reich, 1981), Dutch (Nooteboom, 2005), German (Stemberger, 1984), and Spanish (Hartsuiker et al., 2006). As we will see in the next section, one of the important tests for models of speech production is whether they predict that speakers' errors will be actual words versus nonsense phonological sequences.

Baars et al. (1975) concluded that the lexical bias effect occurred because speakers could edit their speech relatively late during speech planning. The speech editor's job would be similar to quality control, ensuring that the speech contains the speaker's intended message. In their view, during the editing process, non-word speech errors would be caught easily and prevented from being produced. In contrast, errors that involved actual words would be less easily caught. In a subsequent study, they showed that speakers were particularly unlikely to produce an error that created a taboo word, such as swear or curse words or slang words for body parts. Using the phonological bias technique, Motley et al. (1981, 1982) asked participants to pronounce carefully chosen word pairs as quickly as they could. Some of the trials primed participants to produce a speech error containing a vulgar word, while other trials primed participants to produce neutral words. The results showed that errors were significantly less likely to be produced when the error would have resulted in a vulgar word. On the last pair of words, participants were significantly less likely to produce the taboo error *cool tits* for the word pair *tool kits* than a neutral error, such as *barn door*. They concluded that speakers are closely monitoring their planned utterances and have the ability to inhibit an undesirable utterance relatively late in the stages of planning. In a recent brain imaging study, Severens et al. (2012) found that participants' avoidance of taboo words during the SLIP task was associated with activation in the right inferior frontal gyrus for all participants. As we will see in the next section, contemporary models of speech planning incorporate a way for speakers to be able to monitor speech as it is planned; however, the notion of a speech editor continues to be debated (Nozari & Dell, 2009).

Using the SLIP technique in the late 1970s, Motley (1979) appeared to have obtained support for Freud's ([1901] 1971) view that slips of the tongue may reveal one's thoughts (i.e., be related in meaning to the speaker's thoughts or feelings). Freud's view was that it was repressed thoughts, in particular, that led to slips of the tongue. In the experiment, participants were asked to perform a speaking task designed to elicit speech errors some of the time. In the instructions, half of the participants were told that they might receive an electric shock during the task, and the other half did not expect to be shocked. By manipulating the speakers' expectations, Motley (1979) may have led participants in the former group to be concerned more about shocks than the latter group. Recent research by the social psychologist Daniel Wegner and colleagues (Wegner et al., 1987) shows that when we try not to think about something, we actually think about it more rather than less. Indeed, Motley's results showed that there were more slips of the tongue involving shock-related words in the former group.

Subsequent research has shown that some types of words are more likely to be produced with an error than others. Gary Dell (1980) noted that some types of phonemes are more likely to be involved in an error than others. For example, liquids (e.g., /l/ and /r/), fricatives (e.g., /f/ and /v/), and affricates (e.g., /dʒ/, as in *jungle*, and /tʃ/, as in *cheer*) are commonly involved in errors, perhaps because they are inherently more difficulty to produce. Dell (1990) showed that there is a word frequency effect for speech errors. High frequency words were less likely to be produced with an error than low frequency words. There is also convincing evidence that there is a neighborhood effect in speech errors. A word is described as having a "dense" neighborhood when a lot of words sound or look similar to it, and as having a "sparse" neighborhood when it has few similar sounding or looking words. Vitevitch (2002) used two procedures to induce speech errors in the laboratory and compared the rate of speech errors for these two types of words. He found that speakers made more errors for words with sparse neighborhoods.

In this section, you learned about the experiments researchers conducted to capture speech errors in laboratory settings using the SLIP technique. In such experiments, participants see a series of word pairs and rapidly name them. The researcher can create bias by arranging the list of word pairs to repeat specific phonemes or by selecting words that are related in meaning to some aspect of the context. With the technique, Baars et al. (1975) observed the lexical bias effect, when errors are actual words more often than they are nonsense sound sequences. The results revealed patterns of production that will be important in evaluating models of speech production. Before we begin our discussion of models, we must first review the research on sentence production.

Sentence Production

Since the 1970s, researchers have utilized a range of tasks to investigate how speakers plan and produce sentences. We will begin our discussion with the research on the phonological aspects of speech planning and production. Some of the earliest studies in this area involved asking participants to produce novel tongue twister sentences. You may remember tongue twister sentences from childhood, such as *Sally sells seashells by the seashore, or Peter Piper picked a peck of pickled peppers*. Later studies compared errors that speakers made when they said words aloud versus when they only monitored them in their mind. Next, we examine the research on the morphological and syntactic aspects of speech production. Some of this research utilized the visual world paradigm, which you may recall from Chapter 3. The research demonstrates that speakers' eye movements can reveal a great deal about how their utterances are planned.

Phonological Processes

When researchers began investigating the processes involved in the production of sentences, they needed to observe a huge number of errors to make empirical study possible. Some researchers asked participants to recite sentences whose similar sounding words made them challenging to pronounce, a technique known as the **tongue twister paradigm**. Researchers may ask participants to repeat target sentences many times and at a fast rate (Kupin, 1980; Wiltshire, 1998). Depending on the specific question at the heart of the study, the researcher can craft the target sentences to either repeat word-initial phonemes or other targeted segments. Early research using the paradigm showed that the number of errors produced increased as did the number of similar phonemes in the sentences (Butterworth & Whittaker, 1980; Kupin, 1982; Levitt & Healy, 1985). Repeating word-initial consonants led to more errors than repeated consonants in other word positions (Shattuck-Hufnagel, 1992). Other studies showed that speakers made more errors when speaking more quickly (Kupin, 1982; MacKay, 1982). With practice, the number of errors produced when reciting tongue twister sentences decreases (Dell & Repka, 1992; Schwartz et al., 1994). In a recent study, it was shown that drinking alcohol may lead to more speech errors when reciting tongue twisters. A team of Hungarian researchers reported a study in which participants who were sober or intoxicated were asked to repeat tongue twisters (Tisljár-szabó et al., 2014). They found that more errors were produced by the intoxicated speakers. The Research DIY box outlines an experiment to investigate whether fricatives or stop consonants lead to more speech errors when they are repeated in sentences.

 **Research DIY**

Which Types of Phonemes Twist Your Tongue?

Tongue twisters are familiar to most of us, because during childhood they are used to make children more aware of the relationship between the sounds of words and the letters used to spell the words. When you were a child, did you ever try repeating the following sentences over and over as quickly as you could – *How much wood could a woodchuck chuck if a woodchuck could chuck wood?* or *Sally sells seashells by the seashore?*

Sample sentence pairs:

1. a. Tom and Tanya took Timmy's truck on Tuesday.
   b. Frank and Freda found Felix's folder on Friday.
2. a. Cassie carelessly crashed the cab into a canyon in California.
   b. Sarah senselessly sped the Subaru into a sinkhole in Sacramento.
3. a. Benny believed that Brandon would beat Bruce in boxing.
   b. Victor vowed that Vinny would visit Vicki in Vineland.
4. a. Paul put Penny's pants on at Peter's party.
   b. Thad thought Thelma's things were at Theo's theatre
5. a. Last December, David drove Darla around Dallas in the Dodge.
   b. Last September, Steve saw Susan around Savannah in the Scion.

Experiment

You will need blank, unlined index cards. You can print or write one sentence on each index card. Create two sets of cards. Set 1 should contain the sentences with the repeated stop consonants (the "a" versions above). Set 2 should contain the repeated fricative consonants (the "b" versions above). Create a random order of the cards. Use a rubber band to secure the cards in each deck, so that the random order will be preserved. The instructions for the task are as follows. When the card is turned over, say the sentence as quickly as you can six times in a row. If you would like to create additional sentences, more sample sentences can be found in Kennison et al. (2003). Start by creating a sentence that has names or nouns that start with the same stop consonant. The list above does not include /g/ and /d/. In order to create a version of the sentence in which a fricative is repeated, find a replacement word for each of the words beginning with a stop consonant. You may record participants on a recorder or smartphone. Later, you can review the recordings and count the number of errors in each sentence. After you have scored all participants' recordings, you can sum the number of errors for each participant for each type of sentence. Compare the sum for the sentences containing repeated stop consonants and the sum for sentences containing repeated fricatives. Chapter 11 examines the role of phonology in silent reading by skilled and beginning readers.

In his 1980 dissertation, Gary Dell hypothesized that speakers not only make speech errors that others can hear, but they also make errors that only they hear in their minds. The voice we hear in our minds when we are reading or preparing to speak is called "inner speech." Since the early 1900s, researchers have recognized that there is speech heard only in our minds (Huey, [1908] 1968). Most of us have had the occasion in which we are reading a long letter, long text message, or long blog post written by a family member or friend, and as we read along, we hear the person's voice or our own voice in our minds. In an intriguing recent investigation, Filik and Barber (2011) concluded that a person's inner speech sounds like their regional dialect. The existence of inner speech errors was noted previously by Hockett (1967) and Meringer and Meyer (1885, cited in MacKay, 1992). Dell (1980) reasoned that silent speech would be similar to regular speech, but lacking the execution of the motor plans leading to articulation. In Dell's (1980) experiments, participants were instructed to produce speech either aloud or silently. Their spoken errors were noted, and they were asked to report the errors they made in their inner speech. The results indicated that speakers made similar numbers of spoken and unspoken errors. He concluded that it was unlikely that motor planning and articulation aspects of speech were involved in causing speech errors. Chapters 5 and 6 discuss how inner speech is involved in visual word perception and reading comprehension.

Since Dell's (1980) experiments on inner speech and inner speech errors, there have been numerous other investigations. Dell and Repka (1992) investigated the role of practice on overt and inner speech errors and observed that fewer errors occurred after practice. More importantly, they found that inner speech practice reduces errors only for inner speech conditions; thus, the practice that occurred during inner speech was unlikely to involve processes shared by the articulatory aspects of speaking aloud. They concluded that while there are some common aspects of processing for the production of overt and inner speech, producing inner speech does not involve the thorough specification of articulatory features that occurs during the production of audible speech. Oppenheim and Dell (2008) reported evidence for this view in experiments in which they asked participants to recite tongue twister sentences either aloud or silently. The results showed that lexical bias was observed in both spoken errors and inner speech errors; however, phonological bias affected only spoken errors. In a follow-up study, Corley et al. (2011) tested similar conditions as Oppenheim and Dell (2008), but found that phonological bias affected both types of errors. Corley et al. (2011) concluded that inner speech is planned as thoroughly and completely as speech that is articulated. Oppenheim (2012) argued that the data presented by Corley et al. (2011) demonstrated weaker effects of phonological bias for inner speech errors than for regular speech errors, which is consistent with Oppenheim and Dell's (2008) results. Alderson-Day and Fernyhough (2015) provide a more detailed review of this debate.

The level of specification of inner speech has been explored regarding the extent to which inner speech representations are actually phonological in nature. Wheeldon and Levelt (1995) showed a group of Dutch-English bilinguals a series of English words. They instructed participants to respond when they detected a particular phoneme in the Dutch equivalent of the word. The position of the target phoneme in the Dutch word was varied. Participants' response times depended on the position of the phoneme, with shorter times observed when phonemes occurred early in the Dutch word and longer times when phonemes occurred later in the word. The results demonstrated that the words produced in inner speech have a phonological structure. The study was particularly able to demonstrate that participants were planning syllables within the Dutch words. Furthermore, there is other research suggesting that the phonological representations for planned speech (i.e., both inner and overt speech) can influence speech recognition (Roelofs et al., 2007).

An interesting question is how do speakers plan the phonology of their utterances. Are utterances planned phoneme by phoneme or syllable by syllable? Are utterances always planned the same way or can the unit of speech planning (i.e., phoneme versus syllable) vary across utterances? There is mounting evidence that the planning of utterances involves planning whole syllables rather than planning syllables phoneme by phoneme (Cholin et al., 2011; Cholin et al., 2006; Levelt et al., 1999; Levelt & Wheeldon, 1994). These studies found that syllable frequency influences performance in speech production tasks, suggesting that during speech planning individual syllables were retrieved from memory. A recent study suggests that there may be differences in the basic unit of speech planning across languages. A study conducted in Chinese (Mandarin) showed that syllable frequency did not influence how quickly speakers produced utterance (O'Seaghdha et al., 2010).

Laboratory experiments in which participants are asked to name pictures have revealed that semantic and phonological information are activated at different times (Schriefers et al., 1990). Participants listened to a distractor word while carrying out the **picture-naming task**. The distractor word could be semantically related, phonologically related or unrelated to the name of the picture. From trial to trial, the presentation of the distractor varied in terms of time, specifically in how long after the presentation of the picture it was presented. Semantically related distractors had an effect on naming time only when they were presented prior to the presentation of the picture. Phonologically related distractors influenced naming time only on trials in which they were presented around the time the picture was presented. Semantically related distractors resulted in slower naming times on the target (inhibitory effect). Phonologically related distractors resulted in faster naming times on the target (facilitatory effect). The results provided evidence that semantic level of processing during word production precedes the phonological level of processing.

Morphological and Syntactic Processes

An important theoretical question is: how much of an upcoming utterance do speakers plan? When researchers ask this question, they also want to know: what is the smallest unit of planning? Do speakers plan an entire clause at a time, as some have claimed (R. C. Martin et al., 2010; Martin & Freedman, 2001; Martin et al., 2004; Smith & Wheeldon, 1999) or only a word at a time as others have claimed (Griffin, 2003; Griffin & Bock, 2000; Meyer et al., 1998)? The view that speakers plan their utterances clause by clause predicts that before we begin to say an utterance, we have active in memory all the lexical entries for all the words in the utterance (Allum & Wheeldon, 2007; Martin et al., 2004; Smith & Wheeldon, 1999). Research showed that participants took more time to begin speaking when similar sounding words appeared in the clause (Damian & Dumay, 2007; Alario & Caramazza, 2002; Miozzo & Caramazza, 1999).

Heller & Goldrick (2014) investigated the extent to which the grammatical context influenced picture naming. They compared the time taken to name pictures when the picture was named in isolation and when it was preceded by a context. The results showed that speakers took longer to name pictures, due to similar words sharing the same grammatical category as the target (i.e., nouns), when pictures were preceded by context versus when they were named in isolation. The authors claim that phonological processing during picture naming is influenced by contextual grammatical constraints. The results are most compatible with models of speech production in which different sources of information (i.e., grammatical, phonological and phonetic) interact during processing.

Among the most compelling methods used to study speech planning is that involving the recording of eye movements. You may have heard the cliché that *the eyes are the windows to the soul*. In this case, researchers believed that the eyes could serve as windows to the mind. They used the visual world paradigm, a technique you may recall from Chapter 3. In the experiments that support the view that speakers plan their utterances word by word, participants were shown a display of objects and asked to produce utterances related to some of the objects while their eye movements were recorded (Griffin & Bock, 2000; Meyer et al., 1998; Spieler & Griffin, 2006). The researchers found evidence for a word frequency effect, as participants started speaking sooner when the word was higher in frequency. The researchers also analyzed how quickly speakers looked at the objects in the display. Of particular interest was whether they looked at the object just before they said the word that referred to that object. After analyzing the patterns of eye movements during the many trials in which speakers produced utterances containing two of the objects in the display, the authors concluded that speakers planned the two parts of their utterances in succession, rather than simultaneously. Spieler and Griffin (2006) observed similar results in an experiment in which participants produced utterances of the form *the A and the B are above the C*. The results showed that the characteristics related to objects occurring later in the utterance did not influence processing related to the words produced to refer to the object in the A position. It is not clear whether the pattern of results stemmed solely from the nature of the task. It is possible that planning utterances may occur differently in naturalistic settings than in situations arranged by researchers.

Numerous studies have shown that English speakers will produce a subject of a sentence that fails to agree with the following verb. Such errors are called **verb agreement errors**. In a series of experiments by Kay Bock and colleagues, participants were asked to complete sentence fragments (Bock, 1986; Bock & Cutting, 1992; Bock & Eberhard, 1993; Bock & Miller, 1991; Bock et al., 1999). Examples from Bock and Cutting (1992) are provided in 2:

2   a. The report that they controlled the fires were printed in the paper.

      b. The report of the destructive fires were accurate.

They found that participants sometimes produce the incorrect form of the verb *to be* in the past tense (i.e., *was* or *were*). Both 2a and 2b provide examples of this error. The subject of the sentence *the report* is in the singular form and should agree with the verb (i.e., *was*). In the experiment, they have found that speakers produce such errors more often when there is a clause modifying the subject of the sentence, thereby increasing the number of words between the subject noun and the verb with which it must agree in grammatical number. You may notice yourself making this error in conversation and when writing papers for your college courses. It is one of those errors that your word processing software's spell checker will not always catch.

In Bock and Eberhard's (1993) study, participants were asked to complete the fragments in 3a/3b below. The results showed that speakers were more likely to produce a verb agreement error (saying *were* instead of *was*) for the fragment in 3b than in 3a. However, speakers rarely, if ever, produced an error in which the singular form of the verb was substituted for the plural form of the verb. Consider the examples in 4. Bock and Eberhard (1993) concluded that the morphological representation of singular nouns can be more easily overwritten than that of plural nouns:

3   a. the key to the cabinet …

      b. the key to the cabinets …

4   a. the keys to the cabinets …

      b. the keys to the cabinet …

Since these first investigations in English, other researchers have investigated agreement errors in other languages, such as French (Vigliocco et al., 1996b), Spanish (Vigliocco et al., 1996a), Italian (Vigliocco et al., 1995), Dutch (Veenstra et al., 2014), Hebrew (Dank & Deutsch, 2010; Deutsch & Dank, 2011), and Basque (Santesteban et al., 2013). Santesteban et al.'s (2013) experiments with Basque explored the production of agreement errors in a flexible word order language. The typical word order is SOV (also called canonical word order), but sentences may also use an OSV word order (non-canonical word order). Basque also provided an opportunity to compare different types of verb agreement. In Basque, unlike English, the object of the sentence must agree in number with the verb of the sentence. The results showed that more agreement errors occurred in the non-canonical word order. Furthermore, for both subjects and objects, more errors occurred when they appeared in sentence-initial position (i.e., SOV for subject-verb agreement errors and OSV for object-verb agreement errors). Chapter 6 examines how processing involved in subject-verb agreement is carried out during sentence comprehension.

Speakers' selection of a particular syntactic structure has been shown to be influenced by a recently experienced syntactic structure (Bock, 1986; Bock & Cutting, 1992; Bock & Eberhard, 1993; Bock & Miller, 1991; Bock et al., 1999; Loebell & Bock, 2003; see Pickering and Ferreira, 2008 for a review). Some tasks required participants to produce spoken sentences having one of several syntactic structures. Subsequently, participants were shown pictures and asked to describe them. Structures produced in the prime sentences were shown to be used again during the picture descriptions. Loebell and Bock (2003) tested German-English bilinguals and showed that the syntactic structure from one language could influence the selection of a syntactic structure in the other language. Consequently, the representation of the syntactic structure is not language specific, but an abstract form that is language neutral.

To sum up, most of the research conducted on speech production over the past few decades has been conducted in laboratories, where researchers can manipulate variables to measure their effects on speakers and control all aspects of the setting. The resulting research has observed similar types of speech errors as had previously been observed in corpora studies. Furthermore, the research provided insight into the close relationship between overt and inner speech. Numerous studies have shown that speakers plan utterances in terms of phonological, morphological and syntactic structure. In the next section, we examine how these different types of representations are implemented in the different models of speech production.

Models of Speech Production

When we are talking with friends, we usually do not become aware of how much time we take between having something to say and then producing the words. Researchers aim to know what cognitive processes occur from start to finish in speech production – from idea to articulation. Take some time and try to estimate the amount of time that passes for you between having the idea to producing the words. How long does it usually take – one second, half a second, or even less time? Most of the time, the duration is so brief that it is below the threshold of conscious awareness. We cannot reflect on it consciously to describe anything about it. The cognitive processes that occur each time we speak are not observable by our own minds. Consequently, the researchers who have proposed models of speech production must use other types of data in their attempts to describe the intangible details of speech production. In this section, we will begin with the early models, which proposed stages that occurred one at a time with non-overlapping processes. Such models are referred to as **serial processing models**. Next, we will review **parallel processing models**, in which different types of language information can be used simultaneously. Most often, science advances with baby steps, with a new model or approach building closely on earlier models and approaches. This is particularly true of the work on speech production.

Serial Processing Models

Since Fromkin's (1971) work amassing her impressive corpus of speech errors and proposing the first model of speech production, there have been numerous other models using a variety of data sources to improve on Fromkin's framework or develop new frameworks. These data include corpora of speech errors as well as data collected in laboratory experiments. In this section, we start with Fromkin's (1971) model because of its elegance and utility in highlighting the important speech error data that must be accounted for by any successful speech production model. As pointed out by Vigliocco and Hartsuiker (2002), researchers who advocate contemporary models of speech production take differing stances on the issue of modularity. As you recall from previous chapters, some psycholinguistic researchers believe that the brain handles language processing in a modular fashion, with different types of language information handled by independent, non-interactive modules (Fodor, 1983). Other psycholinguistic researchers believe that the brain handles all processing interactively without reliance on modules. Their view is that language processing is carried out like all types of cognitive processing in a brain that processes information in parallel and uses incoming information from all sources as soon as it is available.

In one of the first theories of speech planning, Victoria Fromkin (1973) produced a model in which each utterance is planned in five stages, executed one at a time in sequence. The stages of Fromkin's utterance generation model are given in Table 4.3.

The model was inspired by her analysis of the many types of speech errors collected in her corpus. Consider an exchange error involving content words, as in *Steve put his bag in his book.* The error is likely to result from processing in the fourth stage of processing. A glitch appears to have occurred in the selection of content words for the noun slots in the utterance. An exchange error involving function words, as in *Mary threw in what Bill brought out,* would result from a glitch in processing in the fourth stage. A substitution error involving prefixes, as in *Taniesha was prereading the assigned chapter* instead of *rereading the assigned chapter,* would result from a problem occurring in stage five. An exchange error involving phonemes, as in *Lamar saw the luck troad of books*, would result from a glitch in the processing of the fifth stage. One of the model's advantages is that

Table 4.3 Fromkin's Utterance Generation Model

Stage	Description
1	Select utterance's meaning
2	Select utterance's syntax
3	Select utterance's stress pattern and intonation
4	Select utterance's words (content words then function words)
5	Select utterance's phonemes

Source: Fromkin (1971)

it does describe the planning of prosody for utterance, which can be affected by some types of errors. For example, if one says *the spade of kings* rather than *the king of spades,* as well as the word order being changed, the stress pattern is also changed. In the intended utterance, the stress falls on the first noun *king,* but in the error, the stress falls on the second noun *kings.* The error suggests that the stress pattern of the utterance was planned before the word ordering glitch occurred.

If Victoria Fromkin may be viewed as the grandmother of modern speech production research, then Merrill Garrett can be viewed as the grandfather. His work on speech production in the 1970s and 80s made significant contributions to how researchers view speech production (Garrett, 1975, 1976, 1980, 1988). Garrett's work was informed by his examinations of speech error corpora. He studied numerous examples of exchange errors and observed that most involve elements (phonemes, morphemes, and words) occurring within the same clause. He further noted that morpheme and phoneme exchanges usually involved adjacent elements.

Figure 4.1 Garrett's (1975) Model of Speech Production How quickly do you think you can produce an utterance after you initially think of what you want to say?

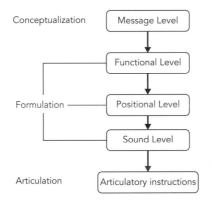

Garrett (1975) put these observations together to propose his own model of speech production. His model could account for how such errors occurred, whereas Fromkin's (1971) model could not. Garrett's (1975) model is shown in Figure 4.1.

In accordance with the model, each utterance we make begins with processing at the conceptual level where the meaning of the message is selected. The speaker selects the sentence structure and the specific words of the utterance in the next three stages, which can be viewed as formulating the utterance in terms of its bits and pieces. The last stage involves selecting the articulatory instructions that will guide muscles and other parts of the vocal tract during the act of speaking. More importantly, Garrett (1975) discussed how different types of speech errors occur during different stages of processing. For example, word exchange errors (saying *put car in my gas,* instead of *put gas in my car*) stem from a glitch happening during the functional level when speakers select the syntactic structure of the utterance. Exchanges involving phonemes occur later in planning at the sound level (saying *luck troad* instead of *truck load*).

In later work, Garrett (1980) observed that in some errors, such as phonological or morpheme exchange, the exchanged elements were usually adjacent. For example, in the error *an anguage lerror,* the phoneme /l/ appears one word later than it should. Interestingly, the article is realized as *an* rather than *a,* suggesting that when the phonology of the article was planned, the following word began with a vowel instead of a consonant. Thus, the planning stage that resulted in the inappropriate placement of the phoneme /l/ must have preceded the planning stage that specified the phonological realization of the article. Also, in the error *the coffee never run outs in the morning,* the present tense verbal suffix /-s/ is not produced on the verb *run,* where it would have been realized as the voiced consonant /z/, but is produced at the end of the verb particle *out,* where it is produced as the voiceless consonant /s/. Garrett used the term "accommodation" to refer to errors in which a moved element is phonologically realized appropriate to the new location in the utterance rather than the source location.

The last serial processing model we discuss is that of Bock and Levelt (1994), which relies on four of the same stages of processing proposed by Garrett (1980, 1982, 1988). These stages are shown in Figure 4.2 and are as follows:

- During the *message stage*, the speaker has something to say (the intention of the utterance).
- The *functional stage* involves the selection of words and determining their syntactic role in the sentence (subject noun phrase or nominative case).
- The *positional stage* involves planning the order of words in the utterance, which includes specifying syntactic and morphology structure.
- The *phonological encoding stage* involves specifying the phonological structure of the utterance, including phonemes and prosody.

As shown in Figure 4.2, exchange errors are believed to stem from processing in the functional level; stranding errors from processing in the positional level; and sound errors from processing in the phonological encoding level. Bock and Levelt (1994) also proposed that just prior to articulation, the speaker is able to monitor the phonetic planning of their speech and filter the utterance, if they deem it desirable.

While the stages of planning proposed by Bock and Levelt (1994) are essentially the same as those proposed by Garrett (1975, 1976), Bock and Levelt (1994) provided more detail about the nature of the processing occurring within the functional and positional stages. In the previous section, you learned about experiments in which speakers' utterances were influenced by prior experience with a specific syntactic structure. These experiments were conducted by Bock and colleagues (Bock, 1986; Bock & Cutting, 1992; Bock & Eberhard, 1993; Bock & Miller, 1991; Bock et al., 1999; Loebell & Bock, 2003) and others (see Pickering and Ferreira, 2008 for a review) and have shown that the positional level of planning can be examined separately from the functional level of processing. These experiments showed that utterances can be produced faster if speakers have previously produced the same syntactic structure even when the words within the structure are different.

Bock and Levelt (1994) further proposed that during the functional stage of processing, speakers access lexical information for the words. They proposed that lexical information about words is stored in memory in a semantic network,

Figure 4.2 Bock and Levelt's Model of Speech Production How do these four stages of processing compare with those proposed by Garrett (1975, 1976)?
Credit: © Elsevier, Gernsbacher, M. A. (1994). Language Production Grammatical Encoding. In Bock. K and Levelt. W (eds) *Handbook of Psycholinguistics* (pp. 945–984).

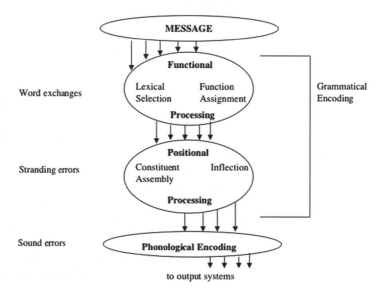

as first described by Collins and Loftus (1975) and Collins and Quillian (1969). Information is stored in a node in the network, and nodes related in meaning are connected. When information is accessed, the node is activated, and the activation can spread along connections, thereby activating related nodes. Bock and Levelt (1994) proposed that there are three levels of nodes involved in lexical access for any word. Figure 4.3 displays the network representing typical knowledge of the words *rooster* and *hen*. The three levels are: the conceptual level; the lemma level, which refers to the syntactic level of word knowledge; and the lexeme level, which refers to information about the morphological and phonological form of the words.

Bock and Levelt's (1994) view of the interconnectedness of different types of information activated during lexical access provided a straightforward way to explain the occurrences of ToT states. Earlier in this chapter, you learned that older adults experience ToT states more often than young adults. In the transmission deficit hypothesis, ToT states are believed to occur because words are not sufficiently activated as a speaker is planning the utterance (Burke et al., 1991; Burke et al., 2000; James & Burke, 2000). The activation levels spreading through the network from the message level down to the functional and positional level do not sufficiently activate the phonological level. Evidence for this theory of ToT states has been obtained in studies in which speakers are tested in a laboratory setting and ToT states are observed. James and Burke (2000) tested older and young adults in a task that involved two activities. The primary activity was naming a target word when presented with its definition (e.g., *This is a type of fruit that is round, can be eaten raw, made into pies, and has a peel that can be red, yellow or green*). The secondary activity was rating a list of words on how easily the words could be pronounced. Unknown to the participants, the researchers varied the relationship between the words rated in the secondary activity and the target words. The results showed that participants produced more correct answers and experienced fewer ToT states on the primary activity when words in the secondary task were phonologically similar to the target words in the primary activity.

Bock and Levelt's (1994) view that the lemma level of representation for a word contains information about morphology and is distinct from the lexeme or phonological level has been supported by ToT studies in languages in which nouns carry morphological gender. Vigliocco et al. (1997) tested native Italian speakers in a ToT elicitation task, in which participants viewed a series of definitions of words and were asked to name each word. All the words had arbitrary gender (e.g., *sedia* means *chair* and is feminine, *tavolo* means *table* and is masculine). When a

Figure 4.3 Bock and Levelt's (1994) Model of Lexical Access This provides greater detail than prior models. At the lemma level, French words would have connections to grammatical gender, but English words do not.
Credit: © Elsevier, Gernsbacher, M. A. (1994). Language Production Grammatical Encoding. In Bock. K and Levelt. W (eds) *Handbook of Psycholinguistics* (pp. 945–984).

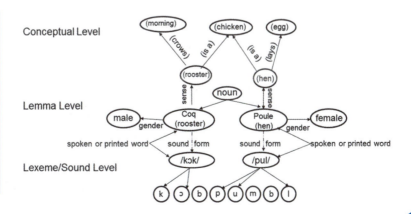

participant could not name the word, they were asked several questions: How well do you know the word?; Can you guess the number of syllables or letters?; Can you guess the gender? When participants reported having a ToT state for a trial, they could report the correct gender of the word 84 percent of the time.

A question you may have is whether the interconnectedness of different types of lexical information is consistent or inconsistent with the view that language is modular (Fodor, 1983). Bock and Levelt's (1984) description of lexical access during speech planning involves interconnectedness between different types of lexical information; however, the model does not permit processing occurring at the positional level to influence processing at the functional level where lexical access occurs. Consequently, modularity is not violated in the model. In the next section, the parallel processing models each violate the assumption of modularity.

Parallel Processing Models

Some researchers have questioned the assumption that the stages involved in the planning of utterances occur in serial, non-overlapping stages. The earliest example of such a model was proposed by Dell (1986, 1988; see also Dell & O'Sheaghdha, 1994). The model utilized connectionist model architecture that you learned about in Chapter 3. The stages of speech planning envisioned by Dell occurred in parallel and processing occurring at each level had the potential to influence processing at every other level. Figure 4.4 displays three levels of nodes involved in producing words. In contrast with the unidirectional connections in the Bock and Levelt (1994) model of lexical processing, the connections in this model are bidirectional with equal weightings. Some believe that the bidirectional connections are desirable, as such models could, at some point in the future, be developed to account for results from speech comprehension as well as speech production (Traxler, 2012).

Dell's model is successful in accounting for the lexical bias effect in speech errors, as are the serial models of Garrett (1975, 1976) and Bock and Levelt (1994). Dell (1985) explains the effect as occurring due to backward activation flowing from the phonological level back to a morphological level. In contrast, in the serial models, the effect occurs due to forward activation flowing from the semantic nodes to the lemma level to the phonological encoding level. The model is also unique in its ability to account for one of the rarest type of speech error – the mixed error, in which an error is related in both sound and meaning

Figure 4.4 Dell's Model of Speech Production
Can you recall from Chapter 3 which model of speech perception was a connectionist model?
Credit: Diagrams based on models by Dell (e.g., Dell et al., 1997)

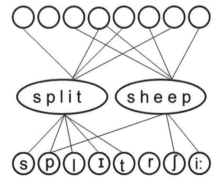

Semantic Nodes

Lexical Nodes

Phonological Nodes

to the intended word (e.g., saying *lobster* instead of *oyster*) (Traxler, 2012). The model cannot account for all research findings in speech production. For example, you may recall the discussion of experiments in the last section, showing that during picture naming, the activation of semantic information occurs earlier than the activation of phonological information (Levelt et al., 1991; Schriefers et al., 1990). It is unclear how the consistent pattern of semantic processing preceding phonological process in planning could be produced.

The shortcomings of Dell and colleagues' (Dell, 1986, 1988; Dell & O'Sheaghdha, 1994) interactive, parallel model served as the impetus for Roelofs' (1997) WEAVER (word-form encoding by activation and verification) model. The model utilizes the interactive framework; however, constraints were added to dictate when various types of processing can occur. For example, activation will not spread to phonological or morphological nodes until a lemma is chosen. Activation flows forward to the phonological and morphological nodes, but does not flow backward from the phonological and morphological nodes to the lemma. One weakness of the model is that the speech monitoring occurs external to the model; thus, it may predict more speech errors than actually occur.

In this section, we reviewed models of speech production, dividing them into two types: serial processing models and parallel processing models. The serial models include those proposed by Fromkin (1971), Garrett (1980), and Bock and Levelt (1994). The interactive, parallel processing models include those proposed by Dell (1986, 1988; Dell & O'Sheaghdha, 1994) and Roelofs (1997). These models provided explanations for the use of top-down processing in speech planning and production.

Time out for Review

Key Terms

Parallel processing models   Serial processing models

Review Questions

1 Compare the features of Fromkin's (1971) model and Garrett's (1975) model. What are the advantages and disadvantages of each?
2 How does Garrett's (1975) model differ from Bock and Levelt's (1994) model?
3 What are the important features of Dell's model of speech production?

Handwriting and Other Forms of Language Production

We produce language in many forms, some of which do not involve speaking. We put our thoughts to paper through handwriting, word processing, and, more recently, texting. Those who use signed language, such as American Sign

Language (ASL), communicate through movements of the hands, face, and body. Relatively few studies have focused on these forms of language production. Although the models of speech production described in this chapter do not aim to account for processes involved in non-speech language production, the approach taken in each model could be used to address one of the other forms of language production. The most obvious area of difference would be the specification of the articulatory stage. Whereas speech involves planning movements in the vocal tract, handwriting, word processing, texting, and using ASL involve planning movements of the hands.

The production of handwriting and word processing (also referred to as typewriting or keyboarding) has received the most attention so far. Early work on the writing process proposed that its planning involves three stages: planning; translating the plan into sentences; and reviewing and editing those (Hayes & Flower, 1980, 1986). The research on handwriting has examined the processes involved in writing single words or word pairs. Van Galen (1991) proposed a model of handwriting production in which the writer is viewed as planning the production of individual letters in a particular serial order. For example, if you were to write *happy*, you would plan *h* in first position, *a* in second position, *p* in third position, a second *p* in fourth position, and y in final position (also represented as $h_1 a_2 p_3 p_4 y_5$). Recent research suggests that handwriting involves planning that is more complex than the production of one letter after the other; rather, handwriting production involves planning pairs of letters (Kandel et al., 2011), three-letter combinations or trigrams (Kandel & Spinelli, 2010), syllable-level planning (Kandel et al., 2006; Kandel et al., 2011), and morpheme-level planning (Kandel et al., 2008). There is not yet a consensus about what the unit of planning is.

There has been a fair amount of research on the planning and production of typewriting, which refers specifically to copy typewriting (i.e., the typist reads the text that must be typed) (Berg, 2002; Logan, 1999). Skilled typists generally are able to type five/six letters per second and up to 200 words per minute (Rumelhart & Norman, 1982). Highly skilled typists who achieve relative high typing rates have been found to make fewer errors involving phonology than less skilled typists (Cooper, 1983). As proficiency in typing increases, the linguistic structure of the text being typed is found to have less and less influence on typing errors. With the proliferation of desktop computers, laptops, and tablets, an increasing number of people routinely use keyboards; however, there appears to be less interest in becoming a fast and accurate typist as in the past. These cultural changes are likely to lead to future research investigating how words and sentences are planned and produced on the various devices.

Photo 4.3 What kinds of errors do you make when you are sending text messages to your friends? Are they similar to the speech errors covered in this chapter?

Review Questions

1 To what extent are the cognitive processes involved in the production of speech similar to the production of typewriting?
2 To what extent are the cognitive processes involved in the production of speech similar to the production of handwriting?

Summary

Formal research on speech production began with the systematic analysis of naturally occurring speech errors (e.g., *I need to put car in my gas.*). Over the past 30 years, laboratory experiments on speech production have shown that speech errors were more likely to form actual words rather than non-word sequences, and speakers can prevent the articulation of an error relatively late in planning, such as when the error would result in a taboo word. Early models of speech planning, which were informed primarily by naturally occurring speech errors, envisioned planning as occurring in a series of non-overlapping stages. More recent models include multiple levels of planning that can influence one another in parallel. These models can account for top-down processing effects, such as phonological and lexical bias. There is a small, but growing literature on the planning and production of handwriting and typewriting. More research is needed in order to determine whether models of speech production will be able to account for the research results on these different forms of language production.

Recommended Books, Films, and Websites

Brown, A. S. (2012). *The Tip of the Tongue State.* New York: Psychology Press.

Goldrick, M., Ferreira, V. & Miozzo, M. (eds) (2014). *The Oxford Handbook of Language Production.* Oxford: Oxford University Press.

Hooper, T. (Director) (2010). *The King's Speech* [Motion picture]. United States: The Weinstein Company.

Jaeger, J. (2005). *Kids' Slips: What Young Children's Slips of the Tongue Reveal about Language Development.* Hove: Psychology Press.

Levelt, W. J. (1989). *Speaking: From Intention to Articulation.* Cambridge, MA: MIT Press.

Lucas, S. (2003). *The Art of Public Speaking.* New York: McGraw-Hill.

Max Planck Institute for Psycholinguistics (n.d.). Fromkin's Speech Error Database – Background. *www.mpi.nl/resources/data/fromkins-speech-error-database.*

Pfau, R. (2009). *Grammar as Processor: A Distributed Morphology Account of Spontaneous Speech.* Amsterdam: John Benjamins.

Schwartz, B. L. & Brown, A. S. (2014). *Tip-of-the-tongue States and Related Phenomena.* Cambridge: Cambridge University Press.

5 HOW ARE WRITTEN WORDS RECOGNIZED?

Chapter Content

Do you consider yourself to be a highly skilled reader? Because you are reading this book and probably enrolled in a university or college course, you are likely to have above-average reading ability. In fact, in industrialized countries today, most people can read and write. This was not always the case. **Literacy** refers to the general state of being able to read and write. Those who can read and write are described as **literate**, and those who cannot are described as **illiterate**. Only about 20 percent of the world's population is illiterate (UNESCO, 2010). Two-thirds of those who are illiterate are girls and women, due to the lack of formal schooling for girls in many parts of the world. Over the past 100 years, the proportion of the world's population that can read and write has dramatically increased, due to formal education becoming common around the world (UNESCO, 2010, 2017). In India, for example, the rate of illiteracy has dropped from about 90 percent for men and over 99 percent for women in 1901 to 29 percent for men and 43 percent for women in 2011 (Census of India, 2013). Reading well is an essential skill for achieving success in industrialized countries. Those who do not become skilled readers during childhood may not finish their education and a significant percentage of them are at risk of future crime-related activities and incarceration (Literacy Project Foundation, 2016). More than two-thirds of the US prison population read so poorly that they are classified as functionally illiterate (Linacre, 1996).

In this chapter, we will begin with the nuts and bolts of literacy, specifically descriptions of the different types of writing systems. **Orthography** refers to writing and spelling conventions in a language. We will see that the relationship between the pronunciation of words and their written form varies a great deal, and that a great deal of attention has been paid to methods of teaching children to read and write. In the second section, we focus on the research into visual word recognition and the factors predicting speed and accuracy. In the last section, we examine the models of visual word recognition and aim to determine which model currently does the best job accounting for the research findings.

The Invention of Writing

Reading and writing are such an integral part of modern life that it is hard to imagine a time when neither activity existed. Archeologists have identified the oldest examples of writing that date as far back as 6600 BC in China (Li et al., 2003). However, examples of well-developed writing systems come later, such as the writing system of 3500 BC Mesopotamia (Bottéro, 1992) and that of 1200 BC China (Boltz, 1986). In the New World, the oldest example has been dated at about 650 BC (Pohl et al., 2002). Historians tend to agree that the evidence suggests that writing in these distant places developed independently, as there is no evidence for extensive contact between the populations (Schmandt-Besserat, 1996).

In Mesopotamia, writing involved marks made into a clay surface that would harden. In China, writing consisted of markings on bone. The prevailing view about why writing developed in Mesopotamia is that there was a need to record financial transactions (Bottéro, 1992). The complexity of the trading relationships increased to the point that it was not possible to keep track of them by relying on individuals' memories. In these different locations around the world, writing came to be used to record other types of events important to the societies, such as documenting historical events, oral histories including those with religious significance, and genealogies. Writing eventually came to be commonplace. People used writing to express personal points of view. For example, the writing and drawing on walls in public places dates back over 1,000 years (Benefiel, 2010), and there are examples of ancient graffiti (written or drawn vandalism) in the ruins of Pompeii and the ancient Roman catacombs.

The fact that reading and writing are relatively recent human innovations means that it cannot be the case that human brains were adapted especially for reading and writing. The areas of the brain involved in reading and writing were originally adapted for other visual and motor tasks. Some of those brain areas have been found to be abnormal in children who exhibit severe problems learning to read. We will learn more about reading development and the factors known to predict reading proficiency in Chapter 11. The topic of reading disorders will be covered in Chapter 14 along with a variety of other types of language processing.

Types of Writing Systems

Systems of writing differ not only in their general appearance, but, more importantly, they differ in how the symbols are related to the sounds and/or meaning of the words they represent. The three types are:

1   the **logographic writing system**, in which the visual form of the word has no predictable relationship with how the word is pronounced

2   the **alphabetic writing systems**, in which words are written as individual characters or letters that correspond to phonemes

3   the **syllabic writing systems**, in which words are written in symbols or letters that correspond to syllables.

The earliest examples of writing were logographic. Photo 5.2 provides an example of logographic symbols preserved from the Qin Dynasty (221–206 BC). The

earliest known writing systems that have been studied are logographic. Most modern languages use alphabetic writing systems. A small number of alphabetic writing systems represent only some of the sounds in the word with characters or letters. For example, in some languages, such as Arabic and Hebrew, some vowels are not usually represented in the written word. These scripts are referred to as **consonantal scripts**. Table 5.1 lists example languages in the writing systems.

Linguists and psycholinguists refer to the written symbols (logograph or letter) as **graphemes**. Depending on the writing system used for a language, a single grapheme may refer to a whole word, syllable or phoneme. Writing systems also vary in the direction in which they are written and read (Coulmas, 2003). The most frequently used direction of writing is left to right, which is used in English, French, Spanish, German, and many other languages around the world. The languages that are written and read right to left include Hebrew and Arabic. Historically, Chinese has been written and read top to bottom and right to left, but there has been a gradual change toward a top-to-bottom,

Table 5.1 Types of Writing Systems with Example Languages

Writing system	Example languages
Logographic	Chinese, Yi, Mayan, Egyptian hieroglyphs
Consonantal	Hebrew, Arabic
Syllabic	Cherokee, Cree, Vai, Central Y'upik
Alphabetic	English, French, German, Italian, Turkish, Russian

Source: Coulmas (2003)

left-to-right pattern. The direction of writing in a culture tends to be correlated with other social norms, such as the pattern of foot traffic into left versus right doors or pathways and how large visual displays, as in a museum, are intended to be processed. In Chapter 11, you will learn about research showing that characteristics of one's language, such as the direction of writing, can influence cognitive processing. Table 5.2 lists the various alphabetic scripts used for writing across the world's languages.

Table 5.2 Most Widely Used Scripts Used for Writing across World Languages

Script	Writing direction	Languages
Arabic	Right to left	Arabic, Persian, Urdu
Canadian Aboriginal script	Right to left	Blackfoot, Chippewa, Cree
Cherokee	Right to left	Cherokee
Cyrillic	Left to right	Russian, Ukrainian, Serbo-Croatian
Devanagari	Left to right	Hindi, Marathi, Nepali, Konkani
Georgian	Left to right	Georgian, Zan, Laz
Greek	Left to right	Greek
Hebrew	Right to left	Hebrew, Bukhori
Roman	Left to right	English, German, French
Tamil	Left to right	Tamil, Badaga, Irula

Source: Coulmas (2003)

Writing and Culture

Writing systems are vehicles of culture. When compared to completely oral traditions in which the history of a community is preserved through stories told again and again, written historical documents are likely to be less prone to error and misremembering. The dominant cultures in the world today have languages that have been written for centuries. Nevertheless, there are numerous languages spoken today that do not have a written form and likely have never been written. Of the 7,097 languages known to still be spoken in the world today, only 3,748 have a known system for writing, leaving 3,349 without one (Lewis et al., 2016). A writing system can be created for a language previously only spoken, if there is a perceived need among the users of that language. One example of a language in which a writing system was created relatively recently is Cherokee. The Cherokee writing system was invented in the early 1800s by then Chief Sequoyah (1770–1843) (Bender, 2002). His work on the writing system began in 1809. He first attempted to develop a logographic system, but decided against that. He knew English and

Photo 5.3 The stop sign from Tahlequah, Oklahoma contains Cherokee writing above the English. Do you know the two states in the USA that are official locations of the Cherokee Indians?

was familiar with the Latin alphabet. After 12 years of work on the project, Sequoyah's syllabary was created. There are 85 symbols, each representing a syllable. By 1824, the majority of the Cherokee people were using the new writing system (Walker & Sarbaugh, 1993). It was used for the *Cherokee Phoenix* newspaper in the 1800s. The newspaper was revived in the 20th century, but is now published in English. The Cherokee syllabary is used for writing documents of tribal significance and children's books.

There are many examples of political leaders changing the writing system. One of the most famous examples occurred in Korea in 1443 (Kim-Renaud, 1997). King Sejong the Great (1397–1450) believed that the logographic writing system, which utilized versions of Chinese symbols, was hard to master and contributed to low levels of literacy in the country. He called together a group of scholars and asked them to create one. The result was a 28-character alphabet called Hangul. Although it took several centuries, it eventually became widely used. Writing systems have also changed due to changes in political governance. Examples of this in the 20th century involved switches from one alphabetic writing system to another. For example, in 1928, Turkey changed its writing system from the Ottoman Turkish alphabet, which is classified as a Perso-Arabic script, to Latin script (Zürcher, 2004). Also, Mongolia switched from the Mongolian script to the Mongolian Cyrillic alphabet in the 1940s (Janhunen, 2012). Cyrillic is the script used for Russian. At the time of the switch, Russia had a great deal of influence over Mongolia.

Changing political conditions over decades or centuries have resulted in some populations utilizing more than one type of writing system for the same language, known as **digraphia** (Dale, 1980). Many instances of digraphia stem from changes in script due to political forces in a country or larger geographic region. Other cases of digraphia involve the contemporary use of multiple scripts by language users. Serbian is such a case, as it uses both the Serbian Cyrillic alphabet and a type of Latin script (Ivković, 2013). Punjabi, spoken in the Punjab area of northern India and eastern Pakistan, is another example. Punjabi has the Gurmukhi script, used by the Sikhs and Hindus, and the Shahmukhi, an Arabic script used by Muslims (Kachru et al., 2008). Interestingly, Gurmukhi is written left to right, but Shahmukhi is written right to left. The Language Spotlight box describes an even more complex example of script mixing.

The Perplexing Orthography of English

Around the world, there are many varieties of English, and those varieties use different spellings for some words. English is the official language in the USA, Canada, the UK, Australia, New Zealand, India, Singapore, numerous Caribbean islands, and several countries in Africa. Across these different regions, there are some vocabulary variations and spelling variations, with many stemming from differences in British and American English usage. English is an alphabetic writing system using Roman script (also called Latin script). Numerous languages use Roman script, including most of the languages of Western Europe (e.g., German, Dutch, Spanish, French, Italian, and others). Unlike many other languages written in Roman script, English spelling does not always provide clear cues to the pronunciation of words. In Spanish, Italian, Finnish, and even Serbo-Croatian,

Writing in Japanese

Japanese is unique because it is written using three types of scripts, two – hiragana and katakana – provide cues to the pronunciation of words and one does not – logographic kanji. The kanji script involves logographic symbols that were borrowed from Chinese; thus, their form provides no information about how the word is pronounced. Numerous kanji symbols exist, but only about 2,000–3,000 are used frequently. Hiragana script involves individual graphemes that provide reliable information about the pronunciation of the letter. It is used for words of Japanese origin. Katakana (also called kana) is used for words borrowed from other languages (Hannas, 1997). There is also some use of rōmaji, a Latin script. For writing words of Japanese origin, language users can use any of the three writing scripts, but the particular choice may be interpreted as having pragmatic significance (Sebba, 2009). For example, writing a word in the non-typical script could be interpreted as having a meaningful significance (e.g., emphasis, contrasting old with new, taking on a slang usage). It is important to note that the three types of scripts can be used within the same discourse and even the same line of text. An analysis of a large corpus of newspaper writing from 1993 revealed that the frequency of kanji and hiragana was 41 percent and 37 percent, respectively (Chikamatsu et al., 2000). Only 6 percent of the corpus was written in katakana. Although traditionally Japanese was written top to bottom, like Chinese, modern Japanese is written left to right without spaces between words. Despite the complexity of the Japanese writing system, 99 percent of the population is literate (UNESCO, 2010).

the graphemes in a word have a predictable pronunciation, thus these languages and many others have **regular spelling** of words. In English, the pronunciations of many words are not predictable from their spelling (e.g., *the*, *one*, and *choir*), which is referred to as **irregular spelling**. Languages with many irregularly spelled words, such as English, are described as having a **deep orthography**, and languages with predictable spelling are described as having a **shallow orthography** (Borleffs et al., 2017; Pollatsek & Treiman, 2015).

As a skilled reader of English, you may not spend much time noticing the many irregularities in English spelling. However, you are likely to remember the many spelling tests you experienced in elementary school. In the USA, the annual Scripps National Spelling Bee showcases the extraordinary skill that it takes to spell unfamiliar and difficult English words that are pronounced and, if requested, defined. The contest is televised nationally on ESPN. In 2015 and 2016, the winning words in the spelling bee were *scherenschnitte* and *nunatak* and *Feldenkrais* and *gesellschaft*, respectively. Both contests ended in a tie, with co-champions. In contrast, in countries in which languages are written with completely regular alphabetic scripts, spelling is easy. Hearing a word pronounced would lead any literate speaker to be able to spell the word.

These are some of the reasons English spelling is so hard:

1   English has many silent graphemes, including word-final silent *e* (*sale* and *lake*), word-initial silent *p* (*pneumonia* and *psychology*), and word-initial silent *k* (*knee* and *knight*). The *h* is silent in *ghost, honest,* and *exhausted*.

2   Some graphemes are pronounced differently in different words. For example, the *c* in *cat* and *cool* is pronounced as a /k/, but the *c* in *ceiling, nice,* and *perceive* is pronounced as a /s/. The *s* in *salt* and *small* is pronounced as a /s/, but the *s* in *was, pause,* and *garages* is pronounced as a /z/. The *g* in *girl* and *green* is pronounced as /g/, but the *g* in *giraffe, general,* and *geography* is pronounced as a /dʒ/.

3   In addition, combinations of graphemes can vary in their pronunciation. The *th* in *Thai* is pronounced differently than the *th* in *the* and *thin*.

4   English vowel combinations have highly variable pronunciation. For example, the spelling of *ou* is pronounced differently in each of the following words: *about, touch, pour, should, soup, soul, delicious, journey,* and *cough*.

The irregularity of English spelling contributes to the many words in English that are pronounced the same way but spelled differently, known as **homophones**. Table 5.3 lists some examples of English homophones. There are also words that are spelled the same way, but have different meanings and, sometimes, different pronunciations (e.g., *lead* as in *to lead* and *lead* as in the metal). This irregularity in English spelling is partly because English has a long history as a written language, dating back to about the 8th century (Baugh & Cable, 2002). Over the centuries, speakers of English had frequent contact with speakers of other languages (e.g., French, German, Norse, Swedish, Greek, and others) (Lass & Hogg, 2000). Thus, English borrowed a large number of words from these other languages. Tilque (2000) estimated that 75 percent of modern English words have non-English origins.

When considering beginning readers, the irregularity of English is particularly frustrating because irregularly spelled words are among the most commonly used words in the language (Francis & Kučera, 1982). Among the top

Table 5.3 Examples of Common Homophones in English

Triplets			Pairs	
buy	by	bye	by	buy
cite	sight	site	cell	sell
flew	flu	flue	foul	fowl
pair	pare	pear	peace	piece
rain	rein	reign	real	reel
rite	right	write	rye	wry
sees	seas	seize	sale	sail
so	sew	sow	sore	soar
there	their	they're	threw	through
vane	vain	vein	tear	tier
way	weigh	whey	waste	waist
you	ewe	yew	yoke	yolk

100 most frequently used words for children are the irregular words *the, you, have, they, were, their, which, when, would, two, people, been, who, down,* and *now* (Stuart et al., 2003). Since the late 1800s, there have been many attempts to reform English spelling in the USA, including an attempt by President Theodore Roosevelt in the 1900s, which was prevented by Congress. In my college courses, when asked if they find English spelling challenging, my students always respond yes. When asked if they would support an effort to regularize how English words are spelled so that children would have an easier time learning to read and write, they usually respond with a resounding no. When I suggest that reforming English spelling would make reading and writing much easier for those who have difficulty, they are not persuaded; rather, they fear the confusion from having to adopt a new system. Chapter 11 discusses how the irregular spelling in English leads to some challenges for beginning readers. Later in this chapter, we discuss the research that shows that the relationship between graphemes and phonemes in a word plays an important role in written word perception.

In this section, we discussed how writing was invented independently in at least three places in the world and the different writing systems that are used in the world's modern languages. These writing systems vary in terms of how the visual symbols correspond to the sounds in the word. Words written in logographic writing systems provide no visual cues as to how the word is pronounced. In syllabic, alphabetic, and consonantal writing systems, the written form of words provides differing amounts of information about pronunciation. Syllabic writing systems provide cues about the syllables in a word. Alphabetic writing systems provide information about individual phonemes, and consonantal writing systems provide information about some, but not all the phonemes in a word. Alphabetic writing systems differ in the extent to which correspondence between graphemes and phonemes is completely predictable (regular), as it is in languages with shallow orthography, or unpredictable (irregular), as it is in languages with deep orthography.

 **Time out for Review**

Key Terms

Alphabetic writing systems	Homophone	Logographic writing system
Consonantal script	Illiterate	Orthography
Deep orthography	Irregular spelling	Regular spelling
Digraphia	Literacy	Shallow orthography
Grapheme	Literate	Syllabic writing system

Review Questions

1 In human history, what was the activity for which writing was believed to be first used?
2 What are the three major types of writing systems used in the world's languages? For each type of writing system, provide an example of a language that uses it.

Recognizing Written Words

For the skilled reader, recognizing a written word occurs automatically. We recognize words without being able to reflect consciously on how we do it. You can test the automaticity of word recognition by taking a few blank index cards and writing a word on each one. Mix the cards up, pick one at random, and quickly bring it to eye level so that you can view the letters of the word. Try as hard as you can to *not* read the word. Tell yourself that it is okay to see the letters, but do whatever you can to prevent the letters from triggering in your mind the awareness of the word. The automaticity of word recognition is also illustrated by the Stroop effect, which you learned about in Chapter 1. Even when the task is to name the color of letters, the meaning of the word that the letters spell is still activated. When the letters spell a color word that is different from the color word to be named, naming time is longer than when the two color words are the same. In our daily lives, we are surrounded by written words not only in books and on computers, but also on street signs and in advertisements in shopping areas. The automatic identification of written words occurs only when you know the language in which the words are written. If you have traveled to a country whose language you do not know, you have experienced the strange feeling of being surrounded by written words you cannot recognize without the help a dictionary. In this section, you will learn about the research that has explored how we perceive written words, highlighting the factors that have been shown in experiments to influence how quickly and/or how accurately words can be perceived visually. We will first review some of the relevant processes involved in visual attention.

Visual Attention and Visual Sensory Memory

As you learned in Chapter 3, the early approach to the perception of spoken words was that listeners engage in a process of pattern recognition, matching the incoming auditory input to memory. Pattern recognition also serves as a good starting point for understanding visual perception generally and visual word perception specifically. In order to fully appreciate the complexity of visual word recognition, it is usual to understand some basic facts about vision, specifically the fact that how well we perceive an object depends on where it is in relation to where we are looking. **Visual acuity** refers to the fact that our vision is best around the point where we are looking. We see objects in the center of our vision clearest. We can make out the smallest of details. Objects that we see to the right or left of the center of vision are perceived less well, with the quality of our vision gradually declining as the distance from the center increases. These differences in visual acuity across our visual field occur because of the characteristics of our visual system, specifically the type of cells within the retina that receive the information. At the center of the visual field, acuity is greatest, because the information is processed by the area of the retina called the **fovea,** which is composed of cone cells that are responsible for crisp, color vision as well as our ability to make out sharp contrasts. The non-central part of the visual field, extending to the left and the right, is processed by the area of the retina called the **parafovea**, which is composed of fewer cones and more rod cells that are incapable of perceiving color and are involved in perceiving information at the periphery of vision. Information is processed by an increasing

Figure 5.1 Trial in the Partial Report Condition in Sperling's (1960) Experiment Participants briefly saw 12 letters, then a masking slide, and then heard a low, medium or high tone. Do you think you could perform well in this type of experiment?

ratio of rods to cones as the distance away from the center of vision increases. When considering what we are able to perceive in a single look in front of us, we can think of our visual field as a large picture window with crisp, clear objects in the middle and very blurry objects at the far left and right edges, with the level of crisp detail declining ever so subtly from the middle to the edges.

During visual processing, as in auditory processing, sensory input is stored briefly in the sensory memory store. Auditory sensory memory is echoic memory. Visual sensory memory is **iconic memory** (Neisser, 1967). In contrast with our echoic memories, which are stored for up to four seconds, iconic memories are short-lived, lasing only about one quarter of a second (i.e., 250 milliseconds). George Sperling (1960) discovered iconic memory in a series of laboratory experiments in which he showed participants groupings of letters for differing amounts of time and asked them to recall as many letters as they could. After varying numerous aspects of the procedure to see how the changes influenced participants' performance, Sperling had evidence that for each image we view, there is a brief memory of the image, stored in a verbatim format. You may find it helpful to think of it as a snapshot identical to the image, only stored in a different form.

Sperling's (1960) experiments, as well as those of others investigating visual perception, used a tachistoscope, so named by combining two Greek root words, *tachys* (swift) and *skopion* (observing instrument). Words were written by hand onto cards and displayed to participants using the tachistoscope which enabled researchers to vary how long a stimulus was available to a participant, with durations as brief as 100 milliseconds (Benschop, 1998; Godnig, 2003). Today, with modern computers and modern software controlling experiments, presentation durations under 100 milliseconds are possible. Researchers now have the ability to display a wide variety of images to participants and to record not only how quickly they respond to the images, but also, in some cases, where on the image the participants actually looked.

Participants in Sperling's (1960) experiments were shown cards each containing a set of 12 letters, which were arranged in three rows. In the initial experiments, participants viewed a set, and after it was removed from view, they recalled as many of the letters as they could. Such trials were called the "whole report condition." The results showed that most participants could report between 25 percent and 33 percent of the letters (3 or 4 out of 12). In subsequent experiments, Sperling instructed participants only to report a particular row from the previously viewed display. On such trials, the letters were displayed, then they were removed from view. Only after the letters were removed, did the participant hear one of three tones. A high tone signaled they should report the first row of letters; a low tone that they should report the bottom row of letters; and a medium tone that they should report the middle row of letters. These trials were called the "partial report condition." Figure 5.1 shows a trial in the partial report condition. Again, the results showed that participants could report between 25 percent and 33 percent of the letters (3 or 4 out of 12). Analyzing participants' performance on the three different types of trials (high, medium, and low tone), Sperling (1960) found that participants were reporting as many as 9 out of 12 letters. The results could only be explained if participants' memory for the letters contained the entire array. For whichever row they were asked to report, participants could recall 3–4 letters before the iconic memory of the letters faded.

For each word that we look at, there is an iconic memory of it that lasts about 250 milliseconds or until we move our eyes to look at something else. Although the majority of the research discussed in this chapter focuses on how we perceive individual words presented alone on a computer screen, in later chapters we will discuss how words are recognized and interpreted within sentence and discourse contexts. The perception of individual words in isolation and in context has been studied through the recording of eye movements (also referred to as eye tracking). Eye movement recording is the state-of-the-art technique for studying visual perception, which was pioneered by Edmund Huey (1870–1913) while he was a professor at Clark University, Worceter, Massachusetts. Huey ([1908] 1968, p. 583) studied eye movements during reading in his laboratory and observed: "the most casual observation showed that the eye moved along the line by little jerks and not with a continuous steady movement." The movements of the eyes are known as **saccades**, and the pauses between saccades are called **fixations**. During reading, each fixation of the eye lasts 250–350 milliseconds, and each saccade moves the eye along approximately five to nine letters in English.

The duration of fixations are related to the difficulty of the text, specifically the word(s) on which the fixation occurs. As the difficulty of the text increases, the duration of fixations increases and the length of saccades decreases. For example, fixations on high frequency (common) words are generally shorter than low frequency (unusual/uncommon) words (Rayner & Duffy, 1986). If you were to examine eye movement behavior for multiple lines of text, you would find that some words are routinely skipped. The most often skipped words are short, high frequency function words. In Chapter 11, we will learn more about eye movement behavior during reading. In the remainder of this chapter, we will focus on studies that have investigated the recognition of individual words using a variety of methodologies.

Before we leave the topic of the visual aspects of processing words, we should touch on processes of selective visual attention. When we discussed spoken word recognition in Chapter 3, you learned about the cocktail party effect, which illustrates how you may hear your name from an area of a room that had not been part of the area you were monitoring. When you detect something that sounds like your name, your attention is immediately drawn to the location. During visual processing, our attention is also attracted to objects in the visual field. William James (1890) is thought of as the first to describe visual attention as functioning as a spotlight. Others have shown in experiments that participants can selectively attend to different parts of the visual field (Eriksen & Hoffman, 1972; Eriksen & St James, 1986). Take a moment, after you finish reading this paragraph, and look up from the book or computer screen you are reading. Look straight ahead. Without moving your eyes, try to make out the far left edge of your visual field. Then try to make out the far right edge, then try the top edge, and then the bottom edge. Another way to experience the varying acuity of your visual field is to look straight ahead and extend both your arms straight out to your sides. Slowly move your hands forward, both arms moving at the same rate. Wiggling your fingers can make it easier to notice them. While you are still looking straight ahead, try to notice the first moment when you perceive your hands moving into the edges of your visual field. As you keep moving your arms forward, the detail of your hands, fingers, and arms should become clearer and clearer.

Eye tracking research has shown that our visual attention is linked to our eye movements. Visual attention shifts immediately before saccades in the direction the eye is moving (Rayner et al., 2012). Readers of languages written left to right shift their attention to the right before a saccade, and readers of languages written right to left shift their attention to the left before a saccade. Readers of languages written top to bottom shift their attention down before a saccade. In the time between the shift of visual attention and the moving of the eye, readers are able to start processing the words or objects to the right of fixation. In experiments in which the researchers controlled the letters at the right of fixation, they found that if words were presented to the right of fixation, they spent less time reading the word when they fixated it than if the letters of the word to the right of fixation had been replaced by random letters. Researchers call this **parafoveal preview benefit** (Kennison & Clifton, 1995; Veldre & Andrews, 2017). Because of the declining visual acuity as distance from the center of vision increases, parafoveal preview tends to permit advanced processing on five to eight letters to the right of fixation, which may include the entire next word if the word is short, or the beginning letters of the next word if the word is long.

Orthographical and Other Visual Form Processes

A reasonable first place to start when considering how readers attempt to search memory for a match to a written word is to assume that the visual input is matched either as a whole or as individual letters with memories. When a match is found in memory, then the spoken word being processed can be identified as the word whose memory representation is the best match. The exact way in which people achieve pattern recognition for spoken words remains unclear, due to the enormous variability in the characteristics of the sound patterns representing words, syllables, and individual phonemes. In contrast, understanding how written words are recognized would be more straightforward, since some of the characteristics of speech that contribute to the difficulty in understanding how spoken words are recognized do not arise during the recognition of written words. For example, while there is a segmentation problem in the recognition of speech (identifying word boundaries), there is rarely a segmentation problem in visual word perception, as words are separated by a space most of the time. Also, while there is co-articulation during the production of phonemes in speech causing a phoneme to be pronounced differently depending on what phonemes are preceding and following it, there is typically no variation in how letters in a word may look depending on the letters that come before or after them.

One of the earliest models of perception aimed to explain how the process of pattern recognition occurs. In a now classic paper, Selfridge (1959) sketched out a framework to explain how the mind might recognize patterns, known as the **pandemonium model**. The model contained *demons* that would be specialized for different parts of the recognition process. Image demons responded to visual input registered by the retina. Feature demons recognized a specific low-level pattern or feature. When the pattern was detected, the demon would become active, triggering additional processing downstream. The numerous demons in the system would work in parallel, detecting whatever feature it was specialized to detect. As well as feature demons, there were also cognitive demons and decision demons. The pandemonium model presumed that the identification of the various parts of an object would occur before the identification of the whole. Interestingly, the experimental evidence disproving this assumption had been obtained in the 1880s. The Classic Research box outlines this evidence.

Over the past 40 years, thousands of experiments have investigated how written words are perceived (Pollatsek & Treiman, 2015). Numerous characteristics of words have been shown to influence how quickly readers can recognize written words. For example, as the number of letters in a word increases, the time taken to recognize the word also increases (Gough, 1972), known as the **word length effect**. In experiments in which participants were asked to recognize written words and quickly judge whether the letters make up a word (lexical decision task), some studies have observed robust effects of word length (Chumbley & Balota, 1984; Whaley, 1978), but others have not (Henderson, 1982). For tasks in which participants are required to produce spoken responses, such as in word naming, there are also conflicting results. Some studies have found that longer words take longer to name (Forster & Chambers, 1973; Eriksen et al., 1970), while others have not (Weekes, 1997).

Classic Research | The Word Superiority Effect

The story of how the **word superiority effect** was first discovered and later confirmed with modern technology is one that demonstrates how advanced psycholinguistics research was in the 1800s. Cattell (1886) was the first to hypothesize that the perception of a whole word occurs more rapidly than the perception of any of the individual letters that make up the word. He devised a task in which participants were shown single letters or words. They were instructed to name the letters or words. Performance was more accurate for words than for letters. Fast forward a little over 80 years when interest in cognitive processes was reinvigorated in the cognitive revolution, and we find Gerald Reicher's (1969) new and improved experiment. Reicher changed the procedure to eliminate the possibility of guessing. Participants viewed one of three types of trials: a single letter; a complete word; or a non-word letter string (e.g., fner). There was a pattern mask presented, then two probe letters appeared, located above and below a particular letter position. Figure 5.2 provides sample stimuli for these three conditions. The participant was instructed to name the letter in that position from the stimulus. The results showed that participants' performance was more accurate and faster when the letter had appeared in a word versus alone or in a non-word letter string.

Figure 5.2 Reicher's (1969) Word Superiority Effect Experiment Reicher showed that letters were recognized more quickly when they occurred in words, as in (a), rather than in isolation, as in (b), or within a non-word, as in (c). Do you find this result counterintuitive?

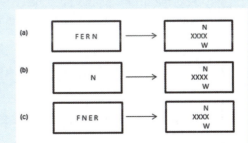

Research on the recognition of Chinese characters has shown that the number of strokes contained in the character is related to how long participants take to recognize the word (Seidenberg, 1985). There are 12 types of strokes (e.g., dot, vertical, horizontal, hooks, rising, turning, etc.) used to write Chinese characters. The most complex Chinese characters can contain up to 64 individual strokes and the least complex a single stroke (Taylor & Taylor, 1995).

Experiments in which the visual forms of words have been manipulated have shown that such manipulations can have strong effects on how quickly words can be recognized (Perea et al., 2015). Recent research has shown that when words are displayed in a mixture of lowercase and uppercase (e.g., sAuSaGe and TOmATo), reader take longer to recognize the words than when cases are not mixed (all lowercase or all uppercase) (Perea et al., 2015). The difficulty experienced when reading mixed-case words appears to be greater for older adults as compared to young adults (Allen et al., 2011). It is important to note that the results obtained for English, which uses lowercase for all words with the exception of the first letter of a word starting a sentence and the first letter of proper names, may differ from those in languages in which uppercase is more frequently used, as in German, which also uses uppercase for the first letter of all nouns.

Other research has confirmed that for typically printed words (i.e., having appropriate case), the physical form of the words also matters (Chung et al., 1998; Moret-Tatay & Perea, 2011; Slattery & Rayner, 2010; Tai et al., 2006). Slattery and Rayner (2010) compared reading times and overall comprehension accuracy for texts presented in different fonts and found that although comprehension did not differ across conditions, reading time did. Moret-Tatay and Perea (2011) tested the view that words printed in serif fonts were easier to process than sans serif fonts. Letters printed in sans serif fonts lack the small lines that appear at the ends of strokes; consequently, some argue that there is less distinction between letters than when using serif fonts. Moret-Tatay and Perea's (2011) results revealed the opposite pattern of processing. Readers took less time recognizing words printed in a Lucinda sans serif font than Lucinda Bright, a serif font. (Lucinda is a family of related typefaces designed in 1985.) Figure 5.3 gives an example of a serif and a sans serif font. In the future, those involved in the printing industry as well as those developing applications for digital presentations will continue to be interested in identifying the font type that facilitates processing in a variety of conditions (e.g., low light, bright light, airplane cockpits, cell phone screens, etc.). Some fonts in some settings may decrease discomfort and eye strain, particularly after long hours of use.

In processing written words, as in processing spoken words, words that are similar to many other words are processed more quickly than others. You may recall the term "neighborhood effect" from Chapter 3. The number of orthographic neighbors (also called neighborhood density) has been found to have a strong

Figure 5.3 A Lucinda Sans Serif and Serif Font Compared Serif fonts include more detail for each letter as compared to sans serif fonts. Do you have a favorite font? Is it a serif or sans serif font?

This is written in Lucinda Bright, a serif font.

This is written in Lucinda sans serif font.

influence on how quickly words are perceived (Andrews, 1989; Havens & Foote, 1963). Researchers continue to debate why words with few neighbors take longer to process. Mounting evidence suggests that processing time is influenced not only by the number of orthographic neighbors a word has, but also by the frequency of occurrence of those neighbors (Bowers, Davis, & Hanley, 2005a, 2005b). Ziegler and Perry (1998) showed that the frequency of words sharing non-initial phonemes with a target word (body neighbors) affected reading time and pointed out that the variance in body neighbor frequency can differ across languages. They suggested that the frequency with which phoneme sequences at the ends of words (word bodies) occur in the language may contribute to word identification more strongly in Spanish and Portuguese than in English.

When there is 100 percent overlap in orthographic form, processing is greatly facilitated, as you might expect. Lexical decision experiments have shown that when participants are asked to judge the same word on two back-to-back trials, they respond faster to the second instance of the same word than they respond to the word when it was immediately preceded by a different word, referred to as **repetition priming** (Schacter & Buckner, 1998). Studies have investigated various aspects of the priming effect. The amount of facilitation that is observed increases with each repetition of the word up to seven repetitions (Maljkovic & Nakayama, 1994). This is observed even when there are subtle changes in the appearance of the word on the computer screen. The amount of time between the repetitions (delay) can influence the size of the facilitation, with shorter delays associated with greater facilitation. The amount of time spent processing the repetitions (stimulus duration) can also influence the size of the facilitation, with longer stimulus durations associated with greater facilitation. When participants view words that are presented rapidly one at a time, a repeated word may not be perceived at all. When participants are presented with two back-to-back trials of the same word (or object), they report seeing only one instance of the word (or object), referred to as **repetition blindness** (Kanwisher, 1987).

Morphological Processes

Research from the 1980s suggested that words are recognized through a process that involves recognizing individual morphemes. Taft (1981) asked participants to perform a lexical decision task. He compared how quickly participants could judge words containing a prefix (e.g., remind) and words whose initial letters resembled a prefix, but were, in fact, not a prefix (e.g., relish). Participants' judgment times were slower for the latter type of word (words with pseudoprefixes). Taft concluded that during word recognition, each morpheme in a word is compared with morphemes in the mental lexicon until a match is found. After the meaning of each morpheme is found, the meanings are combined to yield an understanding of the meaning of the word. This sequence of processing would explain the longer judgment times for *relish*, as the initial treatment of *re* as a prefix led to an initial search of memory for two morphemes. When this search failed, memory was then searched for the single morpheme *relish*, which added to the processing time. In a later experiment in which eye movements were recorded during sentence reading, Lima (1987) also found that words with pseudoprefixes took longer to read than words with actual prefixes.

Since these early studies demonstrating that word recognition involves breaking down words into their morphological parts, numerous experiments have explored how morphologically complex words are recognized across languages. A series of experiments investigated how Finnish readers process multi-morphemic Finnish words during reading (Hyönä & Pollatsek, 1998; Pollatsek et al., 2011; Pollatsek et al., 2000). Finnish is an **agglutinative language**, which means that multiple morphemes can routinely be combined to form very long words (Croft, 2002). In contrast, words in English typically contain relatively few morphemes. English and other languages in which the average number of morphemes per word is low are called **isolating languages**. Hyönä and Pollatsek (1998) compared reading time on words whose word-initial morpheme varied in frequency. They found that reading time was longer when the word-initial morpheme was low frequency. Pollatsek et al. (2000) manipulated the frequency of the second morpheme in a word and found that reading time on the word was longer when the second morpheme was low rather than high frequency. Overall, the results from these studies provide further support for the view that multi-morphemic words are processed not as wholes, but as the sum of their morphemic parts.

Morphemes are categorized into those that can appear as individual words – **free morpheme** – and those that cannot – **bound morphemes**. In English, prefixes and suffixes are examples of bound morphemes. Languages whose morphology is more complex than English not only have prefixes and suffixes that can be added to other morphemes in the forming of new words, but they also have morphemes called **infixes** that can be inserted within a morpheme to change the meaning in a predictable way. Speakers of English can appreciate how an infix would be used by considering the insertion of a curse word into the middle of a word, when the speaker would like to express strong emotion (usually negative), such as *fan-flipping-tastic* or *the whole fam-dam-ily*. In Chickasaw, a Native American language spoken only by a few hundred remaining native speakers in Oklahoma, the negative marker is a glottal stop inserted into a verb stem (Munro & Willmond, 1994). In Tagalog, a language spoken by approximately 28 million people in the Philippines, the infix *-um-* is inserted between the first consonant and vowel of a word and communicates that the word is focused (Gonzales, 1998).

Readers of agglutinative languages, in which words usually contain numerous morphemes, are likely to perceive words through a processing of morpheme deconstruction, with each morpheme undergoing the process of lexical access. The processes involved in psychologically combining the meanings of multiple morphemes within a word in order to arrive at the meaning of the word remain unclear. The processing complexity is likely to vary across different types of morphemes. For example, some morphemes change the part of speech of a word when added. For example, the suffix -er is added to a verb to indicate the one who performs that action denoted by the verb (e.g., bake and baker). Other types of morphemes do not change the part of speech of a word when added. For example, the suffix -ing is added to a verb to indicate the present progressive form of the verb (e.g., sing and singing).

Research suggests that even in the logographic writings systems, such as that used in Chinese, skilled readers are likely to process the logographic symbols as composed of meaningful parts. The subcomponents of Chinese symbols can

Photo 5.4 The *Guinness World Records* lists the above town name from New Zealand as the longest in the world. The English translation from the Maori is "the summit where Tamatea, the man with the big knees, the slider, climber of mountains, the land-swallower who travelled about, played his nose flute to his loved one." How many saccades would it take to read the town's name?

correspond to morphemes, carrying an association with a specific meaning, or a phonological unit (phoneme or syllable) (Norman, 1988). The meaningful elements contained within Chinese logographic symbols are called **radicals**. The location of the radical within a symbol may also convey something about its contribution to the overall meaning of the word. For example, the Chinese characters meaning river (河 hé), lake (湖 hú), stream (流 liú), riptide (沖 chōng), and slippery (滑 huá) contain the three stroke radical meaning water (氵). A growing number of visual word perception experiments demonstrate that Chinese readers do not always process Chinese symbols as wholes; rather, they appear to analyze symbols into radical subcomponents (Feldman & Siok, 1999; Perfetti et al., 2005; Yan et al., 2012).

Phonological Processes

Numerous studies of word recognition and sentence reading have shown that the sounds of words also play an important role in silent reading (Leinenger, 2014). Even during silent reading, when there is no obvious reason to become aware of the sounds of words, we, nevertheless, activate sound codes for words. The experimental evidence for the role of phonology in silent reading is vast and convincing (Rayner et al., 2012). We will review only some of these studies in this section. For example, research from the 1970s and 80s had noted that participants generally take longer to recognize irregularly spelled English words than regularly spelled words that were matched in number of letters and word frequency (Baron & Strawson, 1976; Seidenberg et al., 1984). In addition, research has shown that readers' time to recognize written words is influenced by the syllables within words. In many studies, words were found to be easier to recognize if a syllable within the word has been viewed previously as part of a different word (Ashby & Rayner, 2004; Carreiras et al., 1993).

Coltheart's dual route model claimed that written words can be recognized via two processes that operate in parallel for most readers (Coltheart, 1978; Coltheart & Kohnen, 2012; Coltheart et al., 1993; see also Castles & Coltheart,

1993). **Lexical access** can occur either when pattern matching using the whole word's visual form (whole word route) to access lexical knowledge, or when the phonological representation of a word is computed through the application of the grapheme-to-phoneme rules (grapheme-to-phoneme route). As the two routes operate in parallel, word recognition is viewed as occurring when one of the two processes achieves lexical access. For irregular English words, such as *choir* and *one*, the grapheme-to-phoneme route will fail to access the lexicon with the phonological representations /cho ir/ and /on e/. For these and other irregular words, lexical access is likely achieved first through the whole word route. When lexical access is achieved via the whole word route, participants become aware of the phonological representation of the word (i.e., the pronunciation) only after lexical access. In contrast, the pronunciation of a word is determined prior to lexical access via the grapheme-to-phoneme route. Furthermore, the grapheme-to-phoneme route can explain how readers have no trouble pronouncing letter sequences that do not correspond to known words.

Coltheart's (1978) dual route model elegantly accounted for the symptoms of some individuals with a severe reading disorder known as **dyslexia**. Dyslexia can be categorized into two types:

1   **developmental dyslexia**, which occurs in childhood, in the absence of brain damage and persisting through school when children are learning to read
2   **acquired dyslexia**, which can follow a brain injury in an individual who previously had no problems with reading.

Castles and Coltheart (1993) noted similarities in symptoms experienced by those with forms of developmental and acquired dyslexia. Some individuals have trouble applying the spelling-to-sound rules, but appear only to use the whole word matching route during reading. They are able to read words that are familiar to them, but have trouble reading unfamiliar words or sounding out pronounceable sequences of letters. When this pattern is observed in a child learning to read and the pattern persists over a long time, the child may be described as having **dysphonetic dyslexia**. When the same pattern of performance is observed in a person who once was a skilled reader, but began having reading problems following a brain injury, the person is described as having **phonological dyslexia**. In contrast, other individuals have trouble using the whole word matching route, but they are able to apply the spelling-to-sound route. They have trouble reading irregular words, but can read regular words and also pronounceable non-words. When the symptoms are a form of developmental dyslexia, it is described as **dyseidetic dyslexia**. When the symptoms are a form of acquired dyslexia, it is described as **surface dyslexia**. For both developmental and acquired forms of dyslexia, symptoms are likely to vary widely across individuals.

In the decades since Coltheart (1978) introduced the dual route model of visual word recognition, numerous studies have provided evidence that readers use spelling-to-sound rules (also called assembled phonology) to compute the phonological representations of words. Lesch and Pollatsek (1998) demonstrated that assembled phonology enabled readers to access the meaning of words in an experiment in which participants were asked to judge whether a pair of words was related in meaning (e.g., pillow-bead). In target conditions, one of the words in the pair was a false homophone of a word that was semantically related to the other word (e.g., bed), as the sequence *ead* can be pronounced in two ways (i.e., /ɛd/ and /ed/). They found that participants took significantly longer to respond "no" as compared to a control condition (e.g., pillow-bend). An important theoretical question is whether word recognition always involves the computation of a word's phonological code and to what extent the phonological processing is critical for access to lexical representations. Researchers continue to debate the extent to which readers automatically activate phonological representations for words (Martensen et al., 2005).

Semantic Processes

Characteristics of the meanings of words have been shown to influence how accurately and how quickly written words are recognized. In the 1970s, Paivio and colleagues showed that **concrete words**, which refer to objects that can be visualized through the use of mental imagery, were recognized faster than **abstract words** that refer to abstract concepts (Paivio, 1971; Paivio et al., 1968). This is known as **the concreteness effect**. Paivio (1971) claimed that the effect occurred because of differences in how the two types of words are stored in memory. Both abstract and concrete words have a memory representation in which their meaning is specified as a verbal description (e.g., chair is a piece of furniture for sitting and freedom is a state of being in which one has no restrictions). However, only concrete words have a second type of memory representation in which there is a visual image detailing the appearance of the concept. Later research pointed out that the concreteness effect is also likely influenced by the fact that there are fewer abstract concepts overall in language than concrete concepts (Schwanenflugel, 1991).

The age at which specific words are learned has been shown to influence how quickly the words are recognized (Carroll & White, 1973; Gilhooly & Gilhooly, 1979). This is the **age of acquisition effect** – words learned early in childhood are generally recognized more accurately and faster than words learned later in life (see Juhasz, 2005 for review). Researchers have debated the extent to which age of acquisition effects in word processing may be simply a word frequency effect, since words learned early in life may be used more often over one's lifetime than words learned later (Oldfield & Wingfield, 1965). In a convincing study, Meschyan and Hernandez (2002) demonstrated that the effects of **age of acquisition** and word frequency separately influenced processing time during a word recognition task. In a study of French, Bonin et al. (2004) showed that even when lifetime word frequency is controlled, participants' reaction times are influenced by the word-specific age of acquisition.

The role of meaning in visual word recognition has also been demonstrated in studies in which readers are asked to comprehend sentences containing words that have more than one meaning, known as homographs, which are examples of **lexical ambiguity**. These words are also described as polysemous or examples of polysemy. Table 5.4 lists examples of English homographs. When first introduced to the topic of words having multiple meanings, students often struggle when judging whether a word's many usages are examples of different meanings or merely slight variations of a single meaning. Indeed, there is a continuum of meaning for words (Fillmore & Atkins, 2000), often representing a concrete meaning of a word at one end of the continuum and an abstract meaning of the word at the other end. Consider the word *head*, meaning a part of a body.

Table 5.4 Examples of English Homographs

Homograph	Meanings	
Ball	1. Round object used in sports	2. A formal dance
Band	1. Group of musicians	3. A round object worn on the finger (e.g., ring)
Bank	1. An institution for handling money	2. A natural land formation near a river
Boxer	1. Type of athlete	2. Breed of dog
Bug	1. Insect	2. Listening device used by spies
Cabinet	1. Furniture item used to store objects	2. A president's advisory group
Corn	1. A type of vegetable	2. A formation on the skin
Habit	1. A recurring behavior	2. A nun's clothing
Horn	1. Part of animal's body	2. Object for making sound or music
Page	1. Part of a book	2. Young assistant in Congress
Mint	1. A type of candy	2. A facility for making coins
Pipe	1. An object used to smoke tobacco	2. A round tube used in plumbing
Plant	1. Facility for manufacturing	2. A living organism in the flora category
Scale	1. Part of a fish body	2. Device used for weighing objects
Table	1. Furniture item often used for dining	2. A graphical arrangement in a written work

Sources: Rayner and Duffy (1986); Sereno et al. (2006)

Unlike the different meanings of a word, which are viewed by psycholinguists as part of the same lexical entry in the mental lexicon, the multiple meanings for homographs are viewed as being stored in separate lexical entries. Reading experiments in which participants viewed sentences containing homographs provided evidence that words with multiple meanings take longer to process than other words (Rayner & Duffy, 1986; Sereno et al., 2006).

Research has shown that less time is taken to identify a word if a semantically related word was identified immediately before (Loftus, 1973; Meyer & Schvaneveldt, 1971). This phenomenon is known as **semantic priming**. In a typical semantic priming experiment, participants are asked to perform a lexical decision task. Researchers measured response times as people made lexical decisions (determining whether or not two letter strings, presented simultaneously, were both words). In conditions in which both stimuli were words, some of the pairs were related (e.g. fork and spoon) and others were unrelated (e.g. book and spoon). The key finding from this investigation was that response time was faster for related words than for unrelated words. Words that are strongly related in meaning are referred to as "semantic associates." As you may recall from Chapter 4, researchers envision semantic memory as being organized in a network consisting of nodes, which represent concepts or words, and connections. When a concept is processed, it is activated and sends activation along the connections to other nodes in the network. The more strongly related two concepts are, the more easily one can be activated when the other is activated. It is useful to think of the point at which a word is recognized as the point in which it has been activated enough to trigger lexical access. For words preceded by unrelated words, the amount of activation needed to trigger lexical access is the full amount. For a word that was immediately preceded by a semantically related word, some activation spread to the word already, so the amount of activation needed to reach its threshold is reduced. When the word is viewed and the word receives activation, the threshold needed to trigger lexical access can be reached more quickly. The Research DIY box explores a task that has been used for over a century to explore the interrelationships among words.

Research DIY

What Word Comes to Mind?

Psycholinguists have traditionally identified semantic associates using the word association test, which Sigmund Freud introduced to probe his patients' atypical associations with common concepts. The Freudian version of the word association test involved his asking the patient to say the first word that came to mind after he gave them a particular target word (e.g., *sex*). In contrast, psycholinguists provide participants with a randomized list of words having a variety of meanings and ask participants to provide the first word that comes to mind following the processing of each target word. There is a long tradition in psycholinguistic research in using the word association task to compile the associations for commonly used words (Jenkins & Palermo, 1964; Kiss et al., 1972; Toglia & Battig, 1978). The results of these efforts are descriptive statistics (also called "norms," as in word usage norms) detailing how often a particular response is given for each word. You can carry out your own small-scale study of semantic association norms. Below is a list of words identified as having strong semantic associations and those identified as having only week semantic associations. Recruit between 10 and 20 friends or family members willing to perform the word association test with you. You can either present the list of words to your participants aloud, while you write down the first word they produce for each of the target words, or you may present the participants with a sheet of paper with the list of target words and a blank space next to each one. The list of target words below is presented in alphabetical order. The first step in preparing for your study is to create a randomized list of the target words to present to participants. Compile participants' responses and for each target word, compute the percentage of respondents who provided each of the different responses. For target words with strong semantic associates, you should have most respondents providing the same response. For target words without strong semantic associates, you will have few respondents providing the same response.

1. Words with strong semantic associates

   bread, cat, doctor, man, pen, pot, salt, shoe, spoon, sweet, lock, nose

2. Words with weaker semantic associates

   boot, color, cow, dry, dude, lid, meat, plate, plumber, spice, cord, tongue

In this section, we discussed the methods used to investigate how written words are recognized and the many factors that have been found to influence the time needed to recognize words. Word frequency and neighborhood density influence written and spoken word recognition. Written word recognition is also influenced by the font in which the word is written. Words containing multiple morphemes take longer to recognize than words that contain a single morpheme, suggesting that the recognition of multi-morphemic words begins with the recognition of individual morphemes and ends with the meanings being considered together. The recognition of words involves the activation of the sounds of words. In languages that use logographic writing systems, the phonological representation of the word is activated after lexical access occurs. In languages using alphabetic or syllabic writing systems, the phonological representation may be rapidly computed prior to lexical access. Words that refer to concrete objects are recognized faster than words that refer to abstract words.

 Time out for Review

Key Terms

Abstract word	Fixations	Phonological dyslexia
Acquired dyslexia	Fovea	Radicals
Age of acquisition	Free morpheme	Repetition blindness
Age of acquisition effect	Homograph	Repetition priming
Agglutinative language	Iconic memory	Saccades
Bound morpheme	Infixes	Semantic priming
Concreteness effect	Isolating language	Surface dyslexia
Concrete word	Lexical access	Visual acuity
Developmental dyslexia	Lexical ambiguity	Word length effect
Dyseidetic dyslexia	Pandemonium model	Word superiority effect
Dyslexia	Parafovea	
Dysphonetic dyslexia	Parafoveal preview benefit	

Review Questions

1   What is iconic memory? Describe the experiments that provided evidence for the existence of iconic memory.
2   What evidence is there that words are not recognized letter by letter?
3   Describe Selfridge's pandemonium model. To what extent does the model continue to influence research in word recognition?
4   Describe Coltheart's dual route model of visual word recognition. What pattern of word reading occurs if one of the routes of word recognition is disrupted?
5   To what extent are the sounds of words involved in the recognition of the written form of the word?
6   What are homographs? What has research shown about how such words are recognized within sentence contexts?
7   What evidence is there that the recognition of Chinese logographic symbols involves the recognition of their subcomponent radicals?
8   What evidence is there that the recognition of multi-morphemic words involves the recognition of the individual morphemes within the words?
9   What is the concreteness effect? According to Paivio, why does it occur?
10   How does the age at which one learns a word influence how that word is generally recognized during the adult years?

Contemporary Models of Visual Word Perception

The earliest research on the cognitive processes involved in recognizing written words was conducted in English, and the earliest models were developed with English in mind (Rayner et al., 2012). So far, we have reviewed two models of visual word recognition: Selfridge's pandemonium model and Coltheart's dual route model. In this section, we will review the most influential and useful models attempting to shed additional light on the processes involved in visual word recognition. As we have seen in discussions of the models of spoken word recognition, the distinguishing characteristics include: whether processing occurs serially or in parallel; whether processing occurs in a strict bottom-up manner or allows top-down processing; and whether processing is modular or interactive.

Morton's Logogen Model

You may recall our discussion in Chapter 3 of Morton's (1969, 1979) logogen model, an early model of spoken word recognition. It has served as an important source of inspiration for contemporary visual word recognition models. In the model, the logogens stored in memory can be activated either by auditory or visual input. The model was able to predict word frequency effects. In addition, the model provided a relatively straightforward way to reduce the thresholds by which words could be activated; thus, it provided a way to explain priming effects. The primary shortcoming of the model was its assumption that top-down processing could guide word perception. Numerous experiments have shown that the perception of words, spoken and written, appears to be carried out primarily through bottom-up processing (Rayner et al., 2012).

Forster's Autonomous Serial Search Model

Forster's (1976, 1979) model of visual word recognition is a relatively early model, but one that had a great deal of impact on research that followed. The model proposed that a reader views a word and then initiates a search through the memories of previously experienced words to find a match. We use the metaphor of a dictionary in the mind or **mental lexicon** when envisioning how our knowledge of words and their meanings are stored in our memory. In Forster's model, the search through the mental lexicon was presumed to be serial. It is useful to envision the mental lexicon as a vast library, on which memories of words are arranged on book shelves. Forster used the term "bins" to describe the area in memory where memories for similar words were stored. Certainly, searching through all the words you know each time you see a word would be time-consuming, regardless of how fast each item can be searched. In order to explain how the searching during word identification can be done as quickly as it appears to be done, Forster presumed that our memories of words are organized in a way that leads to rapid memory search. He proposed that our memories for words are organized in bins based on similarity (e.g., word beginnings). Within each bin, the most frequently used words were at the top of the bin, and the least frequently used words at the bottom of the bin. The serial search would locate high frequency words sooner than it would locate low frequency words and would be successfully completed sooner for high versus low frequency words; thus, the model provided an explanation for the well-established word frequency effect.

The model allowed for bottom-up processing of words in multiple modalities (vision, audition, and linguistic), allowing for input of different types to trigger a search of word memories. When identifying written words, readers would search the bins of word memories based on the visual form of the words. Those *orthographic* bins in our memories would be organized based on the visual similarity of word beginnings, and within the bins, memories would be ordered in terms of frequency usage. When identifying spoken words, listeners would search the bins of word memories based on the phonological forms of the words. In the *phonological* bins, words in the same bin would share the same initial phonemes and syllable(s), and within bins, words are ordered, with high frequency words at the top and low frequency words at the bottom.

Forster envisioned the serial memory search to be modular, as top-down processing, such as expectations generated on the basis of contextual information, could not influence how quickly the search for a word would be successfully terminated. The processing involved in lexical access was viewed as distinct from other types of language processing. The clear testable prediction that this stipulation makes is that priming effects would arise from processing involved in lexical access, but not from other types of processing.

There have been criticisms of the model (Harley, 2013). First, it provides no mechanism to account for readers' ability to pronounce non-words (letter or sound sequences without a corresponding memory in the bin), which in daily life would most often be words experienced for the first time. Second, even for the average reader, the model's serial search would have hundreds of thousands of words to search through in memory. The seemingly instantaneous way we recognize words appears inconsistent with a serial, exhaustive search through the entire mental lexicon. Forster's (1994) response to critics addressed the latter issue, suggesting that by assuming that all the bins are searched at the same time, search time could be shortened.

Interactive Activation Models

There are also models of visual word recognition that employ the connectionist architecture you learned about in Chapter 3 during the discussion of the TRACE model of word perception. In the early 1980s, the interactive activation and competition (IAC) model was proposed (McClelland & Rumelhart, 1981; Rumelhart et al., 1986). The IAC model, like the TRACE model, has three layers of nodes, with the input layer representing visual features of letters, the middle layer representing letters, and an output layer representing words. Processing occurring at each level can influence processing in the layer to which it is connected. If the model were presented with the visual input – C A T – the features associated with the three letters would be activated and other letter features would not be activated. Those letter features that are activated send activation to the middle layer, which would result in the activation of the nodes corresponding to the three letters being activated, while other nodes are either not activated or activated at relatively low levels. The activation of the letter nodes flows to the word level, resulting in the node representing the word *cat* being most highly activated.

A later interactive model of word recognition by Seidenberg and McClelland (1989) also had three layers, with each layer containing several hundred nodes. At the input layer, the model could accept visual (orthographic) input or auditory (phonological) input. There was a meaning layer connected to the input layer via three sets of hidden nodes. The hidden nodes are not specified as coding any particular aspect of any word; rather, each learning trial involved the model receiving input, producing output, receiving information about the correct output, and then adjusting the base activations of all nodes, including those in the hidden layers, to make it more likely that the model will produce a correct output on the next trial. There are many types of learning algorithm used in models of this type to make the adjustments in the activation levels of the nodes following an incorrect output (e.g., back propagation). In the testing of the model, there were more than 150,000 learning trials, after which the model was able to *identify* 2,820 words out of 2,897 that had been submitted to the model during the learning trials. Perhaps, a more impressive accomplishment of the model was that it could *identify* novel words (i.e., words that had not been used during the learning trials) and non-words.

 Time out for Review

Key Term

Mental lexicon

Review Questions

1 Describe Morton's logogen model's ability to account for word recognition results. To what extent does the model continue to influence research in word recognition?
2 Describe Forster's autonomous search model of visual word recognition. What are the model's weaknesses?

Summary

Across languages, writing systems differ a great deal, specifically in terms of whether individual symbols correspond to phonemes, syllables or whole words. Most of the research on word recognition has been conducted in English and other languages in which symbols correspond to phonemes. In these languages, there are differences in the amount of irregularity (i.e., when spelling does not completely predict pronunciation). Research has identified the factors that influence how quickly a word is recognized, including: word length in letters, syllables, and number of morphemes; word frequency; neighborhood density (i.e., number of words sharing some of the letters of the word); and the visual form or font of the letter. Further, the stages in visual word recognition involve breaking down words into their morphological and phonological parts. Models of visual word recognition differ in their assumptions about whether processing occurs interactively or in a manner in which lexical access is influenced by contextual information relatively late during processing. Thus far, there is no single model that explains all prior research results.

Recommended Books, Films, and Websites

Adelson, J. S. (2012). *Visual Word Recognition*. vol. 1: *Models and Methods, Orthography and Phonology*. London: Psychology Press.

Adelson, J. S. (2012). *Visual Word Recognition*. vol. 2: *Meaning and Context, Individuals and Development*. London: Psychology Press.

Hustwit, G. (2007). *Helvetica* [Motion Picture]. England: Swiss Dots.

Norris, D. (2013). Models of visual word recognition. *Trends in Cognitive Sciences*, 17(10), 517–24.

Rayner, K., Pollatsek, A., Ashby, J. & Clifton, C. (2012). *The Psychology of Reading* (2nd edn). New York: Psychology Press.

WordNet. A lexical database for English. wordnet.princeton.edu.

6 HOW ARE SENTENCES COMPREHENDED?

Chapter Content

Comprehending sentences usually proceeds rapidly with little or no noticeable effort. Although comprehending the full meaning of a sentence involves determining the syntactic and semantic roles that individual words are serving in the sentence, we are rarely aware that this level of analysis is occurring during processing. Our minds are able to assign words in sentences to their grammatical and semantic roles relatively automatically and without our being consciously aware. It is the rare sentence that leads us to become so consciously confused that we take steps to reread the text or to ask a speaker for clarification. As you will see in this chapter, researchers who aim to understand the cognitive processes involved in sentence comprehension sometimes use confusing sentences to gain insight into how the comprehension mechanisms in the mind work.

In this chapter, we will examine the research on sentence comprehension, including how linguists and psycholinguists envision the syntactic structure of sentences of different types and how comprehenders construct a mental representation of sentences from the beginning of processing to the end. Research in the 1970s focused on how readers determine the syntactic roles of words in a sentence as each newly encountered word is processed, referred to as **syntactic parsing**. In the first section, we review this classic research and the competing theoretical perspectives that were developed later. These theories differ with regard to how different sources of information are believed to be used as each newly encountered word is analyzed. In the second section, we examine the processes involved in comprehending the meaning of sentences. Interestingly, the amount of research on the semantic interpretation of sentences is relatively small compared to that conducted on syntactic parsing. Lastly, we look at how researchers envision sentence processing occurring in real time within **working memory**, which is the type of short-term memory that serves as our mental blackboard (Baddeley, 2012). Because there are individual differences in working memory capacity, there can be individual differences in how sentences are processed.

Syntactic Processing

A fundamental aspect of listening and reading comprehension is that it occurs incrementally. Whether we are listening or reading, we process the speech or text, bit by bit. As you may recall from previous chapters, research has provided some insight into what the bits might be (e.g., phonemes or syllables in speech in Chapter 3 and morphemes during reading in Chapter 5). During listening, we take in the sounds of the sentence as they are produced by a speaker. During reading, we move our eyes to process along a line of text. Since the 1970s, researchers have recognized that comprehenders are analyzing each new word of the input (text or speech) and constructing a mental representation of the sentence in memory (Frazier & Fodor, 1978; Kimball, 1973). In this section, you will learn about different theoretical approaches to parsing. The earliest approaches claimed that comprehenders construct a single analysis of an incoming word, relying first on syntactic information. Alternative approaches emphasized the idea that multiple sources of information could be used in parallel. Two recent proposals, the unrestricted race model and the good enough processing approach, attempt to provide some explanation for conflicting experimental results.

Syntax-first Approaches

Noam Chomsky published his seminal work *Syntactic Structures* in 1957. With it and his 1959 review of B. F. Skinner's book *Verbal Behavior* (1957), he explained the syntactic regularities within and across languages and his view that human language acquisition occurs so rapidly because universal grammar is an innate part of our biological endowment. In 1965, he published *Aspects of the Theory of Syntax* and continued making contributions about the nature of language in later works (Chomsky, 1980, 1981, 1986). Linguists and psycholinguists began representing sentences using phrase structure rules and tree diagrams. Figure 6.1 displays the syntactic phrase structure rules for English and a sample tree diagram. The specifics of each language's syntactic rules can be expressed in terms of phrase structure rules and tree diagrams displaying the hierarchical relationships among elements, such as a sentence node is higher in the tree than a noun phrase (NP) node or verb phrase (VP) node.

Figure 6.1 Phrase Structure Rules for English with an Example Sentence

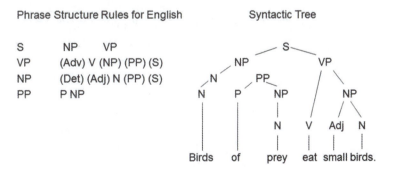

Phrase Structure Rules for English

```
S     NP    VP
VP    (Adv) V (NP) (PP) (S)
NP    (Det) (Adj) N (PP) (S)
PP    P NP
```

Syntactic Tree

S = Sentence; NP = Noun Phrase; VP = Verb Phrase; Adv = Adverb; V = Verb, PP = Prepositional Phrase; Det = Determiner (e.g., the, a(n), this, those, etc.); Adj = Adjective; P = Preposition (e.g., in, on, off, under, etc.)

The phrase structure rules for human languages make it easy to see an important characteristic of languages, one that Chomsky (1957) emphasized. Known as syntactic recursion, it refers to the fact that sentences can, theoretically, be as long as a speaker wants them to be, because the phrase structure rules of languages involve a nesting of syntactic rules, such as a sentence (S) being able to be part of a verb phrase (VP), which itself is part of a sentence (S). One could get a sequence that starts with S → NP VP S NP VP and goes on forever, with the last VP in the sequence containing another S again and again. Similarly, the noun phrase (NP) is nested within the definition of the prepositional phrase (PP), such as in the sequence S → NP VP NP PP NP PP NP PP and so on. Here are examples of these two types of recursion in English:

I thought that I knew that I forgot that he remembered that …
She bought the book about the child with the illness at the hospital …

You may recall the discussion in Chapter 1 of the Pirahã language, spoken by a hunter-gatherer tribe living in the Amazon rainforest. Everett (2008, 2012) has claimed that Pirahã lacks syntactic recursion, making it the only known human language lacking it. Others have disputed Everett's claim on the grounds that insufficient supportive evidence had been presented (Nevins et al., 2009).

Interestingly, around the same time, computer scientists began to envision how computers might be able to interpret speech (Turing, 1950). The subspecialty within computer science is known as **natural language processing** (Hutchins, 1997) and is now considered part of the broader field of artificial intelligence, which involves attempts to create manmade intelligent systems (Sobel & Li, 2013). In 1954, IBM and researchers at Georgetown University attempted to program a computer to translate a corpus of Russian sentences into English. There was a great deal of interest in the promise of one day having a machine-based language translator; however, the task proved more difficult than originally anticipated. After a decade of work on the project, progress was slow (Pierce et al., 1966). Today, smartphones and other electronic gadgets are equipped with voice recognition software that grew from this research in the 1950s. Although a great deal of progress has been made in getting machines to interpret human speech, the performance remains far from perfect. It is important to note that the manner in which these gadgets have been developed to interpret language is not the way in which humans are believed to interpret language. This chapter focuses on the research investigating how people process sentences.

In 1973, John Kimball published an influential paper entitled *Seven Principles of Surface Structure Parsing in Natural Language*. With the principles, Kimball (1973) described how, as we process a sentence in real time, we assign syntactic structure incrementally. His paper built on the earlier work of others, including Chomsky & Miller (1963) and Fodor & Garrett (1967), but rarely gets the recognition it deserves in providing a detailed account of how our knowledge of our language's phrase structure rules can be used to interpret sentences word by word. He argued that the application of our knowledge of phrase structure rules is a form of top-down processing, which, as you may recall, occurs any time prior knowledge is used to interpret an incoming stimulus. At least for native speakers of a language, the knowledge of language is presumed to be retrieved from memory and applied during processing more rapidly than permits conscious reflection; however, as we incrementally interpret sentences, we create a mental representation within our working memory that we are able to consciously monitor. Occasionally, during sentence interpretation, we realize that we have misinterpreted a word or phrase and must backtrack to figure out what, in fact, was the author's intended meaning. The mental representation that the comprehender builds is the **phrase marker**.

Occasionally, we might stumble upon a word or phrase that has more than one interpretation and then we can become consciously aware of the uncertainty. **Syntactic ambiguity** describes sequences of words in sentences that can be analyzed syntactically in more than one way. For example, the phrase *visiting relatives* is syntactically ambiguous. The pair of words may refer to relatives who happen to be visiting, in which case the syntactic analysis would involve analyzing *relatives* as the noun and *visiting* as an adjective, as in *visiting relatives make excellent houseguests*. However, a second possibility is that visiting relatives is an activity in which the noun *relatives* is functioning as object of the verb *visiting* and the subject of the clause is omitted, as in *visiting relatives is something we enjoy*. As you will see, sentences containing ambiguity are frequently used to test different theories of sentence comprehension. It is important to note that as we comprehend sentences in real time, the processing occurs so rapidly that we usually lack conscious awareness of how it occurred. We simply understand what we hear or read.

Garden Path Model

Of the seven principles proposed by Kimball (1973), two were highlighted in Lyn Frazier's dissertation (Frazier, 1979) and provided the foundation of her later work with Janet Fodor (Frazier & Fodor, 1978), Charles Clifton (Frazier & Clifton, 1996), and Keith Rayner (Frazier & Rayner, 1982, 1987, 1990). Her views of the human language parser have become the most prominent of the syntax-first approaches to sentence processing, which is often referred to as the garden path model. This view claimed that in determining the initial analysis or parse of a word, we use only syntactic information about the incoming word's syntactic category (noun, verb, adjective, adverb, etc.) and the syntactic information in the phrase marker up to that point. In cases in which there are many ways in which an incoming word can be incorporated or attached into the phrase marker, parsing principles would guide the decision of which analysis to build. In Frazier's and Kimball's view, the human language parser is a serial processor, constructing a single representation of a sentence at a time. Frazier focused on two syntactic parsing strategies: **minimal attachment**, which applies when the syntactic ambiguity involves two structures that differ in syntactic complexity, and **late closure**, which applies when the syntactic ambiguity involves structures having the same syntactic complexity.

When comprehenders apply minimal attachment, they are believed to select initially the least complex syntactic analysis. When comprehenders apply late closure, they are believed to select initially the syntactic analysis that is part of the most recently processed location in the phrase marker (i.e., low attachment vs. high attachment), which would presumably burden working memory to a lesser degree. Consider the examples in 1. The NP *the girl* is temporarily ambiguous in 1a, as it may be interpreted as the direct object of the preceding verb or the subject NP of the subordinate clause whose main verb is *left*.

1 a. He knew the girl …   Temporarily ambiguous
  b. He knew the girl well.   Direct object continuation
  c. He knew the girl left.   Clause continuation

Constructing a direct object interpretation involves constructing less syntactic structure than constructing a subordinate clause; thus, minimal attachment applies, leading to the syntactically simplest structure being built. In experiments in which participants were asked to read sentences and answer straightforward comprehension questions, reading time was measured to determine when during processing difficulty occurred. As you may recall from Chapter 5, reading time increases as processing difficulty increases. In contrast, when comprehenders apply late closure, they are believed to select the syntactic analysis that can be attached to the most recently processed region of the phrase marker. Consider the examples in 2. In 2a, the relative clause at the end of the sentence (i.e., *who was from Atlanta*) could modify the NP *the son* or the NP the *neighbor* with the same amount of syntactic tree building occurring for each interpretation. Late closure predicts that the comprehender will generally prefer to attach the clause to the right edge of the phrase marker so that it would modify *the neighbor.* In 2b, the NP *the patient* can be analyzed as a direct object of the preceding verb or as the subject of the main clause, which would involve attaching the NP as the subject of the main clause to the most distant part of the phrase marker; thus, late closure predicts that the preferred analysis for the NP would be as a direct object.

2 a. Kim spoke to the son of the neighbor who was from Atlanta.

  b. After the doctor pushed the patient coughed.

The garden path theory of sentence processing predicts that occasionally comprehenders will construct an initial analysis that will later prove to be incorrect and need to be revised (Ferreira & Henderson, 1990; Frazier & Rayner, 1982, 1987). **Syntactic reanalysis** describes instances in which the initial analysis proves not to be the intended analysis. Using eye movement recording, Frazier and Rayner (1982) showed that readers' eye movement patterns during the reading of sentences in which syntactic reanalysis was believed to occur supported the view that a temporary syntactic ambiguity was initially analyzed one way and, later in the sentence, was analyzed in a different way. They measured reading time on sentences similar to those in 3. The NP *the answer* is ambiguous in both sentences. In 3a, the words following the ambiguous NP confirm that the NP serves as the direct object of the verb. In 3b, the sentence continuation confirms that the NP serves as the subject NP of a subordinate clause. Frazier and Rayner (1982) found that reading times were consistent with minimal attachment, as readers spent longer reading *was missing* than reading *by heart.*

3 a. The girl knew the answer by heart.   Direct object
  b. The girl knew the answer was missing.   Clausal subject

They also measured reading time on sentences similar to those in 4. In accordance with late closure, readers were expected to analyze the NP *a mile* as the direct object of the verb *jogs.* Reading time results supported the view that readers analyzed the NP as a direct object, because reading time on the verb *seems* was significantly longer in 4b than in 4a. In both experiments, there was evidence that when readers processed the words that signaled that syntactic reanalysis was needed (*was missing* in 3b and *seems* in 4b), backward eye movements were made to part of the sentence containing the ambiguous phrase.

4   a. Since Jay always jogs a mile it seems like a short distance to him.

b. Since Jay always jogs a mile seems like a short distance to him.

Sentences that have a temporary syntactic ambiguity, which causes the reader to experience temporary confusion, are referred to as **garden path sentences**, as the reader is led down a garden path only to be surprised later that the initial impression of the sentence proved to be incorrect. The classic garden path example is *The horse raced past the barn fell*, in which the verb *raced* is syntactically ambiguous and typically is initially analyzed by readers as serving as a main clause verb whose subject is *the horse*. However, when the reader later encounters a second verb *fell*, the reader figures out that *fell* is the main clause verb and *raced* is a verb of a relative clause, which modifies *horse*, as in *The horse that was raced past the barn fell*. When the verb *ridden* is used instead of *raced*, the ambiguity and the processing difficulty is eliminated, as in *The horse ridden past the barn fell*. Table 6.1 lists some other garden path sentences.

Table 6.1 Examples of Garden Path Sentences

Example	Hint
The old man the boat.	"The old" is the subject and "man" is the verb.
The girl told the story cried.	"told the story" is a relative clause modifying "girl".
We painted the wall with cracks.	The wall with cracks was painted.
When Sue eats food gets thrown.	"eats" is used without a direct object as in "When Sue eats".
He convinced her children are noisy.	Insert "that" between "her" and "children".
She hit the boy with a wart.	The boy had a wart and he was hit.
The cat that Sue had really loved yarn.	Sue had a cat, and it really loved yarn.
Jim gave the boy the dog bit a bandage.	A boy was bit by a dog, and Jim gave him a bandage.
The cotton fabric is usually made of is grown in Egypt.	Insert "that" between "cotton" and "fabric."
Lyn put the book on the shelf in the trash can.	The book was on the shelf, and Lyn put it in the trash can.

Researchers have examined the factors that influence the difficulty that readers experience during syntactic reanalysis. For example, several experiments have found that the processing difficulty occurring during syntactic reanalysis increases as the length of the ambiguous region increases (Ferreira & Henderson, 1991; Frazier & Rayner, 1982; Kennedy & Murray, 1984; Warner & Glass, 1987). The results appear consistent with the review that syntactic reanalysis involves abandoning an initial syntactic analysis and any semantic interpretations that have been built so far as well as constructing a new syntactic analysis. Consider the examples in 5, in which 5a and 5c contain the syntactic ambiguity and 5b and 5d are the unambiguous versions. In 5a, the ambiguity is relatively short (*the cause*), but in 5c, it is longer (*the cause of the deadly helicopter crash*). The typically observed pattern of reading time is that reading time on the disambiguating verb region of the second clause (*was not human error*) is longer in 6b versus 6a and in 6d versus 6c, and the reading time difference between unambiguous and ambiguous versions is larger when the ambiguity is long versus short (i.e., 5d – 5c > 5b – 5a).

5   a. Airline experts established the cause was not human error.

     b. Airline experts established that the cause was not human error.

     c. Airline experts established the cause of the deadly helicopter crash was not human error.

     d. Airline experts established that the cause of the deadly helicopter crash was not human error.

However, in other studies in which the lengths of ambiguous regions were varied, reading time did not differ significantly (Kennison, 2001, 2004). More research is needed to explore possible reasons for the different results. As you will learn in the next section, critics of the syntax-first approaches to sentence processing emphasize our ability to construct multiple analyses in parallel while using multiple sources of information throughout processing. In a later section, you also will learn that researchers still have very little understanding of how semantic interpretation occurs for initial or revised analyses of sentences.

Before we end our examination of the syntax-first approach to sentence processing, we must consider circumstances in which the syntactic category of the incoming word is itself ambiguous. In these circumstances, Frazier and colleagues (Frazier et al., 1999; Frazier & Rayner, 1987, 1990) have argued that the comprehender delays constructing any analysis. Empirical support for their conclusion was obtained in a series of experiments in which they examined instances in which readers encountered a word whose syntactic category (noun, verb, adjective, etc.) was ambiguous. Such words are referred to as examples of **syntactic category ambiguity**. In Frazier and Rayner's (1987) experiments, target words were ambiguous between nouns and verbs. Readers comprehended sentences similar to those in 6 as their eye movements were recorded. The word *trains* is used as a verb in 6a and 6c, but as a noun in 6b and 6d. In 6a and 6b, the use of the word *trains* is initially ambiguous, but readers are able to learn the intended usage when they encountered the words immediately following *trains*. In 6c and 6c, the presence of the words *this* in 6c and *these* in 6d disambiguates the word *trains,* so readers were able to infer which use of the word was intended in the sentence. Frazier and Rayner (1987) compared reading time on the ambiguous sentences (6a and 6b) with the reading time on the unambiguous sentences (6c and 6d), finding that reading time was longer on the words following *trains* in the ambiguous conditions. Of particular interest was the fact that reading time on the words following *trains* in the two types of ambiguous sentences (6a and 6b) did not differ significantly, suggesting that readers did not experience a garden path, presumably because they did not initially construct the NP, following minimal attachment, and then later revise that analysis in sentences like those in 6b. The conclusion was that when an incoming word's syntactic category is ambiguous, the syntactic analysis of the word is delayed, until later disambiguating information is processed.

6   a. I know that the desert trains young people to be especially tough.

b. I know that the desert trains are especially tough on young people.

c. I know that this desert trains young people to be especially tough.

d. I know that these desert trains are especially tough on young people.

The view that the language parser delays analysis under any condition seems at odds with the original motivation for the parsing principle of late closure. The preference for low versus high attachment in cases in which the amount of syntactic structure involved in the two analyses was the same was to reduce the burden on working memory. It seems likely that delaying parsing for any amount of time during processing would place a burden on working memory. We will examine the role of working memory in sentence processing later in this chapter. The Research DIY box examines the extent to which individuals follow late closure consistently when interpreting sentences containing relative clauses similar to the example in 3a.

The Role of Non-syntactic Information

Proponents of the syntax-first approach to sentence processing have argued that comprehenders do not use non-syntactic sources of information initially to analyze incoming words. Investigations providing support for the claim have focused on how comprehenders use three types of non-syntactic information: lexical information associated with verbs (Ferreira & Henderson, 1990; Kennison, 2001); semantic plausibility information (Ferreira & Clifton, 1986); and discourse information (Britt et al., 1992). As you will see later in this chapter, critiques of the syntax-first approach have carried out similar experiments; however, conflicting results have emerged. We will examine the rationale of these studies by focusing on those that have investigated the role of verb information in syntactic ambiguity resolution.

Linguists have noted that our knowledge of verbs includes information about the types of phrases that can be used or must be used with the verb (Kaplan & Bresnan, 1982). For example, the verb *put* requires not just a direct object, but also a prepositional phrase, specifying the location of the action, as in *Jordan put the milk in the refrigerator*. A sentence is ungrammatical when one of the required phrases is missing, as in **Jordan put the milk* or **Jordan put in the refrigerator*. There are other verbs that can occur with a direct object, but do not require one for the sentence to be a grammatical sentence. Consider the examples in 8. Some verbs do not take direct objects, as in 8a, and other verbs always occur with a direct object, as in 8c. These verbs are referred to as "strictly intransitive verbs" and "strictly transitive verbs," respectively. Other verbs can be used with or without a direct object, as in 8b. Such verbs are referred to as "optionally transitive verbs."

Interpreting Ambiguous Relative Clauses

Relative clauses modify NPs, and when they modify NPs serving as direct objects of the sentence, syntactic ambiguity can occur. Consider the examples in 7. The relative clause, which is underlined in the example, can be interpreted as modifying the most recently processed NP, *the actress* in 7a, or a previously processed noun, *the daughter* in 7a. In 7b, because it is unlikely that a son would wear a dress, the relative clause is ultimately resolved as modifying the most recent noun *the actress*. In 7c, because it is unlikely that an actress would have a bushy mustache, the relative clause is resolved as modifying the first noun *the son*.

7   a. The visitor complimented the daughter of the actress who had worn the blue dress. (Ambiguous)

b. The visitor complimented the son of the actress who had worn the blue dress. (Low attachment, preferred by late closure)

c. The visitor complemented the son of the actress who had a bushy mustache. (High attachment)

Recruit between 10 and 20 acquaintances who are native English speakers. Read each of the following sentence pairs aloud to them. You may recall the term "syntactic priming" from Chapter 4 when it was discussed in the context of speech production. There is ample evidence that our processing of a sentence can be influenced by the syntactic structures we have experienced recently. If you construct 12–18 sentences and accompanying comprehension questions to intermix with the sentences below, you can reduce the likelihood that participants' judgments will be strongly influenced by syntactic priming. When unrelated sentences are intermixed with a set of target sentences, they are referred to as filler sentences.

1 Michael admired the son of the doctor who won the award. Who won the award?
2 Janice interviewed the daughter of the actress who made the large donation. Who made the donation?
3 Samuel recognized the mother of the basketball player who was featured in the article. Who was featured in the article?
4 Stephanie met the sister of the senator who recently published a book. Who recently published a book?
5 William read about the attorney of the singer who was arrested. Who was arrested?
6 Linda recalled the news report about the business partner of the millionaire who was murdered. Who was murdered?

For each person you interview, compute the percentage of target sentences to which they responded with an answer consistent with late closure analysis (i.e., the second noun phrase). Across participants, compute the average. If participants consistently apply late closure, the percentage should be above 50 percent.

8   a. The boy yawned the whole day.   Intransitive verb

b. The boy ate the whole day.   Optionally transitive verb

c. The boy gave the whole amount.   Transitive verb

The term **subcategorization frame** refers to different structures that can be used with a verb (Bresnan, 2001; Kaplan & Bresnan, 1982). For most verbs, the subcategorization frames specify optional usages for the verb. For example, the verbs in the examples in 9 subcategorize for both a direct object frame and also sentence (S) (also referred to as a clause) frame. When considering what sources of information comprehenders might use when resolving syntactic ambiguity, researchers recognized that the verb in the sentence can sometimes be helpful in generating expectations about the types of words and phrases that follow it (Clifton et al., 1984). When lexical access occurs, information about the possible uses of a verb can be retrieved from memory following lexical access of the verb and used in the comprehension of the following words and phrases.

9 remembered [NP _____]   believed [NP _____]

          [S _____]   [S _____]

Ferreira and Henderson (1990) investigated how readers use information about verb subcategorization frames (also called "verb bias") to resolve syntactic ambiguity. They investigated the syntactic ambiguity displayed in 10, which is one of the syntactic ambiguities investigated in Frazier and Rayner's (1982) eye movement experiment. The ambiguous NP *the prize* could be analyzed as the direct object of the preceding verb or as the subject NP of a clause that is part of the main clause's VP. Minimal attachment predicts that readers should always interpret this syntactic ambiguity initially as a direct object, because it is less complex in terms of syntactic structure, requiring the fewest nodes and branches to be added to the phrase marker. Ferreira and Henderson (1990) compared reading time on sentences containing one of two types of verbs: verbs used most frequently with direct object NPs (direct object biased verb); and verbs used most frequently with clauses (clausal biased verb). In all sentences, verbs were followed by a clause, as shown in the examples in 11. They recorded eye movements during reading, finding that the initial reading time on the disambiguating verb *would* was longer in ambiguous sentences, as in 11a and 11b, than unambiguous control sentences, as in 11c and 11d, regardless of the type of verb in the sentence. They also found that measures of reading that reflect relatively late stages of processing, such as the number of regressive saccades made from the disambiguating region back to earlier parts of the sentence and total reading time, revealed an effect of verb type, with conditions containing the direct object biased verbs being more difficult to process overall. They concluded that although verb information is not used initially to resolve syntactic ambiguity, it may be used during the process of syntactic reanalysis when it occurs.

10 a. Mia accepted the prize …   Ambiguous

    b. Mia accepted the prize last Saturday.   Direct object NP

    c. Mia accepted the prize would not be hers.   Subject NP in clause

    d. Mia accepted that the prize would be here.   Unambiguous clause

11 a. The director suggested the change   Direct object biased verb
       would …   condition – ambiguous

    b. The director foresaw the change would …   Clausal biased verb
                                                    condition – ambiguous

    c. The director suggested that the change   Direct object biased
       would …   verb condition – control

    d. The director foresaw that the   Clausal biased verb
       change would …   condition – control

As you will see in the next section, researchers disagree about how quickly readers and listeners can use non-syntactic information to make decisions about syntactic ambiguities they encounter during sentence comprehension. The Language Spotlight box examines research investigating how readers process sentences in which the verb always occurs at the end of the sentence.

Language Spotlight

Understanding Hindi

Hindi is one of the official languages of India and among the top five most widely spoken languages in the world today (Lewis et al., 2016). As you may recall from Chapter 1, Hindi belongs to the same Indo-European language family as English. Hindi differs from English in many ways, including the basic ordering of elements in the sentence. Hindi has been described as a free word order language, with SOV being the canonical (preferred) order (Jain, 1995), as the object occurs after the subject and the verb occurs at the end of the sentence. In contrast, in English, word order is fairly inflexible, and the verb typically occurs between the subject and verb (SVO). Theories of sentence parsing that propose that comprehenders use lexical information associated with the verb to analyze words and phrases that follow the verb ("lexical functional grammar") predict that patterns of sentence parsing would vary across languages, because the ordering of the verb relative to the subject and object differs across languages (Kaplan & Bresnan, 1982). There have been relatively few studies of sentence parsing in languages other than English. Among those studies, few have been carried out with languages in which the verb appears in the clause-final position (Mishra et al., 2011). Mishra et al. (2011) explored how rapidly readers of Hindi could detect anomaly in Hindi sentences that varied in word order. Hindi, as many languages with SOV word order, has markings for cases, which distinguish subject noun phrases from object noun phrases as well as other types of noun phrases. Case marking is likely useful to comprehenders in determining the syntactic structure of sentences before the verb is encountered. The semantic compatibility between the subject noun and the verb was either anomalous or non-anomalous in sentences having one of three word orders in which the subject preceded the verb (SOV, SVO, and OSV). Readers could detect the anomaly only at the verb; thus, reading time on the verb was varied for the three word order conditions. The results showed that reading time was significantly longer for anomalous conditions than for non-anomalous conditions. Although the size of the difference between anomalous and non-anomalous conditions varied for the three word order conditions, it is impossible to interpret, as the length and frequency of subject and object nouns were not closely matched and because reading time on the verb would be influenced by the difficulty of the immediately preceding word ("spillover effect"; Rayner et al., 1989).

Interactive Approaches

In the 1980s, researchers rejected the notion that language knowledge and language processing was special or different from other types of knowledge and processing (Rumelhart et al., 1986). Around this time, psycholinguists began to publish attacks on the garden path model, demonstrating that the model's assumptions were incorrect, failing to account for how readers or listeners processed sentences. A prominent alternative to the garden path model was the interactive approach, whose advocates claimed that comprehenders are not limited to constructing a single analysis of a syntactic ambiguity, rather they could construct multiple analyses in parallel; and that comprehenders are not limited to using only syntactic information when constructing the initial analysis of an incoming word, rather they could use any and all types of information they have available (Traxler, 2014). An example of a model included in this approach is the constraint satisfaction model (MacDonald et al., 1994; Tanenhaus et al., 1989).

In numerous studies, proponents of the **constraint satisfaction model** aimed to show that there were circumstances in which readers or listeners would avoid a garden path in a sentence because of their rapid use of non-syntactic information. The conclusions of Ferreira and Henderson (1990) were challenged by Trueswell et al. (1993) who tested the same set of conditions with an improved set of verbs. They improved on the set of verbs compared in sentences, finding that for conditions containing verbs used more often with direct objects, reading time on ambiguous sentences was longer than on unambiguous controls; however, for conditions containing verbs used more often with clauses, reading time on ambiguous and unambiguous sentences did not differ significantly.

Later, Garnsey et al. (1997) investigated how readers resolve the same type of syntactic ambiguity, specifically focusing on how they used information about the semantic plausibility of the noun following the verb in conjunction with verb bias. Unlike earlier studies, Garnsey et al. (1997) included conditions containing verbs used comparably often with each type of subcategorization frame (equi-biased verbs). They observed effects of both verb bias and semantic plausibility on reading times. For conditions containing strongly biased verbs, they observed results similar to Trueswell et al. (1993). They also found that semantic plausibility occurred for equi-biased and direct object biased verb conditions. They found that there was a larger difference in reading time between ambiguous and unambiguous conditions when the noun was plausible as a direct object of the verb versus implausible as a direct object of the verb.

Some of the debate between advocates of the constraint satisfaction and garden path models (Ferreira & Henderson, 1990; Garnsey et al., 1997; Kennison, 2001; Trueswell et al., 1993) has centered on methodological issues, specifically related to the researcher's ability to assess a reader's initial analysis of a word versus processing that includes post-initial processing. Consequently, there was a great deal of excitement surrounding the innovation of a new methodology for investigating sentence processing. The methodology was the visual world paradigm, which you learned about Chapter 3. In 1995, Tanenhaus et al. reported the seminal research in *Science*. They reported results obtained when participants' eye movements were recorded while they listened to instructions that they carried out in the context of a visual display containing physical objects. Through analysis of the participants' saccades to objects in the visual display in conjunction with the speech that they have heard up to that point, they were able to show that participants were able to use information from the visual context when resolving a syntactic ambiguity. Participants heard sentences similar to *Put the apple on the towel in the box.* The prepositional phrase *on the towel* is syntactically ambiguous as it may be specifying the location of the verb *put* or be a modifier of *apple,* indicating which apple to move. The former interpretation has less syntactic complexity, thus would be predicted to be preferred by minimal attachment. In the experiment, Tanenhaus et al. (1995) manipulated the visual context. In one condition, the visual context contained one apple on a towel, a towel with nothing on top of it, an empty box, and an unrelated object. In another condition, the visual context contained two apples, one on a towel and the other on a napkin, a towel with nothing on top of it, and an empty box. During processing, they found that participants made more looks to the empty towel when the visual context contained one apple versus two, suggesting that listeners were able to use information about the visual context to avoid minimally attaching the prepositional phrase (i.e., going down the garden path).

Unrestricted Race Model

Later in the 1990s, Traxler et al. (1998) proposed a new model of syntactic ambiguity resolution, the **unrestricted race approach**. This model claimed that multiple analyses are constructed simultaneously, with the analysis constructed most quickly influencing processing time. The model also stipulated that initial analyses can be influenced by all sources of information. Also, the multiple syntactic analyses constructed in parallel do not compete. Consequently, the approach makes similar predictions as the garden path approach for the processing of the syntactically ambiguous material, but makes similar predictions as the constraint satisfaction approach for the processing of the disambiguating material in a sentence. Recent research by Mohamed and Clifton (2011) yielded results consistent with the unrestricted race model and not consistent with either the garden path or constraint satisfaction approaches. The model has attracted a great deal of interest from other researchers (van Gompel et al., 2005; van Gompel et al., 2001; c.f., Farmer et al., 2007).

Good Enough Processing

One of the more intriguing views of sentence processing was proposed by Ferreira and colleagues (Christianson et al., 2001; Ferreira et al., 2002; Ferreira & Patson, 2007), claiming that during sentence comprehension, readers and listeners do not consistently carry out fine-grained analysis but construct "quick and dirty" interpretations. These interpretations are referred to as *good enough processing,* which involves processing sentences only superficially. The approach was inspired by the conflicting results obtained in experiments testing the garden path and interactive approaches. During good enough processing, comprehenders are viewed as only constructing *good enough* or superficial representations during processing, but failing to take into account the full range of available sources of information. During the processing of sentences containing ambiguity, good enough processing may involve the reader not completely resolving the ambiguity. Evidence for the view has come from sentence processing experiments showing that readers sometimes misinterpret sentences. Ferreira (2003) had participants listen to sentences similar to *the dog was bitten by the man* and then immediately report which word had been the agent or patient. Reaction time and accuracy were recorded. In three experiments, she found that accuracy was significantly lower for non-canonical sentences (passive sentences) than canonical sentences (active sentences). Processing was slower in non-canonical versus canonical sentences. Research conducted by others in the 1990s produced results consistent with the good enough processing approach. For example, Frazier et al. (1999) had participants read sentences similar to *Mary and John saved $100.* The results showed that participants did not resolve the sentences to the point of determining whether each person (Mary and John) saves $100 or whether they together saved $100. The experiment demonstrated that a commitment to a particular interpretation only occurred when following material required it.

As you will learn later in this chapter, research has shown that the meaning of abandoned and revised syntactic analyses may persist in the reader's working memory; thus, in future work, it will be important for researchers to be able to distinguish between a reader's commitment or lack of a commitment to an analysis from the reader having revised one analysis, but the meaning of the initial analysis lingers, later influencing processing. A criticism of the view is that there has not been a full description of the conditions under which comprehenders carry out fully specified processing versus good enough processing. Nevertheless, the good enough processing approach raises the possibility that our patterns of processing may vary not only for a given type of sentence, but also for a given individual across different episodes of processing and possibly across individuals. Later in this chapter, you will learn about studies demonstrating that there are individual differences related to memory that are related to how sentences are processed.

In this section, you learned about the major theoretical approaches to sentence processing. The earliest approaches emphasized initial reliance on syntactic information to analyze words in terms of their syntactic relationship with the preceding context. Later approaches have rejected the notion that syntactic information has a privileged status in processing; thus, other types of information have been argued to play important roles in interpreting words in sentence contexts. Lexical and semantic information have been shown to influence reading time during sentence comprehension; however, debates have arisen regarding how quickly they are used in the analysis of an ambiguous word. The unrestricted race model was proposed to account for conflicting findings from experiments contrasting the predictions of the garden path and interactive approaches. The model has been found to make accurate predictions in one recent study. The conflicting results from prior research have also been addressed by the good enough processing approach, which emphasizes that comprehenders may not always carry out fully specific analyses of sentences and commit to a single interpretation.

Key Terms

Constraint satisfaction model	Natural language processing	Syntactic parsing
Filler sentences	Phrase marker	Syntactic reanalysis
Garden path sentence	Subcategorization frames	Unrestricted race approach
Late closure	Syntactic ambiguity	Working memory
Minimal attachment	Syntactic category ambiguity	

Review Questions

1 What are phrase structure rules? How do syntax-first approaches to parsing believe that phrase structure rules are used during sentence processing?

2 What is syntactic recursion in human language? To what extent do scholars believe that all human languages have this syntactic property?

3 Describe the two parsing strategies – minimal attachment and late closure. When are each believed to be used? When they are used, what type of structure is initially chosen by the comprehender?

4 What is a garden path sentence? How do researchers use garden path sentences to test theories of sentence comprehension?

5 What have experiments shown about comprehenders' use of verb-specific lexical information to resolve temporary syntactic ambiguity?

6 Describe the interactive approach to sentence processing. To what extent is processing presumed to be serial in nature versus parallel?

7 What is the unrestricted race model of syntactic parsing? In terms of empirical evidence from processing experiments, how does the model compare to the garden path and interactive approaches to syntactic parsing?

8 Describe the good enough processing view of sentence comprehension. What evidence supports this view? What are some criticisms of the approach?

Semantic Processing

The processes involved in the comprehension of the meaning of sentences are less well understood than the processes involved in the assignment of the syntactic structure. The topic represents the largest part of the essential question of how sentences are comprehended. This is because there is less agreement among linguists regarding how to represent meaning in natural language than there is about the syntactic representations of sentences. Within the area of formal semantics, there is a lack of a consensus about how to represent meaning as a formal system (Cresswell, 2006; Saeed, 2008). In this section, we will discuss some of the early distinctions that provided insight into the semantic level of processing and how it differs from syntactic processing. We begin our discussion with Chomsky's original insights concerning a semantic level of analysis that is distinct from the syntactic level of analysis. Second, we will examine the classic work suggesting that during comprehension, we must determine who did what to whom where and when by assigning incoming words and phrases their appropriate meaning-based function – thematic role – in the sentence. Lastly, we will explore how comprehenders process sentences.

Semantic Versus Syntactic Representation

Despite the lack of guidance from theoretical linguistics, psycholinguists have moved forward, first building on Chomsky's (1957) original insights about the distinction between the syntactic representation of a sentence and the semantic representation. One of his most famous example sentences is *Colorless green ideas sleep furiously*. The sentence helped illustrate his view. Although the sentence is syntactically well formed (grammatically correct), it is meaningless. Interestingly, it is not possible to have a semantically meaningful sentence that is syntactically incorrect. In his transformational grammar, he further pointed out that sentences with different syntactic structure have similar meanings, as shown in the examples in 12. He argued that the syntactic structure of passive sentences, as in 12b, was generated from corresponding active sentences, as in 12a. Also, the syntactic structure of questions, as in 12d, was generated from corresponding declarative sentences, as in 12c.

12	a.	The child ate the doughnut.	Active
	b.	The doughnut was eaten by the child.	Passive
	c.	Marco went to the airport to pick up someone.	Declarative
	d.	Who did Marco go to the airport to pick up?	Question

An important discovery about our memory for sentence syntax and semantics was made in the 1960s. The Classic Research box explores the fact that our memory for the meaning of the sentence lasts far longer than our memory for the specific words contained in the sentence and their order within the sentence.

Thematic Roles

The prevailing view of how comprehenders carry out the semantic interpretation of sentences is that just as comprehenders interpret sentences word by word and determine the syntactic structure of each incoming word, they must also determine its semantic role. A popular approach is that of Dowty (1990), which was influenced by earlier work by Fillmore (1968), suggesting that comprehenders assign **thematic roles** to words in sentences. The most common thematic roles include:

- *agent*, which refers to the entity performing an action
- *patient*, which refers to the entity that is changed during the action
- *instrument*, which refers to the entity that is used to execute the action
- *location*, which refers to where the action occurs.

The sentences in 14 are examples of an active sentence and its corresponding passive sentences. In active sentences, such as 14a, the subject NP *mechanic* is the

Classic Research — Memory for Sentences

In 1967, Jacqueline Sachs published her dissertation research demonstrating the limits of our memory for sentences. Even today, the results continue to be surprising to those who are not linguists or psycholinguistics and thought-provoking for those who are. Her research initially examined memory for sentences during listening (Sachs, 1967), but later demonstrated similar findings for memory for sentences during reading (Sachs, 1974). Sample sentences from Sachs (1967) are shown in 13. Participants heard one of the sentences embedded in a story. Following the presentation of the sentence, participants' memory for the sentence was assessed either immediately, after 80 additional syllables of the story had been heard (i.e., after about 25 seconds), or after 100 additional syllables of the story had been heard (i.e., after about 50 seconds). Participants were presented with two sentences, the one they just heard and a sentence similar in meaning to the one they heard but with a different word order. The results showed that memory for the specific ordering of words within the sentences decayed rapidly. When participants initially heard the sentence in 13c, they could not correctly judge whether they had heard that sentence or 13a or 13d, which have the same meaning. In contrast, their memory for the meaning of sentences did not decay as rapidly, as they were able to judge correctly that they heard 13a after presented with 13a and 13b.

13 a. He sent a letter about it to Galileo, the great Italian scientist. Original
    b. Galileo, the great Italian scientist, sent him a letter about it. Semantic change
    c. A letter about it was sent to Galileo, the great Italian scientist. Syntactic change
    d. He sent Galileo, the great Italian scientist, a letter about it. Formality change

Later research showed that there are some circumstances in which we are more likely to retain memory for the exact wording of sentences, such as memory for statements made during lectures (Kintsch & Bates, 1977) and statements made during conversations in soap operas (Bates et al., 1978). The results have implications for the criminal justice system. During criminal investigations and legal proceedings, people are routinely asked to report what another person said, despite the fact that scientific studies demonstrate that such memories are prone to error (Campos & Alonso-Quecuty, 2006; Öhman et al., 2013).

agent of the action. In passive sentences, such as 14b and 14c, the subject NP *car* is the patient of the agent, and either the agent appears in a prepositional phrase, as in 14b, or is omitted, as in 14c. Table 6.2 provides examples of thematic roles with examples of English sentences.

14 a. The mechanic repaired the car in the garage. Active
    b. The car was repaired by the mechanic in the garage. Passive
    c. The car was repaired in the garage. Passive

In the 1980s, researchers demonstrated that thematic roles can play a role in how syntactic ambiguity is resolved (Ferreira & Clifton, 1986; Taraban & McClelland,

Table 6.2 Thematic Roles with Sample English Sentences

Thematic role	Description	Sample sentence
Agent	Doer of action	The nurse examined the patient.
		The patient was examined by the nurse.
Patient	Changed by action	The patient pushed the nurse.
		The nurse was pushed by the patient.
Recipient	Receiver in action	The nurse gave the patient the shot.
		The patient handed the nurse the cup.
Location	Place of action	The nurse examined the patient in the hallway.
Instrument	Used for action	The nurse injected the patient with the syringe.
		The patient cleaned the counter with a sponge.

Source: Dowty (1990)

1988). Ferreira and Clifton (1986) investigated readers' use of information about thematic roles in resolving sentences containing syntactically ambiguous relative clauses. Consider the examples in 15. Both 15a and 15b contain a temporarily ambiguous relative clause, which has been reduced through the omission of *that was,* as in 15c and 15d. The construction is referred to as the "reduced relative clause." When comprehenders encounter the verb *examined,* they could analyze it as the verb in the main clause or the verb in a reduced relative clause. In terms of syntactic structure, the former analysis is the less complex and predicted by minimal attachment to always be preferred as the initial parse. Ferreira and Clifton (1986) tested whether readers could use semantic information associated with the subject noun phrase when resolving the following ambiguous verb. In 15b, the noun *evidence* is inanimate and less suitable for the agent thematic role than for the patient thematic role of the verb *examined.* In contrast, in 15a, the noun *defendant* is animate and can be interpreted as an agent of the verb *examined.* They compared reading time on the ambiguous sentences in 15a and 15b with their unambiguous control sentences in which the words *that was* preceded the verb *examined.* They found that although the readers did not use the semantic information to avoid the garden path, their use of semantic information reduced the difficulty experienced during syntactic reanalysis.

15　a. The defendant examined by the lawyer turned out to be unreliable.

　　b. The evidence examined by the lawyer turned out to be unreliable.

　　c. The defendant who was examined by the lawyer turned out to be unreliable.

　　d. The evidence that was examined by the lawyer turned out to be unreliable.

In the past decade, a growing body of literature has explored the relatively elusive semantic level of processing in sentences containing a temporary syntactic ambiguity. Results have shown that when comprehenders carry out syntactic reanalysis, the meaning of the initial, but later abandoned analysis lingers (Cai et al., 2012; Christianson et al., 2001; Christianson et al., 2006; Patson et al., 2009; Patson & Husband, 2016; Sturt, 2007). In the study by Christianson et al. (2001), participants processed sentences word by word and then answered a yes/

no comprehension question. A sample sentence and question are displayed in 16. Readers typically experience a garden path, first analyzing the NP *the deer* as the direct object of *hunt,* but when the verb *ran* is encountered, they realized that the NP is the subject NP of the main clause. Despite the fact that in the syntactically revised analysis, it is not explicitly stated that the man hunted the deer, a large number of participants responded *yes* to the question shown in 16.

16   While the man hunted the deer ran into the woods.

Did the man hunt the deer?

In a later experiment in which eye movements were recorded during reading, Sturt (2007) demonstrated that the lingering meaning from readers' initial parse of a temporary syntactic ambiguity influenced reading time later in the sentence in conditions in which the meaning was incompatible with the overall meaning of the sentence. Sample sentences are displayed in 17. In 17a and 17b, the NP *the South Pole* is temporarily ambiguous, as it may be the direct object of the verb *found* or the subject NP of a subordinate clause. As the former is syntactically less complex, minimal attachment predicts that readers will always construct the direct object analysis. Reading time was measured on 17a and 17b and compared to reading time on the unambiguous control sentences (17c and 17d). The critical comparison was the end of the sentence in which the meaning either conflicted with the meaning of initial, but later revised, parse of the noun phrase, as in 17b, or did not conflict, as in 17a. In measures of second pass and other measures that include time spent rereading, they found that the differences between ambiguous and unambiguous conditions were larger when the meaning of the end of the sentence conflicted with the meaning of the initial parse of the noun phrase.

17   a. The explorers found the South Pole was actually right at their feet.

b. The explorers found the South Pole was actually impossible to reach.

c. The explorers found that the South Pole was actually right at their feet.

d. The explorers found that the South Pole was actually impossible to reach.

Although thematic roles are most often discussed in relation to verbs, other types of words may also assign thematic roles. For example, Grimshaw (1991) proposed that noun phrases describing events (event nominals) differ from noun phrases describing non-events (objects, the result of an event). She argued that event nominals can assign thematic roles to words that complete their meaning just as verbs can. Phrases that receive thematic roles and complete the meaning of predicates are referred to as **arguments**. In contrast, those phrases that do not receive thematic roles and serve in a non-essential aspect of meaning of a preceding predicate are referred to as **adjuncts**. Consider the examples of an event nominal and non-event nominal in 18a and 18b, respectively. The processing prediction of Grimshaw's view of the thematic structure of event and non-event nominals was that the phrase *by the kids* could be read more quickly when functioning as an argument, as in 18a, than when functioning as an adjunct in 18b.

18   a. The frequent collection of butterflies by the kids amazed everyone.

Event nominal

b. The numerous collection of butterflies by the kids amazed everyone.

Non-event nominal

In an eye tracking experiment, Kennison (1999) confirmed the prediction in an experiment in which readers' eye movements were recorded. The results showed that total reading time was significantly longer for sentences containing non-event nominals. These results were consistent with prior research showing that readers generally take less time to process phrases that were arguments of verbs than similar phrases that are adjuncts (Clifton et al., 1991; c.f., Tutunjian & Boland, 2008).

In this section, you learned about Chomsky's classic distinction between the semantic (meaning) and the syntactic (word order) levels of representation in language and the traditional approach to meaning in sentences involving thematic roles (agent, patient, recipient, etc.). You also learned that sentence processing experiments have shown that there is ample evidence showing that in sentences containing syntactic ambiguity, the computed meanings of abandoned syntactic analysis linger. Although thematic roles are most often thought of as an aspect of verb meaning, they can also occur with other types of words (nouns and adjectives), which are derived from verbs.

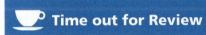 **Time out for Review**

Key Terms

Adjunct   Argument   Thematic roles

Review Questions

1 Describe Noam Chomsky's observations about sentences with similar meanings, but different structures.
2 Identify four thematic roles. For each one, generate a sentence that contains the role and label the word in the sentence as to its thematic role.
3 What evidence is there that the meaning of abandoned syntactic analyses can have an influence on readers' comprehension?

The Role of Working Memory

Chomksy (1986) discussed the role of human memory processes in our comprehension and production of language. He argued that it is useful to distinguish the knowledge of language in the mind of the native speaker and the use of that knowledge. Chomsky referred to the former as language competence and the latter as language performance. Language competence was described as containing knowledge of all the grammar rules that can enable native speakers to produce and comprehend all possible sentences in the language and to provide judgments of grammaticality and/or acceptability for sentences when asked. In contrast, language performance involved the implementation of the *flawless* language knowledge of the native speaker using a biological system that could be flawed due to memory failures, glitches during speaking, and misperceptions during reading. Errors of native speakers that did not appear to be consistent with native speakers having perfect knowledge of their language's grammar could be attributed to glitches occurring during processing. When glitches occur during processing, they are likely to involve a type of memory described as our mental blackboard or working memory. Working memory is also referred to as short-term memory, because information available to the conscious mind may not be retained permanently. Some but not all of the information that makes it into our working memory goes on to be retained in our long-term memory. In this section, we review Baddeley's model of working memory (Baddeley, 2007, 2009, 2012; Baddeley & Hitch, 1974), which is likely the most prominent working memory model today. There have been criticisms of this specific view of working memory (Jones et al., 2004; Nairne, 2002); however, it is useful for our discussion as we focus specifically on how people comprehend sentences. Second, we briefly review studies showing that the phonological representations of words in sentences are activated during comprehension. Third, we examine how comprehenders process sentences containing long distance dependencies (also called filler-gap sentences). Such sentences typically require comprehenders to maintain a word or phrase in memory until a later point in processing when it can be interpreted in relation to the appropriate verb. Lastly, we will review the growing body of research demonstrating that there are individual differences in working memory capacity that can influence sentence processing.

Baddeley's Working Memory Model

A popular approach to working memory has been that of Baddeley and colleagues (Baddeley, 2007, 2009; Baddeley et al., 2009; Baddeley & Hitch, 1974) in which working memory was originally viewed as having three major components; however, recently, a fourth component was added. These are illustrated in Figure 6.2. The parts of the model are:

- the **phonological loop**, which is responsible for storing the sounds of words in short-term memory and carrying out rehearsal of the sounds to prevent the memories of the sounds from decaying
- the **visuospatial sketchpad**, which is responsible for storing visual information in short-term memory
- the **central executive**, which is responsible for managing cognitive processes overall
- the **episodic buffer**, which connects long-term memories of different types (episodic, semantic, linguistic, etc.) with information from the other components of the model (Baddeley, 2000). This is the most recent addition to the model.

Like the phonological loop and the visuospatial sketchpad, the episodic buffer is a *slave system*. Support for this view of working memory has come from experiments in which participants were required to carry out two memory tasks simultaneously. Baddeley (2000) incorporated a third slave component into the model for the processing of episodic memories. During processing, the slave systems operate as short-term storage components with limited capacities, and when an individual

Figure 6.2 Baddeley's Early Working Memory Model Do you have an easier time remembering things you hear or things you see? Credit: AmandaSilver15

carries out more than one task involving one or more of the slave components, the central executive must coordinate the activity, which typically exhibits a pattern of task interference due to working memory having a finite capacity.

A psycholinguist evaluating the model might wonder where representations related specifically to semantics (or meaning) would be handled. Some aspects of meaning for some concepts can be visual in nature, such as words referring to concrete concepts for which one can easily form a mental image (e.g., balloon, sock, pigeon, etc.) (Paivio, 1971). Based on Baddeley's (2000) description of the episodic buffer's role in linking different types of information, including information from long-term **semantic memory**, it may one day be shown that semantic processing during sentence comprehension is the domain of the episodic buffer. Regardless of how semantic representations are viewed as being handled within this and other models of working memory, we have known since the 1970s that semantic representations are part of working memory processing (Wickens, 1972). Using a memory task (Brown, 1958; Peterson & Peterson, 1959), researchers instructed participants to remember a set of words while simultaneously carrying out a mental arithmetic task. The results of studies showed that performance declined over time, presumably because each new trial that participants completed would lead to increased interference among items retained in working memory. This pattern of performance was referred to as **proactive interference**. Wickens (1972) discovered that under certain conditions, participants could experience a release from proactive interference when the semantic category of the words being held in memory from trial to trial was changed. When words on each trial belonged to the same semantic category (e.g., fruit, as in apple, orange, grape, banana, plum, pear, etc.), performance declined with each new trial. After numerous trials using memory items from the same semantic category showed declining performance, participants' performance jumped back to initial level performance when a different semantic category was used on a trial (Wickens, 1972). The results suggested that in tasks requiring maintaining words in memory, there is interference in memory among semantically similar representations. The view that semantic representations, which are distinct from phonological presentations, are an important aspect of working memory is supported by research involving individuals who have experienced brain injury (Martin, 2005; Martin & Tan, 2015; Romani & Martin, 1999).

Phonological Processes

As you learned in Chapter 5, the sounds of words play an important role in reading, even when the reading occurs silently. Research shows that despite the fact that readers have no obvious need to convert the written word into sound, they do so nevertheless. The recognition of individual words involves the activation of their phonological representations, and as you will see, phonological representations play an important role in comprehension (Leinenger, 2014); however, the exact role or roles remain unclear. In terms of Baddeley's (2012) working memory model, the phonological processes involved in sentence comprehension would presumably involve the phonological loop. Other language processes are believed to be handled by the phonological loop, such as learning new words and speech production.

Since the 1960s, researchers have recognized that phonological processes are deeply intertwined with comprehension processing (Garrity, 1977). Studies showed that during silent reading, different parts of readers' vocal tract (larynx, throat, chin, lips, and tongue) were highly activated in terms of electrical activity recorded from the muscles in the neck and head. Readers were described as engaging in subvocalization (Rayner et al., 2012). Early studies suggested that when readers are prevented from subvocalizing (e.g., they repeat aloud a nonsense phrase), comprehension suffers (Slowiaczek & Clifton, 1980), particularly when comprehenders had to answer questions requiring participants to integrate information across the sentence they heard.

The psychological reality of the sounds of words in silent comprehension has been documented in numerous studies showing that processing is slower when sentences contain repeated phonemes (Haber & Haber, 1982; Kennison, 2004; Kennison et al., 2003; McCutchen & Perfetti, 1992; Zhang & Perfetti, 1993). Readers take longer to read tongue twister sentences than control sentences that are similar in meaning, but do not have repeated phonemes. Sample sentences from Kennison et al. (2003) are shown in 19.

19 a. Tina and Todd took the two toddlers the toys.   Tongue twister

   b. Lisa and Chad sent the four orphans the toys.   Control

Zhang and Perfetti (1993) convincingly demonstrated that the slowing in reading time due to phoneme repetition was not completely due to repetition in the orthography. They found that readers of Chinese who were reading silently took longer when sentences contained repeated phonemes. Because Chinese uses a logographic writing system, there are no clues to a word's pronunciation in its visual form.

Research by Acheson and MacDonald (2011) demonstrated that the disrupting effect of repeated phonemes occurs as soon as the first instance of a repeating phoneme is encountered. In a series of experiments, they compared reading time on syntactically complex sentences that either did or did not contain a repeated phoneme. Sample sentences are displayed in 20. All target sentences contained a relative clause that modified the subject NP of the sentence. The sentences in 20a and 20b are examples of subject relative sentences, and the sentences in 20c and 20d are examples of object relative sentences. The results showed that reading time on the region containing *banker* was significantly longer in the repeated phoneme condition (20a vs. 20b). Furthermore, the increase in reading time due to the repeated phoneme was larger when readers processed the more complex object relative conditions (20c and 20d) than the subject relative conditions. Acheson and MacDonald concluded that readers use phonological representations of words in the immediate interpretation of sentences as well as for constructing their memory for what they have read.

20 a. The baker that sought the banker bought   Repeated phoneme
       the house.

   b. The runner that feared the banker bought   Control
       the house.

c. The baker that the banker sought bought the house.　　　Repeated phoneme

d. The runner that the banker feared bought the house.　　　Control

In 2015, Price et al. (2015) showed that there are separate effects for orthographic and phonological similarity leading to longer reading time, with the processing difficulty associated with orthographic similarity occurring earlier in the processing of the sentence than the processing difficulty associated with phonological similarity.

The view that phonological representations are involved in the comprehension occurring relatively late in processing is consistent with research by Kennison and colleagues (Kennison, 2004; Kennison et al., 2003), which has shown that the presence of phonological repetition in sentences increased reading time in the clause following the clause in which the phonological repetition occurred. In the experiment carried out by Kennison (2004), readers comprehended sentences containing or not containing phonological repetition that either contained a temporary syntactic ambiguity or an unambiguous control. Sample sentences are displayed in 21. For syntactically unambiguous condition, as in 21b and 21d, the comma appeared after the verb *to drive*. For the ambiguous garden path conditions, 21a and 21c, the comma was missing, which led readers to temporarily assume that the following noun was the direct object of the verb *to drive*. The temporary analysis would be revised after the reader encountered the word *began*. The results showed that the presence of repeated phonemes in the sentences increased processing time as compared with control sentences without repeated phonemes; however, phonological repetition did not increase the processing difficulty in garden path sentences.

Phonological repetition

21　a. After Dana and David definitely decided to drive the Datsun began to …

　　　b. After Dana and David definitely decided to drive, the Datsun began to …

No phonological repetition

　　　c. After Lea and Michael finally agreed to drive the Nissan began to …

　　　d. After Lea and Michael finally agreed to drive, the Nissan began to …

The fact that the processing difficulty experienced by readers due to the phonological repetition did not interact with the processing difficulty that was due to syntactic complexity can be viewed as support for the two effects being carried out by separate memory systems, which is consistent with Baddeley's (2012) working memory model.

Long Distance Dependencies

Some types of sentences require comprehenders to hold in memory a word or phrase as they process other words in the sentence and can determine how to integrate the word held in memory into the sentence structure. Such sentences are described as containing a **long distance dependency**. Psycholinguists also use the term **filler-gap sentences** in which the **filler** is the word held temporarily in memory and the **gap** is the location later in the sentence where the filler is integrated into the sentence context. Consider the examples in 22. In 22a, the filler *the reporter* can ultimately be associated as the direct object of the verb *attack* (the gap), and in 22b, it is associated as its subject. Dashes have been inserted in the example in 22 to indicate the gap locations. These constructions have also been described as object relative and subject relative clauses, respectively. The distance between the filler and the gap is greater for object relative clauses than for subject relative clauses.

22 a. The reporter that the senator attacked _____ admitted to making an error.

b. The reporter that _____ attacked the senator admitted to making an error.

Studies have shown that processing difficulty is greater for object relative clauses than for subject relative clauses (Gordon et al., 2002; Just & Carpenter, 1992; King & Just, 1991; Wanner & Maratsos, 1978); however, researchers disagree about the factors that contribute to the differences (see Fedorenko et al., 2012). Gibson and colleagues (Gibson, 1998, 2000; Warren & Gibson, 2002) have claimed that the longer an element is held in memory, the more that the memory for the item will become degraded due to memory decay. Gordon et al. (2002) showed that interference among information held in working memory also plays a role. In their experiments, participants read sentences while simultaneously performing a memory task. They read sentences similar to those in 23. In 23a and 23b, the NP *barber* or the proper name *John* must be interpreted as the direct object of the verb *saw*. In 23b and 23d, they are interpreted as the subject of the verb *saw*. The type of words that participants were instructed to hold in memory as they read were either proper names (e.g., *Bill, Ken,* or *Tony*) or noun descriptions (e.g., *poet, cartoonist,* and *voter*). The results showed that participants took longer to process sentences when the type of word held in memory was the same as the filler (proper name or noun description), suggesting that when similar types of words are held in working memory, interference occurs. The results also showed that participants experience more interference when the distance between the filler and gap was greater, as in 23a and 23b.

23 a. It was the barber that the lawyer saw in the parking lot.

b. It was the barber that saw the lawyer in the parking lot.

c. It was John that the lawyer saw in the parking lot.

d. It was John that saw the lawyer in the parking lot.

Individual Differences

Since the 1950s, psycholinguists have recognized that there are individual differences in **working memory capacity**. George Miller (1956) published his groundbreaking paper entitled "The magical number seven, plus or minus two: Some limits on our capacity for processing information." In studies, participants heard or viewed sequences of digits (e.g., 9, 2, 4, 6, etc.) of different lengths in terms of number of digits and were asked to report back the digits in sequence. After a great many tests, the average capacity of working memory was shown to be seven digits (later discussed in terms of seven units of information). Scores followed a normal distribution; thus, when taking the standard deviation of scores into consideration (i.e., SD = two digits), 95 percent of people were predicted to have a working memory capacity between five and nine units of information. In contemporary research, a variety of tasks are used to assess working memory (LaPointe & Engle, 1990).

In the 1980s, research began to demonstrate that individual differences in working memory capacity are related to language processing. Daneman and Carpenter (1980) devised a complex task to assess working memory capacity for sentence comprehension, called the Reading Span Test (RST). Participants were asked to read aloud sentences, while remembering the last word of each sentence. The number of sentences read and the number of words held in memory increased from two to five. They found that participants' ability to hold in memory larger numbers of words while reading sentences aloud correlated positively with performance in the verbal portion of the Scholastic Aptitude Test (SAT) and performance in answering comprehension questions in a separate reading comprehension task (e.g., answering factual questions). The RST continues to be used in contemporary research (Conway et al., 2005).

In the 1990s, Just and colleagues published a series of studies suggesting that readers differing in working memory capacity utilize information sources differently as they process sentences (Just & Carpenter, 1992; King & Just, 1991; MacDonald et al., 1992). They claimed that when resolving a syntactic ambiguity during reading, those with a larger working memory capacity were more likely to use semantic information and to activate multiple syntactic analyses in parallel. In contrast, those with smaller working memory capacity are less likely to maintain in memory all possible syntactic analyses. Consequently, the difference in reading time between syntactically ambiguous and unambiguous sentences (i.e., the effect of ambiguity) was negatively correlated with readers' working memory capacity, with those with the smallest working memory capacity having the largest effect of ambiguity. The results were later shown not to be related to differences in the perceptual abilities of high and low working memory capacity readers (Kennison & Clifton, 1995).

Research has shown that working memory capacity increases during childhood into the teenage years and the twenties and then gradually declines (Alloway & Alloway, 2015). Bopp and Verhaeghen (2005) examined all available prior studies assessing working memory differences between young and older adults, and found a strong linear decline in working memory with increase with age. Insofar as individual differences in working memory capacity influence sentence processing, we would expect to find age-related differences in sentence processing that correspond to age-related changes in working memory capacity. Research with older adults has suggested that a decline in language and other cognitive processing should be considered in relation to the individual's working memory capacity rather than their chronological age (De Beni et al., 2007). In research examining how older versus younger adults comprehend sentences, Christianson et al. (2006) found that older adults more often arrived at incorrect interpretations of sentences, suggesting that they engaged in good enough processing more often than young adults.

Research has also demonstrated that there are differences between how children and adults process sentences containing ambiguity. Trueswell et al. (1999) used the visual world paradigm to examine children's comprehension of short sentences containing a syntactically ambiguous phrase, such as *Put the frog on the napkin in the box.* The phrase *on the napkin* can be interpreted as the location where the child should *put the frog* or as specifying which frog should be moved (i.e., the frog on the napkin versus some other frog). As you may recall from Chapter 3, in experiments using the visual world paradigm, participants are able to see an arrangement of objects in front of them that usually they must manipulate in some way (touch, move, etc.). The instructions to the participants are played via loud speakers. While participants listen and carry out the instructions, their eye movements are recorded. On some of the trials, when children heard the sentence, there was a single frog among the objects in front of them, and on other trials, there were two frogs. The authors expected that the presence of two frogs would lead children to interpret the ambiguous phrase as a modifier of the NP *the frog,* and when the displays contained a single frog, the children would interpret the ambiguous phrase as a location phrase modifying the verb *put.* The results showed that when children were younger than five years, they did not use information from the context when interpreting the ambiguous phrase. They always interpreted the phrase as a location phrase modifying the verb *put.* On trials in which they heard control sentences without ambiguity (e.g., *Put the frog that's on the napkin in the box),* they performed accurately. In another experiment, children who were eight years old were found to use information from the context during comprehension, performing the same as adult participants.

In this section, you learned about the nature of working memory and how it is believed to be involved in sentence processing. One of the subcomponents of working memory is the phonological loop, which is involved in the rehearsal of the sounds of words. Studies have shown that readers activate the phonological representations of words during sentence processing. Phonological processes are likely involved both in the initial identification of words as well as in relatively late-occurring processes involved in comprehending sentences. A complete understanding of how phonological representations serve sentence interpretation remains unknown. Researchers agree that during comprehension, some types of processes, such as comprehending long distance dependencies, place a greater burden on working memory than others. As the distance between the filler and the gap in the long distance dependency increases, burden on working memory also increases.

Key Terms

Central executive	Gap	Semantic memory
Episodic buffer	Long distance dependency	Subvocalization
Filler	Phonological loop	Working memory capacity
Filler-gap sentences	Proactive interference	Visuospatial sketchpad

Review Questions

1 Describe Baddeley's model of working memory and discuss the role working memory plays in sentence comprehension.
2 What is a long distance dependency? How does the distance between the filler and the gap in such sentences influence processing?
3 To what extent do individual differences in working memory capacity influence sentence processing?
4 How does working memory capacity change as we age? How might age-related changes in working memory capacity influence how sentences are processed?

Summary

Theories of sentence comprehension differ in their assumptions about whether syntactic information is used initially to analyze incoming words or whether all types of information can be used simultaneously throughout processing. Researchers also debate whether comprehenders construct a single analysis for the sentence or whether multiple analyses are built and maintained throughout processing. In contrast, research on semantic processing in sentence comprehension has received relatively little attention. Thematic roles describe semantic functions of elements in sentences, which are independent of word order. As the comprehension of sentence unfolds in real time with different information being used and mental representations being built at different times, it is important to take into consideration the nature of human working memory, which likely has multiple components. Baddeley's (2012) view is that working memory has at least four components: a central executive; a phonological loop; a visuospatial sketchpad; and an episodic buffer. The phonological loop is primarily involved in sentence comprehension. Individual differences in sentence comprehension are likely because there are well-established individual differences in working memory capacity.

Recommended Books, Films, and Websites

Baddeley, A. (2012). Working memory: Theories, models, and controversies. *Annual Review of Psychology*, 63(1), 1–29.

Carreiras, M. & Clifton, C. (2004). *The On-line Study of Sentence Comprehension: Eyetracking, ERPs and Beyond*. New York: Psychology Press.

Doolittle, P. (2013). *How your Working Memory Makes Sense of the World* [video file]. Retrieved September 9, 2017 from www.ted.com/talks/peter_doolittle_how_your_working_memory_makes_sense_of_the_world.

Sanz, M., Laka, I. & Tanenhaus, M. K. (2015). *Language down the Garden Path: The Cognitive and Biological Basis for Linguistic Structures*. Oxford: Oxford University Press.

Townsend, D. J. & Bever, T. G. (2001). *Sentence Comprehension: The Integration of Habits and Rules*. Cambridge, MA: MIT Press.

7 HOW DO WE COMPREHEND DISCOURSES?

Chapter Content

Photo 7.1 Many people read for pleasure in their free time. When was the last time you became engrossed in a good book?

When was the last time you heard or read a good story? A good story can be found in a film, book, comic book, or video game. Stories can describe actual events, as when we describe to a friend or family member how it took us longer than usual to get home because there was a terrible accident on the highway, or fictional events that are created to entertain us. Good stories typically have some of the same essential elements: a premise established in a clearly defined space or world; clearly defined characters with a protagonist and an antagonist; and conflict that is responded to through the arc of the story (Goldberg, 2016). Some of your favorite stories may lead you to create detailed images in your mind of the setting and characters. As you experience the story, you are likely to feel the excitement from suspense or other expectations in the story. Among the most memorable stories are those that lead us to generate expectations that turn out to be incorrect, surprising us. The surprising points of stories, whether they occur in books or films, are among the most memorable. Stories are structured similarly whether they are told orally or are written. In prehistory, storytelling, referred to as the **oral tradition**, was the primary means for sharing and remembering events of cultural significance (Ong, 1982). Today, in societies without writing, it is still the primary means of transmitting important cultural information from one generation to another. Following the innovation of writing, communities were able to have longer and more detailed stories preserved for long periods of time. The amount of information transmitted across generations increased tremendously. From the perspective of anthropology and evolutionary psychology, stories have provided humans with opportunities to learn about the dangers and thrills of the world without risk. They have also provided people with opportunities to explore and learn about the complexities of social relationships, as in children's fairy tales (Zipes, 2002).

In this chapter, we will examine how stories and other types of discourses are comprehended. The term **discourse** refers broadly to any written or spoken (or manual, as in signing in a sign language) form of communication. In Chapter 9, you learned about the ways in which psycholinguists analyze conversations and the ways in which what we say is viewed as conforming to the expectations of our listeners. These insights also apply to the topic of discourse, as discourses can be thought of as being either oral or written and short or long. As you will see in this chapter, psycholinguistic researchers consider complex sentences or pairs of sentences as examples of short discourses. In the majority of experiments described in this chapter, the discourses are many paragraphs long. In the first section, we learn about the different types of discourses and examine the terminology used to describe the parts of discourses and how those parts are believed to fit together in an overall discourse structure. In the second section, we examine the research showing how readers form links between different elements in a discourse in real time during discourse processing. Lastly, we review early and contemporary theories of discourse processing. Because a comprehensive theory remains elusive, our discussion will focus on those elements that are likely to be included in future proposals.

Discourses and their Characteristics

The study of discourse processing remains one of the more neglected topics in psycholinguists. The neglect does not result from lack of interest on the part of psycholinguistic researchers. There is a great deal of interest in the topic, because understanding the processing of discourses is the next logical step after understanding the processing involved in sentence comprehension and production. Understanding how discourses are comprehended is the ultimate goal of a complete theory of language processing. Furthermore, educators are particularly interested in assessing differences in the readability of texts; however, the existing techniques for evaluating readability are far from ideal (Benjamin, 2012). If the topic has been neglected by researchers, it is because of the extreme difficulty involved in devising and conducting experiments with discourses. Researchers who study discourse processing often create materials that are long. In experiments in which reading time is measured, the presentation of the discourses must be controlled. When discourses are manipulated for different conditions, the line(s) that are varied must be similar in length and frequency, but also displayed similarly to participants. If you are planning on conducting research in the area of language comprehension, and you have not yet chosen your specific topic, I encourage you to consider discourse processing, as there are many hypotheses that have yet to have been tested and published in research articles. In this section, we will discuss: the different types of discourses that can be studied; the characteristics of discourses that contribute to their being perceived as meaningful, for which the technical description is having coherence; and how we remember information extracted from discourses.

Types of Discourses

If you are in college now or completed college in the past, you are likely to have had a great deal of experience processing different types of discourses. In early childhood, we start out listening to others reading or telling us stories. As you will learn in Chapter 8, we usually are asked to begin making up our own stories when we are still in elementary school. Stories, whether they describe true events or fictional ones, are integral to our daily lives. As we start our exploration of how we process stories, we must begin with some important distinctions that come from different types of scholars, including philosophers, linguists, psycholinguists, but also those specializing in **rhetoric**, the discipline focused on speaking and writing effectively. Table 7.1 lists different types of discourses with brief descriptions and examples. Narration and description may be the most familiar types of discourses. We encounter arguments, which are intended to persuade us, during political seasons leading up to elections and during product demonstrations by those wanting us to purchase their product. Poetic forms of discourse include not only poetry, but also lyrics to your favorite songs and raps.

Table 7.1 Types of Discourses

Discourse type	Description	Example
Description	Describes with physical detail	Anecdotes, newspaper stories
Narration	Tells a story	Anecdotes, short stories, novels
Exposition	Explains or describes	How to essays, textbooks
Argument	Attempts to persuade	Advertisements, political material
Poetic	Conveys emotion and ideas	Poems, prose, song lyrics

Source: Hocking et al. (2003)

In our daily lives, we encounter additional categories of discourse, which have received relatively little attention in psycholinguistic research. If we think of the types of discourses not included in Table 7.1, we may think about the language we experience in religious settings. On one hand, sermons and homilies often contain elegant language that can be compared to poetry. On the other, they usually contain an attempt to persuade. The most memorable sermons and homilies may also contain a story or narration as a subcomponent of the larger message. Another example is small talk or chit chat, which is used by people who do not know each other well and avoids topics of controversy or intimacy (Malinowski, 1923). Then there is humor, which is typically intended to evoke a positive emotion in the reader or listener (Martin, 2006). Chapter 9 covers the topics of small talk and humor.

There are many ways in which the different types of discourses can vary, depending on the particular intentions of the author. The categories that describe these differences are most familiar in the literary world, such as the distinction between non-fiction and fiction. Style is another way in which discourses of the same type can vary. For example, a description may be written in a formal academic style, which is needed at most colleges for written assignments in courses, or may be written in a casual, informal style, which might use non-standard grammar, vocabulary, and spelling. Authors may choose to write in a style that reflects contemporary society or some era in the past. Imagine having to write a dialogue in which a customer orders a cup of coffee at a restaurant, but writing in three different styles: in modern times with words and phrases that a college student might use; Victorian-era England (mid to late 1800s); and the Wild West era of the USA (mid-1800s).

Psycholinguistic research investigating how discourses are processed has traditionally investigated processing during reading comprehension of texts composed of two or more sentences. Most of the investigations have focused on

Figure 7.1 Three-act Structure of Narratives Have you ever written a fictional story as part of an academic assignment or just for fun?
Credit: UfofVincent

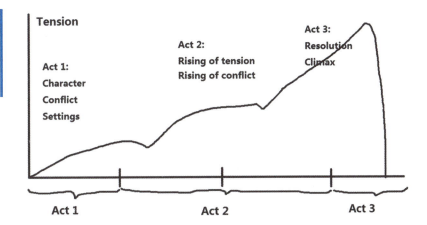

the understanding of **narratives**. Narratives are generally composed of a setting and a plot involving one or more characters. Long narratives, such as plays, novels, and films, are often composed of three parts (or acts) (Abbott, 2009). The first act introduces the characters, the setting, and any elements that will be referred to in the second and/or third parts. The second act typically contains a conflict or problem that is tackled by one or more of the characters, and the third act resolves the conflict, sometimes involving a climax, which is a point of maximum tension in the story that may be surprising. Figure 7.1 illustrates how tension builds over the course of the three acts.

Narratives vary in how the events of the story are arranged in the telling of the story. The most frequently used structure for stories is the **linear narrative**, in which the events of the story are described in the order they occurred (chronological order). A second common structure is the **nonlinear narrative**, in which the events of the story are described in a different order from that in which the events occurred. For example, in a mostly linear narrative, events occurring earlier in time can be presented to the reader or viewer through **flashbacks**. Also, **flash forwards** are sometimes used to insert an event from later in the story in the present time in the flow of the narrative. The amount of nonlinearity in the narrative can vary a great deal, depending on the artistic vision of the writer. Most research studies investigating the comprehension of discourses have used texts with a linear narrative structure. An interesting ramification of stories told using a nonlinear narrative structure is that the comprehender is likely to store in memory information about the story as it occurred in a chronological order, but also retain memory for the specific sequencing of events that was used in the telling of the story. When nonlinear narration is used, the reader or viewer may need to make an effort to determine how each event in the story fits into the chronological timeline of how events presumably occurred.

Coherent Discourses

If you have ever heard someone tell a story particularly badly, you likely experienced a discourse that had a low level of **coherence**, which means that it was difficult to understand or hard to follow. A high level of coherence means that the discourse makes sense in terms of the semantic relationships existing within and between sentences. Discourses with a low level of coherence may contain utterances or sentences that are perceived as only loosely related. If you have had conversations with young children who are still developing their storytelling skills, you are likely to have experienced some discourses with low levels of coherence. By the time children are six, they are usually able to tell a simple story that has at least one setting, one or more central characters, and a goal or plot that one or more characters pursue (Shapiro & Hudson, 1991). For both children and adult storytellers, there are a number of ways in which the coherence in discourses can be increased. We discuss four major techniques that writers and speakers use to make their discourses coherent: aboutness, which refers to the theme or purpose of the discourse; the given-new strategy, which involves giving information that is already known (or given) before information that is new; cohesion, which involves forming links within and across sentences; and semantic similarity among words, which has recently been found to be lacking in poorly written discourses.

Aboutness

The most coherent discourses are those whose themes are clear. Used by linguists and librarians, **aboutness** refers to the fact that written and spoken discourses are always about something, they have a subject or a theme (Fairthorne, 1969; Hjørland, 2001). The success of a writer or speaker can be viewed as how well their audiences are able to arrive at that intended subject or theme. Every choice the author or speaker makes in terms of the ordering of sentences in the discourse and the selection and ordering of words within sentences serves to support the aboutness of the discourse. In a discourse with a high level of coherence, readers or listeners would be able to determine the aboutness of the discourse. In contrast, a discourse with a low level of coherence would leave readers and listeners uncertain about the aboutness of the discourse and/or arriving at the aboutness of the discourse would be difficult.

Meaningful discourses are constructed by speakers and authors so that each utterance or sentence moves the story forward. When understanding long discourses (novels, films, or stories), once the listener ascertains the nature of the

Photo 7.2 Humans throughout history have gathered together, listening to and telling stories to pass the time. Have you ever listened to a ghost story told around a fire at night?
Credit: Jerry Kirkhart

narration, the competence of the author, and the likelihood that the story's narrator is reliable in providing only information that pertains to the story, then each new sentence or utterance is processed with a presumption that the information is important for the overall discourse. You may have had the experience when reading a story or watching a film, when a new detail was presented. At the time, it was not clear how the detail would fit into the overall story later, but you strongly suspected that it would. Authors, filmmakers, and other artists who create discourses to entertain others construct their works to have a particular impact on the audience. Those who are the most skillful in their work are able to bring specific thoughts and emotions to the minds of the reader or viewer. In a recent interview about making the *Godfather* films, Francis Ford Coppola said that he always kept in mind the theme of the story when faced with any decision he had to make, such as should a character have long or short hair (Gross & Shorrock, 2016). He said that in his mind, the theme of the film was succession, as in the transfer of power from one person to another, so each choice he made served that theme. The rest of this chapter reviews the research on discourse processing involving text in which measurements of reading time were used to make inferences about different aspects of reading comprehension.

The Given-New Strategy

Coherent discourses tend to introduce information to the audience in a particular order with familiar or given (i.e., previously mentioned) information coming before new information. The term **given-new strategy** refers to this aspect of discourse structure. First proposed by Clark and Haviland (Clark, 1977; Clark & Haviland, 1977; Haviland & Clark, 1974), the given-new strategy refers to the fact that coherent discourses typically unfold sentence by sentence, with new information being introduced and connecting in some way to previously encountered information, which is considered *old information* (also called *given information*). You may also find the terms "background" and "focus" used to refer to given and new information, respectively (Clark & Haviland, 1977). Consider the sentences in 1. In 1a, all the information is new, because the sentence begins the discourse. In 1b, the sentence begins with information that links back to given information that was introduced in 1a. Similarly, 1c begins with a noun phrase that links back to words in both 1a and 1b. The words in sentences that link to previously mentioned information can be categorized as the *given* information, and the other content is the *new* information.

1 a. Jasmine saw a hamster at the farmer's market.

   b. The farmer's market didn't have many pets for sale, just hamsters and guinea pigs.

   c. Hamsters cost only $2.00, so Jasmine asked her mom if she could buy it with the money she had saved from her allowance.

   d. Jasmine's mom hesitated, but because Jasmine was earning excellent grades in school, she let Jasmine buy the hamster.

In conversations, speakers occasionally violate the given-new strategy when they refer to someone or something as given information, when to the listener the information is new. In college, one of my good friends would do this more than others. He would start a conversation with statements referencing people I did not know and whose names I had never heard him mention before: "Marilyn says that people should bloom where they are planted" or "I heard the funniest joke from Gordon yesterday." As the listener, these statements lacked coherence, as they were difficult to understand. It was not possible to infer whether there was something important about the fact that Marilyn or Gordon said or did what was described or whether the important information that he wanted to share with me would come in a following statement. When a speaker wants to refer to someone in a conversation with a listener who does not know the person, the speaker typically begins with statements of the type: "My old friend from high school Marilyn called yesterday …" or "My best friend from cub scouts, Gordon, emailed me last week …"

Haviland and Clark (1974) proposed that during processing, the reader or listener must determine what information is given and what information is new. The identification of given information involves linking it to information in memory. Subsequently, new information must be linked to given information in the mental representation being constructed during the processing of the discourse. The notion that the given-new strategy may occur across languages is consistent with recent research showing that children as young as three prefer to order given information before new information in sentences (Kizach and Balling, 2013). In processing studies, the proposal was supported, as readers were found to process given information more rapidly than they processed new information (see also Clark & Sengul, 1979; Garrod & Sanford, 1977).

The given-new strategy can give rise to the repetition of one or more concepts, which can lead the reader or listener to perceive the repeated concepts as important. The term **focus** refers to the relative importance of different information in a discourse. Important information is described as being focused. In spoken discourses, focused information is typically pronounced differently to information that is not focused. Words that are focused are emphasized, being spoken with greater stress, higher pitch accent, and longer duration (Selkirk, 1984). Schwarzschild (1999) proposed a narrowing of the definition for given information, suggesting that given information in a sentence is only that information that is semantically inferred by the preceding context (e.g., in the sentence *Melanie sang the song*, the fact that she made a sound is semantically inferred, as singing always involves making a sound). In an eye tracking experiment in which given information was always inferred from the context, Benatar and Clifton (2014) found that given information was consistently read faster than new information. Later in this chapter, we will take a closer look at a wide range of factors that influence how quickly readers can understand discourses.

There has been quite a lot of attention paid to the question of whether the given-new strategy is an aspect of discourse structure across all languages (see Heidinger, 2015). Future research is needed before we can be confident in a conclusion; however, a growing number of studies suggest that the answer may be yes. Thus far, research has demonstrated its importance in English, which has a strict word order, and languages with a more flexible word order, such as Japanese (Ferreira & Yoshita, 2003), Finnish (Chesterman, 1991; Kaiser & Trueswell, 2004), and Russian (Fedorenko & Levy, 2007). Ferreira and Yoshita (2003) investigated how given and new information would be ordered in Japanese sentences. The results showed that in speakers' utterances, given information occurred before new information.

In their examination of the given-new strategy in Finnish, Kaiser and Trueswell (2004) compared self-paced reading times on Finnish sentences that had the canonical SVO order and sentences that had the non-canonical OVS order. They varied the context in which the SVO and OVS sentences occurred, specifically the ordering of given or old information before new information. The results showed that readers processed OVS sentences more slowly when new information preceded given or old information. In contrast, the processing of SVO sentences was not influenced by the ordering of given and new information. They also showed that OVS sentences were processed faster when preceded by supporting context versus inappropriate contexts.

In a similar study conducted with native Russian speakers, Fedorenko and Levy (2007) varied the ordering of given and new information in sentences with canonical SVO order and non-canonical OVS (scrambled) order (c.f., Brown et al., 2012). They found that sentences with given information ordered before new information were easier to process than sentences with new information ordered before given information, and sentences with SVO order were easier to process than sentences with OVS order. Importantly, they found that the two factors did not interact in determining reading time. The results suggest that the role of discourse on the processing of sentences having a non-canonical order is language-specific, rather than the same across languages.

Brown et al. (2012) suggest that readers of Finnish may use statistical information about the particular linear positions of given and new information more so than readers of Russian, because the case-marking system of Finnish permits more local ambiguities than the case-marking system in Russian. To provide support for their speculation about processing in Finnish, Brown et al. (2012) showed that readers of English can use statistical information about the ordering of given and new information. They measured reading time on English sentences containing dative verbs (e.g., give, as in *Betsy gave Brenda a gift*). In Experiment 1, they found that direct object recipients (i.e., *Brenda* in *Betsy gave Brenda a gift*) were more difficult to process when new information was ordered before given information. In conditions in which sentences presented the recipient as a prepositional phrase (e.g., *Betsy gave a gift to Brenda*), readers' processing time was not influenced by the preceding context, which had been varied so that the prepositional phrase was either given information in the context (i.e., inferred) or new information in the context (i.e., not inferred). In Experiment 2, they found that reading time was most consistent with the view that readers use statistical information about word-to-word contingencies. They interpreted the results as indicating that readers' syntactic representations can include information about the linear ordering of arguments.

Cohesion

The third characteristic of coherent discourses is the presence of cohesion, which involves having different parts of the discourse linked through the strategic use of linking words (pronouns, conjunctions, etc.). Table 7.2 lists five cohesion-building devices with sample sentences. Conjunctions are words that provide cohesion between clauses within sentences, and less often, they can provide cohesion between sentences. As you may recall from your English grammar courses from

Table 7.2 Five Cohesion-building Devices with Examples

Category	Example
Conjunction	
and	The server brought the food, **and** the family began eating right away.
but	The server brought the food, **but** the family did not began eating right away.
so	The server brought the food after a long delay, **so** the family complained to the manager.
Ellipsis	Jiang liked the new action movie, and Kim **did** too.
Substitution	Leslie looked for an inexpensive used car, but didn't find **one**.
Reference	
Pronominal	Terrence wanted to win the race. **He** had trained very hard for months.
Demonstrative	Donald denied lying. That puzzled everyone.
Lexical	
Repetition	Juan sang **the ballad**. Everyone knew **the ballad** by heart.
Synonymy	Arnold sang **the ballad**. Everyone knew **the ditty** by heart.
Hyponymy	Callie sang **the ballad**. Everyone knew **the song** by heart.

Source: Halliday and Hasan (1976)

long ago, conjunctions include *and, but, or, however, then, thus, consequently,* and several others. Cohesion can also be created through the repetition of words. Each repetition of a word links back to previous instances of the same word, adding additional information about its role in the discourse. Similarly, reference creates cohesion in a discourse between words that refer to the same discourse entity (pronouns, names, and noun descriptions); however, in the case of reference, different words are used. The most common types of words used in reference relationships are pronouns (*he, she, they, we, you*, etc.); however, proper names (e.g., *Valerie* and *Marlon*) and noun descriptions (e.g., the princess or the king) can also be used. Two additional devices used to create cohesion involve the omission of words, which is then interpreted in relation to previously encountered information in the discourse. These are **ellipsis**, which involves the omission of a portion of a verb phrase that is shared with the preceding clause or sentence (Arregui et al., 2006; Grant et al., 2012), and **substitution**, which involves the substitution of the word *one* for a longer noun phrase mentioned earlier in the discourse (see Table 7.2). As you will learn in Chapter 14, disorders in which semantic knowledge and/or processing are impaired are associated with the production of discourses having low levels of coherence.

Cohesion in written discourses can be increased through the use of words signaling transitions in the discourse. Table 7.3 lists some of the most commonly used transitions. In formal types of writing, such as academic papers and legal documents, these types of transitions are often used, as well as other structural conventions, such as an introduction that previews the topics to be discussed later, and a conclusion that reviews the major points that were made. In some cases, it is possible to increase cohesion in a discourse by using the repetition of an ordering of information. For example, in research articles, authors are likely to discuss the results of a study in the order that was used when the hypotheses or predictions were specified in the introduction.

Semantic Similarity

Some researchers have shown that coherence is highest when there is greater semantic similarity among words in a discourse (Foltz, 2007; Foltz et al., 1998). The approach to

Table 7.3 Commonly Used Transitions in Written Discourses

Type of transition	Example phrases
Coordinating	
Expressing similarity	And, thus, then, similarly, also, too, furthermore, moreover, by the same token
Expressing contrast	But, however, yet, in contrast, on the contrary, on the other hand, nevertheless, besides
Subordinating	
Introducing a list	First, foremost, in the first place, secondly, second, next, then, lastly, finally
Introducing an example	For example, for instance, specifically, namely, that is
Signaling causality	Consequently, thus, hence, so, because, then, since, therefore
Introducing a conclusion	To sum up, finally, in summary, in sum
Temporal	
Specifying sequence	At first, in the beginning, in the meantime, at the same time, simultaneously, in the end
Specifying duration	During, while, for a long time, briefly
Specifying frequency	Frequently, often, day after day, hourly, now and then, occasionally

Source: Weber and Stolley (2016)

discourse coherence grew out of Landauer and Dumais' (1997) latent semantic analysis (LSA) for language. Using complex computational algorithms, the words contained in texts can be represented in terms of relatedness to other words in the same text. Each word in a text is represented in a row, with each column corresponding to a different paragraph in which the word occurs. By taking into account only the co-occurrence of words in the text, without considering their syntactic relations to one another in the text being processed or other texts, LSA appears to be able to distinguish coherent texts from those lacking coherence. The theory has led to the creation of algorithms that are used for grading essays from college and high school courses (Shermis & Burstein, 2013). The coherence scores produced by the algorithm have been found to be highly similar to grades provided on the same essays by human graders (Landauer et al., 2003). For those who are acquiring a second language, being able to produce discourses that are highly similar to those of native speakers can be particularly challenging. Researchers have shown that attending to semantic similarity in second language writing can lead to improvements (Wang et al., 2012).

Memory for Discourses

As you may recall from previous chapters, during language comprehension, we use our working memory to store each incoming word we process as well as the representation of our understanding of the discourse. Some of the information in working memory may be transferred to long-term memory and retained for long periods of time (Goldstein, 2015). It is common for us to store our favorite stories from books, films, and family reunions in our long-term memory. You are likely to have experienced how vulnerable our memory for long discourses is to forgetting. In educational settings, forgetting the information obtained during the reading of discourses is so common that educators have devised techniques to improve students' retention of discourse information, such as the SQ3R method, in which students are instructed to *skim, ask questions, read, recite,* and *review* (Pressley & Hilden, 2005). Have you ever started to tell a familiar story or anecdote to friends, only to find yourself unsure of some of the story's details? Have you ever watched a movie or film and then later realized that you had actually seen it before, but did not remember its details well enough to find it familiar on the second viewing? The Classic Research box highlights an important early demonstration of the fallibility of memory for the content of stories.

Investigations into the role of memory in discourse processing go beyond assessing how people retain the information obtained from discourses in their long-term memory. As you learned in Chapter 6, we construct mental representations of what we are processing using our working memory. During the comprehension of sentences and discourses, we also retrieve information about words from our semantic memory, which is one type of long-term memory, and activate the memory representations of related concepts in long-term memory through processes described as "spreading activation." As we incorporate the meaning of words into the discourse representation we are constructing, we interpret some words as referring to the same discourse entity (pronouns refer to the same characters in stories as proper names). During comprehension, some discourse entities in the discourse representation have greater importance than others, known as **discourse prominence**. Some discourse entities will become the focus of a part of the discourse called the **local level**, which refers to information contained within the same sentence, as opposed to the **global level**, which includes information obtained across multiple sentences, which will either be maintained for the rest of the discourse or changed when another discourse entity becomes the focus. If you take a moment to think about some of the episodic entertainment programs you may have watched on television or other platforms (Internet, Amazon, Netflix, etc.), you may realize that some programs have an element of mystery that spans many episodes and, sometimes, all episodes. As we view each new episode, we retrieve from long-term memory what we remember from prior episodes and use it during our understanding of the new episode.

Some have suggested that our long-term memory system may include processes that resemble aspects of working memory. Research starting in the 1990s pointed out that the traditional conceptualizations of working memory and long-term memory may need to be revised. Ericsson and colleagues claimed that the processes involved in the storage and retrieval of information in long-term memory may result in processing that is similar to the traditional view of how working memory functions, and that processes involved in comprehension typically viewed as involving working memory may involve long-term memory instead (Delaney & Ericsson, 2016; Ericsson & Kintsch, 1995). The research supports the view that there is an aspect of long-term memory that is used for problem-solving. The researchers suggested that the temporary part of working memory is not needed for comprehension, and that the processing typically viewed as occurring in working memory during comprehension (e.g., carrying out processing in real time while maintaining information in consciousness) involves some aspect of long-term memory, referred to as **long-term working memory**. A motivation for the view was the traditional assumption that long-term memory has far greater capacity than working memory and the empirical results showing that experts, such as chess masters, have superior memory abilities for information about their area of expertise versus novices (Chase & Simon, 1973). The theory proposed that, with practice, specific comprehension skills become developed that lead long-term working memory to have much greater capacity than working memory. The three types of skills that can be improved on with practice are: linking cues from current stimulus to stored knowledge; retrieving knowledge; and integrating new knowledge with prior knowledge.

Classic Research

Bartlett's Study of Memory for Narratives

In 1920, Sir Frederic Charles Bartlett (1886–1969) reported his classic studies on how people remember the content of long stories. Consider the story below, which is one of the stories Bartlett (1920) used. Participants were asked to read the story and later were asked to recall the story to the best of their ability.

War of the Ghosts

One night two young men from Equlac went down to the river to hunt seals and while they were there it became foggy and calm. Then they heard war-cries, and they thought: "Maybe this is a war-party." They escaped to the shore, and hid behind a log. Now canoes came up, and they hear the noise of paddles, and saw one canoe coming up to them. There were five men in the canoe, and they said:

"What do you think? We wish to take you along. We are going up the river to make war on the people."

One of the young men said, "I have no arrows."

"Arrows are in the canoe," they said.

"I will not go along. I might be killed. My relatives do not know where I have gone. But you," he said, turning to the other, "may go with them."

So one of the young men went, but the other returned home.

And the warriors went on up the river to a town on the other side of Kalama. The people came home to the water and they began to fight, and many were killed. But presently the young man heard one of the ghosts. He did not feel sick, but they said he had been shot.

So the canoes went back to Equlac and the young man went ashore to his house and made a fire. And he told everybody and said: "Behold I accompanied the ghosts, and we went to fight. Many of our fellows were killed, and many of those who attacked us were killed. They said I was hit, and I did not feel sick."

He told it all, and then he became quiet. When the sun rose he fell down. Something black came out of his mouth. His face became contorted. The people jumped up and cried.

He was dead.

Participants reported that recalling the story was difficult. The results showed that participants tended to remember aspects of the story that were consistent with the overall theme and forgot aspects of the story that were inconsistent with it. Later in this chapter, you will see that Bartlett's observations have figured prominently in some theories of discourse comprehension.

Research has criticized the theory, specifically the prediction that brief interruptions during reading are not expected to disrupt comprehension (Foroughi et al., 2015, 2016). Foroughi et al. (2015) conducted a series of experiments in which participants carried out reading comprehension during which they were interrupted. The experiments were modeled on earlier experiments conducted by Glanzer et al. (1981) and Oulasvirta and Saariluoma (2006), whose results supported Ericsson and Kintsch's (1995) theory of long-term working memory. Unlike prior experiments, those conducted by Foroughi et al. (2015) required readers to integrate information across sentences when answering comprehension questions. The results demonstrated that interruptions caused disruption in comprehension, suggesting that successful comprehension involves the maintenance of information in a transient form of memory, such as working memory. The results refuted the claim that comprehension involves only the permanent memory structures of knowledge contained in long-term working memory. Future research will likely reexamine these experiments that have explored the existence of long-term working memory. The specifics of how long-term working memory is used during comprehension may be changed based on future results. It will be beneficial to the study of discourse processing to advance beyond the traditional view of transient working memory having limited capacity and long-term memory having a large capacity for storage. In the next section, you will learn about different types of processes occurring during discourse comprehension and the experiments that have been conducted to explore them. We will discuss the research without reference to long-term working memory; rather, we will proceed with the traditional distinction between working memory and long-term memory.

In this section, you learned about how linguists and psycholinguists define the term discourse and categorized different types of discourse. You also learned that the most frequently studied type of discourse is the narrative, and narratives can be structured in different ways. Discourses that are meaningful are described as having a high level of coherence. Coherence in a discourse is achieved by having a high level of cohesion in a text. Cohesion is created through the use of words and phrases that provide links between words and phrases within and between sentences.

Photo 7.3 We process discourses when we view films, television programs, and other outlets. Do you prefer films with a lot of action or more conversation?

When computers are used to analyze the characteristics of texts with varying levels of coherence, there is a greater amount of semantic similarity between words in texts high in coherence than those low in coherence. Lastly, you learned about aspects of short-term and long-term memory processing that are likely to be involved in the processing of discourses. Recent research suggests that there is an aspect of long-term memory that operates similarly to working memory, with the information being stored more permanently than that involved in short-term working memory.

 Time out for Review

Key Terms

Aboutness

Coherence

Cohesion

Discourse

Discourse prominence

Ellipsis

Flashbacks

Flash forwards

Focus

Given-new
   strategy

Global level

Linear narrative

Local level

Long-term working
   memory

Narratives

Nonlinear narrative

Oral tradition

Rhetoric

Substitution

Review Questions

1   In narratives, the three-act structure is frequently used. What does each act typically contain?
2   Describe the important differences between linear and nonlinear narratives.
3   What is meant by coherence in a discourse? Describe three ways in which discourses can be created with high levels of coherence.
4   What is the given-new strategy? When comprehending a discourse, how might it be useful in determining which information is old versus new?
5   What are the different ways in which memory processes are involved in discourse comprehension and retaining information obtained from discourses?
6   Describe the different views regarding the roles of working memory versus long-term working memory in comprehension.

Linking Discourse Elements

Compared to the research on word recognition and sentence processing covered in Chapters 5 and 6, the research in discourse processing is relatively small. Of the research that has been done, a great deal of it has focused on how comprehenders form links between discourse elements, such as discourse entities that refer to the same character in a narrative. Psycholinguists refer to this as **referential processing**. In this section, we first review the research on two types of linking that occur frequently in narratives. These are linking pronominal elements (*he, she, himself, herself,* etc.) with proper names (*Mariah, Zachary, Mr. Gordon,* etc.) or noun descriptions (*boy, girl, doctor, nurse,* etc.) and linking non-pronominal elements (*peacock-bird* and *furniture-chair*). Most of the time during comprehension, both types of linking occur rapidly below the level of conscious awareness. Second, we explore comprehenders' ability to acquire information about the discourse when the information is not explicitly stated. This process is referred to as **inferencing** (Noordman & Vonk, 2015)**,** and the specific bits of information that are acquired, **inferences**. For example, when reading that a particular vase is fragile and that it was struck by a heavy stone, the comprehender might make the inference that the vase was broken when it was struck. As you will see, there are some circumstances in which a comprehender could draw an inference, but fails to do so.

Pronouns

A great deal of research has investigated how readers resolve pronouns within and between sentences (Garnham, 2001). As shown in Table 7.2 above, there are many ways to refer to the same discourse entity (e.g., repeating the same name or noun, using a pronoun, or using a different noun to express a variation on the meaning, as in *the robin-the bird*). Most commonly, pronouns are used to refer to discourse entities that have been introduced into the discourse in the form of proper names, noun descriptions, or another pronoun. Examples are displayed in 2. In linguistic and psycholinguistic examples, the subscript is used to show which words refer to the same individual. The term **antecedent** describes the initial mention of a discourse entity to which a pronoun refers back. In a discourse, a referent that refers back to its antecedent is known as an **anaphor**. The term "anaphoric processing" is used to describe the comprehension of an anaphor. The antecedents in 2a and 2d are the proper names *Suzanne* and *Lupita*, and the antecedent in 2b is the noun phrase *the waitress*. Sometimes, the antecedent of a pronoun is another pronoun, as in 2c. Among linguists and psycholinguists, pronouns ending in -*self* (*himself, herself, themselves*, etc.) are distinguished from those that do not (*he, she, they, it, him, her, them*, etc.). The former type of pronoun is referred to as a **reflexive pronoun**.

2   a. Suzanne$_i$ ordered a salad. She$_i$ considered ordering something else.

     b. The waitress$_i$ suggested the steak. She$_i$ also said the salad was good.

     c. She$_i$ asked for a refill for her coffee. She$_i$ also asked for more cream.

     d. Lupita$_i$ treated <u>herself</u>$_i$ to an ice cream sundae.

Reflexive pronouns differ from other pronouns in that they are used to refer back in the discourse (i.e., anaphorically). Another difference between reflexive pronouns and other pronouns involves the syntactic environments in which they occur. Chomsky (1981) described these syntactic differences in his **binding theory**. Chomsky noted that reflexive pronouns and non-reflexive pronouns occurred under different syntactic circumstances, leading to a complimentary distribution (i.e., pronouns could not occur where reflexive pronouns occurred and vice versa). Consider the examples in 3. The reflexive pronoun *himself* can refer to the antecedent *king* in 3a; however, the non-reflexive pronoun *him* in 3b cannot. The non-reflexive pronoun *he* can refer to the antecedent *king* in 2c, but the reflexive pronoun *himself* in 3d cannot. The syntactic position of the reflexive and non-reflexive pronouns relative to their antecedent proved to be the crucial factor.

3 a. The king$_i$ embarrassed himself$_i$.
   b. *The king$_i$ embarrassed him$_i$.
   c. The king$_i$ said that he$_i$ was embarrassed.
   d. *The king$_i$ said that himself$_i$ was embarrassed.
   e. Steve$_i$ smiled when he$_i$ arrived.
   f. He smiled when Steve arrived.

Several studies have investigated how readers resolve pronouns (see Garnham, 2001 for review). Of particular interest has been the question of whether readers rely only on syntactic information to generate a set of possible antecedents from the local and global discourse. Nicol and Swinney (1989) argued that the answer was yes; thus, for reflexive pronouns, only antecedents within the same major phrase unit would be considered as possible antecedents, and for non-reflexive pronouns, only antecedents outside the same major phrase unit would be considered as possible antecedents. Later research proved this view to be incorrect (Badecker & Straub, 2002; Clifton et al., 1997; Kennison, 2003, 2016). There is growing support for the two-stage model of anaphor resolution first described by Simon Garrod and colleagues (Garrod, 1994; Garrod & Sanford, 1994; Garrod & Terras, 2000; Sanford et al., 1983). The model involves binding (linking the pronoun with a preceding entity) and then resolution (evaluating the link for acceptability and integrating the meaning into the mental representation of the discourse).

Noun Descriptions

Noun descriptions (e.g., *the stranger*) may also link back to earlier mentions of the same discourse entity (e.g., *A man walked into the pub*). Although relatively few psycholinguistic studies have investigated how readers link noun descriptions to one another during discourse processing, the research that has been done has revealed some compelling results. The results suggest that the processing noun phrase anaphors can be explained as occurring in the two stages of *bonding* and *resolution*. There are sentences in which a pronoun is followed by material that contains a word that refers to the same discourse entity. Consider the examples in 4.

4 a. He had not lived in the town long. The minister had come to love it.
   b. She ordered the baked ziti for lunch. The judge loved Italian food.

Pronouns used in this way are referred to as **cataphors** and the comprehension of such pronouns is referred to as "cataphoric processing." Research suggests that the time readers take to resolve a noun description (van Gompel & Liversedge, 2003) or name (Kennison et al., 2009; Sun & Kennison, 2015) with a prior pronoun is consistent with the two-stage model of anaphor resolution.

Sometimes, comprehenders link a noun description with a prior noun description. One of the earliest studies by Garrod and Sanford (1977) showed that the amount of time readers took to link words referring to basic level categories (*bird*, *vehicle*, and *flower*) was related to the words' typicality as a member of that basic category. Consider the examples in 5.

5 a. A robin would sometimes wander into the house. The bird was attracted by the food in the pantry.

  b. A goose would sometimes wander into the house. The bird was attracted by the food in the pantry.

In 5a, the nouns *robin* and *bird* refer to the same discourse entity, and in 4b, *goose* and *bird* do. Garrod and Sanford (1977) found that readers spent less time processing the second sentence in 5a than 5b. They reasoned that when readers encountered the word *bird,* they linked it with the previous occurrence of a type of bird (either *robin* or *goose*). As they continued with the linking process and making sense of the discourse with that link established, the processing occurred faster when the previous word was a typical type of bird, such as a robin, than when it was an atypical type of bird, such as a goose. In terms of the two-stage model of anaphor resolution, the processing of resolution could be completed faster when the overlap in meaning and/or semantic features for the two words was higher as opposed to lower.

Later research showed that the distance between the two nouns influenced how rapidly the linking could occur. Duffy and Rayner (1990) recorded eye movements during reading on conditions similar to those tested by Garrod and Sanford (1977) as well as conditions in which the two nouns were farther apart in the discourse. They compared reading time in near and far conditions. The results showed that reading time on material following the word *bird* took longer to read when *robin* or *goose* occurred farther back in the discourse than when the word was shown nearer to the word *bird*. Interestingly, the typicality of the first noun as a bird affected reading time on the word *bird* in the near condition, but not in the far condition. Other research has suggested that the amount of time readers take to link nouns is influenced by other factors, such as focus (Almor, 1999), children's reading skill and working memory (Joseph et al., 2015), and degree of semantic overlap (Cowles & Garnham, 2005).

Research has demonstrated that there are times when comprehenders could link a noun description with a prior discourse element, but fail to do so (Levine et al., 2000). In a series of experiments, Levine et al. (2000) found that when the prior element is not especially important in the part of the discourse being processed and there is a similar type of word in the preceding context, the reader may fail to link the two elements and continue processing the discourse. Other research provides compelling evidence that readers are aware when antecedents are not available in discourses (Cook et al., 2005).

Inferencing

During discourse processing, comprehenders interpret the meaning of noun descriptions and other words with the meaning of the prior context in ways that go beyond referential processing. The way in which comprehenders achieve the integration of meaning in contexts may be the least well understood of all discourse processing. In the 1970s, Clark and colleagues discussed how comprehenders link meaning between sentences (Clark, 1977; Haviland & Clark, 1974). Consider the example in 6. The noun *beer* in the second sentence was not explicitly mentioned in the first sentence, but you might have inferred that the beer was among the supplies Mary took out of the car. These are known as **bridging inferences,** which require comprehenders to use their knowledge of the world to link two or more elements in a discourse. The most common type of inference that has been investigated is similar to that given in 6. It is a **backward inference**, which occurs when the currently processed information is considered in conjunction with preceding information from the discourse (Clark, 1977).

6   Mary got some supplies out of the car. The beer was warm.

Researchers have also investigated cases in which comprehenders use information from the text to generate an inference that leads to a prediction about the resulting state of affairs being described in the text (McKoon & Ratcliff, 1986). These are known as **forward inferences**. Consider the paragraph in 7. After reading the paragraph, did you infer that the swimmer had died due to a shark attack? At which point did you make that inference?

7   The lifeguard saw the swimmer far from shore and then saw the fin of a great white shark. After a few moments, the fin moving in the direction of the swimmer disappeared under the water. The lifeguard could barely see that the swimmer went under the water and did not resurface. No one else on the shore appeared to have noticed the presence of the shark or the disappearance of the swimmer.

Thus far, researchers have investigated a relatively small number of different types of inferences that we routinely make during discourse processing. Future research will likely see researchers include many more types of inferences that can be drawn in a wider range of languages. The types of inferences that can be drawn during discourse processing vary across languages, as the grammatical distinctions that influence how meaning is conveyed in sentences vary. The Language Spotlight box highlights the many types of subjective moods that occur in the Turkish language.

In this section, you learned how comprehenders link discourse elements during processing. Referential processing involves linking pronouns with either preceding or following elements, which can include names, noun descriptions or other pronouns. Far fewer studies have investigated how comprehenders link noun descriptions with other discourse entities; however, the results suggest that comprehenders form the links rapidly and processing is facilitated when semantic similarity is higher versus lower for the elements that are linked. Lastly, you learned about comprehenders' ability to extract meaning from a discourse that is not explicitly stated. Most of the research on inferencing has investigated backward inferencing, but a few studies have demonstrated that forward inferences also occur, but may occur less often.

The Inferential Mood in Turkish

Each language provides ways for speakers to convey to listeners the extent to which the speaker believes the information conveyed is true or likely to be true. Across languages, the options available to speakers vary. Linguists and psycholinguists refer to these options generally as moods typically associated with the verb of a sentence (Palmer, 2001). "Realis moods" refer to those specifying facts or events that are known to be true by the speaker. In contrast, "irrealis moods" refer to those communicating varying degrees of uncertainty about the information convey. One example of an irrealis mood is the subjunctive, which occurs in English, but operates in an optional fashion. Consider the examples in 8. In 8a, the subjective mood conveys that the state of affairs in the sentence does not correspond to reality (i.e., it is a counterfactual).

8 a. If the cake were ready, I would have a   Subjunctive
        big piece.

   b. If the cake was ready, I would have a   Non-
        big piece.   subjunctive

Other languages have multiple irrealis moods (Palmer, 2001). One of the more interesting irrealis moods is one that enables people to describe an event without also implying that the event definitely occurred. This mood is referred to as the "inferential mood" in Turkish. Languages with this mood enable speakers to refer to past events either by implying that the event occurred and was witnessed (i.e., confirmed) or the event occurred and was not witnessed (i.e., not confirmed), leading to certainty regarding the event's occurrence in the former case and uncertainty in the latter case. Consider the examples in 9. In English, the listener has no way of inferring from the sentence whether the speaker witnessed the event described in the sentence or merely heard about it. In Turkish and other languages, the relationship between the speaker and the event can be more precisely specified. Speakers can also use the mood with other verb tenses. For example, when used with the present tense, the speaker may state that a person arrived, but using the irrealis mood would convey that the person's arrival was unknown to the speaker. When used with a verb in the future tense, the speaker can convey doubt that the event could happen.

9 a. When I was in New York City, the Empire State Building caught on fire.

   b. Yesterday, a truck ran over a pedestrian on Main Street.

Theories of Discourse Comprehension

A complete theory of discourse comprehension would ideally be able to explain how people construct mental representations of discourses, whether they be text, auditory, or visually displayed (i.e., film). As you will learn in this section, theories of discourse processing differ in regard to their assumptions about how meaning obtained from discourses is stored in memory and how memory for that meaning is used incrementally as processing occurs. Early theories focused on describing how knowledge obtained from discourses is organized in memory. We examine three types of knowledge structure approaches: the story grammar approach, which claims that discourses can be described with rules; those proposing that the basic unit of meaning obtained from a discourse and stored in memory is a proposition, which is made up of a verb describing a state of being or an event in relation to one or more nouns playing a role in the action described by the verb (Gaskin, 2008); and those emphasizing the role of more complex memory structures referred to as schemas or scripts, which are viewed as organizing not only information obtained in discourses, but also our knowledge about the world. We end with a discussion of contemporary theories of discourse comprehension, which focus on understanding the complex coordination of numerous processes involved in constructing a mental representation of a discourse in real time, retrieving information from memory and storing computed information from the discourse into memory. We examine three promising models: the mental model approach (Carreiras et al., 1996; Johnson-Laird, 2013); Gernsbacher's (1990) structure-building framework; and the RI-Val model proposed by Edward O'Brien and Anne Cook (Cook & O'Brien, 2014; O'Brien & Cook, 2016).

Knowledge Structure Approaches

In the 1970s and 80s, researchers interested in computers and language began examining the fundamental question of how people might store in memory the information they acquire when reading discourses. Only a decade into the cognitive revolution, researchers were quite aware of computers and interested in being able to describe human knowledge as precisely as is required when programming a computer. As you will learn in this section, researchers continue to work on this approach, as no fully implemented model has yet been produced. However, from the work conducted so far, three types of knowledge structures have emerged as likely candidates for inclusion in future models of discourse comprehension. These knowledge structures are: story grammar; propositions; and schemas or scripts.

Story Grammar

An early approach to discourse processing was inspired by Chomsky's (1957) work describing the phrase structure rules for sentences. In the 1970s, researchers argued that the structure of stories could be viewed as part of our knowledge of discourses and that we use that knowledge during comprehension (Mandler & Johnson, 1977; Rumelhart, 1975, 1980; Stein & Glenn, 1979; Thorndyke, 1977). Table 7.4 lists the components of stories as described in **story grammar**.

There were early results supporting the psychological reality of story grammar (Mandler & Johnson, 1977; Stein & Glenn, 1979). Criticisms of the view include that the theory was too vague, making it difficult for researchers to identify testable predictions (Garnham, 1983). Furthermore, demonstrations that recall of discourses was poorer when the order of elements in the story appeared in an atypical order were shown to have a serious confound, specifically referential continuity (Garnham et al., 1982). Despite its intuitive appeal, relatively little attention has been paid to story grammar among psycholinguists conducting research with neurotypical readers. However, a small, but growing literature is investigating story comprehension among individuals who have sustained brain injuries (Coelho, 2002; Mozeiko et al., 2011).

Table 7.4 Components of Story Grammar

Story	involves	A setting, theme, plot, ending in a resolution
Setting	involves	Location, time, and characters specified
Theme	involves	A goal with or without one or more events specified
Plot	involves	One or more episodes
Episode	involves	Subgoals with one or more attempts to achieve goal resulting in an outcome
Resolution	involves	The outcome

Source: Rumelhart (1975)

Propositions

Analyzing meaning obtained in sentences from discourses in terms of **propositions** grew out of work initially published by Charles Fillmore (1968).

Fillmore (1929–2014) was a linguistics professor at the University of California, Berkeley, where he wrote important works in the area of semantics and syntax. His work on semantics formed the basis for the notion of thematic roles, which you learned about in Chapter 6. Propositions are typically characterized as involving a predicate (usually a verb) and its arguments, which you learned about earlier in this chapter (e.g., essential elements involved in the action, agent, patient, etc.). The theory did not distinguish arguments from adjuncts in defining a proposition, so the location of an action would be represented the same whether it occurred with a verb for which it was an argument (e.g., *John put the book in the backpack*) or with a verb for which it was an adjunct (e.g., *John found the book in the backpack*). Importantly, all propositions have a corresponding truth value (i.e., true or false). A proposition is viewed as the smallest unit of meaning that can have a truth value, as a predicate without any arguments (a single verb) or an argument without its predicate (a single noun) cannot have a truth value. It is important to remember that in an author's discourse, a proposition that is not true in the real world can be true within the discourse the author has constructed (e.g., *The little boy could fly*). Among the most prominent theories of discourse comprehension is Kinstch's construction-integration theory (Kintsch; 1974; 1988; Kintsch & van Dijk, 1978), which includes the proposition as the fundamental unit of meaning. The model is recognized as doing an adequate job of accounting for automatic inferences, but failing to explain other types of inferencing during which comprehenders exert conscious effort (Graesser et al., 1994).

Schemas and Scripts

As you recall from the Classic Research box, Bartlett (1920) found that his participants tended to experience similar types of memory errors, specifically, including details related to the theme of the story that were not actually in the story, and omitting details that were unrelated to the theme of the story, which were, in fact, present in the story. From our daily life experiences, we obtain knowledge of the world and store this knowledge in memory. When we process a discourse that involves a familiar setting, situation, or activity, we are likely to activate in memory what we already know about the setting, situation or activity. This type of memory structure was first described by Bartlett (1920) in the context of his studies of people's ability to remember stories. As you recall from earlier in this chapter, he found that people were more likely to forget details of the story that did not fit well with the overall theme of the story and more likely to remember those that did fit well. The term **schema** or **script** refers to memory structures for world knowledge about familiar situations (Goldstein, 2015). For example, most people have experience of having an evening meal at a restaurant. The schema is likely to include entering the restaurant and being met by a host who shows you to a table or seeing a sign that directs you to take any available seat. You get menus from a server or the host, and after some time, a server takes your order. Drinks arrive, appetizers if you ordered them. The meal arrives, and later on, the server asks if you would like dessert. The bill is presented. You pay and leave. Restaurant dining varies around the world, and a person's schema for restaurant dining would include the typical sequence of activities experienced in that culture.

Processing Approaches

By the late 1980s, researchers had routine access to increasingly powerful computers, making it much easier to carry out computer-controlled reaction time language processing experiments. Theories of discourse comprehension, and the experiments designed to support those theories, aimed to explain how readers comprehend discourses in real time, constructing a mental representation in working memory. Into the 1990s, theorizing about discourse comprehension built on earlier notions about how knowledge of discourses may be organized and what information is contained in those structures, and also began to tackle the question of how mental representations of the discourse are constructed in real time as processing occurs. As readers process discourses, they construct in working memory a representation of their understanding of the meaning of the discourse. The emphasis on explaining how comprehension occurs in real time continues today. We review three models of this type: the mental model approach; Gernsbacher's (1990) structure-building approach; and O'Brien and Cook's RI-Val model. Each of these approaches remains incomplete, unable to account for all aspects of discourse processing. As you learn about each one, think about which model is likely to inspire the most future research.

The Mental Model Approach

Advocates of the mental model approach claim that readers use information in the discourse as well as their own world knowledge when constructing mental discourse representations (Bransford et al., 1972; Johnson-Laird, 1983, 2013; van Dijk & Kintsch, 1983; Oakhill & Garnham, 1996). Whenever comprehenders encounter information in the discourse that requires them to update their mental model of the discourse, there is a processing cost that is likely to lead to an increase in reading time. The approach is viewed as being heavily influenced by Kinstch's construction-integration theory (Kintsch (1974, 1988; Kintsch & van Dijk, 1978), but specifically highlighting the fact that discourse comprehension involves the construction of mental representations of information having visual and spatial elements, referred to as **situation models** (Zwaan & Radvansky, 1998).

The approach provides an intuitive explanation for how readers use information about gender and other personal characteristics of story characters in real time as they comprehend discourses. For example, understanding discourses in English and other languages in which the gender of discourse entities is not grammatically marked or lexically specified means that a discourse entity's gender may require updating during processing (Carreiras et al., 1996). Consider the example in 10. In 10a, a reader is likely to interpret the *engineer* as male due to the common **gender stereotype** (Banaji & Hardin, 1996; Kennison & Trofe, 2003). In 10b, when the pronoun *she* is encountered, it is linked with the noun *engineer* and resolved as its antecedent. At that point, the reader is likely to infer that the engineer is, in fact, female. The mental model of the discourse must be updated, which would be reflected in the comprehender taking more time to process that word and some of the following words in the discourse. When the discourse provides disambiguating gender information early, as in *the female engineer* or *the male nurse*, there is no need to update the mental model later, and research has shown that processing time is not increased in such cases (Duffy & Keir, 2004).

10 a. The engineer arrived late to the meeting. He sat in the only available chair.

b. The engineer arrived late to the meeting. She sat in the only available chair.

The mental model approach provides exciting possibilities for future research because of its potential for making clear predictions regarding when, during processing, comprehenders are expected to update their mental model, which corresponds to when they are expected to experience increased processing difficulty (take longer to read). However, researchers have yet to make explicit the nature of the mental representation with which the mental models are constructed in memory. Future research that focuses on how characters are represented in memory is likely to be a productive line of inquiry. During comprehension, one important detail about individuals in a discourse is whether they are male or female. The Research DIY box invites you to explore the extent to which people's associations with gender-neutral terms are actually free of strong gender associations.

Research DIY

How Neutral are Gender-neutral Terms?

Photo 7.5 Some occupations attract workers of one sex more than the other, such as nursing and law enforcement. As you consider your future career possibilities, do you consider the numbers of men and women in each field?
Credit: Chris Yarzab (right photograph)

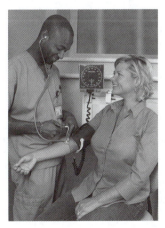

Since the 1970s, there has been a great deal of debate about language and gender (Lakoff, [1975] 2004; Tannen, 2001) and the fact that many terms for occupations contain the word *man* (*policeman, fireman, postman, foreman,* etc.). Not only has gender-biased language been viewed as a product of a gender-biased society, but also as having an influence on people's perception of gender roles, reinforcing those stereotyped roles. Some have advocated the adoption of gender-neutral language in order to reduce gender bias in society. Table 7.5 lists examples of gender-specific job titles and their gender-neutral alternatives. You can ask people to rate each term using the rating scale given below. Lower ratings indicate they believe the term refers mostly to females; higher ratings indicate they believe the term refers mostly to males; and ratings in the middle indicate they believe the term refers to a comparable number of males and females. A similar procedure was used by Kennison and Trofe (2003) for a large set of English terms.

Table 7.5 Gender-specific Job Titles and their Gender-neutral Alternatives

Male term	Gender-neutral term	Female term	Gender-neutral term
Policeman	Police officer	Stewardess	Flight attendant
Fireman	Firefighter	Hostess	Host
Mailman	Mail carrier	Waitress	Server
Foreman	Foreperson	Cleaning lady	Cleaner
Watchman	Guard	Wife	Spouse
Spokesman	Speaker	Maid	Cleaner
Salesman	Salesperson	Seamstress	Stitcher
Weatherman	Meteorologist	Actress	Actor
Anchorman	News anchor	Barmaid	Bartender
Repairman	Technician	Chairwoman	Chairperson

Ask your participants to rate each of the words using the scale below:

1   2   3   4   5   6   7

Refers to mostly males   **Refers to mostly females**

Test at least five men and five women. Compute the average rating provided by men and women for each of the words. The critical comparisons involve the average rating for the male terms and the corresponding gender-neutral terms and the average rating for the female terms and the corresponding gender-neutral terms. Organize these averages in a table like the one below.

	Male terms	Neutral terms	Female terms	Neutral terms
Men	_____	_____	_____	_____
Women	_____	_____	_____	_____
Average	_____	_____	_____	_____

The Structure-building Approach

The structure-building approach to discourse processing was proposed by Gernsbacher (1990) to explain how comprehenders construct mental representations of the details contained in long discourses. The theory has the advantage of explaining how all types of discourses are comprehended (i.e., verbal and nonverbal). She points out that the cognitive processes involved in some of the aspects of discourse comprehension are not central to the human language system and would be used to comprehend meaning that is not expressed with language (e.g., picture books, films, events we watch unfold in our daily lives). The elements that are built in memory when a discourse is processed include a foundation, which would involve information fundamental to the setting, a theme, and characters. There are also two cognitive processes – *mapping*, which involves linking incoming information from the discourse to the foundation if the incoming information is related to the foundation, and *shifting*, which is used when the incoming information is unrelated to the foundation in any clear way. When shifting is used, a new memory structure is built to store the incoming information. The memory representation of a complete discourse would involve a foundation, to which numerous memory structures, referred to as *substructures*, are connected (Gernsbacher, 1995). Substructures may also be connected to other substructures, but not all substructures are connected to the foundation. The substructures are presumed to be stored in memory in the form of memory nodes arranged in a semantic network, in a manner similar to the semantic network proposed by Collins and Quillian (1969). Following the metaphor of spreading activation, Gernsbacher (1990) proposed that nodes that store in memory information processed from a discourse also spread activation to related nodes when activated. Memory nodes storing discourse information may influence other nodes to which they are connected in two ways: *enhancement*, which increases activation of other nodes; and *suppression*, which decreases activation of other notes.

Among the experiments providing empirical evidence for the model are those demonstrating that the discourse entities introduced first in a discourse are processed longer than those introduced later (MacDonald & MacWhinney, 1990; Garnham et al., 1996). This pattern of processing is known as the **advantage of first mention**. Researchers have observed the advantage of first mention in reading experiments (Gernsbacher & Hargreaves, 1988; Gernsbacher et al., 1989). For example, when participants hear the sentence *Mariah played Roberta in several sets of tennis* and are then asked whether the word *Mariah* occurred, they respond faster to say yes than when the sentence was *Roberta played Mariah in several sets of tennis*. In other experiments in which looking time was measured as people comprehended stories told with pictures, comprehenders spent longer processing the first picture in the story than later pictures (Gernsbacher, 1996). The explanation for the advantage of first mention is that those discourse entities are most accessible because they are included in the foundation level of sentence representation rather than in representations that get mapped onto the foundation level.

When discourses lead readers to construct mental representations in which mapping, shifting, enhancement, or suppression have occurred and should not have, the discourse can be perceived as incoherent. Writers who are skilled in anticipating the reader's mind are likely to compose discourses with ample cues for the reader regarding when shifting is needed and the relative importance of discourse elements, which would relate to how activated they should be in memory.

O'Brien and Cook's RI-Val Model

In studies investigating the resolution of noun description anaphors within short discourses, Edward O'Brien and Anne Cook devised the RI-Val model of comprehension, which assumes three prominent processes – activation, integration, and validation (Cook & O'Brien, 2014; O'Brien & Cook, 2016). The model states that when the comprehender processes new information in the discourse, there is an *activation* of related concepts in memory. This is described as the initiation of the resonance signal. Related concepts in the discourse become activated, presumably relative to their level of relatedness to the newly processed information. In order for the newly processed information to be linked with prior information in the discourse, that prior information would have reached a threshold of activation, called the "coherence threshold." The linking process is referred to as *integration*. It is important to note that integration can begin while the resonance process continues, which can result in additional information becoming available after the initiation of integration. The third stage of processing is *validation* and involves the evaluation of the information resulting from the integration on the basis of many sources of knowledge: information from what has been processed in the discourse so far; the comprehender's real-world knowledge; and the relationship between the meaning of the discourse so far and the comprehender's real-world knowledge. In terms of timing, the model assumes that the validation process occurs only after the integration process has begun; however, both the resonance and integration processes can continue after the validation process begins, making additional information available to the comprehender that could be used in the validation process.

The RI-Val model provides a promising model for future development, because it incorporates many of the appealing features of prior approaches, such as the assumption that related concepts can activate one another when one is processed, and the processes resemble the binding and resolution stages of anaphor resolution proposed by Garrod and colleagues (Garrod, 1994; Garrod & Sanford, 1994; Garrod & Terras, 2000; Sanford et al., 1983). The primary challenge for the model is the same challenge faced by all models of discourse comprehension; to be able to make precise predictions about what information obtained from the discourse will lead comprehenders to each of the different types of mental processes that can occur during comprehension (e.g., linking, inferencing, etc.). Perhaps the biggest challenge will be providing parsimonious explanations for individual differences in processing patterns, which have been observed and related to readers' personal characteristics including but not limited to working memory capacity and reading skill (Gernsbacher, 1997), expertise (Rayner et al., 2012), and others.

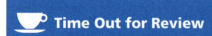

Time Out for Review

Key Terms

Advantage of first mention	Schema	Story grammar
Gender stereotype	Script	
Proposition	Situation model	

Review Questions

1 How is the term "proposition" defined in theories of discourse processing? How do propositional theories of discourse processing differ?
2 What is the mental model approach to discourse processing? Provide an example of an experiment in which the predictions of the mental model approach have been tested.
3 What is a gender stereotype? How are gender stereotypes involved in discourse comprehension?
4 What is the structure-building approach to discourse processing? What research results have provided support for the model?
5 What is the RI-Val model of discourse comprehension? How does the model differ from the structure-building approach?

Summary

Although there are many different types of discourses, research on discourse comprehension has focused primarily on how people comprehend narratives. This research has focused on the characteristics that contribute to discourses being coherent, such as the use of devices (conjunctions, pronouns, and lexical repetition) that increase cohesion and the use of the given-new strategy, which is having new information following familiar (i.e., already given) information. The most well-researched area in discourse processing has been on how readers link words that refer to the same discourse entities (pronouns, names, and noun descriptions) and how readers draw inferences during discourse comprehension. Formal models of discourse processing recognize the proposition as the basic unit of meaning in a mental representation of a discourse, but models differ in terms of how moment-by-moment processing leads to information being stored in memory.

Recommended Books, Films, and Websites

Balnicke, J. & Kennard, D. (1987). *Joseph Campbell: The Hero's Journey* [Motion Picture]. United States: Acorn Media.

Garnham, A. (2001). *Mental Models and the Interpretation of Anaphora*. New York: Psychology Press.

Moder, C. L. & Martinovic-Zic, A. (2004). *Discourse across Languages and Cultures*. New York: John Benjamins.

O'Brien, E. J., Cook, A. E. & Lorch, R. F. (2015). *Inferences during Reading*. Cambridge: Cambridge University Press.

Shermis, M. D. & J. Burstein (eds) (2013). *Automated Essay Scoring: A Cross-disciplinary Perspective*. Mahwah, NJ: Lawrence Erlbaum.

Sparks, J. R. & Rapp, D. (2010). Discourse processing: Examining our everyday language experiences. *WIREs Cognitive Science*, 1(3), 371–81.

Strohner, H. (2012). *Inferences in Text Processing*. Amsterdam: North Holland.

Walker, M. A., Joshi, A. K. & Prince, E. F. (1998). *Centering Theory in Discourse*. Oxford: Clarendon Press.

Chapter Content

When my grandson Logan was about three years old, I asked him if he would like some *water.* I pronounced the word slowly, articulating the /t/ sound very crisply as in the word *turn.* He immediately said, "That's not how you say that." He was right. I had not applied the *flap rule,* which you learned about in Chapter 1. I should have pronounced *water* so that it rhymed with the word *odder.* A few days later, I found myself recalling the interaction and realized that it was relevant to the ongoing debate about how children learn language. On one hand, there is B. F. Skinner's (1957) view that parents and other adults teach children language, and children's speech gets more and more accurate through the application of reinforcements such as praise and other rewards. This view emphasizes the passive role of children as learners whose behaviors are the result of prior learning episodes. On the other hand, Noam Chomsky and others argue that children come into the world with knowledge of what a human language is and acquire language naturally, when they are developmentally ready. They acquire the rules of the language(s) they hear and begin to apply those rules. This view emphasizes the active role of children as the learner, discovering the rules of the language in the environment and using the rules to speak and to understand what is spoken by others. In the case of my grandson, he used his knowledge of language rules to correct me, and he was correct.

In this chapter, you will learn more about how children acquire their first language. Research suggests that the process occurs similarly in all children,

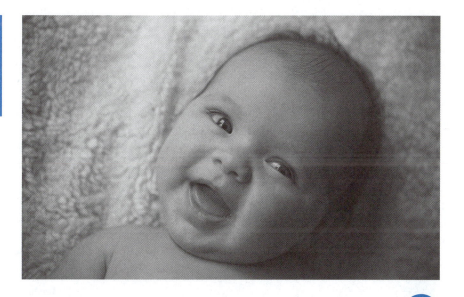

Photo 8.1 An infant typically begins to smile as a form of communication around the age of six weeks. Do you think a parent should be concerned if their infant has not smiled very much by the age of three months?

regardless of where they are raised and which language(s) they are acquiring from birth. This chapter focuses on what is known about children learning one language from birth. In Chapter 10, you will learn more about how multiple languages are acquired and used. The first section describes the opposing theoretical perspectives about how children acquire language. In the second section, we review the variety of methodologies used to study language development. These methodologies overcome serious challenges in studying the knowledge of infants and toddlers who have limited vocabularies and short attention spans. The third section surveys the major milestones in the development of communication from birth to 30 months. The last section explores how children become competent communicators, learning to carry out conversations, make socially appropriate requests, understand narratives, and tell stories themselves.

Theoretical Approaches to Language Development

As you learned in Chapters 1 and 2, the competing theories of language development can be categorized in terms of the nature versus nurture debate. Chomsky's nativist view represents the nature perspective, emphasizing the role of innate knowledge. In contrast, Skinner's (1957) view represents the nurture perspective of the behaviorist approach, emphasizing the role of learning through operant conditioning. Over the past 50 years, there have been other proposals about language development, most of which presume that nurture primarily determines what children learn and when. In this section, we will go deeper into the theoretical claims of the generative approach and examine how it differs from the alternative approaches to language development.

Generative Grammar Approach

Noam Chomsky (1965, 1968, 1986) argued that knowledge of language is innate. All children are born with knowledge that equips them to learn any human language that they might encounter as an infant. This knowledge is referred to as "universal grammar." As they develop, they are able to tap into their knowledge of language to discover the rules of the language or languages they hear spoken around them. The learning involves discovering which rules of language apply. As part of our biology, language emerges in the developing child as naturally as walking does (Searchinger et al., 2005).

The generative approach contrasts sharply with the common myth that children learn language by imitating speakers in their environment, specifically parents and caregivers. Chomsky and others have argued that infants are doing much more during language development than mindlessly imitating others (Searchinger et al., 2005). The strongest body of evidence against imitation as a theory of language development is that children produce utterances that are never produced by parents or caregivers. These novel productions are typically errors that adults do not make. For example, English-speaking children will produce incorrect versions of irregular past tense verbs (e.g., *broked, *goed, and *catched). Children produce these **overregularization errors** by applying the rule for forming past tense verbs (add the suffix -ed) inappropriately. The rule should be applied to some verbs (regular verbs, as in *walk*) and not to others (irregular verbs, *catch*). A second example that is difficult to reconcile with the view that children learn language by imitating others comes from several studies in which children produce questions with a word order adults would never use (de Villiers et al., 1990; Thorton & Crain, 1994). They found some children between the ages of three and four years produced questions, such as *What do you think what is in the bag?* instead of the correct form *What do you think is in the bag?* and *What way do you think how they put out the fire?* instead of *What way do you think they put out the fire?*. Thornton and Crain (1994) argue that children's mastery of this form of question occurs in stages, one of which involves a form that adults never produce, but which are grammatical forms in other languages (Searchinger et al., 2005).

Advocates of the generative approach have pointed out that children generally do not receive adequate exposure to the full range of information about language from the speech of adults to reach the understanding about their language that they ultimately have (Chomsky, 1980; Pinker, [1994] 2007). This observation is known as the **poverty of the stimulus** argument. The language that children hear from parents and others contains almost exclusively grammatically correct forms, which is **positive evidence** for the grammatical rules of the language. Children rarely, if ever, hear examples of ungrammatical forms of their language – **negative evidence**. Yet children end up with a complete understanding of their language's grammar, which enables them to make fine-tuned grammatical judgments about sentences in their language, judging which utterances are and are not grammatically well formed. The Classic Research box reviews a study from the early 1970s showing that young children displayed relatively sophisticated knowledge when judging the grammaticality of sentences.

The generative grammar approach to language development has its critics (Sampson, 2005). The most serious shortcoming of the generative grammar approach to language development is the failure to produce a complete understanding of the nature of universal grammar and information about how

 **Classic Research**

Grammatical Judgments by Young Children

In an early demonstration that young children could judge grammatical sentences from ungrammatical sentences, Gleitman et al. (1972) tested a group of two-year-olds and compared their performance with that of a group of seven- and eight-year-olds. For each group, the children's mothers read sentences aloud to their child in a one-on-one setting with the researcher also present. Sentences were either grammatical (*Open the box*) or ungrammatical (**Box the open*). After a sentence was read aloud by the mother, the child was instructed to respond "good" if the sentence was grammatical or "silly" if the sentence was ungrammatical. The results showed that the age of the child influenced performance. The older group displayed adult-like performance, accurately distinguishing grammatical and ungrammatical sentences. In contrast, the younger group accurately labelled most grammatical sentences and half of the ungrammatical sentences.

children's daily experiences lead to the triggering of innate knowledge. As you learn about alternative approaches, you may find yourself asking whether they too fall short in terms of specificity and details about how children learn what they learn.

Alternative Approaches

Several alternative approaches to the generative approach emphasize the role of learning that is facilitated by parents and other caregivers or learning that occurs unconsciously as infants form and update mental representations of language concepts and structures using aspects of the speech they experience. The social interactionist approach is the oldest and most influential among educators. The second is the statistical learning approach, briefly described in Chapter 1, and currently influential among those interested in computers and computational models of learning. It attempts to explain how statistical learning may occur, leading infants to *chunk* sequences of words and phrases in memory and from those representations create the structures of phrases and sentences.

Social Interactionist Approach

The social interactionist approach to language development emphasizes the role of learning through interactions with others, especially parents and other caregivers. The work of psychologist Lev Vygotsky (1896–1934) provides the foundation for this approach (Vygotsky, 1978, 1987), which focused on understanding how children learn from adults in one-on-one interactions. He viewed most, if not all, learning as occurring through social interaction. The development of language, in particular, occurred through children's interactions with others (Lee & Smagorinsky, 2000). Children's learning is described as beginning with the mastery of simple tasks or skills. More complex tasks or skills are tackled next, followed by even more complex tasks or skills. The term **scaffolding** describes this process of building knowledge or skills by progression through a series of steps that increase in complexity or difficulty (Sawyer, 2006). In terms of learning language, scaffolding is reflected in the mastery of the production of phonemes before the mastery of the production of entire words as well as the mastery of entire words before the production of sentences. Tasks were categorized as those that children could perform without the help of adults – the **zone of proximal development** – and those they could only perform with the help of adults. An important point of contrast between Vygotsky's and Chomsky's view of language is that Vygotsky viewed language as completely external to the child and acquired only through interactions with others. A challenge for the sociocultural approach to language development would be to explain why children produce words and sentences that adults never produce. If language originates external to the child, then there must be experiences with parents where the errors occur and are observed.

Statistical Learning Approach

The statistical learning approach claims that language is not special in any way in terms of how it is acquired. Language is learned just as any other cognitive skill is learned. In particular, the view emphasizes the brain's ability to acquire information implicitly from experience (Saffran, 2003; Saffran et al., 1996; Seidenberg & McClelland, 1989). Through exposure to the language of others, infants passively and unconsciously store bits and pieces of their experiences in memory, which comes to change how infants are able to process and interpret the language around them. Tomasello (2003) proposed that children learn language through statistical learning and rules of thumb processes involving induction and analogy. Children start out chunking sequences of words in sentences heard in adult speech, which enables them to develop mental representations of the chunks. Chunk by chunk, children's mental representations of language become more complex; however, the exact nature of what their mental representations contain remains unclear. Several studies have investigated children's use of phrases involving verbs (Matthews et al., 2007; Tomasello, 2000). The extent to which children's utterances reflect repetitions of phrases they have heard versus novel phrases will be of critical importance. The statistical learning approach predicts that children's speech should exclusively be previously experienced or derived by analogy from previously experienced speech. In contrast, Chomsky's nativist approach predicts that children's productions would not be completely accounted for by previous experience, because children's application of learned language rules regularly results in the production of forms that they may not have encountered in the speech of others.

 Time out for Review

Key Terms

Negative evidence
Overregularization error

Positive evidence
Poverty of the stimulus

Scaffolding
Zone of proximal development

Review Questions

1   What are the major theoretical approaches to language development? What are the differences in their assumptions about language knowledge and their predictions about how children acquire a first language?
2   What evidence is there against the view that children learn language by imitating their parents and/or caregivers?

What Methods are used to Study Language Development?

Conducting research on language development can be challenging, because infants are not ideal test subjects. In studies with adults, a researcher has many ways to obtain data, such as asking questions and recording responses or asking participants to perform a task and recording accuracy and/or response time. With infants as research subjects, the researcher has fewer options. Over the past 100 years or so, researchers have developed a variety of procedures for obtaining and interpreting data from infants. In this section, we review three broad categories of procedures: observational methods; experimental methods; and standardized assessments.

Observational Methods

You may be surprised to learn that the researcher who provided some of the first descriptions of typical child development was none other than Charles Darwin (1809–92). He made careful observations of his children's abilities and behaviors at different ages, referred to as a **baby biography**. Darwin published the baby biography for his oldest child (Darwin, 1877). About a century later, psychologist Jean Piaget (1896–1980) published baby biographies for his three children, covering the first three years of their lives (Piaget, 1957). Piaget went beyond merely being an observer of his children; he set up situations for them and observed how they responded. Contemporary researchers continue to use observation as a method of investigating child development. The behavior of infants and children may be observed as it is occurring and/or videoed for later observation. Typically, many observers are trained to record the behavior of interest. Research teams would aim for observers' judgments to be consistent. In some cases, researchers may also ask others (e.g., parents or teachers) to make careful observations of a child's behavior.

In 1984, Brian MacWhinney and Catherine Snow, two language development researchers, established the Child Language Data Exchange System (CHILDES), which allows researchers to submit transcripts of interactions with children (MacWhinney, 2000). Those transcripts then become available to researchers around the world, who may test hypotheses about language development. There are samples from more than 20 different language and involving children with various developmental disorders. CHILDES has become an important source of observational data for language researchers, now having been cited in over 3,000 research reports. TalkBank (www.talkbank.org) is a multilingual corpus established in 2002 and currently directed and maintained by Brian MacWhinney. CHILDES has been made into a component of the larger corpus TalkBank, which also includes language data from aphasics, second language acquisition, conversation analysis, and classroom language learning.

Experimental Methods

Among the most intriguing and impactful research investigating infant cognition are experiments involving the manipulation of one or more variables that the researcher hypothesizes will cause a change in one or more other variables. We review three of these experimental methods: the habituation paradigm; the preferential looking paradigm; and the head-turn technique. Each technique is used to reach conclusions about what infants perceive and/or remember.

Habituation Paradigm

Habituation paradigm refers to the fact that when people and animals experience a new stimulus (something experienced with one of the senses), there is a strong tendency to become bored with it. After repeatedly experiencing the stimulus, one becomes more and more bored or habituated. By observing how infants change their reactions to repeated stimuli over time, researchers can make inferences about how familiar the stimulus is to them. When a brand new stimulus is experienced, infants tend to respond to it to a greater degree than a stimulus they had experienced before. The infants' heart rate may increase as well as their rate of sucking on a pacifier. When presented with the same stimulus over and over, the infants' heart rate and/or sucking rate decrease. Many studies starting in the 1960s measured infants' sucking rate using pacifiers that could record each time the infant applied pressure on the pacifier (see Jusczyk, 2000, for review). For example, some studies examined infants' perception of phonemes. An infant would be provided with the special pacifier and a baseline level of sucking would be recorded. The first phoneme would be played to the infant. Because it is a new stimulus, the infant may respond fairly strongly to the sound, which would lead to a higher rate of sucking. If the infant is played the same phoneme again and again, the sucking rate would be predicted to decrease, since it is has been heard before and is familiar. If the researcher wants to know whether the infant can tell the difference between two similar sounding phonemes, such as a /p/ and /b/, the researcher could present several instances of the /p/, watch for the sucking rate to decrease, and then play the infant a /b/. If the infant's sucking rate continues to slow, then the researcher would infer that the /b/ is experienced as no different from the /p/. However, infants are excellent at distinguishing all the phonemes of all human languages at birth. When played a /b/ following multiple presentations of /p/, infants would be likely to increase their sucking rate, because they experience it as a new, unfamiliar sound.

Preferential Looking Paradigm

In the 1960s, developmental psychologist Robert Fantz introduced the **preferential looking paradigm** as a method of studying infant cognition (Cohen & Cashon, 2003). The technique was adapted by Roberta Golinkoff, Kathy Hirsh-Pasek, and colleagues, who used it to show that infants are able to comprehend sentences before they are able to produce them (Golinkoff et al., 1987; Golinkoff et al., 2013; Hirsh-Pasek & Golinkoff, 1996). Infants are able to understand language before they are able to speak. Their ability to understand language is their **receptive language ability** and their ability to speak is their **productive language ability**. In a series of studies, infants' receptive language ability was revealed using a laboratory task in which an infant sat on a caregiver's lap and watched videos on two screens, one on the left and one on the right (Golinkoff et al., 1987; Hirsh-Pasek & Golinkoff, 1991). Each screen displayed a different video, but both featuring Cookie Monster and Big Bird from the popular US children's show *Sesame Street*. One video showed Cookie Monster touching Big Bird while Big Bird laughed. The other video showed Big Bird touching Cookie Monster while Cookie Monster laughed. Simultaneously, loudspeakers played a sentence (Where is Cookie Monster tickling Big Bird?). Careful examination of the infants' looking behavior revealed that infants looked more at the display that was similar in meaning to the sentence played over the loudspeakers. The infants tested in this study had only one or two words in their productive vocabularies, yet they seemed to be able to appreciate the meaning of whole sentences. The researchers speculated the infants had developed an appreciation for the pattern in English that nouns occurring first are typically the doers of actions (agents) and the nouns occurring second are typically the objects changed by an action (patient).

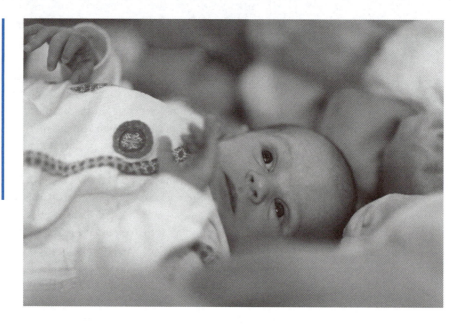

Head-turn Technique

In the late 1970s, researchers developed the **head-turn technique** to enable them to determine whether a child could distinguish between two sounds (Eilers et al., 1977). The technique built on the basic logic of operant conditioning, which, as you learned in Chapter 1, is a powerful form of learning, first proposed by Skinner. Eilers et al. (1977) reasoned that children would find a toy a desirable reward. In fact, just seeing the toy turned out to be very motivating for the child. If they turned their head correctly (when the two sounds were different), then they would be rewarded by being allowed to see the toy. If they turned their head incorrectly (when the two sounds were the same), then they would not be shown the toy. Children could be trained relatively easily to turn their head when they perceived different sounds (Werker et al., 1997). Despite the usefulness of the technique, it is important to note the possibility of false positive responses (a head-turn occurs without different sounds being perceived).

Standardized Assessments

In the field of child language development, a number of measurement tools have an established track record. A review identified 34 assessments (Paul & Norbury, 2012). Assessments are used not only by researchers, but also by speech-language pathologists, who use them to test children for the presence of speech and language disorders. Of the 34 assessments, relatively few can be used with very young children whose comprehension of language is the area of interest.

One of the most commonly used assessments by researchers and speech-language pathologists is the **Peabody Picture Vocabulary Test** (PPVT), which was developed in 1957 by Lloyd and Leota Dunn, who were special education experts and married to one another (Dunn & Dunn, 2007). When children are tested using the PPVT, they hear a target word, such as *bird,* and are shown four pictures, one of which matches the target word and three foils. Over the years, the

PPVT has been revised, with the most recent version, PPTV-4, being published in 2007 (Dunn & Dunn, 2007). The test can be used with children aged two and upward. It is not recommended for use with children who are deaf or blind, as the testing conditions involve pictures and spoken words.

A second popular assessment is the **MacArthur-Bates Communicative Development Inventory** (CDI), which was first described in 1993 (Fenson et al., 1994) and recently revised (Fenson et al., 2007). The original version of the CDI was designed to be used with children between 8 and 30 months and measured a wide range of skills related to language, including letter knowledge, number knowledge, comprehension, speech production, the development of vocabulary, gestures, and grammar. The revised version also includes additional measures that can be used for children between 30 and 37 months. For both versions, responses about children's abilities are obtained by parents and/or other primary caregivers through a series of checklists in which they are asked questions about whether the child understands and/or produces specific words and phrases.

A third assessment is the **Test for Auditory Comprehension of Language** (TACL-4), which measures children's listening comprehension for vocabulary, grammatical morphemes, as well as phrases and sentences (Carrow-Woolfolk & Allen, 2014). In the test, the examiner presents the child with a word or sentence and an array of three drawings, one of which corresponds to the meaning of the word or sentence. One of the other pictures is unrelated to the word or sentence, and the other contrasts in some way with the word or phrase (e.g., is the opposite in meaning). The examiner says the words or phrase and the child is asked to indicate which picture has the same meaning by pointing to the picture. Children are not required to produce a spoken response.

In summary, researchers utilize a variety of methodologies to study language development. These include baby biographies, questionnaires that parents complete regarding their child's abilities and behaviors, experimental procedures that examine children's language comprehension and production in laboratory settings, and standardized assessments used equally often in laboratory research and clinical settings by speech-language pathologists. There are many more experimental techniques and standardized assessments than we had space to cover in this chapter. Furthermore, as researchers and clinicians continue to improve their procedures, more methods are being developed.

 Time out for Review

Key Terms

Baby biography

Habituation paradigm

Head-turn technique

MacArthur-Bates Communicative
   Development Inventory (CDI)

Peabody Picture Vocabulary Test
   (PPVT)

Preferential looking paradigm

Productive language ability

Receptive language ability

Test for Auditory Comprehension
   of Language (TACL)

Review Questions

1 How do researchers conduct experiments to infer what infants are thinking?
2 Define the terms "receptive language ability" and "productive language ability." What evidence is there that one develops before the other?
3 Describe three standardized assessments used to measure language development.

The First 30 Months

Many parents recall eagerly awaiting their child's first word. Will it be *mama* or *dada* or maybe a favorite food? In the first 18 months, infants' ability to communicate increases steadily. Table 8.1 lists milestones in communication and language development from birth to 18 months. The ages provided for each milestone are average. Some children may reach the milestones a little earlier and others a little later while still being viewed as typical. In this section, we examine what research shows about the processes involved in each of these milestones. Our examination begins in a surprising place – in the months before birth, when infants first begin storing memories of sounds. We then review research on how children build their lexicons and how they progress in the production of small sentences.

Table 8.1 Communication and Language Development Milestones from Birth to 24 Months

Communication behavior	Approximate age
Social smile	6 weeks
Babbling	4–6 months
Pointing and other gesturing	8 months
First words	10–12 months
Two-word utterances	14–18 months
Sentences	18 months and upward

Before Birth

Long before an infant has produced their first word, approximately a year's worth of learning related to language has occurred. This learning starts when the fetus's auditory system becomes capable of hearing sounds of events occurring outside of the womb. From this point on, all but those infants with hearing problems are immersed in sound and language. The sounds that reach the fetus pass through the mother's body and, as a result, are quite muffled, much like if you were underwater at your local pool and hearing the conversations and activities of people around the pool. Expectant mothers can attest that the fetus can respond to loud noises, as fetal movement can be felt when such noises are experienced. Such responses have been observed as early as 26 weeks in pregnancy (Kisilevsky et al., 1992).

Photo 8.3 Before we are born, we are able to hear sounds produced outside our mother's womb. Do you think a very loud noise might startle a fetus so much that the mother is able to feel the fetus move?

Research has shown that memories of sound are formed before birth (DeCasper & Fifer, 1980; Kisilevsky et al., 2003). Between this time and birth, the fetus has the opportunity to store experiences involving sound in memory. Researchers have developed methods to obtain evidence for these memories. In studies with very young infants, researchers found that they were able to distinguish the sound of their mother's voice from that of a female stranger. Subsequent studies also found that infants form memories of the sound pattern of the language of the home (the language they have heard through the walls of the womb), as they can distinguish recordings of this language from those of a language they have never heard (Mehler et al., 1988; Moon et al., 1993). In a particularly clever study, DeCasper and Spence (1986) showed that infants could distinguish passages of a storybook that their pregnant mothers had read to them each day during the six weeks prior to birth from a storybook they had never heard. In the test, recordings of the two storybooks being read aloud by their mother were played to the infants. The infants appeared to have stored in memory information about the overall sound pattern of the words in the story when read aloud.

Infants' auditory learning continues after birth, as does their visual and kinesthetic learning (learning through the sense of touch). Infants do not see very well at birth. Technically, they are legally blind (Vital-Durand et al., 1996). Their eye movements are not well coordinated, and they have trouble focusing on individual people or objects. Despite the fact that infants' visual system is still developing in the first few months of life, they demonstrate a remarkable innate ability to imitate facial expressions. Research showed that infants require little or no experience to be able to imitate facial expressions (Meltzoff & Moore, 1977, 1983). Meltzoff and Moore (1977) tested infants who were 12–21 days old, and later Meltzoff and Moore (1983) tested infants who were only minutes old. Both studies demonstrated that infants could copy the expression of another. Three of the expressions were sticking out the tongue, opening the mouth in a small circle, and with the lips protruding forward. The ability to see an expression and imitate it may be useful in language development, because producing certain speech sounds requires precise positioning of the mouth, lips, teeth, and tongue.

The First Year

Most people assume that infants' first communicative act is crying; however, it is likely that crying can occur without a sense on the infants' part that there is another person around to hear the cry. Infants' desire to communicate is clearly seen around the sixth week of life when an infant will catch the gaze of another person and smile, known as the **social smile** (Anisfeld, 1982; Wörmann et al., 2012, 2014). Parents delight in these moments when their infant's face lights up when they enter the room, and they feel that their baby recognizes them and is happy to see them.

Sometime between the fourth and sixth month, infants begin to produce nonsense speech sounds called **babbling**. During this period, the infant blows raspberries and makes other strange sounds, all the while typically producing a fair amount of drool. This is when infants start to learn to use their articulators (the vocal organs above the larynx, including the tongue, lips, teeth, and hard palate). As the weeks pass, infant vocalizations include mostly actual speech sounds, not only from the language(s) they hear every day, but others as well, even speech sounds from languages they have never heard. By the end of the first year, infants' vocalizations include only those speech sounds they hear in their environment. In terms of the structure of the sound sequences that infants babble, two stages exist. Initially, infants' produce **canonical babbling**, with the consonant-vowel syllables repeated (*ba-ba-ba* or *ga-ga-ga*). Over time, the babbling evolves into **variegated babbling**, when the infant produces different syllables in a sequence (*ga-boo-tee* or *poo-ta-mee*). As you may recall from Chapter 2, the rapid production of syllables in language requires the larynx to be relatively low in the throat. When infants are born, the larynx is high in the throat; thus, the infant is limited in what sounds can be produced. Before babbling starts, the larynx lowers in the infant's throat. Prior to this, the infant can drink milk and breathe simultaneously. After the lowering of the larynx, the opening of the windpipe and larynx are close together, increasing the risk of choking (Lieberman et al., 2001). Brown (1958) observed that infants' variegated babbling changes over time, ultimately taking on prosody similar to that of the language(s) spoken in the home. The intonational pattern of the babbling comes to sound more and more like the language(s) the infant is learning (see Boysson-Bardies, 1993). Infants with physical and/or developmental problems may not babble at the typical time in the first year or may babble far less than neurotypical infants. For example, deaf infants will babble; however, the speech sounds they produce may differ from those produced by other infants (Stoel-Gammon, 1988). Infants who learn sign language from birth will produce meaningless sequences of signs (Naeve Velguth, 1996; Petitto & Marentette, 1991).

Infants' vision slowly improves, and by six months, they can see normally, visually exploring their environment and their own bodies. Around this time, they may also be learning to coordinate their arm movements. Sometimes infants may startle themselves when they bring their hands into view from the sides of their bodies. Before infants can speak, they typically attempt to communicate through gestures, such as pointing. Pointing can be observed in infants aged 11–12 months (Leung & Rheingold, 1981). In the months leading up to the use of pointing as a form of communication, infants may point when they are alone (Delgado et al., 2009). Later, infants will point as a way to communicate, as when they draw the attention of a parent to some object (Tomasello et al., 2007). There is some research suggesting that preverbal infants who use gestures to communicate may end up with larger vocabularies than other infants (Iverson & Goldin-Meadow, 2005; Özçaliskan & Goldin-Meadow, 2006) and may begin using two-word utterances earlier than other infants (Goldin-Meadow & Butcher, 2003; Iverson et al., 2008; Iverson & Goldin-Meadow, 2005). Essentially, an infant who demonstrates early communication through pointing and other gestures may also be above average in other ways related to language development. Goldin-Meadow et al. (2007) showed that mothers pay attention to their infants' pointing, interpret it, and carry out actions related to the inferred meaning.

Photo 8.4 Pointing is among the earliest forms of communication, as it emerges before infants produce their first words. When infants point at a toy, what message do you think they might be communicating?

First Words

As infants approach their first birthday, most have produced their first words. Parents eagerly await their child's first words. On YouTube, you can find videos recorded by parents to document the cherished event. Prior to the widespread availability of video recording, parents would record events in scrapbooks or through shared family stories. For example, Picasso's mother reported that Picasso's first word was *piz* (short for *lapiz* meaning pencil) (Wertenbaker, 1967). First words are often *dada* or *mama*. Mothers are sometimes disappointed when *dada* is the first word, but they must remember that the /d/ in *dada* is easier to produce than the /m/ in *mama*.

Those who study infant vocabularies have found a great deal of variation in the first 10 words (Harris et al., 1988). Harris et al. (1988) examined the vocabulary of four children between the ages of 6 and 24 months. Three of the four children had learned *mommy,* and two had learned *hello, bye-bye, go,* and *no.* Other words included onomatopoetic words: *choo-choo, buzz, moo, quack,* and *woof.* As the size of infants' vocabularies grows, nouns appear to outnumber other types of words. For English-speaking infants with a vocabulary of around 50 words, studies have shown that nouns make up 40–60 percent of the total (Bates et al., 1994; Dromi, 1987; Goldin-Meadow et al., 1976). Verbs make up only about 3 percent of the total (Caselli et al., 1995). It remains unclear whether there are universal patterns in infants' early vocabularies. Researchers studying the acquisition of vocabulary by infants have never observed infants who have learned more verbs than nouns (Waxman & Lidz, 2006). However, studies suggest that verbs may be acquired earlier for infants learning Mandarin (Tardif et al., 1999) or Korean (Choi & Gopnik, 1995) than infants learning English.

Invented words, called **protowords** or **idiomorphs**, may be used by some infants. The difference between a protoword and a typical newly acquired word is that the meaning of the protoword is decided by the infant. For a typical newly acquired word, adults and the infant use the same word to refer to an object. But an infant may use the word *lala* to refer to a favorite toy (a car), which others refer to as a car. In order to qualify as a protoword and not merely an error in speaking, the infant must consistently use the protoword to refer to the object. In some families, an infant's protoword may end up as part of the family vocabulary, with each use of the word being a reminder of the child's early years.

Building a Lexicon

Your knowledge of all the words you know is stored in your memory, known as the mental lexicon. We start out with an empty mental lexicon, and we begin to build our vocabulary word by word. Certainly, it is impossible to know exactly how many words a person knows, but it has been estimated that most 18-year-old Americans may know as many as 100,000 words (Nation & Waring, 1997). If you do the math, this corresponds to learning approximately 10 words a day every day up to your 18th birthday (Kennison, 2003). However, **late talker** describes a child who is perceived as not talking as much as other children their age. Researchers have defined late talkers as children 24 months or older who have a relatively small vocabulary (fewer than 50 words) (Kelly, 1998). Recent research suggests that vocabulary is initially harder for children to learn in some languages because of the phonological characteristics of the words in that language. The Language Spotlight box describes research suggesting that certain aspects of the Danish language may be particularly challenging for infants to learn.

 **Language Spotlight**

Danish: A Challenge for Infants

Wherever a child is born in the world, the child will acquire the language(s) spoken in the environment, provided that the child is healthy and typically developing. Infants' ability to master whatever language(s) they experience supports Chomsky's (1965, 1968, 1986) claim that infants are born with an innate knowledge of language that facilitates their language acquisition. However, recent research shows that the rate of language development, specifically with regard to the acquisition of vocabulary, may depend on the language infants are learning. In 2008, Dorothy Bleses and colleagues published a study that compared the vocabulary development of young children learning one of 18 different languages. They included Romance languages (European Spanish, Mexican Spanish, French, Italian, and Galacian), Germanic languages (Swedish, Norwegian, American English, British English, Dutch, and Danish), Slavic languages, Basque, Finnish, and others (Bleses et al., 2008). The results showed that when children were aged 8–15 months, Danish children's language development lagged behind children in the other language groups. The authors suggested that this was because the phonological characteristics of Danish are more challenging to master than those of other languages (Bleses & Basbøll, 2004). Bleses et al. (2011a)

continued

continued

suggest that Danish suffix boundaries may be particularly difficult to perceive. Recent research has shown that Danish suffixes that are not phonologically dropped (pronounced as *schwa*) are learned earlier than suffixes that can be phonologically dropped (Kjaerbaek et al., 2014). Bleses et al. (2011b) showed that the ratio between vowel-like sounds and consonant-like sounds in the 18 languages predicted vocabulary comprehension in children. Higher ratios were related to smaller vocabulary size.

Photo 8.5 Denmark is a Scandinavian country bordered by Germany to the south and separated by water from Sweden to the east and Norway to the north. Do you recall from Chapter 1 whether Danish is in the same or different language family as German, Swedish, and Norwegian? Credit: TUBS

The results suggest that the rate of vocabulary acquisition across languages may be predicted by the phonological patterns of the words in the languages. As you may recall from Chapter 3, the total number of phonemes across all languages is 107 (International Phonetic Association, 1999), but languages vary a great deal in their number of phonemes. Danish has several complex prosodic properties as well, including a suprasegmental feature that some have described as a creaky voice (Titze, 1994), also called vocal fry (Titze, 2008). These and other phonological characteristics of Danish (e.g., consonant weakening) may make syllable boundaries difficult to perceive (Rischel, [1970] 2009).

Although proponents of the nativist view see the role of adults as smaller than advocates of the behaviorist view of language development, there is a role that adults serve. Adults are partners with children in the **original word game** (Brown, 1958), in which children spot something in the environment and ask,

What's that? Adults typically are cooperative and provide the appropriate word. American social psychologist Roger Brown (1925–97) noted that when adults respond to children's questions of this type, they respond with the basic category, rather than the subordinate category (Brown, 1958, 1973). For example, if a toddler sees a parrot and asks *What's that?*, most adults would say *That's a bird* without thinking too much about it. For older children, more detailed answers may be provided.

Research also has shown that adults play an important role in learning even before infants can talk. Baldwin et al. (1996) studied 18-month-old infants, observing how they attended to the environment. They found evidence that infants tended to remember new words only when an adult made it clear to the infant that they should pay attention to the new word. A study comparing 14-month-old and 18-month-old infants showed that word learning was enhanced by the presence of an adult pointing to the object in the environment in 18-month-olds, but not in 14-month-olds (Briganti and Cohen, 2011); thus, infants' ability to use social cues is something that develops over time, after 14 months.

Research has shown that infants learn differently when an adult is physically present. In one experiment, Kuhl et al. (2003) tried to teach Mandarin speech sounds to infants who had been raised in English-speaking homes. The speech sounds were played to the infant in one of three conditions. First, the speech sounds were played to the infant when the experimenter (i.e., tutor) was in the room with the infant. Second, the speech sounds were played to the infant while a video of the experimenter was displayed on a screen. Third, the speech sounds were played to the infant without the experimenter being present or shown in any way. The results showed that the infant learned the speech sounds only when the experimenter was physically present. The researchers concluded that the presence of another person influences infants' attentional processing.

As children acquire words, their learning is described as biased, as they make some inferences in word learning instead of others. For example, children will infer that a new word means the complete object, rather than some part of the object or some aspect of how the object appears (e.g., color or shape). This is known as the **whole object bias**. Philosopher W. V. Quine ([1960] 2016) made a similar observation about word learning in his gavagai problem. His problem begins by asking the listener to imagine walking along with a person who speaks a foreign language. Suddenly, a rabbit darts through the grass. The person who speaks the foreign language points at the rabbit and says, "gavagai." What do you think gavagai means? Quine argues that the number of possible interpretations for gavagai is, in fact, infinite; however, the listener will infer that it means "rabbit."

Research on children's word learning also shows that children typically believe that a new word they have learned refers to a whole category of objects (i.e., a type rather than a token) instead of believing that the new word refers to a particular instance of a category (Markman & Hutchinson, 1984). For example, a child who learns the word *parrot* will infer that the word can refer to all parrots, not just the parrot being discussed at the time the word was learned. This is known as the **taxonomic bias**.

The **mutual exclusivity bias** refers to the tendency in children to assume that an object has one and only one word to describe it. In a study by Markman and Wachtel (1988), three-year-olds were shown two objects. The researchers made sure that one of the objects was familiar to the child (a spoon) and that the other object was something unfamiliar (tongs). The children were then instructed to indicate which of the objects was a *plunk* (or some other invented word). The results showed that the children inferred that the novel word referred to the unfamiliar object instead of the familiar one. The conclusion was that children avoid applying more than one label to an object. Research suggests that humans are not the only species that use the mutual exclusivity bias in learning new words. Pilley and Reid (2011) showed that the Border collie Chaser used it when learning new words.

As children learn new words, they may make errors in using words appropriately. Two of the most common errors are overextensions and underextensions. **Overextensions** occur when a word is used to refer to a broader range of entities than is appropriate. For example, a child might learn the word *bread,* but use it to refer to all types of food (*banana*, *rice*, and *cereal*). **Underextensions** are the opposite type of error. Children use a newly learned word to refer to a smaller range of entities than is appropriate. For example, a child might learn the word *cat,* but use it to refer only to one particular cat. In terms of mental representations of word meaning, children show that these early errors involve them being able to modify initial representations, which are too broad in the case of overextensions and too narrow in the case of underextensions.

After the age of 18 months, children typically experience a phase of rapid vocabulary acquisition – a **word spurt** – in which the number of words they know may quadruple over a period of a few months. There is substantial variation across children as to when the word spurt begins and ends, how quickly the lexicon grows, as well as how many weeks it lasts. Brown (1973) captured this variation when he documented the vocabulary growth in four children. Parents may notice that children begin asking specifically for the names of objects, *What's that?* Children's rapid acquisition of vocabulary is possibly due to their ability to learn a new word after just one exposure, known as **fast mapping** (Carey, 1978; Carey & Bartlett, 1978; Halberda, 2003).

In summary, children begin to rapidly tune up to the phonology of their language in the first year of life and begin producing their first words between the ages of 10 to 12 months. Their vocabulary continues to expand, typically having a period of exponential growth between 18 to 24 months. All children exhibit systematic biases during learning, including the whole object bias, taxonomic bias, and mutual exclusivity bias. Children also make similar errors in word learning. All children have a tendency to first map a word onto a concept that is more broadly or more narrowly defined (overextensions and underextensions errors, respectively).

Building Sentences

When children's utterances contain at least one noun and one verb, they are technically sentences, even if the utterances differ from those typically produced by adults. Long before children produce full sentences, they may attempt to convey sentence-like meaning in their utterances, even when they involve only one or two words. The term **holophrase** refers to children's use of a single word to convey a request or other sentence-like meaning (Dore, 1975; Greenfield & Smith, 1976). For example, a toddler may show mom or dad a broken toy and say *Fix*. The intended meaning behind the utterance can be inferred to be *Fix the toy* or *I would like you to fix my toy*. The sentence-like nature of children's two-word utterances is much clearer, as first pointed out by Brown (1973). He analyzed the two-word utterances of English-speaking toddlers and found that the ordering of the words was consistent with English syntactic rules. Table 8.2 lists some two-word utterances with the relationships contained within each. Brown's data suggested that before children were producing grammatical sentences, their utterances were beginning to conform to the word order rules of the language.

Table 8.2 Examples of Children's Two-word Utterances

Relationship	Utterance
Agent + action	Daddy eat.
Agent + patient	Daddy cookie.
Action + patient	Eat cookie.
Action + location	Eat kitchen.
Patient + location	Cookie kitchen.
Possessor + possession	My cookie.
Patient + attribute	Cookie big.
Demonstrative + patient	That cookie.

Source: Based on Brown (1973)

During the months that children are producing only two words at a time, they are not producing words in random order. There is a regular pattern. The pattern comes from the word order in the language they are learning. For example, when referring to mommy or daddy eating a banana, the English-speaking child would be far more likely to say *mommy eat*, which expresses subject + action, or *mommy banana*, which expresses subject + object, *or eat banana*, which expresses action + object, all in the order that is typical in English, rather than *banana eat,* which expresses object + action.

Between the first and second year, children's utterances increase in number and in complexity, in terms of the types of words produced. Children begin producing words that contain suffixes and, later on, prefixes. Prefixes and suffixes are morphemes, as they are units of meaning that when added to a root word (noun, verb, adjective) lead to a change in meaning. Prefixes and suffixes are referred to as *bound morphemes* because they must be added to a word or another morpheme in order to be used (they do not appear in utterances by themselves). In contrast, morphemes that can appear by themselves are referred to as *free morphemes*, which correspond to whole words. Brown's (1973) study of language development also found that English-speaking children's acquisition of morphemes followed a predictable order. Table 8.3 lists the results in ranked order.

Table 8.3 Typical Order in which Children Acquire Morphemes in English

Order	Morpheme	Function	Example
1	-ing	present progressive	*singing*
2/3	in, on	prepositions	*in bed, on mommy*
4	-s	plural	*blocks*
5		past tense (irregular)	*went, ran*
6	's	possessive	*Daddy's*
7	is	copula	*It is cold*
8	a, the	articles	*a car, the car*
9	-ed	past tense (regular)	*talked, pushed*
10	-s	3rd person, present tense (regular)	*She sleeps*
11	-s	3rd person, present tense (irregular)	*She does*
12	is/was	uncontracted auxiliary	*The dog is barking.*
13	's	contracted *be* verb	*She's a princess.*
14	's	contracted auxiliary	*He's eating.*

Source: Based on Brown (1973)

You may be wondering why children learn morphemes in this particular order. Is there something special about the present progressive suffix -ing that explains why it is the first suffix to be learned? Research in the 1970s and 80s explored how frequency of usage of each of the morphemes was related to its order of acquisition. Brown (1973) examined the relationship between frequency and acquisition and found no evidence for a relationship between the two variables. A later study by Newport et al. (1977) found similar results. The topic is one that merits additional research, especially in languages other than English where the number of bound morphemes may be greater than those in English.

The method most frequently used to measure the grammatical development of children comes to us from the work of Roger Brown (1973). He introduced the notion of **mean length utterance (MLU)**, which refers to the average number of morphemes in children's utterances. In the formal measurement of MLU, Brown used a sample of 100 utterances for the child. Brown's scheme did not count exclamations (*ah*, *oh*, etc.) as morphemes; however, repeated words were counted. Brown's data demonstrated that there is a strong linear relationship between children's age and MLU, as their utterances contain more and more morphemes as they mature. Children's grammatical development can be categorized as belonging to one of five stages, starting with an MLU between 1.0 and 2.0 and increasing 0.5 MLU with each stage. The stages are:

- Children in stage 1 are typically 2–26 months old.
- Children in stage 2 (MLU is 2.0–2.5) are typically 27–30 months old.
- Children in stage 3 (MLU is 2.5–3.0) are typically 31–34 months old.
- Children in stage 4 (MLU is 3.0–3.75) are typically 35–40 months old.
- Children in stage 5 (MLU is 3.75–4.5) are typically 41–46 months old.

Children's productions of complex sentences, such as questions and negatives, initially differ from those produced by adults. Their mastery of complex sentences appears to evolve over time. The production of questions typically occurs between the second and third years, with the first questions being those that can be answered with a yes or no response (*Do you like the puppy?*). Other types of questions begin with words such as *what, where, who, when, which,* or *how*. Sample sentences are provided in 1.

1   a. Who is he?

       b. What is it?

       c. Where are we?

       d. When did she leave?

       e. Which cup is mine?

       f. What is it?

Studies have suggested that children produce questions involving *who, where,* and *what* before other question words because they are the least complex syntactically (Wooten et al., 1979). In a study examining how children understand these different types of questions, Winxemer (1981) found that children's comprehension was better in questions starting with *who, what,* and *where*. Children's first questions typically involve errors, in that the sentences are different from those adults would produce (Klima & Bellugi, 1966). For example, a child might omit the helping verb as in *Where daddy go?* or *What mommy do?* After children begin consistently included the helping verb, they may not produce it in the grammatically correct order (*Where mommy is going?*).

Similarly, children's mastery of negative sentences appears to involve stages (Klima & Bellugi, 1966; see also Bloom, 1970 and de Villiers & de Villiers, 1985). The youngest children's negative sentences involve placing the word *no* at the beginning of the sentence as in *No eat carrot* (I don't want to eat the carrot) or *No go to bed* (I don't want to go to bed). These types of negative sentences are soon replaced with sentences in which the word *no* migrates to a position within the sentence, as in *I no eat carrot* or *I no go to bed*. Later, a third type of negative sentence can be observed, one in which a negative contraction is used, as in *I don't eat the carrot* or *I don't sleep now*. Interestingly, children typically use negative contractions before they produce the positive forms (*I do eat* or *Mommy does eat*).

The Role of Parents and Other Caregivers

Most adults talk to children differently than they talk to someone their own age. Early studies of the speech directed toward children (sometimes called child-directed speech) focused on mothers (Snow, 1972, 1977). **Motherese** describes how mothers talk to babies and small children (see Newport et al., 1977). **Parentese** is also used as a gender-neutral term. Your parents or grandparents may refer to this special way of speaking as *baby talk*. "Who's the good baby? Who's the very good baby? Oh, you are. You are. That's right. You are the best baby in the world." When engaging in this type of communication with a child, we change not only the words we use, but also how the words sound. We use a higher pitched voice. Our intonation can be exaggerated. There is usually a lot of positive emotion in our facial expressions and in the tone of our voice. Some words may be repeated.

Studies of the acoustic properties of parentese have shown that there is valuable information in those speech waves. The speech unfolds more slowly over time than speech adults use with one another, which provides infants with rich information about the vowels in the utterances (Kuhl, 1999). Others have suggested that parentese provides better cues than other speech regarding the beginnings of words (Thiessen et al., 2005) and syllables (Morgan & Demuth, 1996). Research has shown that infants prefer parentese to adult-directed speech (Cooper & Aslin, 1994; Fernald, 1985). It is not clear why infants prefer it; they are too young to be able to tell us. However, it is likely that infants are hardwired to respond positively to the emotional tone of parentese. Fernald (1982) suggested that parentese came about through natural selection, contributing to the survival of humans. Fernald (1989) showed that adults could easily distinguish samples of child-directed speech from adult-directed speech. The innateness of human emotions was first proposed by Darwin ([1872] 2007). Research conducted in the 1970s provided support for this view. Ekman and Friesen (1971) found that across cultures, people are highly accurate in identifying the six universal emotions – anger, disgust, surprise, sadness, fear, and happiness. In a compelling study, Bryant and Barrett (2007) demonstrated that child-directed speech and adult-directed speech sampled from US participants could be reliably distinguished by individuals from a hunter-gatherer culture in Ecuador.

Many cultures routinely use different ways of speaking when talking to children (Bryant & Barrett, 2007; Fernald et al., 1989; Grieser & Kuhl, 1988). Parentese also occurs in signed languages as well as spoken languages (Masataka, 1992). Parentese during signing was shown to involve slower signing, repetition of signs, as well as larger movements of the arms and hands during signing. The research also found that when deaf infants were presented with parentese signing or typical adult-directed signing, the infants preferred the parentese signing.

Language researchers debate the extent to which parentese contributes to language development. Steven Pinker ([1994] 2007) has argued that parentese is not required for language development, because there are cultures where parentese is not used. Despite the lack of parentese in these cultures, children still learn language. Pinker describes the case of the !Kung San people, who make their home in the Kalahari Desert. Children are cared for very well. Most of the time, mothers carry infants or keep them physically close. When an infant cries, the mothers respond quickly. The mother–infant interactions do not involve talking. When the infant begins to talk, which they do around the same time as children in other cultures begin to talk, then adults will talk to them (Konner, 2002; Pinker, [1994] 2007). The Research DIY box invites you to examine how beneficial it is to talk to young children.

How Do Children Become Effective Communicators?

Long after children have mastered the grammar of their native language, they continue to learn how to become effective communicators, which requires learning the social norms of language use. In some settings, more formal language is required. In other settings, it is fine to use informal forms of language, such as slang. It is important to distinguish between children's development in producing speech and children's development as a speaker with an audience. The latter role requires children not only to have the ability to produce utterances, but also to formulate a message that purposely communicates information in a way that is suitable for the

How Beneficial is Talking to Infants?

There is a growing body of evidence showing that talking to children is related to positive outcomes later in childhood (Hurtado et al., 2008; Huttenlocher et al., 1991; Rowe, 2012; Weisleder & Fernald, 2013). Recent research suggests that by the time children first enter school, children from low-income homes may be exposed to about three million fewer words than children from more affluent homes (Hart & Risley, 2003). Earlier research has shown that poor children's language development lags behind that of affluent children (Hoff, 2003; Noble et al., 2005; Whitehurst, 1997). The missing words in their daily experiences may be an important contributing factor. Despite the growing evidence that talking to children is a critical ingredient to healthy language development, young adults appear to vary in their beliefs about how beneficial talking to infants may be for infants and their language development (Kennison & Byrd-Craven, 2015). The research found that in a study of college students (without children of their own), men were less likely than women to believe that talking to infants was beneficial. Further analyses showed that for both men and women, those who reported more negative relationships with their own mother were less likely to believe that talking to infants was beneficial.

If you survey a sample of people you know, what will you find? Below are five questions similar to those used in Kennison and Byrd-Craven's (2015) research. For each statement, ask your volunteer to indicate a level of agreement (1 = Strongly disagree and 7 = Strongly agree, with the intervening numbers representing varying levels of disagreement to agreement). A rating of 4 would reflect "neither disagree nor agree."

Strongly disagree   **Strongly agree**

| 1 | 2 | 3 | 4 | 5 | 6 | 7 |

_____ Talking to infants may help in their development of language.

_____ Infants benefit from listening to the speech of adults even if they cannot understand what is being said.

_____ Parents should be encouraged to talk as much as possible to their infants.

_____ Parentese (the way many people talk to babies) helps babies' language development.

_____ Infants enjoy listening to parentese (the way many people talk to babies).

Give the survey to five men and five women. For each participant, sum the responses for the five items. Compute the average for your sample of five men and compare it to the average for your sample of five women. Did you also find that men reported lower levels of agreement than women? Why do you think that males would be less likely to know that talking to infants promotes healthy language development?

You may find, as the prior research found, that participants who have taken courses in language acquisition, language development, or human development are likely to know that talking to infants is beneficial. It is possible that young women may be more likely to take such courses than men or more likely to remember the content regarding infant care than men. You may also ask participants how much direct experience they have had with infants, using a numerical scale (1 = none, 2 = a small amount, 3 = a moderate amount, and 4 = a lot).

Key Terms

Babbling
Canonical babbling
Fast mapping
Holophrase
Idiomorph

Late talker
Mean length
   utterance
Motherese
Mutual exclusivity bias

Original word game
Overextension
Parentese
Protoword
Social smile

Taxonomic bias
Underextension
Variegated babbling
Whole object bias
Word spurt

Review Questions

1. To what extent does language learning start before birth? Describe a research study that provides evidence for prenatal learning.
2. What are the major communication milestones that children experience by the age of one year? Indicate the approximate age that typical children reach each milestone.
3. What are the characteristics of parentese (also called motherese)? What are the ways in which it aids infants' language development?
4. Describe the biases that children exhibit as they acquire new words in the first three years of life.
5. How does children's production of negative sentences change as they age?
6. How does children's production of questions change as they age?

particular listener. Children begin as speakers who appear oblivious to the needs of the listener, but eventually become able to modify their speech to suit a wide variety of situations. When they are able to communicate effectively in a variety of settings, they have achieved **communicative competence**.

Photo 8.6 Many people experience anxiety when speaking in public. Starting in elementary school, students are given opportunities to practice their public speaking skills. Would you rate yourself as an excellent, good, or fair public speaker?
Credit: Brisbane City Council

Private Speech

Young children typically talk to themselves as they play or perform tasks. The term **private speech** refers to this form of language use (Piaget, 1959; Vygotsky, [1934] 1986). The speech is audible to others, but is not meant to communicate anything to listeners. Children between the ages of two and seven are likely to use private speech when they are alone, engaged in a playtime activity or preparing to fall asleep. In two studies, Berk (1986, 1992) documented that for children in elementary school, between 20 percent and 60 percent of children's speech is private speech. The amount of private speech used by children tends to decrease over time after children begin school. Studies of children's private speech suggest that the speech serves to help children direct their own behavior. Berk and Spuhl (1995) found that when children around the age of five were asked to perform a complex task, the amount of private speech produced by children was positively related to the children's performance on the task. Other studies found relationships between private speech and children's ability to pay attention during a complex task (Behrend et al., 1992; Bivens & Berk, 1990).

Conversations

If you have engaged in conversation with a toddler, you may have noticed that they are not the most skilled conversational partners. Becoming a skilled conversationalist takes quite a bit of experience and children must learn the skills. The building blocks for being able to have a conversation with another person include being able to focus on a topic or an object with another person. This has been referred to as "joint attention" (Moore & Dunham, 2016). Infants demonstrate joint attention between 9 and 15 months. Another basic skill in conversation is turn-taking (Clift, 2016). One person in the conversation speaks, while others listen, and then another person speaks while others listen. Catherine Snow (1977) pointed out that mothers demonstrate turn-taking with their infants from the earliest moments of life, by saying something to the infant, waiting for the infant to make any sound, then saying something else, and so on.

Becoming an effective communicator involves mastering the social rules of language. As you recall from Chapter 1, the social rules of language are known as pragmatic rules. Children must learn how to modify their speech depending on the social status of the person to whom they are talking and also the setting (playground, school, church, government office, etc.). Two examples of polite forms are given in 2. These are versions of the more direct question, "What time is it?"

2 a. I am sorry to bother you, but if it's not too much trouble, could you please tell me what time it is?

   b. If you don't mind, please could you tell me what time it is?

When talking with peers, we tend to use direct and informal speech. We use more polite language when talking to bosses, religious leaders, and others having high status (Brown & Levinson, 1987; Kadar & Haugh, 2013). We also use more polite speech when we may want something from a listener or feel that we are imposing on them.

Children learn the social rules of language by observing others and also by direct instruction. Most of us can remember being reminded about appropriate behavior when we were young, such as speaking quietly in some situations, such as places of worship and hospitals, and minding our manners. Parents begin teaching children social conventions early in life, such as the routines for saying hello and goodbye, for making requests by saying please and for saying thank you when the request has been fulfilled or when receiving something from another person. Early research showed that children as young as two years old produced requests that differed in politeness (Corsaro, 1979). The standard, non-polite request was made to a peer (e.g., Give me car), but a more polite form was made to an adult (e.g., Can I have car?). As children develop, they continue to hone their skills so they are socially appropriate. Studies have suggested that children may continue to work on mastering the particulars of politeness when they are nine years old and older (McTear & Conti-Ramsden, 1992).

Research conducted in the 1970s suggested how this mastery of politeness develops, specifically with regard to children's requests (Bates, 1976). Children start out making the standard non-polite request (e.g., Give it to me.). Around age four, children begin producing more than one type of request sentence structure, but their tone in producing the request retains the directness of the non-polite form. By age five to six, children's polite requests are produced with the appropriate polite tone and non-polite requests are produced with the non-polite direct tone. By age seven to eight, children are further able to soften their request based on the context, such as using indirectness.

Narratives

Most children spend a great deal of time either listening to stories or telling stories about events they experienced or situations they imagined. Stories are more formally referred to as narratives (Schick & Melzi, 2010). Children are not born being able to appreciate what makes a story good or bad or able to tell a story others can understand. The skills of producing and comprehending narratives develop, changing as the child ages (Peterson & McCabe, 1983).

The simplest types of narrative mastered by children refer to familiar, recurring activities, such as eating breakfast or brushing one's teeth. These are known as scripts (Hedberg & Westby, 1993). Two other types of narratives are events, which may include past, future or current events, and fictional stories. Soon after children begin using multiple-word utterances, they begin to describe past events, first using the present tense and then later using the past tense (Hedberg & Stoel-Gammon, 1986). Starting around 24 months of age, their utterances describing events may lack cohesiveness. In the third year, their narratives usually have better cohesiveness, focusing on one topic (event or character). Before the fourth year, children's narratives usually omit information about the temporal relationships between statements. As the child nears the age of five, their narratives may involve many topics, such as settings, events, or characteristics (Shapiro & Hudson, 1991), but they tend to focus on the physical aspects of the topics, rather than the mental states of characters (Kemper & Edwards, 1986).

Children's understanding about the mental states of others is also developed during this time. Most children hold an egocentric perspective before the age of three. As you recall from Chapter 2, theory of mind refers to the understanding that others' knowledge may differ from one's own. Children develop the ability to appreciate the minds of others between their third and fifth year (Birch & Bloom, 2003), although individual differences are possible.

Early work in this area supported the view that there is a relationship between general cognitive development and the development of narrative ability (Applebee, 1978). More recent work has suggested that individual differences in children's narrative ability may predict later language ability (Botting, 2002; Gardner-Neblett & Iruka, 2015; Griffin et al., 2004). Studies have also found that children who had more highly developed narrative skills early in life were more successful later on at school (Bishop & Edmundson, 1987).

Children's interactions with adults can influence the development of children's narrative skills (Melzi et al., 2011). As children engage in storytelling, adults typically are active listeners, sometimes helping them by interjecting important information or asking leading questions. Studies have shown that the ways in which adults interact with children during storytelling varies (Han et al., 1998; Minami & McCabe, 1995; Wiley et al., 1998). Wiley et al. (1998) compared storytelling in working-class and middle-class American families and found that working-class adults contributed more during children's storytelling than middle-class adults. Adult–child interactions in middle-class families involved a focus on children expressing opinions. Comparisons of American and Japanese mother–child interactions have found differences, such as talking less (Han et al., 1998) and questioning children less (Minami & McCabe, 1995) in Japanese families than American families.

 Time out for Review

Key Terms

Communicative competence   Private speech

Review Questions

1   What is communicative competence? How does children's communicative competence change from the second year through later childhood and the teenage years?

Summary

Theories of language development differ in their assumptions about whether innate knowledge exists to support rapid language development and the extent to which language development depends on input from the environment, including input from parents and others. Children's learning of language, specifically the sounds of language, begins before birth. By the 26th week of pregnancy, sounds can be heard through the mother's body and memories of those sounds may begin to be formed. During the first year of life, infants begin communicating through crying, smiling, and pointing. Around four months, infants begin producing random speech sounds or babbling. By the end of the first year, infants begin producing their first words. Children's grammatical development begins before they can speak, as they are able to comprehend the simplest sentences. Their two-word utterances also reflect the ordering rules of their language. As children age, they become more skilled at forming words involving suffixes and sentences. Children must also master the social rules of using language in making requests, participating in conversations and also learning how to understand and tell stories. Becoming an effective communicator is a long-term process that may extend into the teen years and beyond.

Recommended Books, Films, and Websites

Balmès, T. (2010). *Babies* [Motion Picture]. United States: Focus Features.

Brown, R. (1973). *A First Language: The Early Stages*. Cambridge, MA: Harvard University Press.

Gopnik, A., Meltzoff, A. N. & Kuhl, P. K. (2000). *The Scientist in the Crib: Minds, Brains and How Children Learn*. New York: Harper Paperbacks.

Kennison, S. M. (2013). *Introduction to Language Development*. Los Angeles, CA: Sage.

MacWhinney, B. (2000). *The CHILDES Project: Tools for Analyzing Talk*, vols 1 & 2: *The Format and Programs* (3rd edn). Mahwah, NJ: Lawrence Erlbaum.

Piaget, J. & Inhelder, B. (1969). *Psychology of the Child*. New York: Basic Books.

Searchinger, G., Male, M. & Wright, M. (Writers) (2005). *Human Language Series* [DVD]. United States: Equinox Films/Ways of Knowing Inc.

TalkBank. The Talkbank System. talkbank.org.

Vygotsky, L. S. (1978). *Mind in Society*. Cambridge, MA: Harvard University Press.

9 SOCIAL ASPECTS OF LANGUAGE USE

Chapter Content

Photo 9.1 President Barack Obama is talking with the journalist Charlie Gibson. The conversational norms for such a formal setting would differ from the norms of informational conversations we have with our peers. Have you ever had a formal conversation that was videoed?

Talking is an inherently social activity. Talking primarily serves to connect us to others. In daily life, what we say and how we say it depends on the setting and those to whom we are speaking. When we speak to our close friends, our language is less formal than when we speak to our teachers, bosses, or parents. **Sociolinguistics** is the study of the social variation of language use across and within social groups. In psycholinguistics, we approach the variation that occurs in language processing by speakers across different social settings as a fact that must be accounted for by any complete theory of language processing. Furthermore, we must always remember to take into account the fact that speakers' language knowledge and use of that knowledge during processing can be related to social factors such as geographical region, sex, age, socioeconomic status, race/ethnicity, and so on.

In this chapter, we examine the psycholinguistic research on the social aspects of language use. We begin by discussing how different types of verbal interactions have been categorized. The traditional approach categorizes utterances in terms of their intention and the effect they have on the listener. The term speech act is used to characterize an utterance (Austin, 1962; Dore, 1975). We will learn about the extent to which speakers have the listener in mind when planning utterances. Second, we examine some of the important individual differences in language use that have been studied, including geographical dialects and dialects associated with social groups, such as gender, LGBTQ affiliation, ethnicity, social class, and occupation. In the last section, we discuss nonverbal communication, often called body language (Moore, 2010). We communicate our intentions, moods, and states of mind in our body language, through our body posture, the way we hold our bodies when we stand or sit; facial expressions; and gestures, the movements we make with our hands.

Conversations

Face-to-face interactions in which we speak to one another are referred to as conversations (Sidnell, 2010; Thornbury & Slade, 2006). A useful perspective on conversations was provided by linguist Charles Fillmore (1981, p. 152): "the language of face-to-face conversation is the basic and primary use of language, all others being best described in terms of their deviation from that base." Typically, we talk with others, with one person talking and then another. Psycholinguists refer to this aspect of cooperation as **turn-taking**. As you will see in Chapter 10, parents begin socializing infants to take turns during communication long before infants begin speaking. Most of the time, we speak with others, taking turns without noticing that we are planning each utterance, taking into consideration the timing of our partners' utterance. Sometimes, speakers can start speaking before another has finished speaking, called **interruptions**. In this section, you will begin to learn how psycholinguists investigate the cognitive processes involved in conversation and the numerous factors related to how we communicate in face-to-face settings. We begin by examining the ways in which scholars have categorized different types of utterances and the aspects of conversation that appear to be universal, describing conversations across cultures. Second, we examine how languages differ in the extent to which the grammars of languages do or do not require speakers to use different syntactic and morphological rules and sometimes different vocabulary when talking with individuals from different social groups (e.g., elders, higher status people, men vs. women, and specific categories of relatives).

Traditional Perspectives

Since the 1970s, psycholinguists have embraced Grice's (1975) notion that human conversations follow universal principles. He proposed the cooperative principle and the four Gricean maxims of conversations. The cooperative principle proposes that speakers are generally cooperative with one another, producing utterances that serve to facilitate exchanges rather than hinder them (Grice, 1989). The four Gricean maxims believed to hold true for all human conversations are described in Table 9.1.

Table 9.1 The Gricean Maxims of Conversation

Maxim	Description	Violation
Quantity	Contributions have appropriate amount of information	Utterances have too much or too little information
Quality	Contributions are truthful	Utterances are deceptive
Relation	Contributions are relevant	Utterances are off-topic
Manner	Contributions are clear and unambiguous	Utterances are unclear

Source: Grice (1975)

When speakers violate these maxims, others are likely to find the interaction unusual and possibly socially inappropriate, depending on the nature of the violation. We all are likely to know someone who violates one or more of these principles on occasion or perhaps even regularly. As you may recall from earlier chapters, some individuals, such as those with autism spectrum disorders, may have trouble taking the perspectives of others; thus, they may experience difficulty appreciating how much a conversational partner already knows about a particular subject. Other individual differences may affect how likely a person is to violate these conversational norms. For example, there are individuals who engage in deception at a far higher rate than others (Dike, 2008). Habitual lying is a characteristic of antisocial personality disorder, which has been strongly linked to criminal behavior (Patrick, 2005) and impulse control disorders, which are related to shoplifting, pyromania, and pathological gambling.

Research in the 1970s categorized utterances according to the speaker's intention (Austin, 1962; Dore, 1975). Intention varies widely from a speaker saying *hello* or *goodbye* to issuing a proclamation that might affect a country's entire population. The term **speech act** refers to those utterances that are formulated by the speaker with specific intention. Austin (1962) introduced the term **locutionary act** as the production of a given utterance in its final form. The speaker's choices for the syntactic structure, morphemes, phonemes, and articulation make up the final locutionary act. Austin referred to the speaker's goal or intention for a given utterance as its **illocutionary force**. He noted that sometimes listeners do not interpret utterances as speakers intended. He referred to an utterance's effect on a listener as the **perlocutionary act**. When listeners are able to arrive at the speaker's intention behind an utterance, then the illocutionary force and the perlocutionary act of the utterance would be the same. The perlocutionary act of an utterance would differ from the illocutionary force anytime there is an unintended effect of an utterance upon the listener. Speakers whose utterances inadvertently offend listeners would be an example of when an utterance's perlocutionary act differs from its illocutionary force. Table 9.2 lists examples of different types of speech acts. Among the speech acts not discussed by Searle are greetings, congratulations, questions, requests, apologies, humor, and profanity (also called swearing or cursing).

Table 9.2 Types of Speech Acts

Speech act	Description	Example
Declarative	A statement of fact	The cat is sick.
Directive	A direction to a listener	Take out the trash, please.
Expressive	A description of a state of mind	I regret my carelessness.
Representative	A statement of belief or disbelief	I suspect that the milk is spoiled.
Commissive	A promise	I promise to pay you back.

Source: Searle (1975)

There are times when what we say conveys meaning that goes beyond what the words in our utterance mean (Searle, 1975), referred to as **indirect speech acts**. For example, a mother might ask her son, "Can you call me when you get back to your dormitory?" The question literally asks about the son's ability to make a call; however, the question is typically interpreted as a request to call when he arrives at his dormitory. Indirect speech acts are often used to refuse a request. One student asks another, "Would you like to grab lunch?" The response is "I have a class," which does not directly answer the question, but provides a statement from which the listener can infer that because of the class, the request must be refused.

The most extreme example of an indirect speech act is to produce an utterance in which the words together mean the opposite of their intended meaning. Such utterances are examples of verbal **irony** (Gibbs & Colston, 2007). For example, after hearing a confusing presentation, a member of the audience might say, "That was as clear as mud." Speakers sometimes use an indirect speech act to convey a negative attitude or hostility toward others by producing an utterance whose words mean something more positive that the speaker is likely to be thinking. Such utterances are examples of **sarcasm** (Rockwell, 2006). For example, a speaker who has just watched a film she disliked a great deal might sigh and say, "I only fall asleep during the best movies."

Small Talk, Humor, and Cursing

Searle (1975) focused on the speech acts involved in the most formal settings. His list did not include some of the types of discourses that occur in our daily lives. We discuss three topics that were omitted. The first is **small talk** (also called chit chat). Small talk is a particularly interesting speech act, because unlike other speech acts, which have clearly defined purposes, the purpose of small talk appears to be more about social bonding with others rather than the communication of meaning through speaking (Coupland, 2000). In the USA, the topics typically brought up during small talk include the weather, outcomes of recent sporting events in the community or on television, and what one did the previous weekend or will do over the upcoming weekend. The specific content of small talk varies for men and women (Tannen, 1992) and likely differs across cultures (Hofstede, 2000).

The second omission is humor, which is a fundamental element in human interaction (Martin, 2006). The intention of a statement issued in the spirit of humor would be to cause positive affect. The term **mirth** describes the positive affect and/or amusement that is usually the result of humor. Humor also frequently provokes smiling and/or laughter on the part of the listeners. Recent research on the nature of laughter suggests that it occurs as an automatic response to humor (Scott et al., 2014). Martin et al. (2003) have identified four humor styles used in daily life:

- *affiliative*: using humor to create rapport with others
- *self-enhancing*: using humor to make oneself appear more favorably
- *aggressive*: using humor to belittle or humiliate others
- *self-defeating*: using humor to put oneself down.

In broad terms, the affiliative and self-enhancing humor styles are positive uses of humor, and the aggressive and self-defeating humor styles are negative uses of humor. Yip and Martin (2006) found that greater use of the positive humor styles was related to higher levels of social competence and that greater use of the negative humor styles was related to lower levels of social competence. A growing number of studies have shown that use of positive humor styles is associated with higher levels of wellbeing and lower levels of depression (Martin, 2006). Frewen et al. (2008) showed that greater use of the self-defeating humor style and lower use of the affiliative and self-enhancing humor styles predicted higher levels of depression. Chapter 12 explores research investigating the areas of the brain involved in comprehending humorous statements. Individuals who sustain damage to certain right hemisphere brain regions may experience deficits in humor appreciation and/or the ability to produce humorous statements.

A third omission from Searle's (1975) list of speech acts is the use of profanity, which has become synonymous with the use of curse words. The original meaning of the term "cursing" referred to casting a spell or hex. Today, the use of profanity is typically referred to as "cussing." Swearing, or cursing, is a form of language use that has been investigated by psycholinguists (Jay, 1992, 2000, 2009; Jay & Jay, 2013; Kennison & Messer, 2017, 2018). In his book *The Stuff of Thought*, Steven Pinker (2007) described the different functions of using curse words. These are listed in Table 9.3 with examples.

Table 9.3 Pinker's Six Functions of Curse Words

Function	Description	Example
Idiomatic	Swearing that is unrelated to the statement	Damn, man!
Cathartic	Expressing frustration (even when alone)	Damn, that hurt!
Emphatic	Placing emphasis on a statement	Damn, that's impressive!
Abusive	Aggressive verbal abuse toward another	You are a fucking loser.
Dysphemistic	Conveys negativity toward the topic in the statement	He fucks up everything.

Source: Pinker (2007)

Thus far, there have been no studies investigating whether these functions of curse words are used comparably often and to what extent different types of individuals utilize the functions at different frequencies. Timothy Jay (1992, 2000, 2009) has studied cursing behavior for decades. His research has shown that there are individual differences in the frequency of cursing, including the fact that:

- women curse less often than men (Jay, 1996)
- members of high-status groups curse less than members of low-status groups (McEnery, 2006)
- religious individuals curse less often than the non-religious (Jay, 2009)
- prisoners, soldiers, and adolescents curse more than others (Jay, 2009)
- those lower in agreeableness and conscientiousness curse more than others (Mehl et al., 2006).

Recent research by Jay and Jay (2015) suggests that those higher in intelligence curse more than others.

In a study exploring other individual differences predicting the use of curse words, Kennison and Messer (2017) showed that cursing occurred more often in individuals who take more risks in daily life (e.g., cigarette use, alcohol use, drug use, sexual risk). In addition, they found that individuals scoring higher in the sensation-seeking personality trait, which has been shown to predict risk-taking, took more risks and cursed more often than those who scored lower in sensation-seeking. Zuckerman's (1984, 1985) work on sensation-seeking, as well as the work of others (see Roberti, 2004 for review), has found links between types of sensation-seeking and biological processes related to neurotransmitter systems in the brain; thus, future research may be able to show that how often we use curse words in daily language is related to those biological processes. In a follow-up study, Kennison and Messer (2018) found that individual differences in sensation-seeking personality predicted the use of three of the four humor styles in both men and women (aggressive, self-enhancing, and affiliative). They also found that the frequency of using curse words predicted use of the aggressive humor style in men and women and the use of the self-enhancing humor style in men. Future research is likely to review even more connections between different types of utterances and the underlying cognitive and biological factors responsible for the connections.

Social Relationships and Grammar

A fairly large number of languages around the world include information about the social relationship between conversational partners in the grammatical rules of the language. As we noted in Chapter 1, social norms are commonly reflected in the vocabulary, morphology and syntax of speakers' utterances in many languages in Asia (e.g., Japan, Korea, and Vietnam). The extent to which the grammar of the language includes distinctions related to the social rules of language (pragmatic rules) varies a great deal across languages. Languages differ in whether the social relationships between the speaker and listener(s) are related to how an utterance is structured in terms of vocabulary, word order, and morphological composition. In English, speakers tend to use short utterances with peers and others with whom they are familiar, such as family and friends, but use less direct language when attempting to be polite with those of higher status and/or lower familiarity. Consider the examples in 1.

1   a.   Where are the scissors?

      b.   Do you happen to know where the scissors might be?

English speakers commonly use longer utterances when they are trying to be polite (Brown & Levinson, 1987). In other languages, the social relationship between the speaker and the listener(s) is reflected in how the utterance is structured. There are languages whose grammars require speakers to use different pronouns when speaking to peers, friends, or family versus persons of higher status or unfamiliar others. This distinction is known as **social distance** (Brown & Gilman, 1960). Other languages have quite complicated grammatical systems for expressing utterances with different levels of politeness, referred to as "honorifics" (Tsujimura, 2005). We explore examples of each in turn.

Social Distance

Many languages require speakers to use different pronouns when speaking with listeners having different social distances with the speaker. For example, speakers must use different personal pronouns when a listener is not a personal friend of the speaker versus a friend. In French, speakers use the second person singular pronoun *tu* (equivalent to the English *you*) when conversing with a friend, but use *vous* (also *you*) when conversing with others, particularly those who are higher in status (e.g., boss, teacher, judge, etc.). This use of different pronouns to reflect the social distance between the speaker and listener is known as the **t-v distinction**, with the "t" and "v" stemming from the French pronouns (Brown & Gilman, 1960). Similarly, in German, the pronouns *du* and *sie* are used when speaking to friends and non-friends, respectively. In Spanish, the two pronouns are *tú* and *usted*. Other languages in which the t-v distinction is used include Italian, Norwegian, Swedish, Dutch, Russian, Urdu, Persian, Hindi and many others (Helmbrecht, 2005). English had the distinction in the 1200s in the use of the words *ye* and *thou*, but lost the distinction when the pronoun *you* came to be used for both *ye* and *thou* (Crystal, 2004; Crystal & Crystal, 2002). In languages with the t-v distinction, if speakers use the familiar pronoun with someone of higher status (boss, professor, dignitary, etc.), the person being addressed is likely to perceive this as a major social gaffe (also called faux pas from the French meaning *false step* or *stumble*).

Grammars with Honorifics

In many languages, speakers use different morphological forms of verbs to convey information about the social relationship between the speaker and listener(s). In Japanese, speakers modify their speech depending on the status of the person to whom they are speaking. There are four styles of speaking:

- *casual*: used when speaking with peers of the same status level
- *tieneigo*: used to show honor for the listener
- *sonkeigo*: used to show respect for the subject of a sentence, and in business transactions when speaking to customers or those of higher status than the speaker
- *kenjōgo*: used to show respect to an entity of a sentence that occurs in a non-subject position.

"Honorific speech" describes such forms in languages. Tieneigo, the most formal form of Japanese, appears in movies and on television. It involves adding the suffix -desu to nouns and the suffix -masu to verbs. Objects are marked with the suffix -o or -go. In sonkeigo and kenjōgo, different verb forms are used. Table 9.4 lists examples of the same verb expressed in each of the four speaking styles. In Japan, as in the USA, research has found that women are more likely than men to use polite or honorific forms when speaking (Wetzel, 2004). The honorific form of Japanese referred to as teineigo is used by young people when speaking with elders in the family. Do you find that you use more polite language when speaking to your older relatives? As you will see later in this chapter, differences in the language use of men and women have been observed across languages, including English.

Table 9.4 The Four Categories of Polite Language in Japanese

Type	to do	to see
Casual	する suru	見る miru
Teineigo (polite style)	します shimasu	見ます mimasu
Sonkeigo (honorific)	なさる nasaru	ご覧になる go ran ni naru
Kenjōgo (humble)	致す itasu	拝見する haiken suru

Source: Matsumoto (1997)

Native Japanese speakers acquire grammatical rules for the different **politeness** registers early in childhood, but they may not be fully mastered until the teenage years (Cook, 1997; Fukuda, 2005; Nakamura, 2002, 2006). Recent research by Tsuji and Doherty (2014) investigated the extent to which young children's production of polite forms in Japanese reflected conscious awareness of the appropriateness of the forms. They asked children between the ages of three and five to judge the appropriateness of utterances presented in the casual register or an honorific register. Researchers showed each child two dolls and explained that they had different personalities. One was described as kind and the other as mean. Consequently, one used the polite form when speaking and the other did not. Children heard sentences used by each doll, and they had to judge whether the sentence had the appropriate form, given the previous description of the speaker. The results showed that four- and five-year-olds performed well on the judgment task, but three-year-olds did not. The authors further investigated whether children's judgments were related to their theory of mind (i.e., performance on a false belief task). After controlling for the influence of age and word knowledge, they found no relationship between their theory of mind status and performance on the politeness judgment task.

As you may recall from Chapter 1, in some languages, the utterances spoken by men and women differ grammatically. An example language in which there are different grammatical rules for men and women is Yanyuwa, one of the many languages indigenous to Australia. Yanyuwa was widely spoken in northern Australia, but is now in danger of extinction (Kirton, 1988). There are complex grammatical differences in the speech of men and women (Bradley, 1988). Both use the same root words, but differ in morphological markings (e.g., prefixes, suffixes, and infixes). Table 9.5 provides an example of how the same meaning would be conveyed by a male and a female speaker.

Table 9.5 Example Sentences from Men's and Women's Dialect in Yanyuwa

Men's dialect
Jianangu **wukuthu rduwarra** na-**wini wungkurli** ka-**wingka**
This short initiated man his-name Wungkurli go
Women's dialect
Nya-ja nya-**wukuthu** nya-**rduwarra** niya-**wini** nya-**wungkurli** kiwa-**wingka**
This short initiated man his-name Wungkurli go
English translation
The short initiated man whose name is Wungkurli, went down to the sea, taking a harpoon with him for dugong or sea turtle.

Note: Bold morphemes are the same in both dialects

Source: Bradley (1988)

All children initially learn to speak the female version of Yanyuwa grammar, but boys switch to using the male version around puberty. On occasion, when older boys do not use the male version of the grammar, they are corrected, sometimes in a harsh and/or humiliating manner. It is possible to hear a women use the male grammar and vice versa in the context of storytelling, in which the storyteller reports the words of an opposite-sex character in the story.

The Language Spotlight box examines the conversational taboos in Dyirbal, an Aboriginal language spoken in northeastern Australia.

 **Language Spotlight**

Dyirbal and Conversational Taboos

Dyirbal is a language nearing extinction, with only 28 native speakers in existence in 2006 (Schmidt, 1985). The language's many interesting characteristics became known to linguists and psycholinguists following the publication of Robert Dixon's (1972) book, detailing the grammar of the language. One of the most interesting elements is the social customs related to who can and cannot speak to each other within the community. Social customs forbidding certain types of behaviors are called **taboos**. In the Dyirbal-speaking community, people are not supposed to speak to their mothers-in-law or fathers-in-law (Dixon, 1990). They are also not supposed to speak to their mother's brother's children or their father's sister's children. Strictly speaking, people are not supposed to allow even their eyes to meet those of their in-laws. These taboos appear to be related to the fact that marriages occur across generations and are acceptable for cross cousins (the child of a person's parent's opposite-sex sibling), but taboo for parallel cousins (the child of a person's parent's same-sex sibling) (Dixon, 1989). There is a respectful version of the language that people use whenever they are in the presence of someone with whom they are forbidden to speak. It is called Dyalŋuy and has the same syntax and phonemes as Dyirbal, but only four vocabulary items in common, which are the words to refer to maternal and paternal grandparents. The vocabulary of Dyalŋuy is one-quarter the size of Dyirbal; thus, the ability to communicate efficiently is reduced (Dixon, 2000). Speakers deal with the restriction, but use grammatical tricks to convey their meanings, such as using words borrowed by other languages that may be known to both the speaker and the listener and using morphological and/or phonological rules to create novel words.

Dyirbal is among a small number of languages that have conversational taboos for in-laws. Such languages have been referred to as mother-in-law languages and include Aboriginal languages in Australia and also languages in Africa (Anbessa, 1987; Herbert, 1990). You might wonder why languages in such geographically distant parts of the world would share such an unusual custom. Recent DNA research suggests an answer. Aboriginal communities in Australia are likely to have descended from ancestors who migrated out of Africa around 72,000 years ago (Malaspinas et al., 2016). At the time of the migration, the language spoken by the ancestors of the future Australian Aborigines and the ancestors of modern-day Africans may have been the same or quite similar. Over time, the languages of the descendants of the descendants (and so on) changed, retaining some of the same characteristics and losing others.

Common Ground

Beginning in the 1980s, Herbert Clark, a professor of psychology at Stanford University, and some of his graduate students proposed and developed **common ground theory**, which attempted to describe important aspects of conversation that had, up to that point, been neglected (Clark, 1985, 1996; Clark & Brennan, 1991; Clark & Schaefer, 1987; Schober & Clark, 1989). In their view, in order to achieve successful communication, conversational partners must have not only adequate shared knowledge of the situation occurring, but they must also become aware of what knowledge they share. Within the theory, the primary aim of conversation is to expand the conversational partners' common ground or shared knowledge. Furthermore, during conversations, speakers' utterances are formulated taking into direct consideration the information contained in common ground, which would include information about the nature of the relationship the speakers have, as well as social and cultural norms relevant to the situation. For each utterance, the speaker must formulate a specific goal or intention that not only conveys information (not too little and not too much), but does so with the appropriate form, given the speaker's culture and personal relationship. Table 9.6 provides three conversations in which the conversational partners have different common ground. As you learned in previous chapters, some people have difficulty taking into account the perspective of others, which requires people to have a well-developed theory of mind.

Table 9.6 Three Versions of a Conversation Differing in Common Ground

Spouse	Employee–boss	Customer–salesperson
A: Hi, it's me. The train is late. Looks like I won't get there till 7. I'll text you if it will be later.	A: Hello, Manuel. It's Sean. I am down here waiting for the train. There's been some type of accident. Nothing's moving. I'm hoping that I can get to the office by 7. I will call you back if the situation gets worse.	A: Hello, my name is Sean Sims. I called yesterday about picking up the tailored suit around 6 today. I'm not going to be able to make it today. What are your hours for tomorrow?
B: Ok. Love you.	B: Alright. Do your best to get here.	B: 10 a.m. to 7 p.m.
A: Love you.	A: I definitely will.	A: Great. I will see you tomorrow around 6.

In Chapter 4, you learned about the processes involved in speech production. In theories of speech planning, the initial stage is the message level, during which the speaker formulates the semantic content or intention of the utterance. Clark and colleagues' research about the role of common ground during conversation points out more about the processing that must occur at the message stage (Clark, 1985, 1996; Clark & Brennan, 1991; Clark & Schaefer, 1987; Schober & Clark, 1989). Conversational partners bring to an interaction the entirety of their knowledge of the world stored in memory. When the conversation begins, the world knowledge most relevant to the conversational partners' relationship, the setting, and the circumstances may become particularly activated in memory, enabling it to be used in the formation of the message level of speech planning. Common ground is likely to influence the time course of speech planning. Models of speech production could incorporate the activation of common ground prior to the formulation of the message for an utterance. Have you noticed that your utterances to people you know well are typically shorter than those to people you know less well? With more common ground between two conversational partners, utterances may be shorter, as more can be inferred nonverbally.

An interesting question for future research relates to how much the activation of common ground changes throughout the interaction as each utterance is planned and executed. Clark and colleagues advocate the former view, suggesting that common ground increases throughout the interaction (Clark, 1985, 1996; Clark & Brennan, 1991; Clark & Schaefer, 1987; Schober & Clark, 1989). An interesting speculation is that the common ground that conversational partners share would be larger for those who know each other better and for a longer period of time than for conversational partners who are newly acquainted. In Chapter 10, you will learn about language use by people who know multiple languages. Information about the languages your listeners know would definitely be part of the common ground for the conversation.

In this section, you learned about the nature of human conversations and some of the important distinctions that have been made in psycholinguistic research. Conversations are composed of utterances, formulated with a purpose, which may or may not be received by the listener. The formulation of utterances is believed to take into account the knowledge shared by conversational partners as well as the nature of their relationship (intimate, familiar, unfamiliar, etc.). In languages other than English, grammatical rules specify information about the nature of the relationship between the speaker and listener. These rules include the t-v distinction in French, German, and many other languages in which speakers use different pronouns when speaking to a friend and when speaking to someone more socially distant from them.

 Time out for Review

Key Terms

Common ground theory	Mirth	Sociolinguistics
Illocutionary force	Perlocutionary act	Speech act
Indirect speech act	Politeness	Taboos
Interruptions	Sarcasm	Turn-taking
Irony	Small talk	T-v distinction
Locutionary act	Social distance	

Review Questions

1 What is a speech act? What are the five basic categories of speech acts?
2 What are the four Gricean maxims? What type of conversational behavior would violate each one?
3 What are the four humor styles? What has research shown about how the humor styles that people use correspond to health, wellbeing, and other outcomes?
4 According to Steven Pinker, what are the four different functions of curse words?
5 What is common ground theory? Provide an example of a conversation and explain how it would be described within the framework of common ground theory.

Group Differences in Language Use

People who spend a lot of time around each other sometimes develop communication patterns that differ from others, such as heavy reliance on certain words and expressions and possibly the innovation of new words and expressions unknown to others outside the group. If a great deal of time passes, changes in the phonology, morphology, and syntax of the language may occur. This fundamental aspect of language explains why some languages spoken in the world today share the same ancestor language, and why the languages have commonalities. Today, we can find evidence of the same process when we explore the language used by specific social groups within the larger population. In this section, you will learn about how people working in similar occupations or settings often develop specialized terminology and slang that is innovated with each new generation of people in a population (Cole, 2014). You will also learn about research showing that men and women speak differently, having their own gender-specific dialects, called genderlect. Lastly, you will learn about the relatively new area of inquiry called lavender linguistics, which refers to the distinctive types of language use within LGBTQ groups.

Jargon

Members of social groups often develop common vocabulary that is used less frequently by individuals outside the group. For example, specialized vocabulary – **jargon** – is developed by members of the same occupation or profession (e.g., medical personnel, lawyers, military personnel, and police officers). In English, the jargon of certain groups, such as the military and the police, has become commonly understood and used in everyday language. Table 9.7 lists some examples from both groups. It is likely that books, television programs, and movies featuring plots involving these groups have contributed to the familiarity and use of the jargon outside these groups.

Table 9.7 Examples of Military and Police Jargon

Military jargon	Meaning	Police jargon	Meaning
Jeep	vehicle	BOLO	be on the look out
Barracks	living quarters	B&E	breaking and entering
Brig	military jail	CI	confidential informant
Chow	food	DOA	dead on arrival
ASAP	as soon as possible	Heat	police activity
FUBAR	messed up	Junk	Heroin
SNAFU	mistake	Junkie	Heroin addict
Stripes	rank or experience	MO	modus operandi or mode of operating
Grunt	low ranking person	Perp	perpetrator of a crime
Detail	assignment	Priors	previous arrests

Source: Dickson (2011)

Social groups, including those forming around occupations, may create and use jargon with their members as a way of reducing utterances in order to save time. Those sharing the same specialized knowledge may be able to communicate content involving this shared knowledge using fewer words overall and shortened forms of words. Medical professionals regularly use terminology that the rest of us may consider medical jargon, such as *DNR* (i.e., do not resuscitate), *cc* (i.e., cubic centimeters as in a 10 cc dose), and *ENT* (i.e., ear, nose, and throat specialist). Attorneys and judges use words and phrases that others consider legal jargon, such as *a summons* (i.e., order to appear in court), *the bench* (i.e., the judge, the court, or the rulings of a judge or court), and *an exhibit* (i.e., an item introduced as evidence in court). Even the terms used by linguists and psycholinguists can be considered linguistic jargon. Some of the terminology you have learned so far in this textbook may be viewed as jargon by those whose career paths do not involve the topic of language and language processing; however, those who study language-related topics will consider the terms as essential vocabulary of the discipline.

Slang

A second example of how the language use of groups of people can come to differ from others occurs with generational cohorts (baby boomers, gen-Xers, millennials, etc.). Specific words and expressions – **slang** – become associated with specific age groups, with the newest generation of teenagers and young adults innovating new words and expressions (Coleman, 2012). In past decades, some English slang became widely used for a short time. Table 9.8 lists examples of English slang in the USA from selected decades in the 20th century. The slang expressions from earlier decades may sound very peculiar to you. Interestingly, some of the words and expressions you use frequently today will be similarly peculiar when experienced by future generations.

Table 9.8 Examples of 20th-century English Slang in the USA

1920s	Meaning	1930s	Meaning	1940s	Meaning
ritzy	elegant	copper	policeman	dish	cute girl
bimbo	tough guy	grifter	con-man	drip	boring person
dough	money	keen	very good	jalopy	car
gin mill	bar or pub	platter	music record	swell	great
baloney	nonsense	shake a leg	hurry up	jiffy	quick
1950s	**Meaning**	**1960s**	**Meaning**	**1970s**	**Meaning**
square	boring person	groovy	cool	far out	very good
cool	cool	bread	money	boogy	dance
souped up	made to go fast	a gas	fun time	cool	cool
split	leave	burn rubber	go fast	dig	understand
threads	clothing	no sweat	no problem	split	leave

Source: Dalzell and Victor (2008)

Geographical Dialects

The psychological processes that lead to the development of jargon and slang are the same as those that lead to much larger differences in the way people use language somewhat differently in different geographical regions, known as dialect. Geographical dialects are acquired during childhood when we learn the grammar rules without consciously realizing how the learning is happening. We may not even be aware that we are following language rules. This is called "implicit learning." Implicit learning occurs without conscious reflection. The learner cannot explain in words how the learning is happening. In contrast, when people attempt to learn a second language as a teenager or adult as part of a class or on one's own, they are very aware that effort is being exerted and that learning is the goal. There is often conscious realization of how the grammar rules of the first language are similar to or different from the grammar rules of the second language. This conscious, effortful learning is called "explicit learning." People rely on explicit learning to learn the norms for using their first language in formal settings, such as in school. For example, English handbooks of style indicate that a sentence should not end in a preposition (e.g., *Where's he at?).* These types of stylistic, prescriptive grammar rules are needed because there is typically a **standard dialect** of a language, used for formal settings, such as school, government, and business, and a **non-standard dialect** of a language that differs from the standard dialect and can also vary from region to region in a country. For example, speakers who grow up in the southern region of the USA may grow up saying *you was there,* rather than *you were there* (Labov et al., 2006). The mastery of any language involves both implicit and explicit forms of learning. For children who grow up speaking a non-standard dialect, they may not be aware that the way they speak differs from others until they enter a school where instruction is provided in the standard dialect.

As you learned in Chapter 1, the popular theory of how many different languages developed from the same historic language ancestor was that groups of speakers moved to new areas, losing contact with others. Within each group, language conventions changed slowly. The process of groups moving away from each other continued to occur, with language changes occurring within each group. A more recent example of the same process is the English language use at the time that the USA was established. Speakers of *British* English immigrated to North America, then fought a war to gain independence from Britain. A little over 200 years has passed, and although American and British speakers of English can understand each other's language fairly well, there are notable differences. British speakers were also among the founders of what is now Canada, Australia, and New Zealand (Lewis et al., 2016). British speakers also occupied many regions around the globe, such as India and Pakistan where English is still widely spoken as a second and sometimes first language (Lewis et al., 2016). Table 9.9 lists some example vocabulary from five dialects of English.

Dialects can come to be associated with prestige and higher social class, while others can be viewed negatively. When people hold negative attitudes or prejudice toward speakers of specific dialects, they sometimes behave in ways toward those speakers that are unfair or discriminatory. **Linguistic profiling** describes the use of language characteristics (dialect or accent) to stereotype an individual (Baugh, 2003). Scharinger et al. (2011) showed that listeners' detection of dialect differences occurred rapidly (within a tenth of a second after hearing the phoneme with the

Table 9.9 Vocabulary Differences among Dialects of English

British	American	Canadian	Australian	Indian/Pakistani
Lorry	Truck	Truck	Lorry	Lorry
Lift	Elevator	Elevator	LIft	Lift
Flat	Apartment	Apartment	Flat	Flat
Loo	Bathroom	Washroom	Toilet	Toilet
Boot (car)	Trunk	Trunk	Boot	Boot, dicky
Chemist	Pharmacist	Pharmacist	Chemist	Chemist
Torch	Flashlight	Flashlight	Torch	Torch
Nappy	Diaper	Diaper	Nappy	Nappy
Chips	French fries	Fries	Chips	Finger chips
Braces	Suspenders	Suspenders	Braces	Braces

Source: Peters (2004)

dialect variation), as evidenced in their brain activity. The authors concluded that the registering of dialects in speech first occurs unconsciously and categorically (in an all or none fashion, with a dialect either being detected or not detected). Research by Baugh (2003) showed that social stereotyping of speakers can lead to job hunters receiving fewer call-backs about job openings and apartment hunters receiving fewer invitations to visit available apartments than speakers of the standard dialect.

Among speakers of the same geographic area, differences in language use have been observed among individuals from different social groups. The term **social register** describes these shared patterns of language use. Later in this chapter, you will learn about several examples of social registers. The research on social registers became prominent with the research of William Labov, a professor of linguistics at the University of Pennsylvania and prolific researcher in the area of sociolinguistics (Labov, 1966, 1972). The Classic Research box outlines Labov's research exploring phonological aspects of social registers in New York City in the 1960s.

Genderlect

Since the 1970s, linguists have noted that the speech of men and women varies a great deal (Lakoff, [1975] 2004; Tannen, 2001). The original observations involved the speech of men and women in the USA; however, similar differences have been observed in other populations (Hall & Bucholtz, 1995; Holmes & Meyerhoff, 2003). Tannen (2001) referred to gender differences in language use as **genderlect**, which uses the morpheme from *dialect* to create a new word to describe the different dialects used by men and women. Analyses of speech in naturalistic settings have shown that men may tend to produce shorter sentences than women, as men are more likely to produce commands (e.g., *Pass the salt*) and women are more likely to produce requests (e.g., *Could you please pass the salt?*) (Lakoff, [1975] 2004; Mills, 2003). Women also tend to use questions more than men (e.g., *The room feels cold, doesn't it?* and *These grapes aren't very sweet, are they?*). These are known as **tag questions**.

Different Social Registers in a Department Store

In New York City in the 1960s and still today, department stores sell merchandise with a particular group of customers in mind. Some stores sell expensive luxury goods to upper middle-class people, while others sell merchandise to the middle classes and still others sell items at extremely discounted prices. William Labov (1966) devised a field experiment investigating the relationship between the characteristics of speech and the shopping environment. His study focused on three retailers:

- Saks, whose typical customers were relatively high income/upper middle class
- Macy's, whose typical customers were middle income/lower middle class
- S. Klein, whose typical customers were relatively low income/working class.

Working with Labov were research assistants who posed as customers and asked employees in the stores a question that would elicit the answer "the fourth floor." Of particular interest was how employees pronounced the answer. Labov (1966) found that the pronunciation of *r* in *fourth floor* varied, with employees at S. Klein pronouncing the *r* only 21 percent of the time. Employees at Macy's pronounced it more often than employees at S. Klein, but far less often than employees at Saks. The results showed that the dropping of *r* in the New York dialect (e.g., *park* being pronounced as *pahk*) was specifically associated with a register used by lower income people and the pronunciation of *r* was associated with the higher income register. Labov argued that the dialect in which the *r* is dropped is less prestigious than the dialects in which the *r* is pronounced. Historically, the loss of *r* in the New York dialect traces its roots back to the speech of wealthy families in England; thus, it was a prestige dialect at that time. After the Second World War in New York, the dialect in which the *r* is not pronounced gradually acquired a different perception and the dialect in which the *r* was pronounced came to be perceived as prestigious.

There are also differences in the types of words typically used by men and women. Research showed that boys are less likely to use *wow* and *oh* than girls (Ritti, 1973). Men and women tend to use different types of adjectives when speaking (Lakoff, [1975] 2004; Soskin & John, 1963). Women were more likely than men to use *lovely, divine* and *charming*. Men were more likely than women to use *neat, great,* and *terrific*. Another study showed that men and women in Maine used different adjectives when speaking, with numerous descriptive adjectives (e.g., *lovely, pretty, gentle, stylish, little*) used more often by men than women (Hartman, 1976). Work with college students has also documented differences in word usage for men and women. Young men use curse words more often than young women (Mehl & Pennebaker, 2003). In the same study, young men were found to use articles (e.g., *the* and *these*) and words conveying anger more often than young women, while young women used words referring to positive emotions, and *could* and *would*, which were viewed as conveying tentativeness, more often than men. Gender differences in the use of personal pronouns by college students have also been observed, where young women tend to use *my*, *me*, and *I* more often than young men (Pennebaker & King, 1999).

Relatively few laboratory studies have investigated gender differences in language use. In one, however, participants were brought into the laboratory in pairs and asked to select a topic on which to have a conversation (Carli, 1990). The topic was to be one on which their opinions differed. Later, they were asked to evaluate how influential the other person was during the conversation. The researchers tested pairs of participants who were either the same or different gender, with results showing that women used more tentative speech when talking with a man than when talking with another woman. Unsurprisingly, men's ratings of women's level of influence in the conversation were lower when women used tentative speech. Ratings of men's influence during the conversation were found to be unrelated to the language they used.

In a meta-analysis of 30 studies investigating gender differences in language use, 16 types of language use were identified that differed for men and women (Mulac et al., 2001). Women were shown to use negatives (e.g., never, not), intensive adverbs (e.g., really, so), uncertainty verbs (e.g., seems to, maybe), and references to emotions more often than men. In contrast, men were shown to use more commands (e.g., Sit down or Put that away), judgmental adjectives (e.g., stupid, good), and quantity words more often than women. Interestingly, Mulac et al. (2001) did not find evidence that women use tag questions more often than men (cf. Lakoff, [1975] 2004).

Studies have also investigated whether there are differences in the amount that men and women talk. Although many believe that it has been established that women talk more than men, no consensus has been reached in the research literature. In one study, Mehl et al. (2007) used an electronically activated recorder to sample men and women's talking over several days and concluded that the amount women and men talk does not differ. Their results were consistent with earlier research suggesting that the view that women talk more than men is a myth (Cutler & Scott, 1990). Another study has shown that the amount men and women talk may vary depending on setting (Onnela et al., 2014). Onnela et al. (2014) used sensors to assess talkativeness in two contexts: collaborative and non-collaborative. They found no differences in talkativeness for men and women in the non-collaborative context. However, in the collaborative context, they found women to be more talkative than men. The Research DIY box allows you to test the popular view that women like to talk more than men.

Photo 9.2 These girls are talking while looking directly at one another, which is the preferred talking posture for girls and women. Have you ever felt that you prefer talking face to face with others or side by side?

Research DIY

Do Women Like to Talk More than Men?

A common belief is that women talk more than men (Mehl et al., 2007); however, as you just learned, a growing number of empirical studies have found that this belief is a myth. Kennison et al. (2017) have developed a brief questionnaire to assess individual differences in talking enjoyment. The eight-item questionnaire is provided below. For your study, recruit five women and five men to complete the survey. For each statement, they should provide a rating that indicates their level of agreement. For each statement, instruct your volunteer to indicate a level of agreement (1 = strongly disagree and 7 = strongly agree, with the intervening numbers representing varying levels of disagreement to agreement). A rating of 4 would reflect "neither disagree nor agree."

Strongly disagree   **Strongly agree**

| 1 | 2 | 3 | 4 | 5 | 6 | 7 |

1 _____ I enjoy talking.

2 _____ People who know me well would describe me as a person who enjoys talking.

3 _____ I avoid talking when I can.

4 _____ Talking is a fun way to pass the time.

5 _____ Talking is one of my favorite activities.

6 _____ In my free time, I prefer activities that involve little or no talking.

7 _____ People who know me well would describe me as a person who talks a lot.

8 _____ I am one of those people who rarely says very much.

Also ask them their opinion regarding the myth. You can ask them to choose one of the following three statements describing possible gender differences in talking enjoyment.

1 It's generally true that women like to talk more than men.

2 It's generally true that men like to talk more than women.

3 Men and women do not generally differ in how much they like to talk.

Lastly, using the same rating scale as above (1 = strongly disagree, 7 = strongly agree), ask your participants to provide a rating for the following question:

> *When I compare myself to others of my gender, I tend to like talking*
> *more than the average of my gender.*

Before calculating the mean rating score for the eight items for men and women, you must first transform the ratings for items 3, 6, and 8. These items were phrased such that those who enjoy talking more would respond with low rather than high ratings. In survey research, the term "reverse scoring" is used to refer to the transformation of the survey responses to ensure that for all questions, higher ratings always reflect the same relationship. To reverse score items 3, 6, and 8, change all 1 responses to 7, all 2 responses to 6, all 3 responses to 5, all 5 responses to 3, all 6 responses to 2, and all 7 responses to 1. Compute the average rating across the eight items for each participant, then compute the averages for male and female participants. Is the average for women higher than, lower than, or about the same as for men?

African American Vernacular English (AAVE)

Language use also varies across racial and/or ethnic groups. The dialect spoken by many African Americans in the USA is known as **African American Vernacular English** as well as Black English (Baugh, 2002; Green, 2002). The dialect differs from Standard American English in syntax, phonology, and some vocabulary. It shares some grammatical rules with the Southern American English, including use of the double negative. Consider the examples in 2. Speakers of Southern American English and AAVE produce sentences similar to 2a, 2b, and 2c. Each sentence contains two negative words (e.g., not, nobody, hardly, barely, etc.). In contrast, speakers of Standard American English judge these sentences to be ungrammatical. In 2d–2f, the versions in Standard American English contain only one negative word.

2   a. I didn't tell nobody.

   b. He isn't no liar.

   c. She wasn't hardly around today.

   d. I didn't tell anybody.

   e. He isn't a liar.

   f. She was hardly around today.

Table 9.10 lists some AAVE usages that differ from the standard dialect of American English. The dialect is used in many films, television programs, and song lyrics in American music genres, such as blues and hip hop.

Table 9.10 Examples of AAVE Usages that Differ from Standard American English

AAVE	Standard American English
He late.	He is late.
She smart.	She is smart.
She gonna do it.	She is going to do it.
It yours.	It is yours.
He happy.	He is happy (now).
Mary be happy.	Mary is happy (always).

Source: Labov (1969)

Scholars have proposed that the grammatical features of AAVE have their roots in the slavery era, when English-speaking plantation owners controlled indentured servants, who typically spoke low-status English dialects from Ireland, Scotland and England, and slaves stolen from East Africa, who were subjected to a lifetime of forced labor in inhumane conditions (Holm, 1988, 1989). Individuals in the latter group originally spoke a variety of different languages. Over time, individuals developed a way of communicating for work, referred to as **lingua franca**. As the lingua franca became more frequently used, its complexity increased, incorporating more mutually understood vocabulary, but it continued to lack grammatical complexity, which is referred to as **pidgin**. Over time, following the acquisition of pidgin by generations of children, pidgin evolved into **creole**, a language having roots in many other languages, but with its own set of grammatical rules. When compared to other contemporary American English dialects, AAVE is most similar to the Southern American English dialect. It is interesting to note that in the USA today, some speakers of AAVE are not African American. Sweetland (2002) interviewed white Americans who grew up in racially mixed communities and spoke AAVE as their first language.

Speakers of AAVE, Southern American English and other non-standard dialects in the USA grow up using their dialect as their native language, but they begin to acquire the standard dialect in school. They are required to use the standard dialect in educational institutions, most workplaces, and other formal settings; however, they continue to use their native dialect with family and friends. As these individuals move between formal and informal situations in their daily lives, they can find themselves switching between different dialects, described as **code-switching**. Chapter 10 examines the code-switching used by people who speak different languages (e.g., Italian and English). Speakers of multiple dialects also code-switch, although occurrences of code-switching may be less noticeable to listeners than cases in which one is speaking one language and includes a word or phrase in a different language. Much has been written about the code-switching that children who grow up speaking AAVE carry out when they enter school (Baugh, 2002; Wheeler & Swords, 2006).

Lavender Linguistics

Beginning in the 1940s, scholars noted that there were distinctive language and speech characteristics among those identified as homosexual (Kulick, 2000; Legman, 1941). More recent work has shed light on the social norms of lesbian, gay, bisexual, trangender, and queer (LGBTQ) communities (Leap, 1995). Munson and Babel (2007) review research related to the relationship between sexual orientation and speech patterns, known as **lavender linguistics**. Listeners use information that the acoustic properties of consonants and vowels provide to infer the sexual orientation of the speaker. These acoustic properties of speech signaling sexual orientation appear to be acquired through exposure to the speech patterns in daily interactions. This finding does not, however, suggest that every individual who speaks with the specific acoustic cues will identify as part of the group. As pointed out in the documentary film *Do I Sound Gay* (Thorpe, 2014), there are US heterosexual men whose speech patterns are identified by others as *sounding gay,* but they have, in fact, been raised in families with more women than men. The film also points out that the speech patterns used can depend on whether the individual has told family and friends about their sexual orientation.

Worldwide, there are LGBTQ communities where members obtain physical and social help from one another. In the future, these communities are likely to become the focus of sociolinguist studies, exploring how dialects arise and change over time. In the Philippines, the word *sward* is Filipino slang for a homosexual man; hence, swardspeak is the slang used by communities of homosexual men, which incorporates vocabulary from Tagalog, English, Japanese, Spanish, as well as local dialects (Manalansan, 2003). Swardspeak is described as being highly dynamic, regularly innovating new expressions and words. It is used not only by homosexual men, but also by individuals who spend a great deal of time in the community. For example, swardspeak is commonly used in industries that employ many homosexual men, such as fashion and the arts.

In this section, you learned about differences in language use across social groups. Language use can vary across geographic region, between genders, across race/ethnic groups, sexual orientation, as well as occupation. When we interact with others, we rapidly detect the features in their speech that reflect their dialect and use that information to make inferences about their personal characteristics. The research investigating stereotyping of others on the basis of their speech has shown that some groups are systematically discriminated against in the areas of housing and employment.

 Time out for Review

Key Terms

African American Vernacular
    English (AAVE)
Code-switching
Creole
Genderlect

Jargon
Lavender linguistics
Lingua franca
Linguistic profiling
Non-standard dialect

Pidgin
Slang
Social register
Standard dialect
Tag questions

Review Questions

1   How does the speech of men and women differ?
2   What is genderlect? Provide examples and describe the type of person who might use each one.
3   What is linguistic profiling? What dialects are likely to be most profiled linguistically?
4   What do you understand by the term "lavender linguistics"? Give some examples of language use that would be studied by scholars interested in lavender linguistics.

Nonverbal Communication

The social rules of language vary across small social groups and across cultures. Every aspect of verbal interaction can potentially vary across social groups, from how one greets another person to how a person apologizes to another. For example, in many places, a handshake is how people greet one another in a formal setting, whereas in other places, a handshake is not the norm and might be viewed as impolite (e.g., between men and women of the Islamic faith who are unrelated). In this section, you will learn about the nonverbal aspects of communication. We begin with how our body posture can also convey information to our conversational partners and others about our intentions and state of mind. Second, we examine how we use facial expressions when we communicate and the research that sheds light on how facial expressions help us comprehend the others' speech. Lastly, we explore the research on manual gestures, which often accompany speech.

Body Language

The earliest work on **body language** and face-to-face interactions focused on differences in how far away people stand from one another in public spaces and during verbal interactions. The distance at which people feel most comfortable standing next to someone else is referred to as "personal distance" (Hall, 1968). In the 1960s, anthropologist Edward Hall (1914–2009) documented that how close we stand to others in conversations reflects the nature of our relationship, specifically our familiarity, with the person (Hall, 1968). The farther away people stand from one another, the less familiar they are with another. Thus, in situations in which one would be more likely to use polite language when speaking with another person, they would also be more likely to avoid standing too close to the person, which is sometimes referred to as "invading one's personal space" (Navarro & Karlins, 2008). Cultural differences exist in the amount of personal space that is perceived as comfortable when people are standing near those who they do not know well. In our daily life, we sometimes experience an invasion of our personal space, in an elevator or waiting to cross a street. When a stranger stands too close, there is a tendency to take a step away. Many times, we are not even aware why we are stepping away. People living in cities tend to have smaller personal distances than people living in rural areas, which would mean that people from cities are likely to stand closer to you when they are behind you in a line (or queue) than people from rural areas.

Gender differences in body language have been pointed out by researchers (Knapp et al., 2013). Men's postures tend to be more expansive, taking up more room. They may sit with their knees leaning in opposite directions, allowing for their legs to be open wide, sometimes now described as "manspreading". They are comfortable stretching out their arms. In contrast, women's postures tend to take up smaller amounts of space. They tend to sit with knees together, and sometimes with ankles crossed. They avoid large expansions of the arms. The body postures of men tend to fall in the category of dominant postures, which communicate to others that the person is relatively high social status (Knapp et al., 2013). The body postures of women tend to fall into the category of submission postures, signaling a person of lower, non-dominant status. In interactions, dominant or higher status people tend to touch others with whom they are talking more than do lower status people (Jackson, 2010).

Photo 9.3 A man and woman are shown riding a subway train, sitting in the typical way for men and women. Men sit with legs apart and women sit with legs together. How do you typically sit?
Credit: Peter Isotalo

Research has shown that others can infer our emotional states from our body language when we are standing still (Dael et al., 2011) or when walking (Gross et al., 2012). When people are afraid, they may have a defensive posture, crossing their arms and raising their shoulders, while they reduce the amount of space taken up where they stand. When people are angry, their body can take on a fight stance, with shoulders squared and chest out, and fists can be clenched and held out far from the body. Rapid movements of the arms can occur, sometime with pointing of the fingers. The body language of a romantically involved couple differs from that of a couple of friends, with the romantic couple standing closer together, making more physical contact, and holding each other's gaze for longer. The ability to perceive emotions in body language develops early in childhood, becoming accurate for children between the ages of three and five years (Nelson & Russell, 2011).

Facial Expressions

Facial expressions are an important part of body language, which we use especially in our face-to-face interactions with others. They also convey a great deal of information about our emotional state, our level of familiarity with an audience, and how relaxed or nervous we are as we speak. Some aspects of how emotion is conveyed in our facial expressions may be universal (common to all humans). Darwin ([1872] 2007) is credited as being the first person to propose that human emotions are shared by all people, regardless of where they grow up or live. In the 1970s, Darwin's claims were supported in large-scale studies conducted by Ekman and Friesen (1971). They found that across cultures, even in remote regions where the hunter-gatherer lifestyle is still found, people recognized the six basic emotions: fear, anger, sadness, happiness, disgust, and surprise. As you recall from Chapter 8, the ability to imitate the facial expressions of others is present at birth, suggesting that it is an innate ability. Chapter 13 examines the importance of facial expressions during the use of sign languages, such as American Sign Language. Facial expressions and body movements are integral parts of accurate sign production.

One of the most recognizable facial expressions is the natural smile, which is produced when a person experiences something humorous or otherwise pleasant. The Duchenne smile (Martin, 2006) is characterized by the opening and widening of the mouth, which involves the contraction of the zygomatic major muscles, and by closing the opening of the eyes, which involves the contraction of the orbicularis oculi muscles at the sides of the eyes. (The Duchenne smile is named after French neurologist Guillaume Duchenne who identified two distinct smiles in the mid-19th century.) Smiling that occurs without a contraction of the muscles near the eyes is generally interpreted as not genuine (Ekman, 1985). Our ability to maintain a facial expression for an emotion that differs from the emotion we are feeling means that we have the ability to deceive others not only in what we say, but also in how we appear while we say it. Across cultures, there are different interpretations about individuals related to the amount they smile generally, as well as about the context in which the person smiles. People in the USA are described by those from other countries as people who smile a lot (Krys et al., 2016). In Asian countries, too much smiling can be viewed as indicating that the person is superficial and not very intelligent. In Russia and countries sharing a cultural history with Russia, people who smile at those who they do not know well are viewed as untrustworthy or suspect.

Gestures

Although gesturing is commonly used during speaking, the processes involved in planning and coordinating gestures and speech are not completely understood (Abner et al., 2015; McNeill, 2005). A prominent type of body language used during speaking is manual **gestures** (movements of the hands and arms). Gesturing is common across languages and is increasingly viewed as an integral part of speech production. Across cultures, however, gestures vary, and gestures that are offensive in one culture may not be in other cultures (Lefevre, 2011). In some countries, for example Greece, Iran, Nigeria, Afghanistan, and others, the sign that American's use for "thumbs up," which is made by pointing the thumb on one hand straight up, has a similar meaning to that of the offensive sign of the middle finger in the USA. In the Philippines, holding one's palm toward you and moving one's index finger back and forth, as Americans would do to signal to another person to come closer, is considered extremely impolite.

Individual gestures that have symbolic meaning differ from the gestures produced during verbal interactions. McNeill's (1985) early work on these types of gestures demonstrated that 90 percent occur simultaneously with speech. The other 10 percent occurred during silent pauses within or between speakers' utterances. Gestures used in conversations can be divided into two categories. First, there are those that function as beats or break points in the utterance, which are "simple and rapid hand movement of a type that usually accompanies words whose importance depends on multi-sentence text relations" (McNeill, 1985, p. 354). Second, there are conduit gestures, which occur when speakers experience difficulty verbalizing a concept. The gesture serves to maintain the interaction, by signaling to the listener that the speaker is not ready to yield the floor.

The role of gestures in verbal communication has been questioned by other researchers (Krauss, 1998; Krauss et al., 1996, 2000). In a meta-analysis, Hostetter (2011) examined 63 studies that had investigated the role of gestures during speaking. The results confirmed the view that gestures are an important part of verbal communication. Among many findings, she found that children may benefit more from the presence of gestures in conversation than adults. In general, the research found that gestures that depict motor actions are more communicative than those that depict abstract topics, and the effects of gesture on communication are larger when the gestures are not completely redundant with the accompanying speech; effects are smaller when there is more overlap between the information conveyed in the two modalities.

Frick-Horbury and Guttentag (1998) conducted an experiment where participants were presented with definitions for words and asked to name the word. Half the participants had their hands restrained to prevent gesturing. The results showed that those who were able to gesture during the task had significantly better performance than those who could not. McNeill (1985) investigated the coordination of manual gestures and participants' speech as they described a story they viewed in a series of cartoon panels. An example of speech and gestures from the study is presented in 3. The results showed that the production of gestures coincided with speaking 90 percent of the time, with the rest occurring when there was no speaking.

3 a. He tries going up, inside the drainpipe. [hand rises and points upward]

   b. He tries climbing up the drain spout of the building. [hand rises and starts to point upward]

   c. He goes up through the drainpipe this time. [hand rises quickly and fingers open to form a basket]

The view that gestures may play a role in the verbal communication between speaker and listener is also supported by research showing that speakers gesture more and make larger gestures when the speaker knows that listeners can see them (Alibali et al., 2001; Cohen & Harrison, 1973). Research also shows that speakers use gestures more often when they think that the audience will be less attentive (Jacobs & Garnham, 2007) or the audience does not know the topic (Holler & Stevens, 2007).

Researchers have produced compelling evidence that gestures facilitate verbal communication (Rauscher et al., 1996). In the laboratory study, participants were asked to describe the action depicted in a cartoon. The researchers manipulated whether participants were permitted to gesture during the verbal descriptions. To measure whether gestures had or had not been used, researchers had participants touch an electrode throughout the trial. Researchers also gave participants three conditions to describe the cartoon in terms of vocabulary complexity:

1 participants were instructed to describe the cartoon using unfamiliar or obscure words

2 participants were told to avoid words starting with a target phoneme

3 participants were instructed to speak in their natural manner – they were given no special instructions or restrictions.

Participants' fluency of speech was measured and analyzed. The results revealed that for trials on which the cartoon involved a spatial event, participants were more fluent (speech involved less pausing and other dysfluencies) when they were free to gesture. The implication of the results is that gesturing facilitated the planning of speech, perhaps the stage(s) involving retrieving vocabulary from the mental lexicon.

Hostetter and Alibali's (2008) gesture as simulated action theory suggests that gesturing during speaking serves to increase activation within the areas of the mind involved in mental imagery. The theory predicts that it is the involvement of mental imagery during speech planning that increases the speakers' use of gestures, rather than general complexity during the planning of lexical items. Sassenberg and van der Meer (2010) reported evidence supporting the theory from a laboratory experiment. They had individuals who were instructed to be speakers to describe a visual route to participants who were chosen to be listeners. Routes varied in complexity. The results showed that speakers gestured more when the verbal communication was less versus more complex.

Recent research demonstrates that there is a clear link between speech and the planning of gestures (Gonzalez-Fuente et al., 2016; Theocharopoulou et al., 2015). Gonzalez-Fuente et al. (2016) investigated the relationship between speakers' gestures and the production of irony during conversations and the extent to which gesture information assists listeners in identifying irony in others' statements. In Experiment 1, they recorded conversations between pairs of speakers and coded them in terms of the semantic content of the utterances and the presence of gesturing. They found that there were differences in speakers' prosody and gesturing for ironic and non-ironic utterances. In Experiment 2, participants were asked to rate the irony in verbal statements presented in a video showing an ambiguous interaction. In the videos, statements were presented with or without gesturing that was found to occur with ironic statements (gestural coda). The results showed that participants were more accurate detecting irony in verbal statements when they were presented with gesturing.

Research has also investigated the relationship between the areas of the brain involved with language and those areas involved in the production of gestures, finding that the language areas were engaged during the production of gestures (Xu et al., 2009). Participants' brains were imaged using fMRI. The gestures that were tested were those having symbolic meaning, such as a finger placed to the lips to signal that others should be quiet. These results provide support for a view of the evolution of language, which claims that language evolved from an earlier communication system in which gesture played an important role in communication (Corballis, 2009, 2010). The results can also be viewed as evidence against the view that language evolved in a way that was completely unrelated to gestures and their evolution.

Photo 9.4 Chimpanzees' gestures appear to convey information about their states of mind. Estimates suggest that humans and chimpanzees may have shared an ancestor over 6 million years ago. Can you imitate the typical body movements of a chimpanzee?
Credit: Rhys Davenport (right photograph)

 Time out for Review

Key Terms

Body language   Gestures

Review Questions

1   How do people communicate with their body language? What body postures have been discussed in terms of their meaning or interpretations?

2 To what extent does our body language signal to others our level of dominance or social status? Is the dominance signaling similar in the body language of men and women?

3 To what extent do people around the world interpret facial expressions the same? Which facial expressions are most likely to be similar across all societies of people?

4 What has research shown about the use of gestures during speaking? To what extent are gestures and speech planned together versus separately?

5 Describe the gesture as simulated action theory. What evidence has been found to support the theory?

6 What evidence is there that the use of gestures and language may have evolved from similar biological systems?

Summary

Our communication with others can be broadly categorized into those that are verbal, such as conversations, and those that are nonverbal, such as body language, facial expressions, and gestures. Our conversation behavior has been described in terms of speech acts, associated with specific intentions that may or may not be perceived by listeners. There are numerous types of speech acts, many of which have not received much study. How we communicate verbally has been shown to be related to our social groups in the following areas: geographic location; sex; occupation; socioeconomic status; ethnicity; and sexual orientation. Our nonverbal behavior in conversations also serves as a powerful signal to others about our emotional states and possibly our intentions. Emotion can be quickly and accurately perceived from our body postures, facial expressions, and gestures. Research on gesture production shows that their planning and production are linked to the planning of speech and involve brain areas related to language.

Recommended Books, Films, and Websites

Baugh, J. (2002). *Beyond Ebonics: Linguistics Pride and Racial Prejudice*. Oxford: Oxford University Press.

Coulmas, F. (2005). *Sociolinguistics: The Study of Speakers' Choices*. Cambridge: Cambridge University Press.

Eckert, P. & McConnell-Ginet, S. (2003). *Language and Gender*. Cambridge: Cambridge University Press.

Farwell, H. F. & Nicolas, J. K. (2007). *Smokey Mountain Voices: A Lexicon of Southern Appalachian Speech based on the Research of Horace Kephart*. Lexington: University of Kentucky Press.

Green, L. J. (2002). *African American English: A Linguistic Introduction*. Cambridge: Cambridge University Press.

International Dialects of English Archive. www.dialectsarchive.com.

Lakoff, G. (1990). *Women, Fire, and Dangerous Things*. Chicago: University of Chicago Press.

McNeill, D. (2005). *Gesture and Thought*. Chicago: University of Chicago Press.

Martin, R. A. (2006). *The Psychology of Humor: An Integrative Approach*. New York: Academic Press.

Millar, J. (2008). *The Secrets of Body Language*. London: ITV Productions.

Munson, B. & Babel, M. (2007). Loose lips and silver tongues, or, projecting sexual orientations through speech. *Linguistics and Language Compass*, 1(5), 416–69.

Rowe, D. (2011). *Why We Lie?* London: Fourth Estate.

Tannen, D. (2001). *You Just Don't Understand: Women and Men in Conversation*. New York: Quill.

Thorpe, D. (Director) (2014). *Do I Sound Gay?* [DVD] Sundance, Utah: Sundance Selects.

10 HOW ARE TWO OR MORE LANGUAGES PROCESSED?

Chapter Content

Photo 10.1 Many children in Vietnam speak a local language at home and must learn Vietnamese, the country's official language, when they begin elementary school. Have you heard of any of the lesser known languages in Vietnam – Tày, Muong, Cham, and Khmer?
Credit: Mark Knobil

In the world today, the majority of people know more than one language (Grosjean & Li, 2013). A person who knows only one language is **monolingual**. In most countries, it is typical for most people to know at least two languages – **bilinguals** – and often more. The percentage of bilinguals within each country is likely to vary. In countries with numerous bilinguals, children learn second and sometimes even third languages, starting in childhood. In countries with fewer bilinguals, second languages (L2s) may be introduced much later. In this chapter, we examine what is known about the acquisition and use of L2s. In the first section, you will learn the key definitions that are used in bilingual research, starting with the definitions related to bilingualism and other forms of multilingualism. In the second section, you will learn about the developmental aspects of bilinguals, including whether there is a critical period for language learning. In the last section, we review the growing body of research suggesting that bilinguals have a cognitive advantage over their monolingual peers in childhood as well as later in life.

Bilingualism and Other Forms of Multilingualism

Despite all the interest and research on the topic of bilingualism, there is no consensus among researchers regarding the definition of bilingualism (Grosjean & Li, 2013). Similarly, determining who is and who is not bilingual is not as straightforward as one might assume. In psycholinguistic studies of bilinguals, it is common for researchers to rely on participants' self-reported ratings of their own level of proficiency speaking, reading, and listening in their languages

(Marian et al., 2007). Although it is possible to assess participants' abilities in their two languages, doing so would be time-consuming and costly, as the tests are copyrighted products that must be purchased. In studies with bilinguals, researchers typically report a great deal of demographic information about participants, including the age at which they began learning each language and their formal education in each of their languages. In recent years, several questionnaires have been developed to assess language experience in those who know more than one language, such as LEAP-Q (Marian et al., 2007) and language history questions (Li et al., 2014). When bilinguals' self-rated proficiency, language history, and performance in a particular language processing task are considered together, researchers are typically able to make a convincing argument regarding how bilinguals performed differently than monolinguals, or how beginning bilinguals performed differently than advanced bilinguals. Table 10.1 lists questions commonly used to assess language experience and proficiency in research studies.

Table 10.1 Sample Questions Assessing Bilingual Language Experience and Proficiency

Instructions: Please provide information about the languages you know.
Use L1 for first language, L2 for second language, etc.

1 List the languages you know in order of dominance.

2 At what age did you start learning each language?

3 Rate your level of proficiency on a scale from 0 (low) to 10 (high) for each language you know.
   a. Speaking
   b. Understanding speech
   c. Reading
   d. Writing

4 Enter the number of years and months in which you used each language in each of the following circumstances:
   e. Lived in country where it is spoken
   f. Lived with family where primary language was used
   g. Worked or studied in organization where primary language was used

5 Describe the ways in which you have learned the languages you know (e.g., formal classroom learning, self-study, casual exposure to the language, etc.).

Source: Marian et al. (2007)

When considering the regular use of bilinguals' self-reported ratings of proficiency, it is worth noting that bilinguals would likely have difficulty rating their abilities in a language that is not fully known. They can only guess at how they would experience being proficient in the language at the level of a native speaker. Beginning bilinguals are likely to be acutely aware of whether their speaking, reading, and listening skills are comparable. Their judgments of proficiency may be influenced by the extent to which they feel that they fall short of complete comprehension during listening, complete fluency during speaking, and reading without excessive effort. It is possible that the self-ratings for beginning bilinguals are more likely to be good estimates of actual ability than those given by advanced bilinguals. This opinion stems from the numerous highly proficient bilinguals whom I have met, usually in my graduate courses. For most, English is their second, third, fourth or fifth language. Despite their impressive speaking, reading, listening, and academic writing in English, when asked to rate their proficiency in English, none have been willing to rate themselves highly. Their self-ratings tend to be barely above the middle of the rating scale. This anecdotal evidence suggests that in studies with advanced bilinguals, their proficiency self-ratings may underestimate their actual ability.

Research on bilingualism (Myers-Scotton, 2008) has yielded some useful distinctions:

- **Simultaneous bilingualism**: Multiple languages are learned at the same time from childhood.

- **Sequential bilingualism**: An L1 is learned from birth and an L2 is acquired at some point later on. The life experiences that lead to bilingualism may vary widely.

- **Balanced bilinguals**: Some bilinguals feel equally skilled in both their languages.

Other bilinguals report being more highly skilled in one language, referred to as the "dominant language." In such cases, the bilingual's dominant language will often be their L1; however, it may sometimes be L2. For example, L2 may become the dominant language for bilinguals who live and work in the country where they use L2 for most daily interactions. Certainly, maintaining fluency in both L1 and L2 requires regular practice. Some bilinguals report never feeling fully proficient in L2, and after years of living and working in a setting where L1 is rarely used, losing proficiency in their L1.

This loss of a person's first language is known as **L1 attrition** (Linck et al., 2009; Schmid & Jarvis, 2014). Cases of L1 attrition have been documented. For example, Isurin (2000) described the case of an individual born in Russia and adopted in late childhood by an English-speaking couple. By the end of the first year following the adoption, the individual's L1 knowledge of Russian vocabulary had declined by 20 percent. Others have noted that L1 attrition is common for children who are adopted before the age of nine and spend little time using their L1 after the adoption (Pallier et al., 2003). Large-scale investigations of those learning L2 have suggested that learning an L2 contributes to the decline of L1 ability. Linck et al. (2009) compared L1 and L2 language ability for two groups. One group learned L2 in an immersion setting and the other group learned L2 in a traditional classroom. Performance in L2 was better, but L1 ability was worse for those in the immersion group. A personal anecdote about L1 attrition comes from an academic seminar in the 1990s. In a department-wide discussion of research ethics, a professor whose L1 was Chinese, but who spoke excellent English and was published many times over in English-language journals described feeling as though he was not fluent in any language. He remarked that he had never felt that he had fully mastered the intricacies of English, despite having been in the USA for over 20 years, and yet he felt that he had lost a great deal of his native Chinese, because he rarely used it anymore.

As you may be beginning to see, in the research related to **multilingualism**, there are circumstances for individuals and larger populations that make it challenging to create and adhere to firm definitions of bilingual. Another area in which there is substantial ambiguity is how one defines a language as separate from other languages a bilingual may know. Are dialects of the same language counted as one language or multiple languages? For example, Chinese-English bilinguals may report knowing English, Mandarin, and one or more other Chinese dialects. An unresolved question is whether different dialects of a language are considered one or multiple languages (DeFrancis, 1984; Ramsey, 1987). One important criteria that linguists have noted is whether speakers of different dialects can understand one another. If they can understand each other, then the dialects are described as having **mutual intelligibility**. In China, there are more than 200 dialects (Norman, 1988). Some of these are mutually intelligible with Mandarin, which is considered the standard dialect for the country and associated with Beijing, while many others are not. For example, Wu (associated with Shanghai), Min (associated with Taiwan), and Cantonese (associated with South China) are each mutually unintelligible with Mandarin and with each other. It is possible to speculate that it is for political reasons that the populations within China are not usually described in official documents as being linguistically diverse, which, in fact, they are. When an entire population utilizes two dialects of the same language for everyday functions, this is referred to as **diglossia** (Ferguson, 1959; Fishman, 1967). A certain amount of diglossia exists in all language communities, as language use varies for different sexes, ages, and social groups of speakers. Older English speakers may find themselves consulting online dictionaries (e.g., urbandictionary.com) to learn the meanings of words used by teens. The Language Spotlight box examines the extreme example of diglossia in Arabic-speaking communities.

Language Spotlight

Diglossia in the Arabic-speaking World

Photo 10.2 Arabic is the official or co-official language in 26 countries. How many of these countries can you name?
Credit: Paul Andrew Loy

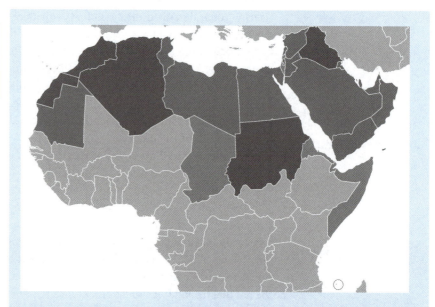

Arabic is one of the most widely spoken languages in the world. Estimates place it in the top five (Lewis et al., 2016), with over 230 million speakers in 26 countries. Table 10.2 lists some of the spoken dialects and where they are spoken.

The written form of the language is Modern Standard Arabic and is largely the same around the world; however, there is wide variation

continued

continued

Table 10.2 Most Widely Spoken Arabic Dialects

Spoken dialect of Arabic	Location of speakers
Egyptian	Egypt
Gulf	The U.A.E., Kuwait, Oman, Qatar, and Bahrain
Hassaniya	Mauritania
Hejazi	Western Saudi Arabia
Iraqi	Iraq
Levantine	Syria, Jordan, Lebanon, and Palestine
Najdi	Central Saudi Arabia
North African	Libya, Morocco, Tunisia, and Algeria
Yemeni	Yemen and southwestern Saudi Arabia

Source: www.myeasyarabic.com

in the spoken language. Modern Standard Arabic is used for all writing and speaking in formal settings, such as courts of law, some news broadcasts, and educational settings. Spoken Arabic varies from country to country and sometimes even across geographic regions within countries. Not all dialects of spoken Arabic are mutually intelligible. There are phonological differences across Arabic dialects as well as differences in vocabulary. Vocabulary differences across Arabic dialects are often related to the influence of other languages spoken in the region in both the distant and the recent past. For example, dialects of spoken Egyptian Arabic include vocabulary from the ancient Egyptian language (known as Coptic), which was used up to the 17th century, and also vocabulary from languages having more recent political and cultural influence, such as Turkish, English, French, and Italian.

Children growing up in Arabic-speaking communities acquire the spoken dialect of their community as an L1 and later learn to read and write Modern Standard Arabic in school. For speakers of Arabic dialects, there may be two or more Arabic words for the same concept – one from the spoken dialect that they rarely see written and one from Modern Standard Arabic that they may rarely hear spoken. Consequently, there is a bigger separation between the written and spoken forms of Arabic than in other languages that have been commonly studied in psycholinguistic research (e.g., English, Dutch, German, Spanish, Italian and French). The vocabulary used in spoken Arabic can be written using the Arabic script. Depending on the region, the spoken dialect may be experienced in written form in popular magazines, books, or song lyrics. For a given individual, their daily experience with the spoken dialect (in spoken and written forms) and their experience with the written form of Modern Standard Arabic would likely influence their language processing.

Trilinguals and Polyglots

Those who know three languages are known as **trilinguals**. Individuals who know five or more language are referred to as **polyglots**, from the Greek *poly* meaning *many* and *glot* meaning *tongue*. In some countries, people commonly learn and routinely use three or more languages (i.e., L3, L4, etc.). Countries in which trilingualism is common are those that have historically had two official languages or one official language and an L2 that is socially, culturally, and politically prominent. In 2012, Sri Lanka, a small island nation located off the southern tip of India, announced that it planned to become a nation of trilinguals by promoting the learning and use of English (Mueller, 2012). The country had two official languages prior to 2012, Sinhala, the historic language of the indigenous people of Sri Lanka, and Tamil, a prominent language in the southern region of India. English is one of the two official languages in India, the country closest to Sri Lanka.

Malaysia is already home to numerous trilinguals. The official language is Malay, and children are required to learn English in school beginning in the elementary grades (Tan, 2005). A significant portion of the population may also be proficient in Chinese or other languages. In Malaysia, 41 different languages are spoken in the peninsula of the country and another 96 languages spoken in the eastern region of Malaysia (also called Malaysian Borneo). Other regions in which trilingualism is common include India, the Philippines, the African continent, and Spain. In India, Hindi and English are the official languages, but approximately 415 languages are spoken in the country (Lewis et al., 2016). In the various regions of the country, there are dominant regional languages as well as minority languages spoken in villages. A person from Chennai may acquire Tamil as L1 and learn Hindi and English as L2 and L3.

Trilingualism is increasingly common in Finland where Finnish and Swedish are the two official languages (Nationmaster, n.d.). Finnish children may acquire Finnish from birth, then acquire Swedish starting in the early elementary school years. Then in middle school or high school, students often acquire English or some other European language. Several minority languages are also spoken in the country, including Sami, Karelian, and Romani. When consulting with a colleague in Finland recently, we found ourselves wondering whether there were any true monolinguals among the younger generations in Finland (S. Vainio, personal communication 2013). In studies of bilingual language processing, it is often useful to include a monolingual group of participants to provide insight into what aspects of processing may be due to knowledge of multiple languages.

Although polyglots are exceedingly rare, some have been featured in newspaper articles and television programs. Many historical figures have been noted for knowing five or more languages:

- Cleopatra VII (69–30 BC) knew nine languages (as reported by Plutarch)
- Elizabeth I of England (1533–1603) knew 10 languages
- English writer J. R. R. Tolkien (1892–1973) spoke 35 languages (Carpenter, 1977)
- Noah Webster (1758–1843) of Webster dictionary fame knew 23 languages
- inventor Nikola Tesla (1856–1943) knew six languages (O'Neill, 2006).

Photo 10.3 Pope Francis, the current pope, is a polyglot who knows at least seven languages. Have you ever heard him give a speech in English?

Credit: Republic of Korea

Emil Krebs (1867–1930), a German lawyer, is a less well-known polyglot who taught himself 63 languages. In 1985, researchers scanned his brain, which had been preserved, and compared it to the brains of individuals who were not polyglots. They found that the speech area known as Broca's area was much larger in Krebs' brain than in the others (Amunts et al., 2004). Of course, it is impossible to determine whether Krebs' Broca's area was unusually large from birth or become larger due to his intensive study of languages. Among the known living polyglots is Pope Francis, the current pope of the Catholic Church, who knows at least seven languages (vatican.com). In his book, *Babel no More: The Search for the World's Most Extraordinary Language Learners*, author, journalist, and linguist Michael Erard (2012) set out to answer the age-old question: What are the upper limits of the human ability to learn, remember, and use languages?

Becoming Multilingual

For many, the journey to becoming multilingual involves spending time in a classroom learning the second or third language. There is a long history of scholarship and research comparing the methods of teaching L2s (Richards & Rodgers, 2001). The most common classroom teaching methods vary in how much L1 is used to aid instruction. **Language immersion** classes prohibit the use of L1 and start students using only L2 from the first day of instruction. In the USA, the **grammar-translation method** is typically used, which emphasizes learning the grammatical structure of L2 through written and oral drills. To this day, I can clearly recall my high school French teacher saying *Répétez s'il vous plait* (*Please repeat*). We repeated phrases again and again each day of the class. Unlike the language learning that occurs during early childhood in which the grammatical rules of the language are unconsciously acquired, the learning of L2s using the grammar-translation method requires learning the grammatical rules of L2 and practicing their use in writing and speaking.

Alternatives to the grammar-translation method have been developed and used throughout the world. The **direct method**, developed early in the 20th century in Europe, uses total immersion in the classroom combined with teaching activities that encourage students to make direct connections between objects and concepts and L2. The **audiolingual method** (Richards & Rodgers, 1987), on the other hand, combines the use of spoken language, grammar quizzes, and behaviorist learning techniques, carried out by an instructor who is a native speaker of the language being learned. Instructors expect students to produce error-free utterances and to become competent communicators. In practice, these techniques may be implemented differently depending on the preferences and experiences of the instructor. Some instructors may stick with complete immersion (i.e., no use of L1), while others may permit L1 to be used on limited occasions.

The past 50 years have seen a proliferation of commercial language learning products; the most familiar are complete self-study courses by Berlitz and Rosetta

Stone. The cell phone application Duolingo also offers self-study lessons that enable users to complete relatively brief interactive lessons on their cell phones. Today, many resources for language learning are also available free on the Internet. There are 130 courses available at the Live Lingua Project (www.livelingua.com), which provides free access to course materials that have been used by the US Foreign Services Institute, Peace Corps, and the Defense Department for training government employees.

In many countries, there are legal provisions to ensure that children entering school without adequate language skills in the language(s) of instruction are provided with extra language support. In the USA, the fight for adequate educational support for bilingual children has been a long battle that has not been completely won. In 1968, the Bilingual Education Act became law in the USA and provided federal funds to assist schools in providing instruction to children for whom English was their L2 (Crawford, 1999; Stewner-Manzanares, 1988). Support for the law originated in Texas where schools were experiencing an increase in the numbers of Spanish-speaking families. The Supreme Court ruling *Lau* v. *Nichols* in 1974 led to the Equal Opportunities Act 1974, which, among other things, mandated for the removal of language barriers preventing students from being able to participate equally in English classes. The case originated in San Francisco where there were many Chinese-speaking families whose children were not receiving adequate support to help them learn English, which was the only language used for instruction (Crawford, 1999). *Lau* v. *Nichols* was a landmark case, which ruled that a school district of San Francisco had violated the Civil Rights Act 1964 in denying some children opportunities to participate in classes. In 2002, the No Child Left Behind (NCLB) Act dramatically changed how schools were required to provide instruction to students for whom English was their L2. NCLB emphasized high-stakes testing in English. Under NCLB, the Bilingual Education Act was retitled the English Language Acquisition, Language Enhancement, and Academic Achievement Act. In recent years, politicians and educators have expressed disappointment with NCLB, and in 2015, it was replaced by the Every Student Succeeds Act.

In Canada, the Official Languages Act named English and French as official languages in 1969 (Office of the Commissioner of Official Languages, www.officiallanguages.gc.ca). The law also provided children with the right to schooling in either language; also, the government funded language learning programs. In those regions in which English was the dominant language, children could receive French immersion classes starting as early as kindergarten. In Quebec and surrounding regions where French was the dominant language, English immersion classes became available for children. The bilingual education efforts in Canada also included languages spoken by indigenous peoples, such as Blackfoot, Cree, Inuktitut, Inuinnaqtun, Mi'kmaq, Mohawk, Ojibwe, and the Pacific Coast Salish languages. In cities with large populations of Chinese, Hindi, Punjabi, and Ukrainian speakers, local schools have developed bilingual education programs for children.

In the European Union (EU), there are 24 official languages, but only three – English, German, and French – are used for conducting day-to-day EU business (Gazzola, 2006). There are approximately 60 other regional languages considered minority languages and an additional 100 languages spoken by immigrants from non-EU countries. Major EU announcements and policies are produced in all 24 official languages. Decisions about the languages used in educational settings are made by the EU's member countries, rather than by any overarching EU policy or body. In 2002, member countries approved recommendations that included the goal of all children achieving proficiency in at least two languages in addition to their mother tongue through the teaching of L2s starting in their childhood (European Union, n.d.).

In many countries, three, rather than two, languages are used for instruction. For example, in India where Hindi and English are official languages, children may start school knowing only their village language. Local school districts are able to determine the order in which Hindi and English will be introduced to children and what subjects will be taught in which language after children have developed proficiency in both languages. In Arabic-speaking countries, schools also commonly utilize three languages for instruction. In Lebanon, Egypt, and Syria, children will start out learning subjects in Arabic, but learn English and French, which may be used as the language of instruction for science and math. As you will see in Chapter 13, countries also vary widely in their laws regarding deaf children's rights to obtain access to learning sign languages and receiving courses in those languages.

In this section, we discussed the prevalence of bilingualism in the world and different types of bilingualism. We also learned about trilinguals and polyglots, who know at least three languages and five or more languages, respectively. In some countries, becoming trilingual is commonplace due to the cultural prominence of three or more languages. Polyglots are rare and a subject of fascination for journalists and television interviewers. Emil Krebs was one of the most well-known polyglots, who taught himself 68 languages.

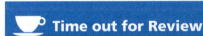 **Time out for Review**

Key Terms

Audiolingual method	Grammar-translation method	Mutual intelligibility
Balanced bilingual	L1 attrition	Polyglots
Bilinguals	Language immersion	Sequential bilingualism
Diglossia	Monolingual	Simultaneous bilingualism
Direct method	Multilingualism	Trilinguals

Review Questions

1 How do simultaneous and sequential bilingualism differ from one another?
2 To what extent are children around the world provided classroom instruction in their first language?
3 What is diglossia? In which countries is diglossia common?
4 What are the different methods that are used to teach L2s? What has research shown about the effectiveness of the different methods?

Developmental Perspectives on Bilingualism

Psycholinguistic research has examined how the acquisition and use of several languages changes across the lifespan. In research that takes a developmental perspective, it is common for researchers to compare performance for groups of participants who differ in age. Studies typically compare groups of children of different ages (five-, six-, or seven-year-olds) or groups of adults (young adults versus older adults). The research can be categorized into four types: early research on the critical period hypothesis; research investigating how age influences the ease versus difficulty of language acquisition, particularly acquiring L2s; research investigating language processing in bilinguals versus monolinguals across the lifespan; and research on how bilingualism may affect thinking, specifically conceptual knowledge.

The Critical Period Hypothesis

As we briefly discussed in Chapter 1, learning language is generally believed to be easier in early childhood than any other time in life (Komarova & Nowak, 2001). A popular explanation for this phenomenon is that for humans, there is a critical period during development in which language can be learned. The view that humans have critical periods of development as other animals do was first discussed by Penfield and Roberts ([1959] 2014). Birds have critical periods for acquiring their species-typical songs (Nottebohm, 1969). Cats have critical periods for developing normal vision (Hubel & Wiesel, 1963). Eric Lenneberg (1964, 1967) proposed that there was a critical period during human development for learning language. Lenneberg specified puberty as the end of the critical period during human development. Consequently, in his view, attempting to acquire a language after puberty was predicted to be unsuccessful.

Support for the critical period hypothesis comes from many sources. There are the anecdotal cases of individuals failing to fully acquire L2 after puberty despite devoting ample amounts of time and effort (Skehan, 1998). There are also cases of individuals who have experienced severe neglect and who failed to master L1 after puberty despite years of effort (Lane, 1975). Throughout history, there have been stories of abandoned children who survived in wilderness settings, living with animals and having little or no contact with humans. As you may recall from Chapter 1, such cases are commonly referred to as feral children. The expression *raised by wolves* stems from the case of twin girls supposedly discovered in the 1920s living with wolves in a forest in Bengal (Singh, 1926). Investigations of the case concluded that it was a hoax (Aroles, 2007). In 1797, a wild boy was first discovered in France in woods near the town of Saint-Sernin-sur-Rance (Lane, 1975). He came to be known as the Wild Boy of Aveyron. He was given the name Victor (1788–1828) by Jean Marc Gaspard Itard, the doctor who cared for him. Itard worked closely with Victor, teaching him the basics of daily living and also attempting to teach him language. Due to Victor's lack of progress in learning language, Itard ended his work with Victor and placed him in the care of a local woman. In 1970, famed French filmmaker François Truffaut released the movie *L'Enfant Savage*

(*The Wild Child*), depicting Victor's case and his time with Itard. The film received praise from critics and garnered many directing awards for Truffaut.

In November 1970, a new case of severe neglect grabbed the world's attention. Child protective authorities in Los Angeles, California rescued a severely neglected 13-year-old girl from her parents' home. She had been found tied to a child-sized toilet. Investigators believed that she spent most of her life tied to the toilet or restrained in a crib. She had had very little social contact, as others were not permitted to see her or interact with her; thus, she had had very little exposure to speech. At the time of her discovery, she did not speak. For the next four years, she received basic medical care and intensive language therapy at the Children's Hospital Los Angeles. Her story was told in the Emmy Award-winning documentary *Genie: Secret of a Wild Child* (1994), although Genie was a pseudonym given to her by the Children's Hospital. The film was based on a journalist's account of the case (Rymer, 1974).

Genie's story and the film describing it are compelling on many fronts, only one of which is relevant to the critical period hypothesis. After four years of intensive language therapy at the Children's Hospital, Genie was unable to master the word order rules of either a spoken or a signed language. She successfully amassed a large vocabulary and became skilled in conveying her intentions through nonverbal communication. Ultimately, many language researchers concluded that Genie's case supported the view that if a language's grammar is not acquired before puberty, then it will not be fully mastered. However, many believe that Genie's failure to learn language was due to an intellectual impairment existing since birth. Ultimately, it is impossible to know which viewpoint is correct. Unfortunately, Genie's case has not been the last instance of severe child neglect in which the critical period hypothesis can be evaluated. Dozens of cases have been reported around the world (https://en.wikipedia.org/wiki/Feral_child).

There is much debate regarding whether the end of the critical period is puberty or some earlier point in childhood (Long, 2005; Rothman, 2008). Some researchers have suggested that different language modules have different critical periods. The most commonly cited module is the one involved in phonology (Fathman, 1975; Hyltenstam, 1992; Hyltenstam & Abrahamsson, 2000; Oyama, 1976; Scovel, 1988). Lee and Schachter (1997) proposed a distinct critical period for the module involved in pronominal reference. Others have completely rejected the notion of an age-related critical period for language learning (Long, 2005; c.f., Rothman, 2008).

Age and Proficiency

In Chapter 5, you learned that the time needed to process individual words during adulthood is influenced by the age at which the word was learned – the age of acquisition effect. Studies have also demonstrated that there is a link between the age at which L2 is acquired and the proficiency achieved in using the language. Across numerous studies, the best predictor of proficiency in L2 has been shown to be the age at which it is acquired (Flege et al., 2002; Hyltenstam & Abrahamsson, 2000; Johnson & Newport, 1989; Kovelman et al., 2008). Some studies have assessed how long participants have lived in the country in which L2 was acquired as a proxy for age of acquisition and have found that longer durations of residence were related to more proficient performance in L2 (Flege et al., 1999). Studies of immigrant children living in the USA and acquiring English as their L2 in school have found relatively rapid progression to proficiency (between three and five years) (Collier, 1989; Hakuta et al., 2000). Children entering school at the earliest ages progressed to high levels of proficiency in English faster than other children. Children's age of acquisition was one of many factors predicting proficiency over time. Other factors included sex, ethnicity, and family income.

As bilingual individuals age, there may be age-related declines observed in L2 proficiency. Hakuta et al. (2003) examined archival data collected as part of the 1990 US census, which obtains information about languages used in the home and respondents' ability levels in those langages. Hakuta et al. (2003) focused their analysis on the 2.3 million respondents whose L2 was English and whose L1 was either Chinese or Spanish. Of particular interest was the extent to which certain factors – age of immigration, years of formal education, family income – predicted proficiency in English. The results showed that for both groups of bilinguals, proficiency in L2 was lowest for those who had immigrated longer ago. The results were later questioned (Stevens, 2004) and were found to be supported (Wiley et al., 2005).

In all the research investigating the relationship between long-term proficiency and L2 and the age at which the individual began learning the language, the variable most likely to be uncontrollable by researchers and important in affecting the outcome is individual motivation (Gardner, 1985; Gardner & Lambert, 1972; Lybeck, 2002). Research by Alene Moyer (1999, 2004, 2007, 2014) in which L2 proficiency has been studied in relation to learners' personal characteristics suggests that those learners who are able to achieve proficiency often demonstrate a high level of engagement with the language, which can translate into useful study strategies (Moyer, 2014). Results from a meta-analysis show that a language learner's aptitude for language learning plays a key role in influencing how likely they are to become proficient in an L2 (Li, 2016), and that the learner's aptitude is independent from their motivation. At least one study has linked brain changes occurring during foreign language immersion to the gene COMT, with different versions of the gene being associated with varying amounts of brain changes due to language experience over time (Mamiya et al., 2016).

Bilingualism across the Lifespan

Studies investigating bilingualism across the lifespan tend to fall into two categories: those that have compared the language development of infants raised in bilingual homes with infants raised with a single language; and those that have compared language processing of bilingual versus monolingual older adults. These studies have dispelled myths that bilingualism can significantly delay infants' language development and create confusion for children learning in school. In this section, you will see that there is increasing scientific evidence that there are numerous advantages to bilingualism for infants, older children, as well as older adults.

The cautions about raising infants with multiple languages are quite familiar. You may have heard people say that raising an infant with two languages is not a good idea, as the infant may become confused by the two languages and end up being slow in the use of both languages. Fortunately, this common fear need not worry anyone. Comparisons of the language development of monolingual and bilingual children have shown that there are no differences that should cause anyone concern. As you recall from Chapter 8, infants typically produce their first words around the age of 12 months. Research shows that bilingual children, like their monolingual peers, produce first words at around 12 months (Genesee, 2003; Patterson & Pearson, 2004; Petitto et al., 2001).

In the past 30 years, numerous studies have investigated infants' perceptual abilities, including infants reared in multilingual environments. These studies demonstrate that the first year of life is a time of substantial perceptual change. Bosch and Sebastián-Gallés (2003) tested the perceptual abilities of infants being raised in monolingual Spanish-speaking homes or bilingual Spanish-Catalan homes. They tested infants at the age of 4, 8, and 12 months on the ability to perceive a particular pair of contrasting vowels. In Spanish, the vowel sounds are perceived as a single vowel. In Catalan, the vowel sounds represent two distinct vowels. At 4 months, all infants were able to distinguish the two vowels. However, infants' performance at 8 and 12 months differed. Monolingual infants' ability to peceive the vowel distinction declined steadily over time, while bilingual infants' performance followed a U-shaped pattern, with a slight decline in performance at 8 months and increased performance back to the baseline level at 4 months (see also Sebastian-Galles & Bosch, 2009).

Studies investigating the perceptual abilities of infants in France have found differences between infants reared in monolingual French homes and infants reared in bilingual (French-English) homes (Burns et al., 2007; Sundara et al., 2008). They examined the infants' ability to distinguish the place of articulation difference between the French /d/ and the English /d/. When the infants were tested at 6 and 8 months, both groups of infants could distinguish the two phonemes; however, by 10 to 12 months of age, only the infants reared in the bilingual homes could. Infants reared in monolingual homes had lost the ability to perceive the distinction due to lack of exposure to the sounds.

Over the first year of life, as infants' perceptual abilities are changing, developing expertise in the sounds they regularly hear and losing the ability to distinguish contrasts they never hear, they are also changing their verbal productions. Infants begin babbling between four and six months. Research showed that infants reared in bilingual homes begin babbling at the same time in development as infants reared in monolingual homes (Oller et al., 1997). Since the work of Brown (1958), researchers have recognized that infants' babbling changes over time. Their utterances increasingly include sounds they regularly hear and gradually cease to include sounds they never hear. Brown (1958) referred to this as **babbling drift** (see also Andruski et al., 2014).

In terms of the major milestones in language development, bilingual children keep pace with monolingual children (Genesee, 2015). The age of first words occurs around 12 months of age for both types of children (Genesee, 2003; Patterson & Pearson, 2004; Petitto et al., 2001). Petitto et al. (2001) found that the use of two-word utterances began around 18 months for both bilingual and monolingual children. Similarly, the word spurt has been found to occur around the same time for bilingual and monolingual children (Pearson & Fernández, 1994; Pearson et al., 1993). Paradis and Genesee (1996) observed that bilingual and monolingual children began producing combinations of words at comparable points in development, around 18 to 24 months.

Research that has compared bilingual and monolingual children's vocabulary has yielded mixed results. Some studies have found that the productive vocabularies of bilingual children are smaller than those of monolingual children (Cote & Bornstein, 2014; Junker & Stockman, 2002; Pearson & Fernández, 1994; Pearson et al., 1993; Oller & Eilers, 2002; Petitto & Kovelman, 2003; Rescorla & Achenbach, 2002; Yan & Nicholadis, 2009). However, methodological issues that may underestimate vocabulary size for bilingual children have been noted (Patterson, 2004). Counting the number of concepts known may underestimate the size of a bilingual's vocabulary, as they may know multiple words for each concept (i.e., one in each language). Other studies have failed to find vocabulary size differences for the two types of children (Bedore et al., 2005). In studies comparing bilingual and monolingual children's receptive vocabularies, the results are also mixed. Some studies have found that bilingual children have smaller receptive vocabularies (Bialystok et al., 2010a, 2010b; Mahon & Crutchley, 2006). Other studies found comparable vocabulary sizes for bilingual and monolingual children (Cromdal, 1999; Yan & Nicholadis, 2009). De Houwer et al. (2014) compared bilingual and monolingual children and found that bilingual children understood more words than monolingual children, but monolingual children knew more total words when production and comprehension were combined.

A substantial portion of a bilingual child's vocabulary involves translation equivalents in their two languages (words in different languages that mean the same thing). Petitto et al. (2001) examined the vocabularies of bilingual children between the ages of one and three. Translation equivalents made up 36–50 percent of the total vocabulary. Genesee and Nicoladis (2007) investigated the vocabularies of young children (8–30 months old) who were raised in homes where English and Spanish were used. Their vocabularies contained 30 percent translation equivalents. The specific languages known by the bilingual child are likely to influence the extent to which there are many versus few translation equivalents with high phonological similarity (see Bosch & Ramon-Casas, 2014).

Research suggests that children differ in how they understand and approach the task of communication, depending on whether they had been exposed to multiple languages or not. In a particularly clever study, Fan et al. (2015) asked children between the ages of four and six to perform a task in which they were required to consider another person's perspective. The task involved children viewing a shelf containing several objects, some that both they and the other person could see, and others that only they could see. They found that bilingual children and those children who were monolingual but had been exposed to multiple languages were more likely to take another's perspective into account during the communication task than monolingual children who had not been exposed to multiple languages. In a follow-up study, Liberman et al. (2016) found similar results with infants as young as 16 months.

Since the 1960s, researchers have argued that there may be cognitive advantages associated with bilingualism. Peal and Lambert (1962) reported among the first evidence that bilingual children may be at an advantage when compared to monolingual children. They investigated children living in Montreal, Canada, comparing those who were French-English bilinguals with monolingual French-speaking children. The results showed that bilingual children exhibited more cognitive flexibility than monolingual children. About 15 years later, Ben-Zeev's

(1977) research demonstrated that Hebrew-English bilingual children between 5 and 8 years of age performed better on a variety of tasks than monolingual children of similar ages. In the study, children were asked to carry out two tasks. One of the tasks required children to use their spatial processing. The experimenter showed them nine cylinders of different sizes arranged in three rows and three columns. First they were asked to describe the arrangement. Then, children were instructed to move the cylinders to a new location while preserving the same arrangement. The second task required children to make judgments about language. For example, the interviewer told children that an *airplane* was a *turtle,* and then asked *can a turtle fly*? Overall, the results suggested that compared to monolingual children, bilingual children were particularly skilled at "seeking out rules and determining which are required by the circumstances" (Ben-Zeev, 1977, pp. 1017–18). In one of the first longitudinal studies, in which bilingual and monolingual children were tested over time, Hakuta and Diaz (1985) observed that bilingual children outperformed monolingual children in tasks involving nonverbal intelligence as well as knowledge of how language works (i.e., metalinguistic awareness). Ricciardelli (1992) found that bilingual children performed better on tasks involving creativity than monolingual children.

Over the past 25 years, the evidence for a **bilingual advantage** in cognitive processing has accumulated (see Ross & Melinger, 2017, for review). Most of the studies have focused on children. For example, children who are bilingual have been shown to outperform monolingual children in tests of grammar and vocabulary (Curtain & Dahlberg, 2004; Dumas, 1999). The bilingual advantage has been observed in children's judgments of grammaticality (Bialystok, 1986, 1988; Bialystok & Majumder, 1998; Galambos & Goldin-Meadow, 1990; Galambos & Hakuta, 1988). The grammaticality task involves participants simultaneously reflecting on the meaning of a sentence and its structure. When the sentence is ungrammatical, the participant likely uses attentional processes to identify the problem. In a study with children aged between five and nine, the researchers found no difference in performance between bilingual and monolingual children when judging sentences that were ungrammatical but meaningful (e.g., *Apples growed on trees*); however, bilingual children were more accurate judging ungrammatical sentences (e.g., *Apples growed on noses*) than monolingual children (Bialystok et al., 2007). Similar results have been observed by others (Cromdal, 1999; Ricciardelli, 1992). The bilingual advantage has also been observed in tests of math and social studies (Andrade et al., 1989; Armstrong & Rogers, 1997; Kretschmer & Kretschmer, 1989; Masciantonio, 1977; Rafferty, 1986; Saunders, 1998). For example, Armstrong and Rogers (1997) examined children's math performance over the course of a semester and found that children who had studied their L2 for 90 minutes each week performed better than children who had not studied an L2. Leikin (2012) found that balanced bilingual children performed better on tasks involving creativity than other children.

Among the most compelling findings are those showing that bilinguals perform better than monolinguals on tasks involving the control of conscious thought and attention (i.e., executive function), such as switching between tasks. For example, Bialystok and colleagues showed that bilingual children performed better on tasks requiring attentional control than monolingual children (Bialystok, 1999, 2005; Bialystok & Majumder, 1998; Bialystok & Martin, 2004). The bilingual advantage in processes involved in attention has been found in infants as young as seven months (Kovács & Mehler, 2009). Carlson and Meltzoff (2008) demonstrated that the differences in attentional processing for bilingual and monolingual children occur only when the task involves concurrent attentional demands (conflict task). In tasks in which children are required to respond after some delay (impulse control task), monolingual children performed just as well as bilingual children.

The bilingual advantage has also been observed for older adults. Intriguing research suggests that being bilingual may be a protection against dementia, which refers to memory loss that occurs in older adults (Bialystok et al., 2007; Craik et al., 2010; Schweizer et al., 2012). Research by Bialystok et al. (2007) found that, on average, bilinguals with dementia received their diagnoses four years later than monolinguals. In a brain imaging study involving older adults, Olsen et al. (2015) found that bilingual participants exhibited differences in frontal and temporal lobe functioning as compared to monolingual participants. Despite the fact that over the past 20 years, a bilingual advantage has generally been accepted, a growing number of studies suggest that the bilingual advantage may not be valid (Antón et al., 2016; Clare et al., 2016; Hilchey & Klein, 2011; Paap & Greenberg, 2013; Paap & Liu, 2014; Zhou & Krott, 2016). Antón et al. (2016) and Clare et al. (2016) failed to find bilingual advantages in studies with older adults. Paap and colleagues argue that the bilingual advantage has, at best, been overestimated, and, at worst, has arisen due to confirmation bias and uncontrolled differences across participants that contribute to performance differences between bilinguals and monolinguals (Paap & Greenberg, 2013; Paap & Liu, 2014). In the future, these contradictory results are likely to be sorted out; however, until then, we can conclude that bilingualism is not a hindrance to children or adults, but we should be cautious about the claim that bilingualism will always lead to measurable cognitive benefits.

Language Effects on Thought in Bilinguals

You may be wondering what affect knowing more than one language has on one's thinking. Chapter 1 discussed the Sapir-Whorf hypothesis, which claimed that the language one speaks can affect thought. Research suggests that the strong version of the hypothesis (linguistic determinism), which suggests language determines what we can perceive and think about, is incorrect. The weak version of the hypothesis (linguistic relativity), which suggests that language can influence the speed and accuracy of our thought processes, is largely supported (Everett, 2013). The Classic Research box highlights the research demonstrating evidence for linguistic relativity in color processing.

Studies have shown that the direction of one's writing system is correlated with how one thinks of a temporal sequence of events (Dobel et al., 2007; Maas & Russo, 2003; Tversky et al., 1991). Tversky et al. (1991) asked participants to organize a set of daily events by arranging a set of physical objects. Arabic speakers organized the events from right to left, which is also the direction in which Arabic is written. Events occurring later in the day were placed to the left of events occurring earlier. In contrast, English speakers ordered the events left to right, with later events being placed to the right of earlier events. Mass and Russo (2003) asked participants to draw an event represented by a sentence. Of interest was where in the drawing the subject/agent and object/patient of the sentence would

Classic Research

Color Processing: Evidence for Linguistic Relativity

In a classic study, Eleanor Heider Rosch (Heider, 1972) tested the strong and weak versions of the Sapir-Whorf Hypothesis, comparing how two groups of participants carried out tasks in which color played a central role. She compared the performance of native English speakers who possess numerous terms to refer to different colors (white, black, red, green, blue, yellow, etc.) and native speakers of Dani (the language of the Dani people of Papua New Guinea), whose language has only two color words, one for black/dark/cool and another for white/light/bright. In the first task, she showed participants color chips, one at a time, and asked them to name the color of the chip. In a second task, she presented a color chip to each participant for five seconds. After removing the color chip, she presented a display showing 40 colors. She asked the participant to point to the color that was the same as the color chip. All participants showed better memory performance when the color chip represented the best example (was prototypical) of the color (e.g., navy blue not sky blue tends to be the best example of blue for English speakers). Heider (1972) concluded that speakers of Dani performed similarly to speakers of English on tests of color perception, contradicting the prediction of the strong version of the Sapir-Whorf hypothesis (linguistic determinism). Subsequent studies have supported the weak version of the Sapir-Whorf hypothesis (linguistic relativity), showing that cognitive processing of color information can be influenced by the number of color terms in participants' native language (Athanasopoulos et al., 2010; Roberson et al., 2000, 2005). Athanasopoulos et al. (2010) found differences in the brain responses to colors for two groups of Greek-English bilinguals, with the color categories for the two languages being more different for bilinguals who had spent less time in an English-speaking country than for other bilinguals. The results demonstrate the dynamic nature of bilinguals' color categories and their influence on cognitive processing.

be drawn. Arabic speakers sketched the event with the subject/agent to the right of the object/patient. In contrast, Italian speakers drew the event with the subject/agent to the right of the object/patient. Italian, as English, is written from left to right. Dobel et al. (2007) showed that before children know how to write, their representation of time is not fixed. They compared the performances of children who spoke German, which is written left to right, with those who spoke Hebrew, which is written right to left, and did not find that language direction predicted their responses. They also tested illiterate adults living in Germany and Israel and found that they produced the same temporal ordering of events as literate adults. Their conclusion was that living in the culture is enough to result in one having the same spatial bias in their thinking about time as regularly writing the language in a particular direction.

For the bilingual, trilingual or polyglot, multiple languages are likely to have some impact on the individual's cognitive processing. There are relatively few studies investigating how an individual's cognition is affected by multiple languages (Athanasopoulous et al., 2010, 2011; Cook et al., 2006; Filipović, 2011).

Cook et al. (2006) compared the performance of two groups of Japanese-English bilinguals who differed in how long they had lived in an English-speaking country. *Short-stay* bilinguals had lived in the English-speaking countries between six months and three years, while *long-stay* bilinguals had lived in English-speaking countries longer than three years. The groups performed similarly on a test of vocabulary knowledge. Both groups performed a task in which they had to categorize novel objects, such as a cork pyramid. After being shown the object, they were shown two other objects and asked to choose the one that was most similar to it. One of the choices was always similar in shape (e.g., plastic pyramid), and the other choice was always similar in materials (e.g., piece of cork). Earlier research had shown that monolingual native Japanese speakers categorized novel objects in this task based on material, while monolingual native English speakers tended to use shape for categorization (Imai & Gentner, 1997). The difference in object classification was attributed to differences in how Japanese and English grammatically encode count versus mass nouns (e.g., pebble versus sand). Cook et al. (2006) found that the long-stay bilinguals performed more similarly to monolingual English speakers and the short-stay bilinguals performed more similarly to monolingual Japanese speakers. The authors concluded that with increased exposure to English, bilinguals' conceptual structure and processing evolves, becoming more similar to that of native L2 speakers.

A compelling question is whether those who know more than one language have associations between their general knowledge and the language that was used when they acquired the knowledge. If a bilingual learns about one topic in French, is the knowledge stored in memory differently than if a bilingual learns about the topic in English? Recent research suggests that once knowledge is acquired by a bilingual, it appears to be stored in a language-free representation (Francis, 1999; Fukumine & Kennison, 2016). In a study of Spanish-English bilinguals, Francis (1999) investigated whether the transfer of knowledge during problem-solving was influenced by the language in which the problems were described. Four groups of participants were asked to solve problems that had similar solutions. The problems were either written in the same language or different languages. For each group, half the participants received the first problem in their L1, and the other half in their L2. The results showed that approximately 70 percent of participants realized that the solution to the first problem could be used to solve the second problem. However, the likelihood of solving the second problem did not significantly depend on whether the two problems were presented in the same or different languages. Consequently, when participants discovered the solution to the first problem and stored that knowledge in memory, the knowledge did not appear to be stored in a language-specific representation. Similar results were obtained by Fukumine and Kennison (2016), who showed that the likelihood of transferring the solution of the first problem to the second problem was higher when participants had better comprehension of the first problem and its solution.

These results showing that knowledge is stored in a language-free representation have implications for classrooms and workplaces. For bilingual students and employees faced with the challenge of acquiring a large amount of knowledge in a short amount of time, it may be more practical to study the material in the language in which they are the most proficient, rather than studying material only in the language in which the test would be given. The results of Francis (1999) and Fukumine and Kennison (2016) provided evidence against the notion that using knowledge gained in one language to perform tasks in a different language would be more difficult or more affected by errors.

In this section, you learned about the development perspectives on bilingualism, beginning with critical period hypothesis. Some cases of feral children support the notion of a critical period for language, as they were unable to learn language fully after puberty. You also learned about the studies showing that learning an L1 or an L2 early in childhood leads to better outcomes, such as higher proficiency. You also learned about the debate in the research literature regarding the cognitive advantages of bilingualism. Studies have shown that bilingual children and adults perform better on cognitive tasks than monolinguals. However, recent failures to replicate past results led some researchers to question whether the bilingual advantage is real. Lastly, you learned about the research on the relationship between language and thought and the possibility that learning an L2 changes the structure of conceptual knowledge.

 Time out for Review

Key Terms

Babbling drift   Bilingual advantage

Review Questions

1 What is the critical period hypothesis? What is the strongest evidence in support of it?
2 What are feral children? How have studies of feral children been used to inform the debate about language development?
3 To what extent do bilingual children reach language development milestones at the same time as monolingual children?
4 What empirical evidence is there that bilingual children are at a cognitive advantage over monolingual children?
5 To what extent does the research support the view that there is a bilingual advantage for older adults, particularly in delaying the onset of dementia?

Bilingual Language Processing

In previous chapters, you have learned about how people perceive speech, produce speech, recognize written words, and comprehend sentences and discourses. Those chapters described models of language processing that were developed using studies involving primarily monolingual participants. Many may assume that it is a safe assumption that those models will be able to accommodate current and future results from bilingual language processing studies. In this section, we will examine the bilingual language processing literature and discover important implications that research with bilinguals has for general models of language processing.

Language Transfer

One of the most robust phenomena in language processing by people who know two or more languages is instances in which one language influences processing of another. The term **language transfer** refers to languages influencing one another during processing (Jarvis & Pavlenko, 2008). Some types of language transfer can facilitate language processing. Any transfer that facilitates the use of another language is called **positive language transfer**. Pairs of words that mean the same thing in a bilingual's two languages are called **translation equivalents**. For many pairs of languages, there are words that are highly similar in spelling and in pronunciation (e.g., the English-German equivalents *friend-freund*). Such pairs are known as **cognates**. When acquiring an L2, cognates can facilitate the building of a vocabulary. The typical relationship between L1 and L2 translation equivalents involves no visual or phonological similarity, as in the English-German pairs *dog-hund*, *question-frage*, and *juice-saft*.

Cases in which there is interference from one language when using the other may be particularly memorable, as they can contribute to the difficulty in mastering an L2. The term **negative language transfer** describes these cases. Here are three examples:

1 Language pairs often have words known as **false cognates** or **false friends** that can confuse the beginning bilingual, as the words have similar spelling and pronunciation but different meanings. For example, some German words that are similar to English words but do not share the same meaning include the German word *gang* (means hallway not group of people), *bad* (means bath not the opposite of good), and *gift* (means poison not something nice that is given to another).
2 The L1 phonology and patterns of articulation can influence how L2 is pronounced, leaving one with accented speech.
3 If a speaker's L1 uses the same word to refer to *he* and *she,* but the L2 uses different words for the two pronouns, there may be difficulty using the correct pronoun in L2.

The Research DIY box explores how the similarity between L1 and L2 words influences the ease with which L2 vocabulary can be acquired.

Organization of Bilingual Memory

An important question in bilingual research relates to how language knowledge is organized in memory. Are a bilingual's two languages stored together or separately? During language processing tasks, does a bilingual activate in memory only the language being used or are memory representations from both languages activated? The **bilingual translation task is** used to investigate the organization of bilingual memory (Heredia et al., 2016). Participants are shown words in one of their languages and they are asked to name its translation equivalent in the other language. Bilinguals' speed and accuracy carrying out translations have been used to inform assumptions about the connections among different types of word knowledge in memory. Kroll and Stewart (1994) pointed out that in bilingual translation tasks, participants generally take more time translating an L1 word into L2 than they take translating an L2 word into L1. They presented a model of bilingual memory that could account for those results and others. This is the **revised hierarchical model** (RHM) (Kroll et al., 2010).

Learning L2 Vocabulary

Research has shown that the difficulty of learning L2 vocabulary can be influenced by the similarity between the L1 and L2 words. Lotto and de Groot (1998) taught L2 vocabulary to participants who studied the L2-L1 word pairs and later were tested. They were provided with the L1 word and participants were asked to produce the appropriate L2 word. The similarity between the L1 and L2 words was varied. Half the items were typical translation equivalents that were not at all similar in spelling or pronunciation. The other half included cognates with a high degree of visual and phonological similarity. The results showed that performance differed for the two types of pairs, with pairs that were visually and phonologically similar being remembered better than pairs that were not.

For this study, use the German-English word pairs below to see how learning L2 vocabulary can be influenced by L1 and L2 word-level (or lexical) similarity. The items below are presented as a group of regular translation equivalents and a group of cognates. More German-English translation equivalents can be obtained from the similarity norms in Friel and Kennison (2001). Recruit up to 10 participants whose L1 is English and who have no prior experience learning German. Create a random order of the word pairs and ask participants to study the list until they feel that they *know* the new L2 words. Prepare three response sheets with the numbers 1–20 and a random ordering of the English word followed by a dash and a space where participants can write the German translation equivalent (e.g., Juice – _____). For each participant, you may provide them three attempts to study the list for up to three minutes and then test. If participants fail to answer all the items correctly on the first attempt, which is very likely, allow a second study session of three minutes followed again by a test. Again, if some items are answered incorrectly, allow participants a final attempt to study the list for three minutes and try the test. You can then calculate the percent correct for translation equivalents and cognates for each participant and overall across the 10 participants.

Translation equivalents		Cognates	
1. Tasse – cup	9. Senf – mustard	17. Butter – butter	25. Insekt – insect
2. Zimmer – room	10. Haut – skin	18. Idee – idea	26. Nummer – number
3. Holz – wood	11. Saft – juice	19. Salat – salad	27. Kaffee – coffee
4. Fenster – window	12. Bein – leg	20. Radio – radio	28. Fisch – fish
5. Pferd – horse	13. Zorn – anger	21. Tiger – tiger	29. Sturm – storm
6. Mantel – coat	14. Kopf – head	22. Korn – corn	30. Haus – house
7. Vogel – bird	15. Spiel – game	23. Werk – work	31. Nest – nest
8. Hemd – shirt	16. Zug – train	24. Braun – brown	32. Wurm – worm

In the RHM, general knowledge was viewed as not being language specific, but connected to the lexical representations stored in memory for L1 and L2. In the model, the memory representations for L1 and L2 vocabulary are separate. The strength of the memory links between knowledge and words differs for L1 and L2. L1 lexical memory representations are more strongly linked to conceptual knowledge than L2 lexical memory representations. The link between L2 lexical representations and knowledge starts out as weak when L2 acquisition begins and becomes stronger over time as the bilingual becomes more skilled in L2. Lastly, the strength of the memory links between L1 and L2 words depends on whether one is given L1 and asked to produce L2 or vice versa. L2 lexical memories are believed to be more strongly linked to L1 lexical memories than vice versa, presumably because acquiring L2 frequently involves the bilingual generating L1 words when L2 words are presented in a classroom setting or other circumstances.

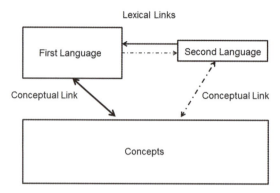

Figure 10.1 The Revised Hierarchical Model (RHM) of Bilingual Memory explains why translating from L2 to L1 is faster than L1 to L2. Do you think some types of words would be easier to translate than others? Credit: Reprinted with permission from Springer Nature, *Journal of Memory & Cognition.* 'Matching words to concepts in two languages: A test of the concept mediation model of bilingual representation' by Dufour, R and Kroll, J. F. (©) 1995.

The notion that memory links differ in strength in bilinguals and increase in strength over time led Bowers and Kennison (2011) to test the hypothesis that the strength of memory links between L1 and L2 words would be influenced by the age of acquisition. In a study with Spanish-English bilinguals, they compared performance in the bilingual translation task for words learned early in childhood (age four or younger) and words learned later in childhood (after age eight). The results showed that for words learned early in childhood, participants translated L2 to L1 faster than L1 to L2. For words learned later in childhood, the direction of translation did not influence response times. They concluded that bilinguals' memory links between L2 and L1 translation equivalents are stronger for those concepts learned very early versus later in childhood.

Criticism of the RHM has come from researchers who view the memory for a bilingual's two languages as being more integrated than in the RHM (Brysbaert & Duyck, 2010; Dijkstra & van Heuven, 2002; Lam & Dijkstra, 2010). An alternative model is the interaction activation plus model (Dijkstra & van Heuven, 2002). Support for this alternative model has come from experiments of visual word perception. You likely recall the neighborhood effect from previous chapters. The time taken to perceive a word is shorter when the word is similar in form to many other words. In experiments with Dutch-English bilinguals, the time taken to perceive an English word is influenced not only by the number of words having a similar form in English, but also by the number of words having a similar form in Dutch (Lam & Dijkstra, 2010; see also Andrews, 1989; Grainger & Segui, 1990; Grainger et al., 1989).

The view that, during language processing, bilingual individuals activate words from both languages may provide insight into the differences observed in prevalence of tip-of-the-tongue (ToT) states for bilingual and monolingual speakers. As you may recall from Chapter 4, research has shown that bilingual speakers experience ToT states more often than monolinguals (Gollan & Acenas, 2004; Gollan & Silverberg, 2001). A study by Gollan et al. (2014) suggests that the increased rate of ToT for bilingual speakers is because during the planning of speech, there is activation of both languages. They tested English-Spanish bilinguals (for whom English was the dominant language) in a task in which they were presented with three semantically or phonologically related words in Spanish and asked to generate a Spanish word that was semantically or phonologically related to the other three. Then they were shown a line drawing and asked to name the object in English. On half the trials, the object's name in Spanish was in the preceding set of three words. The results showed that participants experienced more ToTs when naming the line drawing on trials in which the translation equivalent in Spanish had been experienced. Gollan et al. (2014) conclude that the dual activation of a bilingual's two languages during the naming of the line drawing increased the likelihood of a ToT.

Future research might learn how a bilingual's two languages are activated during processing tasks and whether languages might be activated at different levels in some contexts compared to others. Individual differences in L1 and L2 knowledge and level of proficiency are likely to be related to the activation of both languages during processing. An interesting question is whether both languages are always activated or whether one can be completely inhibited. Thus far, there is no evidence that complete inhibition of a language occurs due to the desire of the individual, the characteristics of a task, or the setting in which a task occurs.

Code-switching

Bilinguals sometimes produce sentences containing words or phrases from both languages, described as code-switching (Poplack, 1980). Chapter 9 examined the term in the context of speakers of multiple dialects of a language in the USA, who use the standard English dialect when at school or work and use a non-standard, lower status dialect when with friends and family (Gumperz & Hymes, 1986). Those who know more than one language may switch between languages within the same conversation as well as within a single utterance (Gumperz, 1971, 1976). Some examples of Spanish sentences containing code-switching in English are provided in 1.

1 a. Leo un magazine.   I read a magazine.
   b. Me iban a lay off.   They were laying me off.

There are several possible reasons why bilingual speakers mix their languages when they speak. The most frequent explanation is that a speaker may experience difficulty finding a word or ToT in the language in which they are speaking and they are able to find the translation equivalent in their other language (Heredia & Altarriba, 2001). It is also possible that code-switched utterances are fulfilling a pragmatic function, having a slightly different intended meaning than the same sentence produced without code-switching. Gumperz (1976) pointed out that the frequency of code-switching among bilingual speakers depends on the social situation (e.g., school, home, church, or work) and the social status of those in the group. Anecdotes from my Spanish-English bilingual students suggest that code-switching is most common when they are speaking to their peers in informal settings and least common in formal settings (e.g., church or work) when they are speaking to higher status people (e.g., family elders or work supervisors).

Bilingual speakers have also been observed using code-switching more often when in discussions involving strong emotions. For example, in counseling sessions, bilingual clients have been observed switching to their L2 to discuss life events or topics with disturbing or embarassing content (Bond & Lai, 1986; Santiago-Rivera & Altarriba, 2002). Santiago-Rivera and Altarriba (2002) proposed that by switching to L2, bilinguals are able to distance themselves from the emotional content of the utterance. They speculated that L1 may have stronger and broader connections to emotional concepts in memory. Further, they suggested that bilinguals' memory for a particular life event may be associated more strongly in memory with the language used during that event (see also Javier, 1996; Rubin et al., 2007). In a recent study with bilingual therapists, Santiago-Rivera and colleagues found that the therapists reported that their bilingual clients used L1 when discussing emotional topics, but switched to L2 when appearing to want distance from the topic (Santiago-Rivera et al., 2009). The therapists reported that their own switching between L1 and L2 was related to attempts to direct clients in their discussion of the topic.

Linguistic analyses of samples of sentences and discourses containing code-switching have revealed that there are syntactic constraints on what words and phrases from one langage are substituted into the utterance of the other language. After examining numerous examples of code-switching across many combinations of speakers, no cases were found in which a bilingual speaker produced a multi-morpheme word in which the morphemes were from different languages. The fact that free morphemes can be code-switched but bound morphemes cannot is referred to as the "free morpheme constraint" (Poplack, 1981). Other examples showing that bilinguals are constrained by syntactic structure when code-switching include noun phrases composed of adjective-noun combinations (Lederberg & Morales, 1985). Languages vary in whether adjectives preceed or follow the nouns they modify. In English, adjectives preceed nouns, but in Spanish, adjectives follow nouns. Lederberg and Morales (1985) showed that when Spanish-English bilinguals code-switch, the placement of the adjective depends on which language is used to produce the adjective. In utterances in which a Spanish adjective is used, it follows the noun (*I want a tomato verde*). In utterances in which an English adjective is used, it preceeds the noun (*Quiero un green tomate*). Using different adjective placements results in code-switched sentences that are considered ungrammatical (**I want a verde tomato* and **Quiero un tomate green*).

In populations with a high percentage of bilinguals, a great many utterances contain elements of the two languages. Over time, the population may use the two languages separately less and less and come to use the two languages intermixed most of the time. This results in a **mixed language** (Bakker & Mous, 1994; Meakins, 2013). An example of a mixed language is Mednyj Aleut, which is spoken in Bering Island in the Bering Sea. This almost extinct language involves the mixing of Aleut and Russian (Bakker & Mous, 1994). Russian verb endings are used on verb stems from Aleut. A second example is Tanglish, a fusion of Tamil and English, used in Tamil Nadu, a state in south India (Cole, 2014). Some have suggested that there is a mixed language spoken in southwestern USA. It is a fusion of English and Spanish referred to as "Spanglish" (Ardila, 2005).

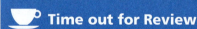

Time out for Review

Key Terms

Bilingual translation task	Language transfer	Positive language transfer
Cognates	Mixed language	Revised hierarchical model
False cognates/false friends	Negative language transfer	Translation equivalents

Review Questions

1 What is positive language transfer? Provide two examples.
2 What is negative language transfer? Provide two examples.
3 How does the revised hierarchical model describe how bilingual memory changes over time as bilinguals become more proficient in L2?
4 To what extent do bilinguals activate both of their languages during visual word perception?
5 What is code-switching? What does the research suggest about why bilinguals code-switch during speaking?

Summary

Bilingualism is common around the world; however, the percentage of bilinguals in a population can vary widely from country to country. There are different types of bilinguals: simultaneous bilinguals who learn multiple languages from birth; and sequential bilinguals who learn one language and then another. A relatively small percentage of people demonstrate the remarkable ability to learn three or more languages, often acquiring some of these as an adult. They seem to contradict the critical period hypothesis, which claims that there is a window of development during childhood in which language learning occurs optimally and after that window closes, language learning is more difficult and will fail to progress to the highest levels of mastery. Evidence for and against the critical period hypothesis has been observed. It remains unclear what evidence would be viewed as sufficient to refute it. Over the past 30 years, research on bilingualism has shown that children who learn two languages from birth reach the language development milestones in step with their monolingual peers. There is some research that suggests that bilingual children may have somewhat smaller vocabularies. Nevertheless, both bilingual children and adults may experience a cognitive advantage leading to enhanced performance on mental processing tasks as compared with monolingual control groups.

Recommended Books, Films, and Websites

Altarriba, J. & Heredia, R. R. (Eds.) (2008). *Introduction to Bilingualism: Principles and Processes*. New York: Psychology Press.

Cook, V. & Bassetti, B. (2010). *Language and Bilingual Cognition*. Hove: Psychology Press.

Erard, M. (2012). *Babel No More: The Search for the World's Most Extraordinary Language Learners*. New York: Free Press.

Grosjean, F. & Li, P. (2013). *The Psycholinguistics of Bilingualism*. Chichester: Wiley-Blackwell.

Köpke, B., Schmid, M. S., Keijzer, M. & Dostert, S. (eds) (2007). *Language Attrition: Theoretical Perspectives*. Amsterdam: John Benjamins.

Kroll, J. & de Groot, A. (2009). *Handbook of Bilingualism*. Oxford: Oxford University Press.

Live Linga Project. www.livelingua.com.

Villeneuve, D. (2016). *Arrival* [Motion Picture]. United States: Paramount.

11 HOW DO WE BECOME SKILLED READERS AND WRITERS?

Chapter Content

Photo 11.1 Bookmobile programs around the USA increase reading by increasing access to books. Does your town have a bookmobile program?

Educators believe that children who are able to find reading pleasurable will become lifelong readers and experience many of the positive outcomes predicted for highly skilled readers, such as academic success and economic prosperity (McKinsey & Co., n.d.). Many of us have fond memories of reading our favorite books during childhood. Do you recall any of the books you enjoyed reading as a child?

In this chapter, we will review what is known about how people acquire reading and writing skills. Most people learn to read and to write as children; thus, we discuss the educational practices used in the classroom as well as those that often occur between parents and children before the children begin formal education. We also discuss the link between learning to write and learning to read. In the second section, we focus on the factors that have been identified as predicting which children will become proficient readers and which children will struggle in reading. In the last section, we learn about reading research that has utilized eye movement recording technology to investigate the work of the eyes during reading and the resulting formal models of eye movement control.

The Development of Reading

Many children are likely to be introduced to reading before they enter formal educational settings. These children start out being read to by parents or other caregivers. Many parents begin this routine with their children between the first and second years. During this period, the child is progressing from producing single words to multiple word utterances. They are also developing better motor skills, which they would need to handle small books and turn pages. The child's ability to sit in one place for an extended time and to focus attention may also influence how easy it is for parents to read with their child. Although reading during the toddler years is increasingly common in industrialized countries where families have access to affordable books, in other parts of the world, there is a lot of variability in how children are first introduced to reading. In this section, we will discuss the latest science and opinion regarding when children learn to read, how reading develops, how reading should be taught, and how learning to write is related to learning to read.

Learning to Read: A Global Perspective

In many places around the world, including low-income homes in the USA and other industrialized countries, children receive very little exposure to books and/or reading at home. Their first experience with reading may not occur until after the age of five or older when they first attend school. In school settings, children may find reading to be more purposeful and stressful, as required reading in school tends to be accompanied by assignments that are graded. The different ways in which reading is introduced to children, either at home in a relaxed, playful setting with parents or at school in a classroom in which the child is graded and whose grades are compared with classmates, are likely to set the tone for the child's future relationship with reading. Those learning to read early in life with parents may be more likely to view reading as an activity carried out for pleasure as well as purpose.

The age at which children are introduced to reading in school varies across countries (Zhang & McBride-Chang, 2014). Some of the variation is likely to be cultural, reflecting differences in attitudes about development, childhood, and work. In the USA and the UK, children are introduced to reading by the age of five, sometimes earlier. In Hong Kong, children begin formally learning to read around age three and a half. In Sweden, children do not begin their reading lessons until around age seven. The cultural attitude is one that views children as needing to master a great deal and beginning sooner rather than later in childhood can only be good. In contrast, in other countries, parents and teachers take a less hurried approach to education. For example, children in France and Japan are around six years old when they begin learning to read. Within countries, there are likely to be differences in when reading is first introduced to children. As there are many different types of schools (public, private, religious, accelerated, etc.), there is likely to be wide variation in children's experiences.

Educators recognize that when children enter their first classroom, they can vary a great deal in how they adjust to the new type of environment and how they perform in mastering the initial tasks that serve as precursors to learning to read, such as following instructions as well as learning the alphabet. Increasingly, teachers and parents are aware that, ideally, children are at an advantage if they have acquired some skills before they receive formal reading instructions. This preparation is referred to as **reading readiness**. Parents of children entering preschool or kindergarten are likely to hear this term during the first few weeks of school as the teachers assess the different ability levels of the children in their class. The US Congress convened a panel of reading development and language experts to review existing research, summarize the findings, and provide recommendations for educators and families for promoting child literacy (National Early Literacy Panel, 2008). The panel identified six skills associated with reading readiness in children younger than five and predictive of future reading performance. These skills are listed in Table 11.1.

Table 11.1 Six Reading Readiness Skills for Children under Five

Skill	Description
Knowledge of alphabet	Can name letters and produce the sounds of letters
Awareness of phonemes	Can pick out and manipulate the sounds and syllables represented in words and parts of words
Rapid naming of numbers and letters	Can name random sequences of numbers and letters quickly
Rapid naming of objects	Can name random sequences of familiar objects or concepts (e.g., colors) when shown as pictures
Writing letters	Can write individual letters when asked and also write the letters in their name
Memory for spoken language	Shows the ability to store and retrieve the speech of others over a short period of time

Source: National Early Literacy Panel (2008)

Parents and caregivers who focus a great deal on teaching the two- or three-year-old child to recognize written words are likely to be placing excess pressure on their toddler for no proven future benefit. The best advice is to let children pick up reading words when they are ready through one-on-one interactions with books assisted by parents and caregivers. Some of the typical recommended activities for parents to introduce to their children younger than three years include handling books during daily routines, talking about the pictures in the books, pretending to read books, beginning to draw and scribble, and gradually paying more and more attention to the printed letters in the book and their connection to the sounds of the words that refer to the characters in the story (DeBruin-Parecki et al., 2000). If you visit the infant section of a department store, you will find waterproof books that infants can play with while taking a bath. Surrounding infants and toddlers with lots of books with colorful covers is the best way to ensure that they will see books and reading as an ordinary part of daily life. By having very young children interact with books and other written materials, you can help them take the first steps toward appreciating the fact that writing is a form of communication, known as **print awareness** (Armbruster et al., 2003). Once young children begin to understand the role of print for communication, they may begin noticing print on objects in the environment, such as food packaging, television, and signs in shopping areas.

Photo 11.2 Children under three years benefit from becoming familiar with books as part of their daily routines. Have you seen the waterproof books that are available for infants to handle during their baths?

Some children may begin reading when they are still quite young and before they enter preschool or kindergarten. It is important to note that there are no documented benefits associated with reading at such young ages, and that children younger than three are not developmentally ready for independent reading (Rayner et al., 2012). A small percentage of very young children appear to develop reading skills without much involvement or encouragement from their parents. To their parents' surprise, they appear to be able to read at a level of a much older child. Some cases are likely to leave parents and family members with the impression that the child is showing early signs of genius-level ability. However, this is not usually the case. Children with exceptional early reading ability are often described as having **hyperlexia**. They typically have IQs that are in the normal range. Some may be above average. Some hyperlexic children tend to be focused on reading words aloud, yet they have poor comprehension for what they read (Frith & Snowling, 1983; Healy, 1982; Snowling & Frith, 1986). Some are also found to have difficulties using language generally and understanding the speech of others. Recent investigations suggest that children with hyperlexia are also likely to be diagnosed with autism spectrum disorder and have trouble with social interactions (Grigorenko et al., 2003; Treffert, 2011). Not every child who exhibits early reading skills will have hyperlexia, but early reading should be viewed by parents and caregivers as a possible early symptom of autism spectrum disorder. Early reading, when it occurs, should be brought to the attention of the child's pediatrician during one of the many check-ups toddlers receive.

Stages of Learning to Read

The 20th century produced numerous scholars of reading development whose work provided useful insights into reading development and the value of reading throughout the lifespan. For example, Jeanne Chall (1921–99) was a prominent Polish-American scholar and expert on reading development who was a professor at Harvard's School of Education from 1965 to 1991, when she retired. She moved to New York with her family at the age of seven knowing only Yiddish. She received all her education in the USA, including a college degree from the City College of New York and a master's and PhD from Ohio State University. Among her family, she was the first to attend college. Friends knew that as a child, she helped her parents learn English well enough to study for their citizenship tests (Institute for Multisensory Education, 2015). She conducted empirical research on the aspects of texts that made them harder or easier to understand (also referred to as "readability") and collaborated on a method for predicting readability (Chall & Dale, 1995; Dale & Chall, 1948). She authored numerous research articles and books. She memorably pointed out that children's reading can be broadly categorized into learning to read, reading to learn, and reading independently (Chall, [1983] 1996). Table 11.2 summarizes Chall's six stages of reading development. As you can see, Chall includes the entire lifespan, rather than limiting the stages to childhood. As we will discuss later in this chapter, Chall was also a prominent figure in the 20th-century debate regarding the best method for teaching reading.

A second prominent American scholar is Linnea Ehri, a professor at the Graduate Center of the City University of New York. Her research has resulted in numerous books and research articles providing insight into how children learn to read words. Among her many contributions to the field is her description of the four stages of learning to read words (Ehri, 1999, 2002, 2005). These are:

1 *Pre-alphabetic phase*, in which children recognize words as whole visual objects.
2 *Partial alphabetic reading phase*, in which children recognize some letters and use them along with other cues to identify words.

Table 11.2 Chall's Six Stages of Reading Development

Stage	Approximate ages	Skills
0 Pre-reading	6 months to preschool	Plays with books and pencils
1 Initial reading/decoding	6–7 years (1st and 2nd grade)	Begins sounding out letters and words
2 Confirmation and fluency	7–8 years (2nd and 3rd grade)	Reading simple, familiar stories
3 Reading to learn	9–13 years (4th to 9th grade)	Reading for acquiring knowledge
4 Multiple viewpoints	15–17 years (10th to 12th grade)	Reading for understanding complex issues
5 Construction-reconstruction	18 years and up	Reading to meet personal and professional needs

Source: Chall ([1983] 1996)

3 *Full alphabetic phase*, in which children compute the sounds of words from their letters, even for words that are unfamiliar.
4 *Consolidated alphabetic phase*, in which readers recognize groups of letters that occur across many words.

It is important to note that she was not the first to point out the importance of learning to identify the phonological correspondence to alphabetic letters (see also Frith, 1985; Gough & Hillinger, 1980). Ehri's (1998, 2002) theory further claims that the phonological representation of a word functions as a critical link between a word's written form and our memory for the word's meaning. She has also pointed out that the ability of skilled readers' ability to recognize so many words (hundreds of thousands of words or more for the 18-year-old English speaker) as rapidly as is common is an amazing feat of memory. The key to our incredible capacity for learning new words and recognizing their written forms appears to be how our minds link phonology, orthography, and memory for word meaning.

An important question that you may be mulling over at this point is whether these stages of learning to read words only apply to languages written in alphabetic scripts, such as English. Is it possible that these stages also apply to all languages, regardless of the type of writing system used? A reasonable assumption would be that learning to read words in a logographic writing system would not involve any alphabetic level of analysis at all. Logographic symbols do not contain information about how the word is pronounced. How can the alphabetic approach be used? However, sometimes our intuition leads us to incorrect assumptions. It is true that learning to read languages that use a logographic writing system, such as Chinese, involves committing to memory thousands of symbols, each representing a word; however, when children (and second language learners) begin learning to read logographic languages, they typically begin using an alphabetic form of writing. After the alphabetic form of writing is mastered, then children progress to learning the logographic symbols.

Beginning readers of Mandarin are first taught the phonologically transparent writing system called **pinyin** (Cheung & Ng, 2003). Pinyin is written in Roman script with a shallow orthography. As you likely recall from Chapter 5, a shallow orthography provides the reader with straightforward cues to the pronunciation of words. Other languages in which there are logographic symbols also use a phonologically transparent writing system to teach children and second language learners to read the language. For example, Japanese is written using a mixed writing system, involving both logographic symbols and a phonologically transparent alphabet. The logographic symbols are referred to as kanji. Kanji symbols were historically those borrowed from Chinese. When Japanese children learn kanji characters, they are provided with the pronunciation of the character written in an alphabet called **furigana**. Teaching children to read a more phonologically transparent version of writing than is used by adults also occurs for languages that use alphabetic scripts. For example, some alphabetic languages, such as Arabic and Hebrew, are written in consonantal scripts, which represent only a subset of the phonemes in a word. In the Language Spotlight box, we take a look at how children around the world learn to read Arabic.

Chinese children learn to read and write pinyin in the first and second grades of elementary school. The logographic Chinese characters are introduced after children become proficient in pinyin, which typically occurs by the second or third grade. Around this time, their task is to learn to recognize the 3,000 or so core symbols that are regarded as necessary for basic proficiency in Chinese (McBride & Wang, 2015). Research has shown that Chinese children's learning of pinyin increases their **phonological awareness** (Cheung et al., 2001; Siok & Fletcher, 2001), which is the understanding that the reader has about sounds of letters and words and the phonological structure of the language. Longitudinal research also shows that children who excel at using pinyin also do well reading regular Chinese characters when tested 12 months later (Lin et al., 2010). As children's expertise in associating Chinese symbols with their meanings and pronunciations, they also come to appreciate subtle consistencies in meaning represented in the visual symbols. In Chapter 5, we also discussed the fact that Chinese symbols are composed of meaningful parts, known as radicals. The highly skilled reading of Chinese is likely to possess both phonological and morphological awareness and use them during word reading specifically and reading comprehension generally.

Methods of Reading Instruction

The debate about the most effective way to teach children to read English is intense and ongoing. Despite numerous studies into the effectiveness of different methods of reading instruction, there is no clear consensus identifying the best method (National Reading Panel, 2000; see also MacGuinness, 2004). In the USA, Congress called on a panel of leading experts, including Linnea Ehri whose research we discussed earlier in this chapter, to review the existing scientific literature and report their findings. The National Reading Panel's (2000) report concluded that too few scientifically rigorous studies had been conducted, and its sole recommendation was that any method of reading instruction that was used should include a component in which students are trained in the spelling-to-sound regularities in language or **phonics**.

Reading methods that explicitly teach children about the spelling-to-sound rules of language use the **phonics method**. Activities and assignments require children

Learning to Read Arabic

Arabic is typically written in a consonantal script, in which only consonants and long vowels are represented. However, there is a way of writing Arabic that shows the short vowels, represented as diacritic marks, which are referred to as ḥarakāt (vowel marks). You may see the two types of Arabic writing referred to as *unvoweled* and *voweled*, as well as *unpointed* and *pointed*. For those learning to read Arabic, ḥarakāt is learned first. The Qur'an is written using ḥarakāt, as are children's books and books for those learning Arabic as a second language. Figure 11.1 shows a sentence written in Arabic with and without the diacritics for the short vowels.

Figure 11.1 Examples of Written Arabic

إذا الشعب يوما أراد الحياة فلابد ان يستجيب القدر

إذا الشَّعْبُ يَوْماً أَرَادَ الْحَيَاةَ فَلا بُدَّ أَنْ يَسْتَجِيبَ الْقَدَر

**If people want to live desirously
fate complies with them willingly.**

The two sentences mean the same thing. The first one is written in the typical manner in Arabic, without the short vowels. The second is written in ḥarakāt, with the short vowels represented. Do you notice the additional diacritic marks?

Becoming a proficient reader in Arabic involves being able to read without having any short vowels explicitly represented in words. However, it is not the case that the short vowels are completely irrelevant to figuring out the meaning of words in a sentence. If they were, there would be no need for beginning readers to start out with ḥarakāt. Skilled readers of Arabic say that when the short vowels are missing, there is much ambiguity. Readers use the context and guesswork to determine which of the possible words the author intended. There are instances in which the context does not provide enough information for the short vowels in the word to be inferred. Similar diacritic marks – referred to as **niqqud** – are optional in the writing of Hebrew, which is also written in a consonantal script.

to identify the sounds of letters and words. Many children's games and nursery rhymes serve to promote phonological awareness. For example, children in the USA often discover Pig Latin, which is a playful way to transform words to obscure their meaning from others. The first sound of each word is moved to the end of the word and then *ay* is added to the end of the word. The Pig Latin version of *College quizzes frighten students* is *ollegecay izzesquay ightenfray udentsstay*. Table 11.3 lists some commonly used tasks to assess the phonological awareness of children.

Table 11.3 Sample Tasks to Assess Children's Phonological Awareness

Question	Possible answer
1 Can you name all the sounds that are in the word *dog*?	/d/ /o/ /g/
2 Can you think of three words that begin with the *s* sound?	see, sing, sit
3 Can you name a word that rhymes with *bat*?	cat
4 Can you pick out the two words in the list that rhyme – blue, mark, hat, glue?	blue, glue
5 Listen to me as I say three words. Two of the words start with the same sound. One word starts with a different sound. Can you tell me the word that starts with the different sound? The words are *lion, mouse,* and *lizard*.	mouse
6 What is the word created when you switch the first sound in the word *bat* with /s/?	sat
7 What would you say if you said the word *hotdog*, but didn't say *dog*?	hot
8 What would you say if you said the word *bedroom*, but you didn't say *bed*?	room
9 What would you say if you said the word *spot*, but you didn't say the /s/?	pot
10 What would you say if you said the word *slip*, but you didn't say the /l/?	sip

Source: Gillon (2012)

The primary alternative to phonics is the **whole language method**, in which instructors place an emphasis on making reading a pleasurable experience and motivating students to spend more time reading (Center for Expansion of Language and Thinking, n.d.; Rayner et al., 2001). The approach has been described as embracing the philosophy of constructivism, as children are believed to construct their knowledge through direct experience. The approach has its roots in the work of Jean Piaget (1967). Students are encouraged to learn new words by reading by sight, rather than sounding out words. The construction of meaning is valued more than the identification of individual words. In classrooms, students may participate in guided reading groups in which material may be read aloud or read by students independently. The teacher can monitor the group's progress and comprehension through individual and/or group discussions of the material being read. Critics of the whole language approach point out that there is a lack of scientific evidence showing that it produces sustained reading proficiency (Hattie, 2009; Moats, 2007). Faust and Kandelshine-Waldman (2011) showed that the benefits of the whole language approach on children's alphabetic skills did not persist beyond third grade.

In my conversations with college students whose schools used the whole language approach, students report rarely using a dictionary to look up the meanings of unfamiliar words; rather, they were taught to guess the meaning from the surrounding context. Similarly, they were never taught about the usefulness of using information about root words to identify connections among words with similar meaning (e.g., root: *duct* meaning to lead or to lead to – *induction, seduction, abduction*, and *production*). Many of these students with interests in attending graduate programs have taken the major standardized test (the Graduate Record Examination, GRE) and have performed lower than they expected on the verbal reasoning section. The questions on the exam require readers to be able to make judgments about some of the most subtle aspects of word meanings. One student remarked after taking the GRE: "I recognized some of the words from the books I have read." I replied: "That's great. You probably got those questions right, since you knew what the words meant?" She said: "No, I recognized them from before, but I never knew what they meant." I must have looked confused, as she explained: "We never had to look up words in a dictionary in school. We were told to use the sentence context to figure out the meaning of the words. So, the meanings just didn't stick with me."

The debate about the best way to teach reading (phonics or whole language) is ongoing, with advocates of each approach sticking to their preferred methods. One benefit of the National Reading Panel's (2000) report is that it raised awareness among educators and parents that the best reading instruction should include phonics. Because curriculum decisions in the USA are usually controlled at the local level by boards of education, teachers themselves may have little or no input into which curriculum their students receive. Teachers may be able to supplement the curriculum with beneficial activities; so teachers in districts in which whole language curriculum is adopted may be able to provide their students with instruction in phonics. Parents should not assume that their child is receiving instruction in phonics in school, but should ask the teacher and/ or school administrators whether reading instruction includes phonics. If the answer is no, parents may wish to work on phonics with their child outside school hours.

Before we leave the topic of reading instruction, we should take note of the fact that the differences of opinion regarding the best way to teach children to read stems, at least in part, from differences in the educational training and philosophical perspectives of the experts. Many advocates of the whole language approach are typically those who have trained in early childhood education, elementary education and literacy (MacGuinness, 2004). Rarely do these experts have substantial coursework in linguistics, psycholinguistics or the broader interdisciplinary area, which aims to understand intelligence in people and in artificial forms (computer technology, robots, etc.). Consequently, college students majoring in education are not routinely exposed to these topics and the latest research advancing our understanding of language processing, particularly regarding the role of the brain in producing and comprehending language. Students in colleges of education have traditionally received training that emphasizes the social and motivational factors in learning. A major inspiration in this area has been the work of Lev Vygotsky ([1934] 1986), who emphasized the role of social processes in development. While the work and insights of Vygotsky were immensely valuable in shaping the 20th-century view of social aspects of learning, the role of biological factors in learning should not be overlooked.

Learning to Write

Children typically begin learning to write around the time they begin reading, and some researchers have suggested that developing writing skills can reinforce skills in reading and vice versa (Domico, 1993; Richgels, 1995). Traditionally, schools have taught handwriting (also called **penmanship**) starting in the first grade or possibly earlier. Physically, children must develop their fine motor skills in order to be able to manipulate crayons and pencils skillfully (Wilson, 2004). Activities that help children improve fine motor skills include using crayons, drawing, using scissors, picking up objects, and using spoons, knives, and forks. Educators have identified several stages in children's development of drawing and writing, beginning with scribbling starting around the age of 15 months, drawing patterns and lines by around 30 months, drawing objects including people by around 36 months, and printing letters also by around 36 months (Zero to Three, 2016). Until the last few decades, children in US schools progressed from learning to print to learning to write in cursive handwriting (also known as joined-up writing). Because cursive handwriting is no longer a requirement in US elementary schools (although several states are fighting to keep cursive on the curriculum), many adults write only using printed block letters, which tends to be slower than using cursive handwriting.

Learning to write is more than merely mastering the physical aspects of manipulating a pen or pencil. It also includes learning how to commit thoughts to paper in the form of correspondence (letters, emails) and narratives. Children's ability to formulate a narrative in speech likely precedes their mastering the writing down of narratives. Snow et al. (1999) described the literacy skills of preschool children in the USA from the age of three through third grade. Table 11.4 shows the typical abilities by age/grade.

Table 11.4 Literacy Abilities of Children in the USA from Preschool through Third Grade

Grade	Age	Skills
Preschool	3 years	Beginning of awareness that writing is a way of communicating
Early kindergarten	4 years	Beginning of writing letters and writing names
Kindergarten	5 years	Beginning to recognize familiar words in print Understanding stories (long and short) that others read aloud
First grade	6 years	Writing for different purposes begins (e.g., lists, stories, correspondence) Narrative structures develop (e.g., *Once upon a time …*)
Second grade	7 years	Increased time reading independently Increased awareness of comprehension strategies Beginning of writing book reports and other formal essays
Third grade and up	8 years and up	Continued development of comprehension strategies Increased awareness of grammatical structure of words and sentences Continued reading and writing over increasing number of subject areas

Source: Snow et al. (1999)

Some children experience more difficulty learning to produce legible handwriting than others. Children with attention deficit hyperactive disorder (ADHD) have been found to write less clearly than other children and to have more error-filled handwriting (Kaisera et al., 2015). Their letter construction and spacing between letters often differ from those of their peers. They also make more errors in spelling, involving the leaving out of letters or inappropriate insertion of letters into words. There is often more correcting of their writing than is observed in children without ADHD.

Children begin with simple descriptions of routines, also called scripts, such as going to the park, eating lunch, and bath time (Hedberg & Westby, 1993). Later, their descriptions focus on events placed in a particular timeframe, occurring in the past, present or future. Later still, they are able to create stories of fiction, which include descriptions of events they understand are not real. As children progress through these stages, their ability to engage in abstract thought and understand the minds of others also improves. Hedberg and Stoel-Gammon (1986) have shown that children as young as two refer to past events, but their descriptions of those events are rudimentary, containing a series of loosely connected statements. Children as young as three begin constructing stories with a clear topic, which might be a character, place, or event. By the age of six, most children are creating adult-like stories in that they have a place, a goal, and one or more characters (Shapiro & Hudson, 1991). Kemper and Edwards (1986) point out that the stories told by young children tend not to contain many descriptions of mental states, but reference to mental states in children's stories increases with the children's age. Some researchers have claimed that individual differences in children's narrative abilities are correlated with their cognitive ability (Applebee, 1978) and can be helpful in predicting future academic achievement (Bishop & Edmundson, 1987) and language ability (Botting, 2002).

In this section, we reviewed how children around the world learn to read, the basic stages of reading development, and research on the best method for teaching children to read. We learned that the sounds of words play a critical role in children learning to read, even when they are learning to read logographic languages, such as Chinese. Children learning to read Chinese are first taught to recognize words written in pinyin, an alphabetic writing system that is a phonologically transparent system. Children learning to read Japanese logographic symbols are also initially taught to read the words written alphabetically. Children learning to read Arabic or Hebrew, which are languages that are typically written with some vowels omitted (i.e., in consonantal writing systems), begin learning to read words with all the phonemes represented. In English-speaking countries, there has been an ongoing vigorous debate about the best method for teaching children to read. Despite the many years of research comparing the effectiveness of different methods to teach reading, there is no consensus about which method is the most effective. The two competing methods are the whole language approach and phonics. The US Congress enlisted the National Reading Panel to investigate the methods used to teach reading and they concluded that reading instruction should include explicit coverage of phonics. As preschoolers become aware of print and letters, they begin learning to write. The development of writing, like the development of reading, continues throughout the elementary years and beyond.

Key Terms

Furigana	Penmanship	Pinyin
Ḥarakāt	Phonics	Print awareness
Hyperlexia	Phonics method	Reading readiness
Niqqud	Phonological awareness	Whole language method

Review Questions

1　What are the six stages of reading development proposed by Jeanne Chall?
2　What are the four stages of learning to read words proposed by Linnea Ehri?
3　What is pinyin? How is it involved in the development of reading?
4　Discuss the characteristics of written Arabic that make learning to read somewhat challenging.
5　What is phonological awareness? What does the research suggest about its role in children becoming skilled readers?
6　What are the advantages and disadvantages of the whole language method of reading instruction?
7　What did the National Reading Panel conclude regarding how best to teach children to read?

Measuring and Predicting Reading Proficiency

Educators and researchers have investigated ways of predicting reading proficiency for children because of the bleak, long-term outcomes associated with failing to become a skilled reader. These outcomes include a higher risk of dropping out of high school, unemployment, homelessness, and incarceration (Literacy Project Foundation, 2016). In this section, you will learn about how educators and researchers measure reading proficiency and what research has shown about the numerous factors that predict reading proficiency in children.

By identifying the factors associated with below average reading proficiency, policy makers and educators may be in a position to take steps to increase reading skills in children and in adults. Such interventions are most easily carried out with children while they are still in elementary or secondary schooling. The typical ways in which children's reading proficiency is measured are listed here (Wren and Litke, 2006):

- Print awareness
- Letter knowledge
- Phonemic awareness
- Vocabulary knowledge
- Background knowledge
- Language comprehension

- Reading comprehension
- Linguistic knowledge – syntax, phonology, semantics.

Print awareness and letter knowledge are typically applicable only to children; however, for illiterate adults, these assessments would also be routine. Vocabulary knowledge and comprehension are routinely assessed in academic settings during regular instruction as well as through standardized examinations that are used to evaluate individual achievement and the quality of the educational setting. Predictors of lower reading proficiency fall into three categories: health problems during childhood, including whether they were born prematurely or full-term and whether they have normal vision; poverty, and genetics.

Health Problems during Childhood

When considering children's long-term reading proficiency, you may not immediately think of general health as an important factor. On further consideration, the notion that less healthy infants may differ from infants born in better health when compared on long-term developmental milestones and academic achievement seems not only plausible, but highly likely. Research supports the relationship between infant health and long-term achievement in reading. A growing number of studies have shown a link between premature and low birth weight babies and learning problems during childhood (Kovachy et al., 2015; Lee et al., 2011; Smith et al., 2014; Waber & McCormick, 1995). In the USA, approximately 500,000 infants are born premature each year (J. A. Martin et al., 2010). A contributing factor to this number is the prevalence of multiples (twins, triplets, etc.), who are rarely carried full term. In some cases, premature infants may be neurologically underdeveloped, which leads to delays in language development and/or reading-specific problems later in childhood.

Hearing and vision problems in childhood have also been found to be related to lower reading proficiency in children (McLachlan et al., 2012). Children who are deaf or who have some hearing impairment have a great deal of difficulty learning to read and achieving a high level of reading proficiency (Goldin-Meadow & Mayberry, 2001). We will examine the case of hearing impairment in depth in Chapter 13. Young children who struggle in the classroom are sometimes found to have vision problems (Thurston, 2014). The longer that vision problems go uncorrected with glasses or contact lenses, the farther behind their peers they lag in reading and other subjects in school. In many industrialized countries, vision screening typically occurs when children are in preschool (Mathers et al., 2010). However, the American Optometric Association (2016a) recommends that children undergo vision screening when they are just six months old and a second one by their third birthday. Children who have trouble seeing may sit close to the television or video game console, tilt or squint to try to see things better, complain of tired eyes, or rub their eyes a great deal. Common vision problems include near-sightedness (myopia), far-sightedness, astigmatism, and crossed eyes (strabismus). Often, children's vision can be corrected with glasses, but in homes with many children, these vision problems can go unnoticed. In middle age, it is common for most adults to require some form of vision correction, as aging tends to cause people to become more far-sighted as they age (American Optometric Association, 2016b). Unfortunately, regular vision exams and glasses that correct the vision to normal or near normal (i.e., 20/20) are still an expensive luxury in many parts of the word (Vision Aid Overseas, n.d.).

Exposure to environmental toxins, such as lead, can cause health problems in children as well as permanent neurological damage. Exposure to lead has devastating consequences for children, including a long-term lowering of IQ and lower academic achievement than children who have not been exposed to lead (MaClain et al., 2013; Silva et al., 1988; Zhang et al., 2013). The dangers of lead exposure received international attention due to the lead contamination in the public water system in Flint, Michigan in the USA (Kennedy, 2016). Due to failures at the state and federal level to ensure that lead levels in public water were below the recommended trace amounts, approximately 100,000 residents of the city received dangerous levels of lead on a daily basis for at least 18 months. Forty percent of the city's majority African American population lives in poverty, leading some to suggest that classism and racism contributed to officials allowing the disaster to occur. It is not known what is in store for those children and adults who were exposed to lead. Studies have found that the level of lead in children's blood was above that considered safe (Hanna-Attisha et al., 2015). The advice to parents of children with high levels of lead in their blood is to spend extra time and effort at school, and to seek the help of school psychologists and/or counselors if problems with learning generally or reading specifically emerge.

Poverty

One of the strongest predictors of children's long-term language development, generally, and reading proficiency, specifically, is family income, with the poorest children having the worst long-term outcomes (McLachlan et al., 2012). The relationship between family income and children's reading proficiency may be influenced by differences in children's general language development. As you learned in Chapter 9, children from low-income families typically have poorer language development skills as compared to children from more affluent families (Hoff, 2003; Noble et al., 2005; Whitehurst, 1997). In addition, studies have found that children from low-income families read less well than other children (Baydar et al., 1993; Reardon, 2011; Reardon et al., 2013; White, 1982). The difference between rich and poor children's reading proficiency is much larger than the differences related to race or ethnicity (Reardon et al., 2013). Many factors may contribute to the relationship between reading proficiency and family income. Low-income families typically have fewer books in the home than higher income families (Levitt & Dubner, 2005). Children in poor families may be read to less often than other children, because parents have less time to spend with children outside paid employment or outside time spent in caretaking activities for other family members. It is important to remember that the link between family income and reading proficiency may stem from factors correlated with family income, such as parents' education level, family dynamics, and neighborhood characteristics (McLanahan, 2004; Murnane et al., 1995; Reardon & Bischoff, 2011; Schwartz & Mare, 2005) as well as the amount of time parents spend carrying out child-centered activities (Molfese & Molfese, 2002). Children from impoverished neighborhoods have been shown to be capable of excelling in reading when schools implement reading programs that involve children spending a lot of time reading both in and outside class and engaging parents in children's homework activities (Cunningham, 2006).

Over the past few decades, educators and researchers have been concerned that disadvantaged children who start school behind their more advantaged peers may never catch up in terms of reading ability. Stanovich (1986) used the term the **Matthew effect** to describe this state of affairs. The term refers to the phrase *the rich get richer and the poor get poorer*, which resembles two verses from Matthew's gospel in the Bible. Advantaged children start school with well-developed vocabularies, which helps with reading. The more time strong readers spend reading, the more words they learn and the better they get at reading. Although longitudinal research has found no statistical evidence for Matthew effects (Pfost et al., 2014), the concept is so intuitively appealing that it may take some time before the idea ceases to influence educators' approach to struggling readers.

The gap in reading proficiency between rich and poor students is likely to be influenced by the sheer difference in the amount that children read. Stanovich and Cunningham (1992, 1993) provided compelling evidence that a primary predictor of reading ability is their lifelong exposure to print. Their estimates of print exposure were obtained in questionnaires in which adults were asked to select authors' names from made-up names (Stephen King and Maya Angelou versus Alexander Marshall and Gloria Tinsley) and to select magazine titles from made-up titles (*Ladies' Home Journal* and *Outdoor Life* versus *Home Life Daily* and *Streams and Trees*). Studies have confirmed that those scoring higher on these measures reflecting exposure to print perform better on a range of reading-related tasks, including homophone spelling (Stanovich & West, 1989), verbal fluency (Stanovich & Cunningham, 1992), naming non-words (McBride-Chang et al., 1993), vocabulary size (Frijters et al., 2000), reading comprehension (Cipielewski & Stanovich, 1992), and time taken to judge words in a lexical decision task (Chateau & Jared, 2000). Because popular authors and magazines change over time, Acheson et al. (2008) updated the questionnaire, adding new author names, magazine names, and questions to assess frequency of daily reading. The Research DIY box enables you to explore the relationship between exposure to print and verbal ability.

Genetics

Perhaps the most surprising revelation about reading proficiency in this chapter is the fact that genetics has a role to play. Over the past few decades, many studies have linked children's reading problems to genetic factors. Dyslexia is a severe reading disorder, described as "a brain-based type of learning disability that specifically impairs a person's ability to read" (National Institute of Neurological Disorders and Stroke, n.d.). Prior to the most recent version of the *Diagnostic and Statistical Manual of Mental Disorders* (DSM-5), the traditional diagnostic criteria of dyslexia was that children with intelligence in the normal range (IQ between 70 and 120) and no known illness or injury that might cause cognitive problems have severe and persistent problems reading.

A child's risk of developing dyslexia has been shown to be related to whether other members in the child's family have dyslexia (Barr & Couto, 2007;

Research DIY

Does Exposure to Print Predict Verbal Fluency?

One of the most widely used tasks to assess individual differences in verbal ability is the verbal fluency task (Shao et al., 2014). Stanovich and West's (1989) tasks for measuring exposure to print are quick and easy to administer, making it possible to test the hypothesis that individuals with very high exposure to print would have higher verbal fluency than others. To test the hypothesis, recruit 10–20 participants. You may wish to recruit half from those you believe to have low exposure to print and half from those you believe to have high exposure to print. For example, you might recruit a young group and an older group, or a group with low interest in books and reading and compare them to a group with high interest in books and reading. For each participant, you should administer the same test of tasks in the same order. These are given below. For the verbal fluency tasks, you will need to time and record participants' responses. Voice recording applications/software are available on many cell phones or computers. You may also use a traditional handheld tape or digital recording device.

For each of the following, instruct the participant to name as many words of the type indicated as they can in one minute:

Verbal fluency task #1	Words beginning with the letter f.
Verbal fluency task #2	Words beginning with the letter a.
Verbal fluency task #3	Words that begin with the letter s.
Verbal fluency task #4	Words that are names for animals
Author recognition task	Circle all authors' names
Magazine recognition task	Circle all the magazine titles

Svensson et al., 2011). Dyslexia, at least in some cases, appears to be highly heritable (Grigorenko, 2001; Wadsworth et al., 2002). Genetic markers for dyslexia have been identified in studies (see Schumacher et al., 2007 for review). So far, nine genes have been associated with dyslexia. The genes are located on different chromosomes – 1, 2, 3, 4, 6, 11, 15, 17, and 18. These early results suggest that just as there is a great deal of variation in the symptoms of dyslexia, there may also be variation in the genetic origins of dyslexia.

The fact that some genes are related to dyslexia in children suggests that dyslexia would occur throughout the world, as humans are genetically highly similar. However, dyslexia tends to disrupt children's word recognition ability. Some have trouble applying the spelling-to-sound rules for their language and others have trouble recognizing words as whole words. You may recall learning about Coltheart's (1978) dual route model of word identification in Chapter 5. Recognizing words as wholes is useful in English in the case of irregularly spelled words (e.g., *choir, the, caught*). An interesting question is whether the rates of dyslexia around the world depend on what language children are trying to learn to read. When the language has relatively few irregularly spelled words, such as languages with very regular spelling systems or shallow orthographies, readers are unlikely to experience problems if they are unable to recognize words as wholes. In logographic languages, in which most words are recognized as whole words, readers are unlikely to experience problems if they are unable to implement the spelling-to-sound rules during word recognition. Studies of individuals with dyslexia who read languages with different writing scripts have shown that the reading problems are influenced by the characteristics of the writing script (McBride-Chang et al., 2011; Ziegler & Goswami, 2005).

The prevalence of dyslexia has been estimated in many industrialized countries, and the percentage of children diagnosed with dyslexia has been found to vary. Tarnopol and Tarnopol (1981) examined rates of dyslexia in 26 countries. The lowest incidence of dyslexia was observed in China and Japan, with the rate of about 1 percent. The rate of dyslexia for countries in which English is spoken was around 20 percent. The highest rate of dyslexia was observed in Venezuela, which had a rate of 33 percent. Other research from the 1980s found low rates of dyslexia in Germany and Scandinavia, with rates of about 5 percent and 10 percent, respectively (Glezerman, 1983, cited in Grigorenko, 2001). More recent research in the USA has found that estimates of the rate of dyslexia also vary from a low rate of 5 percent to a high rate of 17 percent (Shaywitz & Shaywitz, 2004). The incidence among girls and boys does not appear to differ. Goswami (2010) suggests that variations in rates of dyslexia around the world stem from differences across languages in terms of grapheme-to-phoneme correspondences.

A reasonable speculation regarding the role of genes in contributing to children developing dyslexia is that specific genetic variations are related to variations in the development of some brain regions. In the 1980s, comparisons of the brains of men with and without dyslexia occurring during childhood showed that there were differences in the sizes of some brain regions (Booth & Burman, 2001; Deutsch et al., 2005; Galaburda et al., 1985, 1996; Grigorenko, 2001). In the future, it may become possible to screen children for the biological markers of dyslexia through brain imaging or genetic testing.

Research has shown that some, but not all, children with reading problems have dyslexia. Ten percent of students who experience problems reading do not have dyslexia, but have persistent struggles with reading (Nation & Snowling, 1997; Yuill & Oakhill, 1991). Traditional diagnoses of dyslexia have come only after a child is delayed in their reading ability by two grades, such as when the child is in third grade, but reading at first grade level (Rayner et al., 2012). Poor readers may struggle with one or more aspects of reading, such as word meaning, syntax, and general comprehension. Individuals with dyslexia typically have specific problems decoding the meanings of words when perceiving written words. The eye movements of some individuals with dyslexia differ from those readers without dyslexia, stemming from abnormalities in certain pathways in the visual system (Stein, 2001). Readers with dyslexia skip words more often and make more backward saccades than readers without dyslexia. Thus far, investigations of eye movement patterns have not yielded a single eye movement pattern common across individuals with dyslexia (Stein & Kapoula, 2012). The next section examines the research on eye movements during reading.

If children fall behind their peers in reading, they may be referred for a formal assessment by a school psychologist. School psychologists receive extensive training in scientific methods, statistics, psychology, and learning in academic settings, as well as abnormal psychology and counseling techniques (Merrell et al., 2012). In the USA, the primary reference book for matching symptoms to possible diagnoses is the *Diagnostic and Statistical Manual of Mental Disorders* (American Psychiatric Association, 2013). In the most recent revision of the manual, DSM-5, the category dyslexia was removed and replaced with the broader category **specific learning disorder** (SpLD), which may include problems with writing, reading, and/or mathematics. A child that would have been diagnosed with dyslexia in the past would now be diagnosed as having SpLD with reading impairment (Tannock, 2014). Experts in dyslexia have advocated for retaining the distinction between dyslexia and other learning problems (Colker et al., 2016). However, it remains to be seen whether the recommendation will be accommodated in the next revision of the DSM.

Children who exhibit reading problems during their school years often have other conditions, some of which also make learning more challenging. Among healthcare professions, the term **comorbidity** refers to the state of having more than one disease or disorder at the same time. Dyslexia is sometimes comorbid with extreme, persistent difficulty with writing – **dysgraphia** – and extreme, persistent difficulty with mathematical calculations – **dyscalculia** or math disability. Children with reading problems may also have difficulty focusing attention for long periods, which is one of the symptoms of attention deficit disorder (ADD). Other children may experience hyperactivity in addition to attentional problems, which is symptomatic of attention deficit hyperactive disorder (ADHD). Over the past few decades, ADD/ADHD has received a great deal of attention from researchers as well as the general public. Research suggests that 25–55 percent of children with ADD/ADHD are affected by one or more major psychiatric disorders, such as depression or other mood disorder, anxiety disorder, or **conduct disorder**, which is a severe behavioral disorder involving chronic rule-breaking and the violation of social norms (Barkley, 2006). Approximately 30 percent of children with dyslexia also have ADHD (International Dyslexia Association, n.d.). Chapter 14 examines in more detail the symptoms, causes, and treatments of disorders related to language processing.

Before we leave this topic, we should note that individuals who struggle with severe reading problems, regardless of the term used to describe it, can persevere, be successful in life, and make important contributions to their communities. Many celebrities have revealed their personal struggles with reading and academic achievement. Several actors have discussed their dyslexia, such as Henry Winkler (Murfitt, 2008), Tom Cruise (University of Michigan, n.d.), Whoopi Goldberg (Yale Center for Dyslexia & Creativity, n.d.), Salma Hayek (Potter, 2012), and Orlando Bloom (Bloom, 2018). The billionaire Richard Branson (2011), who became well known through his company Virgin Airlines, described his school years as a struggle, but he channeled his creativity outside school. Other businessmen have acknowledged being diagnosed with dyslexia include the investment company CEO Charles Schwab (Yale Center for Dyslexia & Creativity, n.d.), Paul Orfalea, founder of Kinko's, and John Chambers, CEO of Cisco. World leaders who have revealed their dyslexia include Erna Solberg, current prime minister of Norway, and Lee Kuan Yew, founder of Singapore. Because of the stigma that still exists around learning problems, such as dyslexia, there are likely to be others who have not chosen to reveal this aspect of their life.

In this section, you learned about the factors that predict which children will and will not achieve high levels of proficiency in reading. Prematurity, vision problems, and exposure to environmental toxins, such as lead, have been shown to be related to lower reading proficiency in children. Family income is also a major factor. Children raised in poor homes typically have lower reading proficiency than children raised in more affluent homes. Research by Stanovich and colleagues has shown that the amount of print exposure is related to reading proficiency and performance in a range of reading-related tasks. Lastly, genetics can be involved in cases of severe reading problems. So far, nine genes have been linked to reading problems in children and adults.

 Time out for Review

Key Terms

Comorbidity	Dyscalculia	Matthew effect
Conduct disorder	Dysgraphia	Specific learning disorder (SpLD)

Review Questions

1 What are the factors related to children's health and physical abilities that are related to reading proficiency?
2 How has exposure to print been shown to be related to reading development? How has exposure to print been measured?
3 What is the relationship between socioeconomic status and children's reading proficiency?
4 How do the approaches to diagnosing children with reading problems differ in DSM-4 and DSM-5?
5 Are individuals with dyslexia doomed to be unsuccessful in their professional endeavors? What evidence is there to support your answer?

The Work of the Eyes and Mind during Reading

As you likely recall from Chapter 5, the use of eye tracking to understand the cognitive processes occurring during reading began with Huey in the late 1800s. Eye tracking has revealed a great deal about how beginning and skilled readers process texts. Fixations typically last 200–250 milliseconds. Saccades last 20–40 milliseconds (Rayner et al., 2001). Most of the saccades made by readers are **forward saccades**, moving the eye in the direction of reading. A small percentage are **backward saccades** (also called regression or **regressive eye movements**), which move in the opposite direction, presumably to enable the reader to reprocess portions of the text. Readers tend to make more backward saccades when reading difficult texts than when reading easy texts. Backward saccades occur only about 15 percent of the time (Rayner et al., 2010) and may occur more often for some readers than others (Hyönä et al., 2002). For beginning readers, eye movement control during reading is typically consistent by second grade (Blythe, 2014). The time needed for beginning readers to extract meaning from a single fixation has been estimated to be 40–60 milliseconds (Blythe et al., 2009). The Classic Research box examines the first experiment that enabled researchers to estimate the minimum time needed to perceive a word during reading.

Classic Research

How Long Does it Take to Read a Word?

Researchers developed creative techniques for measuring the size of the perceptual span, such as the **moving window paradigm** (McConkie & Rayner, 1975; Reder, 1973), which used state-of-the-art eye tracking equipment that enabled researchers to change the text on a computer screen with each saccade (see also Rayner et al., 1981). While the reader was fixated on a given word in the text, the letters could be changed. In the experiment, researchers varied how long words were visible during each fixation and compared the reading rates of participants. When the reader moved their eye to the next word, the word would be visible for a certain duration and then the letters would be switched to Xs or random letters. The aim was to determine the amount of time readers needed to extract the critical information from the word, as they understood from prior research that readers spend some time during each fixation planning the next saccade (Rayner, 1978). The researchers reasoned that readers' processing of passages would be disrupted if words were shown too briefly for comprehension to be completed before the words disappeared. In those cases, overall reading rate would be slower than in those cases in which words were displayed for the optimal duration. Results showed that normal reading rates were obtained when words were available for just 50 milliseconds. This classic study was just one of hundreds conducted by Keith Rayner (1943–2015). Rayner was a cognitive psychologist best known for pioneering modern eye tracking methodology in reading and visual perception. His work advanced our understanding of how reading occurs under a variety of conditions. His many contributions over his long year career are the focus of an article by some of his collaborators (Clifton et al., 2016).

College students often comment about their reading speed. Most often, they say that they read slowly and they wish they could read faster. One of the most puzzling facts arising from thousands of reading experiments is that there are vast individual differences in average reading rate (Frömer et al., 2015; Rayner et al., 2010; Traxler et al., 2012). Highly skilled readers may read quickly or slowly or somewhere in the middle. Similarly, struggling readers may also read quickly or slowly or somewhere in the middle. Many students seek out formal speed-reading courses that will teach them to read quickly. The claims of these courses vary, but most promise customers that after the course they will be able to read thousands of words per minute. The normal reading rate is 200–400 words per minute. The courses teach students techniques for speeding up their eyes as they move them through a text. For example, students may be told to use their finger as a guide for the eye. They move their finger or a pencil along the line of text as they follow with their eyes. With practice, they are told to move their finger or a pencil faster and faster. Students may also be instructed to *turn off* or inhibit their inner speech. By the end of the typical multiple-week course for which a sizable sum has been paid, most students are likely to feel that they are, indeed, reading faster.

However, empirical research suggests that speed-reading courses are too good to be true. Just et al. (1982) compared reading behavior for a group of speed-readers and a group of typical readers. They recorded their eye movements as they read ordinary texts. Typical readers achieved about 250 words per minute. In contrast, the speed-readers read 600–700 words per minute. However, the reading rate of the speed-readers was comparable to the reading rate of typical readers when they skim read the text. An analysis of how well the two groups of readers understood the material they read suggested that speed-readers sacrificed comprehension for speed. Their comprehension performance was similar to that of typical readers when they skimmed the text. The eye movement record of the speed-readers was quite revealing. Comprehension questions that referred to words viewed directly (fixated) were answered with a high rate of accuracy, but comprehension questions that referred to words that were skipped were frequently answered incorrectly. The researchers concluded that speed-readers were reading more quickly, but their reading comprehension was of a lower quality than typical readers. The findings of Just et al. (1980) and Miyata et al. (2012) have led most reading researchers to conclude that speed-reading is a myth. Readers who would like to increase their reading speed can become more familiar with the subject matter they are reading about and ensure that there are no distractions in the environment when trying to read for understanding.

The Perceptual Span

Research beginning in the 1970s explored the question of how much a reader can perceive on a single fixation, known as **perceptual span** or vision span. The researchers understood the fundamentals of visual perception. Information in the field of vision is processed at different levels of acuity (sharpness and clarity). Research by Keith Rayner and colleagues (see Rayner, 1998 for review) demonstrated that during individual fixations, readers not only extract information about the fixated word, but also about the word to the right of fixation. As you recall from Chapter 5, the center of our vision is processed by the fovea region of our retinas, while the right and the left of our center of vision is processed by the parafovea region of our retinas. A shift of visual attention precedes each saccade, shifting attention in the direction the eye is moving. The objects being processed by the parafovea aided by the applied visual attention can lead to a parafoveal preview benefit, as the time spent fixating the object directly is likely to be shorter than when no parafoveal preview was obtained (Rayner, 1975; Kennison & Clifton, 1995; Pollatsek et al., 1992). The size of the perceptual span would be larger when readers are able to extract more information via parafoveal processing. Recent research by Rayner et al. (2010) determined that a primary contributor to the difference in reading time for fast and slow readers was the size of their perceptual spans. Fast readers had larger perceptual spans than slow readers.

Research with skilled English readers showed that they appear to extract more information to the right of the fixation than from the left of fixation, making the perceptual span asymmetric (Rayner et al., 2012). The asymmetry of the perceptual span changes with the direction of reading; thus, it varies across languages. The perceptual span extends farther to the right for languages that are read left to right and farther to the left for languages that are read right to left. Readers of languages who read from top to bottom have a vertical perceptual span, extending farther below fixation than above fixation. Studies suggest that readers extract information not only from what they are directly looking at, but also from information extending in the direction where the eye will move on the next fixation.

One of the many interesting questions about the perceptual processing that occurs during reading is the lag between visual and cognitive processing – the **eye-mind span**. Just and Carpenter (1980) proposed that the mind processes the word to completion during a fixation, which they referred to as the "immediacy hypothesis." Subsequent research disproved the immediacy hypothesis, showing that the time that words are fixated during reading is influenced by the processing difficulty of an immediately preceding word. For example, several studies have shown that reading time on a word is increased when the word is preceded by a low frequency word versus a high frequency word (Inhoff & Rayner, 1986; Kennison & Clifton, 1995; Rayner et al., 1989). It is highly plausible that the eye-mind span during reading varies across readers as well as across different types of texts (difficult or easy to understand). The eye-mind span is also likely to change as beginning readers develop their reading skills. Research has shown that the perceptual spans of beginning readers start out relatively small, but increase in size as reading skill increases (Häikiö et al., 2009; Rayner, 1986; Sperlich et al., 2016).

The perceptual span of readers has also been studied for a variety of reading situations, including reading by the blind who comprehend texts using Braille and reading sheet music by musicians. **Braille** is a system of writing used by those who are blind or have significant visual impairment (Hampshire, 1981). Specific words are represented by a specific number of dots in a particular arrangement. The reader interprets the word by touching the dots, most often with the right and/or left index fingers. The idea for Braille was inspired by the night writing invented by Charles Barbier, a captain in the French army, which was used by Napoleon's military to communicate at night. Louis Braille, who became blind at age 5, developed and simplified this night writing and turned it into the Braille alphabet still used to this day (Braille, 1829). Highly skilled Braille readers often use both index fingers and can read at a rate of 100–140 words per minute (Bertelson et al., 1985). Some readers will place the index fingers side by side and move them left to right together. Other readers will read with adjacent fingers up to the middle of the line, and then the right index finger will be moved on to the end of the line, while the left index finger will be moved down to the beginning of the next line. Using two fingers may double the size of the perceptual span in Braille; however, empirical studies have not attempted to estimate how many letters or words are typically extracted by each finger. In 2013, the American Foundation for the Blind (2013) reported that the use of Braille in the USA has declined since the 1940s, perhaps due to the availability of technologies that can provide spoken word versions of written materials.

Photo 11.3 Braille enables the blind to read through the sense of touch. Have you noticed Braille in elevators or other public spaces?
Credit: Lrcg2012

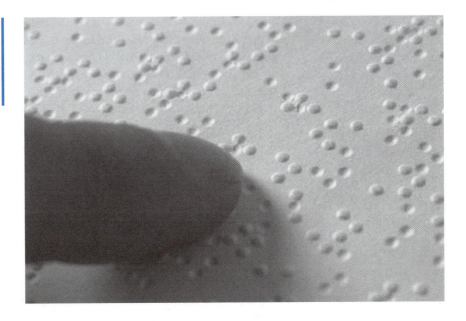

There is a small, but growing literature of studies investigating how novice and expert musicians read written music (see Madell & Hébert, 2008, for review). The graphical representation of music has a long history, with the earliest known examples being found on a tablet found in Sumer (modern-day Iraq) dating back to 2000 BC (Kilmer, 1965; Kilmer & Civil, 1986). Symbols representing musical notes are arranged on two sets of parallel lines (called staves) with the placement of the symbol on the lines indicating the musical note's identity or pitch. Each note is represented with a circle with or without a vertical line (also called stem). The musical note appears differently to indicate the duration of the note (i.e., filled or unfilled circle and type of stem). Figure 11.2 provides an example of musical notation from a composition by Frederic Chopin.

Figure 11.2 Example of Musical Notation
The graphical representation of music includes information about what notes should be played, how long they should last, and how they should be played. Have you ever learned how to read basic musical notation?

Eye movement studies of reading music have shown that the complexity of the material being read affects the pattern of readers' eye movements. When the music being read is higher in complexity, musicians make more fixations, make longer fixations, and make shorter saccades (Smith, 1988; Souter, 2001). Scholars have discussed the positioning of the eye in relation to the hands – **eye-hand span** – during the playing of music that is being read (Furneax & Land, 1999;

Gilman & Underwood, 2003; Slobada, 1974, 1977; Truitt et al., 1997). Truitt et al. (1997) aimed to measure the size of musicians' perceptual spans for reading music. Their results showed that the perceptual span was quite small, on average only one note, but across participants, there was high variability. Individual perceptual spans varied from two notes behind (to the left) of the note being played to 12 notes ahead (to the right) of the note being played. There appears to be growing interest in the perceptual processing of music (Lehmann & Kopiez, 2016; Penttinen & Huovinen, 2011; Penttinen et al., 2013; Rosemann et al., 2016).

Models of Reading

Researchers have attempted to develop formal models of eye movement control during reading, in which the link between the mind and eyes is illuminated. The basic assumption of such models is that cognitive processing influences eye movement behavior during reading. The goal of the models is to explain, as completely as possible, how exactly the mind and the eyes are coordinated. Many questions have yet to be answered regarding eye movement behavior during reading. Of particular interest are: how the reader determines when to move the eye during a fixation; what cognitive processing is occurring during fixations and saccades; and how the destination for the saccade is planned (for both forward and backward saccades). We discuss one of the earliest models, the reader model (Just and Carpenter, 1980), and then a recent model that has received a great deal of attention by reading researchers: the E-Z reader model (Pollatsek et al., 2006; Reichle et al., 2003).

In Just and Carpenter's (1980) reader model, the eyes are presumed to be tightly linked to the processing occurring in the readers' mind. The model incorporates the immediacy hypothesis discussed earlier in this chapter. This hypothesis suggested that during a fixation on a word, the mind is processing that word as completely as possible, and that when the eye moves away from a word, the mind is no longer processing that word. The model can be viewed as a serial, sequential model in which reading occurs fixation by fixation, with the mental processing that occurs during each fixation involving only the information that is currently fixated. The model has been praised for its thoroughness, as it was developed into a computer simulation, and for doing a good job of accounting for some eye movement behaviors, such as increased fixation time on words due to word frequency (Reichle et al., 2003). However, as we learned earlier in this chapter, later experiments provided evidence against the model. Fixation times on words were shown to be influenced by the characteristics (processing difficulty) of immediately preceding words (Inhoff & Rayner, 1986; Kennison & Clifton, 1995; Rayner et al., 1989). In addition, research showed that readers sometimes can begin processing of a word on the fixation just prior to the word itself being fixated when parafoveal preview of a word can be obtained (Rayner, 1975; Kennison & Clifton, 1995; Pollatsek et al., 1992). Reichle et al. (2003) also pointed out that the reader model does not generate accurate predictions about readers' saccades, particularly in terms of which words are fixated or skipped and fixation position (also called landing position) within words.

The E-Z reader model (Reichle et al., 2003; Pollatsek et al., 2006) is currently the most comprehensive and popular of reading models, which appears to be able to account for the widest range of eye movement behavior during reading in the most parsimonious manner. Reichle et al. (2003) describe the model as intending to reflect a *default* reading processing, which occurs when there is no processing difficulty related to linguistic factors, such as syntactic reanalysis. Linguistic factors related to reading comprehension are presumed to influence when or where the eye is moved during reading. Word identification, saccade planning, and saccade production are the three types of processing that determine when and where the eye is moved. In the model, readers carry out an initial familiarity check on a word that they have fixated. When this is complete, they begin planning the next saccade. When lexical access is completed for the word, visual attention shifts in the direction the planned saccade will be made. The process of planning a saccade is described as having two stages, one in which the saccade can be canceled or the saccade's parameters (length) can be modified and a second involving the final planning of the saccade. In the second stage, modification of the saccade is not possible. The saccade plan cannot be modified. When the second stage has been completed, the saccade will be executed. Cancellation of the eye movement is not possible at that point.

The E-Z reader model does a good job of explaining why readers obtain reduced parafoveal preview benefit of a word when the immediately preceding word is low frequency (versus high frequency), which has been demonstrated in several studies (Henderson & Ferreira, 1990; Kennison & Clifton, 1995). The explanation is that the word familiarity check triggers the planning of the next saccade, but lexical access must be achieved before attention shifts to the next word. Lexical access occurs later for low frequency words than high frequency words. The model's two stages of saccade planning also provide an explanation of why some words are skipped. Short, high frequency words are often skipped during reading because they can be perceived completely on the prior fixation (Balota et al., 1985; Pollatsek et al., 1986; Rayner, 1978). When parafoveal preview results in the word to the right of fixation reaching the word familiarity check during the first stage of saccade planning, then the saccade can be modified so that a longer saccade is planned and the word is skipped.

Recent research appears to contradict the E-Z reader model's explanation of word skipping, which is that skipped words are viewed as fully processed. To test this claim, Eskenazi and Folk (2015) conducted an experiment in which participants read sentences in which target three-letter words were unpredictable and low frequency. Following the reading task, they carried out a lexical decision task. The results showed that participants responded faster to words that had been included in the reading task if the word had been fixated by the participant than if the word had been skipped. The authors suggested that the reaction time facilitation reflected repetition priming, a phenomenon we discussed in Chapter 5. Repetition priming was smaller for words that had been skipped during the reading task, indicating that the skipped words had not been fully processed during the reading task. In future research, the E-Z reader model may be revised to incorporate these new results about word skipping and to expand the range of past results that the model can explain. The value of having such models and continuing to improve them is that they may be able to provide insight into the reasons that people experience difficulty learning to read and other reading problems.

Time out for Review

Key Terms

Backward saccade

Braille

Eye-hand span

Eye-mind span

Forward saccade

Moving window paradigm

Perceptual span

Regressive eye movements

Review Questions

1 What is the relationship between the processing difficulty of a text and the characteristics of fixations and saccades?
2 What is the perceptual span? What factors influence the size and shape of a reader's perceptual span?
3 To what extent are there individual differences in reading speed and eye movement behavior for skilled readers?
4 What have eye movement studies shown about how musicians read sheet music? To what extent is eye movement behavior during the reading of music similar to the reading of text?

Summary

Teaching children to read is a core component in most educational systems worldwide. Research suggests that across different types of languages, children benefit from developing phonological awareness about the relationship between the visual form of words (letters or symbols) and their pronunciation. Experts recommend that educators emphasize the relationship between visual form and pronunciation when teaching children to read. While many students will become proficient in reading with little problem, some will struggle. Predictors of lower reading proficiency include early and continuing health problems, family income, and genetic makeup. The use of eye tracking technology has provided an in-depth understanding of how readers extract information from texts and how the cognitive processing occurring during reading influences eye movement behavior. In some cases of children who experience reading problems, there are abnormal patterns of eye movements during reading. The relationship between eye movements and reading comprehension is not fully understood. Models of eye movement struggle to explain how semantic processing influences our decisions about when to move our eyes during a fixation on a word and where to fixate the next word or phrase.

Recommended Books, Films, and Websites

Coulmas, F. (2003). *Writing Systems: An Introduction*. Cambridge: Cambridge University Press.

Gopnik, A., Meltzoff, A. N. & Kuhl, P. K. (2000). *The Scientist in the Crib: What Early Learning Tells us about the Mind*. New York: Harper Perennial.

Moats, L. C. (2007). *Whole-language High Jinks*. Available at http://edex.s3-us-west-2.amazonaws.com/publication/pdfs/Moats2007_7.pdf.

Rayner, K., Pollatsek, A., Ashby, J. & Clifton, C. (2012). *The Psychology of Reading* (2nd edn). New York: Psychology Press.

Rayner, K., Foorman, B., Perfetti, C. A., Pesetsky, D. & Seidenberg, M. S. (2001). How psychological science informs the teaching of reading. *Psychological Science in the Public Interest*, 2(2), 31–74.

Selikowitz, M. (2012). *Dyslexia and Other Learning Difficulties*. Oxford: Oxford University Press.

Von Petzinger, G. (2015). Why are these 32 symbols found in ancient caves all over Europe? Available at www.ted.com/talks/genevieve_von_petzinger_why_are_these_32_symbols_found_in_ancient_caves_all_over_europe.

Wolf, M. & Stoodley, C. J. (2007). *Proust and the Squid: The Story and Science of the Reading Brain*. New York: Harper.

12

WHAT IS THE BRAIN'S ROLE IN LANGUAGE?

Chapter Content

Photo 12.1 Contact sports, such as boxing and American football, cause concussions, which can lead to a wide range of cognitive deficits, including problems using language. Do you believe the rising concerns about concussions in sports are justified?

Brain injury is a leading cause of disability and death around the world. About 138 people die from brain injury every day in the USA (Centers for Disease Control, 2017). Worldwide, millions of individuals live with the after-effects of brain injury that vary from mild to severe. For many, one of the after-effects is permanent changes in language processing. As you may recall from Chapter 1, the term *aphasia* is used to describe any language deficit resulting from brain injury, including brain damage resulting from disease processes, such as infections, and progressive conditions such as dementia. We know that brain injury and aphasia have been known to people for thousands of years, because a reference to aphasia appears in the Edwin Smith Papyrus, an Egyptian document detailing various medical ailments from around the 16th century BC (Minagar et al., 2003). The study of aphasia by Pierre Paul Broca (1824–80) and Carl Wernicke (1848–1905) led to the discovery of brain locations involved in the production and comprehension of language, respectively. Our knowledge of how the brain works and what areas are involved in language processing has advanced a great deal since the time of Broca and Wernicke. Nevertheless, there is an immense amount that we do not know. There are no treatments that can reverse the after-effects of brain injury or cure aphasia.

In this chapter, we will review what is known about the brain's role in language, including how specific brain regions are organized and involved in language processing. We start with a discussion of the localization hypothesis, the view that specific locations in the brain control specific behaviors or functions. Second, we discuss the classic evidence demonstrating that the left hemisphere plays a dominant role in language for the majority of people (approximately 95 percent). In the third section, we discuss research showing that the right hemisphere is involved in certain types of language processing, such as the processing of humor, figurative language, and prosody, especially that involving emotional content. Lastly, we discuss brain plasticity, the brain's ability to reorganize and change how it functions. Our discussion of brain plasticity will focus on how the brain recovers from injury (accidents, illness, and/or surgery), cases of individuals who have recovered after having an entire hemisphere removed (a hemispherectomy), and brain changes across the lifespan.

The Localization Hypothesis

Newspapers and television programs regularly report the discovery of a new brain area that may be responsible for a particular function. Recent technological advances have made studies of brain processing both possible and frequent. New brain imaging innovations are making it possible to understand what specific regions do and how complex behaviors are carried out by the coordination of multiple brain areas. One of the ironies in science is that the **localization hypothesis** traces its roots back to those who, in the 1800s, promoted the well-known pseudoscience of **phrenology,** which claimed that personality traits could be determined through the examination of bony bumps on the head (Wickens, 2015). In the early 1800s, phrenologists, led by Franz Joseph Gall (1758–1828) and Johann Spurzheim (1776–1832), erroneously believed that the bumps on the scalp were caused by enlarged brain regions beneath, and that larger brain regions associated with a specific personality trait would lead to more of that trait being exhibited by the person.

Today, phrenology is recognized as a pseudoscience, which is a set of practices incorrectly portrayed as following the scientific method. In its day, phrenology was sold to the masses as a way to find out more about themselves, perhaps in a manner similar to how people seek personal information in astrological horoscopes. In the 1800s, phrenology became popular among the highest social classes, and newly engaged couples would seek out phrenological exams in order to determine their compatibility (Fowler, 1848). Despite the false premises on which phrenology was founded, it turns out to be true that specific locations of the brain are responsible for specific functions. In the following section, we discuss some of the earliest and most convincing evidence for the localization hypothesis. The fad of phrenology eventually waned, and by the end of the 1800s, there were large-scale studies postulating not one, but two, brain areas involved in language, which are still referred to by the scientists who discovered them.

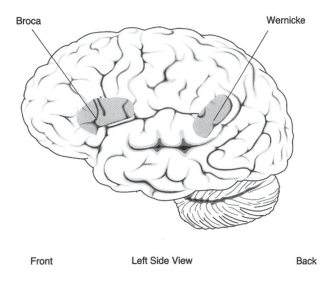

Figure 12.1 Broca's and Wernicke's Areas
Would you be able to add to the drawing the left eye and left ear?
Credit: National Institute of Mental Health, National Institutes of Health, Department of Health and Human Service

Broca

Wernicke

Front   Left Side View   Back

Broca's and Wernicke's Areas

Working separately, Broca and Wernicke studied patients with language deficits and identified the affected brain regions through **postmortem autopsy**, the examination of the body, in this case the brain, following death (LaPointe, 2012). The patients in the hospitals where Broca and Wernicke worked were often destitute, without immediate family. In those days, doctors had unfettered access to patients' bodies after death. Both men's research involved the examination of multiple patients' brains and recording of the patients' language deficits. Figure 12.1 shows the locations of Broca's and Wernicke's regions in the brain. **Broca's area** is located in the left frontal lobe of the brain, while **Wernicke's area** is located in the left hemisphere, in the posterior area of the temporal lobe. These areas continue to be recognized as major brain regions involved in language processing.

The symptoms of Broca's and Wernicke's aphasia differ, with each type of aphasia involving a loss of language ability that is preserved in the other aphasia. Those with **Broca's aphasia** have difficulty physically producing speech, but are able to comprehend what is said to them. Those with **Wernicke's aphasia** have little trouble producing speech, but they typically have trouble understanding speech. Those with Broca's aphasia produce speech that contains content words (nouns, verbs, adjectives), but tends to lack function words (prepositions, pronouns, helping verbs, suffixes and prefixes). Those with Wernicke's aphasia produce speech that lacks content words, but contains function words. Their speech may also contain **neologisms** or nonsense, made-up words. Those with Wernicke's aphasia may show little to no awareness that they are unable to communicate with others, either by understanding what is said to them or conveying meaning in their own speech. In contrast, those with Broca's aphasia typically experience high levels of frustration when they struggle to produce speech and struggle to be understood by others. Those with Broca's aphasia exhibit **insight** into their condition, while those with Wernicke's aphasia often do not. Table 12.1 summarizes the symptoms of Broca's and Wernicke's aphasia.

Table 12.1 Symptoms of Broca's and Wernicke's Aphasia

Broca's aphasia	Wernicke's aphasia
Problems producing speech	No problems producing speech
Some problems comprehending speech	Problems comprehending speech
Speech contains content words	Speech lacks content words
Speech lacks function words	Speech contains function words
Has insight of the problem	Little or no insight of the problem

Recent research using modern brain imaging techniques has shed light on the organization within Broca's and Wernicke's areas. Within Broca's area, three subareas have been identified, each associated with a different type of language deficit:

1 The **pars triangularis** is the intermediate region. Damage to this area can result in deficits in semantic processing (Devlin et al., 2003; Gold & Buckner, 2002) and syntactic processing (Hagoort, 2005).
2 The **pars orbitalis** is located near the front of the brain. Damage to this area can result in deficits in semantic processing (Hagoort, 2005).
3 The **pars opercularis** is the most posterior region. Damage to this region has been found to result in deficits in phonological processing (Gold & Buckner, 2002; Nixon et al., 2004) and syntactic processing (Hagoort, 2005).

Research suggests that Broca's area plays no role in comprehending sentences (Rogalsky & Hickok, 2011). Research has also shown that Broca's area receives input from the sensory areas and then word representations associated with articulatory plans, which were transmitted to the motor areas (Flinker et al., 2015).

Wernicke's area is located in the superior temporal gyrus. Research into the subdivisions within Wernicke's area has yielded some surprising results (Binder, 2015). Despite the fact that Wernicke's area has been viewed as primarily involved in language comprehension, mounting research shows that the area is critically involved in the retrieval of phonological information, the repetition of speech, and word retrieval. The job of Wernicke's area appears to be more related to sound processing than the processing of meaning. Studies of the subdivisions within Wernicke's area have identified a major subarea called the **planum temporale**, a triangular area located just posterior to the auditory cortex and believed to play an important role in language acquisition. In a study in which brain activity was recorded using functional magnetic resonance imaging (fMRI), the triangular region was found to be activated in the brains of infants when they listened to speech, but it was not activated when they listened to music (Dehaene-Lambertz et al., 2010). Since the 1960s, researchers had noted that for most people the region was larger in the left hemisphere than the right hemisphere (Geschwind & Levitsky, 1968). Reduced or absent asymmetry in the planum temporale has been observed in individuals with dyslexia (Elnakib et al., 2014). The planum temporale has also been associated with non-speech functions, such as spatial hearing (Hickok, 2009).

Since the discovery of Broca's and Wernicke's areas, there has been a great deal of interest about how they are connected and how information flows between them. The bundle of axons that connects the two areas is referred to as

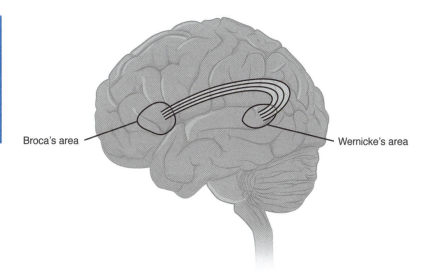

Broca's area   Wernicke's area

the **arcuate fasciculus** (Catani & de Schotten, 2012). Figure 12.2 shows how the arcuate fasciculus connects Broca's and Wernicke's regions in the left hemisphere. Individuals who experience damage to the arcuate fasciculus may develop a particularly rare form of aphasia known as **conduction aphasia**. These individuals have difficulty repeating words and phrases, make frequent errors when speaking spontaneously, but are able to understand others' speech (Manasco, 2014). The existence of conduction aphasia demonstrates a separateness of the systems in the brain that enable the production of speech from those involved in the comprehension of speech. Research suggests that the arcuate fasciculus may play a role in stuttering (Cieslak et al., 2015). The volume of **white matter** in the area, which includes the myelin-covered axons, was significantly reduced in those who were affected by stuttering as compared to unaffected control participants. There were no significant differences in the **gray matter** in the region, which includes the cell bodies and dendrites.

Understanding how specific brain areas contribute to our abilities and behaviors provides physicians with the ability to predict how people will be affected by brain damage. There are numerous types of aphasia. For each type of aphasia, the typical areas of brain damage causing it have been identified. Chapter 14 details the most common language disorders along with descriptions of some of the most common treatments. There can be a great deal of variability in the cases of aphasia. No two individuals are likely to sustain the same pattern of brain injury. Furthermore, there can be variability in how people recover from brain injury, as we will discuss later in this chapter. In the next section, we will discuss the major parts of the brain, their organization, and their role in producing behavior. Each of these parts of the brain are involved in multiple aspects of language processing as well as other types of complex human behavior.

Four Lobes and Two Hemispheres

Over the past 150 years, research has yielded an immense amount of knowledge about how different parts of the brain are involved in producing specific human behaviors. Understanding the basic organizational features of the brain will

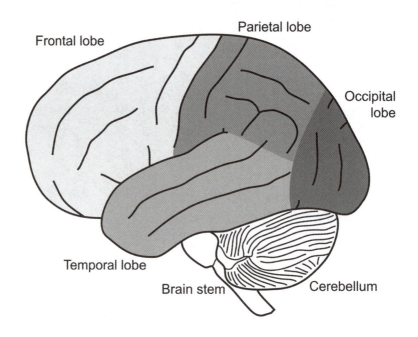

assist us later in this chapter when we focus specifically on functions related to language. The brain has four primary lobes and two hemispheres or halves, which are connected by a bundle of fibers referred to as the **corpus callosum**. It is the largest structure composed of white matter in the brain, containing 200–250 million axons connecting the two lobes of the brain (Fitsiori et al., 2011). Figure 12.3 displays the four major lobes of the brain. From research conducted in the 20th century, we know many of the functions of each lobe of the brain. Visual processing is carried out predominantly in the occipital lobe. Memory processing occurs in the temporal lobe. Spatial processing, particularly that involving the sense of touch, occurs in the parietal lobes. Planning and the regulation of behavior occur in the frontal lobe. When considering the numerous types of processing involved in perceiving, producing, and recalling language, we can identify ways in which each of the four lobes plays a role. The totality of language processing certainly involves many regions of the brain; however, some locations have been found to be involved in particularly critical functions.

Some of what we have learned about what different parts of the brain do is derived from **case studies** of individuals who sustained damage to the brain. In a case study, it is possible to compare a patient's abilities before and after a brain injury to develop hypotheses about how the region of the brain generally functions. The hypotheses can be tested through the examination of additional cases of individuals with brain injury in the same area. The limitation of a single case study is that it is never possible to rule out the possibility that a particular finding will be true only for that person. Multiple case studies are needed to confirm that a particular brain area is always involved in a specific function. The research is particularly challenging to carry out, as injuries rarely produce identical regions of damage. Furthermore, the sizes and shapes of people's brains vary widely. As a methodological approach to understanding human behavior, case studies are well known to be among the most exploratory and the least conclusive of all methods in behavioral science (Yin, 2014). Nevertheless, they continue to provide compelling evidence about the functions of specific locations in the brain. In the 20th century, we learned a great deal about the functioning of the brain through two of the most famous case studies in the history of neuropsychology. The Classic Research box outlines the first of these case studies.

The second case study that provided critical new knowledge about brain function was the case of Henry Molaison, who, prior to his death in 2008, had been referred to in the academic literature only as H. M. He underwent surgery as a treatment for his severe epileptic seizures. The surgeons removed a portion of his temporal lobe where the seizures were forming. The surgery removed most of the area now known as the **hippocampus**. The surgery proved to be a success in reducing the number and severity of his seizures; however, it left him with an inability to form long-term memories for events that he experienced after the surgery. Now, we know that the hippocampus is vital in the formation of long-term memories (Corkin, 2013). The term **amnesia** is generally used to refer to any loss of memory. Henry Molaison's memory loss is called **anterograde amnesia**. In contrast, **retrograde amnesia** refers to memory loss for events that precede an injury or stressful event. Anterograde amnesia has been depicted in films, including the thriller *Memento* (Nolan, 2000) and the goof-ball comedy *Fifty First Dates* (Segal, 2004).

In the 20th century, the functions of the left and right hemispheres of the brain were explored using a variety of methods. Among the earliest observations about the localization of function in the brain were differences in the functions of the left and right hemispheres. For example, the left hemisphere controls movements and receives sensory information from the right side of the body, and the right hemisphere controls movements and receives sensory information from the left side of the body. The brain's control of the body has been described as **contralateral control**, as contralateral means *opposite side.* Individuals who experience a brain injury on the right side of the brain may suffer some paralysis on the left side of the body and vice versa. Hippocrates (460–370 BC), the ancient Greek scholar recognized as the founder of western medicine, noted that paralysis on the right side of the body accompanies loss of language (Finger, 2000). The next section examines the functions of these brain areas and what has been discovered about them since their discovery.

What are the Brodmann Areas?

In the past 150 years, there have been remarkable advances in technology to investigate how the brain functions (Gazzaniga et al., 2013). The research that has been produced and continues to be produced provides enormous detail about brain regions and possible associations with functions. Korbinian Brodmann (1868–1918), German anatomist, is best known for mapping the brain based on its cellular composition or **cytoarchitecture** (Brodmann, 1909; see also Finger, 2001). The map was based on cellular analysis of brains from humans, other primates, and other animal species obtained from postmortem autopsies; however, the numbering system frequently appears in articles and textbooks discussing brain

Classic Research

The Case of Phineas Gage

Photo 12.2 Phineas Gage lived for more than a decade after his accident with some changes to his personality and physical abilities. Do you know anyone who has suffered a traumatic brain injury from an accident or stroke?
Credit: Originally from the collection of Jack and Beverly Wilgus, and now in the Warren Anatomical Museum, Harvard Medical School

The first case study was on the functioning of the frontal lobes, and concerned Phineas Gage (1823–60), a US railroad worker who sustained damage to his brain when an explosion sent a pipe into and through his skull (MacMillan, 2002). The accident happened on September 13, 1848, 13 years before Broca's research was published. Comparisons of Gage's personality and usual behavior before and after the accident led to speculation about the functioning of the frontal lobe (Damasio et al., 1994). Before the injury, Gage had been described as a mild and religious man. After the injury, Gage was described as prone to outbursts. MacMillan (2002) points out that we must consider with caution the anecdotes about Gage's behavior before and after the accident, as there is a lack of credible evidence on the subject beyond the personal perceptions of previous biographers. The case of Gage will likely continue to fascinate students and researchers alike for decades to come. Gage's skull is now housed at the Harvard Medical School and has been featured in an episode of the Scientific American series *Frontiers* (Chedd, 2002).

From a scientific perspective, the case of Phineas Gage became a reference point for all subsequent cases of brain injury treatment and recovery (Bigelow, 1850; Harlow, 1848; Luria, 1963). In 1940, Stanley Cobb, once called the father of biological psychiatry (White, 1984), created a sketch of Phineas Gage's skull based on his examination of the skull. Tyler and Tyler (1982) made images of the skull using computerized axial tomography (CAT scan) and hypothesized that specific regions of brain tissue were totally destroyed. Damasio et al. (1994) used computer technology to create a model of the skull to identify the locations of the brain that were damaged by the rod passing through the skull. The model suggested that the damage occurred to the right of the midline of the brain. Later research contradicted these findings, supporting the view that all the damage was left of the midline (Ratiu & Talos, 2004; van Horn et al., 2012). Van Horn et al. (2012) estimated that 11 percent of brain white matter in the left hemisphere was lost in addition to 3.97 percent brain gray matter. Specific regions that were estimated to be most damaged included the left orbital sulcus (91 percent lost), the left middle frontal sulcus (80 percent lost), the horizontal ramus of the anterior segment of the lateral sulcus (71 percent lost), and the anterior segment of the circular sulcus of the insula (62 percent lost). Van Horn et al. (2012) pointed out that the damage severed the connections between the frontal and temporal lobes in the left hemisphere as well as connections between frontal regions and the limbic system, which is known to be involved in emotional processing. Further, the authors point out that the behavioral changes reported in Phineas Gage are commonly observed in contemporary cases of traumatic brain injury.

areas. Remarkably, the labeling system that Brodmann invented is still used today. Figure 12.4 shows the Brodmann areas that were identified on the brain's surface of the left hemisphere. For each region, there is a corresponding region in the right hemisphere.

Broca's area corresponds to Brodmann's areas 44 (pars opercularis), 45 (pars triangularis), and 47 (pars orbitalis). Wernicke's area corresponds to Brodmann's area 22 (superior temporal gyrus). One of Brodmann's interests was the possibility that the difference observed in the structure of brain regions stemmed from their evolutionary origins (Garey, 2006). Researchers engaged in brain imaging work continue to use the Brodmann labeling system, but some have noted that there may be a need for a new labeling system in light of the fact that additional cellular distinctions are being discovered even within the Brodmann areas (Geyer et al., 2011).

Research from the early 20th century provides insight into how brain regions involved in producing movement and receiving sensory input are organized. The earliest evidence for this was provided by the use of **electrical brain stimulation (EBS)**. A small stream of electricity was directed to a specific region of the brain, and the effects were observed. EBS was first used by the neurosurgeon Wilder Penfield (1891–1976) to reduce seizures in those suffering from epilepsy. Brain tissue that caused electrical misfiring and seizures was destroyed using carefully directed electrical currents into the brain tissue (Jasper & Penfield, 1954; Penfield, 1958, 1972; Penfield & Roberts, [1959] 2014). Over many years, Penfield and his colleagues used EBS to investigate the function of brain regions in patients when they were prepared for brain surgery. The patients were conscious and able to respond to questions. Penfield would stimulate different parts of the brain and observe the effect on patients' behavior (whether the stimulation interfered with speech or caused random speech to occur). He would ask patients if there were any sensations or memories triggered by the stimulation. Even today, patients undergoing brain surgery will have EBS in order to determine the locations of their language areas, which can vary somewhat across individuals. Surgeons use the results of the EBS to avoid removing or damaging brain regions involved in language, because any loss of language function, however small, can greatly reduce patients' quality of life.

Figure 12.4 Brodmann Areas of the Left Hemisphere
Broca's area corresponds to areas 44, 45 and 47 and Wernicke's area corresponds to area 22. Do you think that brain imaging research may lead to a revision of these areas?

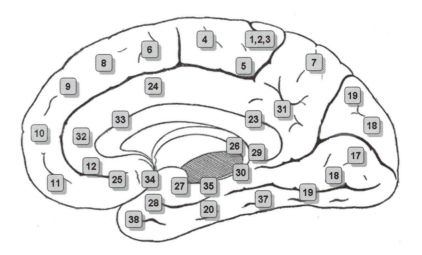

Penfield's work led to the original topographical map of the motor cortex (Brodmann area 4), called the "cortical homunculus," shown in Figure 12.5. The diagram shows how the different parts of the human body are controlled by the different regions within the motor cortex. The word "topographical" is used to describe the type of organization of the areas of the brain controlling movement and sensory processing, as it can be graphically represented as a map. You are likely familiar with the topographical maps of the earth's surface, showing detailed aspects of the hills, valleys, rivers, and other physical features. Similarly, topographical maps of brain regions are used to display how different regions of the brain are involved in movement or sensory input from different parts of the body. The parts of the motor cortex involved in controlling the movement of the feet are distinct from the parts involved in controlling the hands.

An important contributor to the understanding of how the brain is organized was John Hughlings Jackson (1835–1911), a physician specializing in neurology who worked in the National Hospital for Diseases of the Nervous System including Paralysis and Epilepsy (now called the National Hospital for Neurology and Neurosurgery) in London, England. He is most famous for his contributions to understanding epilepsy (Balcells Riba, 1999). Jackson observed the seizures of patients with epilepsy and began to formulate a hypothesis about why there were systematic patterns of body movements as a seizure progressed. The random body movements caused by a seizure would begin to affect one body part and then spread along the same side of the body in a predictable pattern ending up affecting the face. Now known as Jacksonian seizures (a type

Figure 12.5 The Cortical Homunculus
Different amounts of brain area in the primary motor cortex are involved in controlling each body part. The larger the body part in the drawing, the more brain area involved in controlling the body part. Why do you think the face and the hands would be controlled by such a large amount of brain area?
Credit: OpenStax College

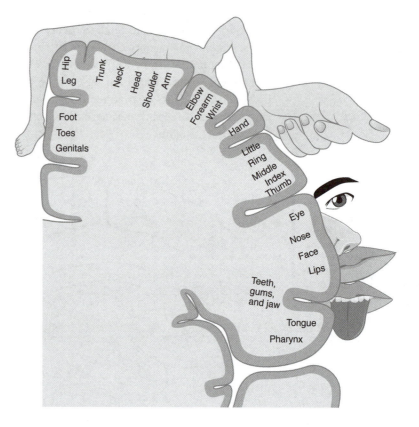

of focal partial seizure), this spreading is referred to as a "Jacksonian march." Jackson speculated that the pattern of how the seizure spread across the body reflected something about the organization of the brain. Decades later, he was proven correct.

A second brain area that has been found to be topographically organized is the primary auditory cortex (Brodmann areas 41, 42, and part of 22). Figure 12.6 displays the organization of the auditory cortex. Different regions of the brain areas are involved in processing different frequencies of sound. In the cochlea of the ear, different hair cells respond to different frequencies of sound. Hair cells located in the front respond to sounds 500 Hz or below. The hair cells located behind these respond to sounds between 500 and 1000 Hz. Moving farther back, hair cells respond to sounds of higher and higher frequency to the maximum of human hearing 20,000 Hz. Within the auditory cortex, populations of neurons respond to certain frequencies of sound with regions toward the front of the auditory cortex responding to low frequencies of sound and regions moving back responding to increasingly higher frequencies

Figure 12.6 The Auditory Cortex
Different frequencies of sound are processed by different regions of the cochlea and the auditory cortex. Do you think people with an *ear* for music have brains that are different from others individuals?
Credit: PLOS

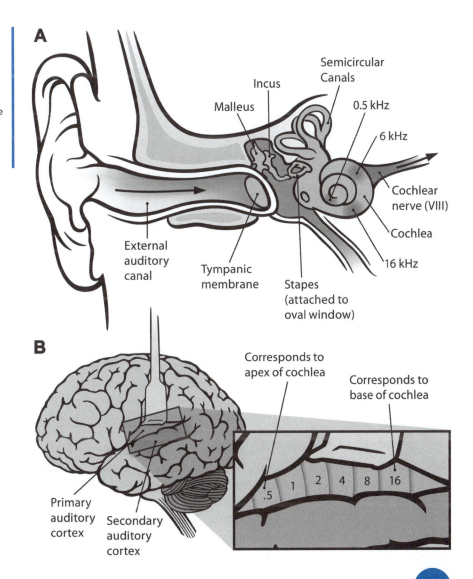

Figure 12.7 The Relaying of Visual Information to the Two Hemispheres
How would an injury to the left occipital lobe affect what one could perceive in the visual field?
Credit: Busey, T. A. , Motz, B.A., & James, K. H. (2012). The Lateralizer: a tool for students to explore the divided brain. *American Physiological Society*, 36, 2.

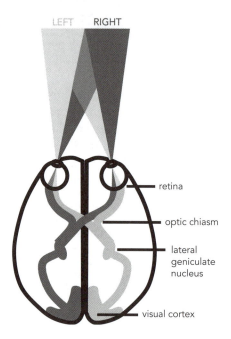

LEFT   RIGHT

retina

optic chiasm

lateral geniculate nucleus

visual cortex

of sound. Topographic organization is also found in the visual system, the olfactory (smell) sensory system, and the gustatory (taste) sensory system.

Many areas of the brain can be graphically represented in topographic maps. For example, the occipital lobe is organized such that visual information located in different locations of the visual field is processed by distinct locations in the occipital lobe. Figure 12.7 displays how visual information processed in different regions of the field of vision is transmitted to different regions of the brain.

In Figure 12.7, information in the lighter shade of gray is viewed in the left visual field, but is processed by a portion of the occipital lobe in the right hemisphere. Information in the darker shade of gray is viewed in the right visual field, but is processed by a portion of the occipital lobe in the left hemisphere. Individuals who sustain brain damage in the occipital lobe may experience blindness in the corresponding area of the visual field. Because the visual field changes when a person moves their eyes and/or body position, when the damage affects only a small portion of the occipital lobe, it is possible to cope with the partial blindness. Perceiving the entire visual field would require making more scans of the scene than made by a normally sighted person.

The efforts to map the brain and discover how each area is involved in producing and comprehending language are ongoing. New discoveries are being made regularly, and new techniques to explore brain processing are being developed. An important avenue of research is investigating the extent to which the Brodmann areas, which were documented using postmortem examinations, correspond to location distinctions in the brains of healthy individuals as they carry out tasks as their brain activity is recorded. Further research is needed to investigate the extent to which there are individual differences in size and composition of the Brodmann areas. Although brain imaging is much more common than it was just ten years ago, it remains the case that relatively few individuals have participated in brain imaging studies. The diversity of brain architecture that exists remains unknown.

In summary, the localization hypothesis is the view that specific brain locations are responsible for specific functions. Although the localization hypothesis has its origins in the pseudoscience of phrenology, it is supported by a wealth of evidence, including the evidence that Broca's and Wernicke's areas are involved in different aspects of language processing. The brain is composed of four lobes and two hemispheres, each associated with specific functions. An early attempt to catalogue the distinct regions of the brain resulted in the identification of the Brodmann areas, which continue to be used by brain researchers. In the past century, research has shown that within brain areas involved in producing movement and processing sensory information, there is systematic organization that can enable physicians to predict deficits for patients based on the location of the brain damage.

 Time out for Review

Key Terms

Amnesia
Anterograde amnesia
Arcuate fasciculus
Broca's aphasia
Broca's area
Case studies
Conduction aphasia
Contralateral control
Corpus callosum

Cytoarchitecture
Electrical brain
   stimulation (EBS)
Gray matter
Hippocampus
Insight
Localization hypothesis
Neologism
Pars opercularis

Pars orbitalis
Pars triangularis
Phrenology
Planum temporale
Postmortem autopsy
Retrograde amnesia
Wernicke's aphasia
Wernicke's area
White matter

Review Questions

1 What is the localization hypothesis? What group of scholars first proposed it?
2 What is Broca's aphasia? What are the symptoms? What are its causes?
3 What is Wernicke's aphasia? What are the symptoms? What are its causes?
4 What are the Brodmann areas? To what extent are they still used by contemporary brain imaging researchers? Which Brodmann areas represent Broca's and Wernicke's areas?
5 What is meant by topographical organization? What areas of the brain have been described as being topographically organized?

Language and the Left Hemisphere

The consensus following more than a century of research using a variety of methods is that, for most people, language processing occurs in the left hemisphere. The term "lateralized for language" describes the fact that language processing is associated with one side of the brain. In anatomy, the term *lateral* refers to *side*. Knowing this can be helpful in remembering that **lateralization of language** means that language processing is generally controlled on the left side of the brain. The evidence that language function is lateralized in the brain has been generated not only from case studies showing that injury to the left hemisphere is more likely to result in aphasia than injury to the right hemisphere, but also from multiple lines of research relying on different research methodologies. We will review these in the next section.

Evidence for Lateralization

Penfield's EBS technique produced compelling demonstrations that the left hemisphere controlled speech (Penfield & Roberts, [1959] 2014). Stimulation to the left hemisphere could interfere with speaking, while stimulation to the right hemisphere would not. A second methodology that convincingly showed that, for most people, the left hemisphere is critical in language production and processing was **Wada testing** (Wada, 1949, 1997) a technique invented by Japanese Canadian neurologist Juhn Atsushi Wada (1949–97). The technique involved paralyzing one hemisphere at a time to explore what functions were present and likely handled by the non-paralyzed hemisphere and what functions were eliminated and likely handled by the paralyzed hemisphere. Studies using the technique showed that the left hemisphere controlled language, because left hemisphere paralysis would result in language disruption (Branch et al., 1964; Wada & Rasmussen, 1960). The effects of the anesthesia were short-lived, lasting only five to ten minutes (Bradshaw & Nettleton, 1983).

A third source of information about the different functions of the left and right hemisphere is likely the most intriguing. This is research investigating the abilities of individuals who have had their left and right hemispheres disconnected in a procedure known as a "split-brain operation" that severs the corpus callosum, which enables the two hemispheres to communicate. This drastic procedure is carried out on individuals with severe seizures due to intractable epilepsy, in the hope of reducing the severity of their seizures. Individuals who have undergone this treatment are referred to as **split-brain patients** (Gazzaniga, 2005; Sperry, 1964). Numerous laboratory experiments have been conducted with split-brain patients to understand the different processing of the left and right hemispheres of the brain (Gazzaniga, 2005). In 1981, neuropsychologist Roger Sperry (1913–94) won the Nobel Prize in Psychology and Medicine for his research on the topic. His student Michael Gazzaniga continued the work.

Many of the laboratory studies with split-brain patients have used the **divided visual field (DVF) paradigm**, which enables researchers to present words or pictures directly to one hemisphere only (Mishkin & Foroays, 1952). The organization of the human visual system makes this possible. Information to the right of the center of vision is processed by the left hemisphere only. Information to the left of the center of vision is processed by the right hemisphere only. When split-brain patients were tested using the DVF paradigm, it was found that words presented to the right visual field (left hemisphere) could be verbalized, because the brain areas involved in the production of speech are located in the left hemisphere. When split-brain patients viewed words presented to the left visual field (right hemisphere), the words could not be verbalized. When they are asked to draw the object referred to by the word, they performed well. With the right hand, the object referred to by a word presented to the left visual field can be drawn. With the left hand, the object referred to by a word presented to the right visual field can be drawn. The results suggest that the process of naming an object initially processed by the right hemisphere requires the transfer of information about the object to the left hemisphere, where the language production system is located. Those of us with an intact corpus callosum can transfer information from the right to the left hemisphere and vice versa. Split-brain patients cannot.

In other demonstrations, split-brain patients were asked to close their eyes while an object was placed in either their right or left hand. They were asked to name the object using only their sense of touch from the hand in which the object was placed. For example, when a comb was placed in the right hand of a split-brain patient, the object could be named, because the right hand is controlled by the left hemisphere, which is where the mechanism for the language production resides. In contrast, when a comb was placed in the left hand, the object could not be named. The left hand is controlled by the right hemisphere. The information received by the left hand and right hemisphere would need to be sent across the corpus callosum to the speech mechanism in the left hemisphere to be named. For neurologically intact individuals, objects placed in the left hand can be named without any problem or delay. Studies with split-brain patients advanced our understanding of the major functions of the left and right hemispheres. Table 12.2 lists the functions carried out by each hemisphere.

Table 12.2 Selected Functions of the Left and Right Hemispheres Identified in Split-brains Studies

Left hemisphere functions	Right hemisphere functions
Producing speech	Spatial processing
Mathematical processing	Recognizing faces
Analytical processing	Music processing
Direction of conscious processing	Emotional processing

Source: Agrawal et al. (2014)

The lateralization of language has also been studied for listening. Research shows that the lateralization of language influences which ear we prefer to use when talking on the telephone. The Research DIY box outlines a study you can carry out in any busy public location where you can observe cell phone use as it occurs. Of interest is whether the use of cell phones supports prior research showing that there is a preference to use the right ear for listening to language.

 **Research DIY**

The Right Ear Advantage for Language

Since the 1960s, researchers have known that, for most people, there is a **right ear advantage (REA)** for processing language (Blumstein et al., 1975; Kimura, 1961; Shankweiler & Studdert-Kennedy, 1975). Each ear sends information to both hemispheres of the brain. One pathway involves contralateral control and one **ipsilateral control** (information is sent to the same side of the brain, such that the right ear sends information to the right hemisphere and the left ear sends information to the left hemisphere). The REA reflects the fact that our brains process language in the left hemisphere, and the pathways from our right ear to our left hemisphere are stronger than the pathways from our left ear to our right hemisphere. In Kennison and Bowers (2011), students were asked to investigate whether the REA for language processing could be observed when people used cell phones.

Photo 12.3 A women sits at a cafe using a cell phone. She is listening with her right ear, but holding the phone with her left hand. Which ear do you typically use?
Credit: © Jorge Royan

Naturalistic Observation

In the activity, you should find a public location on the campus or in the nearby community where you can sit and watch people going about their daily activities. It is recommended that you observe for 30 minutes or until you have collected 30 observations of passersby who were talking on a cell phone. As in research studies, before you begin collecting your observations, it is important to count only those instances when you observe someone holding the phone up to their ear as they listen. Other examples of listening (e.g., using a speakerphone where the phone is held away from the head) should not be included on your data sheet. On your scoring sheet, also note the sex of the person (male or female), the ear that was being used to listen (left or right), and the hand that was used to hold the phone (left, right, or none, as when cradling the phone between the head and shoulder or having a friend hold up the phone). Although it is not easy to determine individuals' handedness in a naturalistic observation, it may be possible to observe participants writing before or after they are observed using the phone. Below is a sample scoring sheet you can use for your data collection.

Sample Scoring Sheet for Naturalistic Observation of Ear Preference

Listener #	Listener sex		Hand holding phone		Listening ear	
1	M	F	L	R	L	R
2	M	F	L	R	L	R
3	M	F	L	R	L	R
4	M	F	L	R	L	R
5	M	F	L	R	L	R
6	M	F	L	R	L	R
7	M	F	L	R	L	R
8	M	F	L	R	L	R
9	M	F	L	R	L	R
10	M	F	L	R	L	R

Individual Differences

The evidence regarding hemispheric specialization that we have discussed so far has referred to the patterns of performance observed in a majority of cases. Individual differences in hemispheric specialization have been observed. For example, there have been individuals who have experienced language deficits following injury to the right hemisphere. These cases of **crossed aphasia** are rare (de Witte et al., 2008). The rarest of all cases are those involving right-handed individuals. In this section, we will discuss the research examining the factors shown to predict greater right hemisphere involvement in language than is typical. Such individuals have been described as not being lateralized for language in the left hemisphere. The three factors that have received the most attention are handedness, sex, and bilingualism.

The Role of Handedness

Since the early 20th century, researchers have recognized that a person's handedness is a predictor of whether their left hemisphere will be dominant for language. Most of the world's population, 88–90 percent, is right-handed (Papadatou-Pastou et al., 2008). Studies showed that between 84 and 94 percent of people identify as right-handed (Gilbert & Wysocki, 1992; Hardyck & Petrinovich, 1977). Among those who are left-handed, there are more men than women (Gilbert & Wysocki, 1992). Researchers and physicians measure handedness using questionnaires. Table 12.3 provides a commonly used handedness questionnaire. Those who perform all tasks using their right hand are the most strongly right-handed. Those who perform all tasks using their left hand are the most strongly left-handed. Many may perform one or more tasks using their non-dominant hand. One study suggests that approximately 96 percent of right-handed individuals are lateralized for language in the left hemisphere (Pujol et al., 1999). The remaining 4 percent of right-handers used their right hemispheres for language. In contrast, for left-handed people, only about 76 percent are lateralized for language in the left hemisphere. Of the remaining, 14 percent relied on both hemispheres for language and 10 percent are lateralized for language in the right hemisphere. The study showed that it was extremely rare for language to involve only the right hemisphere. This occurred in only 2 percent of the left-handers.

Research suggests that there may be slight variations in the numbers of left-handed people in different regions of the USA (Ingraham, 2015); however, estimates suggest that 10–12 percent of people are left-handed. The causes of handedness are not fully known, but most agree that both genetic and environmental factors are involved (Llaurens et al., 2009; McManus, 2002). An intriguing relationship

Table 12.3 Sample Questions to Assess Degree of Handedness

Instructions: For each activity listed below, indicate which hand you prefer for that activity. Do you ever use the other hand for the activity?

	Left	No Pref	Right	Do you ever use other hand?	
Writing	___	___	___	yes	no
Drawing	___	___	___	yes	no
Throwing	___	___	___	yes	no
Using scissors	___	___	___	yes	no
Using a toothbrush	___	___	___	yes	no
Using a knife (without a fork)	___	___	___	yes	no
Using a spoon	___	___	___	yes	no
Using a broom (upper hand)	___	___	___	yes	no
Striking a match	___	___	___	yes	no
Opening a box (holding the lid)	___	___	___	yes	no

Source: Oldfield (1971)

between the percentage of left-handers in a population and its historic rates of homicide suggest that left-handedness may have been advantageous in cultures where violence was common (Faurie & Raymond, 2005). Where violence has been historically common, the prevalence of left-handedness is higher in the population than where violence has been less common. In the former population, being able to throw a powerful left-handed punch against a right-handed opponent may have led to higher rates of survival for them and their descendants.

Recent research suggests that the phenomenon of handedness is not unique to humans. One study compared hand use of human infants, adult baboons, and adult capuchin monkeys for two laboratory tasks (Meunier et al., 2013). The results showed a preference for right-handedness in all species, suggesting that the preference for right-handedness and possibly lateralization in humans may arise from a lateralized gestural system present in a common ancestor of humans, apes, and monkeys. Research focusing on vertebrates suggests asymmetry in limb preference, but non-human species appear to be more variable in limb preference as a result of task demands than humans (Ströckens et al., 2013). It is likely that research will continue to investigate the relationship between handedness in humans and hemispheric specialization and limb preferences in animals and brain development. That research will provide an important missing piece to the puzzle of why the brains of left-handers differ so much from those of right-handers.

In an intriguing study by Papadatou-Pastou and Sáfár (2016), deaf individuals were found to be 2.25 times more likely to be left-handed than non-deaf individuals. The investigation was a statistical analysis of four sets of prior studies (31 datasets), involving 4,606 deaf participants and 786 individuals with normal hearing. The authors suggest that left-handedness among the deaf may be related in part to their delay in acquiring language, implying that early childhood experiences with language may contribute to the lateralization of language and the development of right-handedness.

Other research that supports the view that life experiences may predispose individuals to left-handedness comes from a study of military personnel in

Sweden. The study involved 180,000 male recruits whose medical records contained information about their mother's prenatal care. The incidence of left-handedness was significantly higher among recruits had their mothers received a sonogram (an image produced by ultrasound) during their pregnancy (Kieler et al., 2001; Salvesen, 2011). For males, the trend was strongest for those mothers who had the sonogram between 19 and 22 weeks of the pregnancy. While it is a compelling finding, it is unclear how handedness and exposure to sonogram imaging are linked.

An intriguing body of research suggests that among right-handers, there may be variation in brain organization related to whether the person has biological relatives who are left-handed. Research by Bever and colleagues showed that differences in language processing were observed between right-handers reporting only right-handed biological relatives and right-handers who reported one or more left-handed biological relatives (Bever et al., 1989; Ross & Bever, 2004; Townsend et al., 2001). The implication is that there may be brain differences related to having left-handedness in the family tree. Evidence from a brain imaging study provided support for this claim (Newman et al., 2014). Participants carried out a language comprehension task while their brain activity was recorded using fMRI. Individual differences in the degree of right-handedness predicted activity in brain regions known to be involved in language comprehension – the anterior temporal cortex, which corresponds approximately to Wernicke's area.

While the causes of handedness are still unclear, research on the topic can be challenging. Because left-handers are relatively rare, making up only 10–12 percent of the population, they are routinely excluded from empirical studies in cognitive neuroscience (Willems et al., 2014). The justification is that researchers desire samples with the least amount of variability. To make their samples as homogeneous as possible, researchers typically test only right-handed individuals. Willems et al. (2014) called for researchers to abandon the practice of excluding left-handed participants, as it may lead to a more complete understanding of the biological basis of human behavior. Ideally, studies would compare similar sized groups of right-handed and left-handed people.

Sex Differences

There is an ongoing debate about whether there are sex differences in language, particularly in how language is processed by the brain (Wallentin, 2009). The rate of left-handedness in men is about twice the rate in women (Faurie & Raymond, 2004). Since the 1980s, the view that there are sex differences in lateralization has been generally accepted (Bryden, 1982; Harris, 1980; Hirnstein et al., 2013; McGlone, 1980; Voyer, 2011). These early studies showed that the brains of men are more lateralized for language than women, suggesting that women may rely more on the right hemispheres for language processing than men. A recent study examining lateralization for different age groups of boys and girls between 4 and 18 years showed that sex differences in lateralization were largest in early childhood and were reduced by adulthood (Yu et al., 2014). Nevertheless, it is possible to find relatively old and newer studies in which sex differences in lateralization were not observed (Boles, 1984; Sommer et al., 2008).

Geschwind and Galaburda (1987) proposed that brain lateralization could be influenced by prenatal hormones, such as testosterone. Males are exposed to higher levels of prenatal testosterone than girls, perhaps explaining the trend for men to be more lateralized than women. Studies have also demonstrated that sex differences in lateralization may be related to individuals' exposure to hormones before birth. Lust et al. (2010) showed that prenatal exposure to testosterone was related to differences in lateralization for children at the age of six. For girls, those who experienced higher levels of prenatal testosterone had better left hemisphere processing of language than girls who had been exposed to lower levels. For boys, higher levels of prenatal testosterone were related to differences in interhemispheric transfer of information via the corpus callosum. A growing body of research has shown that the degree of lateralization for women fluctuates across the monthly hormone cycle, with less lateralization being observed when estradiol levels are high (Cowell et al., 2011; Hjelmervik et al., 2012; Hodgetts et al., 2015).

A number of studies have revealed sex differences in the sizes and characteristics of brain regions, specifically those involved in language (Harasty et al., 1997; Knaus et al., 2004). Nevertheless, a competing view is that sex differences in laterality and the sizes of brain regions associated with language processing are not supported by the evidence (Wallentin, 2009). The future will, no doubt, provide new research findings on this topic. However, any discussion of differences between groups of people should recognize that the amount of difference that is observed between the groups' averages is typically smaller and less impressive than the amount of difference observed within each group. The amount that each group's brains differ from one another is larger and more impressive than the average amount that the two groups differ on average.

Bilingualism

Research has also shown that the number of languages that a person speaks may determine the extent to which language function is lateralized in the brain. Research with bilinguals has shown that the right hemisphere may play a greater role than for monolinguals (see Vaid, 2008 for a review). Studies suggest that the age of acquisition is an important determinant of whether a bilingual's second language will be lateralized. The earlier in life that the second language was learned, the more likely that the language will be processed by the left hemisphere (Hull & Vaid, 2007). There is some evidence that different brain regions are involved in processing the different languages a person knows. Aphasia studies have shown that bilinguals and trilinguals may suffer impairment in just one of the languages they know, rather than in all the languages they know (Nilipour & Ashayeri, 1989; Paradis & Goldblum, 1989).

Research suggests that it is when a second language is learned that may influence how the language is handled by the brain. There is more bilateral and frontal activity during the processing of second languages that are learned later in life versus early in childhood (Dehaene et al., 1997; Hahne & Friederici, 2001; Hernandez et al., 2000; Kim et al., 1997; Marian et al., 2003; Weber-Fox & Neville, 1999, 2001).

Additional studies have provided evidence that individual differences in proficiency in a second language are related to brain differences. In these studies, the age at which individuals began learning the second language was also an important variable (Chee et al., 2004; Kim et al., 1997; Wartenburger et al., 2003). Wartenburger et al.'s (2003) study showed that brain differences were related to both second language proficiency and the age at which participants first began learning the second language. In Chee et al.'s (2004) study, differences in brain organization were related only to proficiency and not to the age at which participants began learning the second language. In a study comparing differences for bilinguals whose age of first exposure to a second language differed, Kim et al. (1997) recorded brain activity while participants were instructed to use either their first or second language for a task. The results showed that during the use of either language, there was an area of activity in the left inferior frontal gyrus. Further analyses showed that the brain areas involved in the use of the second and first languages for each participant appeared to be influenced by the age at which the second language was learned. When the second language had been learned in childhood, there was more overlap in the brain areas activated during the use of the first and second language. When the first and second language had been learned at different times of life, there was less overlap in the brain areas activated during the use of the two languages. Other researchers have pointed out that the results should be considered with caution because participants' language proficiency was not measured and there may be other variables that vary between the two groups of bilinguals, such as method of instruction in the second language (Abutalebi et al., 2005).

Research has shown that there are differences in brain density for bilinguals and monolinguals (Mechelli et al., 2004). Three groups of adult participants were tested: monolinguals, bilinguals who learned their second language before age 5, and bilinguals who learned their second language between the ages of 10 and 15. Both groups of bilinguals reported using their second language frequently. The results showed that for bilinguals, gray matter was denser in the left parietal lobe than for monolinguals. Those bilinguals who had learned their second language early in childhood had the densest gray matter. Further, the density of the gray matter in the parietal lobe was positively correlated with the bilinguals' language proficiency.

 Time out for Review

Key Terms

Crossed aphasia
Divided visual field paradigm
Ipsilateral control

Lateralization of language
Right ear advantage (REA)
Split-brain patient

Wada testing

Review Questions

1   Describe at least two types of research that provided evidence for the lateralization of language.
2   What is a split-brain patient? What have studies with split-brain patients shown about the functioning of the left and right hemispheres?
3   How is handedness related to brain organization?
4   What sex differences have been found in brain structures and brain organization?
5   What evidence is there that lateralization may differ between individuals who know more than one language versus individuals who know one language?

Language and the Right Hemisphere

An increasing number of studies are providing evidence that the right hemisphere participates in certain aspects of language processing (Federmeier et al., 2008; Johns et al., 2008; Kaplan et al., 1990; Lindell, 2006). The evidence comes from studies using a variety of methods, including evidence from patients with damage to the right hemisphere, brain imaging studies, as well as experiments using the divided visual field paradigm with healthy adults. In this section, we will review selected research showing that the right hemisphere plays a role in comprehending and producing prosody, using figurative language, understanding humor, and processing pragmatic and narrative information.

Prosody

As we learned in Chapter 3, the melody of speech is referred to as prosody. Prosody contains not only information about the stress pattern of the words in an utterance, but also the emotional state of the speaker. **Affective prosody** communicates the speaker's emotional state (sad or happy) (Pell, 1999), whereas **linguistic prosody** conveys aspects of the meaning of an utterance – whether an utterance is a question rather than a statement using an intonational contour that rises at the end of the utterance. Research relying on brain imaging of healthy individuals has shown that the comprehension of linguistic prosody involves the left rather than the right hemisphere (Kreitewolf et al., 2014). The Language Spotlight box discusses how native speakers of the Shona language are affected by damage to the left or right hemisphere.

Language Spotlight

Processing Lexical Tone in Shona Following Brain Damage

Photo 12.4 Shona is a Bantu language spoken in Zimbabwe and the neighboring regions in Botswana and Mozambique. How many languages do you think are spoken on the continent of Africa? Credit: *TUBS*

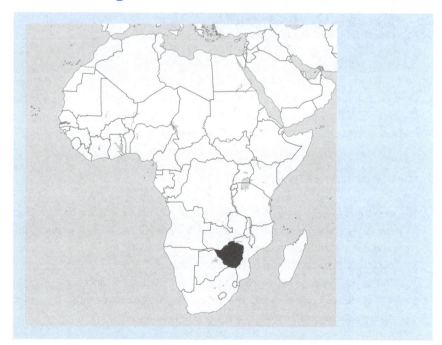

continued

continued

Shona is a Bantu language spoken in Africa, with about 10 million speakers who live in Zimbabwe, Botswana, and Mozambique (Lewis et al., 2016). Shona is one of the rare tonal languages (e.g., Chinese, Thai, Swedish, and Norwegian) in which there are words containing the same order of phonemes whose meaning is differentiated by being produced with different accenting or tonal pattern (Yip, 2002). Words are generally multi-syllabic and composed of tones in addition to consonants and vowels. Tones, which can be high (H) or low (L), occur in four pairings: HH, LL, HL, and LH. The HL sequence is described as a falling tone, and LH, as a rising tone. The majority of words in the language have at least one other word that differs from it in the tonal pattern as well as meaning. For example, the word for *bee* is /zana/ with a LH tonal pattern, whereas /zana/ with an LL tonal pattern means *one hundred* (Hannan, 2000). For a small number of words in the language, one word has the same sequence of consonants and vowels, but differs in tonal pattern, and thus in meaning. Consider the words shown in 1.

1 a. /ndere/   HH   self-willed person
   b. /ndere/   LL   day flying chafer
   c. /ndere/   HL   the sound of stinging
   d. /ndere/   LH   clean person

In the first known study of the processing of tone by Shona native speakers following left or right hemisphere brain damage, McLoddy et al. (2011) tested participants' ability to discriminate words that varied only in tone. In addition, they tested participants' ability to perceive tone in samples of words that had been low-pass filtered. A low-pass filter removes acoustic information about the individual phonemes in a word. Of particular interest was whether filtered and unfiltered words were processed differently by the two hemispheres. The results showed that, on both tasks, individuals with left hemisphere damage performed significantly worse than individuals with right hemisphere damage. These results are consistent with the view that the sounds of words that are related to a word's lexical status is the domain of the left hemisphere, even when the sounds involve pitch changes (Eng et al., 1996; Moen & Sundet, 1996; Yiu & Fok, 1995).

Studies have shown that the ability to understand and produce affective prosody can be impaired following damage to the right hemisphere (Pell, 1999, 2006). In a study that statistically analyzed the results from numerous prior studies investigating the relationship between prosodic processing and brain damage, evidence for a link between the right hemisphere and affective prosody was confirmed (Witteman et al., 2011). Research with married individuals found decreased marital satisfaction following a right hemisphere stroke due to problems processing affective prosody, but also in interpreting facial expressions (Blonder et al., 2012).

Figurative Language

Figurative language includes idioms, proverbs, metaphors, irony, sarcasm, as well as other forms of usage in which the meaning of the utterance cannot be constructed through a word-by-word decoding and combining of meaning. There is convincing evidence that the right hemisphere plays an important role in the comprehension of figurative language. Some studies with patients who have experienced brain damage have found that right hemisphere damage can lead to problems comprehending idiomatic expressions (see Kasparian, 2013 for review). However, there are also studies in which individuals with right hemisphere brain damage show no reduction in their ability to comprehend idioms. In one of the earliest studies, Winner and Gardner (1977) asked patients who had either left or right hemisphere damage to match the meaning of an idiom to one of two pictures. One picture was a representation of the meaning of the idiom, and the second picture was a representation of the literal meaning of the words in the idiom. They found that individuals with right hemisphere brain damage tended to interpret the words in the idiom literally. For example, when they were asked to select the picture with the same meaning as the sentence *the man had a heavy heart,* they were more likely to select a picture of a man holding a heart-shaped object than a picture of a man crying. Similar results were obtained by van Lancker and Kempler (1987). In a study comparing idiom comprehension in adults and children with right and left hemisphere brain damage, Kempler et al. (1999) found that while adults with right hemisphere damage performed more poorly than adults with left hemisphere damage, children with right hemisphere damage performed as well as children with left hemisphere damage.

The processing of metaphors has been found to be impaired in individuals with right hemisphere damage (Schmidt et al., 2010; Thoma & Daum, 2006). However, in a meta-analysis of 23 brain imaging studies, Bohrn et al. (2012) concluded that greater right versus left hemisphere involvement occurs only for novel metaphors. They also found that the processing of irony and sarcasm involved greater right versus left hemisphere involvement.

Humor

Although there are relatively few studies investigating hemispheric differences in the processing of humor, research has provided evidence that the right hemisphere plays a critical role. Heath and Blonder (2005) studied a group of individuals with damage either to the right or left hemisphere following a stroke. They found that the individuals with right hemisphere damage and their spouses reported less appreciation of humor following the stroke versus before the stroke. In contrast, the orientation toward humor did not change for individuals with left hemisphere damage and their spouses. Shammi and Stuss (1999) found that patients with frontal right hemisphere damage were the most impaired in appreciating humor when compared to others with damage to the frontal left hemisphere, non-frontal left hemisphere, or non-frontal right hemisphere.

Comprehending humor has been characterized as involving multiple stages of processing, including detecting a surprising element and then integrating it into the context. Studies have found that the comprehension of humor can be impaired following right hemisphere damage (Bihrle et al., 1986; Cheang & Pell, 2006).

Bihrle et al. (1986) investigated the understanding of cartoons for patients with left or right hemisphere damage. In one experiment, each person viewed the first three panels of a cartoon followed by two panels from which they were asked to select the one that would complete the cartoon humorously. One of the two panels was the original concluding panel and led to a funny resolution. The other panel contained a surprising resolution for the preceding panels, resulting in a less humorous effect. Patients whose brain injury was located in the right hemisphere were less likely to choose the humorous concluding panel for the cartoon than patients whose brain injury was located in the left hemisphere. In a second experiment, patients were tested on their understanding of verbal humor (jokes) and the results were similar. Patients with right hemisphere damage were less likely to select the correct punchline for jokes than patients with left hemisphere damage.

In a brain imaging study, Marinkovic et al. (2011) found evidence that healthy participants showed two distinct patterns of humor processing, one in the left hemisphere and one in the right hemisphere. They asked participants to rate jokes as funny or not funny. The punchlines for the jokes were varied such that they were funny, sensible but not funny, or nonsensical. For example, "What fish will make you an offer you can't refuse?" The punchline is "the codfather." The activity observed in the right hemisphere appeared to occur when participants were detecting the punchline of the joke and searching semantic memory for alternative interpretations. The "getting of a joke" can be thought of as realizing the one interpretation of the punchline that can be integrated with the first part of the joke for the most humorous effect.

The right hemisphere's role in the processing of humor continues to attract the attention of brain imaging researchers (Chan et al., 2012, 2013; Shibata et al., 2014). The research shows that there are multiple brain areas in both hemispheres differently involved in comprehending humorous, non-humorous, and nonsensical material. In the right hemisphere, the middle gyrus and middle frontal gyrus played a key role in processing humorous material. Chan et al. (2013) proposed a neutrally based model of humor processing involving three stages. In the first stage, incongruity is detected using processes related to semantic processing and involving right hemisphere locations (the right middle gyrus and the right frontal gyrus). The second stage involves incongruity resolution, involving regions in the left hemisphere. The third stage is humor elaboration, which results in "a feeling of amusement" and involves the **amygdala**, a brain area known to play a central role in emotional processing.

Pragmatic and Narrative Processing

Individuals with damage to the right hemisphere may also have difficulty interpreting social situations. Baldo et al. (2016) presented individuals with left or right hemisphere damage with a set of cartoons, which were not related to one another. Participants provided statements about what they believed the character in the cartoon was thinking or saying. Later, participants' statements were rated in terms of social appropriateness. Statements from individuals with right hemisphere damage were rated as significantly less appropriate than statements from individuals with left hemisphere damage. Brain imaging results showed that while the understanding of narratives involved both the left and right hemispheres, the production of narratives involved only the left hemisphere (AbdulSabur et al., 2014). However, a study of individuals with brain damage found that in a narrative production task, individuals with damage to the frontal right hemisphere made more errors related to global coherence than did other participants with frontal left hemisphere damage (Marini, 2012).

 **Time out for Review**

Key Terms

Affective prosody   Amygdala   Linguistic prosody

Review Questions

1 Discuss the distinction that researchers make between affective prosody and linguistic prosody. How do they differ in terms of brain processing?
2 What evidence is there that the right hemisphere plays a role in language processing? What types of language processing have been shown to involve the right hemisphere?

Brain Plasticity

Recent research has shed light on the brain's remarkable ability to respond to trauma. However, the mechanisms involved in the brain's response are not yet fully known. In this section, we first examine how the brain reorganizes following an injury, such as an amputation, loss of vision, or hearing. Research on these topics demonstrates that the brain is not a static organ, but a dynamic one. We then discuss what is known about individuals who have recovered from the removal of an entire hemisphere of the brain. Lastly, we learn about recent work showing that **brain plasticity** occurs throughout the lifespan, even in the brains of older adults. Brain plasticity is also known as neuroplasticity: where *neuro* refers to neurons, the nerve cells that are the building blocks of the brain and nervous system, and *plasticity* refers to the brain's malleability.

Cortical Reorganization

Since the 1990s, our understanding of the dynamic nature of brain organization advanced due to the work of V. S. Ramachandran and colleagues, whose studies of individuals with recent amputations who feel sensations and/or pain in the missing limb – **phantom limb syndrome** – led to the discovery of cortical reorganization in some cases (Ramachandran & Blakeslee, 1998; Ramachandran et al., 1992). After an individual loses a limb, the areas of the brain that once controlled the movement of the limb and processed the sensory input from the limb are left unutilized. Ramachandran and colleagues' studies of phantom limb patients showed that there is reorganization of function by the brain, such that those areas previously used in sensing and moving the lost limb come to be used in the service of other body parts. Although there has been some debate regarding the cause of sensations and/or pain experienced in the phantom limb, there is a consensus that cortical reorganization occurs (Flor et al., 2006). Similarly, after an individual becomes blind, cortical reorganization can occur involving the visual areas of the brain (Sabbah et al., 2016). In the next section, we discuss cases of plasticity occurring following the removal of an entire hemisphere.

Recovery from Hemispherectomy

Each year, a small number of individuals, typically children, undergo a **hemispherectomy**. Some of these children are diagnosed with **Rasmussen's syndrome**, a metabolic disorder that causes severe, unrelenting seizures. The condition is rare, and so is the treatment – the hemisphere of the brain found to be the source of the seizures is removed. Parents whose children undergo hemispherectomy are likely frozen with fear that the procedure will leave their child with permanent and severe disability. Surprisingly, case studies of children who have received the treatment show that recovery from hemispherectomy is not only possible, but common. When such a drastic surgery is performed on a young child, the brain shows a remarkable ability to recover, such that the remaining hemisphere takes over some of the functions of the removed hemisphere. Recovery from hemispherectomy is generally believed to be related to the age of the child at the time of surgery. Younger children recover better than older children, as brain plasticity is higher in younger brains. The procedure is typically only performed on children; however, there are now circumstances in which the procedure may be recommended for some adults (McClelland and Maxwell, 2007).

Researchers have studied the patterns of recovery in children who have undergone hemispherectomy. Of particular interest has been language development following left hemispherectomy (Curtiss & de Bode, 2003; Curtiss & Schaeffer, 2005; Liegeois et al., 2008; Vanlancker-Sidtis, 2004). In a study of eight patients, Curtiss and de Bode (2003) found the children's utterances to be highly similar to the utterances of children at the same stage of development in terms of mean length utterance. There was no evidence of grammatical deficits in the children who were missing their left hemisphere. A similar conclusion was drawn by Curtiss and Schaeffer's (2005) study of ten more patients who had left or right hemispherectomy. However, they reported finding that more grammatical errors were produced by those without a left hemisphere than without a right hemisphere.

Younger brains demonstrate remarkable plasticity, as cases of hemispherectomy have shown. In a television interview in the 1990s (Downs & Walter, 2008), the experience of Brandi was described. At the age of four years, she had a right hemispherectomy to treat a severe seizure disorder that caused her to have hundreds of seizure per day. She had little quality of life living with the seizures. Doctors cautioned her family that because the right hemisphere controls the left side of the body and also musical processing, Brandi would likely be paralyzed and unable to walk. Further, she would likely lose the ability to appreciate music. Brandi was interviewed while at middle school, able to walk with a slight limp and also able to dance to her favorite music. Her parents describe the intense process of rehabilitation and constant stimulation that Brandi received from professionals as well as her family. She was a straight A student, because of hours of extra tutoring each day. Brandi's case is an inspiration, showing the power of brain plasticity and hard work.

Brain Changes across the Lifespan

The age at which a brain injury occurs, either through an accident or necessary surgery, is an important factor that predicts how well the person will recover from the injury. Older brains recover less well than younger brains. Older brains are far less able to recover function following brain injury. Physicians typically suggest that the period of time that an older adult is likely to recover function following a brain injury, including a stroke, is six months following the injury. One of the most compelling stories of recovery from brain injury has been described by neuroscientist Judy Bolte Taylor in her book *My Stroke of Insight* (2008a). At the age of 37, when she was a neuroscience researcher at the Harvard Medical School, she suffered a major stroke (a rupture of a blood vessel in the brain). Her book describes her experience of having the stroke as well as her long road to recovery. When the book was written, she reported experiencing recovery of functions eight years after the stroke. Her experience provides hope for others who now know that continuous work trying to regain both physical and cognitive functions can lead to long-term benefits. You can see her TED talk on the topic (Bolte Taylor, 2008b).

The view that older brains are capable of new neuronal growth and creating new neural pathways is a relatively recent one (Eriksson et al., 1998, 2011; Kleemeyer, 2016). Earlier research emphasized the difference in plasticity between younger and older brains, with younger brains capable of far greater recovery than older brains. Recent research, however, has revealed that although recovery from brain injury is slower and smaller in older brains than younger brains, older brains are capable of regaining functioning. New neuron growth continues throughout the lifespan as does the creation of new neural pathways. Furthermore, the common assumption was that the recovery of functioning that individuals experience occurred within the first six months after the injury and that additional recovery of functioning was unlikely to occur. This assumption is also being called into question by recent evidence.

 Time out for Review

Key Terms

Brain plasticity

Hemispherectomy

Phantom limb syndrome

Rasmussen's syndrome

Review Questions

1 What is brain plasticity? What types of brains are likely to be the most *plastic*?
2 What has the study of individuals who have experienced amputations revealed about the ability of the brain to reorganize?
3 What is a hemispherectomy? What type of person may receive this surgery? What has research shown about brain plasticity generally and about the brain's control of language specifically?
4 What evidence is there that it is possible for new neurons to grow in the brains of older adults?

Summary

The idea that specific areas of the brain are responsible for producing specific functions dates back to the early 1800s. Early case studies documenting loss of function and brain regions were those involving Broca's aphasia and Wernicke's aphasia. The physician John Hughlings Jackson was the first to suggest that the parts of the brain controlling body movement had a systematic organization such that body parts were controlled by regions of the brain located close together. Later in the 20th century, researchers discovered that the left and right hemispheres of the brain were responsible for different functions. In most people, the left hemisphere is involved in speaking and the right hemisphere involved in the recognition of faces. The specialization of function of the two hemispheres is called lateralization. There are individual differences in lateralization with deviations from the typical pattern being observed in left-handed individuals, women, and bilinguals. The functions of the right hemisphere in language processing are less clear. Research confirms that the right hemisphere plays a critical role in processing related to prosody, figurative language, humor, and narratives. There have been recent studies pointing out brain functions related to language change following brain injury and across the lifespan.

Recommended Books, Films, and Websites

Battro, A. M. (2001). *Half a Brain is Enough: The Story of Nico*. Cambridge: Cambridge University Press.

Bolte Taylor, J. (2008). *My Stroke of Insight: A Brain Scientist's Personal Journey*. New York: Viking.

Bolte Taylor, J. (2008). *My Stroke of Insight* [video]. Available at www.ted.com/talks/jill_bolte_taylor_s_powerful_stroke_of_insight?language=en.

Calvin, W. H. & Ojemann, G. A. (1994). *Conservations with Neil's Brain: The Neural Nature of Thought and Language*. New York: Addison-Wesley.

Gazzaniga, M. S. (2005). Forty-five years of split-brain research and still going strong. *Nature Reviews Neuroscience*, 6(8), 653–9.

Hickok, G. (2009). The functional neuroanatomy of language. *Physics of Life Reviews*, 6(3), 121–43.

Lewis, J. (1981). *Something Hidden: A Biography of Wilder Penfield*. New York: Doubleday.

MacMillan, M. (2002). *An Odd Kind of Fame: Stories of Phineas Gage*. Cambridge, MA: MIT Press.

The Human Brain Atlas. https://msu.edu/~brains/brains/human/index.html.

The Split Brain Experiments. www.nobelprize.org/educational/medicine/split-brain.

13

WHAT ARE SIGN LANGUAGES AND HOW ARE THEY USED?

Chapter Content

Over the past two decades, the use of sign language interpreters on television has become more common. It is routine to see sign language interpreters during speeches and press conferences of national and international significance. You may even see a sign language interpreter at a rap concert. In 2013, interpreter Amber Galloway Gallego gained national attention when she was recorded signing at Kendrick Lamar's performance at Lollapalooza (*Huffington Post*, 2013). In the USA, having sign language interpreters available during public events increased dramatically after the Americans with Disabilities Act became law in 1990, which makes discrimination against the deaf and others with disabilities illegal. Similar laws have been passed in other countries. These laws have been beneficial for the relatively high number of individuals and families affected by deafness and who rely on sign languages. There are estimated to be 137 sign languages in the world, used by approximately 70 million individuals (Lewis et al., 2016). In the USA, sign language is the dominant mode of communication for more than 300,000 people (Emmorey, 2002). The number of sign language users grows each year, as the number of infants who are born with profound deafness is estimated to be 6 in 1,000 births (Kemper & Downs, 2000).

In this chapter, we look at the historical origins of sign languages and the psycholinguistic perspectives on the acquisition and use of sign language. In the first section, we review the origins of modern sign languages, how they are related, and how they are used by millions of people worldwide today. We will see that modern sign languages can be traced back to signing systems developed and used by communities of deaf people. Interestingly, these early gesturing systems were more complex than those used by deaf individuals in their homes to facilitate basic communication with those who can hear (called home sign). We explore the 20th-century movement in deaf education called oralism, which forbade the use of sign language and required the use of spoken language and lip-reading (see Baynton, 1996), and how it contributes to the modern debate within deaf communities regarding whether deafness should be viewed as a disorder (one that can be cured with a medical electronic implant, such as a cochlear implant). In the second section, we investigate how sign languages are described in terms of their grammatical rules (syntax, phonology, morphology, and semantics) and how these rules differ from those of spoken languages. In the final section, we review the research on the acquisition and use of sign language, both as a first language and a second language.

Historical Perspectives

Historical records dating back to the 16th century BC document that there was an awareness about deafness. A papyrus from Ancient Egypt discussed deafness and pointed out that there were many words in the language meaning *to be deaf* (Nunn, 1996). We can speculate that deafness has always been a part of the human condition, since genetics plays a role in approximately half the contemporary cases of childhood deafness (Rehm et al., 2003). We can also speculate that deaf individuals have used their hands to facilitate communication throughout history. Egyptian papyri from around 1200 BC also make reference to deaf people communicating with their hands (Gardiner, 1911; c.f., Caminos, 1954). It is interesting to note that the Ancient Egyptians are described as being tolerant of individuals with disabilities (Hubert, 2000). In contrast, in Ancient Greece, those with disabilities, including the deaf, received far less compassion. Aristotle's (384 BC–322 BC) view of the deaf is often cited as an example: "The deaf are born incapable of reason" (Moore & Bruder, 2013). More recently, historical records from the Ottoman Empire dating between 1500 and 1700 provide evidence that deaf servants were preferred over their hearing counterparts, because they were viewed as being quiet and trustworthy (Miles, 2000).

The historical record also tells us that sign language was useful not only for deaf individuals, but also for groups of people who spoke different languages. There are multiple references to gestural forms of communications being used by groups for trading transactions and other negotiations as a lingua franca. As we saw in Chapter 9, a lingua franca is a human communication system involving forms from many language sources, but lacking strict grammatical rules. One example of this type of sign language is **Plains Indian Sign Language** used by the indigenous tribes in North America (Wurtzburg & Campbell, 1995). There are reports of it being used in the 1500s when Spanish conquerors encountered the native peoples of the New World. The scant descriptions of Plains Indian Sign Language suggest that it was not merely a translation of spoken words into signs, but rather a stand-alone form of communication. It is not known whether it contained the grammatically complexity of modern sign languages. Its use was widespread in the geographic regions corresponding to contemporary northern Mexico, the USA, and Canada. In a second example, historians made note of gestural communication being used to facilitate trading arrangements by speakers of different languages in Africa during the 1500s (Blake, [1942] 2006; Grierson, 1903–1928).

The Origins of Modern Sign Language

Today's modern sign languages can trace their origins back to the first efforts to educate the deaf. The first instance of formal schooling for the deaf is believed to have occurred in 1550 in Spain (Daniels, 1997). Pedro Ponce de Leon (1520–84), a Benedictine monk, founded a school for the deaf at the San Salvador Monastery in central Spain. He is often referred to as the first teacher of the deaf. His students were from wealthy families who paid to attend the school. He is credited with successfully teaching his deaf students to speak. Some students also learned to write and read. He also developed the first system of manual signs for spelling. All modern sign languages have signs to represent alphabetic letters, which can be used to spell the names of people and places for which there is not a sign. Spelling with these signs is called **fingerspelling**. In most sign languages, including **American Sign Language** (ASL), fingerspelling is done with one hand, but in others, such as **British Sign Language** (BSL), Auslan, and New Zealand Sign Language, two hands are used. Across communities of sign language users, the frequency of fingerspelling varies and likely reflects social norms within dialects of sign languages. In ASL, fingerspelling may be used to spell English words for which there is no translation equivalent in ASL. Words may be also be spelled for emphasis. Studies of the frequency of signs used in sign language suggest that fingerspelling makes up less than 10 percent of ASL conversations (Morford & MacFarlane, 2003). It is also common for hearing children to learn fingerspelling during elementary school lessons about deafness and sign languages. Hearing children typically learn to spell their names and/or common greetings (How are you? What is your name?). Figure 13.1 shows the fingerspelling alphabet for ASL and the sign for *I love you*.

Around the same time that Pedro Ponce de Leon was establishing his school for the deaf in Spain, a community of deaf people in Scotland was using a form of manual communication (Kyle & Woll, 1988). The signs grew organically out of the interactions among deaf individuals in the area. It was refined and further developed by Thomas Braidwood (1715–1806), who founded Braidwood's Academy for the Deaf and Dumb in 1760 in Edinburgh, Scotland. Recognized as the first school for the deaf in Britain, the students were sons from prominent families with the ability to pay for schooling. His early use of a form of sign

Figure 13.1 The ASL Alphabet for Fingerspelling Did you learn any form of sign language fingerspelling in elementary school?

language, the combined system, was the first codification of what was to become British Sign Language. At least two other sign languages got their start from BSL. These include Auslan, which is used in Australia, and New Zealand Sign Language. Trevor Johnston (2002) has suggested that it is appropriate to refer to BSL, Auslan, and New Zealand Sign Language as dialects of the same language, for which Johnston and Adam Schembri coined the term BANZSL.

French Sign Language has influenced the largest number of modern sign languages (Lane, 1984). There was a deaf community in Paris using manual signs to communicate (Old French Sign Language). In the 1700s, this deaf community came to the attention of Charles-Michel de l'Épée (1712–89), who was from a wealthy family and interested in philanthropy and education. He became fascinated with the sign language and learned it himself. In 1755, he established a school for the deaf that was free for students to attend. It is unclear how much of the resulting French Sign Language was due to his contribution and how much was already developed by the community with whom he began to work. The influence of French Sign Language on the development of sign languages in other countries cannot be overstated. It strongly influenced many other sign languages: Irish Sign Language (Leeson & Saeed, 2012a), Flemish Sign Language, Belgian-French Sign Language, Dutch Sign Language, German Sign Language, Russian Sign Language, and American Sign Language and Quebec (aka French Canadian) Sign Language.

Sign language was first brought to the USA by Thomas Hopkins Gallaudet (1787–1851). Founded in 1864, Gallaudet University, the first university for the deaf and currently still one of a few universities for the deaf in the world, was named after him. Gallaudet had planned to pursue a career as a minister when he became a tutor for Alice Cogswell, a nine-year-old deaf girl (Gallaudet, 1888). Mason Cogswell, Alice's father, sent Gallaudet to Europe to learn the cutting-edge techniques being used to teach the deaf. Gallaudet traveled to England and met with Braidwood and Abbé Sicard. Gallaudet found Braidwood unwelcoming; however, Sicard invited him to his school for the deaf in Paris, the Institution Nationale des Sourds-Muets à Paris. Here, Gallaudet learned the manual sign language used in the school and the techniques used to teach it. In 1817, having returned to the USA, Gallaudet, along with Mason Cogswell and Laurent Clerc, who had been trained by Sicard in France, started a school in Hartford, Connecticut for educating the deaf. The sign language that developed at Gallaudet's school, now called the American School for the Deaf, is referred to as American Sign Language (ASL). In the early days of ASL, the majority of its signs were borrowed from the Old French Sign Language used by Sicard's students. Today, approximately 60 percent of the signs in ASL are the same as French Sign Language. ASL is used not only in the USA and Canada, but also in numerous countries in Africa and Southeast Asia. Table 13.1 lists the most widely used sign languages in the world.

Psycholinguists still do not understand how new signing systems are created within communities, but they do know that it was a common occurrence in the past and that it continues to happen today. Such cases of geographic communities developing their own signing systems have been referred to as **village sign language** (Meir et al., 2010). In the USA, there was a vibrant community of deaf people on the island Martha's Vineyard, located just off the coast of Massachusetts, who had developed their own signing system between the early 1800s and the middle of the 20th century (Groce, 1988). Due to a form of inherited deafness that was prevalent in families on the island, approximately 1 in 150 islanders were born deaf. The rate

Table 13.1 Most Widely Used Sign Languages in the World

Sign language	Estimated native users	Countries
Chinese Sign Language	exact number unknown	China
Brazilian Sign Language	3,000,000	Brazil
Indo-Pakinstani Sign Language	2,700,000	India, Bangladesh, Nepal, Pakistan
American Sign Language	500,000	U.S., Canada, countries in Africa, Southeast Asia
Hungarian Sign Language	350,000	Hungary
Kenyan Sign Language	300,000	Kenya
Japanese Sign Language	320,000	Japan
Ecuadorian Sign Language	180,000	Ecuador
Norwegian-Malagasy Sign Language	185,000	Norway, Madagascar
French Sign Language	150,000	France, Switzerland, Mali, Rwanda, Togo, Vietnam
British Sign Language	125,000	United Kingdom
Russian Sign Language	121,000	Russia, Ukraine, Belarus, Kazakhstan
Philippine Sign Language	100,000	Philippines
Spanish Sign Language	100,000	Spain
Mexican Sign Language	100,000	Mexico
German Sign Language	50,000	Germany
Greek Sign Language	43,000	Greece
Italian Sign Language	40,000	Italy
Irish Sign Language	40,000	Ireland
Yugoslav Sign Language	30,000	Slovenia, Croatia, Bosnia, Serbia
New Zealand Sign Language	24,000	New Zealand

Source: Lewis et al. (2016)

at the time in the rest of the USA was 1 in 6,000. The sign system used on the island came to be known as **Martha's Vineyard Sign Language (MVSL)**. When the last user of MVSL passed away in the 1950s, the language became extinct. In Martha's Vineyard, as well as other places in which a village sign language exists, hearing people learned and used the language as well as those who were deaf. Even hearing fishermen were known to use the sign language to communicate with each other when it was inconvenient to use spoken language. Today, village sign languages are known to be in use in several places in the world, including Bali, Ghana, India, and Jamaica (de Vos & Zeshan, 2012; Meir et al., 2010).

Schools for the deaf are also locations where deaf people, sometimes from different linguistic backgrounds, develop a manual system for communication, referred to as **deaf community sign languages**. They are used only by the deaf individuals who initially meet as strangers. The signs that come to be used by the community appear to be influenced by home signs, used by the individuals in the community. Some of the sign languages in Table 13.1 are likely to have started with a deaf community sign language, arising in an educational setting (Meir et al., 2010). However, for others, the details of their origins are not completely known. For example, Chinese Sign Language (CSL), which is likely the most widely used of all the sign languages, has received very little attention from scholars (Fischer & Gong, 2010). It is believed to have originated in 1887 at a deaf school started by

Nellie Thompson Mills, the wife of C. R. Mills, a missionary from the USA. In China today, there are approximately 20 million deaf people who use different dialects of CSL; a northern dialect is associated with Beijing and a southern dialect is associated with Shanghai.

There has been research comparing the characteristics of deaf community sign languages and **home signs**, which can be thought of as the idiosyncratic gestures that a deaf child may invent over time to communicate with their hearing parents. The invention of home signs by deaf children and sometimes adults occurs quite commonly (Frishberg, 1987; Goldin-Meadow, 2003). A famous case of the use of home signs is that of Helen Keller (1880–1968). You may have learned about her from the films depicting her experiences with her teacher Anne Sullivan (Penn, 1962; Tass, 2001). In 1882, around the age of 19 months, Keller became blind and deaf. Her parents struggled to control her, as her behavioral problems were difficult to manage, and they could not communicate with her. When Keller was six years old, her parents hired the teacher Anne Sullivan to work with Keller. Eventually, Sullivan led Keller to make tremendous progress. Before learning fingerspelling, Keller had invented about 60 home signs to communicate with Sullivan and others (Keller et al., 2004). Keller went on to college, becoming the first deaf-blind person to receive a bachelor's degree. She mastered Braille and ASL. In her autobiography, she described how another teacher helped her learn to speak by allowing Keller to place her hand inside the teacher's mouth as she spoke. She became a world famous public speaker, traveling frequently to give speeches about rights for the disabled, women's suffrage, and workers' issues (Einhorn, 1998).

An important distinguishing characteristic of home signs generally is that they are used by one person to communicate with another person (child to parent) and are not used by a larger community of people. Frishberg (1987) examined many home sign systems and proposed a framework with which home sign can be identified and distinguished from modern sign languages. The home signs of an individual are generally not passed along unchanged to a new generation of people. In addition, the relationship between individual home signs and meaning is not as consistent as it is in formal sign languages. Comparisons of home signs used by children and parents in different countries reveal some striking similarities (Goldin-Meadow, 2003; Zheng & Goldin-Meadow, 2002). For example, Zheng and Goldin-Meadow (2002) compared home signs of children in the USA and China and found similarities. As you will learn later in this chapter, the grammatical complexity found in modern sign languages is far greater than that observed in home signing. It remains unclear how the grammatical complexity evolves over time from the less complex home signing systems to the fully complex deaf community signing systems. We can gain some insight into this by examining one of the most publicized, recent cases of home signs being developed into a deaf community sign language. The Language Spotlight box explores one of the first documented cases of a new sign language invented in the 20th century by deaf children in a government school in Nicaragua.

Sign Language in 20th-century Deaf Education

Despite the prevalence with which deaf individuals and communicates have used gestures to communicate, there was a time in the 19th and 20th centuries when educators of the deaf forbad the use of gestures and the learning of sign languages

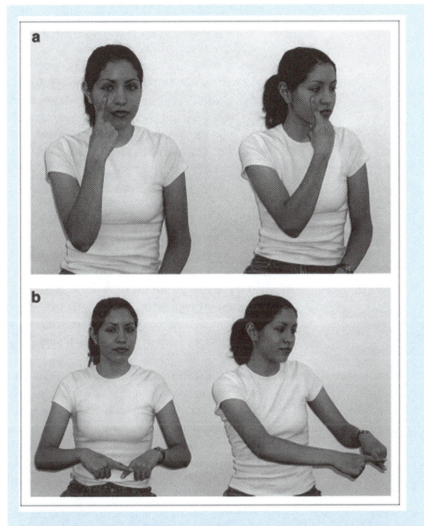

Language Spotlight

Nicaraguan Sign Language

Photo 13.2 A woman demonstrates the Nicaragua Sign Language signs. In the upper panel, she demonstrates the sign for the verb *to see*. In the lower panel, she demonstrates the sign *to pay*. Does one of these signs violate the principle of arbitrariness you learned about in Chapter 2? Credit: Ann Senghas, Copyright © 2010 by S. Karger AG, Basel

In the 1980s, children in a school for the deaf in Nicaragua were discovered to be communicating with one another using a new language they had invented themselves (Kegl et al., 1999). Teachers in the school were unaware of the meaning in the signs that children were making. The history of deaf education in the country provides a partial explanation for how the new language began. Prior to 1980, the government made no provisions for the education of deaf children. In 1980, a school for the deaf was formed in Managua. However, rather than teaching students a form of sign language, the school's curriculum focused on teaching children spoken language. For the next few years, the children made little progress learning to speak, but the use of gestures developed as children interacted with one another after school and on weekends. By 1986, the children's ability to communicate with one another was detected by teachers, but they had no way of knowing what the gestures meant or how to

continued

continued

learn. The Ministry of Education asked Judy Kegl, a psycholinguist from MIT, to study the children's new sign language. Following Kegl's first reports of her analyses, which suggested that the children's signing did, indeed, show signs of an independent language (Kegl, 2002), others visited the school to conduct their own research (e.g., Senghas & Coppola, 2001). Since the discovery of Nicaraguan sign language, other newly invented sign languages have been identified. Senghas (2005) describes one that was developed in southern Israel by deaf Bedouin children. The invention of sign languages by children in deaf communities supports the view of Chomsky and Pinker that humans are hardwired for language.

and required all deaf students to learn to speak and lip-read. The advocates of **oralism** were also proponents of using aids for hearing and having deaf people assimilate into the world of the hearing. After the American Civil War in the 1860s, advocates of oralism began to actively criticize the teaching of sign language and argue strongly for the complete assimilation of deaf people into the world of the hearing. In the 1880s, an international conference was organized by advocates of oralism. Subsequently, teachers in schools for the deaf who advocated sign language were replaced by advocates of oralism.

In Spain, oralism became the dominant approach in the education of the deaf as early as the 1500s. During that time, the Catholic Church refused to allow the deaf to receive communion because they could not make spoken confessions (Fox, 2007). The use of signing by the deaf community came to be viewed as having lower social status, particularly after word had spread among the higher social classes that a deaf person had been successfully taught to speak by Pedro Ponce de Leon at San Salvador Monastery. Wealthy families with a deaf child could send the child to the monastery to be kept away from the influence of the signing deaf community.

In the late 1800s, one of the most influential advocates of oralism was the inventor Alexander Graham Bell (1847–1922), who was born in Edinburgh, Scotland and migrated to Canada with his family in 1870 (Bruce, 1990; Petrie, 1975). His work as an inventor was greatly influenced by the fact that both his mother and his wife were deaf. His father, brother, and grandfather were experts on speech processing. His father Alexander Melville Bell was a professor of phonetics and communication disorders, serving as a lecturer at several universities including the University of Edinburgh and the University of London. He developed a system to represent speech sounds with written symbols to help individuals learn to speak. The system was called "visible speech" (Bell, 1867) and can be thought of as similar to the currently used International Phonetic Alphabet. Alexander Graham Bell's early tinkering included devices that could be used as hearing aids. One of his 30 patents was for a device that could be used to detect hearing impairment. Like many people at the time, he believed that deafness should be eliminated, if possible, and that deaf individuals should learn to speak. Bell was known to discourage deaf people from using sign language, as he believed that this excluded them from mainstream society (Miller & Branson, 2002). He delivered a speech to the National Academy of Sciences in 1883 in which he cautioned that because deaf people tend to marry other deaf people, the human race could be split into a hearing group and a deaf group. He noted that elements of **deaf culture** (schools, social clubs, magazines, newspapers, etc.) promoted the marriage of the deaf to one another, which could ultimately lead to deaf offspring due to inherited conditions, which we now know are relatively rare. In his view, hereditary deafness should be prevented, if possible.

In 1867, Alexander Graham Bell, and other advocates of oralism, criticized Edward Gallaudet, the son of Thomas Gallaudet and the president of Gallaudet University, for not emphasizing oralism more at the university. Gallaudet advocated the use of ASL in the education of the deaf, called **manualism**, and argued that oralism would deprive deaf students of deaf culture and their identities as deaf individuals (Winefield, 1987). In 1880, the 2nd International Congress on the Education of the Deaf was held in Milan, Italy. Here, the number of advocates of oralism outnumbered advocates of manualism. Many of the presentations advocated the complete elimination of manualism in favor of oralism. The conference concluded with eight resolutions voted on by the attendees, including the recommendation that oralism, rather than manualism, be the core curriculum in deaf education. Following the conference, schools for the deaf in Europe and the USA embraced oralism completely (Cohen, 1995). For the next century, schools for the deaf prevented students from learning sign languages. They required students to receive primarily spoken lessons that they comprehended through lip-reading. Then, in 1965, the US Congress examined the state of deaf education, producing the Babbidge Report (Babbidge, 1965), which concluded that oralism in deaf education had been a failure. Finally, in 1980, at the 15th International Conference on the Education of the Deaf, the 1880 resolutions were voted down in favor of a curriculum tailored to the individual, which could include training in sign language. One of the most influential advocates for manualism in the 1960s and 70s was William Stokoe (1919–2000), a linguistics professor at Gallaudet University whose work on the grammatical structure of ASL led to sign languages being given status as languages on par with spoken languages. Today, Gallaudet University is officially a bilingual institution, as ASL and English are used by instructors and students (Gallaudet University, n.d.).

Deaf Rights, Deaf Culture, and Cochlear Implants

Today, there are advocacy organizations for deaf individuals and their families to raise awareness about deafness, provide resources for families, and to provide input on public policy. The largest of these organizations is the World Federation of the Deaf, which works to promote the human rights of deaf people, with the goal that all deaf people should be able to "exercise civil, political, social, economic and cultural rights on an equal basis with everyone else" (https://wfdeaf.org/human-rights/). Despite the strides made over the past century, approximately 80 percent of deaf people around the world still do not receive basic education. Of those who receive education, 98 percent do not receive instruction in sign language. In some countries, the deaf are not considered equal to hearing citizens in terms of basic rights (Haualand & Allen, 2009). In many countries, the deaf are not allowed to obtain a driver's license. Many countries do not have laws against discriminating against the deaf in the workplace. In the USA, the National Association of the

Deaf (www.nad.org) points out that some of the common old-fashioned language (*deaf-mute* or describing a person as *deaf* and *dumb*) used to refer to members of their community in the 20th century is now thought to be insulting and should be avoided.

In many countries, including the USA, deaf people have become entitled to services through the passing of laws requiring accommodations for individuals with disabilities. The USA passed the Americans with Disabilities Act (ADA) in 1990. As a result, employers could no longer discriminate against the deaf or other individuals with disabilities. Deaf students were entitled to sign language interpreters in schools. Corporations controlling commercial communications were required to provide the deaf with access to communication technology comparable to that provided to the hearing public. This led to the development of machines that transfer messages either in typewritten form or as a video relay service by which a caller's message is delivered to a deaf person through a sign language interpreter (Strauss, 2006).

Just as Alexander Graham Bell had noted, deaf communities also have strong cultural identities in which deafness is viewed not as a disability or disease, but as one of the many ways in which people differ from one another (Lane et al., 2011; Padden & Humphries, 2006). As with any cultural group, the members share life experiences, social norms, and cultural values with similar others, so deafness and being part of a deaf community are viewed as a source of pride. Many deaf individuals do not feel as strong an affinity to the hearing culture of their geographical region. Research by Jambor (2005) has found that deaf individuals who are part of a deaf community benefit in terms of self-esteem. Mindess (2006) examined the cultural ties among deaf African Americans and found that they felt stronger ties to the deaf community than the hearing African American community.

Within deaf communities, there has been a great deal of resistance to **cochlear implants** for children, which have the potential to be a cure for deafness for some (Padden & Humphries, 2006). For families with multiple deaf family members, deaf culture touches every aspect of their daily lives. Consequently, curing deafness in the younger generation potentially means the eventual end to the rich, supportive culture of the deaf community (Padden & Humphries, 1988). At minimum, curing deafness in a family's new arrival will lead to the hearing child having vastly different experiences than the deaf family members, identifying as hearing rather than deaf, and not being part of deaf culture. The documentary film *Sound and Fury* (Aronson, 2002) is a compelling account of the emotional debate within a deaf family regarding a child's desire to have a cochlear implant. Those interested in preserving deaf culture fear that the complete elimination of deafness in the world will be the equivalent to a cultural genocide (Nevala, 2000).

For most hearing individuals, the technological advances that have led to implants are welcome innovations. A cure for deafness means that a child will have fewer obstacles to overcome in life. The cochlear implant is among the most successful (Niparko, 2009). The cochlear implant is an electronic device that can allow some deaf individuals to hear, specifically those without nerve damage. The device is able to transfer energy from sound directly to the auditory nerve, which then relays the signal to the auditory processing areas in the brain. Electronic aids for the hearing impaired were first introduced in the 1950s (Clark et al., 1990).

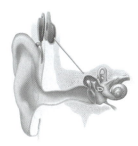

Figure 13.2 A Cochlear Implant
Does anyone in your family have a hearing impairment?
Credit: NIH Medical Arts

In 1972, the first cochlear implant was marketed by the company House 3M. The ideal recipients are those who are profoundly deaf in both ears with intact and functioning auditory nerves. Figure 13.2 is a photograph of a typical cochlear implant. As of December 2012, cochlear implants have been acquired by 324,200 people worldwide (National Institute on Deafness and Other Communication Disorders, 2017). Parents of deaf infants are now routinely informed about the benefits of a cochlear implant, which can be implanted in a child as young as 12 months (Spencer & Marschark, 2003). Geers and Nicholas (2013) found that children who received implants before 18 months did not differ in later language development from a comparison group of hearing children.

Approximately 50 percent of the cases of infants born with complete or significant hearing loss are due to genetics (Smith et al., 1999). The developmental causes include maternal illness or exposure to toxins during pregnancy. In some cases, the inner ear does not develop normally. Incomplete or abnormal development of any of the parts of the inner ear can often be detected through medical imaging. After birth, hearing loss can be due to recurrent infection of the ear (Bluestone, 2005). **Otitis media** is a group of inflammatory diseases of the middle ear, which can lead to hearing loss. This hearing loss is mainly due to fluid in the middle ear or rupture of the tympanic membrane. Symptoms of otitis media in infants include crying, trouble sleeping, and sometimes fever (Centers for Disease Control, n.d.). Older children may pull at their ears. Otitis media is more common for children under two years of age, and is slightly more common for boys than for girls.

In this section, we discussed the historical origins of modern sign languages and how attitudes toward the use of sign language have changed over the past few centuries. There are numerous modern sign languages, all of them having their origins in deaf communities in which deaf members developed manual forms of communication over time. Schools for the deaf began teaching sign languages to deaf students, and in some cases, had an influence on the language that is now used. Despite the popularity and usefulness of sign language among the deaf, the use of sign language fell out of favor among educators for about a century starting from about 1880. During this time, deaf individuals were typically taught to speak and to understand spoken language through lip-reading. Learning sign language was not encouraged. Understanding the discrimination and marginalization of deaf people in history sheds light on why deaf people and their families often feel strongly about preserving their deaf communities and resist completely assimilating into and becoming invisible in the hearing culture. Around 1980, the failure of oralism was acknowledged and the teaching of sign language was again promoted. Deaf communities have experienced marginalization and discrimination, which has led to advocacy efforts to protect the civil rights of deaf people. There are strong cultural ties to deaf communities, which some believe are threatened by the possible elimination of deafness in the world through cochlear implants. The end of deafness will also mean an end of deaf culture; consequently, many families find their members divided on whether the younger generation should have their deafness cured.

Key Terms

American Sign Language (ASL)
British Sign Language (BSL)
Cochlear implant
Deaf community sign language
Deaf culture

Fingerspelling
French Sign Language
Home sign
Manualism
Martha's Vineyard Sign Language

Oralism
Otitis media
Plains Indian Sign Language
Village sign language

Review Questions

1 In your own words, describe how sign languages have been developed in history, leading up to the modern versions of ASL.
2 Discuss the oralism movement in deaf education. How did the oralism movement affect the use of sign language in the USA and other countries?
3 What led to the end of the oralism approach in deaf education? To what extent did the oralism succeed or fail in its goal of ensuring that deaf people become integrated into the hearing culture?
4 How are village sign languages and deaf community sign languages similar and different? Provide an example of each one.
5 What is a home sign? How is it different from ASL and other commonly used sign languages, such as British Sign Language or French Sign Language?
6 What is a cochlear implant? Why would some parents decide against allowing their deaf children to have a cochlear implant?

Linguistic Analysis of Sign Languages

Sign languages are now recognized by linguists and psycholinguists as having the same status as spoken languages in terms of their complexity and grammatical structure. Your college may even allow students to satisfy their foreign language requirement by taking sign language classes. The view that sign languages are, indeed, natural human languages is relatively recent. This modern view traces its origin back to William Stokoe. He was the first to argue that sign languages should be regarded as equivalent to spoken languages, rather than a form of a spoken language implemented with hand gestures (Stokoe, 1960). Stokoe's work changed the way scholars thought about sign languages (Stokoe, 1978; Stokoe et al., 1965). He is revered as a hero in deaf communities, as his work helped promote sign languages in educational settings. In 1972, he founded the academic journal *Sign Language Studies*. He also developed the first system for writing down sign language, a phonemic script referred to as **Stokoe notation**. However, its usage is limited, and mostly restricted to linguists and academics. There have been other writing systems for sign languages, but none of these have been widely adopted either. In this section, we examine aspects of sign language grammar that Stokoe and others have compared to the grammars of spoken languages. First, we focus on the phonology, syntax, and morphology of sign languages. Second, we review how sign language vocabulary compares to the vocabulary in spoken languages. Lastly, we discuss the use of figurative language and other creative forms of usage.

Phonology

As phonology refers to the rules of language involving sound, you may be wondering how a sign language can have phonology when it does not have sounds. In spoken languages, phonological rules pertain to how the forms in the language are produced, so in sign languages, there are rules pertaining to how signs are produced in terms of hand and finger locations (place of articulation), hand configuration, hand motion (path, e.g., straight, circle, or arc), hand direction (from body forward or toward body), and number of repetitions of the sign. Linguists and psycholinguists still refer to these rules as *phonological*. In sign languages, an important aspect of phonology is how signers use the area around the body – the **signing space** – during signing. During signing, specific locations come to be associated with specific discourse entities or actions. Signing may point to the locations to refer back to the entity or action. Further, there are signs formed using only one hand, signs formed using two hands, and signs formed using two hands, in which one hand is more dominant in the signing than the other. Stokoe (1960) distinguished 19 phonemes (handshapes). Among contemporary linguists, sign languages are also recognized as possessing prosody, produced by movements of the face, head, and body (Brentari, 1999; Liddell, 2003). The tone of the message can be communicated through differing facial expressions (happy, sad, angry, frightened, etc.) and through the speed of the signing. Interestingly, just as users of spoken languages can modulate the loudness of their utterances, users of sign languages can modulate the size of their signs. Whispering in sign language may be achieved by signing to a person using small signs concealed from the view of others. Yelling in sign language can be achieved by raising the hands up so that the signing can be easily seen from those across the room.

In sign languages, words with similar meaning are often phonologically similar. In English, there are numerous words to refer to the act of thinking. They include: *to think, to consider, to ponder, to mull over, to contemplate, to reflect, to ruminate, to cogitate, to study*, and *to rack one's brain*. Each word denotes a slightly different manner of thinking. Languages differ in the number of words to refer to thinking, and those words differ in their phonological representation. In ASL, there may be fewer synonyms for common verbs and nouns, and for the signs with similar meaning, there is often similar phonological structure. For example, in ASL, the sign meaning *to think* is formed using the index finger of the right hand starting a few inches from the forehead and moved in to touch the forehead (American Sign Language University, www.lifeprint.com). The sign meaning *to think about* or *to ponder* is formed with the index finger pointed toward the head at the side, and the finger is moved in a circle near the forehead. The sign meaning *to mull over* is formed with the hand forming the sign for *and* close to the forehead and the fingers opening and closing in a fluttering movement to represent mental activity. The sign meaning *to think so, but to be unsure* is formed with the same hand-finger positioning and movement combined with a facial expression of uncertainty.

The phonological similarity among words similar in meaning appears to be common in sign languages. Consider the verbs related to the meaning *to see* in English. In ASL, the sign for *to see* is formed with the right hand forming a V with the index and middle fingers and the palm of the hand toward the face. The V is moved forward, away from the body. The sign for *to watch* is formed with the right hand position with the palm toward the face and the thumb and index finger forming a wide U. The sign for *to look at* is formed similarly to the sign for *to see*, but the hand forms the V with the index and middle fingers with the palm facing away from the signer and the hand is moved forward away from the body. The sign can be directed to an object in the signing space as in *look at that* or *look at her*. The fingers are angled in the direction of the object and moved forward in that direction. The signer would typically also look in that direction. The sign for *to look around* is formed by using both hands, each forming a V with the index and middle fingers, and moving forward together three times moving around the signing space first toward the right side of the body, then the middle, then the left.

Syntax

As you recall from earlier chapters, languages vary in terms of their basic word order, specifically the ordering of the subject (S), verb (V), and object (O) of a sentence. English uses SVO, while Japanese and Hindi use SOV. In sign languages, we also see variation in the basic word order. Although debated, the word order of ASL is considered to be SVO (Leeson & Saeed, 2012b). Other sign languages with SVO word order include Brazilian Sign Language and Hong Kong Sign Language. Sign languages that use an SOV word order include Japanese Sign Language, Italian Sign Language, and German Sign Language. ASL differs from English in the ordering of nouns and adjectives within noun phrases. In English, an adjective precedes the noun (the red car), but in ASL, an adjective follows the noun (car red), as it does in other spoken languages, such as Spanish.

As in spoken languages, the word order in the utterances of sign languages may be changed through grammatical processes, such as word movement. In English, the formation of questions involves syntactic and phonological changes to the corresponding declarative sentence. Consider the examples in 1. When a speaker produces a statement of fact, as in 1a, the intonation falls, reaching a low point by the end of the utterance. In contrast, a question having similar meaning to 1a is formed by adding the *wh*-word to the beginning of the utterance, as in 1b, and producing the utterance with rising intonation throughout, with the highest intonation at the end.

1 a. The stranger asked something.   Statement, falling intonation

   b. What did the stranger ask?   Question, rising intonation

Questions also differ phonologically from their declarative versions, with intonation rising at the end of questions, but falling at the end of statements. In ASL, signers also form questions by modifying the word order and phonology of corresponding statements. In ASL, there are three types of questions: yes/no questions, *wh*-questions, and rhetorical questions, which do not require an answer. When asking a yes/no question in ASL, signers produce a statement while tilting their heads and bodies forward, widening their eyes, raising their eyebrows, and pursing their lips throughout the entire question. When asking *wh*-questions, the *wh*-word (*who, what, when, where, why,* or *how*) is signed either at the beginning of the statement (*what Steve ate?*) or at the end of the statement (*Steve ate what?*) or signed in both locations (*what Steve ate what?*). When producing rhetorical questions in ASL, signers used raise eyebrows. Rhetorical questions are used much more frequently in ASL than in English. A common type of rhetorical question is followed by an explanatory statement (Juan likes who[rhetorical] Marcella).

In ASL, syntactic movement occurs in the ordering of signs to highlight the topic of the sentence for the observer. A signer may wish to communicate that the girl photographed the dog, and *dog* is the topic of the conversation. The signer can produce the signs for *photographed dog* or *dog photographed*. The latter order makes it clear that the dog is the topic of the utterance. Moving a topic word from a later point in a sentence to an earlier point in a sentence is known as **topicalization**. In cases in which the event occurred in the past, the signer often signs the time first, then the topic word, then the remainder of the sentence, as in *photographed-past dog girl*. For these types of sentences, the word order is VOS, an order that never occurs in English.

Some words that appear in sentences in English and in other spoken languages are omitted in ASL, such as *the* in the previous examples. Klima and Bellugi (1979, p. 189) described ASL as having "economy of expression." For example, ASL does not have the verb form *to be* (Chen Pichler, 2001), which linguists refer to as the **copula**. In English, an example of a sentence with a copula is *The cake is delicious*. In ASL, this sentence would be signed as *cake delicious*. Another example of a type of word omitted in ASL is the pronoun. Pronouns are omitted in some spoken languages – referred to as **pro-drop languages** – such as Spanish, Chinese, Japanese, Arabic, for example, but are rarely omitted in English (*Love you* versus *I love you*). In English, we would say *They have cookies*, whereas in ASL, the sentence would be signed as *have cookies*. When pronouns are not omitted in sign language, they are commonly communicated by the signer pointing in the signing space to indicate which of the discourse entities is involved in the action (Cormier et al., 2013).

Morphology

Sign languages also follow morphological rules. As in spoken languages, morphemes can be added to words to alter word meaning in predictable ways. In sign languages, morphemes are movements added to another sign or sign sequence. In English, the suffix *-less* can be added to nouns to form an adjective that means to have none of the noun. In ASL, there is a similar morpheme that when added to a noun or adjective also results in the formation of an adjective that means to have none of the noun or adjective quality. In ASL, there are morphemes that are added to verbs. For example, one morpheme specifies that the action is occurring *over and over*. After the sign for the verb is made, it is followed by a circular motion in front of the body, rotating high to low.

Sign repetition is something that occurs across languages, both spoken and signed, and is referred to as **reduplication**. In English, reduplication occurs when a word is repeated and there is a different meaning intended compared with the utterance with the single instance of the word, as in *I know she likes him, but does she like like him* and also in *Technically, I hit him, but I didn't hit hit him*. In sign languages, reduplication of signs is prevalent. For example, a singular noun (e.g., house) may be communicated by signing the word once and the plural version of the noun (e.g., houses) may be communicated by signing twice in quick succession (Wilbur, 2005; Wilbur & Petersen, 1997). Bergman and Östen (1994) discuss sign repetition in Swedish Sign Language, showing that how long the signer takes to complete the sign, which is a phonological difference, changes the meaning of the sign. For example, when the sign meaning to wait is repeated at a typical signing speed, the meaning is generally interpreted as wait for a while. In contrast, when the same sign is repeated slowly, the meaning is generally interpreted as wait for a long time. The signer may use facial expression during the slow repetition of the sign to further modify the meaning, such as communicating that the waiting time was exceedingly long. Interestingly, ASL does not distinguish the gender of nouns, as in Romance language (e.g., Spanish and Italian) and other languages (e.g., Arabic). In this way, ASL is similar to spoken languages that do not specify gender grammatically (e.g., Chinese and Finnish).

In some, but not all sign languages, signers use their mouth to communicate meaning. You may have seen sign language interpreters, mouthing words from the spoken language from which they are translating. This form of mouthing does not have a grammatical function in ASL. In contrast, there are specific syllables that are mouthed during sign production that function as morphemes, predictably changing the meaning of the sequence of signs. In ASL, mouthing the syllable *cha* while signing functions as an **intensifier** of meaning. For example, when a signer produces *stranger tall* while mouthing *cha*, the meaning is *the stranger is VERY tall*. Table 13.2 provides examples of other mouthed morphemes in ASL. My colleagues who have acquired ASL as a second language report that the face, mouth, and body phonology of ASL is the most challenging aspect of the language to master.

Table 13.2 Examples of Mouthed Morphemes in ASL

Mouthed morpheme	Function
1. CHA	intensifier
2. Puffed cheeks	large amount or size
3. OO	small in size
4. MM	medium, normal
5. AHH	far, far away
6. PAH	finally
7. FISH	finish, stop
8. EEK	yuck, despise, hate
9. AF-FO	have to, must
10. SAM	same
11. CS	nearby in time or space
12. BRR	great magnitude

Source: Bridges and Metzger (1996)

Dialects and Social Registers

In previous chapters, we discussed the fact that in spoken languages, geographic or social communities develop dialects that differ from the standard form of the language in vocabulary and/or in grammatical rules. Sign languages also have dialects (Lucas et al., 2001, 2002). For example, users of ASL living in Philadelphia have been described as having a distinct dialect (Fisher, 2015), which involves differences in vocabulary and phonology. Jami Fisher, a lecturer at the University of Pennsylvania, and Meredith Tamminga, her collaborator, aim to document the dialect before it disappears.

In at least one sign language, there is evidence for gender differences in language use. The term "genderlect" describes differences in how men and women use language. Barbara LeMaster (1990, 1997, 2000; LeMaster & Dwyer, 1991) was the first to study genderlect among users of Irish Sign Language, leading others to also examine the phenomenon (Leeson & Grehan, 2004; Leeson & Saeed, 2012a, 2012b). The genderlect differences exist among older adults who attended single-sex schools in the 20th century. Some aspects of the genderlect (e.g., vocabulary) are not commonly understood by the opposite gender. There are also some phonological differences. There is the strong possibility that other examples of genderlect in sign language may exist in other places in the world where deaf education was carried out in single-sex institutions for a long period of time.

Dialect differences in ASL have also been documented among African American signers, which developed in the segregated schools for the deaf in the southern USA (McCaskill et al., 2011). African schools for the deaf remained racially segregated until around the 1970s or later. Interestingly, the oralism movement in the 19th and 20th centuries was not always incorporated into the curriculum of deaf schools for African Americans, as it was in deaf schools for white American children. The dialect is referred to as **Black American Sign Language** (BASL). Due to the lack of frequent interaction between the populations using BASL and ASL, the normal processes of language change have resulted in both vocabulary differences and differences in phonology (how signs are executed) in the two dialects. For example, signers of BASL use a larger signing space than signers in ASL. In BASL, there are also more signs involving two hands and more frequent use of repetition of signs than in ASL. Users of BASL report also being proficient in ASL and using the two dialects in different situations in much the same way that speakers of the African American Vernacular English (AAVE) also use Standard American English (Lewis et al., 1995). Recent research suggests that idioms and other vocabulary have been borrowed by BASL from AAVE (Lucas et al., 2015).

In this section, we learned that William Stokoe was the first to argue convincingly that sign languages are comparable to spoken languages in terms of grammatical structure and complexity. We reviewed some of the grammatical rules in ASL comparing them to the rules in English and other spoken languages. Sign languages have *economy of expression,* in that the number of signs per utterance is typically less than the number of spoken words per utterance in spoken languages. Some sign languages allow pronouns to be omitted. Sign languages vary in their basic word order; ASL is viewed as having SVO word order. The phonological rules of sign languages pertain to the production of signs by the hands, but also include movements of the mouth, face, and body. Lastly, we learned about the existence of dialects and social registers in sign languages. Dialects related to geographic regions of the country have been observed as well as dialects related to gender and ethnicity.

Key Terms

Black American Sign Language
  (BASL)
Copula

Intensifier
Pro-drop language
Reduplication

Signing space
Stokoe notation
Topicalization

Review Questions

1 What are the phonological aspects of signs in sign language?
2 To what extent are sign languages complete languages like spoken languages, with grammatical rules involving syntax, morphology, and phonology?
3 Discuss the basic word order in ASL as compared with other sign languages and English.
4 Discuss the extent to which words in spoken and sign languages differ with regard to the relationship between the phonological representations and the meanings of words.

Sign Language Processing

Previous chapters covered the various aspects of language processing, such as language production (Chapter 4), language comprehension (Chapters 3, 5, 6, and 7), and language development (Chapter 8). In this section, we will review the most notable findings so far in the areas of the acquisition of sign languages, comprehension, and production. We also discuss bilingualism among sign language users, as there are many sign language users who learn a sign language as L1, but learn to read a spoken language, such as English, as their L2. There also those for whom a spoken language is their L1 who learn a sign language as their L2. Unlike the bilinguals you read about in Chapter 10 who know two spoken languages, bilinguals for whom a sign language is one of their languages are unique in that their two languages utilize different sensory modalities (e.g., speaking-hearing or manual signing-seeing). The term **bimodal bilingual** refers to those whose two languages utilize different modalities. Unlike bilinguals of spoken languages, research has shown that bimodal bilinguals can produce different words in their two languages at the same time (Casey & Emmorey, 2008; Marian & Shook, 2012; Shook & Marian, 2012). In this section, we will examine the relatively small literature on the acquisition, comprehension and production of sign languages.

Acquisition

Researchers now recognize that sign languages are acquired as first languages in a manner highly similar to the acquisition of spoken languages (Petitto, 2000). Infants acquiring sign languages reach the typical language development milestones at comparable ages (Meier, 1991). Consequently, when hearing parents of deaf infants are approached about having their infants learn sign language soon after birth, they are assured that there is no reason to fear that the infant will experience delays in language development. Parents and their infants may use a tutor to introduce sign language to the parents and infants at the same time. Research by Kluwin and Gaustad (1991) found that the three most important factors in parents' choice about how to communicate with their deaf infants (sign language or speech lip-reading) were:

1 Child's degree of hearing impairment; the more severe the hearing impairment, the more likely parents are to use sign language with the infant.
2 Child's involvement in preschool and the communication norms there; when preschools are familiar with sign language, parents are more likely to use sign language with their infants.
3 Mother's level of education; mothers with higher levels of education are more likely to use sign language with their infant.

Infants who begin acquiring sign language soon after birth exhibit similar behaviors as hearing infants learning spoken languages. As you may recall from Chapter 8, hearing infants acquiring spoken languages will begin producing random speech sounds (or babbling) around four to six months. Signing infants also engage in **manual babbling**, producing random hand and arm movements (Naeve Velguth, 1996; Petitto & Marentette, 1991). The average ages at which deaf and hearing children produce their first words, two-word utterances, and longer utterances are comparable (Corina & Sandler, 1993; Meier & Newport, 1990; Slobin, 1985). When deaf children's two-word utterances in sign language are analyzed in terms of the semantic relations expressed, they are similar to those observed in hearing children's two-word utterances in spoken language (Newport & Ashbrook, 1977; Slobin, 1985). Adults' interactions with signing infants also include a signed form of parentese or motherese (Masataka, 1992), which involves signing slowly, repeating signs, using larger hand and arm movements, and exaggerated facial and body gestures.

Just as spoken languages are learned better early in childhood versus later in life, learning sign languages also appears to be learned best during early childhood. As you learned in Chapter 10, the critical period hypothesis explains that early childhood is the optimal developmental time for acquiring language. In a study by Cormier et al. (2012), users of BSL (the ages they first began learning BSL varied) were asked to judge the grammaticality of sentences. The results showed that those who had begun learning BSL prior to age eight were indeed accurate in judging the grammaticality of sentences, but the most accurate were those who had learned BSL very early in childhood. In a study of ASL users who had learned ASL at differing points in childhood, Mayberry and Eichen (1991) found better performance on a range of language processing judgments for those who had learned ASL at younger ages. Hall et al. (2012) compared the performance of two groups of ASL users who acquired the language either as their L1 or L2 in a task in which they evaluated the phonological similarity of signs. They found better performance for those for whom ASL was L1. Sign languages contain slightly more words that are similar in appearance to what they mean (they are iconic). Such words are exceptions to the principle of arbitrariness, which states that for most words in human languages, the form of the word (sound or visual appearance) has no relationship with the word's meaning. The Research DIY box looks at iconic signs in ASL and the procedure for determining which signs are and are not iconic.

Iconic Signs in ASL

Words for which there is a relationship between form and meaning are referred to as "iconic." Sign languages have been recognized as having more iconicity than spoken language (Perry et al., 2015). For the iconic signs, those with little or no knowledge of sign language would be able to guess the meaning of the sign. However, just because a sign is iconic in one sign language, such as ASL, does not mean that the same iconic sign would be used in other sign languages (e.g., BSL). In this study, you can test the iconicity of the following 20 ASL signs. The ASL signs in the left column have a high level of iconicity, and those in the right column have a low level of iconicity (www.signingsavvy.com). You can download a brief video for each of the signs at the student resources website for this textbook (www.macmillanihe.com/kennison-psychology-of-language). You can insert the videos into a PowerPoint slideshow presentation.

Stimuli list

1 tree	11 house
2 telephone	12 ambulance
3 eat	13 cook
4 ball	14 cow
5 walk	15 run
6 time	16 door
7 baby	17 dog
8 book	18 flower
9 piano	19 church
10 drink	20 pretend

Ask 10 participants who have no experience with ASL to guess the meaning of each sign. Ask them to write down their guesses on a sheet of paper. For the non-iconic signs, they may have trouble coming up with the guess. Reassure them that this is normal and to make their best guess without spending too much time. Compile the responses to determine how many correct guesses there are. For each sign, calculate the percentage of correct guess (100 x # of correct guesses/# of total guesses). Were any signs guessed correctly 100 percent of the time? Those signs that were guessed correctly over 75 percent of the time may be considered strongly iconic.

There is ample scientific evidence that introducing deaf infants to sign language as early as possible leads to long-term benefits for the child. Because the vast majority of infants who are born deaf are born to parents with normal hearing (Meier & Newport, 1990), there is often a delay in exposing the infant to sign language. As you learned in Chapter 8, even before hearing infants produce their first spoken word around the age of 12 months, their brains are busy learning the sounds of phonemes, syllables, words, and sentences. For deaf infants, any delay in introducing sign language has the potential to lead to delays in later language milestones (Cooper, 1967; Quigley & King, 1982), such as delays in grammatical development (Cooper, 1967; Elfenbein et al., 1994; Presnell, 1973).

Over the past 20 years, some parents of hearing infants have tried teaching them some manual signs in the early months before infants are able to speak. The commonly used signs are for basic vocabulary (e.g., *all done*, *more*, *drink*, *eat*, and *sleep*), referred to as **baby signs**. An interesting question is whether there are any measurable benefits of baby sign language for hearing infants' later language development. Studies of hearing infants' acquisition of baby sign language have confirmed that the signs are easily acquired (Acredolo et al., 1999; Goodwyn et al., 2000). There was some speculation that there may be a cognitive benefit for infants who learn to use baby sign language prior to being able to speak; however, thus far, there are no convincing studies in which families were randomly assigned to use baby sign language with their infants (Johnston et al., 2005).

Comprehension

The number of studies investigating sign language processing is still relatively low compared to studies of processing in spoken languages; however, there has been a noticeable increase in the past decade (Carreiras, 2010). Of the language processing phenomena that have been investigated in sign language, the results suggest that the processing that occurs is similar to that observed for spoken languages. For example, studies in which ASL users were asked to perform a lexical decision task for a randomized order of actual signs and non-signs, which were created by changing one feature (i.e., handshape, location or movement) from an actual sign, showed that correct responses to non-signs were significantly longer than correct responses to signs, as has been shown in spoken languages (Carreiras et al., 2008; Emmorey, 1991). An explanation for the pattern of results in all languages is that during lexical decision, participants search memory until a match is found. Matches are found for actual words, resulting in a "yes" response. For "no" responses, memory is presumably exhaustively searched without a match being found. Carreiras et al. (2008) also demonstrated that signs with a high level of familiarity (likely due to high frequency of use) were judged more quickly in a lexical decision task than signs with lower familiarity. Due to the lack of word frequency norms for ASL (or other sign languages), the pattern cannot strictly be described as evidence for a word frequency effect, which has been demonstrated in numerous studies involving spoken languages. Nevertheless, in research with spoken languages, familiarity has been shown to be highly correlated to word frequency (Gernsbacher, 1984; see also Balota et al., 2001).

The phenomenon of phonological priming was documented in sign language in a series of experiments reported by Carreiras et al. (2008). They found that the time participants took to process a sign was shorter when immediately preceded by a non-sign that had the same handshape versus different handshape. For cases in which signs were preceded by non-signs that either did or did not share the same location, they found that participants took longer to process signs preceded by related primes versus unrelated ones. The authors noted that there are cases in spoken languages in which relatedness between two words judged back to back leads to inhibition rather than facilitation. It remains unclear how the process of sign recognition is carried out with different aspects of a sign (hand location and handshape) being stored separately in memory.

Comprehension of ASL has also been studied in bimodal bilinguals (Emmorey & McCullough, 2009; Morford et al., 2011; Swanwick, 2016). Emmorey and McCullough (2009) compared the brain scans of monolingual speakers of English, monolingual users of ASL who were deaf, and a group of bimodal bilinguals who knew spoken English and ASL. As their brains were scanned, participants viewed photos of a person signing as well as photos of faces with emotional expressions, such as anger, fear, or disgust. For the bimodal bilinguals and the monolingual users of ASL, the superior temporal sulcus, which is located below Wernicke's area, was activated when they watched signing. For monolingual users of ASL, there was activation in the left hemisphere during the perception of emotional facial expressions; however, bimodal bilinguals did not show this pattern of brain activation. Because signed and spoken languages are distinct languages with unique grammatical rules and vocabulary, deaf users of ASL in the USA may not be bilingual in English. Consequently, learning to read English can be challenging (Goldin-Meadow & Mayberry, 2001). The Classic Research box explores a series of reading experiments that revealed how deaf readers differ from hearing readers.

Classic Research

A Comparison of Deaf and Hearing Readers

Treiman and Hirsh-Pasek (1983) wanted to compare the performance of deaf and hearing readers. Earlier research has shown that deaf individuals who were skilled in the use of ASL and reading English showed activation of the muscles in the hands and fingers when they read English silently (McGuigan, 1971). This result was seen as demonstrating that manual *subvocalization* occurs during reading for ASL users. In Treiman and Hirsh-Pasek's (1983) first experiment, both groups of participants read target sentences that contained phonologically similar words (e.g., *She chose three shows to see at the theater*) and control sentences, which were similar in meaning to the target sentences, but did not contain the phonological repetition (e.g., *She picked two movies to see with her friend*). Participants were asked to indicate whether the sentences were grammatically correct. The researchers confirmed their prediction that hearing participants would make more errors on sentences containing phonological repetition than deaf participants, as deaf participants may be less likely to activate the phonological representations of the words, or activate the phonological representations to a lesser extent than hearing participants. In their second experiment, Treiman and Hirsh-Pasek tested the hypothesis that deaf readers may activate ASL signs when reading English sentences. They constructed sentences that contained several words whose ASL translations involved similar handshapes. For example, in the sentence *I ate the apples at home yesterday*, there are four words that, when signed in ASL, involve forming a fist and placing the hand near the face. As predicted, deaf readers may make more errors on sentences containing handshape repetition than on control sentences that were similar in meaning, but did not contain handshape repetition. In contrast, hearing participants performed similarly for both types of sentences. Since the publication of this classic research, numerous other studies have shown that learning to read a spoken language is challenging for those who are deaf (see Goldin-Meadow & Mayberry, 2001).

Researchers have come to recognize how challenging it is for deaf individuals to learn to read a spoken language. As you may recall from previous chapters, readers automatically activate the phonological representation of words and are likely to use the phonological information during comprehension and the storage of meaning in working memory. When those who have been profoundly deaf since birth learn to read a spoken language, they do not have access to phonology. Consequently, they have difficulty developing the phonological awareness that is needed for reading comprehension in a spoken language (Sterne & Goswami, 2000; Transler et al., 1999, 2001). Research has shown, however, that with appropriate training, it is possible for the profoundly deaf to achieve a high level of phonological awareness and reading skill in English (Furlonger et al., 2014). Individual differences in phonemic awareness, as reflected in fingerspelling ability, has been found to predict English reading proficiency (Stone et al., 2015).

Research has also shown that for deaf individuals for whom a sign language is L1, learning to read a spoken L2 is related to their language ability in L1 (Andrew et al., 2014; Aura et al., 2016). In a study of deaf children and adolescents who had acquired ASL as L1 and had learned to read English as L2, Andrew et al. (2014) found that proficiency in ASL predicted performance in the reading task. The results support the view that L1 acquisition influences L2 acquisition. Aura et al. (2016) demonstrated a link between L1 ability in Kenyan Sign Language and L2 reading proficiency in English. As we look to the future, we will likely see more research on this topic, as there are many questions worthy of examination. Some interesting questions include: How does the age at which the sign language L1 is acquired influence the relationship between L1 proficiency and reading in L2? Do differences in the amount of L1 experiences or types of L1 experiences occurring early in childhood predict L1 ability, proficiency in reading in L2 and/or the relationship between L1 ability and reading in L2?

Due to the relatively small number of studies on the acquisition of sign languages by young children, there is much yet to be learned about how the acquisition of sign languages may differ from the acquisition of spoken language, particularly the role of the home environment (whether parents are deaf or hearing, number of family members using sign versus spoken language, number of deaf children in the home, etc.). Goldstein and Bebko (2003) noted the potential complexity involved in the acquisition of language by deaf children and presented a new measure, the Profile of Multiple Language Proficiencies (PMLP), to assess children's abilities in both signed and spoken languages. The measure was designed to assess three categories of signers' communications: ASL; signed English, which typically occurs with fingerspelling; and spoken English. They demonstrated the usefulness of the PMLP by having raters use it to assess the skills of a small group of profoundly deaf children between the ages of 7 and 13 years. The PMLP can be used to classify each of the three language abilities into eight levels, from pre-linguistic skills only to fluency. Others have noted that there continue to be substantial differences between how signers' language skills are assessed in research settings versus other settings (Bennett et al., 2014).

Production

There is a growing body of research demonstrating that the processes used in the production of sign language are similar to those identified in studies of spoken languages. As you learned in previous chapters, speakers sometimes experience difficulty finding a word, referred to as tip-of-the-tongue (ToT) states. Speakers may be able to identify some characteristics of the elusive word, such as the initial phoneme or syllable, the number of syllables, and part of speech. Typically, the speaker will think of the elusive word some time later.

Research by Thompson et al. (2005) showed that users of ASL also experience temporary word-finding difficulty, described as **tip-of-the-fingers** (ToF) **states**. While struggling to identify the word, signers are often able to report some characteristics of the word (hand location, hand shape, and movement type). As with speakers in studies of ToT states, ASL users were typically able to retrieve the word eventually. Thompson et al. (2005) concluded that the results support a model in which the retrieval of signs during signing occurs in two stages. The first stage involves semantics, and the second, phonology. However, they argued that during the retrieval of signs, the stages of semantics and phonology are more overlapping than in spoken word retrieval.

The view that word production, in both spoken and sign language, involves an early stage of semantic processing followed by a later stage of phonological processing was demonstrated in Chapter 4 during the discussion of picture-naming experiments (Schriefers et al., 1990). As participants viewed a picture and prepared their spoken response, a distractor word was played that the participant could hear. The researchers varied the relatedness between the distractor word and the name of the picture as well as the timing of the presentation of the distractor word (early or later in the period when the participant prepared to say the name of the picture). Distractor words could be semantically related, phonologically related, or unrelated to the name of the picture. The results showed that distractors that were semantically related to the picture name affected processing only when they were presented soon after the picture and early in the participant's word planning. Also, distractors that were phonologically related to the picture name affected processing relatively late in the participant's word planning and production.

Baus et al. (2008) reported the sign language version of this research with a group of participants who were fluent in Catalan Sign Language, which is used in eastern regions of Spain where there are large populations of Catalan speakers. Participants were asked to name pictures (with a signed word) that were projected on a screen superimposed on a video of a person signing in Catalan Sign Language. The images were presented to participants at the same time. Participants were instructed to name the picture and ignore the signing in the background. The researchers varied the relatedness between the distractor signing in the background and the sign that participants were expecting. The distractor could be: phonologically related by sharing location, handshape, or movement; semantically related sharing meaning, but not sharing any phonological features (location, handshape, or movement); or unrelated in terms of both phonology and semantics. The results showed the familiar pattern for some, but not all, of the conditions. When the distractor was semantically related to the target, there was inhibition of target signing time (slower responding versus unrelated condition). When the distractor was phonologically related to the target in handshape or movement, there was facilitation of target signing time (faster responding versus unrelated condition). The novel result was that when the distractor shared the phonological feature of location, there was inhibition of target signing time. These results, considered in conjunction with the lexical decision task results of Carreiras et al. (2008), suggest that in contrast to the features of handshape and movement, the feature of location plays a different, but unknown role in the process of lexical access for signs in sign languages.

In this section, we learned that the research on the acquisition, comprehension and production of sign languages has revealed similarities between the processing of spoken and sign languages. Sign languages tend to have more signs that resemble their meaning (making the sign for *tree* looks like the hand taking the shape of a tree) than spoken languages have words with sounds that indicate their meaning (onomatopoeia as in *drip* or *boom*). The stages in the acquisition of sign languages appear similar to the stages observed in the acquisition of spoken language. Lastly, the approaches that have been used in the study of the comprehension and production of spoken languages have been successfully applied to understanding the comprehension and production of sign languages.

 Time out for Review

Key Terms

Baby signs   Manual babbling
Bimodal bilingual   Tip-of-the-fingers state

Review Questions

1   What are baby signs? Why might hearing parents teach their hearing infants baby sign language? Have studies found any long-term benefits of teaching hearing infants baby signs?
2   Most sign languages have some iconic signs. What does this mean? Why would sign languages typically contain some iconicity?
3   What has the research shown about the benefits of teaching deaf children sign language very early in life?
4   Describe the differences between ASL and BASL. What group(s) of people typically use BASL? Why have the two forms of ASL developed into different dialects?

Summary

ASL and other modern sign languages have relatively long histories, beginning with innovations in deaf communities. Often, the early signing of a deaf community came to be refined and further developed in an educational setting for the deaf. Recently, new sign languages have been developed by deaf communities in Nicaragua and Israel. In terms of grammatical structure, sign languages can be described using the same categories of language rules as spoken language (phonology, syntax, and morphology). The phonological structure involves aspects of the production of signs with the hands and the location of the hands around the body during the execution of a sign. Sign languages can be acquired as first languages. Children who acquire a sign language as a native language (L1) have been shown to reach language development milestones at the same ages as hearing children acquiring spoken languages. Individuals who know a sign language in addition to a spoken language are referred to as bimodal bilinguals. Although earlier research showed that profoundly deaf individuals struggle to achieve proficiency in reading a spoken L2, recent research showing that fingerspelling ability is related to the reading proficiency of deaf individuals implies that it may be possible to increase phonological awareness and reading proficiency by improving fingerspelling ability through instruction and practice.

Recommended Books, Films, and Websites

Acredolo, L. P., Goodwyn, S. W. & Abrams, D. (2002). *Baby Signs*. New York: McGraw-Hill.

Aronson, J. (2002). *Sound and Fury* [Motion picture]. United States: New Video Group.

Aronson, J. (2006). *Sound and Fury: 6 Years Later* [Motion picture]. United States: New Video Group.

Black ASL Project. http://blackaslproject.gallaudet.edu/BlackASLProject/Welcome.html.

Brentari, D. (2010). *Sign Languages*. Cambridge: Cambridge University Press.

Fox, M. (2007). *Talking Hands: What Sign Language Reveals About the Mind*. New York: Simon & Schuster.

Gary, D. & Hott, L. R. (Directors) (2007). *Through Deaf Eyes* [DVD]. Available from www.pbs.org.

Haines, R. (Director) (1986). *Children of a Lesser God* [Motion picture]. United States: Paramount.

Keller, H., Shattuck, R. & Herrmann, D. (2004). *The Story of My Life: The Restored Classic*. New York: W. W. Norton.

Sandler, W. & Lillo-Martin, D. (2006). *Sign Language and Linguistic Universals*. Cambridge: Cambridge University Press.

Scarl, H. (Producer/Director) (2011). *See What I Am Saying* [Documentary]. United States: New Video Group.

World Federation of the Deaf (n.d.). Who we are? Available at https://wfdeaf.org/who-we-are.

14 HOW CAN LANGUAGE BECOME DISORDERED?

People of all ages, nationalities, ethnicities, and socioeconomic levels can be affected by language disorders. You may have a friend or family member who is affected. Children may be identified as having a language disorder if their problem with language interferes with their performance in school. In contrast, adults with no history of language problems may acquire one due to brain injury. The cause of many language problems in older adults is a **stroke**, a condition that causes bleeding in the brain and damage to brain tissue (Johnson et al., 2016). Our risk of stroke increases as we get older. Because the percentage of the population over 65 years of age worldwide is expected to continue to rise in the coming decades, the numbers of people experiencing strokes and aphasia are also expected to increase. In this chapter, we explore the complexities of language disorders, with a particular focus on the language systems involved. In section one, we distinguish between speech disorders and language disorders, and go on to examine the prevalence of language disorders, the different types of professionals who treat language disorders, some of the obstacles encountered when individuals pursue a diagnosis, and a brief note about treatments. In section two, we examine severe disorders in which syntactic processing is impaired. Lastly, we discuss disorders involving non-syntactic processing, including disorders with lexical, phonological, and semantic/pragmatic information deficits.

Speech versus Language Disorders

As a psycholinguist, I use the phrase *speech disorders* to refer to those communication processes primarily involving articulation or speech processes, and *language disorders* to refer to processes involving one or more of the language systems or processes. You may find that others use the phrases interchangeably or use the phrase "speech processes" to broadly cover all the processes involved in human communication in which speech is involved (Oyer et al., 2000). Examples of speech disorders that predominantly involve articulation include:

- **dysarthria**: speech is unclear, but linguistically correct
- **apraxia of speech**: speech errors caused by glitches in the planning of articulation
- **speech impediment**: a consistent type of error in articulation that can cause speech to be difficult to perceive, as in stuttering and difficulty producing specific phonemes like *s* or *r*.

In addition, **voice disorders** involve severe problems speaking, due to the speaker's inability to produce and/or control the loudness and quality of the sound produced by the larynx (Verdolini et al., 2006). For this chapter, we will focus exclusively on disorders suspected to involve one or more language systems.

Prevalence of Language Disorders

An important first step in identifying and classifying language disorders is determining how many people experience problems with language. Currently, we have no reliable way to estimate the worldwide prevalence of language problems experienced by children or adults, as there is no organization responsible for compiling the data. The World Health Organization is an excellent source of numerous types of global health statistics; however, it currently does not compile statistics related to speech and language-related disorders. In our discussion, we examine estimates of language disorders by considering separately those affecting children and those affecting older adults. Healthcare professionals classify language disorders into two broad categories:

1 **Developmental disorders**: the disorder is present from birth in individuals who have no evidence of brain injury.
2 **Acquired disorders**: the disorder emerges only after some form of brain injury.

Research has identified forms of dyslexia in which there are developmental and acquired forms that share symptoms (Castles & Coltheart, 1993; Coltheart & Kohnen, 2012), as well as the inability to recognize faces, also called prosopagnosia or face blindness (Grüter et al., 2008). When similarities between developmental and acquired disorders exist, it is possible that the brain areas known to be involved in the acquired disorder may prove to be involved in the developmental disorder with similar symptoms. Consequently, identifying similarities between the two types of language disorders can be an impetus for future research.

While we lack statistics regarding the numbers of older adults with aphasia worldwide, there are statistics about the prevalence of stroke, the major cause of acquired language problems or aphasia. Stroke ranks second on the list of top ten causes of death worldwide and ranks sixth in the top ten causes of disability (Johnson et al., 2016). The lifetime risk of stroke has been estimated to be slightly higher for women than men, at 20 percent and 14 percent respectively (Seshadri et al., 2006). Age is a major factor in the risk for stroke, with the risk increasing steadily after the age of 55 years (National Stroke Association, n.d.). Approximately 19 percent of those who survive a stroke are left with language problems (Mozaffarian et al., 2015). Other types of brain injury (car accidents, falls, brain diseases that lead to brain degeneration, etc.) can also lead to aphasia. In the USA, nearly 800,000 people experience a stroke every year (National Stroke Association, n.d.). The total number of people estimated to be living with aphasia in the USA is 1 in 250 or around 1 million (American Speech-Language-Hearing Association, n.d.). For reasons that remain unknown, men appear more likely to suffer from Broca's aphasia and women from Wernicke's aphasia (Hier et al., 1994).

As we aim to estimate the prevalence of children's speech and language-related problems, we can look to data provided in published academic articles. Such studies typically focus on a single country or a small number of countries whose residents share a common dominant language. Nevertheless, few, if any, provide comprehensive examinations of language ability and processing; rather, they typically test children on one or more assessments designed to identify specific types of disorders commonly observed in clinical settings in which speech therapy with children is provided. In the studies conducted in different countries, it may be the case that different assessments are used; thus, the different prevalence rates of child language problems observed for different countries may not be strong evidence for actual cross-national differences in how often children in those countries experience language problems. In 2015, the American Speech-Language-Hearing Association (ASHA) reported the results of the first national study in the USA aiming to estimate the prevalence of communication or swallowing problems in children. The results suggested that 7.7 percent or 1 in 12 children between the ages of 3 and 17 had problems with communication and/or swallowing in the previous year (*ASHA Leader*, 2015). Speech problems affected 5 percent of children, and language problems affected 3.3 percent. A little more than half of children with a problem received treatment for the problem. Overall, boys were slightly more likely to be affected than girls. Other studies focusing on children between the ages of 5 years and 6 have estimated the prevalence of a specific language impairment, which is just one type of language disorder affecting children, to be 12.6 percent of Canadian children (Beitchman et al., 1986) and 7.4 percent of US children (Tomblin et al., 1997).

Looking to the future, our understanding of language disorders will be greatly enhanced by new systematic efforts to estimate numbers of individuals across different age groups who experience problems with language. Large-scale studies will be the most useful, requiring financial commitment and one-on-one contact with affected individuals. Until such studies have been conducted, the prevalence of language disorders will remain unknown.

The Professional Labyrinth

For those who experience a problem using language and seek out professional experts for a diagnosis, they may embark on a journey that will involve consulting more than one type of professional. The professionals who diagnose and treat language disorders are specialists, whose area of expertise and training can vary widely. Furthermore, the professional roles vary from country to country. Some of the professional areas of expertise commonly involved in either identifying or evaluating language problems include neurology, speech-language pathology, school psychology, clinical psychology, educational psychology, and educators specializing in early childhood. It is important to note that the amount of training each type of professional might have received on linguistics or psycholinguistics will vary widely. Individuals who are seeking a diagnosis might initially encounter other professionals. For those with acquired language disorders, these intermediaries are likely to be healthcare professionals (doctors, nurses, physician assistants, emergency medical technicians, etc.). For children showing signs of a developmental language disorder, the intermediaries are likely to be teachers and/or school counselors.

Among the professionals involved in the diagnosis and treatment of language disorders, those who have the most formal education in terms of number of years are **neurologists,** who are experts in the functioning of the nervous system and the disorders affecting it. Neurologists complete four years of undergraduate courses, four years of medical school, a year of internship, and three additional years of training in neurology, learning about a wide variety of neurological conditions. As in many professions, neurologists may develop a more narrow expertise within neurology by obtaining experience treating patients with a particular type of disorder. Medical doctors with specialties in areas other than neurology and clinical psychologists receive slightly less formal training in terms of years. Medical doctors receive the same length of college and medical training, but their training in their specialty beyond the internship differs across specialty. In the USA, medical students complete undergraduate work usually with an emphasis on the sciences and then complete four years of medical school. In the fifth year, medical students gain experience in their specialty. Professional psychologists have typically completed four to six years of graduate school, which includes a year of internship that is predominantly clinical practice. These include clinical psychologists and school psychologists. It is sometimes the case that professional psychologists will have had additional postdoctoral training, but it is not a norm. Commonly, the roles of professional psychologists are confused with the work of **psychiatrists,** who are medical doctors with a specialty in mental health disorders and typically emphasizes pharmaceutical treatments over talk and/or behavioral therapies. Individuals with degrees in educational psychology complete college and graduate programs. Elementary educators receive the least amount of training, typically completing a college major in elementary education and experience as a student teacher.

For children with language problems, elementary educators and others involved in school systems, who may have degrees in education (principals and other administrators), are likely to be among the first individuals with whom parents discuss their children's symptoms. Because educators, even those who teach reading and/or language, typically do not receive extensive training in linguistics, psycholinguistics or the biological basis of behavior, they will encourage parents to consult their pediatrician first to rule out the possibility of a health condition that may be contributing to cognitive and/or speech problems. Assuming that the pediatrician's examination leads to the child being deemed healthy, parents are likely to be encouraged to consult a psychologist to

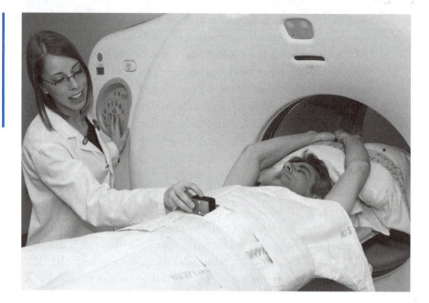

seek formal assessment of their child's cognitive abilities. If the child's cognitive functioning is in the normal range, parents will be referred to a speech-language pathologist to obtain formal assessment of their child's speech-related abilities and problems. Parents may feel it is reasonable to skip the consultations with doctors and psychologists when they believe that they have a healthy, intelligent child; however, they may find later that the speech-pathologist recommends these consultations, if only to rule out possible causes of a language problem (a pediatrician can rule out a brain tumor and a psychologist can rule out anxiety disorder).

Obstacles to Diagnosis

In some circumstances, there can be challenges in obtaining a diagnosis from the appropriate professional experts. We will focus on a few of these, which can complicate the process of diagnosis for both acquired and developmental forms language disorders. First, there is the ever present issue of individual differences. In cases of acquired disorders, the brain injury leading to the disorder is unlikely to be identical in size and effect to any other individual. For those with developmental disorders, the severity of symptoms and the circumstances in which symptoms occur can vary widely. Similarly, children with the same language or learning problem can exhibit a wide range of symptoms, causing different cases to appear, at least on first examination, as highly different from others. Consequently, in most settings where diagnosis and treatment are the focus, the emphasis is typically centered on the individual, reducing the individual's distress and increasing the individual's ability to function well in daily life.

A second obstacle is the fact that individuals are often affected by more than one condition, disease or disorder – comorbidity – making the presentation of symptoms difficult to interpret. For example, a person with a form of cancer may also have type II diabetes. With regard to language problems, problems producing and/or comprehending speech can be temporarily caused by other health conditions. As you may recall from earlier chapters, developmental forms of dyslexia can be comorbid with ADHD and/or other learning problems. Among older adults who have suffered a stroke causing some form of aphasia, it would be rare if other health conditions were not present, as our risk of suffering from a major health problem related to mortality increases as we age.

The third and final obstacle relates specifically to language differences between the professional involved in the evaluation and diagnosis of language problems and the individual seeking a diagnosis. Arriving at a diagnosis can be more difficult when the person seeking a diagnosis is a speaker of a non-standard dialect (Southern American English, African American Vernacular English, Appalachian English, etc). For the professional making a diagnosis, sentences that are grammatically correct within the non-standard dialect may be evaluated as incorrect and produced due to a disordered process. Similarly, multilingualism on the part of the person seeking a diagnosis presents a unique problem, as the assessments used in the diagnosis of both acquired and developmental disorders are typically normed on large numbers of healthy participants, who happen to be monolingual. Normative data for bilingual and multilingual individuals are lacking; thus, some aspects of normal language use in bilingual and multilingual individuals may be perceived by those involved in the diagnostic process as disordered (Tetnowski et al., 2012). For example, research with healthy participants suggests that bilingual adults may experience ToT states more often than monolinguals (Gollan & Acenas, 2004; Gollan & Silverberg, 2001), and older adults experience ToT states more often than younger adults (Burke et al., 1991; James & Burke, 2000). It is possible that bilingual older adults who experience ToTs regularly may be perceived as displaying disordered word-finding performance.

Treatments

For conditions in which language is disordered, there are no known cures. The specifics of the treatment will vary across the different types of language disorders. Approaches to treatment typically take the form of speech therapy, in which the patient/client is provided with drills to repeat, sometimes with positive reinforcement, which, for children, might be stickers or prizes. Depending on the type of deficit, the drills will vary. Some activities may involve putting the skill to use in a real-world setting. The activities are typically modified to suit the age and other personal characteristics of the person. Because of recent research demonstrating the plasticity of the brain in both children and adults, those receiving speech therapy may find that improvements increase as their time and effort spent performing the speech exercises increase.

In this section, you learned about the lack of data about the prevalence of language disorders affecting children and adults. Future research is needed in which the same types of assessments are used to screen individuals within and across countries sharing the same dominant language. You also learned about the different types of professionals involved in the diagnosis and treatment of language disorders and about factors that make receiving a diagnosis more difficult, including comorbidity, differences between non-standard dialects (spoken by the person being assessed) and standard dialects (typically being used by the person performing the assessment), and multilingualism.

Syntactic Language Disorders

As you have learned, the syntactic rules of language pertain to the ordering of words in sentences, and the morphological rules of language pertain to the formation of words through the combinations of morphemes (root words/stems, prefixes, suffixes, etc.). When the syntactic rules of language are disrupted, the effects are noticeable in the speech and writing of the person affected. First, we examine the acquired form of agrammatism that leaves individuals unable to produce grammatical utterances and sentences consistently (Bastiaanse & Thompson, 2012). We go on to discuss Parkinson's disease and Huntington's disease, in which those affected commonly develop symptoms similar to those observed in agrammatism. We then take a look at specific language impairment, which can be viewed as a developmental form of agrammatism, as well as developmental disorders in which individuals are significantly delayed in their syntactic development.

Agrammatism

An early description of **agrammatism** dates back to the late 1800s, when Adolph Kussmaul (1822–1902), a German doctor, described a patient whose brain injury left him unable to produce grammatically correct sentences (Kussmaul, 1877). In the 1970s, agrammatism was more formally characterized as the omission of morphological units (suffixes, prefixes, etc.), conjunctions (and, but, or, etc.), and auxiliary verbs (*do, has, is,* etc.) (Goodglass, 1976). A subset of the symptoms in classic Broca's aphasia are those found in agrammatism (Tesak & Code, 2008; Wepman & Jones, 1964), such as speech that contains mostly content words (nouns, verbs, adverbs, etc.) and lacks function words (helping verbs, prepositions, pronouns, etc.), prefixes, and suffixes. The level of severity varies across individuals. Because the prevalence and use of these types of morphemes vary across languages, the symptoms of agrammatism depend on the characteristics of a patient's language(s) (Menn, 2001; Tzeng et al., 1991). For example, Tzeng et al. (1991) described a case study of agrammatism in a native speaker of Chinese, a language that lacks many of the grammatical markers that occur in English. In languages that have more grammatical markers than English, errors often involve the omission of inflectional morphology on words (Luzzatti et al., 2012; Niema & Laine, 2012). Many brain areas have been linked to syntactic processing, including the left pars opercularis and pars triangularis, which you learned about in Chapter 12 (e.g., Longoni et al., 2005; Heim, 2008), the superior and middle frontal gyri and posterior parietal regions (e.g., Kielar et al., 2011), the middle frontal gyrus (Indefrey et al., 2001), the left anterior superior temporal gyrus (Friederici et al., 2003), and the left caudate nucleus and insula (Cappa, 2012).

Parkinson's Disease

Syntactic deficits are known to occur and gradually worsen during the progression of **Parkinson's disease** (PD), which is primarily recognized as a movement disorder (Elgh et al., 2009). Those who are diagnosed with PD are, on average, 60 years old. There are approximately 10 million people in the world today living with PD (Parkinson's Foundation, n.d.). The disorder is caused by the loss of neurons in the dorsal striatum, which is located in the basal ganglia in the midbrain. Several cognitive functions and processes are associated with the striatum, foremost among them is planning and executing pathways of movement. Both Parkinson's and Huntington's disease are associated with degeneration of the **striatum**. By the time an individual begins to experience problems controlling movements, 70 percent of the dopaminergic cells in the substantia nigra have already degenerated. Michael J. Fox has publicized the fact that he was diagnosed with Parkinson's while he was still in his thirties. Developing the disorder before age 40 is fairly uncommon. The cause of Parkinson's disease is not completely understood. Most cases do not appear to be inherited; however, a genetic link may be involved in a small percentage of cases (Gasser, 2005). Recent research established a link between gut bacteria and protein changes in the brain and the development of Parkinson's symptoms (Sampson et al., 2016).

Photo 14.3 Several celebrities have been diagnosed with Parkinson's disease, including Michael J. Fox (left), actor and philanthropist, and Mohammed Ali (right), late boxer and activist.

As Parkinson's progresses, working memory capacity declines. Research suggests that the working memory deficits occur due to the loss of connectivity between the frontal lobe and posterior regions of the brain (Gilbert et al., 2005; Monetta & Pell, 2007). Research by Bocanegra et al. (2015) showed that in patients with PD, syntactic deficits were present even when there was no evidence of mild cognitive impairment; thus problems with language can be observed during the early stages of PD before cognitive problems become detectable in daily life. In the research, syntactic processing was assessed using a task in which the patient heard a sentence as they were shown four pictures. They were instructed to point to the picture that was the closest match with the meaning of the sentence. Pictures contained multiple objects in a particular arrangement or people carrying out an activity and spoken sentences would describe the objects (*he is touching the spoon and the scissors*). When compared with heathy individuals, those with PD performed less accurately overall, and those with more advanced PD performed less accurately than those in the early stages of PD.

Huntington's Disease

Huntington's disease (HD), also referred to as Huntington's chorea, is an inherited disorder that causes degeneration of brain cells in the motor control regions of the brain, ultimately leading to death (National Institute of Neurological Disorders and Stroke, n.d.). HD is caused by a genetic defect in the HTT gene, which is located on chromosome 4 (Genetics Home Reference, n.d.). If one parent has HD, the children have a 50 percent chance of inheriting HD (Dayalu & Albin, 2015). There are 30,000 individuals living with the disease in the USA, with men and women affected at comparable rates. People with Asian or African ancestors are affected least often, and those with ancestors from Europe are at highest risk. People are usually diagnosed with HD between age 30 and 50, but a particularly rare form can emerge in childhood. Adults with HD can live for 15–20 years. Those with HD experience uncontrollable movements, which become progressively worse, decreasing coordination, problems walking, and frequent falls. In the late course of the disorder, dementia is common. There is no cure for HD.

As the disorder progresses, there are other symptoms, including problems understanding and producing grammatical sentences, compulsivity, anxiety, depression, and aggression. Early cognitive problems include forgetting and a difficulty maintaining attentional focus. As the disease progresses, people experience more and more difficulty in solving problems and making decisions. Language problems include word production and forming sentences (Ho et al., 2002). Syntactic and morphological errors occur increasingly frequently as more and more neurons in the striatum are destroyed (Teichmann et al., 2005, 2008). De Diego-Balaguer et al. (2008) compared the performance of healthy controls, individuals who had not yet developed symptoms of HD although they had the genetic mutation, and patients with advanced and intermediate HD on rule learning and word learning tasks. They found that rule learning was poorer among all three groups of patients affected by HD, even those who had not begun to show classic motor symptoms.

In a study that compared those who were in the early stage of HD with healthy control participants, Sambin et al. (2012) assessed sentence comprehension for sentences that varied the syntactic relationship between a name and a pronoun within a sentence composed of two clauses. Consider the examples in 1. In 1a, the pronoun *he* and the preceding name *Steve* can refer to the same person. Recall Chomsky's (1981) binding theory from Chapter 7, in which he described the syntactic relationships that occur for reflexive and non-reflexive pronouns. In 1b, the pronoun *he* and the name *Steve* cannot refer to the same person. Healthy controls understand that the pronoun and name are referring to the same person in 1a, but not in 1b. However, participants with HD interpreted the pronoun and name as referring to the same person in both 1a and 1b.

1   a. Steve$_i$ smiled when he$_i$ arrived.   Co-reference possible

   b. He smiled when Steve arrived.   Co-reference not possible

Because the authors controlled the extent to which sentences placed demands on working memory, they concluded that the comprehension errors were due to a syntactic deficit, stemming from damage to the striatum. Syntactic deficits in the early stage of HD have also been observed among native speakers of Hungarian, which is an agglutinative language with extensive affixation (Nemeth et al., 2012).

Specific Language Impairment

Specific language impairment (SLI) is a disorder characterized by impaired use of syntactical and morphological rules in individuals with normal range IQ (Gopnik, 1990; Gopnik & Crago, 1991). For example, errors include the use of verbal and nominal suffixes (e.g., *He sing in the church* and *She bought three flower*). Awareness about SLI is not widespread. Individuals with SLI may never receive a definitive diagnosis, because educators, speech therapists, and physicians may not be familiar with the symptoms of the disorder (Rice, 1997). When SLI was first identified in the 1980s, the most prominent feature was that it was inheritable. Children who exhibited syntactic and grammatical problems at school often had adult family members who exhibited similar symptoms. In a study of one extended family with some members affected by SLI and others without the disorder, it was found that SLI is unrelated to sex. This family of over 30 members representing three generations is referred to as the KE family.

Genetic studies of families in which SLI occurs have been conducted (Vargha-Khadem et al., 2005). The results show that as one's genetic relationship to someone with SLI increases, the chance of the person also having SLI increases (Tomblin et al., 1996). If one identical twin has SLI, the chance of the other twin having SLI is around 71 percent. In the past decade, attempts to identify the part of the genome affected in those with SLI were successful (Fisher, 2006; Vargha-Khadem et al., 2005). DNA was analyzed in a number of families in which SLI occurred, which revealed a mutation on chromosome 7 involved in the control of the **FoxP2** protein controlled by the FoxP2 gene. When the discovery was initially made, there were news headlines proclaiming the discovery of the language gene, followed by clarifications that the discovery of the source of the problem shared by

KE family members did not explain the entirety of the genetic basis of language. The research created interest in the genetics of language (Estruch et al., 2016; Fisher, 2006; Marcus & Fisher, 2003; Ramus & Fisher, 2009).

Using brain imaging techniques, Watkins et al. (2002) found that the left hemisphere caudate nucleus was smaller in those with SLI than those without SLI. More recent studies examining volume of brain areas also found smaller volumes in the caudate nucleus for those with SLI than for control participants (Badcock et al., 2012; Soriano-Mas et al., 2009). Future research is needed to determine how variations in language symptoms are related to variations in the sizes of particular brain regions. In the research so far, the variation in symptoms for individuals with SLI has been described as on a continuum from normal to disordered (Dale & Cole, 1991). Furthermore, researchers have discussed the issue of comorbidity in those diagnosed with SLI. Most also exhibit symptoms compatible with autism spectrum disorders (ASD) (Bishop & Snowling, 2004) and developmental dyslexia (Bishop, 2008). Those with SLI also have been found to have impairments in working memory (Archibald & Gathercole, 2006), executive function (Henry et al., 2012), statistical learning (Evans et al., 2009), and learning involving operant conditioning (reinforcement) (Lee & Tomblin, 2012).

As with agrammatism, SLI has been examined in numerous languages, having a variety of morphological characteristics, including Swedish (Hansson & Nettelbladt, 1995), German (Clahsen, 1989), Spanish (Bedore & Leonard, 2001), French (Hamann et al., 2003; Jakubowicz & Nash, 2001), Italian (Leonard & Bortolini, 1998), Greek (Dalalakis, 1999), Japanese (Fukuda & Fukuda, 2001), Inuktitut (Crago & Allen, 2001), and Hebrew (Dromi et al., 1999). The Language Spotlight box explores the symptoms of specific language impairment among children acquiring sign language as their first language.

Other Developmental Disorders

There are several other developmental disorders in which significant delays occur in syntactic processing, and for many individuals affected by these disorders, syntactic processing never fully develops (Oetting & Hadley, 2009). In this section, we will focus on three of these disorders: **Down syndrome, Fragile X syndrome**, and **autism spectrum disorder** (ASD). The causes of Down syndrome and Fragile X have been established. Down syndrome is caused by a copying glitch during development of chromosome 21 (Patterson, 2009; National Down Syndrome Society, n.d). Fragile X is caused by individuals inheriting a defective FRM1 gene, which occurs on the X chromosome (Loomis et al., 2012). There is mounting evidence that genetics strongly influence many cases of ASD (Rutter, 2000). Research has documented comorbidity occurring for individuals with Fragile X, with around 30 percent of children with Fragile X also diagnosed with ASD (Genetics Home Reference, n.d.; Hagerman & Silverman, 1996).

The specific deficits in syntactic processing vary somewhat across disorders. For children with Down syndrome, there are delays in learning syntactic and morphological knowledge (Eadie et al., 2002; Fletcher, 2009; Fowler, 1990; Laws & Bishop, 2003; Price et al., 2008). In the production of speech, utterances typically are missing free grammatical morphemes (Eadie et al., 2002). The production of

SLI in Children Acquiring Sign Language

Sign languages differ from spoken languages in that the phonological processes correspond to physical movements of the hands, face, and body rather than the production of sounds via the vocal tract. Syntactic and morphological processes involve the order in which signs are performed and how the sign is performed in the space between the signer and audience. Because of the fundamental differences between spoken and sign languages, researchers have raised the question of whether SLI might affect spoken languages, but not sign languages. Research has found evidence that a small percentage of deaf children acquiring sign language from birth experience persistent problems with the grammatical aspects of language (Mason et al., 2010). Chapter 13 explored the characteristics of sign languages and what is known about how sign languages are acquired and used by children and adults. The challenge in diagnosing deaf children with SLI is being certain that the errors in sign language production are due to a grammatical deficit and not to some consequence of profound deafness. Mason et al. (2010) tested a group of 50 deaf children who were native users of British Sign Language and who had been referred for speech/language services. The 50 children were tested on a range of tasks assessing their BSL language ability, narrative ability, and nonverbal intelligence. Of these 50, 13 were found to be severely impaired in the use of BSL grammar and narrative ability as compared to age-matched and BSL-experience control participants. The 13 scored in the normal range for nonverbal intelligence. These results are consistent with recent research showing that attempts to teach individuals with SLI to use sign language as a form of augmentative communication proved unsuccessful (van Berkel-van Hoof et al., 2016).

Photo 14.4 Individuals with Down syndrome are increasingly visible in the media. Chris Burke (left) and Jamie Brewer (right) are accomplished actors who are helping raise awareness about the condition and reduce the stigma that exists in society.
Credit: Christopher Voelker (left), RedCarpetReport (right)

bound inflectional morphemes (plural -s, verb endings, such as -ed, -ing, etc.) is typically impaired (Fowler, 1990; Laws & Bishop, 2003). During comprehension, errors occur when interpreting passive sentence (*the spy was seen by the cop* versus *the cop saw the spy*) and interpreting pronouns in relation to antecedents (Ring & Clahsen, 2005; Perovic, 2006).

Individuals with Fragile X also show a variety of language deficits, including vocabulary development and syntactic processing. Research showed that the ability to comprehend syntactic relations was significantly poorer than for typically development children. Performance for girls with Fragile X was significantly better than for girls with Down syndrome. Particularly poor performance was observed for both children with Fragile X and Down syndrome for syntactically complex sentences (e.g., relative clauses) (Oakes et al., 2013). A recent study in which children with Fragile X were subcategorized into those with and without ASD symptoms showed similar results, with both groups of children with Fragile X performing better on syntactic processing than children with Down syndrome (Martin et al., 2013).

Typically, ASD is characterized as involving communication deficits, particularly problems acquiring and using social and/or pragmatic information. The language-specific deficits commonly experienced by individuals with ASD are less well known. There is wide variation in the severity of each of these types of deficits, with the group of individuals who self-identify as having Asperger's syndrome, which is typically associated with an IQ in the normal range, showing little or no evidence of language deficits (National Institute of Neurological Disorders and Stroke, n.d.). In contrast, children diagnosed as having ASD and with lower than average age IQ show deficits in syntactic processing (Brynskov et al., 2017; Eigsti & Bennetto, 2009; Perovic et al., 2013). Brynskov et al. (2017) compared syntactic processing for children with and without ASD, who were matched on nonverbal abilities (nonverbal mental age) and between the ages of four and six. The study was conducted in Denmark, where the Danish language has slightly more grammatical markings than English (gender marking on nouns). The results showed that children with ASD made more errors related to syntactic and morphology than the other children. When the performance was compared with children with ASD who were grouped according to whether they had exhibited a language delay, the results showed syntactic impairment for both groups, suggesting that children with ASD who are labeled as high functioning may have syntactic deficits that go unnoticed in daily life.

In the past decade, awareness about ASD has grown, and it appears to be more prevalent now; however, there is a debate about whether the increase is due to more frequent diagnoses (Newschaffer et al., 2007). Studies documenting the link between the incidence of autism and environmental factors (Arndt et al., 2005) cause understandable concern among adults planning families and policy makers who foresee the future costs to governments in providing health and social services to larger numbers of their populations. These environmental factors include exposure to pollution (Flores-Pajot et al., 2016; Weisskopf et al., 2015), maternal illness and/or related immune response during pregnancy (Fox et al., 2012), and maternal stress, which can lead to epigenetic changes in the fetus (Miyake et al., 2012). The Research DIY box explores the extent to which people are familiar with the common symptoms of ASD.

Awareness of Symptoms in Autism Spectrum Disorder

Given the attention the media has shown to the topic of autism spectrum disorder, you might assume that the general public is now familiar with the symptoms of those *on the spectrum*. How familiar with the symptoms are you? The symptoms related to impaired social functioning are frequently discussed in the media, as a lack of interest in others can be fairly easily detected in the behavior of young children. Other symptoms related to delayed language may be generally less familiar. In this activity, you can explore how familiar young adults are with the different symptoms of ASD. Below is a list of 20 symptoms. Half are actual symptoms of ASD and half are not. They are symptoms of other disorders and are not diagnostically important with regard to ASD. Recruit 10 participants (five men and five women) and ask them to circle the 10 symptoms most commonly associated with ASD.

1 Does not respond to their name	11 Smiles too much
2 Has unusual posture and body movements	12 Imitates others' facial expressions
3 Enjoys the company of others	13 Does not like to be touched
4 Hates loud noises	14 Expresses feelings easily
5 Avoids making eye contact	15 Makes grammatical errors
6 Speaks using baby talk	16 Has nightmares frequently
7 Has difficulty interpreting figurative language	17 Produces repetitive behaviors
8 Enjoys telling jokes	18 Likes to sing
9 Repeats words spoken by others	19 Stutters often
10 Does not gesture very much	20 Notices if someone is hurt

For each participant, calculate the number of mistakes (number of times they incorrectly circled a symptom not associated with ASD plus the number of times they failed to circle an ASD symptom. Participants should circle items 1, 2, 4, 5, 7, 9, 10, 13, 15, and 17. You may reveal the correct answers to your participants. By noting their reactions to their performance, you may be able to determine whether they expected to perform well or poorly on the task. Make a note of whether respondents frequently missed the symptoms related to language processing (7 and 15).

In this section, we examined examples of syntactic and/or morphological disorders. You learned about the oldest known type of acquired syntactic disorders known as agrammatism, as well as the disordered syntax typically observed in individuals with Parkinson's disease and Huntington's disease, both of which occur in older adults, are progressive, and have no cure. You also learned about the developmental disorders in which there are syntactic deficits. These include specific language impairment, an inherited language disorder, caused by a mutation on the FoxP2 gene on chromosome 7, Down syndrome, Fragile X syndrome, and autism spectrum disorder (ASD). Future research is needed to determine to what extent differences in brain regions known to be involved in syntactic processing differ in these disorders as compared with typically developing individuals.

Key Terms

Agrammatism
Autism spectrum disorder (ASD)
Down syndrome
FoxP2

Fragile X syndrome
Huntington's disease
Parkinson's disease

Specific language impairment
(SLI)
Striatum

Review Questions

1 Describe the symptoms and causes of agrammatism. How is it related to Broca's aphasia?
2 Describe the syntactic deficits often observed in patients with Parkinson's and Huntington's disease.
3 What are the symptoms of specific language impairment? What causes it? Does it occur among speakers of languages other than English?
4 To what extent are deficits in syntactic and morphological processing observed in individuals with Down syndrome, Fragile X, and autism spectrum disorder?

Non-syntactic Language Disorders

Impairments related to non-syntactic types of language processing can also reduce individuals' ability to communicate. The effects on communication overall may be larger for non-syntactic than for syntactic disorders for languages similar to English where there are a relatively small number of function words, prefixes, and suffixes. In this section, we examine disorders that can be categorized broadly as lexical, phonological and semantic/pragmatic disorders. For each of these discussions, we will begin considering deficits that are acquired, resulting from a known brain injury.

Lexical Disorders

Lexical disorders are those affecting the processing of individual words. Among the classic symptoms of Broca's aphasia is word-finding difficulty, also known as **anomia** (from *nom* meaning *name* and the prefix *a* meaning *without*). Anomia occurs in all forms of aphasia (Dick et al., 2001). Individuals with anomia are unable to produce words during speaking or during tasks in which they are shown objects and asked to name them. They know the meaning of the word they cannot produce in conversation and know the identity of objects they cannot name. For example, when shown a comb, an individual with anomia might take the object and use it appropriately, smoothing out their own hair, but would not be able to produce the word *comb* reliably either through speaking or writing. As we saw in Chapter 4, a common type of speech disfluency is a temporary form of word-finding difficulty known as tip-of-the-tongue (ToT). ToT experiences occur more frequently during normal aging and are experienced more often in bilinguals as compared with monolinguals. A person with acquired anomia may fail to produce

80 percent of the words they attempt to say in conversation (Butterworth, 1989, 1992; Levelt, 1989).

Mendez (2000) reported a case study of a 71-year-old Spanish-English bilingual man who had experienced a stroke causing damage to his posterior left temporal lobe. Interestingly, the patient experienced anomia when using English, but not when using Spanish. He began to learn English at age seven when he started school where English was the language of instruction. He reported being ambidextrous before going to school, but having to learn to write with his right hand. Mendez (2000) concluded that lexical deficits can be language specific, indicating that the storage, or the neural pathways involved in accessing the storage, of lexical knowledge in the brain exists for each language that an individual speaks.

Anomia is routinely observed in individuals with Alzheimer's dementia. The word dementia comes from *mens*, which means *mind*, and the prefix *de-*, which means *without*. The gradual loss of mental ability is referred to as dementia (Burns & Iliffe, 2009). The most familiar type of dementia may be Alzheimer's dementia, a form of memory loss caused by the gradual loss of brain cells (World Health Organization, 2017). Alzheimer's may account for 60–70 percent of all cases of dementia. The cause of Alzheimer's is not completely understood; however, it appears to be related to the development of plaques and tangles of neural cells in the brain. The symptoms of Alzheimer's include forgetting how to carry out daily activities, forgetting recent experiences, and loss of vocabulary for familiar concepts. As the disease progresses, language problems worsen (Convit et al., 2000; Grober & Kawas, 1997; Small et al., 1997). Cognition is increasingly impaired, speech becomes more and more unintelligible (Murdoch et al., 1987), problems with spelling and writing worsen (Forbes et al., 2004; Glosser et al., 1999), and the ability to understand of the speech of others declines and is eventually completely lost (Groves-Wright et al., 2004).

Photo 14.5 Alzheimer's dementia took the lives of former President Ronald Regan (left), former Prime Minister Margaret Thatcher (middle), and singer Glen Campbell (right). Do you know anyone who has Alzheimer's disease?
Credit: Chris Collins of the Margaret Thatcher Foundation (middle photograph)

A particular lexical deficit in Alzheimer's was investigated in a large study of verb processing conducted by Ullman et al. (1997). They compared how well different types of patients performed on a task requiring the production of verbs. As noted in Chapter 8, English verbs can be categorized as regular verbs, for which speakers apply rules to form different tenses, and irregular verbs, whose various forms are exceptions to the rule and must be learned. Producing a particular tense of an irregular verb involves retrieving from memory the exception, which is stored as part of the lexical knowledge for that verb. Ullman et al. (1977) found that individuals with Alzheimer's dementia performed poorly when naming irregular verb forms, but performed better when naming verbs with a regular past tense form (e.g., *walk, walked*). In those patients, the deterioration of brain tissue corresponded to posterior regions roughly corresponding to Wernicke's area.

Due to difficulty finding words when speaking, someone with Alzheimer's may engage in circumlocution, which is a roundabout manner of speaking, taking more time to express themselves than is normal (Nebes, 1989). For example, they may want to say: "The dog is wanting to take its bone outside." Instead, they may say: "That little animal, the one that barks, and digs, is trying to go now. It's trying to take that item that it likes through there, outside." Their speech may also contain more pronouns than is typical (Kempler & Zelinski, 1994; Nebes, 1989; Ripich & Terrell, 1988). Pronouns may be easier to retrieve from memory than the corresponding full noun phrase.

Phonological Disorders

The sounds of words and sentences are processed by the phonological processing system of language. As you may recall from Chapter 12, a great deal has been learned about how brain injury, usually to the right hemisphere, can lead to impairments in people's ability to interpret the emotional content in speech. In this section, we will restrict our discussion to disorders specifically affecting people's ability to apply phonological rules; thus, we will avoid disorders in which the deficit appears to be limited to articulatory processes. However, it is important to remember that it is not always clear whether a disorder affecting speech is completely articulatory in nature. We first consider a disorder involving the production of speech, and then a disorder involving the perception of speech.

Foreign Accent Syndrome

Considered one of the rarest phonological disorders, **foreign accent syndrome** occurs when a person's speech changes from normal to having the superficial characteristics of a foreign accent (Ryalls & Miller, 2015). The syndrome has most often been observed following brain injuries caused by stroke and head trauma, but cases have been observed in children with no known brain injury. Among individuals diagnosed with foreign accent syndrome, the accents observed include German, Chinese, and Jamaican (Mariën et al., 2009). Mariën et al. (2009) stated that fewer than 100 cases have been observed worldwide. It is not a new phenomenon, however; the first reported case was described in 1907 by French neurologist Pierre Marie (1907). The speech characteristics of those with foreign accent syndrome do not resemble the speech characteristics of the language identified as the closest to the accent (Ryalls & Miller, 2015). The perception of speech as having a "foreign" accent may be a perceptual illusion on the part of listeners. The disordered stress patterns create highly ambiguous input, which the listener associates with a vaguely similar sounding language accent.

Foreign accent syndrome occurs because people become unable to produce normal intonation when speaking. The term **dysprosody** describes the condition of speaking with abnormal intonational patterns. Close examination of the speech of those with foreign accent syndrome indicates abnormalities in their speech sounds. Vowels can be lengthened and/or distorted during production. Voicing errors occur during the production of consonants (*grape* for *crepe*). Consonants and vowels may be substituted. Consonants may be omitted and/or produced with distortions. Multi-syllabic words may be produced with too much stress or unusual stress patterns. Words may be produced with "uh" in word-internal positions. Interviews of individuals with foreign accent syndrome revealed that speaking with the accent requires no extra effort. They report viewing their condition as a speech disorder (Miller et al., 2011).

Auditory Verbal Agnosia

Following brain injury, some people are left unable to understand speech, a condition known as **auditory verbal agnosia**. The word *agnosia* comes from the Greek *gnos* meaning *to know* and the prefix *a-* meaning *without*. For example, individuals with auditory verbal agnosia (also known as pure word deafness) are unable to recognize spoken words, yet are able to read, write, speak, and hear normally (Ingram, 2007). Most cases occur following damage to both left and right temporal lobes, either due to an injury or a disease process. They can show that they know the meaning of the word that cannot be heard and can identify manual signs (using sign language that they learn), but cannot recognize the auditory form of the word. Consonants are perceived less well than vowels (Ackermann & Mathiak, 1999). Although the condition is most often observed in adults who have experienced some brain injury, which would include any progressive brain disease, children may also be affected. For example, children with the very rare Landau Kleffner syndrome (also called acquired epileptic aphasia) may also develop it.

Semantic/Pragmatic Disorders

Disorders of semantics and pragmatics affect the processing of meaning beyond the level of the word, either how meaning is interpreted for groups of words (word pairs, phrases or sentences) or how meaning is interpreted in discourses. In this section, we first discuss category-specific semantic impairment, one of the rarer forms of aphasia, which involves individuals losing the ability to comprehend and produce words in a specific semantic category (living things, animals, pieces of furniture, etc.), while retaining the ability to comprehend and produce words in other categories. We then discuss a compelling new theory claiming that schizophrenia, the mental health disorder in which individuals have difficulty discerning reality from unreality, is a disorder of the semantic language system. Last, we discuss the mounting evidence that children with severe behavioral problems, which when severe enough can be diagnosed as conduct disorder, have deficits in pragmatic language processing.

Category-specific Semantic Impairment

Warrington and Shallice (1984) reported six cases studies of patients whose brain damage led to different types of **category-specific semantic impairment**. Four patients were able to recognize words referring to non-living things, but were not able to recognize words referring to living things, while for the other two patients, knowledge of abstract words was intact, but knowledge of concrete words was lost. Garrard et al. (2001) investigated semantic processing in two groups of patients with Alzheimer's dementia, finding that one group performed poorly on a task requiring words referring to living things to be named, but well on a task naming words referring to non-living things. The other group showed the reverse performance (poorly naming words referring to non-living things and better naming words referring to living things). Numerous cases of category-specific semantic impairment have been observed in individuals with herpes simplex virus encephalitis (Lambon Ralph et al., 2007). Jefferies et al. (2011) reported two case studies in which individuals' loss of semantic category information appeared to be influenced by their level of expertise on different topics before the brain injury, with conceptual knowledge being retained for concepts associated with the most recent knowledge. The Classic Research box outlines case studies showing that brain injuries can result in a person having a deficit in one type of information, while a similar type of information is left unaffected.

Classic Research

Selective Impairment of Nouns and Verbs

In a paper published in the prestigious journal *Nature,* Caramazza and Hillis (1991) reported the language abilities of two individuals with different symptoms of aphasia. They also had damage to different locations in their brains after suffering strokes. After extensive testing, the two patients' patterns of deficits revealed something new about the organization of healthy brains. Patient A performed fairly well using language in writing, but was severely impaired using language when speaking, while Patient B made many errors in writing and relatively few errors when speaking. Close analysis revealed something even more surprising. Patient A performed much more poorly saying verbs than saying nouns, but performance on nouns and verbs did not differ when written down. In contrast, Patient B performed much more poorly writing verbs than nouns but showed no difference in producing nouns and verbs when speaking. The two case studies taken together provided an example of a **double dissociation**, which means that two processes are independent of one another (they do not depend on one another). The double dissociation is represented in the table below.

Performance	Patient A	Patient B
Writing nouns	intact	impaired
Writing verbs	impaired	intact
Reading nouns	impaired	intact
Reading verbs	intact	impaired

The results indicated that in healthy brains, the processes used to write nouns and verbs and to speak nouns and verbs were independent, since one process could be impaired without the other being impaired. In terms of the representation of linguistic knowledge in the mind, the study showed that for the two output systems (speaking and writing), information about the grammatical category of words (noun or verb) is in both. Caramazza and Hillis (1991) ruled out an alternative explanation for the results. Because verbs tend to be more abstract in meaning, the authors further demonstrated that both patients had higher error rates for abstract versus concrete words when asked to speak or write a special set in which the abstract and concrete words had been matched on length and printed frequency. They concluded that the patients' different performance on nouns and verbs was due to their brain damage.

Schizophrenia

Schizophrenia is one of the most severe and debilitating psychological disorders, causing those who are affected to confuse reality and unreality and in some cases experience visual and auditory hallucinations, paranoia and false beliefs (also called delusions) (Kurtz, 2016; National Institute of Mental Health, n.d.). It is relatively rare, affecting between 0.3 and 0.7 percent of the population (van Os & Kapur, 2009), with men more likely to have it than women. Symptoms typically emerge between the ages of 16 and 30; however, research has shown that developmental abnormalities can occur much earlier (Lewis & Levitt, 2002). There are different types of schizophrenia, which vary in symptom type and severity. Across the types of schizophrenia, symptoms are categorized as:

- positive symptoms, such as visual and/or auditory hallucinations, agitated body movements, paranoia, and delusions negative symptoms, such as apathy, problems beginning and completing tasks, reduced talking, and inability to find pleasure in activities that others find pleasurable.

The symptoms for a given individual with schizophrenia vary, and it is rare for someone to exhibit all major symptoms. The causes of schizophrenia are not well understood; however, experts believe that there are both genetic and environmental factors that increase an individual's likelihood of developing the disorder (Kurtz, 2016). There is no cure. The primary course of treatment usually involves the use of antipsychotic medication to reduce the positive symptoms; however, it is recommended that, where possible, drug therapy be combined with behavioral treatments that emphasize social functioning.

The speech of individuals with schizophrenia – **schizophasia** – is particularly distinctive. Schizophasia includes a variety of unusual features, such as made-up words, called neologisms (e.g., *paperskate* to refer to a *pen*) (Andreasen, 1986, p. 478) and repetition of irrelevant words with similar phonology, known as clang associations – "I'm not trying to make noise. I'm trying to make sense. If you can try to make sense out of nonsense, well, have fun" (Andreasen, 1986, p. 478). Overall, the speech of individuals with schizophrenia lacks coherence. Links between utterances may be loose or lacking, hence the alternative name "word salad," suggesting that the collection of words in sentences are tossed together without achieving meaning that is easily determined by the listener. Examples of word salad produced by individuals with schizophrenia are given here:

> *If we need soap when you can jump into a pool of water, then when you go to buy your gasoline, my folks always thought they should get pop, but the best thing is to get motor oil. (Andreasen, 1979, p. 477)*

Table 14.1 lists the verbal and nonverbal symptoms observed across the different forms of schizophrenia.

Traditionally, schizophrenia has been viewed as a thought disorder that results in disordered language (Jablensky, 2010). In the past decade, an alternative view has been advanced, specifically that schizophrenia is a language disorder, operating at the level of semantic concepts leading to disorganized thought and behavior (Brown & Kuperberg, 2015; Hinzen & Rosselló, 2015; Kuperberg, 2010a,

Table 14.1 Verbal and Nonverbal Symptoms in Individuals with Schizophrenia

Verbal symptoms	Nonverbal symptoms
Poverty of speech	Hallucinations (visual and/or auditory)
Neologisms	Perceptual abnormalities
Clang associations	Delusions
Loose associations	Memory problems
Lack of coherence (word salad)	Distractibility
Non-logical statements	Apathy
Unusual syntax	Lack of motivation
Repetition	Lack of emotion

Source: Covington et al. (2005)

2010b). This view is somewhat consistent with Crow's (2000, 2008) theory that schizophrenia is the unfortunate byproduct of how language evolved (see also Priddle & Crow, 2013). Research by Gina Kuperberg and colleagues suggests that schizophrenia is a language disorder stemming from abnormal activation of concepts in memory and abnormal spreading of activation between concepts (Ditman et al., 2011; Kuperberg, 2010a, 2010b; Brown & Kuperberg, 2015; Kuperberg et al., 2008; Sitnikova et al., 2010; Thermenos et al., 2013). This view is called the **semantic hyperactivity theory**. Evidence for the theory has come from experiments in which reaction times were recorded in a semantic priming task, in which target word pairs were related (*bread – butter*, also called direct priming). Individuals with schizophrenia showed larger priming effects than healthy controls (Manschreck et al., 1988; Moritz et al., 2001; Spitzer et al., 1994). Other studies have shown that individuals with schizophrenia demonstrated priming effects for word pairs that were only weakly related (bread and cream) due to having a priming word in common (butter), which was not presented (*lion – stripes* are each related to *tiger*, also called mediated priming) (Moritz et al., 2001; Spitzer, 1993; Weisbrod et al., 1998). The results suggest that there are differences in how concepts are activated in memory for those with and without schizophrenia. Individuals with schizophrenia appear to experience stronger activation of concepts in memory than healthy controls. Research has also shown abnormal semantic priming in the family members of an individual with schizophrenia who themselves do not have the disorder (Thermenos et al., 2013). Nevertheless, there is reason not to accept the theory prematurely. Others have found that the semantic priming patterns in individuals with schizophrenia may not be stable over repeated testing episodes (Besche-Richard et al., 2014). Future research is needed to provide additional tests and refinements, if needed, to the theory.

With regard to treatments, Joyal et al. (2016) conducted a review of the literature and found that there is some evidence that the communication abilities, specifically related to discourse coherence and pragmatics, can be improved through speech therapy involving traditional positive reinforcement procedures (operant conditioning). These results provide some hope for an illness that typically offers little hope for improvement of symptoms. Using fMRI brain imaging, Palaniyappan et al. (2013) found abnormal asymmetries in language regions of the brain in adolescents with schizophrenia. They compared images of the region taken soon after diagnosis and then again two years later, which they also compared to images from a group of same-age healthy control participants. The images taken soon after diagnosis showed left asymmetries where healthy controls showed little asymmetry, and the images taken two years later showed reduced asymmetry where healthy controls showed increased asymmetry.

Conduct Disorder in Children

Research suggests that some behavioral problems in children may be linked to problems comprehending semantic and pragmatic language (Donno et al., 2010; Norbury, 2014; Oliver et al., 2011). Children diagnosed with dyslexia, ADHD, and/or other learning problems are at a higher risk of exhibiting severe behavioral problems, such as disobeying commands, skipping school, getting into arguments and fights with others, infringing on the rights of others (Frick et al., 1991; Waschbusch, 2002). In the most severe cases, a child's misbehavior may warrant a diagnosis of conduct disorder, which is usually diagnosed before the age of 10 (Berkout et al., 2011). In Oliver et al.'s (2011) study, children diagnosed with conduct disorder completed two measures assessing communication: the Social and Communication Disorders Checklist, comprising just 12 questions (Skuse et al., 2005) and the Children's Communication Checklist (Bishop, 1998). The latter 70-item questionnaire screens for communication problems in children aged 4–16 years. It measures children's abilities in establishing rapport through the use of nonverbal communication (body language, smiling, etc.), adherence to social norms, clear verbal communication, as well as understanding the speech of others. The results showed that children with conduct disorder had significant deficits in pragmatic processing when compared to other children.

In this section, we discussed disorders in which there are deficits in the non-syntactic aspects of language. We discussed disorders that impair language at the lexical or word level. These included word-finding problems, which in the severest cases are referred to as anomia, and category-specific impairments in which an individual loses the ability to use words from a semantic category (living things). Second, we examined disorders that involve phonological processing, such as foreign accent syndrome and auditory agnosia. Lastly, we learned about disorders related to semantic and/or pragmatic processing, such as schizophrenia and conduct disorder.

 Time out for Review

Key Terms

Anomia
Auditory verbal agnosia
Category-specific semantic
   impairment

Dysprosody
Double dissociation
Foreign accent syndrome
Schizophasia

Semantic hyperactivity theory

Review Questions

1 Provide two examples of disorders in which lexical knowledge is impaired. Describe the symptoms and the causes of each of your examples.
2 What lexical deficits are commonly observed in individuals with Alzheimer's dementia?
3 What are the symptoms and the causes of dysprosody? Provide an example of a rare disorder that is classified as an example of dysprosody.
4 What evidence is there that schizophrenia may be a language disorder?
5 What evidence is there that children diagnosed with conduct disorder may have problems with the semantic and pragmatic aspects of language?

Summary

There are many disorders affecting people's ability to learn and/or use language; however, due to the lack of adequate statistics, their prevalence remains uncertain. Disorders are broadly classified as acquired, resulting from a brain injury, and developmental, emerging in childhood or adolescence without known brain injury. Those seeking a diagnosis for a language disorder may seek the expertise of speech-language pathologists and/or neurologists. Some disorders involve syntactic deficits, including Broca's aphasia, diseases in which there is neural degeneration (Parkinson's disease and Huntington's disease), and developmental disorders, such as Down syndrome, Fragile X, and autism spectrum disorder. Other disorders involve deficits in other aspects of language. Lexical deficits occur in cases of severe word-finding difficulty or anomia, which are known to occur in individuals with Alzheimer's dementia. Phonological deficits may be involved in the mysterious foreign accent syndrome. Semantic/pragmatic deficits may underlie schizophrenia and conduct disorder in children.

Recommended Books, Films, and Websites

Codina, A. (Director) (2009). *Monica and David* [Documentary]. United States: Home Box Office.

Daheane, S. (2009). *Reading in the Brain.* New York: Viking.

Davis, R. D. & Braun, E. M. (2003). *The Gift of Dyslexia, Revised and Expanded: Why Some of the World's Smartest People Can't Read … and How They Can Learn.* Bel Air, CA: Perigee Books.

Eide, B. L. & Eide, F. F. (2011). *The Dyslexic Advantage: Unlocking the Hidden Advantage of the Dyslexic Brain.* New York: Penguin.

Harris, M. & Hatano, G. (eds) (1999). *Learning to Read and Write: A Cross-linguistic Perspective.* Cambridge: Cambridge University Press.

Human Genome Project (n.d.). Human Genome Project Information. Available at www.ornl.gov/sci/techresources/Human_Genome/home.shtml.

Johns, C. L., Tooley, K. M. & Traxler, M. J. (2008). Discourse impairments following right hemisphere brain damage: A critical review. *Language and Linguistics Compass,* 2(6), 1038–62.

Leong, C. K. & Joshi, R. M. (eds) (1997). *Cross Language Studies of Learning to Read and Spell.* Dordrecht: Kluwer Academic.

Menn, L. (2001). Comparative aphasiology: Cross-language studies of aphasia. In R. S. Berndt (ed.) *Handbook of Neuropsychology:* vol. 3, *Language and Aphasia* (2nd edn, pp. 51–68). Amsterdam: Elsevier Science.

GLOSSARY

Aboutness refers to the subject, as in the aboutness of a discourse.

Abstract words refer to concepts that are generally not tangible objects and for which people cannot easily form mental images.

Acquired disorders occur following physical injury and generally involve a person losing an ability they had prior to the injury.

Acquired dyslexia is a severe reading disorder occurring in a person who could read normally prior to experiencing a brain injury.

Active sentences are those in which the subject of the sentence functions as the agent/doer/experiencer of the action.

Adjunct is a syntactic type of phrase that is optional.

Advantage of first mention refers to the fact that during comprehension, discourse entities introduced first are accessed faster than other discourse entities.

Affective prosody is the aspect of the intonational pattern of speech that conveys the speaker's emotion or mood.

African American Vernacular English (AAVE) is a dialect of American English spoken by African Americans and those living in African American communities.

Age of acquisition is the age at which a language or a specific word is learned.

Age of acquisition effect refers to the fact that words that are learned earlier in life are remembered better and perceived faster than words of similar length and frequency that are learned later in life.

Agglutinative languages are those whose words contain a relatively high number of morphemes involving the presence of prefixes, infixes, and suffixes with root words.

Agrammatism refers to being unable to use grammatical rules in the production and comprehension of sentences.

Alarm call is a vocalization made by animals in response to perceiving a threat, such as a predator.

Alex was an African gray parrot owned and trained by Irene Pepperberg to perform a variety of impressive feats in the production and comprehension of human language.

Alphabetic writing systems are those having symbols that represent phonemes.

American Sign Language (ASL) is the sign language used most often in the USA and Canada.

Amnesia is the loss of memory due to brain injury.

Amygdala is the part of the brain contained in the limbic system and involved in emotional processing.

Anaphor is a discourse entity that refers back to a word that introduced the same discourse entity, such as a pronoun referring back to a proper name.

Anomia refers to severe word-finding difficulty that can occur following brain injury.

Antecedent is a word or name that precedes a pronoun and is interpreted as referring to the same entity in the discourse.

Anterograde amnesia is the inability to form new long-term memories following a brain injury (surgery or other trauma).

Anthropomorphism refers to attributing human thoughts, motives, or feelings to non-human animals.

Aphasia is a language deficit due to brain injury.

Apraxia of speech refers to a disorder in which a person has trouble with articulation.

Arbitrariness refers to the fact that, in human language, how a word sounds or looks usually has no relationship to what the word means.

Arcuate fasciculus is the region of the brain partially connecting Broca's and Wernicke's areas.

Argument refers to a phrase in a sentence that has a thematic role (agent, patient, recipient, etc.).

Audiolingual method is a method of teaching a second language that involves the use of spoken language, grammar quizzes, and behaviorist learning techniques, taught by an instructor who is a native speaker of the language being learned.

Audiologists are individuals trained in the diagnosis of hearing impairment who are also experts in hearing enhancement devices.

Auditory verbal agnosia occurs following a brain injury, leaving the individual able to physically hear sounds, but unable to interpret the meaning of the sound.

Augmentative and alternative communication refers to assisting individuals with communication problems to communicate better through the use of technological devices and/or people.

Autism spectrum disorder (ASD) is a developmental disorder characterized by social deficits and acquiring and using language.

Babbling refers to infants' production of random phonemes aged around four to six months.

Babbling drift refers to the fact that the phonemes contained in infants' babbling change over time so that they reflect those heard in the environment.

Baby biography refers to an early research methodology used by Darwin and Piaget involving the careful recording of observations of children as they develop from infancy.

Baby signs are a small set of gestures that are taught to nonverbal infants to improve communication with caregivers.

Backward inference occurs when the comprehender links incoming material with previously encountered material and generates information that is not present in the material, but is viewed as likely from the material.

Backward saccades are eye movements made to previously processed information.

Balanced bilinguals   are those who are comparably proficient in both languages they know.

Behaviorism   is an approach to psychology popular from 1911 to 1959 that focused primarily on observable behavior that could be explained through classical or operant conditioning.

Bilingual advantage   refers to the fact that research, in which cognitive performance is compared for bilinguals and monolinguals, has confirmed that there are cognitive benefits associated with being bilingual.

Bilinguals   are those who know two languages.

Bilingual translation task   is a laboratory procedure used with participants who know more than one language. Upon seeing a word in one language, they are asked to produce its equivalent in another language as quickly as possible.

Bimodal bilinguals   are people who know languages that involve different modalities (speech and signs).

Binding theory   is Chomsky's theory about the syntactic relationships between pronouns (*him, his, her*) and reflexive pronouns (*himself, herself*) and their antecedents.

Black American Sign Language (BASL)   is a dialect of ASL used predominantly by African Americans in the southern region of the USA.

Body language   refers to nonverbal communication involving movements of the body (face, hands, torso, etc.) as well as posture.

Bonobo   refers to one of the species of non-human primate in the great ape category along with chimpanzees, gorillas, orangutans, and gibbons.

Bottom-up processing   is processing involving just the information contained in the stimulus.

Bound morpheme   refers to a morpheme that cannot be used in utterances on its own; rather, it must be used with other morphemes (e.g., -ing, -ed).

Bow-wow theory   of language evolution claims that language began when people started using words that sounded like what they mean (onomatopoeia).

Braille   is a system for writing and reading in which words are represented as patterns of raised dots on the page, used by individuals with complete or partial visual impairment.

Brain plasticity   is the ability of the brain to repair itself, to recover lost functions after brain injury through the creation of new connections and/or the growth of new neurons.

Bridging inference   refers to an elaboration that comprehenders generate during discourse processing in which they use their knowledge of the world to link two or more elements in the discourse.

British Sign Language (BSL)   is the form of signed language that developed in Britain and now taught to deaf individuals and their families.

Broca's aphasia   is a language disorder occurring after a brain injury in which the person has difficulty producing speech, some comprehension problems, and the lack of function words in utterances.

Broca's area   is located in the left frontal hemisphere of the brain, and when damaged results in Broca's aphasia.

Canonical babbling   is the earliest stage of babbling in which infants repeat the same phoneme in sequence, as in *ba-ba-ba*.

Case studies are investigations of a single person or event conducted to explore some aspect of the person or event for research purposes.

Cataphors are referents, such as pronouns, that are introduced before the name or noun that refers to the same discourse entity.

Categorical perception is the perceptual ability of organisms to distinguish between categories of sounds.

Category-specific semantic impairment is a rare form of aphasia in which a person loses the ability to use words from a semantic category (e.g., living things). Across cases, impairment may affect a broad category (e.g., living things) or a narrow category (e.g., furniture).

Central executive is a component of Baddeley's model of working memory, which coordinates memory processing across the three other components – phonological loop, visuospatial sketchpad, and episodic buffer.

Chaser is a dog that has been taught to identify more than 1,000 spoken words and understand short sentences.

Classical conditioning is a form of learning described by John Watson and Ivan Pavlov, which involves learning to produce a response after hearing or seeing a stimulus that previously became associated with a stimulus that naturally produced the response (e.g., salivating after hearing a bell after the bell became associated with a bowl of food).

Clever Hans was a horse whose trainer showcased the horse's seemingly extraordinary ability to remember names, carry out basic math computations, and other feats of cognitive ability.

Cluttering is a speech disorder that involves rapid speech with unusual speech rhythms and high amounts of co-articulation.

Co-articulation is the production of multiple phonemes simultaneously during speaking.

Cochlear implant is an electronic device that includes an implant into the brain, enabling those who are deaf or severely hearing impaired to hear.

Cocktail party effect is people's ability to perceive a meaningful stimulus even in the context of high levels of extraneous sounds, such as when people hear their name called from across the room at a party.

Code-switching refers to using words or phrases from different dialects or different languages within the same utterance.

Cognates are words in two languages that are similar in meaning as well as sound and, in many cases, written form.

Cognitive psychology is focused on understanding human cognition, which includes thinking, memory, and language.

Cognitive science is the study of human, animal, and artificial intelligence, drawing on interdisciplinary contributions from psychology, philosophy, computer science, linguistics, and neuropsychology.

Coherence refers to making sense, being logical and consistent, as in a discourse.

Cohesion refers to the extent to which the elements in the discourse are linked.

Common ground theory is the view that for successful communication, conversational partners must have not only adequate shared knowledge of the situation occurring, they must also be aware of the knowledge they share.

Communicative competence refers to one having a high level of skill in exchanging information with others.

Comorbidity refers to having more than one disease or disorder at the same time.

Concreteness effect is the fact that words that refer to objects that are easy to represent as pictures are remembered better and perceived more quickly than words that refer to abstract concepts.

Concrete words are those that refer to tangible objects for which people can easily form a mental image.

Conditioned response is a behavior that is produced following the presentation of a conditioned stimulus during classical conditioning.

Conditioned stimulus is an element in classical conditioning whose presentation leads to the production of a conditioned response after conditioning has occurred.

Conduct disorder is a severe behavioral disorder involving chronic rule-breaking and the violation of social norms.

Conduction aphasia is a form of aphasia in which the individual has trouble repeating words and phrases and makes frequent errors when speaking spontaneously, but is able to understand others' speech.

Connectionism is an approach to understanding human cognition, involving models in which there are nodes and connections whose processing occurs in parallel and interactively.

Connections are part of a connectionist model, which connect nodes.

Consonantal scripts are writing systems in which vowels are omitted.

Consonants are phonemes that are produced with some amount (complete or partial) of interruption in the airflow.

Constraint satisfaction model is a model of language processing in which information is believed to be used interactively through parallel processing.

Contralateral control describes the fact that the brain's control of the body involves the "opposite side", with the left hemisphere controlling the movement and sensing of the right side of the body and the right hemisphere controlling the movement and sensing of the left side of the body.

Copula refers to the verb *to be*, which serves to connect a subject and a predicate.

Corpus callosum is the bundle of fibers that connect the left and right hemispheres of the brain.

Creole is a human language created from two or more source languages, but having its own set of grammatical rules.

Critical period hypothesis is the view that there is a window of opportunity when language can be acquired completely and that learning language after that results in incomplete mastery of the language.

Crossed aphasia is a language deficit that occurs following damage to the right hemisphere.

Cross modal task refers to a laboratory technique in which participants process stimuli in two modalities, usually visual and auditory presentation.

Cytoarchitecture refers to the arrangement of cells in tissues.

Deaf community sign language refers to the communication sign system that develops through necessity among deaf individuals living in the same community.

Deaf culture refers to the social norms of communities of deaf people, which some believe to be threatened by the increasing use of cochlear implants.

Deep orthography describes languages, such as English, in which there are many irregularly spelled words.

Developmental disorders occur in the absence of brain injury and are present from birth.

Developmental dyslexia is a severe reading disorder first observed in childhood and not related to brain injury.

Dichotic listening task involves presenting participants with different sounds to different ears through headphones during laboratory studies.

Digit span refers to a common test of working memory capacity that involves a person seeing or hearing a sequence of numbers and being asked to report back the sequence.

Diglossia occurs when a population uses two dialects of the same language for everyday functions.

Digraphia occurs when a population uses more than one type of writing system for the same language.

Direct method is a method for teaching second languages in a classroom setting, which uses total immersion combined with teaching activities that encourage students to make direct connections between objects and concepts and L2.

Discourse refers to communication, which is written, spoken, signed, or otherwise produced, that is longer than a sentence.

Discourse prominence refers to the relative importance of different entities in a discourse.

Discreteness is a characteristic of language, specifically the fact that utterances are composed of smaller parts – morphemes, syllables, and phonemes.

Disfluency refers to utterances in which there is a reduction in the normal flow of speech, as when one pauses or stutters or makes an error.

Displacement is a characteristic of human language, but not most forms of animal communications, in which utterances can refer to events in the past and future, as well as the present.

Distraction displays are animal behaviors that appear to be produced to misdirect the attention of a threat, such as a predator.

Divided visual field (DVF) paradigm refers to a technique used in laboratory studies of visual perception in which stimuli are presented so that they are processed exclusively by one hemisphere of the brain.

Double dissociation refers to a circumstance when two systems can be shown to be independent, because each can be impaired without affecting the processing of the other system.

Down syndrome is a developmental disorder caused by a chromosomal copying error of chromosome 23. The disorder is characterized by lower than normal IQ, language delays, distinctive physical features, and chronic health problems.

Dysarthria occurs when speech is unclear, but linguistically correct.

Dyscalculia is a disorder characterized by an inability to carry out mathematical calculations.

Dyseidetic dyslexia is a developmental form of dyslexia in which individuals have trouble reading irregular words (e.g., *the* and *choir*), but can read regular words (e.g., *walk*) and also pronounceable non-words (e.g., *plore*).

Dysgraphia is a disorder that affects a person's ability to physically write and also to express thoughts in writing.

Dyslexia is a severe problem reading, either first observed when a person begins to learn to read or occurring in literate adults who have sustained a brain injury.

Dysphonetic dyslexia is a developmental reading disorder in which individuals are able to read words that are familiar to them, but have trouble reading unfamiliar words or sounding out pronounceable sequences of letters.

Dysprosody occurs when one is unable to produce speech normally; although the words and phonemes of the speech are correct, the intonational pattern of the utterance overall is abnormal.

Early European Modern Human (EEMH) is an extinct species of humans, who co-existed with Neanderthals for at least 15,000 years and lived as recently as 45,000 years ago.

Echoic memory is the brief sensory memory for what we hear, lasting three to four seconds.

Electrical brain stimulation (EBS) is a technique developed by Wilder Penfield to explore the function of brain areas.

Ellipsis occurs when words that can be inferred from the context are omitted from a sentence or utterance.

Episodic buffer is a component of Baddeley's model of working memory, which connects long-term memories of different types (episodic, semantic, linguistic, etc.) with information from the other components of the model.

Etymology refers to the historical origin of a word.

Eye-hand span is the position of the eye in relation to the hands during the playing of music that is being read.

Eye-mind span refers to how closely linked a person's eye position during reading is to their mental processing of the text.

False belief test assesses the presence of theory of mind in children and adults and involves presenting a scenario in which one person must describe the likely behavior of another person.

False cognates or **false friends** refer to words that appear similar in terms of spelling and sound in two languages, but have different meanings.

Fast mapping refers to children's ability to learn a new word after a single learning experience.

Feral children are those who experience severe neglect and/or isolation early in life. Examples include Genie and the French boy Victor.

Filled pauses are hesitations during speaking in which *um* or *uh* are produced.

Filler-gap sentences are those containing a long-distance dependency.

Filler sentences are the non-target items used in language experiments to ensure that the participant receives a variety of stimuli.

Fingerspelling is a feature of signed languages in which names can be spelled using finger gestures. The fingerspelling alphabet is used to spell names of people and places for which there is not a sign.

First responders are individuals employed in emergency services fields, such as police, firefighters, and emergency medical personnel.

Fixation refers to the phase during seeing when the eye is held still (between eye movements) when visual input is actively processed.

Flashbacks are parts of narratives, involving events that occur chronologically earlier in the narrative.

Flash forwards are parts of narratives, involving events that occur chronologically later in the narrative.

Focus is the level of importance of different information in a discourse. Information that is in focus is of higher importance than information that is not in focus.

Foreign accent syndrome refers to an acquired condition (after brain trauma) in which one appears to speak their L1 in the accent of another (foreign) language.

Formants are complex sound patterns associated with the production of vowels.

Forward inference refers to the generation of a prediction during discourse processing using information from the discourse, but also world knowledge.

Forward saccade refers to a movement of the eyes in the direction of processing.

Fovea is the region on the retina containing more cones than rods, resulting in sharp visual acuity.

FoxP2 is a gene and corresponding protein that has been discussed as possibly related to an inherited language disorder in which an individual has difficulty producing speech.

Fragile X syndrome is a developmental disorder characterized by intellectual delay, distinctive physical characteristics, and sometimes chronic health problems.

Free morphemes are those that can occur in utterances without other morphemes attached to them (e.g., suffixes, prefixes).

French Sign Language originated in France and is used by the deaf community for communication.

Freudian slip (also called slip of the tongue) refers to a speech error.

Fricatives are consonants produced with partial closure of the vocal tract, allowing some air to flow out during the production of the phoneme, such as the /f/ in *fun* or the /s/ in *sit*.

Furigana is the alphabetic writing system used to assist beginning readers of Japanese.

Ganong effect is a phenomenon of speech perception in which listeners perceive incomplete or ambiguous speech.

Gap is the location in a sentence containing a long-distance dependency, where the filler is integrated with the sentence meaning during processing. The location is also viewed as where the filler originated prior to the application of a syntactic movement rule.

Garden path sentences contain a temporary syntactic ambiguity, which causes the reader to experience a conscious confusion because an initial interpretation of the ambiguity turns out not to be the intended one.

Gating paradigm is used to investigate spoken word recognition. In this task, a spoken word stimulus is presented to listeners in segments of increasing duration in order to determine how much of the word has to be presented in order for the word to be recognized.

Genderlect refers to the distinct patterns of language use produced by men and women.

Gender stereotype is when a word or phrase becomes strongly associated with men or women, rather than being equally likely to be associated with either sex.

Generative approach refers to Chomsky's view of language, which emphasizes the facts that languages can be characterized by a set of rules, which can be used to generate all forms of the language, and that we acquire grammar early in childhood.

Gestures are movements of the body, usually hand movements.

Given-new strategy refers to the ordering of information that is already known (or given) before information that is new.

Global level refers to information in a discourse that occurs outside the sentence being processed.

Grammar refers to all the rules involved in using a language correctly that are acquired by children unconsciously during childhood.

Grammar-translation method is a popular method in teaching second languages in which learning the grammatical structure of L2 is emphasized.

Grapheme is a written symbol used to represent a letter, syllable, or word in a language.

Gray matter is the tissue in the brain composed primarily of cell bodies, which are gray in color, rather than axons, which are white in color due to the myelin covering.

Gua was a chimpanzee adopted and raised for a short time by a couple in an attempt to teach Gua to learn language.

Habituation paradigm is a laboratory technique used to investigate infant cognition, in which infants' responses to familiar and unfamiliar stimuli are examined in order to infer whether infants process them as the same or a different category.

Ḥarakāt is the form of writing in Arabic that involves including the vowels in words in the form of diacritic marks.

Head-turn technique is a laboratory technique that involves operant conditioning to investigate infant comprehension by training the infant to produce a head-turn when a particular target stimuli is perceived.

Hemispherectomy refers to the surgical removal of one hemisphere of the brain. It is used as a treatment for some cases of Rasmussen's syndrome.

Hippocampus is the horseshoe-shaped part of the brain involved in forming long-term conscious memories.

Holophrase refers to when infants appear to attempt to communicate a sentence-level amount of meaning in the utterance of a single word.

Home sign refers to the relatively small number of gestures invented by deaf individuals for rudimentary communication with family members and friends.

Homographs are words that are spelled the same, but have different meanings and may have different pronunciations.

Homophones are words that are pronounced the same, but have different meanings and sometimes different spellings (e.g., *sole* and *soul*).

Human factors refer to the field that is concerned with optimal technology design through understanding how people use the technology and analyzing any errors or problems they may have when using it.

Huntington's disease   is an inherited disorder typically emerging at age forty, characterized by progressive inability to control movements as well as worsening cognitive impairment.

Hyperlexia   refers to very early reading ability in some children.

Iconic memory   refers to the brief sensory memory that people have for what they see. Its approximate duration is 250 milliseconds.

Idiomorphs   are among infants' first words; they are sound sequences used consistently with the same apparent meaning, but are not used by adults.

Illiterate   describes a person who is unable to read and write.

Illocutionary force   refers to the speaker's intention of an utterance.

Imprinting   occurs in some animals, such as birds, when after hatching a bird tends to follow whatever individual is present, even if that individual belongs to another species.

Indirect speech act   refers to utterances in which the meaning includes a message not present in the individual words used in the utterance (e.g., *Where have you been?* to communicate unhappiness about the person being late).

Inference   refers to the new information that is generated mentally during discourse processing using information in the discourse.

Inferencing   is the process of generating information mentally that is not present in a discourse, but may be suggested by the discourse.

Infixes   are bound morphemes that are inserted into a root word to form a new word whose meaning is a combination of the root word and the infix.

Inner speech   is the voice heard in a person's mind during reading or thinking.

Insight   refers to the awareness that an individual who has an illness or disorder has about how the illness or disorder is affecting them.

Intensifier   is a gesture in a signed language, which increases the importance of the sign.

Interruptions   occur during conversations when one speaker produces an utterance before another speaker in the conversation has finished speaking.

Introspection   is a research methodology closely associated with Wundt's structuralism in which participants are asked to reflect on and report aspects of their experience.

Ipsilateral control   refers to the fact that some systems of the brain receive input from "the same side" of the body, such as the olfactory system.

Irony   is a type of figurative language in which a statement is intended to mean the opposite of what the words in the statement mean.

Irregular spelling   describes words whose pronunciations are not fully indicated by the spelling, because the word is an exception to the typical spelling-to-sound rules of the language.

Isolating languages   are those that have a relatively low number of morphemes per word.

Jargon   refers to forms of language (words and expressions) developed and used by members of a social group, such as occupational groups, but also those sharing the same special interest.

Kanzi   is a bonobo that has been learning to communicate with trainers using a board containing picture symbols.

Koko   is a gorilla that has been learning to use American Sign Language and understand spoken English since the 1970s.

L1 attrition   is the loss of one's first language, which can occur when one or more other languages are acquired and used more frequently than one's first language.

Labials   are consonants that are produced with an obstruction of airflow (partial or complete) involving the lips.

Language acquisition device   refers to Chomsky's notion about what is contained in the brain that is responsible for children's rapid acquisition of language.

Language competence   refers to Chomsky's view that speakers have access to knowledge of language rules that they use in the processing of language and can use to make judgments about the grammaticality of sentences.

Language family   refers to languages that evolved from the same ancestor language.

Language immersion   refers to a method of teaching a second language in which the learner must use only the language being acquired for all interactions.

Language performance   refers to Chomsky's view that the use of language involves one's knowledge of language or language competence and mental processes involved in physically comprehending and/or producing language.

Language transfer   occurs when the rules of one language that a person knows well influence the acquisition of a new language.

Larynx   refers to the voice box.

Late closure   refers to a syntactic parsing principle that applies when the two possible analyses for a temporary syntactic ambiguity are comparable in syntactic complexity. According to the principle, comprehenders select the analysis associated with the most recently processed part of the sentence.

Lateralization of language   refers to the fact that, for most people, language is processed primarily by the left hemisphere.

Late talker   refers to a child whose first words, two-word utterances, and complex sentences occur much later than is typical for their age.

Lavender linguistics   refers to the area of studying the sociolinguistic patterns among LGBTQ individuals.

Lexical access   is the process of recognizing a morpheme or word by retrieving all that is known about the word from semantic memory.

Lexical ambiguity   is a word that has more than one meaning (e.g., pen is a writing utensil or a place to keep a pig).

Lexical bias effect   refers to the fact that speech errors are more likely to result in actual words versus combinations of phonemes that do not correspond to a word.

Lexical decision task   is a task used to measure how quickly people can recognize words. Typically, letter sequences are presented and participants are asked to respond "yes" if they make up a real word or "no" if they do not.

Linear narratives   describe elements of the story in the order that they occurred chronologically.

Lingua franca   refers to a form of communication developed by speakers of different languages for the purposes of carrying out daily tasks.

Linguistic determinism   refers to the strong version of the Sapir-Whorf hypothesis, which claims that the language a person speaks determines what they can think.

Linguistic profiling   refers to using someone's linguistic characteristics (e.g., dialect and/or accent when speaking) to stereotype the individual.

Linguistic prosody   refers to when the sound of a word or sentence conveys a meaning that is distinct from the phonemes and syllables.

Linguistic relativity   refers to the weak version of the Sapir-Whorf hypothesis, which claims that the language people speak can influence their cognitive processing.

Linguistics   is the scientific study of language(s) as a formal system.

Lip-reading   is a technique for a person who is deaf or hearing impaired to comprehend the speech of others by guessing the phonemes and words from how the speakers' lips move while speaking.

Literacy   is an individual's ability to read and write.

Literate   describes a person as being able to read and write.

Localization hypothesis   refers to the view that specific locations in the brain are responsible for specific functions.

Local level   refers to information in a discourse that occurs within the sentence being processed.

Locutionary act   refers to an utterance's final form – the words it contains and how the words are produced.

Logogen   refers to the memory representations of words in the logogen model.

Logogen model   was one of the earliest models of word recognition, in which the memory representations of words are referred to as logogens.

Logographic writing system   has symbols to refer to words and the visual form of the word has no predictable relationship with how the word is pronounced.

Long distance dependency   occurs in sentences in which a word or phrase is interpreted in relation to a word that occurs relatively far away in the sentence (e.g., Which *sandwich* did the new exchange student from China *order* at the restaurant?).

Long-term working memory   refers to a possible component of working memory, which is used for problem-solving that occurs over long periods of time.

Lying   refers to stating information known not to be true.

MacArthur-Bates Communicative Development Inventory (CDI)   refers to an assessment of child language development used with children aged 8–30 months.

McGurk effect   refers to an auditory illusion that occurs when one listens to a stop consonant while viewing the face of someone producing a different stop consonant. The listener perceives the sound to be a third stop consonant.

Malapropism   is a type of speech error in which the speaker produces a word that is similar in sound to the intended word but has a different meaning, and the speaker has confused as meaning the same thing as the intended word (e.g., saying *prostrate* when you actually mean *prostate*).

Manner of articulation   refers to how a consonant is produced, specifically whether the airflow is completely or incompletely interrupted.

Manual babbling   is the random gestures made by infants who are acquiring sign language.

Manualism   refers to the use of signed languages in the education of the deaf.

Martha's Vineyard Sign Language is a form of village sign language that developed on Martha's Vineyard, Massachusetts and is now extinct.

Matthew effect refers to the controversial pattern found in literacy research, in which *the rich get richer*; the most skilled readers continue to excel in reading and the least skilled readers progress less quickly, never catching up to the most skilled readers.

Mean length utterance (MLU) is a common measurement of utterance length first introduced by Roger Brown. It is calculated by examining a speaker's 100 utterances, identifying the number of morphemes in each, and computing the average.

Mental lexicon is the part of long-term memory involved in the storage of information about words.

Mind blindness is synonymous with theory of mind and refers to individuals' failure to appreciate that others have different thoughts and feelings from themselves.

Minimal attachment refers to a syntactic parsing strategy that leads the comprehender to construct the least syntactically complex analysis in the case of ambiguity.

Mirror neurons are cells in the brain that fire when the organism views an action being performed or when the organism performs the action itself.

Mirror self-recognition test involves placing a mark on the forehead of animals or young children without their being aware and allowing them to explore their reflection in a mirror. Noticing the mark and attempting to remove it is interpreted as comprehending the image in the mirror as oneself.

Mirth is a word to refer to amusement.

Mixed language refers to a form of communication in which a population uses words and phrases from multiple languages (usually two) in most utterances in daily life.

Modularity is the view that the mind is composed of independent, distinct modules (e.g., visual processing).

Monolingual is a person who knows one language.

Morphemes are the smallest unit of meaning in a language – suffix, prefix, and, in many cases, a whole word.

Morpheme stranding errors are errors in which a prefix or suffix or other type of morpheme is produced in an utterance attached to the wrong root word, as in the error *Turking talkish*.

Morphological rules are those involved in forming new words through the combining of words, prefixes, suffixes, and other types of morphemes.

Motherese (also called parentese) refers to the nurturing manner of speaking that adults use with babies and toddlers.

Moving window paradigm is a technique used to investigate reading comprehension, which allows participants to view only a subset of the text at a time.

Multilingualism involves using two or more languages in daily life.

Mutual exclusivity bias refers to young children's ability to infer that an object has one name or label, not two, so when the child hears an unfamiliar label in the context of a familiar object and an unfamiliar object, the child infers that the new word is the label for the unfamiliar object.

Mutual intelligibility   refers to dialects of the same language having enough similarity that speakers of different dialects can understand one another.

Narratives   are a type of discourse in which there is a setting and one or more characters and usually a plot.

Nativist view of language   refers to Chomsky's view that infants are born with knowledge of universal grammar, which enables relatively rapid language acquisition.

Naturalistic observation   is a research methodology that involves the collection of data while watching one or more research subjects going about their normal activities, typically carried out in public locations.

Natural language processing   refers to the processing of human language (either by humans or computers) that has been produced in naturalistic situations.

Neanderthal   refers to an extinct species living as recently as 35,000 years ago.

Negative evidence   refers to the information about the ungrammatical forms in a language that might aid children in learning their L1 grammar, but which occurs infrequently.

Negative language transfer   occurs when the rules of one of the languages a person knows impede the acquisition and/or correct use of another language.

Neighborhood effect   refers to the fact that the time taken to recognize a word is influenced by the finding that words sharing phonemes with other words (e.g., *trap* share letters with *rap*, *tap*, *pat*, *rat*, *par*, and *part*) are recognized faster than words sharing no or few phonemes with other words (e.g., *elk*).

Neologisms   are new words, which can be created by combining existing root words with prefixes and/or suffixes. When first used, they may seem nonsensical.

Neurologists   specialize in the treatment of diseases and/or disorders of the central nervous system, including the brain.

Niqqud   refers to the diacritic marks used to represent vowels in Hebrew.

Nodes   are part of connectionist models, representing information stored in memory.

Nonlinear narrative   refers to a story in which the elements are conveyed in an order that does not correspond to how they occurred chronologically.

Non-standard dialect   refers to a dialect of a language that has some rules making it different from the dialect of the language that is considered to be how the language should be spoken.

Normalization   refers to our ability to adjust our perception of speech.

Observer bias   refers to inaccuracy that can be introduced into data stemming from the observer's beliefs and/or expectations.

Onomatopoeia   refers to words whose meaning is related to how they sound (e.g., zip and buzz) and/or appear in print.

Onset   is the beginning of a syllable composed of a single consonant or consonant cluster.

Operant conditioning   is a form of learning described by B. F. Skinner leading to the increase or the decrease of behaviors through the application or withdrawal of reinforcement or punishment.

Oralism   is the view that deaf individuals should be taught to use spoken language and to lip-read to comprehend speech.

Oral tradition   refers to the use of storytelling as the primary means of communicating information about events of cultural significance from the past.

Original word game   refers to the back and forth of children and parents during word learning in which the child asks, "What's that?" and parents provide the word.

Orthography   refers to the writing and spelling conventions in a language.

Otitis media   is inflammation of the middle ear.

Overextensions   are examples of young children's early word learning errors when they use a word to refer more broadly than is correct (e.g., calling all animals *cows*).

Overregularization error   is a type of error made by children, in which a morphological rule is applied incorrectly (e.g., *broked and *catched).

Pandemonium model   was proposed by Selfridge to describe how humans recognize visual patterns, with demons serving as feature detectors that would become active when the visual pattern contains the particular feature.

Parafovea   is the region of the retina, which contains more rods than cones, causing the vision to be unclear, mostly shades of gray.

Parafoveal preview benefit   is the amount of facilitation that a reader experiences during the processing of a word due to having perceived the word in the periphery during the immediately preceding fixation.

Parallel processing models   allow for individual processes to occur simultaneously.

Parentese   (also called motherese) refers to the nurturing manner of speaking that adults use with babies and toddlers.

Parkinson's disease   is caused by the degeneration of the dopamine-producing cells of the substantia nigra, leaving people with tremors, trouble controlling movement, and cognitive problems.

Pars opercularis   is a subsection of Broca's area that is closest to Wernicke's area, which has been shown to be involved in phonological processing.

Pars orbitalis   is a subsection of Broca's area closest to the front, which has been shown to be involved in semantic processing.

Pars triangularis   is the middle part of Broca's area, which has been shown to be involved in syntactic and semantic processing.

Passive sentences   are sentences in which the entity that is changed by the action of the sentence or patient appears in the subject position.

Pattern recognition   refers to the view of perception in which one compares an incoming stimulus to patterns stored in memory.

Peabody Picture Vocabulary Test (PPVT)   is a standardized assessment of children's vocabulary.

Penmanship   refers to handwriting.

Perception   refers to the interpretation of some input entering the sensation, as occurs when one realizes that a loud bang is the backfiring of an automobile.

Perceptual span   refers to the amount of information that can be perceived in a single fixation during visual processing or during a single touch during the reading of Braille.

Perfect pitch   is the ability to recognize any musical note's pitch and to produce the corresponding musical tone when provided with its pitch.

Perlocutionary act   refers to the utterance's effect on the listener.

Phantom limb syndrome   refers to the phenomenon in which a person with an amputated limb perceives sensations in the missing body part.

Phoneme   refers to the smallest unit of sound in a language.

Phonemic restoration effect   refers to the perceptual illusion that leads people to hear phonemes within words that have been removed from the speech sample.

Phonics   refers to a method of teaching reading that focuses on teaching the correspondences between the letters used to spell words and the sounds making up the words.

Phonics method   is the method for teaching reading in which the correspondences between letters and sounds are emphasized.

Phonological awareness   refers to the understanding that the reader has about sounds of letters and words and the phonological structure of the language.

Phonological dyslexia   is an acquired reading disorder in which individuals are able to read words that are familiar to them, but have trouble reading unfamiliar words or sounding out pronounceable sequences of letters.

Phonological liaison   refers to a phonological process in some languages, such a French, in which the word-final phoneme is sometimes pronounced as the beginning of the following word.

Phonological loop   is the component within Baddeley's model of working memory involved in the storage of sound and believed to be involved in language comprehension.

Phonological rules   are rules pertaining to the sounds of words and sentences.

Phrase marker   refers to the mental representation that comprehenders construct during syntactic parsing.

Phrenology   is a pseudoscientific belief that personal characteristics could be determined from the location of bumps on the skull.

Picture-naming task   is a common laboratory procedure used to study speech production in which participants are shown pictures and asked to produce the word that describes the picture.

Pidgin   is a system of communication that enables speakers of different native languages to understand one another, but lacks regular grammatical rules.

Pinyin   is the alphabetic writing system used to teach children and second language learners to read Chinese characters.

Place of articulation   is the location in the vocal tract at which the airflow is interrupted during the production of a consonant.

Plains Indian Sign Language   is a sign language that was used as a lingua franca by indigenous tribes in North American who spoke different languages.

Planum temporale   is a subregion within Wernicke's area believed to play an important role in language acquisition.

Politeness   refers to behaviors, including language, that are considerate and respectful toward others.

Polyglots   are individuals who know many languages.

Pooh-pooh theory of language evolution claims that the first utterances of humans were exclamations (e.g., *oh, mmm, ouch*, etc.).

Positive evidence refers to information about the grammatical forms in a language that might aid children in learning their L1 grammar.

Positive language transfer occurs when the rules in a person's native language facilitate the acquisition of a second language.

Postmortem autopsy is the methodology used to investigate brain locations and their functions involving brain dissection after death. It was used to identify Broca's and Wernicke's areas.

Poverty of the stimulus refers to the nativist view that what is contained in adult speech to children generally cannot explain how children acquire grammar fully.

Pragmatic rules are the rules governing the use of language in socially appropriate ways.

Preferential looking paradigm is a technique for investigating infant comprehension, in which the researcher makes inferences about what the infant perceives based on the infant choosing to look at one of two objects or scenes.

Presbycusis refers to the fact that our ability to adapt to the variation in speech changes as we age.

Print awareness refers to the understanding that develops in childhood that written symbols are used to communicate.

Private speech occurs in children when they talk to themselves during play or problem-solving.

Proactive interference occurs when memory for a new item to be remembered is reduced due to previous trials on which words with similar meanings were processed.

Problem of invariance refers to the fact that phonemes are not associated with one unchanging pattern in the speech signal.

Pro-drop language refers to any language in which pronouns can be omitted from sentences, such as Spanish.

Productive language ability is infants' and children's ability to produce speech.

Productivity is a characteristic of human languages, as users of the language can create novel words and sentences using the grammatical rules of the language.

Proposition refers to the basic unit of meaning obtained from a discourse and stored in memory.

Prosody refers to the pattern of stress and rhythm of speech.

Protowords are among infants' first words; they are sound sequences used consistently with the same apparent meaning, but are not used by adults.

Psychiatrists are medical doctors who specialize in the diagnosis and treatment of mental health disorders.

Psycholinguistics is the scientific study of how language is acquired and used.

Punishment is a concept from operant conditioning that refers to any action that aims to reduce the frequency of a behavior.

Radicals are the subcomponents of Chinese characters, which may be associated with a particular meaning, such as *water*, and occur in the Chinese words that involve some aspect of that meaning.

Rasmussen's syndrome is a rare, metabolic disorder affecting young children, causing seizures and sometimes leading to a hemispherectomy as treatment.

Reading readiness refers to an individual, usually a child, having learning experiences that prepare them to learn to read.

Receptive language ability refers to the ability to comprehend language, usually speech.

Recognition point refers to a concept within the cohort model of spoken word recognition, which means the point during listening to the word when the listener identifies what the word is.

Reduplication is the repetition of a morpheme or word to express a meaning that is usually greater in amount or intensity than when the single morpheme or word is used.

Referential processing refers to a process during comprehension in which words and phrases that represent the same discourse entity are linked.

Reflexive pronouns are those containing the suffix -self, as in himself, herself, themselves, myself, etc.

Regressive eye movement refers to a saccade that is made to view previously processed information; also referred to as a backward saccade.

Regular spelling describes words whose pronunciations are clearly indicated by the spelling of the word.

Reinforcement is anything that serves to make a behavior more likely to occur within the operant conditioning framework.

Repair refers to when the speaker notices that an error has been made during speaking and corrects their error.

Repetition blindness refers to a perceptual phenomenon when an individual is presented with two instances of a stimulus back to back, but perceives the stimulus occurring only once.

Repetition priming refers to the fact that a word is recognized faster the second time it is presented than when the word is immediately preceded by a different word.

Retrograde amnesia refers to the loss of memory for events occurring before the event in which the brain was damaged (trauma, stroke, etc.)

Revised hierarchical model refers to a model of bilingual memory in which L2 words are strongly linked to L1 words, which are strongly linked to concepts, and L2 words are more weakly linked to concepts.

Rhetoric refers to the discipline focused on speaking and writing effectively.

Right ear advantage (REA) refers to the fact that words are perceived better in the right ear than the left ear because the left hemisphere is dominant for language and the pathway from the right ear and the left hemisphere is stronger than the pathway from the left ear and the right hemisphere.

Rime is a part of a syllable, distinguished from the onset and occurring at the end of the syllable.

Root words are words that can appear with suffixes and/or prefixes resulting in words that share a core aspect of meaning.

Saccade refers to a movement of the eyes.

Sarcasm refers to statements that express hostility in an indirect way.

Sapir-Whorf hypothesis claims that the language a person speaks influences their thinking.

Scaffolding   refers to the process through which children increase their knowledge and/or skills by progression through a series of steps that increase in complexity or difficulty.

Schema   refers to a memory structure in which we store information about what is typical (e.g., contents of an office).

Schizophasia   refers to the manner of speaking that occurs in individuals with schizophrenia, including loosely connected sentences, jumping from topic to topic, and made-up words.

Script   refers to a memory structure in which we store the typical steps involved in a particular type of interaction (e.g., going to a restaurant involves reviewing a menu, ordering, getting the order, eating, and paying).

Segmentation problem   refers to the fact that speech does not typically contain silences between words, making it difficult to perceive word boundaries.

Selective attention   is the fact that we are able to focus our attention on one stream of input among multiple streams.

Semantic hyperactivity theory   claims that schizophrenia is a language disorder stemming from abnormally high activation of concepts in memory and abnormal spreading of activation between concepts.

Semanticity   is a characteristic of communication systems in which each word in human language or call in other species is associated with a different meaning.

Semantic memory   is the part of long-term memory involved in storing factual knowledge and word meanings.

Semantic priming   refers to the fact that one can recognize a word faster if the word is immediately preceded by a semantically related word.

Semantic rules   are language rules governing meaning.

Sensation   refers to the registering of input into one or more of the five senses. Sensation generally does not involve interpreting the input.

Sensory memory   is the brief memory for information registered in the senses – vision, hearing, smell, touch, and taste.

Sequential bilingualism   occurs when people learn a second language after fully acquiring a first language.

Serial processing models   are those in which processes are carried out one at a time.

Shallow orthography   is a writing system that provides clear clues to pronunciation.

Signing space   is the area around the body of someone who is using sign language where the hands move during the process of signing.

Simultaneous bilingualism   occurs when one learns two languages at the same time during life, such as early childhood.

Situation model   refers to the mental representation of information that contains both visual and spatial elements.

Slang   refers to informal language use often considered nonstandard in the language. Sometimes, over time, words and phrases first considered slang become part of the broadly used language and considered part of the standard dialect.

Slip of the ear   refers to misperceiving the speech of another.

Slip of the finger   refers to an error made when using a signed language; analogous to slips of the tongue made during speaking.

Slip of the hand   refers to a language production error made by users of signed languages.

Slip of the tongue   is synonymous with speech error and spoonerism.

SLIP technique   refers to the procedure used in a laboratory setting to elicit speech errors from research participants.

Small talk   (also called chit chat) refers to the language use typically produced between strangers or acquaintances on emotionally neutral topics and topics least likely to lead to strong opinions.

Social distance   refers to the difference in social status between a speaker and a listener.

Social register   refers to the dialect that a person speaks, associated with their socioeconomic level in society.

Social smile   first emerges in infants around six weeks of age and provides the first form of communication between the infant and another, signaling that the infant recognized the individual.

Sociolinguistics   is the study of the social variation of language use across and within social groups.

Sound symbolism   refers to when words having similar meaning share some phonological features (e.g., words related to *nose* often begin with /sn/).

Specific language impairment (SLI)   is an inherited language disorder that involves frequent syntactic and/or morphological errors.

Specific learning disorder (SpLD)   refers to a category in the DSM-5, which includes problems with writing, reading, and/or mathematics.

Speech act   refers to an utterance having a particular intention.

Speech error   (also called slip of the tongue) is a mistake made when the sound, word or phrase produced is not what was intended by the speaker.

Speech fluency   refers to the degree to which speech is produced without hesitations or errors.

Speech impediment   refers to an error in articulation that can cause speech to be difficult to perceive, such as stuttering and difficulty producing specific phonemes as in *s* or *r*, which is produced by a speaker on a regular basis.

Speech-language pathologists   are professionals trained in the treatment of speech disorders.

Speech spectrograms   display speech and other sounds in terms of the frequency (or energy) of sound waves as they unfold over time, usually milliseconds.

Split-brain patients   are those whose left and right hemispheres have been surgically separated through the severing of the corpus callosum in the brain.

Spoonerism   is a speech error or slip of the tongue, in which a speaker accidentally transposes the initial sounds or letters of two or more words, often to humorous effect, as in the sentence *you have hissed the mystery lectures*.

Standard dialect   refers to the form of a language that is used for governmental and educational functions and considered to be the correct way to speak.

Statistical learning approach   refers to the view that language is learned through experience only and not through reliance on innate knowledge.

Individuals' brains are able to build mental representations of language based on the statistical properties of languages (e.g., how often a word occurs with other words).

Stokoe notation refers to the writing system invented to represent ASL graphically.

Stop consonants are phonemes produced with some amount of obstruction (partial or complete) in the airflow through the vocal tract.

Story grammar claims discourses can be described with rules, as sentences are described by phrase structure rules. Story grammar would contain settings, themes, plots and resolutions.

Stress is the emphasis placed on a syllable during articulation.

Striatum is an area of the basal ganglia in the brain, which degenerates in Parkinson's and Huntingon's disease and appears to be related to problems with language processing.

Stroke is a brain hemorrhage that can result in brain injury.

Structuralism is an early approach to psychology emphasizing the study of the parts of the mind, developed by Wilhelm Wundt in 1879 in Leipzig, Germany.

Stuttering is a speech disorder in which a person's speech contains disfluencies, such as repeated phonemes, hesitations, and/or periods of undesirable silences.

Subcategorization frames are associated with individual verbs and contain information about the different types of syntactic structures that can occur with the verb.

Substitution in discourses occurs when the word *one* is used instead of a longer noun phrase, as in *Seppo examined all the fishing lures, before picking one to buy.*

Subvocalization involves the activation of speech sounds when someone is reading silently.

Surface dyslexia is an acquired form of dyslexia in which individuals have trouble reading irregular words (e.g., *the* and *choir*), but can read regular words (e.g., *walk*) and also pronounceable non-words (e.g., *plore*).

Syllabic writing system are those having symbols that represent syllables.

Syllables are groups of phonemes making up a word or part of a word containing at least a vowel and often surrounded by consonants.

Syntactic ambiguity refers to a word or phrase that can be interpreted as more than one syntactic structure in the context of a sentence.

Syntactic category ambiguity refers to a word that can be used in more than one syntactic category (noun, verb, adjective, etc.).

Syntactic parsing refers to the process of assigning syntactic structure to words in sentences as soon as they are processed.

Syntactic reanalysis refers to the process of realizing that a syntactic ambiguity has been initially misanalyzed, which results in the first analysis being abandoned and another analysis constructed.

Syntactic recursion refers to the characteristic of human languages that enables sentences to be theoretically infinitely long because the phrase structure rules of human languages involve a nesting of syntactic rules (e.g., an S contains a VP, which is able to contain another S).

Syntactic rules in a language govern word order and other aspects of the positioning of morphemes and words in a sentence.

Taboo   refers to anything that is viewed as socially unacceptable to acknowledge or discuss.

Tag questions   are statements that include a question at the end communicating tentativeness on the part of the speaker and a validating response from the listener (e.g., *It's cold in here, isn't it?*).

Taxonomic bias   refers to children's bias in word learning in which they infer that the term for a member of a category (e.g., parrot) refers to all members of that category (i.e., all parrots).

Test for Auditory Comprehension of Language (TACL)   is a standardized assessment of children's language development which measures children's listening comprehension for vocabulary, grammatical morphemes, as well as phrases and sentences.

Thematic roles   are the meaning-based functions of a phrase within a sentence.

Theory of mind   is the ability to infer that others can have different thoughts and feelings than one's own; it develops in children between the ages of three and four.

Tip-of-the-fingers state   refers to the temporary word-finding difficulty experienced by sign language users who cannot produce a well-known sign when signing.

Tip-of-the-tongue (ToT) state   refers to the temporary difficulty we experience when we cannot produce a word or name we know during speaking.

Tongue twister paradigm   is a technique used to investigate the role of phonology in sentence comprehension, involving the comprehension of sentences containing repeated phonemes.

Top-down processing   refers to processing that utilizes information contained in the stimulus as well as other information, such as that stored in memory.

Topicalization   refers to a movement process in some languages in which a phrase is moved to the beginning of a sentence to indicate that it is important.

TRACE model   is one of the models of the recognition of spoken words, which has a connectionist architecture and interactive, parallel processing.

Translation equivalents   are words from different languages that are generally viewed as having the same meaning.

Trilinguals   are those who know three languages.

True experiment   is the only methodology that enables a researcher to establish a cause-and-effect relationship; at least one variable is manipulated, there must be a control and an experimental group, and random assignment.

Turn-taking   refers to the back and forth pattern that occurs in conversations when one person speaks, then the other, then back to the first speaker, and so on.

T-v distinction   is used in languages in which speakers use the second person plural form when speaking with a single person with whom the speaker is not familiar or is of lower status. So called because in French, *vous* is used instead of *tu* if the speaker is addressing someone higher in social status.

Underextension   refers to a common error made by children who are producing their first words. They use a word to mean something more restrictive (more narrow in meaning) than adults would.

Uniqueness point is a concept in the cohort model of speech perception that means the point in spoken word recognition at which a single remaining candidate is left and all other possible candidates are no longer being considered

Universal grammar is Noam Chomsky's notion of innate knowledge of human language that enables children to learn any language to which they are exposed relatively rapidly.

Unrestricted race approach is a model of syntactic ambiguity resolution in which multiple analyses are constructed simultaneously, with the analysis constructed most quickly influencing processing time; initial analyses can be influenced by all sources of information.

Uptalk refers to a dialect of American English in which statements are produced with rising intonation rather than falling intonation.

Urgency is a characteristic of an animal's communication, which communicates the level of fear.

Variegated babbling is the type of babbling that infants do after they have been babbling for a while when they use different syllables together, as in *ba-ga-da*.

Verb agreement errors occur when the incorrect form of a verb is used with a subject in a clause (e.g., *the basket of candies were …*).

Viki was a chimpanzee that was raised for two years by the Hayes in the 1950s.

Village sign language refers to a signed form of communication developed by deaf individuals within a single community for the purpose of communication outside an academic setting.

Visual acuity refers to the quality of vision, with the highest acuity experienced for information looked at directly (the center of vision).

Visual world paradigm is a methodology used to investigate the processes involved in speech comprehension, using an array of objects, instructions that participants hear, and the recording of their eye movements as they comprehend and follow the instructions.

Visuospatial sketchpad refers to a component in Baddeley's model of working memory, which handles mental imagery.

Voice disorders involve severe problems speaking, stemming from the inability to control voice production.

Voice onset time (VOT) is the amount of time that passes between a consonant's release during production and the beginning of the vibration of the vocal cords.

Voicing is a feature of phonemes, involving the presence of vocal cord vibration during the production of the phoneme.

Vowels are speech sounds that are produced without obstruction of the airflow.

Wada testing is a technique used to investigate hemispheric differences in processing involving the administration of a drug that paralyzed one hemisphere at a time.

Waggle dance is the communication system used by bees to inform hive mates about the location of distant food sources.

Washoe was a chimpanzee taught to use American Sign Language by the Gardners.

Wernicke's aphasia   is a form of language deficit occurring after damage to Wernicke's area in the brain, involving nonsensical speech with a lack of content words that is produced fluently.

Wernicke's area   is located in the temporal lobe of the left hemisphere (for most individuals) and is involved in language processing, specifically the use of content words, such as nouns, verbs, adjectives, and adverbs.

White matter   is the tissue in the brain composed of axons, which are covered with myelin, a white covering.

Whole language method   is a method of teaching reading that emphasizes extracting meaning from texts using strategies and generally avoids focus on the relationship between sounds and letters.

Whole object bias   refers to children's tendency during word learning to infer that a new word refers to an entire object in the context rather than one or more parts of the object or some superficial aspect of the object (e.g., color, shape, or texture).

Withholding information   refers to a form of tactical deception involving not communicating something to others.

Word frequency effect   refers to the fact that people process frequently used words more quickly than infrequently used words.

Word length effect   refers to the fact that people take longer to process longer words (in terms of number of syllables or number of letters) than shorter words.

Word spurt   is a time of rapid word learning, in which the vocabulary of a child may quadruple in a matter of 12 weeks. Most children experience this between 18 months and 24 months of age.

Word superiority effect   refers to the fact that people recognize whole words faster than they can recognize any single letter within the word.

Working memory   is one type of memory that serves as our mental blackboard storing information for a relatively short period of time.

Working memory capacity   refers to the amount of information that individuals can store in working memory. The average working memory capacity is 7 ± 2 units of information.

Yo-he-ho theory   of language evolution claims that humans' first utterances were noises made during hard work, as in *heave-ho*.

Zone of proximal development   refers to the difference between what children are able to do without help from adults and what they can do with help.

REFERENCES

Abbott, H. P. (2009). *The Cambridge Introduction to Narrative* (2nd edn). Cambridge: Cambridge University Press.

AbdulSabur, N. Y., Xu, Y., Liu, S., Chow, H. M., Baxter, M. et al. (2014). Neural correlates and network connectivity underlying narrative production and comprehension: A combined fMRI and PET study. *Cortex*, 57, 107–27.

Abner, N., Cooperrider, K., & Goldin-Meadow, S. (2015). Gesture for linguists: A handy primer. *Language and Linguistics Compass*, 9(11), 437–51.

Abutalebi, J., Cappa, S. F., & Perani, D. (2005). Functional neuroimaging of the bilingual brain. In J. F. Kroll & A. M. de Groot (eds) *Handbook of Bilingualism: Psycholinguistic Approaches*. Oxford: Oxford University Press.

Acheson, D. J., & MacDonald, M. C. (2011). The rhymes that the reader perused confused the meaning: Phonological effects during on-line sentence comprehension. *Journal of Memory and Language*, 65(2), 193–207.

Acheson, D. J., Wells, J. B., & MacDonald, M. C. (2008). New and updated tests of print exposure and reading abilities in college students. *Behavior Research Methods*, 40(1), 278–89.

Ackermann, H., & Mathiak, K. (1999). Symptomatology, neuroanatomical correlates and pathomechanisms of central hearing disorders (pure word deafness, verbal/nonverbal auditory agnosia, cortical deafness). *Fortschritte der Neurologie-Psychiatrie*, 67(11), 509–23.

Acredolo, L. P., Goodwyn, S. W., Horobin, K., & Emmons, Y. (1999). The signs & sounds of early language development. In L. Balter & C. Tamis-LeMonda (eds) *Child Psychology* (pp. 116–39). New York: Psychology Press.

Agrawal, D., Mohanty B. B., Kumar S., & Chinara, P. K. (2014). Split brain syndrome: One brain but two conscious minds? *Journal of Health Research and Reviews*, 1(2), 27–33.

Aitchison, J. (1998). On discontinuing the continuity-discontinuity debate. In J. R. Hurford, M. Studdert-Kennedy & C. Knight (eds) *Approaches to the Evolution of Language* (pp. 17–29). Cambridge: Cambridge University Press.

Alario, F. X., & Caramazza, A. (2002). The production of determiners: Evidence from French. *Cognition*, 82, 179–223.

Alderson-Day, B., & Fernyhough, C. (2015). Inner speech: Development, cognitive functions, phenomenology, and neurobiology. *Psychological Bulletin*, 141(5), 931–65.

Alibali, M. W., Heath, D. C., & Myers, H. J. (2001). Effects of visibility between speaker and listener on gesture production: Some gestures are meant to be seen. *Journal of Memory and Language*, 44, 169–88.

Allen, P. A., Bucur, B., Grabbe, J., Work, T., & Madden, D. J. (2011). Influence of encoding difficulty, word frequency, and phonological regularity on age differences in word naming. *Experimental Aging Research*, 37(3), 261–92.

Allopenna, P. D., Magnuson, J. S., & Tanenhaus, M. K. (1988). Tracking the time course of spoken word recognition using eye movements: Evidence for continuous mapping models. *Journal of Memory and Language*, 38, 419–39.

Alloway, R. G., & Alloway, T. P. (2015). Working memory benefits of proprioceptively demanding training: A pilot study. *Perceptual and Motor Skills*, 120(3), 766–75.

Allum, P. H., & Wheeldon, L. R. (2007). Planning scope in spoken sentence production: The role of grammatical units. *Journal of Experimental Psychology: Learning, Memory, and Cognition*, 33, 791–810.

Almor, A. (1999). Noun-phrase anaphora and focis: The informational load hypothesis. *Psychological Review*, 106(4), 748–65.

American Foundation for the Blind (2013). School experience for children and youth with vision loss. Retrieved July 23, 2017 from www.afb.org/info/blindness-statistics/children-and-youth/school-experience/235.

American Optometric Association (2016a). Recommended eye examination frequency for pediatric patients and adults. Retrieved October 6, 2016 from www.aoa.org/patients-and-public/caring-for-your-vision/comprehensive-eye-and-vision-examination/recommended-examination-frequency-for-pediatric-patients-and-adults?sso=y.

American Optometric Association (2016b). Adult vision: 41 to 60 years of age. Retrieved October 6, 2016 from www.aoa.org/patients-and-public/good-vision-throughout-life/adult-vision-19-to-40-years-of-age/adult-vision-41-to-60-years-of-age?sso=y.

American Psychiatric Association (2013). *Diagnostic and Statistical Manual of Mental Disorders: DSM-5*. Washington, D.C.: APA.

American Speech-Language-Hearing Association (n.d.). Aphasia. Retrieved April 14, 2017 from www.asha.org/PRPSpecificTopic.aspx?folderid=8589934663&section=Incidence_and_Prevalence.

Amunts, K., Schleucher, A., & Zilles, K. (2004). Outstanding language competence and cytoarchitecture in Broca's speech region. *Brain and Language*, 89, 346–53.

Anbessa, T. (1987). Ballissha: Women's speech among the Sidama. *Journal of Ethiopian Studies*, 20, 44–59.

Andrade, C., Kretschmer, R. R., & Kretschmer, L. W. (1989). Two languages for all children: Expanding to low achievers and the handicapped. In K. E. Muller (ed.) *Languages in the Elementary Schools* (pp. 177–203). New York: American Forum.

Andreasen, N. C. (1986). The scale for assessment of thought, language and communication (TLC). *Schizophrenia Bulletin*, 12, 473–82.

Andrew, K. N., Hoshooley, J., & Joanisse, M. F. (2014). Sign language ability in young deaf signers predicts comprehension of written sentences in English. *PLoS One*, 9(2), e89994.

Andrews, S. (1989). Frequency and neighborhood effects on lexical access: Activation or search? *Journal of Experimental Psychology: Learning, Memory and Cognition*, 15, 802–14.

Andruski, J. E., Casielles, E., & Nathan, G. (2014). Is bilingual babbling language-specific? Some evidence from a case study of Spanish-English dual acquisition. *Bilingualism: Language and Cognition*, 17(3), 660–72.

Anisfeld, E. (1982). The onset of social smiling in preterm and full-term infants from two ethnic backgrounds. *Infant Behavior & Development*, 5(4), 387–95.

Antón, E., García, Y. F., Carreiras, M., & Duñabeitia, J. A. (2016). Does bilingualism shape inhibitory control in the elderly? *Journal of Memory and Language*, 90, 147–60.

Applebee, A. N. (1978). *The Child's Concept of Story: Ages Two to Seventeen*. Chicago: University of Chicago Press.

Archibald, L. M., & Gathercole, S. E. (2006). Short-term memory and working memory specific language impairment. In T. P. Alloway & S. E. Gathercole (eds) *Working Memory and Neurodevelopmental Conditions* (pp. 139–60). Hove: Psychology Press.

Ardila, A. (2005). Spanglish: An Anglicized Spanish dialect. *Hispanic Journal of Behavioral Sciences*, 27(1), 60–81.

Armbruster, B. B., Lehr, F., & Osborn, J. (2003). A child becomes a reader: Birth through preschool. National Literacy Institute. Retrieved September 27, 2016 from https://lincs.ed.gov/publications/html/parent_guides/birth_to_pre.html.

Armstrong, P. W., & Rogers, J. D. (1997). Basic skills revisited: The effects of foreign language instruction on reading, math and language arts. *Learning Languages*, 20–31.

Arndt, T. L., Stodgell, C. J., & Rodier, P. M. (2005). The teratology of autism. *International Journal of Developmental Neuroscience*, 23(2/3), 189–99.

Aroles, S. (2007). *L'énigme des enfants-loups: Une certitude biologique mais un déni des archives, 1304–1954.* Paris: Publibook.

Aronson, J. (2002). *Sound and Fury* [Motion picture]. United States: New Video Group.

Arregui, A., Clifton, C. J., Frazier, L., & Moulton, K. (2006). Processing elided verb phrases with flawed antecedents: The recycling hypothesis. *Journal of Memory and Language*, 55(2), 232–46.

ASHA Leader (2015). Almost 8 percent of U.S. children have a communication or swallowing disorder. *The ASHA Leader*, 20(10). Retrieved April 14, 2017 from http://leader.pubs.asha.org/article.aspx?articleid=2423605.

Ashby, J., & Rayner, K. (2004). Representing syllable information during silent reading: Evidence from eye movements. *Language and Cognitive Processes*, 19(3), 391–426.

Athanasopoulos, P., Damjanovic, K., Krajciova, A., & Sasaki, M. (2011). Representation of colour concepts in bilingual cognition: The case of Japanese blues. *Bilingualism: Language and Cognition*, 14, 9–17.

Athanasopoulos, P., Dering, B., Wiggett, A., Kuipers, J., & Thierry, G. (2010). Perceptual shift in bilingualism: Brain potentials reveal plasticity in pre-attentive colour perception. *Cognition*, 116(3), 437–43.

Aura, L. J., Venville, G., & Marais, I. (2016). The relationship between Kenyan sign language and English literacy. *Issues in Educational Research*, 26(2), 165–81.

Austin, J. L. (1962). *How to do Things with Words*. New York: Oxford University Press.

Baars, B. J. (1980). On eliciting predictable speech errors in the laboratory. In V. A. Fromkin (ed.) *Errors in Linguistic Performance* (pp. 307–18). New York: Academic.

Baars, B. J., & Motley, M. T. (1976). Spoonerisms as sequencer conflicts: Evidence from artificially elicited errors. *American Journal of Psychology*, 89, 467–84.

Baars, B. J., Motley, M. T., & MacKay, D. (1975). Output editing for lexical status in artificially elicited slips of the tongue. *Journal of Verbal Learning & Verbal Behavior*, 14, 382–91.

Bachem, A. (1955). Absolute pitch. *Journal of the Acoustical Society of America*, 27, 1180–5.

Babbidge, H. D. (1965). *Education of the Deaf in the United States: A Report to the Secretary of Health, Education and Welfare by his Advisory Committee of Education of the Deaf*. Washington, D.C.: United States Government Printing Office.

Badcock, N. A., Bishop, D. M., Hardiman, M. J., Barry, J. G., & Watkins, K. E. (2012). Co-localisation of abnormal brain structure and function in specific language impairment. *Brain and Language*, 120(3), 310–20.

Baddeley, A. D. (2000). The episodic buffer: A new component of working memory? *Trends in Cognitive Science*, 4(11), 417–23.

Baddeley, A. D. (2007). *Working Memory, Thought and Action*. Oxford: Oxford University Press.

Baddeley, A. D. (2009). What's it for? Why ask? *Applied Cognitive Psychology*, 23, 1045–9.

Baddeley, A. D. (2012). Working memory: Theories, models, and controversies. *Annual Review of Psychology*, 63, 1–29.

Baddeley, A. D., & Hitch, G. (1974). Working memory. In G. H. Bower (ed.) *The Psychology of Learning and Motivation: Advances in Research and Theory* (vol. 8, pp. 47–89). New York: Academic Press.

Baddeley, A. D., Eysenck, M., & Anderson, M. C. (2009). *Memory*. New York: Psychology Press.

Badecker, W., & Straub, K. (2002). The processing role of structural constraints on the interpretation of pronouns and anaphors. *Journal of Experimental Psychology: Learning, Memory, and Cognition*, 28, 748–69.

Bakker, P., & Mous, M. (1994). *Mixed Languages: 15 Case Studies in Language Intertwining*. Amsterdam: IFOTT.

Balcells Riba, M. (1999). Contribution of John Hughlings Jackson to the understanding of epilepsy. *Neurología*, 14(1), 23–8.

Baldo, J. V., Kacinik, N. A., Moncrief, A., Beghin, F., et al. (2016). You may now kiss the bride: Interpretation of social situations by individuals with right or left hemisphere injury. *Neuropsychologia*, 80, 133–41.

Baldwin, D. A., Markman, E. M., Bill, B., Desjardins, N., Irwin, J. M. et al. (1996). Infants' reliance on a social criterion for establishing word–object relations. *Child Development*, 67, 3135–53.

Balota, D. A., Pilotti, M., & Cortese, M. J. (2001). Subjective frequency estimates for 2,938 monosyllabic words. *Memory and Cognition*, 29, 639–47.

Balota, D. A., Pollatsek, A., & Rayner, K. (1985). The interaction of contextual constraints and parafoveal visual information in reading. *Cognitive Psychology*, 17, 364–90.

Banaji, M. R., & Hardin, C. D. (1996). Automatic stereotyping. *Psychological Science*, 7, 136–41.

Barkley, R. A. (2006). *Attention Deficit Hyperactivity Disorder: A Handbook for Diagnosis and Treatment* (3rd edn). New York: Guilford Press.

Baron, J., & Strawson, C. (1976). Use of orthographic and word-specific knowledge in reading words aloud. *Journal of Experimental Psychology: Human Perception and Performance*, 2, 386–93.

Baron-Cohen, S. (1990). Autism: A specific cognitive disorder of mind-blindness. *International Review of Psychiatry*, 2, 81–90.

Baron-Cohen, S. (2009). Autism: The emphathizing-systemizing (E-S) theory. *Annals of New York Academy of Science*, 1156, 68–80.

Baron-Cohen, S., Leslie, A. M., & Frith, U. (1985). Does the autistic child have a "theory of mind"? *Cognition*, 21, 37–46.

Barr, L., & Couto, M. (2007). Molecular genetics of reading. In E. Grigorenko & A. J. Naples (eds) *Single Word Reading: Behavioural and Biological Perspectives* (pp. 255–81). New York: Psychology Press.

Bartlett, J. C. (1920). Some experiments on the reproduction of folk-stories. *Folklore*, 31(1), 30–47.

Basbøll, H. (2005). *The Phonology of Danish*. Oxford: Oxford University Press.

Bastiaanse, R., & Thompson, C. K. (2012). *Perspectives on Agrammatism*. New York: Psychology Press.

Bates, E. (1976). Pragmatics and sociolinguistics in child language. In D. Morehead & A. Morehead (eds) *Normal and Deficient Child Language* (pp. 247–307). Baltimore: University Park Press.

Bates, E., Masling, M., & Kintsch, W. (1978). Recognition memory for aspects of dialogue. *Journal of Experimental Psychology: Human Learning and Memory*, 4, 187–97.

Bates, E., Marchman, V., Thal, D., Fenson, L., Dale, P. et al. (1994). Developmental and stylistic variation in the composition of early vocabulary. *Journal of Child Language*, 21(1), 85–124.

Baugh, A. C., & Cable, T. (2002). *A History of the English Language*. New York: Psychology Press.

Baugh, J. (2002). *Beyond Ebonics: Linguistic Pride and Racial Prejudice*. Oxford: Oxford University Press.

Baugh, J. (2003). Linguistic profiling, in black linguistics. *Language, Society, and Politics in Africa and the Americas*, 155, 155–63.

Baus, C., Gutiérrez-Sigut, R., Quer, J., & Carreiras, M. (2008). Lexical access in Catalan Signed Language (LSC) production. *Cognition*, 108, 856–65.

Baydar, N., Brooks-Gunn, J., & Furstenberg, F. F. (1993). Early warning signs of functional illiteracy: Predictors in childhood and adolescence. *Child Development*, 64, 815–29.

Baynton, D. (1996). *Forbidden Signs*. Chicago, IL: University of Chicago Press.

Beattie, G., & Butterworth, B. (1979). Contextual probability and word-frequency as determinants of pauses in spontaneous speech. *Language & Speech*, 22, 201–21.

Beck, H. P., Levinson, S., & Irons, G. (2009). Finding Little Albert: A journey to John B. Watson's infant laboratory. *American Psychologist*, 64(7), 605–14.

Bedore, L., & Leonard L. (2001). Grammatical morphology deficits in Spanish-speaking children with specific language impairment. *Journal of Speech, Language, and Hearing Research*, 44, 905–24.

Bedore, L., Peña, E., Garcia, M., & Cortez, C. (2005). Conceptual versus monolingual scoring: When does it make a difference? *Language, Speech, and Hearing Services in Schools*, 36, 188–200.

Beekes, R. S. (1995). *Comparative Indo-European Linguistics*. Amsterdam: John Benjamins.

Behrend, D., Rosengren, K. S., & Perlmutter, M. A. (1992). Parental scaffolding and children's private speech: Differing sources of cognitive regulation. In R. M. Diaz & L. E. Berk (eds) *Private Speech: From Social Interaction to Self-regulation*. Hillsdale, NJ: Erlbaum.

Beitchman, J. H., Nair, R., Clegg, M., & Patel, P. G. (1986). Prevalence of speech and language disorders in 5-year-old kindergarten children in the Ottawa-Carleton region. *Journal of Speech and Hearing Disorders*, 51, 98–110.

Bell, A. M. (1867). *Visible Speech: The Science of Universal Alphabetics*. London: Simkin, Marshall & Co.

Benatar, A., & Clifton, C. J. (2014). Newness, givenness and discourse updating: Evidence from eye movements. *Journal of Memory and Language*, 71(1), 1–16.

Bender, M. (2002). *Signs of Cherokee Culture: Sequoyah's Syllabary in Eastern Cherokee Life*. Chapel Hill, NC: University of North Carolina Press.

Benefiel, R. R. (2010). Dialogues of ancient graffiti in the house of Maius Castricius in Pompeii. *American Journal of Archaeology*, 114(1), 59–101.

Benjamin, C. F., Walshaw, P. D., Hale, K., Gaillard, W. D., Baxter, L. C. et al. (2017). Presurgical language fMRI: Mapping of six critical regions. *Human Brain Mapping*, 38(8), 4239–55.

Benjamin, L. T. Jr. (2007). *A Brief History of Modern Psychology*. Malden, MA: Blackwell.

Benjamin, R. G. (2012). Reconstructing readability: Recent developments and recommendations in the analysis of text difficulty. *Educational Psychology Review*, 24(1), 63–88.

Bennett, J., Gardner, R. I., & Rizzi, G. L. (2014). Deaf and hard of hearing students' through-the-air English skills: A review of formal assessments. *American Annals of the Deaf*, 158(5), 506–21.

Benschop, R. (1998). What is a tachistoscope? Historical explorations of an instrument. *Science in Context*, 11, 23–50.

Bensky, M. K., Gosling, S. D., & Sinn, D. L. (2013). *The World from a Dog's Point of View: A Review and Synthesis of Dog Cognition Research*. San Diego, CA: Elsevier Academic Press.

Ben-Zeev, S. (1977). The influence of bilingualism on cognitive strategy and cognitive development. *Child Development*, 48, 1009–18.

Berg, T. (2002). Slips of the typewriter key. *Applied Psycholinguistics*, 23(2), 185–207.

Bergman, B. & Östen, D. (1994). Ideophones in sign language? The place of reduplication in the tense-aspect system of Swedish Sign Language. In C. Bache, H. Basbøll & C. E. Lindberg (eds) Tense, *Aspect and Action: Empirical and Theoretical Contributions to Language Typology* (pp. 397–422). New York: Mouton de Gruyter.

Berk, L. (1986). Relationship of elementary school children's private speech to behavioral accompaniment to task, attention, and task performance. *Developmental Psychology*, 22, 671–80.

Berk, L. (1992). Children's private speech: An overview of theory and the status of research. In R. M. Diaz & L. E. Berk (eds) *Private Speech: From Social Interaction to Self-regulation* (pp. 17–53). Hillsdale, NJ: Erlbaum.

Berk, L., & Spuhl, S. (1995). Maternal interaction, private speech, and task performance in preschool children. *Early Childhood Research Quarterly*, 10, 145–69.

Berko, J. (1958). The child's learning of English morphology. *Word*, 14, 150–77.

Berkout, O. V., Young, J. N., & Gross, A. M. (2011). Mean girls and bad boys: Recent research on gender differences in conduct disorder. *Aggression and Violent Behavior*, 16(6), 503–11.

Berlin, B., & Kay, P. (1969). *Basic Color Terms: Their Universality and Evolution*. Berkeley, CA: University of California Press.

Bernstein, R. N. (2005). Evidence-based practice in stuttering: Some questions to consider. *Journal of Fluency Disorder*, 30(3),163–88.

Bertelson, P., Mousty, P., & D'Alimonte, G. (1985). A study of Braille reading: 2. Patterns of hand activity in one-handed and two-handed reading. *Quarterly Journal of Experimental Psychology A*, 37, 235–56.

Besche-Richard, C., Iakimova, G., Hardy-Baylé, M., & Passerieux, C. (2014). Behavioral and brain measures (N400) of semantic priming in patients with schizophrenia: Test–retest effect in a longitudinal study. *Psychiatry and Clinical Neurosciences*, 68(5), 365–73.

Beukelman, D., Miranda, P., Garrett, K., & Light, J. (2012). *Augmentative and Alternative Communication: Supporting Children and Adults with Complex Communication Needs*. Baltimore, MD: Paul H. Brookes.

Bever, T. G., Carrithers, C., Cowart, W., & Townsend, D. J. (1989). Language processing and familial handedness. In A. Galaburda (ed.) *From Neurons to Reading* (pp. 331–60). Cambridge, MA: MIT Press.

Bialystok, E. (1986). Children's concept of word. *Journal of Psycholinguistic Research*, 15(1), 13–32.

Bialystok, E. (1988). Levels of bilingualism and levels of linguistic awareness. *Developmental Psychology*, 24(4), 560–67.

Bialystok, E. (1999). Cognitive complexity and attentional control in the bilingual mind. *Child Development*, 70, 636–644.

Bialystok, E. (2005). Consequences of bilingualism for cognitive development. In J. F. Kroll & A. M. de Groot (eds) *Handbook of Bilingualism: Psycholinguistic Approaches* (pp. 417–32). New York: Oxford University Press.

Bialystok, E., & Majumder, S. (1998). The relationship between bilingualism and the development of cognitive processes in problem solving. *Applied Psycholinguistics*, 19, 69–85.

Bialystok, E., & Martin, M. M. (2004). Attention and inhibition in bilingual children: Evidence from the dimensional change card sort task. *Developmental Science*, 7, 325–39.

Bialystok, E., Craik, F., & Freedman, M. (2007). Bilingualism as a protection against the onset of symptoms of dementia. *Neuropsychologia*, 45, 459–64.

Bialystok, E., Barac, R., Blaye, A., & Poulin-Dubois, D. (2010a). Word mapping and executive functioning in young monolingual and bilingual children. *Journal of Cognition and Development*, 11, 485–508.

Bialystok, E., Luk, G., Peets, K. F., & Yang, S. (2010b). Receptive vocabulary differences in monolingual and bilingual children. *Bilingualism: Language and Cognition*, 13, 525–31.

Bigelow, H. J. (1850). Dr. Harlow's case of recovery from the passage of an iron bar through the head. *American Journal of the Medical Sciences*, 20, 13–22.

Bihrle, A. M., Brownell, H. H., & Powelson, J. A. (1986). Comprehension of humorous and nonhumorous materials by left and right brain-damaged patients. *Brain and Cognition*, 5(4), 399–411.

Binder, J. R. (2015). The Wernicke area: Modern evidence and a reinterpretation. *Neurology*, 85(24), 2170–5.

Birch, S. A., & Bloom, P. (2003). Children are cursed: An asymmetric bias in mental state attribution. *Psychological Science*, 14, 283–6.

Bishop, D. V. (1998). Development of the Children's Communication Checklist (CCC): A method for assessing qualitative aspects of communicative impairment in children. *Journal of Child Psychology and Psychiatry*, 39, 879–92.

Bishop, D. V. (2008). Specific language impairment, dyslexia, and autism: Using genetics to unravel their relationship. In C. F. Norbury, J. B. Tomblin & D. V. Bishop (eds) *Understanding Developmental Language Disorders: From Theory to Practice* (pp. 67–78). Hove: Psychology Press.

Bishop, D. V., & Edmundson, A. (1987). Specific language impairment as a maturational lag: Evidence from longitudinal data on language and motor development. *Developmental Medicine and Child Neurology*, 29, 442–59.

Bishop, D. V., & Snowling, M. J. (2004). Developmental dyslexia and specific language impairment: Same or different? *Psychological Bulletin*, 130(6), 858–86.

Bivens, J. A., & Berk, L. E. (1990). A longitudinal study of the development of elementary school children's private speech. *Merrill Palmer Quarterly*, 36, 443–63.

Blake, J. W. ([1942] 2006). *Europeans in West Africa 1450–1560*. London: Hakluyt Society.

Bleses, D., & Basbøll, H. (2004). The Danish sound structure: Implications for language acquisition in normal and hearing impaired populations. In E. Schmidt, U. Mikkelsen, I. Post, J. B. Simonsen & K. Fruensgaard (eds) *Brain, Hearing and Learning* (pp.165–90). Denmark: Holmen Center Tryk.

Bleses, D., Basbøll, H., & Vach, W. (2011a). Is Danish difficult to acquire? Evidence from Nordic past-tense studies. *Language and Cognitive Processes*, 26(8), 1193–231.

Bleses, D., Basbøll, H., Lum, J., & Vach, W. (2011b). Phonology and lexicon in a cross-linguistic perspective: The importance of phonetics – a commentary on Stoel-Gammon's "relationships between lexical and phonological development in young children". *Journal of Child Language*, 38(1), 61–8.

Bleses, D., Vach, W., Slott, M., Wehberg, S., Thomsen, P. et al. (2008). Early vocabulary development in Danish and other languages: A CDI-based comparison. *Journal of Child Language*, 35(3), 619–50.

Block, M. (2006). Teens turn "repeller" into adult-proof ringtone. National Public Radio. Retrieved July 14, 2017 from www.npr.org/templates/story/story.php?storyId=5434687.

Blonder, L. X., Pettigrew, L. C., & Kryscio, R. J. (2012). Emotion recognition and marital satisfaction in stroke. *Journal of Clinical & Experimental Neuropsychology*, 34(6), 634–42.

Bloom, L. (1970). *Language Development: Form and Function in Emerging Grammars*. Cambridge, MA: MIT Press.

Bloom, O. (2018). Orlando Bloom on dyslexia. Retrieved July 14, 2017 from https://childmind.org/article/orlando-bloom-on-dyslexia/.

Bluestone, C. D. (2005). *Eustachian Tube: Structure, Function, Role in Otitis Media*. Hamilton: PMPH-USA.

Blumstein, S., Goodglass, H., & Tartter, V. (1975). The reliability of ear advantage in dichotic listening. *Brain and Language*, 2, 226–36.

Blumenthal, A. L. (1970). *Language and Psychology: Historical Aspects of Psycholinguistics*. New York: Wiley.

Blythe, H. I. (2014). Developmental changes in eye movements and visual information encoding associated with learning to read. *Current Direction in Psychological Science*, 23, 201–7.

Blythe, H. I., Liversedge, S. P., Joseph, H. S., White, S. J., & Rayner, K. (2009). Visual information capture during fixations in reading for children and adults. *Vision Research*, 49, 1583–91.

Blumenthal, A. L. (1970). *Language and Psychology*. Wiley: New York.

Bocanegra, Y., García, A. M., Pineda, D., Buriticá, O., Villegas, A. et al. (2015). Syntax, action verbs, action semantics, and object semantics in Parkinson's disease: Dissociability, progression, and executive influences. *Cortex*, 69, 237–54.

Bock, J. K. (1986). Syntactic persistence in language production. *Cognitive Psychology*, 18, 355–87.

Bock, K., & Cutting, J. C. (1992). Regulating mental energy: Performance units in language production. *Journal of Memory and Language*, 31, 99–127.

Bock, K., & Eberhard, K. M. (1993). Meaning, sound, and syntax in English number agreement. *Language and Cognitive Processes*, 8(1), 57–99.

Bock, K., & Levelt, W. J. (1994). Language production: Grammatical encoding. In M. A. Gernsbacher (ed.). *Handbook of Psycholinguistics* (pp. 741–79). New York: Academic Press.

Bock, K., & Miller, C. A. (1991). Broken agreement. *Cognitive Psychology*, 23, 45–93.

Bock, K., Nicol, J. L., & Cutting, J. C. (1999). The ties that bid: Creating number agreement in speech. *Journal of Memory and Language*, 40, 330–46.

Bohrn, I. C., Altmann, U., & Jacobs, A. M. (2012). Looking at the brains behind figurative language: A quantitative meta-analysis of neuroimaging studies on metaphor, idiom, and irony processing. *Neuropsychologia*, 50(11), 2669–83.

Boles, D. B. (1984). Sex in lateralized tachistoscopic Word recognition. *Brain and Language*, 23(2), 307–17.

Bolte Taylor, J. (2008a). *My Stroke of Insight: A Brain Scientist's Personal Journey*. New York: Viking.

Bolte Taylor, J. (2008b). *My Stroke of Insight* [video]. Available at www.ted.com/talks/jill_bolte_taylor_s_powerful_stroke_of_insight?language=en.

Boltz, W. G. (1986). Early Chinese writing. *World Archaeology*, 17(3), 420–36.

Bond, M., & Lai, T. (1986). Embarrassment and code-switching into a second language. *Journal of Social Psychology*, 126(2), 179–86.

Bonin, P., Barry, C., Méot, A., & Chalard, M. (2004). The influence of age of acquisition in word reading and other tasks: A never ending story? *Journal of Memory and Language*, 50(4), 456–76.

Booth, J. R., & Burman, D. D. (2001). Development and disorders of neuro-cognitive systems for oral language and reading. *Learning Disabilities Quarterly*, 24, 205–15.

Bopp, K. L., & Verhaeghen, P. (2005). Aging and verbal memory span: A meta-analysis. *Journal of Gerontology: Series B: Psychological Sciences and Social Sciences*, 60(5), P223–33.

Borleffs, E., Maassen, B. M., Lyytinen, H., & Zwarts, F. (2017). Measuring orthographic transparency and morphological-syllabic complexity in alphabetic orthographies: A narrative review. *Reading and Writing*, 30(8), 1617–38.

Bortfeld, H., Leon, S. D., Bloom, J. E., Schober, M. F., & Brennan, S. E. (2001). Disfluency rates in conversation: Effects of age, relationship, topic, role, and gender. *Language and Speech*, 44(2), 123–47.

Bosch, L., & Ramon-Casas, M. (2014). First translation equivalents in bilingual toddlers' expressive vocabulary: Does form similarity matter? *International Journal of Behavioral Development*, 38(4), 317–22.

Bosch, L., & Sebastián-Gallés, N. (2003). Simultaneous bilingualism and the perception of a language specific vowel contrast in the first year of life. *Language and Speech*, 46, 217–43.

Bottéro, J. (1992). *Mesopotamia: Writing, Reasoning, and the Gods*. Chicago: University of Chicago Press.

Botting, N. (2002). Narrative as a tool for the assessment of linguistic and pragmatic impairments. *Child Language Teaching and Therapy*, 18(1), 1–22.

Bowers, J. M., & Kennison, S. M. (2011). The role of age of acquisition in bilingual translation. *Journal of Psycholinguistic Research*, 40, 279–89.

Bowers, J. S., Davis, C. J., & Hanley, D. A. (2005a). Automatic semantic activation of embedded words: Is there a "hat" in "that"? *Journal of Memory and Language*, 52, 131–43.

Bowers, J. S., Davis, C. J., & Hanley, D. A. (2005b). Interfering neighbours: The impact of novel word learning on the identification of visually similar words. *Cognition*, 97, 45–54.

Boysson-Bardies, B. de (1993). Ontogeny of language-specific syllabic productions. In B. de Boysson-Bardies, S. de Schonen, P. Jusczyk, P. McNeilage & J. Morton (eds) *Developmental Neurocognition: Speech and Face Processing in the First Year of Life* (pp. 353–63). Dordrecht: Kluwer.

Bradbury, J. W., & Vehrencamp, S. L. (2011). *Principles of Animal Communication* (2nd edn). Sunderland, MA: Sinaur.

Bradley, J. (1988). Yanyuwa: Men speak one way, women speak another. *Aboriginal Linguistics*, 1, 126–34.

Bradshaw, J. L., & Nettleton, N. C. (1983). *Human Cerebral Asymmetry*. Englewood Cliffs, NJ: Prentice Hall.

Braille, L. (1829). *Method of Writing Words, Music, and Plain Songs by Means of Dots, for Use by the Blind and Arranged for them*. Paris: Institute for Blind Youth.

Branch, C., Milner, B., & Rasmussen, T. (1964). Intracarotid sodium amytal for the lateralization of cerebral speech dominance. *Journal of Neurosurgery*, 21(5), 399–405.

Bransford, J. D., Barclay, R. J., & Franks, J. J. (1972). Sentence memory: A constructive versus interpretive approach. *Cognitive Psychology*, 3, 193–209.

Branson, R. (2011). *Losing my Virginity: How I've Survived, Had Fun, and Made a Fortune Doing Business My Way*. New York: Crown Business.

Brentari, D. (1999). *A Prosodic Model of Sign Language Phonology*. Cambridge, MA: MIT Press.

Bresnan, J. (2001). *Lexical-functional Syntax*. Oxford: Blackwell.

Bridges, B., & Metzger, M. (1996). *Deaf Tend your: Non-manual Signals in ASL*. Silver Spring, MD: Calliope Press.

Briganti, A. M., & Cohen, L. B. (2011). Examining the role of social cues in early word learning. *Infant Behavior Development*, 34(1), 211–14.

Bristow, D., Dehaene-Lambertz, G., Mattout, J., Soares, C., Gliga, T. et al. (2009). Hearing faces: How the infant brain matches the face it sees with the speech it hears. *Journal of Cognitive Neurosciences*, 21(5), 905–21.

Britt, A., Perfetti, C. A., Garrod, S., & Rayner, K. (1992). Parsing in discourse: Context effects and their limits. *Journal of Memory and Language*, 31, 293–314.

Broadbent, D. (1958). *Perception and Communication*. London: Pergamon Press.

Broecke, M. V. & Goldstein, L. (1980). Consonant features in speech errors. In V. A. Fromkin (ed.) *Errors in Linguistic Performance* (pp. 47–65). San Diego: Academic Press.

Brodmann, K. (1909) *Vergleichende Lokalisationslehre der Grosshirnrinde in ihren Prinzipien dargestellt auf Grund des Zellenbaues*. Leipzig: Johann Ambrosius Barth.

Brown, A. S. (1991). A review of the tip-of-the-tongue experience. *Psychological Bulletin*, 109, 204–23.

Brown, J. (1958). Some tests of the decay theory of immediate memory. *Quarterly Journal of Experimental Psychology*, 10(1), 12–21.

Brown, M., & Kuperberg, G. R. (2015). A hierarchical generative framework of language processing: Linking language perception, interpretation, and production abnormalities in schizophrenia. *Frontiers in Human Neuroscience*, 9, 643.

Brown, M., Savova, V., & Gibson, E. (2012). Syntax encodes information structure: Evidence from on-line reading comprehension. *Journal of Memory and Language*, 66(1), 194–209.

Brown, P., & Levinson, S. C. (1987). *Politeness: Some Universals in Language Usage*. Cambridge: Cambridge University Press.

Brown, R. (1958). *Words and Things*. New York: Simon & Schuster.

Brown, R. (1973). *A First Language: The Early Stages*. Cambridge, MA: Harvard University Press.

Brown, R., & Gilman, A. (1960). The pronouns of power and solidarity. In T. A. Sebeok (ed.) *Style in Language* (pp. 253–76). Cambridge, MA: MIT Press.

Bruce, R. V. (1990). *Bell: Alexander Bell and the Conquest of Solitude*. Ithaca, NY: Cornell University Press.

Bryant, G. A., & Barrett, H. C. (2007). Recognizing intentions in infant-directed speech: Evidence for universals. *Psychological Science*, 18(8), 746–51.

Bryce, T. R. (1999). *The Kingdom of the Hittites*. Oxford: Oxford University Press.

Bryden, M. P. (1982). *Laterality: Functional Asymmetry in the Intact Brain*. New York: Academic Press.

Bryden, M. P. (1988). Does laterality make any difference? Thoughts on the relation between cerebral asymmetry and reading. In D. L. Molfese & S. J. Segalowitz (eds) *Brain Lateralization in Children: Developmental Implications* (pp. 509–26). New York: Guilford Press.

Brynskov, C., Eigsti, I., Jørgensen, M., Lemcke, S., Bohn, O. et al. (2017). Syntax and morphology in Danish-speaking children with autism spectrum disorder. *Journal of Autism and Developmental Disorders*, 47, 373–83.

Brysbaert, M., & Duyck, W. (2010). Is it time to leave behind the revised hierarchical model of bilingual language processing after fifteen years of service? *Bilingualism: Language and Cognition*, 13(3), 359–71.

Brysbaert, M., Buchmeier, M., Conrad, M., Jacobs, A. M., Bölte, J., et al. (2011). The word frequency effect: A review of recent developments and implications for the choice of frequency estimates in German. *Experimental Psychology*, 58(5), 412–24.

Bureau of Labor Statistics (2015). *Occupational Outlook Handbook: Speech-Language Pathologists*. Retrieved September 19, 2015 from www.bls.gov/ooh/healthcare/speech-language-pathologists.htm.

Burke, D. M., & MacKay, D. G. (1997). Memory, language and ageing. *Philosophical Transactions of the Royal Society: Biological Sciences*, 352, 1845–56.

Burke, D. M., MacKay, D. G., & James, L. E. (2000). Theoretical approaches to language and aging. In T. Perfect & E. Maylor (eds) *Models of Cognitive Aging* (pp. 204–37). Oxford: Oxford University Press.

Burke, D. M., MacKay, D. G., Worthley, J. S., & Wade, E. (1991). On tip-of-the-tongue: What causes word finding failures in young and older adults? *Journal of Memory and Language*, 30, 542–79.

Burnham, D., & Brooker, R. (2002). Absolute putch and lecical tones: Tone perception by non-musician, musician, and absolute pitch non-tonal language speakers. In J. Hansen & B. Pellom (eds) *The 7th International Conference on Spoken Language Processing* (pp. 257–60). Denver.

Burnham, D., & Dodd, B. (2004). Auditory-visual speech integration by prelinguistic infants: Perception of an emergent consonant in the McGurk effect. *Developmental Psychobiology*, 45(4), 204–20.

Burns, A., & Iliffe, S. (2009). Alzheimer's disease. *British Medical Journal*, 338, 466–71.

Burns, T. C., Yoshida, K. A., Hill, K., & Werker, J. F. (2007). Bilingual and monolingual infant phonetic development. *Applied Psycholinguistics*, 28(3), 455–74.

Busnel, R.-G., & Classe, A. (1976). *Whistled Languages*. New York: Springer.

Butterworth, B. (1989). Lexical access in speech production. In W. Marslen-Wilson (ed.) *Lexical Representation and Process* (pp. 108–35). Cambridge, MA: MIT Press.

Butterworth, B. (1992). Disorders of phonological encoding. *Cognition*, 42, 261–86.

Butterworth, B., & Whittaker, S. (1980). Peggy Babcock's relatives. In G. E. Stelmach & J. Requin (eds) *Tutorials in Motor Behavior*, vol. 1 (pp. 657–77). Amsterdam: Holland.

Bybee, J. L., Perkins, R., & Pagliuca, W. (1994). *The Evolution of Grammar: Tense, Aspect, and Modality in the Languages of the World*. Chicago, IL: University of Chicago Press.

Cai, Z. G., Sturt, P., & Pickering, M. J. (2012). The effect of nonadopted analyses on sentence processing. *Language and Cognitive Processes*, 27(9), 1286–311.

Call, J., & Tomasello, M. (1999). A nonverbal theory of mind test: The performance of children and apes. *Child Development*, 70, 381–95.

Camerer, C., Loewenstein, G., & Weber, M. (1989). The curse of knowledge in economic settings: An experimental analysis. *Journal of Political Economy*, 97, 1232–54.

Caminos, R. A. (1954). *Late-Egyptian Miscellanies*. London: Oxford University Press.

Campbell, S. (2008). Now crime gadget can annoy us all. BBC. Retrieved July 14, 2017 from http://news.bbc.co.uk/2/hi/uk_news/7759818.stm.

Campos, L., & Alonso-Quecuty, M. L. (2006). Remembering a criminal conversation: Beyond eyewitness testimony. *Memory*, 14(1), 27–36.

Cappa, S. F. (2012). Neurological accounts of agrammatism. In R. Bastiaanse & C. K. Thompson (eds) *Perspectives on Agrammatism* (pp. 49–59). New York: Psychology Press.

Caramazza, A., & Hillis, A. E. (1991). Lexical organization of nouns and verbs in the brain. *Nature*, 349(6312), 788–90.

Carey, S. (1978). The child as a word learner. In M. Halle, J. Bresnan & G. Miller (eds) *Linguistic Theory and Psychological Reality* (pp. 264–93). Cambridge, MA: MIT Press.

Carey, S., & Bartlett, E. (1978). Acquiring a single new word. *Proceedings of the Stanford Child Language Conference*, 15, 17–29.

Carli, L. L. (1990). Gender, language, and influence. *Journal of Personality and Social Psychology*, 59, 941–51.

Carlson, N., & Buskist, W. (1997). *Psychology: The Science of Behavior* (5th edn). Boston: Allyn & Bacon.

Carlson, S. M., & Meltzoff, A. N. (2008). Bilingual experience and executive functioning in young children. *Developmental Science*, 11, 282–98.

Carpenter, H. (1977). *Tolkien: A Biography*. London: Allen & Unwin.

Carreiras, M. (2010). Sign language processing. *Language and Linguistics Compass*, 4(7), 430–44.

Carreiras, M., Álvarez, C. J., & de Vega, M. (1993). Syllable frequency and visual word recognition in Spanish. *Journal of Memory and Language*, 32, 766–80.

Carreiras, M., Garnham, A., Oakhill, J., & Cain, K. (1996). The use of stereotypical gender information in constructing a mental model: Evidence from English and Spanish. *Quarterly Journal of Experimental Psychology A: Human Experimental Psychology*, 49A(3), 639–63.

Carreiras, M., Gutierrez, E., Baquero, S., & Corina, D. P. (2008). Lexical processing in Spanish Sign Language (LSE). *Journal of Memory and Language*, 58, 100–22.

Carreiras, M., Lopez, J., Rivero, F., & Corina, D. (2005). Neural processing of a whistled language. *Nature*, 433(7021), 31–2.

Carroll, J. B., & White, M. N. (1973). Word frequency and age of acquisition as determiners of picture naming latency. *Quarterly Journal of Experimental Psychology*, 25, 85–95.

Carrow-Woolfolk, E. & Allen, E. A. (2014). *The Test of Expressive Language*. Austin, TX: Pro-Ed.

Case, L. K., Pineda, J., & Ramachandran, V. S. (2015). Common coding and dynamic interactions between observed, imagined, and experienced motor and somatosensory activity. *Neuropsychologia*, 79, 233–45.

Casey, S., & Emmorey, K. (2008). Co-speech gesture in bimodal bilinguals. *Language and Cognitive Processes*, 24, 290–312.

Caselli, M. C., Bates, E., Casadio, P., Fenson, J., Fenson, L. et al. (1995). A cross-linguistic study of early lexical development. *Cognitive Development*, 10, 159–99.

Castles, A., & Coltheart, M. (1993). Varieties of developmental dyslexia. *Cognition*, 47(2), 149–80.

Castro, N. (2014). What turns speech into song? Investigations of the speech-to-song illusion. Unpublished Master's thesis. University of Kansas.

Catani, M., & de Schotten, M. T. (2012). *Atlas of Human Brain Connections*. Oxford: Oxford University Press.

Cattell, J. M. (1886). The time taken up by cerebral operations. *Mind*, 11, 220–42.

CBS News (2014). iPads may help kids with autism communicate. Retrieved June 15, 2017 from www.cbsnews.com/videos/ipads-may-help-kids-with-autism-communicate.

Census of India (2013). State of literacy. Retrieved September 16, 2016 from http://censusindia.gov.in/2011-prov-results/data_files/india/Final_PPT_2011_chapter6.pdf.

Center for Expansion of Language and Thinking (n.d.). What whole language is not: Commom myths and misunderstandings. Retrieved July 22, 2017 from www.celtlink.org/fact-sheet-6-myths-and-misunderstandings.

Centers for Disease Control (n.d.). Ear Infection. Retrieved October 8, 2016 from www.cdc.gov/getsmart/community/for-patients/common-illnesses/ear-infection.html.

Centers for Disease Control (2017) Traumatic Brain Injury & Concussion: TBI: Get the Facts. Retrieved July 19, 2017 from www.cdc.gov/traumaticbraininjury/get_the_facts.html.

Chall, J. ([1983] 1996). *Learning to Read: The Great Debate*. Fort Worth: Harcourt Brace.

Chall, J., & Dale, E. (1995). *Readability Revisited: The New Dale-Chall Readability Formula*. Northampton, MA: Brookline Books.

Chan, Y. C., Chou, T. I., Chen, H. C., & Liang, K. C. (2012). Segregating the comprehension and elaboration processing of verbal jokes: An fMRI study. *NeuroImage*, 61(4), 899–906.

Chan, Y. C., Chou, T. I., Chen, H. C., Yeh, Y. C., Lavallee, J. P. et al. (2013). Towards a neural circuit model of verbal humor processing: An fMRI study of neural substrates of incongruity detection and resolution. *NeuroImage*, 66C, 169–76.

Chase, W. G., & Simon, H. A. (1973). The mind's eye in chess. In W. G. Chase (ed.) *Visual Information Processing* (pp. 215–81). New York: Academic Press.

Chateau, D., & Jared, D. (2000). Exposure to print and word recognition process. *Memory & Cognition*, 28, 143–53.

Cheang, H. S., & Pell, M. D. (2006). A study of humour and communicative intention following right hemisphere stroke. *Clinical Linguistics & Phonetics*, 20(6), 447–62.

Chedd, G. (2002). *Make up your Mind. Scientific American Frontiers*, Season 13, Episode 2. Retrieved July 22, 2017 from www.chedd-angier.com/frontiers/season13.html.

Chee, M. W., Soon, C. S., Lee, H. L., & Pallier, C. (2004). Left insular activation: A marker for language attainment in bilinguals. *Proceedings of the National Academy of Sciences, USA*, 101, 15265–70.

Chen Pichler, D. (2001). Word Order Variation and Acquisition in American Sign Language. Doctoral dissertation, University of Connecticut.

Cherry, E. C. (1953). Some experiments on the recognition of speech, with one and with two ears. *Journal of the Acoustical Society of America*, 25(5), 975–9.

Chesterman, A. (1991). *On Definiteness. A Study with Special Reference to English and Finnish*. Cambridge: Cambridge University Press.

Cheung, H., & Ng, L. (2003). Chinese reading development in some major Chinese societies: An introduction. In C. McBride-Chang & H. C. Chen (eds) *Reading Development in Chinese Children* (pp. 3–17). Westport, CT: Praeger.

Cheung, H., Chen, H.-C., Lai, C. Y., Wong, O. C., & Hills, M. (2001). The development of phonological awareness: Effects of spoken-language experience and orthography. *Cognition*, 81, 227–41.

Chikamatsu, N., Yokoyama, S., Nozaki, H., Long, E., & Fukuda, S. (2000). A Japanese logographic character frequency list for cognitive science research. *Behavior Research Methods, Instruments, & Computers*, 32(3), 482–500.

Ching, M. (1982). The question intonation in assertions. *American Speech*, 57, 95–107.

Choi, S., & Gopnik, A. (1995). Early acquisition of verbs in Korean. *Journal of Child Language*, 22, 297–531.

Cholin, J., Dell, G. S., & Levelt, W. J. (2011). Planning and articulation in incremental word production: Syllable-frequency effects in English. *Journal of Experimental Psychology: Learning, Memory, and Cognition*, 37, 109–22.

Cholin, J., Levelt, W. J., & Schiller, N. O. (2006). Effects of syllable frequency in speech production. *Cognition*, 99, 205–35.

Chomsky, N. (1957). *Syntactic Structures*. Cambridge, MA: MIT Press.

Chomsky, N. (1959). Review of B. F. Skinner's verbal behavior. *Language*, 35, 26–58.

Chomsky, N. (1965). *Aspects of the Theory of Syntax*. Cambridge, MA: MIT Press.

Chomsky, N. (1968). *Language and Mind*. New York: Harcourt, Brace & World.

Chomsky, N. (1980). *Rules and Representations*. Oxford: Basil Blackwell.

Chomsky, N. (1981). *Lectures on Government and Binding: The Pisa Lectures*. Holland: Foris.

Chomsky, N. (1986). *Knowledge of Language: Its Nature, Origin, and Use*. New York: Praeger.

Chomsky, N. A., & Miller, G. (1963). Introduction to the formal analysis of natural languages. In R. D. Luce, R. R. Bush and E. Galanter (eds) *Handbook of Mathematical Psychology* (vol. 2). New York: Wiley.

Christianson, K., Hollingworth, A., Halliwell, J. F., & Ferreira, F. (2001). Thematic roles assigned along the garden path linger. *Cognitive Psychology*, 42(4), 368–407.

Christianson, K., Williams, C., Zacks, R., & Ferreira, F. (2006). Younger and older adults' good enough interpretations of garden-path sentences. *Discourse Processes*, 42(2), 205–38.

Chumbley, J. I., & Balota, D. A. (1984). A word's meaning affects the decision in lexical decision. *Memory & Cognition*, 12(6), 590–606.

Chung, S. T., Mansfield, J. S., & Legge, G. E. (1998). Psychophysics of reading. XVIII. The effect of print size on reading speed in normal peripheral vision. *Vision Research*, 38(19), 2949–62.

Cieslak, M., Ingham, R., Ingham, J., & Grafton, S. (2015). Anomalous white matter morphology in adults who stutter. *Journal of Speech, Language, and Hearing Research*, 58(2), 268–77.

Cipielewski, J., & Stanovich, K. E. (1992). Predicting growth in reading ability from children's exposure to print. *Journal of Experimental Child Psychology*, 54, 74–89.

Clahsen, H. (1989). The grammatical characterization of developmental dysphasia. *Linguistics*, 27, 897–920.

Clare, L., Whitaker, C. J., Martyr, A., Martin-Forbes, P. A., Bastable, A. M. et al. (2016). Executive control in older Welsh monolinguals and bilinguals. *Journal of Cognitive Psychology*, 28(4), 412–26.

Clark, G. M., Tong, Y. C., & Patrick, J. F. (eds) (1990). *Cochlear Prostheses*. Melbourne: Churchill Livingstone.

Clark, H. H. (1977). Inferences in comprehension. In D. LaBerge & S. J. Samuels (eds) *Basic Processes in Reading: Perception and Comprehension* (pp. 243–63). Hillsdale, NJ: Lawrence Erlbaum.

Clark, H. H. (1985). Language use and language users. In G. Lindzey & E. Aronson (eds) *Handbook of Social Psychology* (3rd edn, pp. 179–231). New York: Harper & Row.

Clark, H. H. (1996). *Using Language*. Cambridge: Cambridge University Press.

Clark, H. H. & Brennan, S. E. (1991). Grounding in communication excerpt. In L. B. Resnick, J. M. Levine & S. D. Teasley (eds) *Perspectives on Socially Shared Cognition* (pp. 127–49). Washington: APA.

Clark, H. H., & Haviland, S. E. (1977). Comprehension and the given-new contract. In R. O. Freedle (ed.) *Discourse Production and Comprehension* (pp. 1–40). Hillsdale, NJ: Erlbaum.

Clark. H. H., & Schaefer, E. F. (1987). Collaborating on contributions to conversations. *Language and Cognitive Processes*, 2(1), 19–41.

Clark, H. H. & Sengul, C. (1979). In search of referents for nouns and pronouns. *Memory and Cognition*, 7, 35–41.

Clark, H. H., & Fox Tree, J. E. (2002). Using uh and um in spontaneous speech. *Cognition*, 84, 73–111.

Clift, R. (2016). *Conversational Analysis*. Cambridge: Cambridge University Press.

Clifton, C., Jr, Ferreira, F., Henderson, J. M., Inhoff, A. W., Liversedge, S. et al. (2016). Eye movements in reading and information processing: Keith Rayner's 40 year legacy. *Journal of Memory and Language*, 86, 1–16.

Clifton, C., Frazier, L., & Connine, C. (1984). Lexical expectations in sentence comprehension. *Journal of Verbal Learning & Verbal Behavior*, 23(6), 696–708.

Clifton, C., Kennison, S. M., & Albrecht, J. (1997). Reading the words "her", "his", and "him": Implications for parsing principles based on frequency and on structure. *Journal of Memory and Language*, 36, 276–92.

Clifton, C., Speer, S., & Abney, S. P. (1991). Parsing arguments: Phrase structure and argument structure as determinants of initial parsing decisions. *Journal of Memory and Language*, 30(2), 251–71.

Cloherty, M. (2017). 911 dispatcher sends ambulance to wrong address. https://wtop.com/dc/2017/04/struggling-child-waited-20-minutes-for-ambulance-dispatched-to-wrong-address/.

Coelho, C. A. (2002). Story narratives of adults with closed head injury and non-brain-injured adults: Influence of socioeconomic status elicitation task and executive functioning. *Journal of Speech, Language, and Hearing Research*, 45, 1232–48.

Cohen, A. (1966). Errors in speech and their implication for understanding the strategy of languages. *Zeitschrtft fir Phonetik*, 21, 177–81.

Cohen, A. A., & Harrison, R. P. (1973). Intentionality in the use of hand illustrators in face-to-face communication situations. *Journal of Personality and Social Psychology*, 28, 276–9.

Cohen, L. B., & Cashon, C. H. (2003). Infant perception and cognition. In R. M. Lerner et al. (eds) *Handbook of Psychology*: vol. 6, *Developmental Psychology* (pp. 65–89). Hoboken, NJ: Wiley & Sons.

Cohen, L. H. (1995). *Train Go Sorry: Inside a Deaf World*. New York: First Vintage Books.

Colapinto, J. (2007). The Interpreter: Has a remote Amazonian tribe upended our understanding of language. *The New Yorker*, 16 April. Retrieved June 16, 2017 from www.newyorker.com/magazine/2007/04/16/the-interpreter-2.

Cole, J. (2014). *Global English Slang: Methodologies and Perspectives*. Abingdon-on-Thames: Routledge.

Coleman, J. (2012). *The Life of Slang*. Oxford: Oxford University Press.

Colflesh, G. J., & Conway, A. R. (2007). Individual differences in working memory capacity and divided attention in dichotic listening. *Psychonomic Bulletin & Review*, 14(4), 699–703.

Colker, R., Shaywitz, S., Shaywitz, B., & Simon, J. A. (2016). Comments on proposed DSM-5 criteria for specific learning disorder from a legal and medical/scientific perspective. Retrieved July 23, 2017 from http://dyslexia.yale.edu/CommentsDSM5ColkerShaywitzSimon.pdf.

Collier, V. P. (1989). How long? A synthesis on academic achievement in a second language. *TESOL Quarterly*, 23, 509–31.

Collins, A. M., & Loftus, E. F. (1975). A spreading activation theory of semantic processing. *Psychological Review*, 82, 407–28.

Collins, A. M., & Quillian, M. R. (1969). Retrieval time from semantic memory. *Journal of Verbal Learning and Verbal Behavior*, 8(2), 240–7.

Collins, B., & Mees, I. (2013). *Practical Phonetics and Phonology: A Resource Book for Students* (3rd edn). New York: Routledge.

Coltheart, M. (1978). Lexical access in simple reading tasks. In G. Underwood (ed.) *Strategies of Information Processing*. London: Academic Press.

Coltheart, M., & Kohnen, S. (2012). Acquired and developmental disorders of reading and spelling. In M. Faust (ed.) *The Handbook of the Neuropsychology of Language* (pp. 892–920). Chichester: Wiley-Blackwell.

Coltheart, M., Curtis, B., Atkins, P., & Haller, M. (1993). Models of reading aloud: Dual-route and parallel-distributed-processing approaches. *Psychological Review*, 100(4), 589–608.

Convit, A., de Asis, J., de Leon, M. J., Tarshish, C. Y., de Santi, S. et al. (2000). Atrophy of the medial occipitotemporal, inferior, and middle temporal gyri in non-demented elderly predict decline to Alzheimer's disease. *Neurobiology of Aging*, 21, 19–26.

Conway, A. R., Cowan, N., & Bunting, M. F. (2001). The cocktail party phenomenon revisited: The importance of working memory capacity. *Psychonomic Bulletin & Review*, 8, 331–5.

Conway, A. A., Kane, M. J., Bunting, M. F., Hambrick, D. Z., Wilhelm, O. et al. (2005). Working memory span tasks: A methodological review and user's guide. *Psychonomic Bulletin & Review*, 12(5), 769–86.

Cook, A. E., & O'Brien, E. J. (2014). Knowledge activation, integration, and validation during narrative text comprehension. *Discourse Processes*, 51(1/2), 26–49.

Cook, A. E., Myers, J. L., & O'Brien, E. J. (2005). Processing an anaphor when there is no antecedent. *Discourse Processes*, 39(1), 101–20.

Cook, H. M. (1997). The role of the Japanese masu form in caregiver–child conversation. *Journal of Pragmatics*, 28, 695–718.

Cook, V., Bassetti, B., Kasai, C., Sasaki, M., & Takahashi, J. (2006) Do bilinguals have different concepts? The case of shape and material in Japanese L2 users of English. *International Journal of Bilingualism*, 10(2), 137–52.

Coolin, A., Fischer, A. L., Aβfalg, A., Thornton, W. L., Sommerville, J. A. et al. (2017). Decomposing false-belief performance across the life span. In J. A. Sommerville and J. Decety (eds) *Social Cognition: Development across the Life Span* (pp. 280–302). New York: Routledge/Taylor & Francis.

Cooper, R. (1967). The ability of deaf and hearing children to apply morphological rules. *Journal of Speech and Hearing*, 10, 77–86.

Cooper, R. M. (1974). Control of eye fixation by meaning of spoken language: New methodology for real-time investigation of speech perception, memory, and language processing. *Cognitive Psychology*, 6, 84–107.

Cooper, R. P., & Aslin, R. N. (1994) Developmental differences in infant attention to the spectral properties of infant-directed speech. *Child Development*, 65(6), 1663–77.

Cooper, W. E. (1983). *Cognitive Aspects of Skilled Typewriting*. New York: Springer.

Corballis, M. C. (2009). Language as gesture. *Human Movement Science*, 28(5), 556–65.

Corballis, M. (2010). The gestural origins of language.WIREs *Cognitive Science*, 1, 2–7.

Corina, D. P., & Sandler, W. (1993) On the nature of phonological structure in sign language. *Phonology*, 10, 165–207.

Corkin, S. (2013). *The Permanent Present Tense: The Unforgettable Life of the Amnesic Patient, H. M.* New York: Basic Books.

Corley, M., Brocklehurst, P. H., & Moat, H. S. (2011). Error biases in inner and overt speech: Evidence from tongue twisters. *Journal of Experimental Psychology: Learning, Memory, and Cognition*, 37(1), 162–75.

Cormier, K., Schembri, A., & Woll, B. (2013). Pronouns and pointing in sign languages. *Lingua*, 137, 230–47.

Cormier, K., Schembri, A., Vinson, D., & Orfanidou, E. (2012). First language acquisition differs from second language acquisition in prelingually deaf signers: Evidence from sensitivity to grammaticality judgement in British sign language. *Cognition*, 124(1), 50–65.

Corsaro, W. A. (1979). "We're friends, right?" Children's use of access rituals in nursery school. *Language & Society*, 8, 315–36.

Cote, L. R., & Bornstein, M. H. (2014). Productive vocabulary among three groups of bilingual American children: Comparison and prediction. *First Language*, 34(6), 467–85.

Coulmas, F. (2003). *Writing Systems: An Introduction*. Cambridge: Cambridge University Press.

Coupland, J. (ed.) (2000). *Small Talk*. London: Longman.

Covington, M. A., He, C., Brown, C., Naçi. L., McClain, J. T. et al. (2005). Schizophrenia and the structure of language: The linguist's view. *Schizophrenia Research*, 77(1), 85–98.

Cowell, P. E., Ledger, W. L., Wadnerkar, M. B., Skilling, F. M., & Whiteside, S. P. (2011). Hormones and dichotic listening: Evidence from the study of menstrual cycle effects. *Brain and Cognition*, 76(2), 256–62.

Cowles, H. W., & Garnham, A. (2005). Antecedent focus and conceptual distance effects in category noun-phrase anaphora. *Language and Cognitive Processes*, 20(6), 725–50.

Crago, M., and Allen, S. (2001). Early finiteness in Inuktitut: The role of language structure and input. *Language Acquisition*, 9(1), 59–111.

Craik, F. I., Bialystok, E., & Freedman, M. (2010). Delaying the onset of Alzheimer's disease: Bilingualism as a form of cognitive reserve. *Neurology*, 75(19), 1726–19.

Crawford, J. (1999). *Bilingual Education: History, Politics, Theory and Practice*. Los Angeles, CA: Bilingual Education Service.

Cresswell, M. (2006). Formal semantics. In M. Devitt & R. Hanley (eds) *The Blackwell Guide to the Philosophy of Language* (pp. 131–46). Oxford: Wiley-Blackwell.

Croft, W. (2002). *Typology and Universals* (2nd edn). Cambridge: Cambridge University Press.

Cromdal, J. (1999). Childhood bilingualism and metalinguistic skills: Analysis and control in young Swedish-English bilinguals. *Applied Psycholinguistics*, 20, 1–20.

Crow, J. F. (2002). Unequal by nature: A geneticist's perspective on human differences. *Dedalus*, 131, 81–8.

Crow, T. J. (2000). Schizophrenia as the price that Homo Sapiens pays for language: A resolution of the central paradox in the origin of the species. *Brain Research Reviews*, 31, 118–29.

Crow, T. J. (2008). The "big bang" theory of the origin of psychosis and the faculty of language. *Schizophrenia Research*, 102(1/3), 31–52.

Crystal, D. (2004). *The Stories of English*. New York: Overlook Press.

Crystal, D., & Crystal, B. (2002). *Shakespeare's Words: A Glossary and Language Companion*. New York: Penguin Books.

Cunningham, P. M. (2006). High-poverty schools that beat the odds. *Reading Teacher*, 60, 382–5.

Curtain, H., & Dahlberg, C. A. (2004). *Languages and Children: Making the Match: New Languages for Young Learners, Grades K–8* (3rd edn). New York: Longman.

Curtiss, S. (1977). *Genie: A Psycholinguistic Study of a Modern-day "Wild Child."* New York: Academic Press.

Curtiss, S., & de Bode, S. (2003). How normal is grammatical development in the right hemisphere following hemispherectomy? The RI stage and beyond. *Brain and Language*, 86, 193–206.

Curtiss, S., & Schaeffer, J. (2005). Syntactic development in children with hemispherectomy: The I-, D-, and C-systems. *Brain and Language*, 94, 147–66.

Cutler, A. (1994). Segmentation problems, rhythmic solutions. *Lingua*, 92, 81–104.

Cutler, A., & Norris, D. (1979). Monitoring sentence comprehension. In W. E. Cooper & E. C. Walker (eds) *Sentence Processing: Psycholinguistic Studies Presented to Merrill Garrett* (pp. 113–34). Hillsdale, NJ: Erlbaum.

Cutler, A., & Norris D. (1988). The role of strong syllables in segmentation for lexical access. *Journal of Experimental Psychology: Human, Perception, and Performance*, 14, 113–21.

Cutler, A., & Scott, D. R. (1990). Speaker sex and perceived apportionment of talk. *Applied Psycholinguistics*, 11(3), 253–72.

Dael, N., Mortillaro, M., & Scherer, K. R. (2011). Emotion expression in body action and posture. *Emotion*, 12(5), 1085–101.

Dahlgren, D. J. (1998). Impact of knowledge and age on tip-of-the tongue rates. *Experimental Aging Research*, 24, 139–53.

Dalalakis, J. E. (1999). Morphological representation in specific language impairment: Evidence from Greek word formation. *Folia Phoniatrica et Logopaedica*, 51, 20–35.

Dale, E., & Chall, J. (1948). A formula for predicting readability. *Educational Research Bulletin*, 27(11), 20–8.

Dale, I. R. (1980). Digraphia. *International Journal of the Sociology of Language*, 26, 5–13.

Dale, P. S., & Cole, K. N. (1991). What's normal? Specific language impairment in an individual differences perspective. *Language, Speech and Hearing Services in Schools*, 22, 80–3.

Dalla Bella, S., Peretz, I., & Aronoff, N. (2003). Time-course of melody recognition: A gating paradigm study. *Perception & Psychophysics*, 65(7), 1019–28.

Dallet, L. (2014). This communication quirk could cost you a promotion. *Business Insider,* January 25. Retrieved June 21, 2017 from www.businessinsider.com/how-uptalk-could-cost-you-a-promotion-2014-1.

Dalzell, T., & Victor, T. (2008). *The Concise New Patridge Dictionary of American Slang.* New York: Routledge.

Damasio, H., Grabowski, T., Frank, R., Galaburda, A. M., & Damasio, A. R. (1994). The return of Phineas Gage: Clues about the brain from the skull of a famous patient. *Science,* 264(5162), 1102–5.

Damian, M. F., & Dumay, N. (2007). Time pressure and phonological advance planning in spoken production. *Journal of Memory and Language,* 57, 195–209.

Daneman, M., & Carpenter, P. A. (1980). Individual differences in working memory and reading. *Journal of Verbal Learning and Verbal Behavior,* 19(4), 450–66.

Daniels, M. (1997). *Benedictine Roots in the Development of Deaf Education: Listening with the Heart.* Westport, CT: Bergin & Garvey.

Dank, M., & Deutsch, A. (2010). The role of morpho-phonological factors in subject-predicate gender agreement in Hebrew. *Language and Cognitive Processes,* 25(10), 1380–410.

Danziger, K. (1980). The history of introspection reconsidered. *Journal of the History of the Behavioral Sciences,* 16, 241–62.

Danzger, M., & Halpern, H. (1973). Relation of stuttering to word abstraction, part of speech, word length, and word frequency. *Perceptual Motor Skills,* 37, 959–63.

Darwin, C. (1871). *The Descent of Man, and Selection in Relation to Sex.* London: Murray.

Darwin, C. ([1872] 2007).*The Expression of the Emotions in Man and Animals.* New York: Filiquarian.

Darwin, C. (1877). Biographical sketch of an infant. *Mind,* 2, 285–94.

Dawson, M. R. (2004). *Minds and Machines: Connectionism and Psychological Modeling.* Malden: Blackwell.

Dayalu, P., & Albin, R. L. (2015). Huntington's disease: Pathogenesis and treatment. *Neurologic Clinics,* 33(1), 101–14.

De Beni, R., Borella, E., & Carretti, B. (2007). Reading comprehension in aging: The role of working memory and metacomprehension. *Aging, Neuropsychology, and Cognition,* 14, 189–212.

DeBruin-Parecki, A., Perkinson, K., & Ferderer, L. (2000). *Helping Your Child Become A Reader.* U.S. Department of Education.

DeCasper, A. J., & Fifer, W. P. (1980). Of human bonding: Newborns prefer their mothers' voices. *Science,* 208, 1174–6.

DeCasper, A. J., & Spence, M. J. (1986). Prenatal maternal speech influences newborns' perception of speech sounds. *Infant Behavior and Development,* 9, 133–50.

De Diego-Balaguer, R., Couette, M., Dolbeau, G., Dürr, A., Youssov, K. et al. (2008). Striatal degeneration impairs language learning: Evidence from Huntington's disease. *Brain: A Journal of Neurology,* 131(11), 2870–81.

Deese, J. (1978). Thought into speech. *American Scientist,* 66(3), 314–21.

Deese, J. (1984). *Thought into Speech: The Psychology of a Language.* Englewood Cliffs, NJ: Prentice-Hall.

DeFrancis, J. (1984). *The Chinese Language: Fact and Fantasy*. Honolulu, HI: University of Hawaii Press.

Dehaene, S., Dupoux, E., Mehler, J., Cohen, L., Paulesu, E. et al. (1997). Anatomical variability in the cortical representation of first and second language. *NeuroReport*, 8, 3809–15.

Dehaene-Lambertz, G., Montavont, A., Jobert, A., Allirol, L., Dubois, J. et al. (2010). Language or music, mother or Mozart? Structural and environmental influences on infants' language networks. *Brain and Language*, 114, 53–65.

De Houwer, A., Bornstein, M. H., & Putnick, D. L. (2014). A bilingual-monolingual comparison of young children's vocabulary size: Evidence from comprehension and production. *Applied Psycholinguistics*, 35(6), 1189–211.

Delaney, P. F., & Ericsson, K. A. (2016). Long-term working memory and transient storage in reading comprehension: What is the evidence? Comment on Foroughi, Werner, Barragán, and Boehm-Davis (2015). *Journal of Experimental Psychology: General*, 145(10), 1406–9.

Delfour, F., & Marten, K. (2001). Mirror image processing in three marine mammal species: Killer whales (Orcinus orca), false killer whales (Pseudorca crassidens) and California sea lions (Zalophus californianus). *Behavioural Processes*, 53(3), 181–90.

Delgado, B., Gómez, J. C., & Sarriá, E. (2009). Private pointing and private speech: Developing parallelisms. In A. Winsler, C. Fernyhough & I. Montero (eds) *Private Speech, Executive Functioning, and the Development of Verbal Self-regulation*. Cambridge: Cambridge University Press.

Dell, G. S. (1980). Phonological and Lexical Encoding: An Analysis of Naturally Occurring and Experimentally Elicited Speech Errors. Doctoral dissertation, University of Toronto.

Dell, G. S. (1985). Positive feedback in hierarchical connectionist models: Applications to language production. *Cognitive Science*, 9, 3–23.

Dell, G. S. (1986). A spreading-activation model of retrieval in sentence production. *Psychological Review*, 93, 283–321.

Dell, G. S. (1988). The retrieval of phonological forms in production: Tests of predictions from a connectionist model. *Journal of Memory and Language*, 27, 124–42.

Dell, G. S. (1990). Effects of frequency and vocabulary type on phonological speech errors. *Language and Cognitive Processes*, 5(4), 313–49.

Dell, G. S., & O'Seaghdha, P. G. (1994). Inhibition in interactive activation models of linguistic selection and sequencing. In D. Dagenbach & T. H. Carr (eds) *Inhibitory Processes in Attention, Memory, and Language* (pp. 409–51). San Diego: Academic Press.

Dell, G. S., & Reich, P. A. (1981). Stages in sentence production: An analysis of speech error data. *Journal of Verbal Learning and Verbal Behavior*, 20(6), 611–29.

Dell, G. S., & Repka, R. J. (1992). Errors in inner speech. In B. J. Baars (ed.) *Experimental Slips and Human Error: Exploring the Architecture of Volition* (pp. 237–62). New York: Plenum.

DePaulo, B. M., Kashy, D. A., Kirkendol, S. E., Wyer, M. M., & Epstein, J. A. (1996). Lying in everyday life. *Journal of Personality and Social Psychology*, 70, 979–95.

Desalles, J. (2007). *Why We Talk*. Oxford: Oxford University Press.

Deutsch, A., & Dank, M. (2011). Symmetric and asymmetric patterns of attraction errors in producing subject-predicate agreement in Hebrew: An issue of morphological structure. *Language and Cognitive Processes*, 26(1), 24–46.

Deutsch, D. (2002). The puzzle of absolute pitch. *Current Directions in Psychological Science*, 11, 200–4.

Deutsch, D. (2013). *Psychology of Music* (3rd edn). New York: Academic Press.

Deutsch, D., Henthorn, T., & Dolson, M. (2004). Absolute pitch, speech, and tone language: Some experiments and a proposed framework. *Music Perception*, 21, 339–56.

Deutsch, D., Henthorn, T., and Lapidis, R. (2011). Illusory transformation from speech to song. *Journal of the Acoustical Society of America*, 129, 2245–52.

Deutsch, D., Dooley, K., Henthorn, T., & Head, B. (2009). Absolute pitch among students in an American music conservatory: Association with tone language fluency. *Journal of the Acoustical Society of America*, 125, 2398–403.

Deutsch, D., Henthorn, T., Marvin, E., & Xu, H. S. (2006). Absolute pitch among American and Chinese conservatory students: Prevalence differences, and evidence for a speech-related critical period. *Journal of the Acoustical Society of America*, 119, 719–22.

Deutsch, G. K., Dougherty, R. F., Bammer, R., Siok, W. T., Gabrieli, J. D. et al. (2005). Children's reading performance is correlated with white matter structure measured by diffusion tensor imaging. *Cortex*, 41, 354–63.

Deutscher, G. (2010). *Through the Language Glass: Why the World Looks Different in Other Languages*. New York: Macmillan.

De Villiers, J. G., & de Villiers, P. A. (1985). The acquisition of English. In D. I. Slobin (ed.) *The Crosslinguistic Study of Language Acquisition*. Hillsdale, NJ: Erlbaum.

De Villiers, J., Roeper, T., & Vainikka, A. (1990). The acquisition of long distance rules. In L. Frazier (ed.) *Language Processing and Language Acquisition* (pp. 257–97). Dordrecht: Kluwer.

Devlin, J. T., Matthews, P. M., & Rushworth, M. F. (2003). Semantic processing in the left inferior prefrontal cortex: A combined functional magnetic resonance imaging and transcranial magnetic stimulation study. *Journal of Cognitive Neurosciences*, 15, 71–84.

De Vos, C., & Zeshan, U. (2012). Introduction: Demographic, sociocultural, and linguistic variation across rural signing communities. In C. de Vos and U. Zeshan (eds) *Sign Languages in Village Communities: Anthropological and Linguistic Insights* (pp. 2–24). Berlin: De Gruyter Mouton.

De Waal, F. (1997). Are we in anthropodenial? *Discover*, 18, 50–3.

De Witte, L., Verhoeven, J., Engelborghs, S., de Deyn, P. P., & Mariën, P. (2008). Crossed aphasia and visuo-spatial neglect following a right thalamic stroke: A case study and review of the literature. *Behavioural Neurology*, 19(4), 177–94.

Dick, F., Bates, E., Wulfeck, B., Utman, J., Dronkers, N. et al.. (2001). Language deficits, localization, and grammar: Evidence for a distributive model of language breakdown in aphasic patients and neurologically intact individuals. *Psychological Review*, 108(4), 759–88.

Dickson, P. (2011). *War Slang: American Fighting Words & Phrases since the Civil War* (3rd edn). New York: Dover.

Diehl, R. L., & Kluender, K. R. (1989). On the objects of speech perception. *Ecological Psychology*, 2, 121–44.

Diehl, R. L., Walsh, M. A., & Kluender, K. R. (1991). On the interpretability of speech/nonspeech comparisons: A reply to Fowler. *Journal of Acoustic Society of America*, 89, 2905–9.

Dijkstra, A., & van Heuven, W. J. (2002). The architecture of the bilingual word recognition system: From identification to decision. *Bilingualism: Language and Cognition*, 5, 175–97.

Dike, C. (2008). Pathological lying: symptom or disease? Lying with no apparent motive or benefit. *Psychiatric Times*, 25(7), 67–73.

Di Pellegrino, G., Fadiga, L., Fogassi, L., Gallese, V., & Rizzolatti, G. (1992). Understanding motor events: A neurophysiological study. *Experimental Brain Research*, 91(1), 176–80.

Ditman, T., Goff, D., & Kuperberg, G. R. (2011). Slow and steady: sustained effects of lexico-semantic associations can mediate referential impairments in schizophrenia. *Cognitive, Affective, & Behavioral Neuroscience*, 11, 245–58.

Dixon, R. M. (1972). *The Dyirbal Language of North Queensland*. Cambridge: Cambridge University Press.

Dixon, R. M. (1989). The Dyirbal kinship system. *Oceania*, 59(4), 245–68.

Dixon, R. M. (1990). The origin of "mother-in-law vocabulary" in two Australian languages. *Anthropological Linguistics*, 32(1/2), 1–56.

Dixon, R. M. (2000). A typology of causatives: Form, syntax, and meaning. In R. M. Dixon & A. Y. Aikhenvald (eds) *Changing Valency: Case Studies in Transitivity* (pp. 39–40). Cambridge: Cambridge University Press.

Dobel, C., Diesendruck, G., & Bölte, J. (2007). How writing system and age influence spatial representations of actions: A developmental, cross-linguistic study. *Psychological Science*, 18(6), 487–91.

Domico, M. (1993). Patterns of development in narrative stories of emergent writers. In C. Kinzer & D. Leu (eds) *Examining Central Issues in Literacy Research, Theory, and Practice* (pp 391–404). Chicago: National Reading Conference.

Donno, R., Parker, G., Gilmour, J., & Skuse, D. H. (2010). Social communication deficits in disruptive primary-school children. *British Journal of Psychiatry*, 196, 282–89.

Donolato, E., Giofrè, D., & Mammarella, I. C. (2017). Differences in verbal and visuospatial forward and backward order recall: A review of the literature. *Frontiers in Psychology*, 8, 663–70.

Dore, J. (1975). Holophrases, speech acts, and language universals. *Journal of Child Language*, 2, 21–40.

Dorey, N. R., Conover, A. M., & Udell, M. A. (2014). Interspecific communication from people to horses (equus ferus caballus) is influenced by different horsemanship training styles. *Journal of Comparative Psychology*, 128(4), 337–42.

Downs, H., & Walter, B. (2008). *Brandi's Miracle* (Television program). New York: ABC News.

Dowty, D. (1990). Thematic proto-roles and argument selection. *Language*, 67(3), 547–619.

Dromi, E. (1987). *Early Lexical Development*. London: Cambridge University Press.

Dromi, E., Leonard, L., Adam, G., & Zadunaiscy-Ehrlich, S. (1999). Verb agreement in Hebrew-speaking children with specific language impairment. *Journal of Speech, Language, and Hearing Research*, 42, 1414–31.

Duffy, S. A., & Keir, J. A. (2004). Violating stereotypes: Eye movements and comprehension processes when text conflicts with world knowledge. *Memory & Cognition*, 32(4), 551–9.

Duffy, S. A., & Rayner, K. (1990). Eye movements and anaphor resolution: Effects of antecedent typicality and distance. *Language and Speech*, 33(2), 103–19.

Dumas, L. S. (1999). Learning a second language: Exposing your child to a new world of words boosts her brainpower, vocabulary & self-esteem. *Child*, 72(74), 76–7.

Dunbar, R. I. (1996). *Grooming, Gossip, and the Evolution of Language*. London: Faber and Faber.

Dunn, L. M., & Dunn, D. M. (2007). *Manual: Peabody Picture Vocabulary Test* (4th edn). Bloomington, MN: Pearson Assessments.

Eacker, J. N. (1975). *Problems of Philosophy and Psychology*. Oxford: Nelson-Hall.

Eadie, P. A., Fey, M. E., Douglas, J. M., & Parsons, C. L. (2002). Profiles of grammatical morphology and sentence imitation in children with specific language impairment and Down syndrome. *Journal of Speech Language and Hearing Research*, 45(4), 720–32.

Eckstein, G. (1949). Concerning a dog's word comprehension. *Science*, 13, 109.

Economist, The (2007). Alex the African grey: Science's best known parrot died on September 6th, aged 31. *The Economist*, September 20. Retrieved May 6, 2012, from www.economist.com/node/9828615.

Ehri, L. (1998). Grapheme-phoneme knowledge is essential for learning to read words in English. In J. Metsala & L. Ehri (eds) *Word Recognition in Beginning Literacy* (pp. 3–40). Mahwah, NJ: Erlbaum.

Ehri, L. (1999). Phases of development in learning to read words. In J. Oakhill & R. Beard (eds) *Reading Development and the Teaching of Reading: A Psychological Perspective* (pp. 79–108). Oxford: Blackwell.

Ehri, L. (2002). Phases of acquisition in learning to read words and implications for teaching. *British Journal of Educational Psychology: Monographs Series*, 1, 7–28.

Ehri, L. (2005). Learning to read words: Theory, findings, and issues. *Scientific Studies of Reading*, 9(2), 167–88.

Eigsti, I.-M., & Bennetto, L. (2009). Grammaticality judgments in autism: Deviance or delay. *Journal of Child Language*, 36(5), 999–1021.

Eilers, R. E., Wilson, W. R., & Moore, J. M. (1977). Developmental changes in speech discrimination in infancy. *Journal of Speech and Hearing Research*, 20, 766–80.

Einhorn, L. J. (1998) *Helen Keller, Public Speaker: Sightless but Seen, Deaf but Heard*. Santa Barbara, CA: Greenwood Press.

Eisenstein, E. L. (2005). *The Printing Revolution in Early Modern Europe* (2nd edn). Cambridge: Cambridge University Press.

Ekman, P. (1985). *Telling Lies: Clues to Deceipt in the Marketplace, Marriage, and Politics*. New York: W. W. Norton.

Ekman, P., & Friesen, W. (1971). Constants across cultures in the face and emotion. *Journal of Personality and Social Psychology*, 17(2), 124–9.

Elfenbein, J. L., Hardin-Jones, M. A., & Davis, J. M. (1994). Oral communication skills of children who are hard of hearing. *Journal of Speech and Hearing Research*, 37, 216–26.

Elgh, E., Domellof, M., Linder. J., Edstrom. M., Stenlund, H. et al. (2009). Cognitive function in early Parkinson's disease: A population-based study. *European Journal of Neurology*, 16, 1278–84.

Ellis, I., Derbyshire, A. J., & Joseph, M. E. (1971). Perception of electronically gated speech. *Language and Speech*, 14, 229–40.

Elman, J. L., & McClelland, J. L. (1988). Cognitive penetration of the mechanisms of perception: Compensation for coarticulation of lexically restored phonemes. *Journal of Memory and Language*, 27(2), 143–65.

Elnakib, A., Soliman, A., Nitzken, M., Casanova, M. F., Gimel'farb, G. et al. (2014). Magnetic resonance imaging findings for dyslexia: A review. *Journal of Biomedical Nanotechnology*, 10(10), 2778–805.

Emmorey, K. (1991). Repetition priming with aspect and agreement morphology in American Sign Language. *Journal of Psycholinguistic Research*, 20(5), 365–88.

Emmorey, K. (2002). *Language, Cognition, and the Brain: Insights from Sign Language Research*. Mahwah, NJ: Lawrence Erlbaum.

Emmorey, K., & McCullough, S. (2009). The bimodal brain: Effects of sign language experience. *Brain and Language*, 110(2), 208–21.

Eng, N., Obler, L. K., Harris, K. S., & Abramson, A. S. (1996). Tone perception deficits in Chinese-speaking Broca's aphasics. *Aphasiology*, 10(6), 649–56.

Engbert, R., & Kliegl, R. (2011). Parallel graded attention models of reading. In S. P. Liversedge, I. D. Gilchrist & S. Everling (eds) *Oxford Handbook of Eye Movements* (pp. 787–800). Oxford: Oxford University Press.

Engbert, R., Nuthmann, A., Richter, E. M., & Kliegl, R. (2005). SWIFT: A dynamical model of saccade generation during reading. *Psychological Review*, 112(4), 777–813.

Erard, M. (2012). *Babel No More: The Search for the World's Most Extraordinary Language Learners*. New York: Free Press.

Ericsson, A. K., & Kintsch, W. (1995). Long-term working memory. *Psychological Review*, 102(2), 211–45.

Eriksen, C., & Hoffman, J. (1972). Temporal and spatial characteristics of selective encoding from visual displays. *Perception & Psychophysics*, 12(2B), 201–4.

Eriksen, C., & St. James, J. (1986). Visual attention within and around the field of focal attention: A zoom lens model. *Perception & Psychophysics*, 40(4), 225–40.

Eriksen, C., Pollack, M., & Montague, W. (1970). Implicit speech: Mechanism in perceptual encoding? *Journal of Experimental Psychology*, 84, 502–7.

Eriksson, K. I., Voss, M. W., Prakash, R. S., Basak, C., Szabo, A. et al. (2011). Exercise training increases size of hippocampus and improves memory. *Proceedings of the National Academy of Sciences of the United States of America*, 108(7), 3017–22.

Eriksson, P. S., Perfilieva, E., Björk-Eriksson, T., Alborn, A. M., Nordborg, C. et al. (1998). Neurogenesis in the adult human hippocampus. *Nature Medicine*, 4(11), 1313–17.

Eskenazi, M. A., & Folk, J. R. (2015). Skipped words and fixated words are processed differently during reading. *Psychonomic Bulletin & Review*, 22(2), 537–42.

Estes, R. D. (1992). *The Behavior Guide to African Mammals: Including Hoofed Mammals, Carnivores, Primates*. Berkeley, CA: University of California Press.

Estruch, S. B., Graham, S. A., Chinnappa, S. M., Deriziotis, P., & Fisher, S. E. (2016). Functional characterization of rare FOXP2 variants in neurodevelopmental disorder. *Journal of Neurodevelopmental Disorders*, 8, 19–38.

Estival, D., Farris, C., & Moleworth, B. (2016). *Aviation English: A Lingua Franca for Pilots and Air Traffic Controllers*. New York: Routledge.

European Union (n.d.). Multilingualism. Retrieved October 22, 2016 from https://ec.europa.eu/education/policy/multilingualism_en.

Evans, J. L., Saffran, J. R., & Robe-Torres, K. (2009). Statistical learning in children with specific language impairment. *Journal of Speech, Language, and Hearing Research*, 52, 321–35.

Everett, C. (2013). *Linguistic Relativity: Evidence across Languages and Cognitive Domains*. Berlin: De Gruyter Mouton.

Everett, D. L. (2005). Cultural constraints on grammar and cognition in Pirahã: Another look at the design features of human language. *Current Anthropology*, 46, 621–46.

Everett, D. L. (2007). Challenging Chomskyan linguistics: The case of Pirahã. *Human Development*, 50, 297–9.

Everett, D. L. (2008). *Don't Sleep, There Are Snakes*. New York: Pantheon Books.

Everett, D. L. (2012). What does Pirahã grammar have to teach us about human language and the mind? *WIREs Cognitive Science*, 3(6), 555–63.

Fahle, M. (1994). Human pattern recognition: Parallel processing and perceptual learning. *Perception*, 23(4), 411–27.

Fairthorne, R. A. (1969). Content analysis, specification and control. *Annual Review of Information Science and Technology*, 4, 73–109.

Falk, S., & Rathcke, T. (2010). On the speech-to-song illusion: Evidence from German. In *5th Conference on Speech Prosody*. Chicago, IL: Speech Prosody Interest Group.

Fan, S. P., Liberman, Z., Keysar, B., & Kinzler, K. D. (2015). The exposure advantage: Early exposure to a multilingual environment promotes effective communication. *Psychological Science*, 26(7), 1090–7.

Farmer, T. A., Cargill, S. A., Hindy, N. C., Dale, R., & Spivey, M. J. (2007). Tracking the continuity of language comprehension: Computer mouse trajectories suggest parallel syntactic processing. *Cognitive Science*, 31, 889–910.

Fathman, A. (1975). The relationship between age and second language productive ability. *Language Learning*, 25, 245–53.

Faurie, C., & Raymond, M. (2004) Handedness frequency over more than ten thousand years. *Proceedings of the Royal Society of London Series B*, 271, 43–5.

Faurie, C., & Raymond, M. (2005). Handedness, homicide, and negative frequency-dependent selection. *Proceedings of the Royal Society of London Series B*, 272, 25–8.

Faust, M., & Kandelshine-Waldman, O. (2011) The effects of different approaches to reading instruction on letter detection tasks in normally achieving and low achieving readers. *Reading and Writing: An Interdisciplinary Journal*, 24(5), 545–66.

Fay, R. R., & Popper, A. N. (eds) (1994). *Comparative Hearing: Mammals*. New York: Springer.

Federmeier, K. D., Wlotko, E. W., & Meyer, A. M. (2008). What's "right" in language comprehension: Event-related potentials reveal right hemisphere language capabilities. *Language and Linguistics Compass*, 2(1), 1–17.

Fedorenko, E., & Levy, R. (2007). Information structure and word order in Russian sentence comprehension. Poster presented at the 20th CUNY Conference on Human Sentence Processing, La Jolla, CA.

Fedorenko, E., Piantadosi, S., & Gibson, E. (2012). The interaction of syntactic and lexical information sources in language processing: The case of the noun-verb ambiguity. *Journal of Cognitive Science*, 13(3), 249–85.

Feldman, L. B., & Siok, W. W. (1999). Semantic radicals contribute to the visual identification of Chinese characters. *Journal of Memory & Language*, 40, 559–76.

Feldman, R. S., Forrest, J. A., & Happ, B. R. (2002). Self-presentation and verbal deception: Do self-presenters lie more? *Basic & Applied Social Psychology*, 24, 163–70.

Fenson, L., Dale, P. S., Reznick, S., Bates, E., Thal, D. et al. (1994). Variability in early communicative development. *Monographs of the Society for Research in Child Development*, 59(5), 1–173.

Fenson, L., Marchman, V. A., Thal, D. J., Dale, P. S., Reznick, J. S. et al. (2007). *MacArthur–Bates Communicative Development Inventories: User's Guide and Technical Manual* (2nd edn). Baltimore, MD: Brookes.

Ferguson, C. (1959). Diglossia. *Word*, 15, 325–40.

Fernald, A. (1982). Acoustic Determinants of Infant Preference for "Motherese". Doctoral dissertation, University of Oregon.

Fernald, A. (1985). Four-month-old infants prefer to listen to motherese. *Infant Behavior and Development*, 8, 181–95.

Fernald, A. (1989). Intonation and communicative intent in mother's speech to infants: Is the melody the message? *Child Development*, 60(6), 1497–510.

Fernald, A., Taeschner, T., Dunn, J., Papousek, M., de Boysson-Bardies, B. et al. (1989). A crosslanguage study of prosodic modifications in mothers' and fathers' speech to preverbal infants. *Journal of Child Language*, 16, 477–501.

Ferreira, F. (2003). The misinterpretation of noncanonical sentences. *Cognitive Psychology*, 47, 164–203.

Ferreira, F., & Clifton, C. (1986). The independence of syntactic processing. *Journal of Memory and Language*, 25(3), 348–68.

Ferreira, F., & Henderson, J. (1990). Use of verb information during syntactic parsing: Evidence from eye tracking and word by word self-paced reading. *Journal of Experimental Psychology: Learning, Memory, & Cognition*, 16, 555–68.

Ferreira, F., & Henderson, J. (1991). Recovery from misanalyses of garden-path sentences. *Journal of Memory & Language*, 30, 725–45.

Ferreira, F., & Patson, N. (2007). The good enough approach to language comprehension. *Language and Linguistics Compass*, 1, 71–83.

Ferreira, F., Bailey, K. D., & Ferraro, V. (2002). Good-enough representations in language comprehension. *Current Directions in Psychological Science*, 11(1), 11–15.

Ferreira, V. S., & Yoshita, H. (2003). Given-new ordering effects on the production of scrambled sentences in Japanese. *Journal of Psycholinguistic Research*, 32, 669–92.

Filik, R., & Barber, E. (2011). Inner speech during silent reading reflects the reader's regional accent. *PLoS One*, 6(10), e25782.

Filipović, L. (2011). Speaking and remembering in one or two languages: Bilingual vs. monolingual lexicalisation and memory for motion events. *International Journal of Bilingualism*, 15, 466–85.

Fillmore, C. J. (1968). The case for case. In E. Bach and R. T. Harms (eds) *Universals in Linguistic Theory* (pp. 1–88). New York: Holt, Rinehart & Winston.

Fillmore, C. J. (1981). *Conversational Organization: Interactions between Speakers and Hearers.* New York: Academic Press.

Fillmore, C. J., & Atkins, B. T. (2000). Describing polysemy: The case of craw. In Y. Ravin & C. Leacock (eds) *Polysemy: Theoretical and Computational Approaches* (pp. 91–110). Oxford: Oxford University Press.

Finger, S. (2000). *The Minds behind the Brain.* Oxford: Oxford University Press.

Finger, S. (2001). *Origins of Neuroscience: A History of Explorations into Brain Function.* Oxford: Oxford University Press.

Fischer, L. B., & Kennison, S. M. (2007). Detecting lies told by friends and strangers. *Psi Chi Journal of Psychological Research*, 12, 173–8.

Fischer, S., & Gong, Q. (2010). Variation in East Asian sign language structures. In D. Brentari (ed.) *Sign Languages* (pp. 502–21). Cambridge: Cambridge University Press.

Fisher, J. (2015). A researcher is trying to document Philadelphia's ASL accent, before it disappears. Retrieved October 7, 2016 from www.pri.org/stories/2015-12-04/researcher-trying-document-philadelphias-asl-accent-it-disappears.

Fisher, S. E. (2006). Tangled webs: Tracing the connections between genes and cognition. *Cognition*, 101, 270–97.

Fishman, J. (1967). Bilingualism with and without diglossia; diglossia with and without bilingualism. *Journal of Social Issues*, 23(2), 29–38.

Fishman, J. (1980). Bilingualism and biculturism as individual and as societal phenomena. *Journal of Multilingual and Multicultural Development*, 1(1), 3–15.

Fitch, W. T., Hauser, M. D., & Chomsky, N. (2005). The evolution of the language faculty: Clarifications and implications. *Cognition*, 97, 179–210.

Fitch, W. T., Huber, L., & Bugnyar, T. (2010). Social cognition and the evolution of language: Constructing cognitive phylogenies. *Neuron*, 65, 795–814.

Fitsiori, A., Nguyen, D., Karentzos, A., Delavelle, J., & Vargas, M. I. (2011). The corpus callosum: White matter or terra incognita. *British Journal of Radiology*, 84, 5–18.

Fivaz, D. (1970). *Shona Morphophonemics and Morphosyntax.* Johannesburg: University of the Witwatersrand Press.

Flanagan, J. L. (1972). *Speech Analysis, Synthesis and Perception*. New York: Springer.

Flege, J., MacKay, I. R., & Piske, T. (2002). Assessing bilingual dominance. *Applied Psycholinguistics*, 23(4), 567–98.

Flege, J., Yeni-Komshian, G., & Liu, S. (1999). Age constraints on second language learning. *Journal of Memory and Language*, 41, 78–104.

Fletcher, P. (2009). Syntax in child language disorders. In R. G. Schwartz (ed.) *Handbook of Child Language Disorders* (pp. 388–405) New York: Psychology Press.

Flinker, A., Korzeniewska, A., Shestyuk, A. Y., Franaszczuk, P. J., Dronkers, N. F. et al. (2015). Redefining the role of Broca's area in speech. *PNAS Proceedings of the National Academy of Sciences of the United States of America*, 112(9), 2871–5.

Flor, H., Nikolajsen, L., & Jensn, T. (2006). Phantom limb pain: A case of maladaptive CNS plasticity? *Nature Reviews Neuroscience*, 7, 873–81.

Flores-Pajot, M. C., Ofner, M., Do, M. T., Lavigne, E., & Villeneuve, P. J. (2016). Childhood autism spectrum disorders and exposure to nitrogen dioxide, and particulate matter air pollution: A review and meta-analysis. *Environmental Research*, 151, 763–76.

Fodor, J. A. (1983). *Modularity of Mind: An Essay on Faculty Psychology*. Cambridge, MA: MIT Press.

Fodor, J. A., & Garrett, M. (1967). Some syntactic determinants of sentential complexity. *Perception & Psychophysics*, 2(7), 289–96.

Fogassi, L., & Ferrari, P. F. (2007). Mirror neurons and the evolution of embodied language. *Current Directions in Psychological Science*, 16, 136–41.

Foltz, P. W. (2007). Discourse coherence and LSA. In T. K. Landauer, D. S. McNamara, S. Dennis, W. Kintsch & T. K. Landauer (eds) *Handbook of Latent Semantic Analysis* (pp. 167–84). Mahwah, NJ: Lawrence Erlbaum.

Foltz, P. W., Kintsch, W., & Landauer, T. K. (1998). Analysis of text coherence using latent semantic analysis. *Discourse Processes*, 25(2/3), 285–307.

Forbes, K. E., Shanks, M. F., & Venneri, A. (2004). The evolution of dysgraphia in Alzheimer's disease. *Brain Research Bulletin*, 63, 19–24.

Foroughi, C. K., Werner, N. E., Barragán, D., & Boehm-Davis, D. A. (2015). Interruptions disrupt reading comprehension. *Journal of Experimental Psychology: General*, 144(3), 704–9.

Foroughi, C. K., Werner, N. E., Barragán, D., & Boehm-Davis, D. A. (2016). Multiple interpretations of long-term working memory theory: Reply to Delaney and Ericsson (2016). *Journal of Experimental Psychology: General*, 145(10), 1410–11.

Forster, K. I. (1976). Accessing the mental lexicon. In F. Wales & E. Walker (eds) *New Approaches to Language Mechanisms* (pp. 257–87). Amsterdam: North Holland.

Forster, K. I. (1979). Levels of processing and the structure of the language processor. In W. Cooper & E. Walker (eds) *Sentence Processing: Psycholinguistics Studies Presented to Merrill Garrett*. Hillsdale, NJ: Erlbaum.

Forster, K. I. (1994). Computational modeling and elementary process analysis in visual word recognition. *Journal Of Experimental Psychology: Human Perception And Performance*, 20,6, 1292–310.

Forster, K. I., & Chambers, S. M. (1973). Lexical access and naming time. *Journal of Verbal Learning & Verbal Behavior*, 12, 627–35.

Fouts, R. S., Fouts, D. H., & van Cantfort, T. E. (1989). The infant Loulis learns signs from cross-fostered chimpanzees. In R. Gardner, B. T. Gardner & T. van Cantfort (eds) *Teaching Sign Language to Chimpanzees* (pp. 280–92). Albany: SUNY Press.

Fowler, A. (1990). Language abilities in children with Down syndrome: Evidence for a specific syntactic delay. In D. Cicchetti & M. Beeghly (eds) *Children with Down Syndrome: A Developmental Perspective*. New York: Cambridge University Press.

Fowler, L. N. (1848). *Marriage: Its History and Ceremonies with a Phrenological and Physiological Exposition of the Functions and Qualifications for Happy Marriages*. New York: Fowlers & Wells.

Fox, E., Amaral, D., and van de Water, J. (2012). Maternal and fetal antibrain antibodies in development and disease. *Developmental Neurobiology*, 72, 1327–34.

Fox, M. (2007) *Talking Hands: What Sign Language Reveals About the Mind*. New York: Simon & Schuster.

Fox Tree, J. E. (1995). The effects of false starts and repetitions on the processing of subsequent words in spontaneous speech. *Journal of Memory and Language*, 34, 709–38.

Francis, W. N., & Kučera, H. (1982). *Frequency Analysis of English Usage: Lexicon and Grammar*. Boston: Houghton Mifflin.

Francis, W. S. (1999). Analogical transfer of problem solutions within and between languages in Spanish-English bilinguals. *Journal of Memory and Language*, 40(3), 301–29.

Frank, M., Everett, D., Fedorenko, E., & Gibson, E. (2008). Number as a cognitive technology: Evidence from Pirahã language and cognition. *Cognition*, 108, 819–24.

Frazier, L. (1979). On Comprehending Sentences: Syntactic Parsing Strategies. Unpublished doctoral dissertation, University of Connecticut.

Frazier, L. (1990). Exploring the architecture of the language-processing system. In G. T. Altmann (ed.) *Cognitive Models of Speech Processing: Psycholinguistic and Computational Perspectives* (pp. 409–33). Cambridge, MA: MIT Press.

Frazier, L., & Clifton, C. Jr. (1996). *Construal*. Cambridge, MA: MIT Press.

Frazier, L., & Fodor, J. D. (1978). The sausage machine: A new two stage parsing model. *Cognition*, 6, 1–34.

Frazier, L., & Rayner, K. (1982). Making and correcting errors during sentence comprehension: Eye movements in the analysis of structurally ambiguous sentences. *Cognitive Psychology*, 14(2), 178–210.

Frazier, L., & Rayner, K. (1987). Resolution of syntactic category ambiguities: Eye movements in parsing lexically ambiguous sentences. *Journal of Memory and Language*, 26(5), 505–26.

Frazier, L., & Rayner, K. (1990). Taking on semantic commitments: Processing multiple meanings vs. multiple senses. *Journal of Memory and Language*, 29(2), 181–200.

Frazier, L., Pacht, J. M., & Rayner, K. (1999). Taking on semantic commitments, II: Collective versus distributive readings. *Cognition*, 70(1), 87–104.

Freud, S. ([1901] 1971). *The Psychopathology of Everyday Life*. New York: W. W. Norton.

Frewen, P., Brinker, J., Martin, R., & Dozois, D. (2008). Humor styles and personality-vulnerability to depression. *Humor*, 2(21), 179–95.

Frick, P. J., Lahey, B. B., Christ, M. A., Loeber, R., & Green, S. M. (1991). History of childhood behavior problems in biological relatives of boys with attention-deficit hyperactivity disorder and conduct disorder. *Journal of Clinical Child Psychology*, 20, 445–51.

Frick-Horbury, D., & Guttentag, R. E. (1998). The effects of restricting hand gesture production on lexical retrieval and free recall. *American Journal of Psychology*, 111(1), 43–62.

Friederici, A. D., Rüschemeyer, S.-A., Hahne, A., & Fiebach, C. J. (2003). The role of left inferior frontal and superior temporal cortex in sentence comprehension: Localizing syntactic and semantic processes. *Cerebral Cortex*, 13, 170–77.

Friel, B. M., & Kennison, S. M. (2001). Identifying German-English cognates, false cognates, and non-cognates: Methodological issues and descriptive norms. *Bilingualism: Language and Cognition*, 4, 249–74.

Frijters, J. C., Barron, R. W., & Brunello, M. (2000). Direct and mediated influences of home literacy and literacy interest on prereaders' oral vocabulary and early written language skill. *Journal of Educational Psychology*, 92, 466–77.

Frishberg, N. (1987). Home sign. In J. van Cleve (ed.) *Gallaudet Encyclopedia of Deaf People and Deafness* (vol. 3, pp. 128–31). New York: McGraw Hill.

Frith, U. (1985). Beneath the surface of developmental dyslexia. In K. E. Patterson, J. C. Marshall & M. Coltheart (eds) *Surface Dyslexia* (pp. 301–22). London: Lawrence Erlbaum.

Frith, U., & Snowling, M. (1983). Reading for meaning and reading for sound in autistic and dyslexic children. *British Journal of Developmental Psychology*, 1, 329–42.

Frömer, R., Dimigen, O., Niefind, F., Krause, N., Kliegl, R. et al. (2015). Are individual differences in reading speed related to extrafoveal visual acuity and crowding? *Plos One*, 10(3), e0121986.

Fromkin, V. A. (1971). The non-anomalous nature of anomalous utterances. *Language*, 47(1), 27–52.

Fromkin, V. A. (ed.) (1973). *Speech Errors as Linguistic Evidence*. The Hague: Mouton.

Fromkin, V. A. (1988). Grammatical aspects of speech errors. In F. J. Newmeyer (ed.) *Linguistics: The Cambridge Survey:* vol. II: *Linguistic Theory: Extensions and Implications* (pp. 117–38). Cambridge: Cambridge University Press.

Fromkin, V. A., Rodman, R., & Hyams, N. (2013). *An Introduction to Language* (10th edn). Belmont, CA: Wadsworth.

Fukuda, C. (2005). Children's use of the masu form in play scenes. *Journal of Pragmatics*, 37, 1037–58.

Fukuda, S., & Fukuda, S. E. (2001). The acquisition of complex predicates in Japanese specifically language-impaired and normally developing children. *Brain and Language*, 77, 305–20.

Fukumine, E., & Kennison, S. M. (2016). Analogical transfer in Spanish-English bilinguals. *Journal of Latinos and Education*, 15(2), 134–9.

Furlonger, B., Holmes, V. M., & Rickards, F. W. (2014). Phonological awareness and reading proficiency in adults with profound deafness. *Reading Psychology*, 35(4), 357–96.

Furneax, S., & Land, M. F. (1999) The effects of skill on the eye-hand span during musical sight-reading. *Proceedings: Biological Sciences*, 266, 2435–40.

Galaburda, A. M., Schrott, L. S., Sherman, G. F., Rosen, G. D., & Denenberg, V. H. (1996). Animal models of developmental dyslexia. In C. Chase, G. D. Rosen & G. F. Sherman (eds) *Developmental Dyslexia: Neural, Cognitive, and Genetic Mechanisms* (pp. 1–14). Timonium, MD: York Press.

Galaburda, A. M., Sherman, G. F., Rosen, G. D., Aboitiz, F., & Geschwind, N. (1985). Developmental dyslexia: Four consecutive patients with cortical anomalies. *Annals of Neurology*, 18(2), 222–33.

Galambos, S. J., & Goldin-Meadow, S. (1990). The effects of learning two languages on levels of metalinguistic awareness. *Cognition*, 34, 1–56.

Galambos, S. J., & Hakuta, K. (1988). Subject-specific and task-specific characteristics of metalinguistic awareness in bilingual children. *Applied Psycholinguistics*, 9, 141–62.

Galantucci, B., Fowler, C. A., & Turvey, M. T. (2006). The motor theory of speech perception reviewed. *Psychonomic Bulletin & Review*, 13(3), 361–77.

Gallaudet, E. M. (1888). *Life of Thomas Hopkins Gallaudet: Founder of Deaf-Mute Instruction in America*. New York: H. Holt and Co.

Gallaudet University (n.d.). *Bilingual Education*. Retrieved July 8, 2017 from www.gallaudet.edu/academic-catalog/about-gallaudet/bilingual-education.

Gallese, V., Fadiga, L., Fogassi, L., & Rizzolatti, G. (1996). Action recognition in the premotor cortex. *Brain*, 119, 593–609.

Gallup, G. G., Jr. (1970). Chimpanzees: Self recognition. *Science*, 167(3914), 86–7.

Gandour, J. (1977). Counterfeit tones in the speech of southern Thai bidilectals. *Lingua*, 41, 125–43.

Ganong, W. F. (1980). Phonetic categorization in auditory word recognition. *Journal of Experimental Psychology*, 6, 110–25.

Gardiner, A. H. (1911). *Egyptian Hieratic Texts, Transcribed, Translated and Annotated.* series I: *Literary Texts of the New Kingdom*. Hildesheim: Georg Olms.

Gardner, B. T., & Gardner, R. A. (1975). Evidence for sentence constituents in the early utterances of child & chimpanzee. *Journal of Experimental Psychology: General*, 104, 244–67.

Gardner, R. C. (1985). *Social Psychology and Second Language Learning: The Role of Attitudes and Motivation*. London: Edward Arnold.

Gardner, R. C., & Lambert, W. E. (1972). *Attitudes and Motivation in Second-language Learning*. Rowley, MA: Newbury House.

Gardner-Neblett, N., & Iruka, I. U. (2015). Oral narrative skills: Explaining the language-emergent literacy link by race/ethnicity and SES. *Developmental Psychology*, 51(7), 889–904.

Garey, L. J. (2006). *Brodmann's Localisation in the Cerebral Cortex*. New York: Springer.

Garmon, L. (Producer) (2007). *Secret of the Wild Child* [DVD]. NOVA. Boston: WGBH Educatonal Foundation.

Garnham, A. (1983). What's wrong with story grammars. *Cognition*, 15, 145–54.

Garnham, A. (2001). *Mental Models and the Interpretation of Anaphora*. New York: Psychology Press.

Garnham, A., Oakhill, J. V., & Johnson-Laird, P. N. (1982). Referential continuity and the coherence of discourse. *Cognition*, 11, 29–46.

Garnham, A., Traxler, M. J., Oakhill, J., & Gernsbacher, M. A. (1996). The locus of implicit causality effects in comprehension. *Journal of Memory and Language*, 35, 517–43.

Garnsey, S. M., Pearlmutter, N. J., Myers, E., & Lotocky, M. (1997). The contributions of verb bias and plausibility to the comprehension of temporarily ambiguous sentences. *Journal of Memory & Language*, 37, 58–93.

Garrard, P., Lambon Ralph, M. A., Watson, P. C., Powis, J., Patterson, K. et al. (2001). Longitudinal profiles of semantic impairment for living and nonliving concepts in dementia of Alzheimer's type. *Journal of Cognitive Neuroscience*, 13(7), 892–909.

Garrett, M. F. (1975). The analysis of sentence production. In G. H. Bower (ed.) *The Psychology of Learning and Motivation: Advances in Research and Theory* (vol. 9, pp. 133–77). New York: Academic Press.

Garrett, M. F. (1976). Syntactic processes in sentence production. In R. J. Wales & E. C. T. Walker (eds) *New Approaches to Language Mechanisms* (pp. 231–56). Amsterdam: North-Holland.

Garrett, M. F. (1980). Levels of processing in sentence production. In B. Butterworth (ed.) *Language Production*: vol. 1. *Speech and Talk* (pp. 177–220). London: Academic Press.

Garrett, M. F. (1988) Process in language production. In F. J. Newmeyer (ed.) *Linguistics: The Cambridge Survey: III. Language: Psychological and Biological Aspects* (pp. 69–96). Cambridge: Cambridge University Press.

Garrity, L. I. (1977). Electromyography: A review of the current status of subvocal speech research. *Memory and Cognition*, 5, 615–22.

Garrod, S. (1994). Resolving pronouns and other anaphoric devices. In C. Clifton, L. Frazier & K. Rayner (eds) *Perspectives on Sentence Processing* (pp. 339–59). Englewood, NJ: Erlbaum.

Garrod, S., & Sanford, A. J. (1977). Interpreting anaphoric relations: The integration of semantic relations while reading. *Journal of Verbal Learning and Verbal Behavior*, 16, 77–90.

Garrod, S., & Sanford, A. J. (1994). Resolving sentences in a discourse context: How discourse representation affects language understanding. In M. A. Gernsbacher (ed.) *Handbook of Psycholinguistics* (pp. 675–98). San Diego, CA: Academic Press.

Garrod, S., & Terras, M. (2000). The contribution of lexical and situational knowledge to resolving discourse roles: Bonding and resolution. *Journal of Memory and Language*, 42, 526–44.

Gaskin, W. (2008). *The Unity of the Proposition*. Oxford: Oxford University Press.

Gasser T. (2005). Genetics of Parkinson's disease. *Current Opinion in Neurology*, 18(4), 363–9.

Gazzaniga, M. S. (2005). Forty-five years of split-brain research and still going strong. *Nature Reviews Neuroscience*, 6(8), 653–9.

Gazzaniga, M. S., Ivry, R. B., & Magnun, G. R. (2013). *Cognitive Neuroscience: The Biology of the Mind*. New York: W. W. Norton.

Gazzola, M. (2006). Managing multilingualism in the European Union: Language policy evaluation for the European Parliament. *Language Policy*, 5(4), 393–417.

Geers, A. E., & Nicholas, J. G. (2013). Spoken language benefits of extending cochlear implant candidacy below 12 months of age. *Otology & Neurotology*, 34(3), 532–8.

Genesee, F. (2003). Rethinking bilingual acquisition. In J. M. Dewaele, A. Housen & L. Wei (eds) *Bilingualism: Beyond Basic Principles* (pp. 204–28). Clevedon: Multilingual Matters.

Genesee, F. (2015). Myths about early childhood bilingualism. *Canadian Psychology*, 56, 6–15.

Genesee, F., & Nicoladis, E. (2007). Bilingual first language acquisition. In E. Hoff & M. Shatz (eds) *Blackwell Handbook of Language Development* (pp. 324–42). Malden, MA: Blackwell.

Genetics Home Reference (n.d.). Huntingdon disease. Retrieved December 20, 2017 from https://ghr.nlm.nih.gov/condition/huntington-disease#genes.

Genetics Home Reference (n.d.). Fragile X syndrome. Retrieved February 4, 2017 from https://ghr.nlm.nih.gov/condition/fragile-x-syndrome.

Gernsbacher, M. A. (1984). Resolving twenty years of inconsistent interactions between lexical familiarity and orthography, concreteness, and polysemy. *Journal of Experimental Psychology: General*, 113, 256–81.

Gernsbacher, M. A. (1990). *Language Comprehension as Structure Building*. Hillsdale, NJ: Erlbaum.

Gernsbacher, M. A. (1995). The structure building framework: What it is, what it might also be, and why. In B. K. Britton & A. C. Graesser (eds) *Models of Text Understanding* (pp. 289–311). Hillsdale, NJ: Erlbaum.

Gernsbacher, M. A. (1996). Coherence cues mapping during comprehension. In J. Costermans & M. Fayol (eds) *Processing Interclausal Relationships in the Production and Comprehension of Text* (pp. 3–21). Hillsdale, NJ: Erlbaum.

Gernsbacher, M. A. (1997). Two decades of structure building. *Discourse Processes*, 23, 265–304.

Gernsbacher, M. A., & Hargreaves, D. (1988). Accessing sentence participants: The advantage of first mention. *Journal of Memory and Language*, 27, 699–717.

Gernsbacher, M. A., Hargreaves, D., & Beeman, M. (1989). Building and accessing clausal representations: The advantage of first mention versus the advantage of clause recency. *Journal of Memory and Language*, 28, 735–55.

Geschwind, N., & Galaburda, A. M. (1987). *Cerebral Lateralization: Biological Mechanisms, Associations and Pathology*. Cambridge, MA: MIT Press.

Geschwind, N., & Levitsky, W. (1968). Human brain: Left-right asymmetries in temporal speech region. *Science*, 161(3837), 186–7.

Geyer, S., Weiss, M., Reimann, K., Lohmann, G., & Turner, R. (2011). Microstructural parcellation of the human cerebral cortex: From Brodmann's post-mortem map to in vivo mapping with high-field magnetic resonance imaging. *Frontiers in Human Neuroscience*, 5, 19.

Gibbs, W. G., & Colston, H. L. (2007). *Irony in Language and Thought: A Cognitive Science Reader.* New York: Routledge.

Gibson, C. J., & Gruen, J. R. (2008). The human lexinome: Genes of language and reading. *Journal of Communication Disorders*, 41(5), 409–20.

Gibson, E. (1998). Linguistic complexity: Locality of syntactic dependencies. *Cognition*, 68, 1–76.

Gibson, E. (2000). The dependency locality theory: A distance-based theory of linguistic complexity. In Y. Miyashita, A. Marantz & W. O'Neil (eds) *Image, Language, Brain* (pp. 95–126). Cambridge, MA: MIT Press.

Gilbert, A. N., & Wysocki, C. J. (1992). Hand preference and age in the United States. *Neuropsychologia*, 30, 601–8.

Gilbert, B., Belleville, S., Bherer, L., & Chouinard, S. (2005) Study of verbal working memory in patients with Parkinson's disease. *Neuropsychology*, 19, 106–14.

Gilhooly, K. J., & Gilhooly, M. L. (1979). Age-of-acquisition effects in lexical and episodic memory tasks. *Memory & Cognition*, 7, 214–23.

Gill, S. A., & Bierema, A. M. (2013). On the meaning of alarm calls: A review of functional reference in avian alarm calling. *Ethology*, 119(6), 449–61.

Gillon, S. (2012). *Phonological Awareness: From Research to Practice.* New York: Guilford Press.

Gilman, E., & Underwood, G. (2003). Restricting the field of view to investigate the perspectual spans of pianists. *Visual Cognition*, 10, 201–32.

Glanzer, M., Dorfman, D., & Kaplan, B. (1981). Short-term storage in the processing of text. *Journal of Verbal Learning and Verbal Behavior*, 20, 656–70.

Gleitman, L. R., Gleitman, H., & Shipley, E. F. (1972). The emergence of the child as grammarian. *Cognition*, 1(2/3), 137–64.

Glosser, G., Grugan, P. K., & Friedman, R. B. (1999). Comparison of reading and spelling in patients with probable Alzheimer's disease. *Neuropsychology*, 13, 350–8.

Godnig, E. C. (2003). The tachistoscope: Its history and uses. *Journal of Behavioral Optometry*, 14(2), 39–42.

Gold, B. T., & Buckner, R. L. (2002). Common prefrontal regions coactivate with dissociable posterior regions during controlled semantic & phonological tasks. *Neuron*, 35, 803–12.

Goldberg, N. (2016). *Writing down the Bones: Freeing the Writer Within.* New York: Shambhala.

Goldinger, S. D., Luce, P. A., & Pisoni, D. B. (1989). Priming lexical neighbors of spoken words: Effects of competition and inhibition. *Journal of Memory and Language*, 28, 501–18.

Goldin-Meadow, S. (2003). *The Resilience of Language: What Gesture Creation in Deaf Children Can Tell Us About How All Children Learn Language.* New York: Psychology Press.

Goldin-Meadow, S., & Butcher, C. (2003). Pointing toward two-word speech in young children. In S. Kita (ed.) *Pointing: Where Language, Culture, and Cognition Meet* (pp. 85–107). Mahwah, NJ: Erlbaum.

Goldin-Meadow, S. & Mayberry, R. I. (2001). How do profoundly deaf children learn to read? *Learning Disabilities Research & Practice*, 16(4), 222–9.

Goldin-Meadow, S., Seligman, M. E. P., & Gelman, R. (1976). Language in the two-year-old: Receptive and productive stages. *Cognition*, 4(2), 189–202.

Goldin-Meadow, S., Goodrich, W., Sauer, E., & Iverson, J. (2007). Young children use their hands to tell their mothers what to say. *Developmental Science*, 10, 778–85.

Goldman-Eisler, F. (1958a). The predictability of words in context and the length of pauses in speech. *Language and Speech*, 1, 226–31.

Goldman-Eisler, F. (1958b). Speech production and the predictability of words in context. *Quarterly Journal of Experimental Psychology*, 10, 96–106.

Goldman-Eisler, F. (1968). *Psycholinguistics: Experiments in Spontaneous Speech*. London: Academic Press.

Goldstein, E. B. (2015). *Cognitive Psychology* (4th edn). Belmont, CA: Wadsworth.

Goldstein, G., & Bebko, J. M. (2003). The profile of multiple language proficiencies: A measure for evaluating language samples of deaf children. *Journal of Deaf Studies and Deaf Education*, 8(4), 452–63.

Goldstone, R. L., Medin, D. L., & Schyns, P. G. (1997). *Perceptual Learning*. San Diego, CA: Academic Press.

Golinkoff, R. M., Hirsh-Pasek, K., Cauley, K., & Gordon, L. (1987). The eyes have it: Lexical & syntactic comprehension in a new paradigm. *Journal of Child Language*, 14, 23–46.

Golinkoff, R. M., Ma, W., Song, L., & Hirsh-Pasek, K. (2013). Twenty-five years using the intermodal preferential looking paradigm to study language acquisition: What have we learned? *Perspectives on Psychological Science*, 8(3), 316–39.

Gollan, T. H., & Acenas, L. A. (2004). What is ToT? Cognate and translation equivalent effects on tip-of-the-tongue states in Spanish-English and Tagalog-English bilinguals. *Journal of Experimental Psychology: Learning, Memory, and Cognition*, 30, 246–69.

Gollan, T. H., & Silverberg, N. B. (2001). Tip-of-the-tongue states in Hebrew-English bilinguals. *Bilingualism: Language and Cognition*, 4, 63–83.

Gollan, T. H., Ferreira, V. S., Cera, C., & Flett, S. (2014). Translation-priming effects on tip-of-the-tongue states. *Language, Cognition and Neuroscience*, 29(3), 274–88.

Gonzales, A. (1998). Language planning situation in the Philippines. *Journal of Multilingual and Multicultural Development*, 19(5), 487–525.

Gonzalez-Fuente, S., Escandell-Vidal, V., & Prieto, P. (2016). Gestural codas pave the way to the understanding of verbal irony. *Journal of Pragmatics*, 90, 26–47.

Goodall, J. (1986). *The Chimpanzees of Gombe: Patterns of Behavior*. Cambridge, MA: Harvard University Press.

Goodglass, H. (1976). Agrammatism. In H. Whitaker & H. A. Whitaker (eds) *Studies in Neurolinguistics,* vol. 1. New York: Academic Press.

Goodwyn, S., Acredolo, L., & Brown, C. A. (2000). Impact of symbolic gesturing on early language development. *Journal of Nonverbal Behavior*, 24, 81–103.

Gopnik, M. (1990). Genetic basis of grammar defect. *Nature*, 347, 26.

Gopnik, M., & Crago, M. B. (1991). Familial aggregation of a developmental language disorder. *Cognition*, 39(1), 1–50.

Góral-Półrola, J., Zielińska, J., Jastrzebowska, G., & Tarkowski, Z. (2016). Cluttering: Specific communication disorder. *Acta Neuropsychologica*, 14(1), 1–15.

Gordon, P. (2004). Numerical cognition without words: Evidence from Amazonia. *Science*, 306, 496–9.

Gordon, P. C., Hendrick, R., & Levine, W. H. (2002). Memory-load interference in syntactic processing. *Psychological Science*, 13, 425–30.

Gorney, C. (1985). When the gorilla speaks. Retrieved September 9, 2017 from www.washingtonpost.com/archive/lifestyle/1985/01/31/when-the-gorilla-speaks/d0552651-a7d6-4003-a395-bf8f4dfbb7a6/?utm_term=.0ecb892846d3.

Goswami, U. (2010). A psycholinguistic grain size view of reading development across languages. In N. Brunswick, S. McDougall & D. P. de Mornay (eds) *Reading and Dyslexia in Different Orthographies* (pp. 23–42). Hove: Psychology Press.

Gough, P. B. (1972). One second of reading. In J. F. Kavanagh & I. G. Mattingly (eds) *Language by Ear and by Eye* (pp. 331–58). Cambridge, MA: MIT Press.

Gough, P. B., & Hillinger, M. L. (1980). Learning to read: an unnatural act. *Annals of Dyslexia*, 30, 179–96.

Graesser, A. C., Singer, M., & Trabasso, T. (1994). Constructing inferences during narrative text comprehension. *Psychological Review*, 101, 371–95.

Grainger, J., & Segui, J. (1990). Neighborhood frequency effects in visual word recognition: A comparison of lexical decision and masked identification latencies. *Perception and Psychophysics*, 47, 191–8.

Grainger, J., O'Regan, J. K., Jacobs, A. M., & Segui, J. (1989). On the role of competing word units in visual word recognition: The neighborhood frequency effect. *Perception and Psychophysics*, 45, 189–95.

Grant, M., Clifton, C. J., & Frazier, L. (2012). The role of non-actuality implicatures in processing elided constituents. *Journal of Memory and Language*, 66(1), 326–43.

Gray, G., & Wedderburn, A. (1960). Grouping strategies with simultaneous stimuli. *Quarterly Journal of Experimental Psychology*, 12, 180–5.

Green, L. J. (2002). *African American English: A Linguistic Introduction*. Cambridge: Cambridge University Press.

Greenberg, J. (1966). *Universals of Language*. Cambridge, MA: MIT Press.

Greenfield, P. M., & Savage-Rumbaugh, E. S. (1991). Imitation, grammatical development, and the invention of protogrammar by an ape. In N. Krasnegor, D. M. Rumbaugh, M. Studdert-Kennedy & R. L. Schiefelbusch (eds) *Biological and Behavioral Determinants of Language Development* (pp. 235–58). Hillsdale, NJ: Erlbaum.

Greenfield, P. M., & Smith, J. H. (1976). *The Structure of Communication in Early Language Development*. New York: Academic Press.

Grice, P. (1975). Logic and conversation. In D. Davidson & G. Harman (eds) *The Logic of Grammar* (pp. 64–75). Encino, CA: Dickenson.

Grice, P. (1989). *Studies in the Way of Words*. Cambridge, MA: Harvard University Press.

Grieser, D. L., & Kuhl, P. K. (1988). Maternal speech to infants in a tonal language: Support for universal prosodic feature in motherese. *Developmental Psychology*, 24, 14–20.

Grierson, G. A. (1903–1928) *Linguistic Survey of India*. Calcutta: Government of India, Central Publication Calcutta Branch.

Griffin, Z. M. (2003). A reversed word length effect in coordinating the preparation and articulation of words in speaking. *Psychonomic Bulletin and Review*, 10(3), 603–9.

Griffin, Z. M., & Bock, K. (2000). What the eyes say about speaking. *Psychological Science*, 11, 274–9.

Griffin, T. M., Hemphill, L., Camp, L., & Wolf, D. P. (2004). Oral discourse in the preschool years and later literacy skills. *First Language*, 24, 123–47.

Grigorenko, E. L. (2001). Developmental dyslexia: An update on genes, brains, and environments. *Journal of Child Psychology and Psychiatry and Allied Disciplines*, 42(1), 91–125.

Grigorenko, E. L., Klin, A., & Volkmar, F. (2003). Annotation: Hyperlexia: disability or superability? *Journal of Child Psychology and Psychiatry*, 44(8), 1079–91.

Grimshaw, J. (1991). *Extended Projection*. Waltham, MA: Brandeis University.

Grober, E., & Kawas, C. (1997). Learning and retention in preclinical and early Alzheimer's disease. *Psychology of Aging*, 12, 183–8.

Groce, N. E. (1988). *Everyone Here Spoke Sign Language: Hereditary Deafness on Martha's Vineyard*. Cambridge, MA: Harvard University Press.

Grønnum, N. (1998). Illustrations of the IPA: Danish. *Journal of the International Phonetic Association*, 28(1/2), 99–105.

Grosjean, F. (1980). Spoken word recognition processes and the gating paradigm. *Perception and Psychophysics*, 28, 267–83.

Grosjean, F. (1996). Living with two languages and two cultures. In I. Parasnis (ed.) *Cultural and Language Diversity and the Deaf Experience*. Cambridge: Cambridge University Press.

Grosjean, F., & Li, P. (2013). *The Psycholinguistics of Bilingualism*. Chichester: Wiley-Blackwell.

Gross, M. M., Crane, E. A., & Fredrickson, B. L. (2012). Effort-shape and kinematic assessment of bodily expression of emotion during gait. *Human Movement Science*, 31(1), 202–21.

Gross, T., & Shorrock, R. (2016). To make *The Godfather* his way, Francis Ford Coppola waged a studio battle [Radio series episode]. In D. Miller, *Fresh Air*. Los Angeles, CA: National Public Radio.

Groves-Wright, K., Neils-Strunjas, J., Burnett, R., & O'Neill, M. J. (2004). A comparison of verbal and written language in Alzheimer's disease. *Journal of Communication Disorders*, 37, 109–30.

Grüter, T., Grüter, M., & Carbon, C. C. (2008). Neural and genetic foundations of face recognition and prosopagnosia. *Journal of Neuropsychology*, 2(1), 79–97.

Gumperz, J. J. (1971). *Language in Social Groups*. Stanford, CA: Stanford University Press.

Gumperz, J. J. (1976). The sociolinguistic significance of conversational code-switching. Working papers of the Language Behavior Research Laboratory, No. 46. Berkeley: University of California.

Gumperz, J. J., & Hymes, D. H. (1986). *Directions in Sociolinguistics: The Ethnography of Communication*. Oxford: Basil Blackwell.

Haber, L. R., & Haber, R. N. (1982). Does silent reading involve articulation? *American Journal of Psychology*, 95, 409–19.

Hagerman, R. J., & Silverman, A. C. (1996). *Fragile X Syndrome: Diagnosis, Treatment, and Research* (2nd edn). Baltimore: Johns Hopkins University Press.

Hagoort, P. (2005). Broca's complex as the unification space for language. In A. Cutler (ed.) *Twenty-first Century Psycholinguistics: Four Cornerstones* (pp. 157–73). Mahwah, NJ: Erlbaum.

Hahne, A., & Friederici, A. D. (2001). Processing a second language: Late learners' comprehension mechanisms as revealed by event-related brain potentials. *Bilingualism: Language and Cognition*, 4, 123–41.

Häikiö, T., Bertram, R., Hyönä, J., & Niemi, P. (2009). Development of the letter identity span in reading: Evidence from the eye movement moving window paradigm. *Journal of Experimental Child Psychology*, 102, 167–81.

Hakuta, K., & Diaz, R. (1985). The relationship between degree of bilingualism and cognitive ability: A critical discussion and some new longitudinal data. In K. E. Nelson (ed.) *Children's Language* (pp. 319–44). Hillsdale, NJ: Erlbaum.

Hakuta, K., Bialystok, E., & Wiley, E. (2003). Critical evidence: A test of the critical period hypothesis for second language acquisition. *Psychological Science*, 14, 31–8.

Hakuta, K., Butler, Y. G., & Witt, D. (2000). How long does it take English learners to attain proficiency? University of California Linguistic Minority Research Institute Policy Report 2000–1.

Halberda, J. (2003). The development of a word-learning strategy. *Cognition*, 87, B23–4.

Hall, E. T. (1968). Proxemics. *Current Anthropology*, 9(2/3), 83–108.

Hall, K., & Bucholtz, M. (1995). *Gender Articulated: Language and the Socially Constructed Self.* New York: Routledge.

Hall, M. L., Ferreira, V. S., & Mayberry, R. I. (2012). Phonological similarity judgments in ASL: Evidence for maturational constraints on phonetic perception in sign. *Sign Language & Linguistics*, 15(1), 104–27.

Halliday, M. A., & Hasan, R. (1976). *Cohesion in English*. London: Longman.

Halliwell, J. O. (1846). *The Nursery Rhymes of England: Collected Chiefly from Oral Tradition* (4th edn). London: John Russell Smith.

Hamann, C., Cronel-Ohayon, S., Dubé, S., Frauenfelder, U., Rizzi, L. et al. (2003). Aspects of grammatical development in young French children with SLI. *Developmental Science*, 6(2), 151–8.

Hampshire, B. (1981). *Working with Braille*. Paris: Unesco.

Han, J. J., Leichtman, M. D., & Wang, Q. (1998). Autobiographical memory in Korean, Chinese and American children. *Developmental Psychology*, 34(4), 701–13.

Hanna-Attisha, M., LaChance, J., Sadler, R. C., & Champney Schnepp, A. (2015). Elevated blood lead levels in children associated with the flint drinking water crisis: A spatial analysis of risk and public health response. *American Journal of Public Health*, 106(2), 283–90.

Hannas, W. C. (1997). *Asia's Orthographic Dilemma*. Honolulu, HI: University of Hawaii Press.

Hannan, S. J. (2000). *Standard Shona Dictionary*. Harare: College Press.

Hansson, K., & Nettelbladt, U. (1995). Grammatical characteristics of Swedish children with SLI. *Journal of Speech and Hearing Research*, 38, 589–98.

Harasty, J., Double, K. L., Halliday, G. M., Kril, J. J., & McRitchie, D. A. (1997). Language-associated cortical regions are proportionally larger in the female brain. *Archives of Neurology*, 54(2), 171–6.

Hardcastle, W., & Hewlett, N. (2006). *Coarticulation: Theory, Data, and Techniques*. Cambridge: Cambridge University Press.

Hardyck, C., & Petrinovich, L. F. (1977). Left-handedness. *Psychological Bulletin*, 84, 385–404.

Harley, T. A. (2013). *The Psychology of Language: From Data to Theory* (4th edn). New York: Psychology Press.

Harley, T. A., & Brown, H. E. (1998). What causes a tip-of-the-tongue state? Evidence for lexical neighbourhood effects in speech production. *British Journal of Psychology*, 89, 151–74.

Harlow, J. M. (1848). Passage of an iron rod through the head. *Boston Medical & Surgical Journal*, 39(20), 389–93.

Harris, B. (2011). Letting go of Little Albert: Disciplinary memory, history, and the uses of myth. *Journal of the History of the Behavioral Sciences*, 47(1), 1–17.

Harris, L. J. (1980). Lateralized sex differences: Substrate and signifance. *Behavior Brain Sciences*, 3, 236–7.

Harris, M., Barrett, M., Jones, D., & Brookes, S. (1988). Linguistic input and early word meaning. *Journal of Child Language*, 15, 77–94.

Hart, B., & Risley, T. R. (2003). The early catastrophe: The 30 million word gap by age 3. *American Educator*, 27(1), 4–9.

Hartman, M. A. (1976). Descriptive study of the language of men and women born in Maine around 1900 as it reflects the Lakoff hypotheses in language and woman's place. In B. L. Dubois & I. Crouch (eds) *The Sociology of the Languages of American Women*. San Antonio, TX: Trinity University Press.

Hartsuiker, R. J., Anton-Mendez, I., Roelstraete, B., & Costa, A. (2006). Spoonish Spanerisms: A lexical bias effect in Spanish. *Journal of Experimental Psychology: Learning, Memory, & Cognition*, 32, 949–53.

Hattie, J. A. (2009). *Visible Learning*. London: Routledge.

Haualand, H., & Allen, C. (2009). *Deaf People and Human Rights*. World Federation of the Deaf. www.rasit.org/files/Deaf-People-and-Human-Rights-Report.pdf.

Hauser, M. D., Chomsky, N., & Fitch, W. T. (2002). The faculty of language: What is it, who has it, and how did it evolve? *Science*, 298(5598), 1569–79.

Havens, L. L., & Foote, W. E. (1963). The effect of competition on visual duration thresholds and its independence of stimulus frequency. *Journal of Experimental Psychology*, 65, 6–11.

Haviland, S. E., & Clark, H. H. (1974). What's new? Acquiring new information as a process in comprehension. *Journal of Verbal Learning and Verbal Behavior*, 13, 512–21.

Hayes, C. (1951). *The Ape in our House*. New York: Harper.

Hayes, J., & Flower, L. (1980). Identifying the organization of writing processes. In L. Gregg & E. Steinberg (eds) *Cognitive Processes in Writing: An Interdisciplinary Approach* (pp. 3–30). Hillsdale, NJ: Lawrence Erlbaum.

Hayes, J., & Flower, L. (1986). Writing research and the writer. *American Psychologist*, 41, 1106–13.

Hayes, K. L., & Nissen, C. H. (1971). Higher mental functions of a home-raised chimpanzee. In A. Schrier and F. Stollnitz (eds) *Behavior of Nonhuman Primates* (pp. 60–114). New York: Academic Press.

Hayter, W. (1977). *Spooner: A Biography*. London: W. H. Allen.

Hayward, R. (2000). Afroasiatic. In B. Heine & D. Nurse (eds) *African Languages: An Introduction* (pp. 74–98). Cambridge: Cambridge University Press.

Healy, J. M. (1982). The enigma of hyperlexia. *Reading Research Quarterly*, 17(3), 319–38.

Heath, R. L., & Blonder, L. X. (2005). Spontaneous humor among right hemisphere stroke survivors. *Brain and Language*, 93(3), 267–76.

Hedberg, N. L., & Stoel-Gammon, C. (1986). Narrative analysis: Clinical procedures. *Topics in Language Disorders*, 7, 58–69.

Hedberg, N. L., & Westby, C. E. (1993). *Analyzing Storytelling Skills: Theory to Practice*. Tucson, AZ: Communication Skill Builders.

Heider, E. (1972). Universals in color naming and memory. *Journal of Experimental Psychology*, 93,10–20.

Heidinger, S. (2015). The information status and discourse anchorage of non-nominal constituents: A case study on Spanish secondary predicates. *Journal of Pragmatics*, 81, 52–73.

Heim, S. (2008). Syntactic gender processing in the human brain: A review and a model. *Brain and Language*, 106, 55–64.

Heller, J. R., & Goldrick, M. (2014). Grammatical constraints on phonological encoding in speech production. *Psychonomic Bulletin & Review*, 21(6), 1576–82.

Helmbrecht, J. (2005). Politeness distinctions in pronouns. In M. Haspelmath et al. (eds) *The World Atlas of Language Structures* (pp. 186–90). Oxford: Oxford University Press.

Henderson, L. (1982). *Orthography and Word Recognition in Reading*. New York: Academic Press.

Henderson, J. M., & Ferreira, F. (1990). Effects of foveal processing difficulty on the perceptual span in reading: Implications for attention and eye movement control. *Journal of Experimental Psychology: Learning, Memory, and Cognition*, 16, 417–29.

Henry, L., Messer, D. J., & Nash, G. (2012). Executive functioning in children with specific language impairment. *Journal of Child Psychology & Psychiatry*, 53, 37–45.

Herbert, R. K. (1990). Hlonipha and the ambiguous woman. *Anthropos*, 85, 455–73.

Heredia, R. R., Cieślicka, A. B., & Altarriba, J. (2016). *Methods in Bilingual Comprehension Research*. Berlin: Springer.

Heredia, R. R., & Altarriba, J. (2001). Bilingual language mixing: Why do bilinguals code-switch? *Current Directions in Psychological Science*, 10(5), 164–8.

Herman, L. M. (1980). Cognitive characteristics of dolphins. In L. M. Herman (ed.) *Cetacean Behavior: Mechanisms and Functions* (pp. 363–429). New York: Wiley Interscience.

Herman, L. M. (2010). What laboratory research has told us about dolphin cognition. *International Journal of Comparative Psychology*, 23, 310–30.

Herman, L. M. (2012). Body and self in dolphins. *Consciousness and Cognition: An International Journal*, 21(1), 526–45.

Herman, L. M., & Uyeyama, R. K. (1999). The dolphin's grammatical competency: Comments on Kako (1998). *Animal Learning & Behavior*, 27, 18–23.

Herman, L. M., Richards, D. G., & Wolz, J. P. (1984). Comprehension of sentences by bottlenosed dolphins. *Cognition*, 16, 129–219.

Hernandez, A. E., Martinez, A., & Kohnert, K. (2000). In search of the language switch: An fMRI study of picture naming in Spanish–English bilinguals. *Brain and Language*, 73, 421–31.

Hess, E. (2008). *Nim Chimpsky: The Chimp Who Would Be Human*. New York: Bantam.

Hickok, G. (2009). The functional neuroanatomy of language. *Physics of Life Reviews*, 6(3), 121–43.

Hicks, R. G. (1974). The duration of echoic memory. *Journal of Auditory Research*, 14(2), 125–32.

Hier, D. B., Yoon, W. B., Mohr, J. P., & Price, T. R. (1994). Gender and aphasia in the stroke bank. *Brain and Language*, 47, 155–67.

Hilchey, M. D., & Klein, R. M. (2011). Are there bilingual advantages on nonlinguistic interference tasks? Implications for the plasticity of executive control processes. *Psychonomic Bulletin & Review*, 18(4), 625–58.

Hill, H. M., Webber, K., Kemery, A., Garcia, M., & Kuczaj, S. A. (2015). Can sea lions (zalophus californianus) use mirrors to locate an object? *International Journal of Comparative Psychology*, 28(1), 1–12.

Hinton, L., Nichols, J., and Ohala, J. J. (eds) (1994). *Sound Symbolism*. Cambridge: Cambridge University Press.

Hinzen, W., & Rosselló, J. (2015). The linguistics of schizophrenia: Thought disturbance as language pathology across positive symptoms. *Frontiers in Psychology*, 6, 971.

Hirnstein, M., Westerhausen, R., Korsnes, M. S., & Hugdahl, K. (2013). Sex differences in language asymmetry are age-dependent and small: A large-scale, consonant-vowel dichotic listening study with behavioral and fMRI data. *Cortex*, 49(7), 1910–21.

Hirsh-Pasek, K., & Golinkoff, R. (1991). Language comprehension: A new look at some old themes. In N. Krasnegor, D. Rumbaugh, M. Studdert-Kennedy & R. Schiefelbusch (eds) *Biological and Behavioral Aspects of Language Acquisition*. Hillsdale, NJ: Erlbaum.

Hirsh-Pasek, K., & Golinkoff, R. (1996). *The Origins of Grammar*. Cambridge, MA: MIT Press.

Hjelmervik, H., Westerhausen, R., Osnes, B., Endresen, C. B., Hugdahl, K. et al. (2012). Language lateralization and cognitive control across the menstrual cycle assessed with a dichotic-listening paradigm. *Psychoneuroendocrinology*, 37(11), 1866–75.

Hjørland, B. (2001). Towards a theory of aboutness, subject, topicality, theme, domain, field, content … and relevance. *Journal of the American Society for Information Science and Technology*, 52(9), 774–8.

Ho, A. K, Sahakian, B. J., Robbins, T. W., Barker, R. A., Rosser, A. E. et al. (2002). Verbal fluency in Huntington's disease: A longitudinal analysis of phonemic and semantic clustering and switching. *Neuropsychologia*, 40, 1277–84.

Hockett, C. F. (1960). The origin of speech. *Scientific American*, 203, 89–97.

Hockett, C. F. (1967). Where the tongue slips, there slip I. In *To Honor Roman Jakobson*. vol. 2 (pp. 910–36). The Hague: Mouton.

Hocking, J. E., Stacks, D. W., & McDermott, S. T. (2003). *Communication Research*. (3rd edn). Boston: Allyn & Bacon.

Hodgetts, S., Weis, S., & Hausmann, M. (2015). Sex hormones affect language lateralisation but not cognitive control in normally cycling women. *Hormones and Behavior*, 74, 194–200.

Hoff, E. (2003). The specificity of environmental influence: Socioeconomic status affects early vocabulary development via maternal speech. *Child Development*, 74, 1368–78.

Hoffman, J. (2013). Overturning the myth of valley girl speak. *The New York Times,* December 23. Retrieved June 21, 2017 from https://well.blogs. nytimes.com/2013/12/23/overturning-the-myth-of-valley-girl-speak.

Hofstede, G. (2000). *Culture's Consequences*, rev. edn. Beverly Hills, CA: Sage.

Holm, J. (1988). *Pidgins and Creoles:* vol. 1. Cambridge: Cambridge University Press.

Holm, J. (1989). *Pidgins and Creoles:* vol. 2. Cambridge: Cambridge University Press.

Holmes, J., & Meyerhoff, M. (eds) (2003). *The Handbook of Language and Gender*. Malden: Blackwell.

Holler, J., & Stevens, R. (2007). An experimental investigation into the effect of common ground on how speakers use gesture and speech to represent size information in referential communication. *Journal of Language and Social Psychology*, 26, 4–27.

Holt, L. L., & Lotto, A. J. (2014). Commentary: The alluring but misleading analogy between mirror neurons and the motor theory of speech. *Behavioral and Brain Sciences*, 37, 204–5.

Hostetter, A. B. (2011). When do gestures communicate? A meta-analysis. *Psychological Bulletin*, 137(2), 297–315.

Hostetter, A. B., & Alibali, M. W. (2008). Visible embodiment: Gestures as simulated action. *Psychonomic Bulletin & Review*, 15, 495–514.

Hubbard, C. P., & Prins, D. (1994). Word familiarity, syllabic stress pattern, and stuttering. *Journal of Speech and Hearing Research*, 37, 564–71.

Hubel, D. H., & Wiesel, T. N. (1963). Receptive fields of cells in striate cortex of very young, visually inexperienced kittens. *Journal of Neurophysiology*, 26, 994–1002.

Hubert, J. (2000). *Madness, Disability, and Social Exclusion: The Archaeology and Anthropology of "Difference"*. London: Routledge.

Huettig, F., Rommers, J., & Meyer, A. S. (2011). Using the visual world paradigm to study language processing: A review and critical evaluation. *Acta Psychologica*, 137(2), 151–71.

Huey, E. ([1908] 1968). *The Psychology and Pedagogy of Reading*. Cambridge, MA: MIT Press.

Huffington Post (2013). Kendrick Lamar sign language interpreter at Lollapalooza is our hero. August 16. Retrieved October 7, 2016 from www.huffingtonpost.com/2013/08/16/kendrick-lamar-sign-langu_n_3769343.html.

Hugdahl, K. (1988). *Handbook of Dichotic Listening: Theory, Methods and Research*. New York: Wiley.

Hull, R., & Vaid, J. (2007). Bilingual language lateralization: A meta-analytic tale of two hemispheres. *Neuropsychologia*, 45, 1987–2008.

Human Genome Project. (n.d.). Human Genome Project information. Retrieved June 15, 2017 from www.ornl.gov/sci/techresources/Human_Genome/home.shtml.

Hunt, E., & Agnoli, F. (1991). The Worfian hypothesis: A cognitive psychology perspective. *Psychological Review*, 98(3), 377–89.

Hurtado, N., Marchman, V. A., & Fernald, A. (2008). Does input influence uptake? Links between maternal talk, processing speed and vocabulary size in Spanish-learning children. *Developmental Science*, 11, 31–9.

Hutchins, J. (1997). From first conception to first demonstration: The nascent years of machine translation, 1947–1954. A chronology. *Machine Translation*, 12, 195–252.

Huttenlocher, J., Haight, W., Bryk, A., Seltzer, M., & Lyons, T. (1991). Early vocabulary growth: Relation to language input and gender. *Developmental Psychology*, 27, 236–48.

Hyltenstam, K. (1992). Non-native features of non-native speakers: On ultimate attainment of childhood L2 learners. In R. J. Harris (ed.) *Cognitive Processing in Bilinguals* (pp. 351–68). Amsterdam: Elsevier.

Hyltenstam, K., & Abrahamsson, N. (2000). Who can become native-like in a second language? All, some, or none? On the maturational constraints controversy in second language acquisition. *Studia Linguistica*, 54, 150–66.

Hyönä, J., & Pollatsek, A. (1998). Reading Finnish compound words: Eye fixations are affected by component morphemes. *Journal of Experimental Psychology: Human Perception & Performance*, 24, 1612–27.

Hyönä, J., Lorch, R. J., & Kaakinen, J. K. (2002). Individual differences in reading to summarize expository text: Evidence from eye fixation patterns. *Journal of Educational Psychology*, 94(1), 44–55.

Imai, M., & Gentner, D. (1997). A cross-linguistic study of early word meaning: Universal ontology and linguistic influence. *Cognition*, 62, 169–200.

Indefrey, P., Brown, C. M., Hellwig, F., Amunts, K., Herzog, H. et al. (2001). A neural correlate of syntactic encoding during speech production. *Proceedings of the National Academy of Sciences*, 98(10), 5933–6.

Ingraham, C. (2015). The surprising geography of American left-handedness. *Washington Post*. Retrieved July 20, 2015 from www.washingtonpost.com/news/wonk/wp/2015/09/22/the-surprising-geography-of-american-left-handedness/.

Ingram, J. C. (2007). *Neurolinguistics: An Introduction to Spoken Language Processing and its Disorder*. Cambridge: Cambridge University Press.

Inhoff, A. W., & Rayner, K. (1986). Parafoveal word processing during eye fixations in reading: Effects of word frequency. *Perception & Psychophysics*, 40(6), 431–9.

Institute for Multisensory Education (2015). Stages of reading development. Retrieved September 27, 2016 from https://journal.orton-gillingham.com/stages-of-reading-development/.

International Dyslexia Association (n.d.). Attention-deficit/hyperactive disorder (AD/HD) and dyslexia. Retrieved September 4, 2016 https://dyslexiaida.org/attention-deficithyperactivity-disorder-adhd-and-dyslexia/.

International Phonetic Association (1999). *Handbook of the International Phonetic Association: A Guide to the Use of the International Phonetic Alphabet*. Cambridge: Cambridge University Press.

Irwin, J. R., Whalen, D. H., & Fowler, C. A. (2006). A sex difference in visual influence on heard speech. *Perception and Psychophysics*, 68(4), 582–92.

Isurin, L. (2000). Deserted island or a child's first language forgetting. *Bilingualism: Language and Cognition*, 3(2), 151–66.

Iverson, J. M., & Goldin-Meadow, S. (2005). Gesture paves the way for language development. *Psychological Science*, 16, 367–71.

Iverson, J. M., Capirci, O., Volterra, V., & Goldin-Meadow, S. (2008). Learning to talk in a gesture-rich world: Early communication in Italian vs. American children. *First Language*, 28, 164–81.

Ivković, D. (2013). Pragmatics meets ideology: Digraphia and non-standard orthographic practices in Serbian online news forums. *Journal of Language and Politics*, 12, 335–56.

Jablensky, A. (2010). The diagnostic concept of schizophrenia: Its history, evolution, and future prospects. *Dialogues in Clinical Neuroscience*, 12, 271–87.

Jackson, R. L. (2010). *Encyclopedia of Identity*, vol. 1. London: Sage.

Jacobs, N., & Garnham, A. (2007). The role of conversational hand gestures in a narrative task. *Journal of Memory and Language*, 56(2), 291–303.

Jaeger, J. (1992). Not by the chair of my hinny hin hin: Some general properties of slips of the tongue in young children. *Journal of Child Language*, 19(2), 335–66.

Jaeger, J. (2005). *Kids' Slips: What Young Children's Slips of the Tongue Reveal about Language Development*. Hove: Psychology Press.

Jaensch, E. R. (1929). *Grundformen menschlichen Seins*. Berlin: Otto Elsner.

Jain, U. R. (1995). *Introduction to Hindi Grammar*. Berkeley, CA: University of California Press.

Jakubowicz, C., & Nash, L. (2001). Functional categories and syntactic operations in (ab)normal language acquisition. *Brain and Language*, 77, 321–39.

Jambor, E. (2005). Self-esteem and coping strategies among deaf students. *Journal of Deaf Studies and Deaf Education*, 10(1), 63–81.

James, W. (1890). *The Principles of Psychology*. I. New York: Dover.

James, L. E., & Burke, D. M. (2000). Phonological priming effects on word retrieval and tip-of-the-tongue experiences in young and older adults. *Journal of Experimental Psychology*, 26, 1378–91.

Janhunen, J. A. (2012). *Mongolian*. Amsterdam: John Benjamins.

Janik, V. M. (2009) Acoustic communication in delphinids. *Advances in the Study of Behavior*, 40, 123–57.

Janik, V. M. (2013). Cognitive skills in bottlenose dolphin communication. *Trends in Cognitive Sciences*, 17(4), 157–9.

Janik, V. M. (2014). Cetacean vocal learning and communication. *Current Opinion in Neurobiology*, 28, 60–5.

Jarvis, S., & Pavlenko, A. (2008). *Crosslinguistic Influence in Language and Cognition*. Abingdon: Routledge.

Jasper, H., & Penfield, W. (1954). *Epilepsy and the Functional Anatomy of the Human Brain* (2nd edn). New York: Little, Brown.

Javier, R. (1996). In search of repressed memories in bilingual individuals. In R. Foster, M. Moskowitz & R. Javier (eds) *Reaching across Boundaries of Culture and Class: Widening the Scope of Psychotherapy* (pp. 225–41). Northvale, NJ: Jason Aronson.

Jay, K. L., & Jay, T. B. (2013). A child's garden of curses: A gender, historical, and age-related evaluation of the taboo lexicon. *American Journal of Psychology*, 126(4), 459–75.

Jay, K. L., & Jay, T. B. (2015). Taboo word fluency and knowledge of slurs and general pejoratives: Deconstructing the poverty-of-vocabulary myth. *Language Sciences,* 52, 251–9.

Jay, T. (1992). *Cursing in America*. Philadelphia: John Benjamins.

Jay, T. (1996). Cursing: A damned persistent lexicon. In D. Hermann et al. (eds) *Basic and Applied Memory Research: Practical Applications,* vol. 2 (pp. 301–13). Mahwah, NJ: Erlbaum.

Jay, T. (2000). *Why we Curse*. Philadelphia, PA: John Benjamins.

Jay, T. (2009). The utility and ubiquity of taboo words. *Perspectives on Psychological Science*, 4, 153.

Jefferies, E., Rogers, T. T., & Lambon Ralph, M. A. (2011). Premorbid expertise produces category-specific impairment in a domain-general semantic disorder. *Neuropsychologia*, 49(12), 3213–23.

Jenkins, J. J., & Palermo, D. S. (1964). *Word Association Norms*. Minneapolis, MN: University of Minnesota Press.

Jensen, A. R., & Rohwer, W. D. (1966). The Stroop color-word test: A review. *Acta Psychologica*, 25(1), 36–93.

Jerger, J., Jerger, S., Oliver, T., & Pirozzolo, F. (1989). Speech understanding in the elderly. *Ear and Hearing*, 10, 79–89.

Johns, C. L., Tooley, K. M., & Traxler, M. J. (2008). Discourse impairments following right hemisphere brain damage: A critical review. *Language and Linguistics Compass*, 2(6), 1038–62.

Johnson, J. S., & Newport, E. L. (1989). Critical period effects in second language learning: The influence of maturational state on the acquisition of English as a second language. *Cognitive Psychology*, 21, 60–99.

Johnson, W., Onuma, O., Owolabi, M., & Sachdev, S. (2016). Stroke: A global response is needed. *Bulletin of the World Health Organization*, 94(9), 634–634A.

Johnson-Laird, P. N. (1983). *Mental Models*. Cambridge: Harvard University Press.

Johnson-Laird, P. N. (2013). The mental models perspective. In D. Reisberg (ed.) *The Oxford Handbook of Cognitive Psychology* (pp. 650–67). New York: Oxford University Press.

Johnston, T. (2002). BSL, Auslan and NZSL: Three sign languages or one? In A. Baker, B. van den Bogaerde & O. Crasborn (eds) *Cross-linguistic Perspectives in Sign Language Research: Selected Papers from TISLR 2000* (pp. 47–69). Hamburg: Signum.

Johnston, J., Durieux-Smith, A., & Bloom, K. (2005). Teaching gestural signs to infants to advance child development. *First Language*, 25, 235–51.

Jolly, A. (1972). *The Evolution of Primate Behavior*. New York: Macmillan.

Jones, D. M., Macken, W. J., & Nicholls, A. P. (2004). The phonological store of working memory: Is it phonological and is it a store? *Journal of Experimental Psychology: Learning, Memory, and Cognition*, 30, 656–74.

Joseph, H. L., Bremner, G., Liversedge, S. P., & Nation, K. (2015). Working memory, reading ability and the effects of distance and typicality on anaphor resolution in children. *Journal of Cognitive Psychology*, 27(5), 622–39.

Joyal, M., Bonneau, A., & Fecteau, S. (2016). Speech and language therapies to improve pragmatics and discourse skills in patients with schizophrenia. *Psychiatry Research*, 240, 88–95.

Juhasz, B. (2005). Age-of-acquisition effects in word and picture identification. *Psychological Bulletin*, 131, 684–712.

Junker, D. A., & Stockman, I. J. (2002). Expressive vocabulary of German-English bilingual toddlers. *American Journal of Speech-Language Pathology*, 11(4), 381–95.

Jusczyk, P. W. (1999). How infants begin to extract words from speech. *Trends in Cognitive Sciences*, 3(9), 323–8.

Jusczyk, P. W. (2000). *The Discovery of Language*. Cambridge, MA: MIT Press.

Just, M. A., & Carpenter, P. A. (1980). A theory of reading: From eye fixations to comprehension. *Psychological Review*, 87(4), 329–54.

Just, M. A., & Carpenter, P. A. (1992). A capacity theory of comprehension: Individual differences in working memory. *Psychological Review*, 99(1), 122–49.

Just, M. A., Carpenter, P. A., & Masson, M. E. (1982). What eye fixations tell us about speed reading and skimming. Unpublished technical report, Department of Psychology, Carnegie Mellon University, Pittsburgh, PA.

Kachru, B. B., Kachru, Y., & Sridhar, S. N. (2008). *Language in South Asia*. Cambridge: Cambridge University Press.

Kadar, D., & Haugh, M. (2013). *Understanding Politeness*. Cambridge: Cambridge University Press.

Kaiser, E., & Trueswell, J. C. (2004). The role of discourse context in the processing of a flexible word-order language. *Cognition*, 94(2), 113–47.

Kaisera, D. M., Schoemaker, M. M., Albaretc, J.-M., & Geuze, R. H. (2015). What is the evidence of impaired motor skills and motor control among children with attention deficit hyperactivity disorder (ADHD)? Systematic review of the literature. *Research in Developmental Disabilities*, 36, 338–57.

Kandel, S., & Spinelli, E. (2010). Processing complex graphemes in handwriting production. *Memory & Cognition*, 38, 762–70.

Kandel, S., Alvarez, C., & Vallée, N. (2006). Syllables as processing units in handwriting production. *Journal of Experimental Psychology: Human Perception and Performance*, 32, 18–31.

Kandel, S., Alvarez, C., & Vallée, N. (2008). Morphemes also serve as processing units in handwriting production. In M. Baciu (ed.) *Neuropsychology and Cognition of Language: Behavioral, Neuropsychological and Neuroimaging Studies of Spoken and Written Language* (pp. 87–100). Kerala: Research Signpost.

Kandel, S., Peereman, R., Grosjacques, G., & Fayol, M. (2011). For a psycholinguistic model of handwriting production: Testing the syllable-bigram controversy. *Journal of Experimental Psychology: Human Perception and Performance*, 37(4), 1310–22.

Kantor, J. ([1935] 1952). *An Objective Psychology of Grammar.* Bloomington, IN: Indiana University Press.

Kanwisher, N. (1987). Repetition blindness: Type recognition without token individuation. *Cognition*, 27, 117–43.

Kaplan, R., & Bresnan, J. (1982). Lexical functional grammar: A formal system of grammatical representation. In J. Bresnan (ed.) *The Mental Representation of Grammatical Relations* (pp. 173–281). Cambridge, MA: MIT Press.

Kaplan, J. A., Brownell, H. H., Jacobs, J. R., & Gardner, H. (1990). The effects of right hemisphere damage on the pragmatic interpretation of conversational remarks. *Brain and Language*, 38(2), 315–33.

Kasparian, K. (2013). Hemispheric differences in figurative language processing: Contributions of neuroimaging methods and challenges in reconciling current empirical findings. *Journal of Neurolinguistics*, 26(1), 1–21.

Kegl, J. (2002). Language emergence in a language-ready brain: Acquisition issues. In G. Morgan and B. Woll (eds) *Language Acquisition in Signed Languages* (pp. 207–54). Cambridge: Cambridge University Press.

Kegl, J., Senghas, A., & Coppola, M. (1999). Creation through contact: Sign language emergence & sign language change in Nicaragua. In M. DeGraff (ed.) *Comparative Grammatical Change: The Intersection of Language Acquisition, Creole Genesis, and Diachronic Syntax* (pp. 179–237). Cambridge, MA: MIT Press.

Keller, H., Shattuck, R., & Herrmann, D. (2004). *The Story of my Life: The Restored Classic.* New York: W. W. Norton.

Kellogg, W. N., & Kellogg, L. A. (1933). *The Ape and the Child: A Comparative Study of the Environmental Influence upon Early Behavior.* New York: Hafner.

Kelly, D. J. (1998). A clinical synthesis of the "late talker" literature: Implications for service delivery. *Language, Speech, and Hearing Services in Schools*, 29, 76–84.

Kemper, A. R., & Downs S. M. (2000). A cost-effectiveness analysis of newborn hearing screening strategies. *Archives of Pediatric and Adolescent Medicine*, 154, 484–8.

Kemper, S., & Edwards, L. L. (1986). Children's expression of causality and their construction of narratives. *Topics in Language Disorders*, 7(1), 11–20.

Kempler, D., & Zelinski, E. M. (1994). Language function in dementia and normal aging. In F. A. Huppert, C. Brayne & D. O'Connor (eds) *Dementia and Normal Aging* (pp. 331–65). Cambridge: Cambridge University Press.

Kempler, D., van Lancker, D., Marchman, V., & Bates, E. (1999). Idiom comprehension in children and adults with unilateral brain damage. *Developmental Neuropsychology*, 15(3), 327–49.

Kennedy, M. (2016). Lead-laced water in flint: A step-by-step look at the makings of a crisis. Retrieved October 13, 2016 from www.npr.org/sections/thetwo-way/2016/04/20/465545378/lead-laced-water-in-flint-a-step-by-step-look-at-the-makings-of-a-crisis.

Kennedy, A., & Murray, W. S. (1984). Inspection times for words in syntactically ambiguous sentences under three presentation conditions. *Journal of Experimental Psychology: Human Perception & Performance*, 10, 833–47.

Kennison, S. M. (1999) Processing agentive 'by'-phrases in complex event and non event nominals. *Linguistic Inquiry*, 30, 502–8.

Kennison, S. M. (2001). Limitations on the use of verb information in sentence comprehension. *Psychonomic Bulletin & Review*, 8, 132–38.

Kennison, S. M. (2003). Comprehending the pronouns her, him, and his: Implications for theories of referential processing. *Journal of Memory and Language*, 49, 335–52.

Kennison, S. M. (2004). The effect of phonemic repetition on syntactic ambiguity resolution: Implications for models of working memory. *Journal of Psycholinguistic Research*, 33, 493–516.

Kennison, S. M. (2016). The role of discourse prominence in antecedent search: The case of genitive NPs. *Discourse*, 18, 1–14.

Kennison, S. M., & Bowers, J. M. (2011). Illustrating brain lateralization in a naturalistic observation of cell phone use. *Psychology Learning & Teaching*, 10, 46–51.

Kennison, S. M., & Byrd-Craven, J. (2015). Gender differences in the beliefs about infant-directed speech: A role for family dynamics. *Child Development Research*, www.hindawi.com/journals/cdr/2015/871759.

Kennison, S. M., & Clifton, C. (1995). Determinants of parafoveal preview benefit in high and low working memory capacity readers: Implications for eye movement control. *Journal of Experimental Psychology: Learning, Memory, and Cognition*, 21, 68–81.

Kennison, S. M., & Messer, R. H. (2017). Cursing as a form of risk-taking. *Current Psychology*, 119–26.

Kennison, S. M . & Messer, R. H. (2018, in press). Humor as social risk-taking: The relationships among humor styles, sensation-seeking, and use of curse words. *Humor: International Journal of Humor Research*.

Kennison, S. M., & Trofe, J. L. (2003). A role for gender stereotype information in language comprehension. *Journal of Psycholinguistic Research*, 32, 355–78.

Kennison, S. M., Byrd-Craven, J., & Hamilton, S. L. (2017) Individual differences in talking enjoyment: The roles of life history strategy and mate value. *Evolutionary Psychology*, www.cogentoa.com/article/10.1080/23311908.2017.1395310.pdf.

Kennison, S. M., Fernandez, E. C., & Bowers, J. M. (2009). Processing differences for anaphoric and cataphoric pronouns: Implications for theories of referential processing. *Discourse Processes*, 46, 25–35.

Kennison, S. M., Sieck, J. P., and Briesch, K. A. (2003). Evidence for a late occurring effect of phoneme repetition in silent reading. *Journal of Psycholinguistic Research*, 32, 297–312.

Kielar, A., Milman L., Bonakdarpour B., & Thompson C. K. (2011). Neural correlates of covert and overt production of tense and agreement morphology: Evidence from fMRI. *Journal of Neurolinguistics*, 24, 183–201.

Kieler, H., Cnattingius, S., Haglund, B., Palmgren, J., & Axelsson, O. (2001). Sinistrality – a side-effect of prenatal sonography: A comparative study of young men. *Epidemiology*, 12, 618–23.

Kilmer, A. D. (1965). The strings of musical instruments: Their names, numbers, and significance. In H. G. Güterbock and T. Jacobsen (eds) *Studies in Honor of Benno Landsberger on His Seventy-fifth Birthday, April 21, 1965* (pp. 261–8). Chicago: University of Chicago Press.

Kilmer, A. D., & Civil, M. (1986). Old Babylonian musical instructions relating to hymnody. *Journal of Cuneiform Studies*, 38(1), 94–8.

Kim, H. S., Relkin, N. R., Lee, K. M., & Hirsch, J. (1997). Distinct cortical areas associated with native and second languages. *Nature*, 388, 171–4.

Kimball, J. (1973). Seven principles of surface structure parsing in natural language. *Cognition*, 2,15–47.

Kim-Renaud, Y. (1997). *The Korean Alphabet: Its History and Structure*. Honolulu, HI: University of Hawaii Press.

Kimura, D. (1961). Cerebral dominance and the perception of verbal stimuli. *Canadian Journal of Psychology*, 15, 166–71.

King, J., & Just, M. A. (1991). Individual differences in syntactic processing: The role of working memory. *Journal of Memory & Language*, 30, 580–602.

King, S. L., & Janik, V. M. (2013). Bottlenose dolphins can use learned vocal labels to address each other. *PNAS Proceedings of the National Academy of Sciences of the United States of America*, 110(32), 13216–21.

Kintsch, W. (1974). *The Representation of Meaning in Memory*. Hillsdale, NJ: Erlbaum.

Kintsch, W. (1988). The role of knowledge in discourse comprehension: A construction-integration model. *Psychological Review*, 95, 163–82.

Kintsch, W., & Bates, E. (1977). Recognition memory for statements from a classroom lecture. *Journal of Experimental Psychology: Human Learning and Memory*, 3, 150–9.

Kintsch, W., & van Dijk, T. A. (1978). Toward a model of text comprehension and production. *Psychological Review*, 85, 363–94.

Kircher, T. T., Brammer, M. J., Levelt, W., Bartels, M., & McGuire, P. K. (2004). Pausing for thought: Engagement of left temporal cortex during pauses in speech. *NeuroImage*, 21, 84–90.

Kiriazis, J., & Slobodchikoff, S. N. (2006). Perceptual specificity in the alarm calls of Gunnison's prairie dogs. *Behavioural Processes*, 73, 29–35.

Kirton, J. F. (1988). Men's and women's dialect. *Aboriginal Linguistics*, 1, 111–25.

Kisilevsky, B. S., Muir, D. W., & Low, J. A. (1992). Maturation of human fetal responses to vibroacoustic stimulation. *Child Development*, 63, 1497–508.

Kisilevsky, B. S., Hains, S. M., Lee, K., Xie, X., Huang, H. et al. (2003). Effects of experience on fetal voice recognition. *Psychological Science*, 14(3), 220–4.

Kiss, G. R., Armstrong, C. A., & Milroy, R. (1972). *An Associative Thesaurus of English* (microfilm version). Wakefield: E. P. Microforms.

Kizach, J., & Balling, L. W. (2013). Givenness, complexity, and the Danish dative alternation. *Memory & Cognition*, 41(8), 1159–71.

Kjaerbaek, L., Christensen, R. D., & Basboell, H. (2014). Sound structure and input frequency impact on noun plural acquisition: Hypotheses tested on Danish children across different data types. *Nordic Journal of Linguistics*, 37(1), 47–86.

Kleemeyer, M. M., Kühn, S., Prindle, J., Bodammer, N. C., Brechtel, L. et al. (2016). Changes in fitness are associated with changes in hippocampal microstructure and hippocampal volume among older adults. *NeuroImage*, 131, 155–61.

Klein, R. G., & Edgar, B. (2002). *The Dawn of Human Culture*. New York: John Wiley.

Klima, E. S., & Bellugi, U. (1966). Syntactic regularities in the speech of children. In J. Lyons & R. J. Wales (eds) *Psycholinquistic Papers: The Proceedings of the 1966 Edinburgh Conference* (pp. 183–219). Edinburgh: Edinburgh University Press.

Klima, E. S., & Bellugi, U. (1979). *The Signs of Language*. Boston: Harvard University Press.

Kluwin, T. N., & Gaustad, M.G. (1991). Predicting family communication choices. *American Annals of the Deaf*, 136, 28–33.

Knapp, M. L., Hall, J. A., & Horgan, T. G. (2013). *Nonverbal Communication in Human Interaction*. New York: Cengage.

Knaus, T. A., Bollich, A. M., Lemen, L. C., Corey, D. M., & Foundas, A. L. (2004). Sex-linked differences in the anatomy of the perisylvian language cortex: A volumetric MRI study of gray matter volumes. *Neuropsychology*, 18(4), 738–47.

Kolb, B., & Wishaw, I. Q. (2009). *Fundamentals of Human Neuropsychology* (7th edn). New York: Worth.

Komarova, N. L., & Nowak, M. A. (2001). Natural selection of the critical period for language acquisition. *Proceedings: Biological Sciences*, 268(1472), 1189–96.

Konner, M. (2002). *The Tangled Wing: Biological Constraints on the Human Spirit*. New York: Times Books.

Koren, M. (2013). B. F. Skinner: The man who taught pigeons to play ping-pong and rats to pull levers. Retrieved September 20, 2015 from www. smithsonianmag.com/science-nature/bf-skinner-the-man-who-taught-pigeons-to-play-ping-pong-and-rats-to-pull-levers-5363946/?no-ist.

Kovachy, V. N., Adams, J. N., Tamaresis, J. S., & Feldman, H. M. (2015). Reading abilities in school-aged preterm children: A review and meta-analysis. *Developmental Medicine & Child Neurology*, 57(5), 410–19.

Kovács, A. M., & Mehler, J. (2009). Cognitive gains in 7-month-old bilingual infants. *Proceedings of the National Academy of Sciences of the United States of America*, 106, 6556–60.

Kovelman, I., Baker, S. A., & Petitto, L. A. (2008). Age of first bilingual language exposure as a new window into bilingual reading development. *Bilingualism: Language and Cognition*, 11(2), 203–23.

Kraft, S. J., & Yairi, E. (2011). Genetic bases of stuttering: The state of the art. *Folia Phoniatrica et Logopaedica*, 64(1), 34–47.

Krauss, R. M. (1998). Why do we gesture when we speak? *Current Directions in Psychological Science*, 7(2), 54–60.

Krauss, R. M., Chen, Y., & Chawla, P. (1996). Nonverbal behavior and nonverbal communication: What do conversational hand gestures tell us? In M. Zanna (ed.) *Advances in Experimental Social Psychology* (pp. 389–450). San Diego, CA: Academic Press.

Krauss, R. M., Chen, Y., & Gottesman, R. F. (2000). Lexical gestures and lexical access: A process model. In D. McNeill (ed.) *Language and Gesture* (pp. 261–83). New York: Cambridge University Press.

Kreitewolf, J., Friederici, A. D., & von Kriegstein, K. (2014). Hemispheric lateralization of linguistic prosody recognition in comparison to speech and speaker recognition. *NeuroImage*, 102, 332–44.

Kretschmer, R., & Kretschmer, L. (1989). Second language teaching and the handicapped child. In D. Nielsen (ed.) *Two Languages for all Children*. New York: Addison.

Kroll, J. F., & Stewart, E. (1994). Category interference in translation and picture naming: Evidence for asymmetric connection between bilingual memory representations. *Journal of Memory & Language*, 33, 149–74.

Kroll, J. F., van Hell, J. G., Tokowicz, N., & Green, D. W. (2010). The revised hierarchical model: A critical review and assessment. *Bilingualism: Language and Cognition*, 13, 373–81.

Krys, K., et al. (2016). Be careful where you smile: Culture shapes judgments of intelligence and honesty of smiling individuals. *Journal of Nonverbal Behavior*, 40, 101–16.

Kuhl, P. K. (1987). The special-mechanisms debate in speech perception: Nonhuman species & nonspeech signals. In S. Harnad (ed.) *Categorical Perception: The Groundwork of Cognition* (pp. 355–86). New York: Cambridge University Press.

Kuhl, P. K. (1999). Speech, language, and the brain: Innate preparation for learning. In M. D. Hauser & M. Konishi (eds) *The Design of Animal Communication* (pp. 419–50). Cambridge, MA: MIT Press.

Kuhl, P. K. (2007). Is speech learning "gated" by the social brain? *Developmental Science*, 10, 110–20.

Kuhl, P. K., Tsao, F.-M., & Liu, H.-M. (2003). Foreign-language experience in infancy: Effects of short term exposure & social interaction on phonetic learning. *Proceedings of the National Academy of Sciences, USA*, 100, 9096–101.

Kuhl, P. K., Stevens, E., Hayashi, A., Deguchi, T., Kiritani, S. et al. (2006). Infants show a facilitation effect for native language perception between 6 and 12 months. *Developmental Science*, 9, F1–9.

Kulick, D. (2000). Gay and lesbian language. *Anthropology Annual Review*, 29, 243–85.

Kuperberg, G. R. (2010a). Language in schizophrenia part 1: An introduction. *Language and Linguistics Compass*, 4(8), 576–89.

Kuperberg, G. R. (2010b). Language in schizophrenia part 2: What can psycholinguistics bring to the study of schizophrenia … and vice versa? *Language and Linguistics Compass*, 4(8), 590–604.

Kuperberg, G. R., West, W. C., Lakshmanan, B. M., & Goff, D. (2008). Functional magnetic resonance imaging reveals neuroanatomical dissociations during semantic integration in schizophrenia. *Biological Psychiatry*, 64(5), 407–18.

Kupin, J. J. (1980). Tongue Twisters as a Source of Information about Speech Production. (Order No. 8103189). Available from ProQuest Dissertations & Theses A&I.

Kupin, J. J. (1982). *Tongue Twisters as a Source of Information about Speech Production*. Bloomington: Indiana University Linguistics Club.

Kurtz, M. M. (2016). *Schizophrenia and its Treatment: Where is the Progress?* New York: Oxford University Press.

Kussmaul, A. (1877). *Die Störungen der Sprache: Versuch einer Pathologie der Sprache*. Leipzig: Vogel.

Kyle, J. G., & Woll, B. (1988). *Sign Language: The Study of Deaf People and Their Language*. Cambridge: Cambridge University Press.

Labov, W. (1966). *The Social Stratification of English in New York City*. Washington, D.C.: Center for Applied Linguistics.

Labov, W. (1969). *The Study of Nonstandard English*. Washington, D.C.: Center for Applied Linguistics.

Labov, W. (1972) *Language in the Inner City: Studies in the Black English Vernacular*. Philadelphia: University of Pennsylvania Press.

Labov, W., Ash, S., & Boberg, C. (2006). *The Atlas of North American English*. Berlin: Mouton de Gruyter.

Ladefoged, P. (2006). *A Course in Phonetics* (5th edn). Fort Worth: Harcourt College.

Lakoff, R. ([1975] 2004). *Language and Woman's Place: Text and Commentaries*. Oxford: Oxford University Press.

Lam, K., & Dijkstra, T. (2010). Modeling code-interactions in bilingual word recognition: Recent empirical studies and simulations with BIA+. *International Journal of Bilingual Education and Bilingualism*, 13, 487–503.

Lambon Ralph, M., Lowe, C., & Rogers, T. T. (2007). Neural basis of category-specific semantic deficits for living things: Evidence from semantic dementia, HSVE and a neural network model. *Brain*, 130(4), 1127–37.

Lamy, D., Leber, A. B., & Egeth, H. E. (2013). Selective attention. In A. F. Healy, R. W. Proctor, I. B. Weiner, A. F. Healy, R. W. Proctor et al. (eds) *Handbook of Psychology: Experimental Psychology*, vol. 4, 2nd edn (pp. 267–94). Hoboken, NJ: John Wiley & Sons.

Landauer, T. K., & Dumais, S. T. (1997). A solution to Plato's problem: The latent semantic analysis theory of acquisition, induction, and representation of knowledge. *Psychological Review*, 104(2), 211.

Landauer, T. K., Laham, D., & Foltz, P. (2003). Automatic essay assessment. *Assessment in Education: Principles, Policy & Practice*, 10(3), 295–308.

Lane, H. L. (1975). *The Wild Boy of Aveyron*. Cambridge, MA: Harvard University Press.

Lane, H. L. (ed.) (1984). *The Deaf Experience: Classics in Language and Education*. Cambridge, MA: Harvard University Press.

Lane, H. L., Pillard, R., & Hedberg, U. (2011). *The People of the Eye: Deaf Ethnicity and Ancestry*. Oxford: Oxford University Press.

LaPointe, L. B., & Engle, R. W. (1990). Simple and complex word spans as measures of working memory capacity. *Journal of Experimental Psychology: Learning, Memory, and Cognition*, 16, 1118–33.

LaPointe, L. L. (2012). *Paul Broca and the Origins of Language in the Brain*. San Diego: Plural.

Lass, R., & Hogg, R. M. (2000). *The Cambridge History of the English Language*. Cambridge: Cambridge University Press.

Laws, G., & Bishop, D. V. (2003). A comparison of language abilities in adolescents with Down syndrome and children with specific language impairment. *Journal of Speech, Language and Hearing Research*, 46, 1324–39.

Leap, W. L. (1995). *Beyond the Lavender Lexicon*. Newark: Gordon & Breach.

Leblanc, M. (2013). *The Mind of the Horse: An Introduction to Equine Cognition*. Cambridge, MA: Harvard University Press.

Lederberg, A. R., & Morales, C. (1985). Code switching by bilinguals: Evidence against a third grammar. *Journal of Psycholinguistic Research*, 14(2), 113–36.

Lee, C. D., & Smagorinsky, P. (eds) (2000). *Vygotskian Perspectives on Literacy Research: Constructing Meaning through Collaborative Inquiry*. New York: Cambridge University Press.

Lee, D., & Schachter, J. (1997). Sensitive period effects in binding theory. *Language Acquisition*, 6(4), 333–62.

Lee, E. S., Yeatman, J. D., Luna, B., & Feldman, H. M. (2011). Specific language and reading skills in school-aged children and adolescents are associated with prematurity after controlling for IQ. *Neuropsychologia*, 49(5), 906–13.

Lee, J. C., & Tomblin, J. B. (2012). Reinforcement learning in young adults with developmental language impairment. *Brain and Language*, 123, 154–63.

Leeson, L., & Grehan, C. (2004). To the lexicon and beyond: Gender as a variable affecting variation in Irish Sign Language. In M. van Herreweghe & M. Veermerbergen (eds) *The Sociolinguistics of European Sign Languages*. Washington, D.C.: Gallaudet University Press.

Leeson, L., & Saeed, J. (2012a) *Irish Sign Language*. Edinburgh: Edinburgh University Press.

Leeson, L., & Saeed, J. (2012b). Word order. In R. Pfau, M. Steinbach & B. Woll (eds) *Sign Language: An International Handbook* (pp. 245–64). Berlin: Mouton de Gruyter.

Lefevre, R. (2011). *"V". Rude Hand Gestures of the World: A Guide to Offending Without Words*. San Francisco, CA: Chronicle Books.

Legman, G. (1941). The language of homosexuality: An American glossary. In G. W. Henry (ed.) *Sex Variants*. New York: Paul B. Hoeber.

Lehmann, A. C., & Kopiez, R. (2016). Sight-reading. In S. Hallam, I. Cross & M. Thaut (eds) *The Oxford Handbook of Music Psychology*, 2nd edn (pp. 547–57). New York: Oxford University Press.

Leikin, M. (2012). The effect of bilingualism on creativity: Developmental and educational perspectives. *International Journal of Bilingualism*, 17(4), 431–77.

Leinenger, M. (2014). Phonological coding during reading. *Psychological Bulletin*, 140(6), 1534–55.

LeMaster, B. (1990). The Maintenance and Loss of Female and Male Signs in the Dublin Deaf Community. Doctoral Dissertation. Los Angeles, CA: UCLA.

LeMaster, B. (1997). Sex differences in Irish Sign Language. In J. H. Hill, P. J. Mistry & L. Campbell (eds) *The Life of Language: Papers in Linguistics in Honor of William Bright*. Berlin: Mouton de Gruyter.

LeMaster, B. (2000). Reappropriation of gendered Irish Sign Language in one family. *Visual Anthropology Review*, 15(2), 1–15.

LeMaster, B., & Dwyer, J. P. (1991). Knowing and using female and male signs in Dublin. *Sign Language Studies*, 73, 361–96.

Lenneberg, E. H. (1964). The capacity for language acquisition. In J. A. Fodor & J. J. Katz (eds) *The Structure of Language: Readings in the Philosophy of Language* (pp. 579–603). Englewood Cliffs, NJ: Prentice Hall.

Lenneberg, E. H. (1967). *Biological Foundations of Language*. New York: Wiley.

Leonard, L. B., & Bortolini, U. (1998). Grammatical morphology and the role of weak syllables in the speech of Italian speaking children with specific language impairment. *Journal of Speech, Language, and Hearing Research*, 41, 1363–74.

Lesch, M. F., & Pollatsek, A. (1998). Evidence for the use of assembled phonology in accessing the meaning of printed words. *Journal of Experimental Psychology: Learning, Memory, and Cognition*, 24, 573–92.

Leung, E. H., & Rheingold, H. L. (1981). Development of pointing as a social gesture. *Developmental Psychology*, 17, 215–20.

Levelt, W. J. (1983). Monitoring and self-repair in speech. *Cognition*, 14, 41–104.

Levelt, W. J. (1989). *Speaking: From Intention to Articulation*. Cambridge, MA: MIT Press.

Levelt, W. J., & Wheeldon, L. R. (1994). Do speakers have access to a mental syllabary? *Cognition*, 50, 239–69.

Levelt, W. J., Roelofs, A., & Meyer, A. S. (1999). A theory of lexical access in speech production. *Behavioral and Brain Sciences*, 22, 1–38.

Levelt, W. J., Schriefer, H., Vorberg, D., Meyer, A. S., Pechmann, T. et al. (1991). The time course of lexical access in speech production: A study of picture naming. *Psychological Review*, 98(1), 122–42.

Levine, W. H., Guzmán, A. E., & Klin, C. M. (2000). When anaphor resolution fails. *Journal of Memory and Language*, 43(4), 594–617.

Levitt, A. G., & Healy, A. F. (1985). The roles of phoneme frequency, similarity, and availability in the experimental elicitation of speech errors. *Journal of Memory and Language*, 24, 717–33.

Levitt, S., & Dubner, S. J. (2005). *Freakonomics: A Rogue Economist Explores the Hidden Side of Everything*. New York: William Morrow/HarperCollins.

Lewis, D. A., & Levitt, P. (2002). Schizophrenia as a disorder of neurodevelopment. *Annual Review of Neuroscience*, 25, 409–32.

Lewis, J., Palmer, C., & Williams, L. (1995). Existence of and attitudes towards black variations of sign language. *Communication Forum*, 4, 17–48.

Lewis, M. P., Simons, G. F., & Fennig, C. D. (eds) (2016). *Ethnologue: Languages of the World*, 18th edn. Dallas, TX: SIL International.

Li, P., Zhang, F., Tsai, E., & Puls, B. (2014). Language history questionnaire (LHQ 2.0): A new dynamic web-based research tool. *Bilingualism: Language and Cognition*, 17(3), 673–80.

Li, S. (2016). The construct validity of language aptitude: A meta-analysis. *Studies in Second Language Acquisition*, 38(4), 801–42.

Li, X., Harbottle, G., Zhang, J., & Changsui, W. (2003). The earliest writing? Sign use in the seventh millennium BC at Jiahu, Henan Province, China. *Antiquity*, 77(295), 31–45.

Liberman, A. M., & Mattingly, I. G. (1985). The motor theory of speech perception revised. *Cognition*, 21(1), 1–36.

Liberman, A. M., Cooper, F. S., Shankweiler, D. P., & Studdert-Kennedy, M. (1967). Perception of the speech code. *Psychological Review*, 74(6), 431–61.

Liberman, Z., Woodward, A. L., Keysar, B., & Kinzler, K. D. (2016). Exposure to multiple languages enhances communication skills in infancy. *Developmental Science*, 20(1), 1–11.

Liddell, S. K. (2003). *Grammar, Gesture, and Meaning in American Sign Language*. Cambridge: Cambridge University Press.

Lieberman, D. E., McCarthy, R. C., Hiiemae, K. M., & Palmer, J. B. (2001). Ontogeny of larynx and hyoid descent in humans: Implications for deglutition and vocalization. *Archives of Oral Biology*, 46, 117–28.

Lieberman, P. (2007). The evolution of human speech: Its anatomical and neural bases. *Current Anthropology*, 48(1), 39–66.

Liederman, J., Gilbert, K., Fisher, J. M., Mathews, G., Frye, R. E. et al. (2011). Are women more influenced than men by top-down semantic information when listening to disrupted speech? *Language and Speech*, 54(1), 33–48.

Liegeois, F., Cross, H. J., Polkey, C., Harkness, W., & Vargha-Khadem, F. (2008). Language after hemispherectomy in childhood: Contributions from memory and intelligence. *Neuropsychologia*, 46(13), 3101–7.

Lima, S. D. (1987). Morphological analysis during sentence reading. *Journal of Memory and Language*, 26, 84–99.

Lin, D., McBride-Chang, C., Shu, H., Zhang, Y. P., Li, H. et al. (2010). Small wins big: Analytic Pinyin skills promote Chinese word reading. *Psychological Science*, 21, 1117–22.

Linacre, J. M. (1996). The prison literacy problem. *Rasch Measurement Transactions*, 10(1), 473–4.

Linck, J., Kroll, J. F., & Sunderman, G. (2009). Losing access to the native language while immersed in a second language: Evidence for the role of inhibition in second language learning. *Psychological Science*, 20, 1507–15.

Lindell, A. K. (2006). In your right mind: Right hemisphere contributions to language processing and production. *Neuropsychology Review*, 16(3), 131–48.

Literacy Project Foundation (2016). Staggering illiteracy statistics. Retrieved October 2, 2016 from http://literacyprojectfoundation.org/community/statistics/.

Llaurens, V., Raymond, M., & Faurie, C. (2009). Why are some people left-handed? An evolutionary perspective. *Philosophical Transactions of the Royal Society of London. Series B Biological Sciences,* 364, 881–94.

Loebell, H., & Bock, K. (2003). Structural priming across languages. *Linguistics*, 41, 791–824.

Loftus, E. F. (1973). Category dominance, instance dominance and categorization time. *Journal of Experimental Psychology*, 97, 70–74.

Logan, F. A. (1999). Errors in copy typewriting. *Journal of Experimental Psychology: Human Perception and Performance*, 25(6), 1760–73.

Long, M. (2005). Problems with supposed counter-evidence to the critical period hypothesis. *International Review of Applied Linguistics*, 43(4), 287–317.

Longoni, F., Grande, M., Hendrich, V., Kastrau, F., & Huber, W. (2005). An fMRI study on conceptual, grammatical, and morpho-phonological processing. *Brain and Cognition*, 57, 131–4.

Loomis, E. W., Eid, J. S., Peluso, P., Yin, J., Hickey, L. et al. (2012). Sequencing the unsequenceable: Expanded CGG-repeat alleles of the Fragile X gene. *Genome Research*, 23(1),121–8.

Lotto, L., & de Groot, A. M. (1998). Effects of learning method and word type on acquiring vocabulary in an unfamiliar language. *Language Learning*, 48, 31–69.

Lucas, C., Bayley, R., & Valli, C. (2001). *Sociolinguistic Variation in American Sign Language*. Washington, D.C.: Gallaudet University Press.

Lucas, C., Bayley, R., McCaskill, C., & Hill, J. (2015). The intersection of African American English and Black American Sign Language. *International Journal of Bilingualism*, 19, 156–68.

Lucas, C., Bayley, R., Rose, M., & Wulf, A. (2002). Location variation in American Sign Language. *Sign Language Studies*, 2, 407–40.

Luce, P. A., Pisoni, D. B., & Goldinger, S. D. (1990). Similarity neighborhoods of spoken words. In G. Altmann (ed.) *Cognitive Models of Speech Processing* (pp. 122–47). Cambridge: MIT Press.

Luria, A. R. (1963). *Restoration of Function after Brain Injury* (trans. O. L. Zangwill). New York: Pergamon Press.

Lust, J. M., Geuze, R. H., Van, B. B., Cohen-Kettenis, P., Groothuis, A. G. et al. (2010). Sex specific effect of prenatal testosterone on language lateralization in children. *Neuropsychologia*, 48(2), 536–40.

Luzzatti, C., Mondini, S., & Semenza, C. (2012). Lexical impairment in agrammatism. In R. Bastiaanse & C. K. Thompson (eds) *Perspectives on Agrammatism* (pp. 60–74). New York: Psychology Press.

Lybeck, K. (2002). Cultural identification and second language pronunciation of Americans in Norway. *Modern Language Journal*, 86, 174–91.

Lyons, M. T., & Hughes, S. (2015). Malicious mouths? The dark triad and motivations for gossip. *Personality and Individual Differences*, 78, 1–4.

Ma, X., Jin, Y., Luo, B., Zhang, G., Wei, R. et al. (2015). Giant pandas failed to show mirror self-recognition. *Animal Cognition*, 18(3), 713–21.

Maas, A., & Russo, A. (2003). Directional bias in the mental representation of spatial events: Nature or culture? *Psychological Science*, 14(4), 296.

McBride, C., & Wang, Y. (2015). Learning to read Chinese: Universal and unique cognitive cores. *Child Development Perspectives*, 9(3), 196–200.

McBride-Chang, C., Liu, P. D., Wong, T., Wong, A., & Shu, H. (2011). Specific reading difficulties in Chinese, English, or both: Longitudinal markers of phonological awareness, morphological awareness, and RAN in Hong Kong Chinese children. *Journal of Learning Disabilities*, 45(6), 503–14.

McBride-Chang, C., Manis, F. R., Seidenberg, M. S., Custodio, R. G., & Doi, L. M. (1993). Print exposure as a predictor of word reading and reading comprehension in disabled and nondisabled readers. *Journal of Educational Psychology*, 85, 230–8.

McCaskill, C., Lucas, C., Bayley, R., & Hill, J. (2011) *The Hidden Treasure of Black ASL, its History and Structure*. Washington, D.C.: Gallaudet University Press.

McClain, D. A., Abuelgasim, K. A., Nouraie, M., Salomon-Andonie, J., Niu, X. et al. (2013). Decreased serum glucose and glycosylated hemoglobin levels in patients with Chuvash polycythemia: A role for HIF in glucose metabolism. *Journal of Molecular Medicine*, 91(1), 59–67.

Maclay, H., & Osgood, C. E. (1959). Hesitation phenomena in spontaneous English speech. *Word*, 15, 19–44.

McClelland, J. L., & Elman, J.L. (1986). The TRACE model of speech perception. *Cognitive Psychology*, 18, 1–86.

McClelland, J. L., & Rumelhart, D. E. (1981). An interactive activation model of context effects in letter perception: I. An account of basic findings. *Psychological Review*, 88, 375–407.

McClelland, J. L., Rumelhart D. E. and the PDP Research Group (1986). *Parallel Distributed Processing: Explorations in the Microstructure of Cognition*. vol. 2: *Psychological and Biological Models*. Cambridge, MA: MIT Press.

McClelland, S., & Maxwell, R. E. (2007). Hemispherectomy for intractable epilepsy in adults: The first reported series. *Annals of Neurology*, 61(4), 372–6.

McConkie, G. W., & Rayner, K. (1975) The span of the effective stimulus during a fixation in reading, *Perception & Psychophysics*, 17, 578–86.

McCutchen, D., & Perfetti, C. A. (1982). The visual tongue-twister effect: Phonological activation in silent reading. *Journal of Verbal Learning and Verbal Behavior*, 21, 672–87.

MacDonald, M., & MacWhinney, B. (1990). Measuring inhibition and facilitation from pronouns. *Journal of Memory and Language*, 29, 469–92.

MacDonald, M. C., Just, M. A., & Carpenter, P. A. (1992). Working memory constraints on the processing of syntactic ambiguity. *Cognition*, 24, 56–98.

MacDonald, M. C., Pearlmutter, N. J., & Seidenberg, M. S. (1994). The lexical nature of syntactic ambiguity resolution. *Psychological Review*, 101, 676–703.

McEnery, T. (2006). *Swearing in English*. New York: Routledge.

McGlone, J. (1980). Sex differences in the human brain: A critical survey. *Behavioral Brain Sciences*, 3, 215–63.

McGuigan, F. J. (1971). Covert linguistic behavior in deaf subjects during thinking. *Journal of Comparative and Physiological Psychology*, 75, 417–20.

MacGuinness, D. (2004). *Early Reading Instruction: What Science Really Tells Us about How to Teach Reading*. Cambridge, MA: MIT Press.

McGurk, H., & MacDonald, J. (1976). Hearing lips and seeing voices. *Nature*, 264(5588), 746–8.

McHenry, H. M. (2009). Human evolution. In M. Ruse & J. Travis (eds) *Evolution: The First Four Billion Years*. Cambridge, MA: Belknap Press.

Mackay, D. G. (1973). Aspects of the theory of comprehension, memory and attention. *Quarterly Journal of Experimental Psychology*, 25(1), 22–48.

MacKay, D. G. (1982). The problems of flexibility, fluency, and speed-accuracy trade-off in skilled behavior. *Psychological Review*, 89(5), 483–506.

MacKay, D. G. (1992). Constraints on theories of inner speech. In D. Reisberg (ed.) *Auditory Imagery* (pp. 121–49). Hillsdale, NJ: Erlbaum.

McKinsey and Co. (n.d.). Engaging teachers to advance childhood literacy. Retrieved July 22, 2017 from www.mckinsey.com/industries/social-sector/how-we-help-clients/engaging-teachers-to-advance-childhood-literacy.

McKoon, G., & Ratcliff, R. (1986). Inferences about predictable events. *Journal of Experimental Psychology: Learning, Memory, and Cognition*, 12, 82–91.

McLachlan, C., Nicholson, T., Fielding-Barnsley, R., Mercer, L., & Ohi, S. (2012). *Literacy in Early Childhood and Primary Education: Issues, Challenges, Solutions.* Cambridge: Cambridge University Press.

McLanahan, S. (2004). Diverging destinies: How children are faring under the second demographic transition. *Demography*, 41(4), 607–27.

MacLeod, C. M. (1991). Half a century of research on the Stroop effect: An integrative review. *Psychological Bulletin*, 109(2), 163–203.

MacLeod, C. M. (1992). The Stroop task: The "gold standard" of attentional measures. *Journal of Experimental Psychology: General*, 121(1), 12–14.

McLoddy, R. K., Bleser, R. D., & Mayer, J. (2011). Lexical tone disruption in Shona after brain damage. *Aphasiology*, 25(10), 1239–60.

McManus, C. (2002). *Right Hand, Left Hand: The Origins of Asymmetry in Brains, Bodies, Atoms and Cultures.* Cambridge, MA: Harvard University Press.

MacMillan, M. (2002). *An Odd Kind of Fame: Stories of Phineas Gage.* Cambridge, MA: MIT Press.

McNeill, D. (1985). So you think gestures are non-verbal? *Psychological Review*, 92, 350–71.

McNeill, D. (2005). *Gesture and Thought.* Chicago: University of Chicago Press.

McQueen, J. M. (1998). Segmentation of continuous speech using phonotactics. *Journal of Memory Language*, 39, 21–46.

McTear, M. F., & Conti-Ramsden, G. (1992). *Pragmatic Disability in Children.* London: Whurr.

MacWhinney, B. (2000). *The CHILDES Project: Tools for Analyzing Talk,* vols 1 & 2: *The Format and Programs* (3rd edn). Mahwah, NJ: Lawrence Erlbaum.

Madell, J., & Hébert, S. (2008). Eye movements and music reading: Where do we look next? *Music Perception*, 26(2), 157–70.

Magnotti, J. F., Basu Mallick, D., Feng, G., Zhou, B., Zhou, W., et al. (2015). Similar frequency of the McGurk effect in large samples of native Mandarin Chinese and American English speakers. *Experimental Brain Research*, 233(9), 2581–6.

Mahon, M., & Crutchley, A. (2006). Performance of typically-developing school-age children with English as an additional language on the British Picture Vocabulary Scales II. *Child Language Teaching and Therapy*, 22(3), 333–51.

Malaspinas, A., Westaway, M. C., Muller, C., Sousa, V. C., Lao, O., et al. (2016). A genomic history of Aboriginal Australia. *Nature*, 538(7624), 207–14.

Malinowski, B. (1923). The problem of meaning in primitive languages. In C. Ogden & I. Richards (eds) *The Meaning of Meaning.* London: Routledge.

Maljkovic, V., & Nakayama, K. (1994). Priming of pop-out: I. Role of features. *Memory & Cognition*, 22, 657–72.

Mallick, D. B., Magnotti, J., & Beauchamp, M. (2015). Variability and stability in the McGurk effect: Contributions of participants, stimuli, time, and response type. *Psychonomic Bulletin & Review*, 22(5), 1299–307.

Mamiya, P. C., Richards, T. L., Coe, B. P., Eichler, E. E., & Kuhl, P. K. (2016). Brain white matter structure and COMT gene are linked to second-language learning in adults. *PNAS Proceedings of the National Academy of Sciences of the United States of America*, 113(26), 7249–54.

Manasco, M. H. (2014). *Introduction to Neurogenic Communication Disorders.* Burlington, VT: Jones & Bartlett Learning.

Manalansan, M. F. (2003). *Global Divas: Filipino Gay Men in the Diaspora.* Durham, NC: Duke University Press Books.

Mandler. J. M., & Johnson, N. S. (1977). Remembrance of things parsed: Story structure and recall. *Cognitive Psychology*, 9, 111–91.

Manschreck, T. C., Maher, B. A., Milavetz, J. J., Ames, D., Weisstein, C. C. et al. (1988). Semantic priming in thought disordered schizophrenic patients. *Schizophrenia Research*, 1(1), 61–6.

Manser, M. B. (2001) The acoustic structure of suricates' alarm calls varies with predator type and the level of response urgency. *Proceedings of the Royal Society B*, 268, 2315–24.

Manser, M. B., Bell, M. B., & Fletcher, L. B. (2001). The information that receivers extract from alarm calls in suricates. *Proceedings B (The Royal Society)*, 268 (1484).

Manser, M. B., Seyfarth, R. M., & Cheney, D. L. (2002) Suricate alarm calls signal predator class and urgency. *Trends in Cognitive Sciences*, 6(2), 55–7.

Mansson, H. (2000). Childhood stuttering: Incidence and development. *Journal of Fluency Disorders*, 25(1), 47–57.

Marcus, G. F., & Fisher, S. E. (2003). FOXP2 in focus: What can genes tell us about speech and language? *Trends in Cognitive Sciences*, 7(6), 257–62.

Marian, V., & Shook, A. (2012). The cognitive benefits of being bilingual. *Cerebrum*. Available at http://dana.org/Cerebrum/2012/The_Cognitive_Benefits_of_Being_Bilingual.

Marian, V., Blumenfeld, H. K., & Kaushanskaya, M. (2007). The Language Experience and Proficiency Questionnaire (LEAP-Q): Assessing language profiles in bilinguals and multilinguals. *Journal of Speech Language and Hearing Research*, 50(4), 940–67.

Marian, V., Spivey, M., & Hirsch, J. (2003). Shared and separate systems in bilingual language processing: Converging evidence from eyetracking and brain imaging. *Brain and Language*, 86, 70–82.

Marie, P. (1907). Presentation de malades atteints d'anarthrie par lesion de l'hemisphere gauche du cerveau. *Bulletins et memoires de la Société médicale des hôpitaux de Paris*, 1, 158–60.

Mariën, P., Verhoeven, J., Wackenier, P., Engelborghs, S., & de Deyn, P. P. (2009). Foreign accent syndrome as a developmental motor speech disorder. *Cortex*, 45, 870–8.

Marini, A. (2012). Characteristics of narrative discourse processing after damage to the right hemisphere. *Seminars in Speech and Language*, 33(1), 68–78.

Marinkovic, K., Baldwin, S., Courtney, M. G., Witzel, T., Dale, A. M. et al. (2011). Right hemisphere has the last laugh: Neural dynamics of joke appreciation. *Cognitive, Affective & Behavioral Neuroscience*, 11(1), 113–30.

Markman, E. M., & Hutchinson, J. E. (1984). Children's sensitivity to constraints on word meaning: Taxonomic vs. thematic relations. *Cognitive Psychology*, 16, 1–27.

Markman, E. M., & Wachtel, G. F. (1988). Children's use of mutual exclusivity to constrain the meaning of words. *Cognitive Psychology*, 20, 121–57.

Marks, J. (2002). *What it Means to be 98% Chimpanzee: Apes, People, and Their Genes.* Berkeley, CA: University of California Press.

Marslen-Wilson, W. (1987). Functional parallelism in spoken word recognition. *Cognition*, 25, 71–102.

Marslen-Wilson, W. (1989). *Lexical Representation and Process.* Cambridge, MA: MIT Press.

Marslen-Wilson, W. (1990). Activation, competition, and frequency in lexical access. In G. T. Altmann (ed.) *Cognitive Models of Speech Processing* (pp. 148–72). Cambridge, MA: MIT Press.

Marslen-Wilson, W., & Tyler, L. K. (1980). The temporal structure of spoken language understanding. *Cognition*, 8, 1–71.

Marslen-Wilson, W., & Warren, P. (1994). Levels of perceptual representation and process in lexical access: words, phonemes, and features. *Psychological Review*, 101(4), 653–75.

Marslen-Wilson, W., & Welsh, A. (1978). Processing interactions and lexical access during word recognition in continuous speech. *Cognitive Psychology*, 10(1), 29–63.

Marten, K., & Psarakos, S. (1995). Evidence of self-awareness in the bottlenose dolphin (Tursiops truncatus). In S. T. Parker, R. Mitchell and M. Boccia (eds) *Self-awareness in Animals and Humans: Developmental Perspectives* (pp. 361–79). Cambridge: Cambridge University Press.

Martensen, H., Dijkstra, A., & Maris, E. (2005). A werd is not quite a word: On the role of sublexical phonological information in visual lexical decision. *Language and Cognitive Processes*, 20, 513–52.

Martin, G. E., Losh, M., Estigarribia, B., Sideris, J., & Roberts, J. (2013). Longitudinal profiles of expressive vocabulary, syntax and pragmatic language in boys with fragile X syndrome or Down syndrome. *International Journal of Language & Communication Disorders*, 48(4), 432–43.

Martin, J. A., Hamilton, B. E., Sutton, P. D., Ventura, S. J., Mathews, T. J., et al. (2010). Births: final data for 2008. *National Vital Statistics Report*, 59(1), 3–71.

Martin, R. A. (2006). *The Psychology of Humor: An Integrative Approach.* New York: Academic Press.

Martin, R. A., Puhlik-Doris, P., Larsen, G., Gray, J., & Weir, K. (2003). Individual differences in uses of humor and their relation to psychological well-being: Development of the Humor Styles Questionnaire. *Journal of Research in Personality*, 37(1), 48–75.

Martin, R. C. (2005). Components of short-term memory and their relation to language processing: Evidence from neuropsychology and neuroimaging. *Current Directions in Psychological Science*, 14(4), 204–8.

Martin, R. C., & Freedman, M. (2001). Short-term retention of lexical-semantic representations: Implications for speech production. *Memory*, 9, 261–80.

Martin, R. C., & Tan, Y. (2015). Sentence comprehension deficits: Independence and interaction of syntax, semantics, and working memory. In A. E. Hillis (ed.) *The Handbook of Adult Language Disorders* (2nd edn) (pp. 303–27). New York: Psychology Press.

Martin, R. C., Miller, M. D., & Vu, H. (2004). Lexical-semantic retention and speech production: Further evidence from normal and brain-damaged participants for a phrasal scope of planning. *Cognitive Neuropsychology*, 21, 625–44.

Martin, R. C., Crowther, J. E., Knight, M., Tamborello, F. P., & Yang, C. L. (2010). Planning in sentence production: Evidence for the phrase as a default planning scope. *Cognition*, 116, 177–92.

Masataka, N. (1992). Pitch characteristics of Japanese maternal speech to infants. *Journal of Child Language*, 19, 213–23.

Masciantonio, R. (1977). Tangible benefits of the study of Latin: A review of research. *Foreign Language Annals*, 10, 375–82.

Mason, K., Rowley, K., Marshall, C. R., Atkinson, J. R., Herman, R. et al. (2010). Identifying specific language impairment in deaf children acquiring British Sign Language: Implications for theory and practice. *British Journal of Developmental Psychology*, 28, 33–49.

Massaro, D. W., & Chen, T. H. (2008). The motor theory of speech perception revisited. *Psychonomic Bulletin & Review*, 15, 453–57.

Massaro, D. W., & Oden, G. C. (1995). Independence of lexical context and phonological information in speech perception. *Journal of Experimental Psychology: Learning, Memory, and Cognition*, 21, 1053–64.

Mathers, M., Keyes, M., & Wright, M. (2010). A review of the evidence on the effectiveness of children's vision screening. *Child: Care, Health and Development*, 36(6), 756–80.

Matsumoto, Y. (1997). The rise and fall of Japanese nonsubject honorifics: The case of "o-verb-suru." *Journal of Pragmatics*, 28(6), 719–49.

Matthews, D. E., Theakston, A., Lieven, E., & Tomasello, M. (2006). The effect of perceptual availability and prior discourse on young children's use of referring expressions. *Applied Psycholinguistics*, 27, 403–22.

Mattys, S. L., Barden, K., & Samuel, A. G. (2014). Extrinsic cognitive load impairs low-level speech perception. *Psychonomic Bulletin & Review*, 21(3), 748–54.

Mayberry, R. I., & Eichen, E. B. (1991). The long-lasting advantage of learning sign language in childhood: Another look at the critical period for language acquisition. *Journal of Memory and Language*, 30(4), 486–512.

Meakins, F. (2013). Mixed languages. In P. Bakker & M. Yaron (eds) *Contact Languages: A Comprehensive Guide* (pp. 159–228). Berlin: Mouton de Gruyter.

Mechelli, A., Crinion, J. T., Noppeney, U., O'Doherty, J., Ashburner, J. et al. (2004). Structural plasticity in the bilingual brain. *Nature*, 431, 757.

Mefferd, A. S., & Corder, E. E. (2014). Assessing articulatory speed performance as a potential factor of slowed speech in older adults. *Journal of Speech, Language, and Hearing Research*, 57, 347–60.

Mehl, M. R., & Pennebaker, J. W. (2003). The sounds of social life: A psychometric analysis of students' daily social environments and natural conversations. *Journal of Personality and Social Psychology*, 84(4), 857–70.

Mehl, M. R., Gosling, S., & Pennebaker, J. (2006). Personality in its natural habitat: Manifestations and implicit folk theories of personality in daily life. *Journal of Personality and Social Psychology*, 90, 862–77.

Mehl, M. R., Vazire, S., Ramírez-Esparza, N., Slatcher, R. B., & Pennebaker, J. W. (2007). Are women really more talkative than men? *Science*, 317(5834), 82.

Mehler, J., Jusczyk, P. W., Lambertz, G., Halsted, N., Bertoncini, J. et al. (1988). A precursor of language acquisition in young infants. *Cognition*, 29, 143–78.

Meier, R. P. (1991). Language acquisition by deaf children. *American Scientist*, 79, 60–70.

Meier, R. P., & Newport, E. L. (1990). Out of the hands of babes: On a possible sign advantage in language acquisition. *Language*, 66, 1–23.

Meir, I., Sandler, W., Padden, C., & Aronoff, M. (2010). Emerging sign languages. In M. Marschark & P. Spencer (eds) *Oxford Handbook of Deaf Studies, Language and Education*, vol. 2. Oxford: Oxford University Press.

Melzi, G., Schick, A., & Kennedy, J. (2011). Narrative participation and elaboration: Two dimensions of maternal elicitation style. *Child Development*, 82(4), 1282–96.

Meltzoff, A. N., & Moore, M. K. (1977). Imitation of facial & manual gestures by human neonates. *Science*, 198, 75–8.

Meltzoff, A. N., & Moore, M. K. (1983). Newborn infants imitate adult facial gestures. *Child Development*, 54, 702–9.

Mendez, M. F. (2000). Language-selective anomia in a bilingual patient. *Journal of Neuropsychiatry and Clinical Neuroscience*, 12, 515–16.

Menn, L. (2001). Comparative aphasiology: Cross-language studies of aphasia. In R. S. Berndt, F. Boller & J. Grafman (eds) *Handbook of Neuropsychology*: vol. 3, *Language and Aphasia* (pp. 51–68). Amsterdam: Elsevier Science.

Meringer, R. (1908). *Aus dem Leben der Sprache*. Berlin: B. Behr.

Meringer, R., & Mayer, C. ([1895] 1978). *Versprechen und Verlesen: Eine Psychologisch-linguistische Studie*. Stuttgart: G. J. Goschen. (Reprint with an introduction by A. Cutler & D. A. Fay, Amsterdam: J. Benjamins.)

Merrell, K. W., Ervin, R. A., & Gimpel, G. A. (2012). *School Psychology for the 21st Century: Foundations and Practices* (2nd edn). New York: Guilford.

Meschyan, G., & Hernandez, A. (2002). Is native-language decoding skill related to second-language learning. *Journal of Educational Psychology*, 94(1), 14–22.

Meunier, H., Fagard, J., Maugard, A., Briseño, M., Fizet, J. et al. (2013). Patterns of hemispheric specialization for a communicative gesture in different primate species. *Developmental Psychobiology*, 55(6), 662–71.

Meyer, A. S., Sleiderink, A. M., & Levelt, W. J. (1998). Viewing and naming objects: Eye movements during noun phrase production. *Cognition*, 66, B25–33.

Meyer, D. E., & Schvaneveldt, R. W. (1971). Facilitation in recognizing pairs of words: Evidence of a dependence between retrieval operations. *Journal of Experimental Psychology*, 90, 227–34.

Meyer, D. E., Schvaneveldt, R. W., & Ruddy, M. G. (1975). Loci of contextual effects on visual word recognition. In P. Rabbitt & S. Dornic (eds) *Attention and Performance V* (pp. 98–118). London: Academic Press.

Meyer, J. (2008). Typology and acoustic strategies of whistled languages: Phonetic comparison and perceptual cues of whistled vowels. *Journal of the International Phonetic Association*, 38, 1, 69–94.

Miles, M. (2000). Signing in the Seraglio: Mutes, dwarfs, and jestures in the Ottoman Court 1500–1700. *Disability & Society*, 15, 115–34.

Miller, D., & Branson, J. (2002). *Damned for their Difference: The Cultural Construction of Deaf People as Disabled: A Sociological History.* Washington, D.C.: Gallaudet University Press.

Miller, G. A. (1956). The magical number seven, plus or minus two: Some limits on our capacity for processing information. *Psychological Review*, 63(2), 81–97.

Miller, N., Taylor, J., Howe, C., & Read, J. (2011). Living with foreign accent syndrome: Insider perspectives. *Aphasiology*, 25(9), 1053–68.

Mills, S. (2003). *Gender and Politeness.* Cambridge: Cambridge University Press.

Minagar, A., Ragheb, J., & Kelley, R. E. (2003). The Edwin Smith surgical papyrus: Description and analysis of the earliest case of aphasia. *Journal of Medical Biography*, 11(2), 114–17.

Minami, M., & McCabe, A. (1995). Rice balls and bear hunts: Japanese and North American family narrative patterns. *Journal of Child Language*, 22, 423–45.

Mindess, A. (2006). *Reading between the Signs: Intercultural Communication for Sign Language Interpreters.* London: Nicholas Brealey.

Miozzo, M., & Caramazza, A. (1999). The selection of determiners in noun phrase production. *Journal of Experimental Psychology: Learning, Memory, and Cognition*, 25, 907–22.

Mishkin, M., & Foroays, D. G. (1952). Word recognition as a function of retinal focus. *Journal of Experimental Psychology*, 43, 43–8.

Mishra, R. K., Pandey, A., & Srinivasan, N. (2011). Revisiting the scrambling complexity hypothesis in sentence processing: A self-paced reading study on anomaly detection and scrambling in Hindi. *Reading and Writing*, 24(6), 709–27.

Mitchell, R. J., Williamson, A. M., Molesworth, B., & Chung, A. Z. (2014). A review of the use of human factors classification frameworks that identify causal factors for adverse events in the hospital setting. *Ergonomics*, 57(10), 1443–72.

Mithen, S. (2006). *The Singing Neanderthals: The Origins of Music, Language, Mind, and Body.* Cambridge, MA: Harvard University Press.

Miyake, K., Hirasawa, T., Koide, T., & Kubota, T. (2012). Epigenetics in autism and other neurodevelopmental diseases. *Advanced Experimental Medicine and Biology*, 724, 91–8.

Miyata, H., Minagawa-Kawai, Y., Watanabe, S., Sasaki, T., & Ueda, K. (2012). Reading speed, comprehension and eye movements while reading Japanese novels: Evidence from untrained readers and cases of speed-reading trainees. *PLoS One*, 7(5), e36091.

Moats, L. C. (2007). *Whole-language High Jinks.* Available at http://edex. s3-us-west-2.amazonaws.com/publication/pdfs/Moats2007_7.pdf.

Moen, I., & Sundet, K. (1996). Production and perception of word tones (pitch accents) in patients with left and right hemisphere damage. *Brain and Language*, 53, 267–81.

Mohamed, M. T., & Clifton, C. J. (2011). Processing temporary syntactic ambiguity: The effect of contextual bias. *Quarterly Journal of Experimental Psychology*, 64(9), 1797–820.

Molfese, V., & Molfese, D. (2002). Environmental and social influences as indexed by brain and behavioral responses. *Annals of Dyslexia*, 52, 121–37.

Moller, A. R. (2006). *Hearing: Anatomy, Physiology, and Disorders of the Auditory System* (2nd edn). New York: Academic Press.

Monetta, L., & Pell, M. D. (2007). Effects of verbal working memory deficits on metaphor comprehension in patients with Parkinson's disease. *Brain & Language*, 101, 80–9.

Moon, C., Cooper, R. P., & Fifer, W. P. (1993). Two day old infants prefer native language. *Infant Behavior and Development*, 16, 495–500.

Moore, B. N., & Bruder, K. (2013). *Philosophy: The Power of Ideas* (9th edn). New York: McGraw-Hill.

Moore, C., & Dunham, P. J. (2016). *Joint Attention: Its Origins and Role in Development*. New York: Psychology Press.

Moore, N. (2010). *Nonverbal Communication: Studies and Applications*. New York: Oxford University Press.

Moray, N. (1969). *Listening and Attention*. New York: Penguin.

Moret-Tatay, C., & Perea, M. (2011). Do serifs provide an advantage in the recognition of written words? *Journal of Cognitive Psychology*, 23(5), 619–24.

Morford, J. P., & MacFarlane, J. (2003). Frequency characteristics of American Sign Language. *Sign Language Studies*, 3(2), 213–25.

Morford, J. P., Wilkinson, E., Villwock, A., Piñar, P., & Kroll, J. F. (2011). When deaf signers read English: Do written words activate their sign translations? *Cognition*, 118(2), 286–92.

Morgan, J., & Demuth, K. (eds) (1996). *Signal to Syntax: Bootstrapping from Speech to Grammar in Early Acquisition*. Mahwah, NJ: Erlbaum.

Moritz, S., Mersmann, K., Kloss, M., Jacobsen, D., Wilke, U. et al. (2001). Hyper-priming in thought-disordered schizophrenic patients. *Psychological Medicine*, 31, 221–9.

Morrell, C. H., Gordon-Salant, S., Pearson, J. D., Brant, L. J., & Fozard, J. L. (1996). Age- and gender-specific reference ranges for hearing level and longitudinal changes in hearing level. *Journal of the Acoustical Society of America*, 100, 1949–67.

Morton, J. (1969). The interaction of information in word recognition. *Psychological Review*, 76, 165–78.

Morton, J. (1979). Facilitation in word recognition: Experiments causing change in the logogen model. In P. A. Kolers, M. E. Wrolstad & H. Bouma (eds). *Processing Visible Language* (pp. 259–68). New York: Plenum Press.

Motley, M. T. (1979). Personality and situational influences upon verbal slips: A laboratory test of freudian and prearticulatory editing hypotheses. *Human Communication Research*, 5(3), 195–202.

Motley, M. T., Camden, C. T., & Baars, B. J. (1981). Toward verifying the assumptions of laboratory induced slips of the tongue: The output-error and editing issues. *Human Communication Research*, 8, 3–15.

Motley, M. T., Camden, C. T., & Baars, B. J. (1982). Covert formulation and editing of anomalies in speech production: Evidence from experimentally elicited slips of the tongue. *Journal of Verbal Learning and Verbal Behaviour*, 21, 578–94.

Moyer, A. (1999). Ultimate attainment in L2 phonology: The critical factors of age, motivation, and instruction. *Studies in Second Language Acquisition*, 21, 81–108.

Moyer, A. (2004). *Age, Accent, and Experience in Second Language Acquisition: An Integrated Approach to Critical Period Inquiry*. Tonawanda, NY: Multilingual Matters.

Moyer, A. (2007). Do language attitudes determine accent? A study of biilnguals in the USA. *Journal of Multilingual and Multicultural Developments*, 28, 1–17.

Moyer, A. (2014). Exceptional outcomes in L2 phonology: The critical factors of learner engagement and self-regulation. *Applied Linguistics*, 35(4), 418–40.

Mozeiko, J., Le, K., Coelho, C., Krueger, F., & Grafman, J. (2011). The relationship of story grammar and executive function following TBI. *Aphasiology*, 25, 826–35.

Mozaffarian, D., Benjamin, E. J., Go, A. S., Arnett. D. K., Blaha, M. J. et al. (2015). Heart disease and stroke statistics 2016 update: A report from the American Heart Association. *Circulation*, 131(4), e29–322.

Mueller, M. (2012). Sri Lanka launches plan to become trilingual nation. The Asia Foundation, Retrieved September 3, 2016 from http://asiafoundation. org/2012/03/28/sri-lanka-launches-plan-to-become-trilingual-nation/.

Mulac, A., Bradac, J. J., & Gibbons, P. (2001). Empirical support for the "gender as culture" hypothesis: An intercultural analysis of male/female language differences. *Human Communication Research*, 27, 121–52.

Müller, F. M. ([1861] 1996). The theoretical stage, and the origin of language. Lecture 9 from Lectures on the Science of Language. Reprinted in R. Harris (ed.) *The Origin of Language* (pp. 7–41). Bristol: Thoemmes Press.

Murfitt, N. (2008). "I was called Dumb Dog": Henry Winkler's happy days as The Fonz were blighted by condition undiagnosed for 35 years. *Daily Mail*. Retrieved January 31, 2013, from www.dailymail.co.uk/health/article-1092477/I-called-Dumb-Dog-Henry-Winklers-happy-days-The-Fonz-blighted-condition-undiagnosed-35-years.html.

Munro, P., & Willmond, C. (1994). *Chickasaw: An Analytical Dictionary*. Norman: University of Oklahoma Press.

Munson, B., & Babel, M. (2007). Loose lips and silver tongues, or, projecting sexual orientations through speech. *Linguistics and Language Compass*, 1(5), 416–69.

Murdoch, B. E., Chenery, H. J., Wilks, V., & Boyle, R. S. (1987). Language disorders in dementia of the Alzheimer type. *Brain and Language*, 31, 122–37.

Murnane, R., Willett, J., & Levy, F. (1995) The growing importance of cognitive skills in wage determination. *Review of Economics and Statistics*, 77(2), 251–66.

Myers, S. (1987). Tone and the structure of words in Shona. Doctoral dissertation, University of Massachusetts, Amherst.

Myers-Scotton, C. (2008). *Multiple Voices: An Introduction to Bilingualism*. Oxford: Wiley-Blackwell.

Naeve Velguth, S. (1996). Prelinguistic Gestures in a Deaf and a Hearing Infant. Doctoral dissertation, University of Minnesota.

Nails, D. (2006). The life of Plato of Athens. In H. A. Benson (ed.) *Companion to Plato* (pp. 1–12). Malden, MA: Blackwell.

Nairne, J. S. (2002). Remembering over the short-term: The case against the standard model. *Annual Review of Psychology*, 53, 53–81.

Nakamura, K. (2002). Polite language usage in mother-infant interactions: A look at language socialization. In Y. Shirai, H. Kobayashi, S. Miyata, K. Nakamura, T. Ogura et al. (eds) *Studies in Language Sciences*, vol. 2 (pp. 175–91). Tokyo: Kuroshio.

Nakamura, K. (2006). The acquisition of linguistic politeness in Japanese. In M. Nakayama, R. Mazuka, Y. Shirai & P. Li (eds) *The Handbook of East Asian Psycholinguistics*, vol. 2 (pp. 110–15). Cambridge: Cambridge University Press.

Nation, K., & Snowling, M. J. (1997). Assessing reading difficulties: The validity and utility of current measures of reading skill. *British Journal of Educational Psychology*, 67, 359–70.

Nation, P., & Waring, R. (1997). Vocabulary size, text coverage, and word lists. In N. Schmitt & M. McCarthy (eds) *Vocabulary: Description, Acquisition, Pedagogy* (pp. 6–19). New York: Cambridge University Press.

National Down Syndrome Society (n.d.). Down syndrome facts. Retrieved August 12, 2015 from www.ndss.org/Down-Syndrome/Down-Syndrome-Facts/.

National Early Literacy Panel (2008). *Developing Early Literacy: Report of the National Early Literacy Panel*. Washington, D.C.: National Institute for Literacy.

National Institute on Deafness and Other Communication Disorders (2017). Cochlear implants. Retrieved July 9, 2017 from www.nidcd.nih.gov/health/cochlear-implants.

National Institute of Mental Health (n.d.). Schizophrenia. Retrieved April 21, 2017 from www.nimh.nih.gov/health/topics/schizophrenia/index.shtml.

National Institute of Neurological Disorders and Stroke (n.d.). Dyslexia Information Page. Retrieved September 23, 2016 from www.ninds.nih.gov/disorders/dyslexia/dyslexia.htm.

National Institute of Neurological Disorders and Stroke (n.d.). Huntington's Disease Information Page. Retrieved 19 July 2016 from www.ninds.nih.gov/Disorders/All-Disorders/Huntingtons-Disease-Information-Page.

National Institute of Neurological Disorders and Stroke (n.d.). Asperger's Syndrome Information Page. Retrieved April 21, 2017 from www.ninds.nih.gov/Disorders/All-Disorders/Asperger-Syndrome-Information-Page.

National Institutes of Health (2017). Age-related hearing loss. Retrieved July 14, 2017 from www.nidcd.nih.gov/health/age-related-hearing-loss.

National Reading Panel (2000). *Teaching Children to Read*. Retrieved July 23, 2017 from www.nichd.nih.gov/publications/pubs/nrp/Documents/report.pdf.

National Stroke Association (n.d.). Uncontrollable risk factors. Available at www.stroke.org/understand-stroke/preventing-stroke/uncontrollable-risk-factors.

Nationmaster (n.d.). Finland language stats. Retrieved July 17, 2017 from www.nationmaster.com/country-info/stats/Language/English/Conversational-English-prevalence.

Navarro, J., & Karlins, M. (2008). *What Every Body is Saying*. New York: William Morrow Paperbacks.

Nebes, R. D. (1989). Semantic memory in Alzheimer's disease. *Psychological Bulletin*, 106, 377–94.

Neisser, U. (1967). *Cognitive Psychology*. New York: Appleton-Century-Crofts.

Nelson, N. L., & Russell, J. A. (2011). Preschoolers' use of dynamic facial, bodily, and vocal cues to emotion. *Journal of Experimental Child Psychology*, 110(1), 52–61.

Nemeth, D., Dye, C. D., Sefcsik, T., Janacsek, K., Turi, Z. et al. (2012). Language deficits in pre-symptomatic Huntington's disease: Evidence from Hungarian. *Brain and Language*, 121(3), 248–53.

Nevala, A. E. (2000). Not everyone is sold on the cochlear implant. *Seattle Post-Intelligencer*, September 28.

Nevins, A., Pesetsky, D., & Rodrigues, C. (2009). Evidence and argumentation: A reply to Everett (2009). *Language*, 85(3), 671–81.

Newkirk, D., Klima, E. S., Pedersen, C. C., & Bellugi, U. (1980). Linguistic evidence from slips of the hand. In V. Fromkin (ed.) *Errors in Linguistic Performance: Slips of the Tongue, Ear, Pen, and Hand*. New York: Academic Press.

Newman, R. S. (2004). Perceptual restoration in children versus adults. *Applied Psycholinguistics*, 25(4), 481–93.

Newman, R. S. (2006). Perceptual restoration in toddlers. *Perception & Psychophysics*, 68(4), 625–42.

Newman, S., Malaia, E., & Seo, R. (2014). Does degree of handedness in a group of right-handed individuals affect language comprehension? *Brain and Cognition*, 86, 98–103.

Newport, E. L., & Ashbrook, E. (1977). The emergence of semantic relations in American Sign Language. *Papers and Reports on Child Language*, 13, 16–21.

Newport, E. L., Gleitman, H., & Gleitman, L. R. (1977). Mother, I'd rather do it myself: Some effects and noneffects of maternal speech style. In C. Snow & C. Ferguson (eds) *Talking to Children: Language Input and Acquisition*. Cambridge: Cambridge University Press.

Newschaffer, C. J., Croen, L. A., Daniels, J. et al. (2007). The epidemiology of autism spectrum disorders. *Annual Review of Public Health*, 28, 235–58.

Nicol, J., & Swinney, D. (1989). The role of structure in co-reference assignment during sentence comprehension. *Journal of Psycholinguistic Research*, 18, 5–19.

Niema, J., & Laine, M. (2012). Lexical, inflectional, and clitic morphology: Evidence from an agrammatic aphasic individual. In R. Bastiaanse & C. K. Thompson (eds) *Perspectives on Agrammatism* (pp. 106–19). New York: Psychology Press.

Nilipour, R., & Ashayeri, H. (1989). Alternating antagonism between two languages with successive recovery of a third in a trilingual aphasic patient. *Brain and Language*, 36, 23–48.

Nip, I. S., & Green, J. R. (2013). Increases in cognitive and linguistic processing primarily account for increases in speaking rate with age. *Child Development*, 84(4), 1324–37.

Niparko, J. K. (2009). *Cochlear Implants: Principles and Practices*. Philadelphia, PA: Lippincott, Williams & Wilkins.

Nixon, P., Lazarova, J., Hodinott-Hill, I., Gough, P., & Passingham, R. (2004). The inferior frontal gyrus & phonological processing: An investigation using rTMS. *Journal of Cognitive Neuroscience*, 16, 289–300.

Noble, K. G., Norman, M. F., & Farah, M. J. (2005). Neurocognitive correlates of socioeconomic status in kindergarten children. *Developmental Science*, 8(1), 74–87.

Nolan, C. (2000). *Memento*. [Motion Picture]. England: Summit Entertainment.

Noordman, L. G., & Vonk, W. (2015). Inferences in discourse, psychology of. In J. D. Wright (ed.) *International Encyclopedia of the Social and Behavioral Sciences*, vol. 12 (2nd edn) (pp. 37–44). Amsterdam: Elsevier.

Nooteboom, S. G. (1967). *Some Regularities in Phonemic Speech Errors. Annual Progress Report, 2.* Eindhoven: Instituut voor Perceptie Onderzoek.

Nooteboom, S. G. (1969). The tongue slips into patterns. In A. G. Sciarone et al. (eds) *Nomen: Leyden Studies in Linguistics and Phonetics.* The Hague: Mouton.

Nooteboom, S. G. (1973). The perceptual reality of some prosodic durations. *Journal of Phonetics,* 1, 25–45.

Nooteboom, S. G. (1980). Speaking and unspeaking: Detection and correction of phonological and lexical errors of speech. In V. A. Fromkin (ed.) *Errors in Linguistic Performance: Slips of the Tongue, Ear, Pen, and Hand* (pp. 87–96). New York: Academic Press.

Nooteboom, S. G. (1981). Speech rate and segmental perception or the role of words in phoneme identification. In T. Myers, J. Laver & J. Anderson (eds) *The Cognitive Representation of Speech* (pp. 143–50). Amsterdam: North-Holland.

Nooteboom, S. G. (2005). Listening to one-self: Monitoring speech production. In R. Hartsuiker, Y. Bastiaanse, A. Postma & F. Wijnen (eds) *Phonological Encoding and Monitoring in Normal and Pathological Speech* (pp. 167–86). Hove: Psychology Press.

Norbury, C. F. (2014). Atypical pragmatic development. In D. Matthews (ed.) *Pragmatic Development in First Language Acquisition* (pp. 343–61). Amsterdam: John Benjamins.

Norman, J. (1988). *Chinese.* Cambridge: Cambridge University Press.

Nottebohm, F. (1969). The song of the chingolo, Zonotrichia capensis, in Argentina: Description and evaluation of a system of dialects. *Condor,* 71(3), 299–315.

Nozari, N., & Dell, G. S. (2009). More on lexical bias: How efficient can a "lexical editor" be? *Journal of Memory and Language,* 60(2), 291–307.

Nunn, J. F. (1996). *Ancient Egyptian Medicine.* London: British Museum.

Oakes, A., Kover, S. T., & Abbeduto, L. (2013). Language comprehension profiles of young adolescents with Fragile X syndrome. *American Journal of Speech-Language Pathology,* 22(4), 615–26.

Oakhill, J., & Garnham A. (eds) (1996). *Mental Models in Cognitive Science.* Hove: Psychology Press.

O'Brien, E. J., & Cook, A. E. (2016). Coherence threshold and the continuity of processing: The RI-Val model of comprehension. *Discourse Processes,* 53(5/6), 326–38.

Obusek, C. J., & Warren, R. M. (1973). Relation of the verbal transformation and phonemic restoration effects. *Cognitive Psychology,* 5, 97–107.

Oden, G. C., & Massaro, D. W. (1978). Integration of featural information in speech perception. *Psychological Review,* 85, 172–91.

Oetting, J. B., & Hadley, P. A. (2009). Morphosyntax in child language disorders. In R. G. Schwartz (ed.) *Handbook of Child Language Disorders* (pp. 341–64). New York: Psychology Press.

Öhman, L., Eriksson, A., & Granhag, P. A. (2013). Enhancing adults' and children's earwitness memory: Examining three types of interviews. *Psychiatry, Psychology and Law,* 20(2), 216–29.

Oldfield, R. (1971). The assessment and analysis of handedness: The Edinburgh inventory. *Neuropsychologia,* 9, 97–113.

Oldfield, R. C., & Wingfield, A. (1965). Response latencies in naming objects. *Quarterly Journal of Experimental Psychology*, 4, 272–81.

Oliver, B. R., Barker, E. D., Mandy, W. P., Skuse, D. H., & Maughan, B. (2011). Social cognition and conduct problems: A developmental approach. *Journal of the American Academy of Child Adolescent Psychiatry*, 50(4), 385–94.

Oller, D. K., & Eilers, R. E. (2002). *Language and Literacy in Bilingual Children*. Clevedon: Multilingual Matters.

Oller, D. K., Eilers, R. E., Urbano, R., & Cobo-Lewis, A. B. (1997). Development of precursors to speech in infants exposed to two languages. *Journal of Child Language*, 27, 407–25.

Olsen, R. K., Pangelinan, M. M., Bogulski, C., Chakravarty, M. M., Luk, G. et al. (2015). The effect of lifelong bilingualism on regional grey and white matter volume. *Brain Research*, 1612, 128–39.

O'Neill, J. J. (2006). *Prodigal Genius: The Life of Nikola Tesla*. New York: Cosimo.

Ong, W. J. (1982). *Orality and Literacy: The Technologizing of the Word*. London: Methuen.

Onnela, J., Waber, B. N., Pentland, A., Schnorf, S., & Lazer, D. (2014). Using sociometers to quantify social interaction patterns. *Scientific Reports*, 4, 5604.

Oppenheim, G. M. (2012). The case for subphonemic attenuation in inner speech: Comment on Corley, Brocklehurst, and Moat (2011). *Journal of Experimental Psychology*, 38(2), 502.

Oppenheim, G. M., & Dell, G. S. (2008). Inner speech slips exhibit lexical bias, but not the phonemic similarity effect. *Cognition*, 106(1), 528–37.

O'Seaghdha, P. G., Chen, J.-Y., & Chen, T.-M. (2010). Proximate units in word production: Phonological encoding begins with syllables in Mandarin Chinese but with segments in English. *Cognition*, 115, 282–302.

Osgood, C. E., & Seboek, T. A. (eds) (1954). *Psycholinguistics: A Survey of Theory and Research Problems* (pp. 93–101). Bloomington, IN: Indiana University Press.

Oulasvirta, A., & Saariluoma, P. (2006). Surviving task interruptions: Investigating the implications of long-term working memory theory. *International Journal of Human-Computer Studies*, 64, 941–61.

Oyama, S. (1976). A sensitive period for the acquisition of a nonnative phonological system. *Journal of Psycholinguistic Research*, 5(3), 261–83.

Oyer, H. J., Hall, B. J., & Haas, W. H. (2000). *Speech, Language, and Hearing Disorders*. Boston: Allyn & Bacon.

Özçaliskan, S., & Goldin-Meadow, S. (2006). X IS LIKE Y: The emergence of similarity mappings in children's early speech and gesture. In G. Kristianssen, M. Achard, R. Dirven & F. Ruiz de Mendoza (eds) *Cognitive Linguistics: Foundations and Fields of Application* (pp. 229–60). Berlin: Mouton de Gruyter.

Paap, K. R., & Greenberg, Z. I. (2013). There is no coherent evidence for a bilingual advantage in executive processing. *Cognitive Psychology*, 66(2), 232–58.

Paap, K. R., & Liu, Y. (2014). Conflict resolution in sentence processing is the same for bilinguals and monolinguals: The role of confirmation bias in testing for bilingual advantages. *Journal of Neurolinguistics*, 27(1), 50–74.

Padden, C., & Humphries, T. (1988). *Deaf in America: Voices from a Culture*. Cambridge, MA: Harvard University Press.

Padden, C., & Humphries, T. (2006). *Inside Deaf Culture*. Cambridge, MA: Harvard University Press.

Paivio, A. (1971). *Imagery and Verbal Processes*. New York: Holt, Rinehart & Winston.

Paivio, A., Yuille, J. C., & Madigan, S. A. (1968). Concreteness, imagery, and meaningfulness values for 925 nouns. *Journal of Experimental Psychology*, 76(1), 1–25.

Palaniyappan, L., Crow, T. J., Hough, M., Voets, N. L., Liddle, P. F. et al. (2013). Gyrification of Broca's region is anomalously lateralized at onset of schizophrenia in adolescence and regresses at 2 year follow-up. *Schizophrenia Research*, 147(1), 39–45.

Pallier, C., Dehaene, S., Poline, J.-B., LeBihan, D., Argenti, A.-M. et al. (2003). Brain imaging of language plasticity in adopted adults: Can a second language replace the first? *Cerebral Cortex*, 13, 155–61.

Palmer, F. R. (2001). *Mood and Modality*. Cambridge: Cambridge University Press.

Papadatou-Pastou, M., & Sáfár, A. (2016). Handedness prevalence in the deaf: Meta-analyses. *Neuroscience & Biobehavioral Reviews*, 60, 98–114.

Papadatou-Pastou, M., Martin, M., Munafò, M. R., & Jones, G. V. (2008). Sex differences in left-handedness: A meta-analysis of 144 studies. *Psychological Bulletin*, 134(5), 677–99.

Paradis, J., & Genesee, F. (1996). Syntactic acquisition in bilingual children: Autonomous or interdependent? *Studies in Second Language Acquisition*, 18, 1–25.

Paradis, M., & Goldblum, M. C. (1989). Selective crossed aphasia in a trilingual aphasic patient followed by reciprocal antagonism. *Brain and Language*, 36, 62–75.

Pardo, J. S., & Remez, R. E. (2006). The perception of speech. In M. Traxler and M. A. Gernsbacher (eds) *The Handbook of Psycholinguistics* (2nd edn) (pp. 201–48). New York: Academic Press.

Parkinson's Foundation (n.d.). Statistics. www.parkinson.org/Understanding-Parkinsons/Causes-and-Statistics/Statistics.

Partee, M. H. (1972). Plato's theory of language. *Foundations of Language*, 8(1), 113–32.

Patrick, C. J. (2005). *Handbook of Psychopathy*. New York: Guilford Press.

Patson, N. D., & Husband, E. M. (2016). Misinterpretations in agreement and agreement attraction. *Quarterly Journal of Experimental Psychology*, 69(5), 950–71.

Patson, N. D., Darowski, E. S., Moon, N., & Ferreira, F. (2009). Lingering misinterpretations in garden-path sentences: Evidence from a paraphrasing task. *Journal of Experimental Psychology: Learning, Memory, and Cognition*, 35(1), 280–5.

Patterson, D. (2009). Molecular genetic analysis of Down syndrome. *Human Genetics*, 126, 195–214.

Patterson, J. (2004). Comparing bilingual and monolingual toddlers' expressive vocabulary size: Revisiting Rescorla and Achenbach (2002). *Journal of Speech, Language and Hearing Research*, 47, 1213–15.

Patterson, J. L., & Pearson, B. Z. (2004). Bilingual lexical development: Influences, contexts, and processes. In B. Goldstein (ed.) *Bilingual Language Development and Disorders in Spanish-English Speakers* (pp. 77–104). Baltimore: Paul Brookes.

Paul, R., & Norbury, C. (2012). *Language Disorders from Infancy through Adolescence*. St. Louis, MI: Elsevier.

Peal, E., and Lambert, W. E. (1962). The relation of bilingualism to intelligence. *Psychological Monographs*, 76(27), 1–23.

Pearson, B. Z., & Fernández, S. (1994). Patterns of interaction in the lexical development in two languages of bilingual infants. *Language Learning*, 44, 617–53.

Pearson, B. Z., Fernández, S., & Oller, D. K. (1993). Lexical development in simultaneous bilingual infants: Comparison to monolinguals. *Language Learning*, 43, 93–120.

Pell, M. D. (1999). The temporal organization of affective and non-affective speech in patients with right-hemisphere infarcts. *Cortex: A Journal Devoted to the Study of the Nervous System and Behavior*, 35(4), 455–77.

Pell, M. D. (2006). Cerebral mechanisms for understanding emotional prosody in speech. *Brain and Language*, 96(2), 221–34.

Pellis, S. M., & Pellis, V. C. (2010). Social play, social grooming, and the regulation of social relationships. In A. V. Kalueff (ed.) *Neurobiology of Grooming Behavior* (pp. 66–87). New York: Cambridge University Press.

Penfield, W. (1958). Some mechanisms of consciousness discovered during electrical stimulation of the brain. *Proceedings of the National Academy of Sciences U.S.A*, 44, 51–66.

Penfield, W. (1972). The electrode, the brain & the mind. *Journal of Neurology*, 201, 297–309.

Penfield, W., & Roberts, L. ([1959] 2014). *Speech and Brain Mechanisms*. Princeton, NJ: Princeton University Press.

Penn, A. (Director) (1962). *The Miracle Worker* [Motion picture]. United States: United Artists.

Pennebaker, J. W., & King, L. A. (1999). Linguistic styles: Language use as an individual difference. *Journal of Personality and Social Psychology*, 77, 1296–312.

Penttinen, M., & Huovinen, E. (2011). The early development of sight-reading skills in adulthood: A study of eye movements. *Journal of Research in Music Education*, 59(2), 196–220.

Penttinen, M., Huovinen, E., & Ylitalo, A. (2013). Silent music reading: Amateur musicians' visual processing and descriptive skill. *Musicae Scientiae*, 17(2), 198–216.

Pepperberg, I. M. (1981). Functional vocalizations by an African grey parrot (Psittacus erithacus). *Zeitschrift für Tierpschologie*, 55, 139–60.

Pepperberg, I. M. (1983). Cognition in the African grey parrot: Preliminary evidence for auditory/vocal comprehension of the class concept. *Animal Learning and Behavior*, 11, 179–85.

Pepperberg, I. M. (1987). Acquisition of the same/different concept by an African grey parrot (Psittacus erithacus): Learning with respect to categories of color, shape, and material. *Animal Learning and Behavior*, 14, 423–32.

Pepperberg, I. M. (1998). Talking with Alex: Logic and speech in parrots. *Scientific American Presents: Exploring Intelligence*, 9(4), 60–5.

Pepperberg, I. (2009). *Alex and Me: How a Scientist and a Parrot Discovered a Hidden World of Animal Intelligence and Formed a Deep Bond in the Process*. New York: Harper Paperbacks.

Perea, M., Vergara-Martínez, M., & Gomez, P. (2015). Resolving the locus of cAsE aLtErNaTiOn effects in visual word recognition: Evidence from masked priming. *Cognition*, 142, 39–43.

Perez, E., Santiago, J., Palma, A., & O'Seaghdha, P. G. (2007). Perceptual bias in speech error data collection: Insights from Spanish speech errors. *Journal of Psycholinguistic Research*, 36(3), 207–35.

Perfetti, C. A., Liu, Y., & Tan, L. H. (2005). The lexical constituency model: Some implications of research on Chinese for general theories of reading. *Psychological Review*, 112, 43–59.

Perovic, A. (2006). Syntactic deficit in Down syndrome: More evidence for the modular organization of language. *Lingua*, 116(10), 1616–30.

Perovic, A., Modyanova, K., & Wexler, K. (2013). Comprehension of reflexive and personal pronouns in children with autism: A syntactic or pragmatic deficit? *Applied Psycholinguistics*, 34(4), 813–35.

Perry, L. K., Perlman, M., & Lupyan, G. (2015). Iconicity in English and Spanish and its relation to lexical category and age of acquisition. *PLoS ONE*, 10(9), e0137147.

Peters, P. (2004). *The Cambridge Guide to English Usage*. Cambridge: Cambridge University Press.

Petersen, N. (2008). *Embracing the Edge*. Bothell, WA: Book Publishers Network.

Peterson, C., & McCabe, A. (1983). *Developmental Psycholinguistics: Three Ways of Looking at a Child's Narrative*. New York: Plenum Press.

Peterson, L. R., & Peterson, M. J. (1959). Short-term retention of individual verbal items. *Journal of Experimental Psychology*, 58(3), 193–8.

Petitto, L. A. (2000). The acquisition of natural signed languages: Lessons in the nature of human language and its biological foundations. In C. Chamberlain, J. P. Morford & R. I. Mayberry (eds) *Language Acquisition by Eye* (pp. 41–50). Mahwah, NJ: Lawrence Erlbaum.

Petitto, L. A., & Kovelman, I. (2003). The bilingual paradox: How signing-speaking bilingual children help us to resolve it and teach us about the brain's mechanisms underlying all language acquisition. *Learning Languages*, 8(3), 5–19.

Petitto, P. F., & Marentette, L. A. (1991). Babbling in the manual mode: Evidence for the ontogeny of language. *Science*, 251(5000), 1493–6.

Petitto, L. A., Katerelos, M., Levy, B. G., Gauna, K., Tetreault, K. et al. (2001). Bilingual signed and spoken language acquisition from birth: Implications for the mechanisms underlying early bilingual language acquisition. *Journal of Child Language*, 28, 453–96.

Petrie, A. R. (1975). *Alexander Graham Bell*. Don Mills, Ontario: Fitzhenry & Whiteside.

Pfost, M., Hattie, J., Dörfler, T., & Artelt, C. (2014). Individual differences in reading development: A review of 25 years of empirical research on Matthew effects in reading. *Review of Educational Research*, 84(2), 203–44.

Pfungst, O. ([1911] 1965). *Clever Hans (The Horse of Mr. von Osten): A Contribution to Experimental Animal and Human Psychology* (trans. C. L. Rahn). New York: Henry Holt.

Phillips, F. (Director/Writer/Producer) (2009). *Written in the Wind*. Retrieved June 18, 2017 from www.francescaphillips.com/whistling-language.

Piaget, J. (1957). *Construction of Reality in the Child*. London: Routledge & Kegan Paul.

Piaget, J. (1959). *The Language and Thought of the Child*. New York: Psychology Press.

Piaget, J. (1967). *Six Psychological Studies*. New York: Random House.

Pickering, M. J., & Ferreira, V. S. (2008). Structural priming: A critical review. *Psychological Bulletin*, 134, 427–59.

Pierce, J. R. et al. (1966). *Language and Machines: Computers in Translation and Linguistics*. ALPAC report. Washington, D.C.: National Academy of Sciences/National Research Council.

Pilley, J. W. (2013). Border collie comprehends sentences containing a prepositional object, verb, and direct object. *Learning and Motivation*, 44(4), 229–40.

Pilley, J. W, & Reid, A. K. (2011). Border collie comprehends object names as verbal referents. *Behavior Processes*, 86, 184–95.

Pinker, S. ([1994] 2007). *The Language Instinct*. New York: Harper.

Pinker, S. (2007). *The Stuff of Thought: Language as a Window into Human Nature*. New York: Penguin.

Pisoni, D. B. (1993). Long-term memory in speech perception: Some new findings on speaker variability, speaking rate, and perceptual learning. *Speech Communications*, 13, 109–25.

Plotnik, J. M., de Waal, F. B., & Reiss, D. (2006). Self-recognition in an Asian elephant. *Proceedings of the National Academy of Sciences of the United States of America*, 103(45), 17053–7.

Pohl, M. E., Pope, K. O., & von Nagy, C. (2002). Olmec origins of Mesoamerican writing. *Science*, 298(5600),1984–7.

Pollatsek, A., & Treiman, R. (2015). *Oxford Handbook of Reading*. Oxford: Oxford University Press.

Pollatsek, A., Bertram, R., & Hyönä, J. (2011). Processing novel and lexicalised Finnish compound words. *Journal of Cognitive Psychology*, 23(7), 795–810.

Pollatsek, A., Hyönä, J., & Bertram, R. (2000). The role of morphological constituents in reading Finnish compound words. *Journal of Experimental Psychology*, 26(2), 820–33.

Pollatsek, A., Rayner, K., & Balota, D. A. (1986). Inferences about eye movement control from the perceptual span in reading. *Perception & Psychophysics*, 40, 123–30.

Pollatsek, A., Reichle, E. D., & Rayner, K. (2006). Tests of the E-Z Reader model: Exploring the interface between cognition and eye movements. *Cognitive Psychology*, 52, 1–56.

Pollatsek, A., Lesch, M., Morris, R. K., & Rayner, K. (1992). Phonological codes are used in integrating information across saccades in word identification and reading. *Journal of Experimental Psychology: Human Perception and Performance*, 18(1), 148–62.

Poplack, S. (1980). Sometimes I'll start a sentence in Spanish y termino en español: Toward a typology of code-switching. *Linguistics*, 18(7/8), 581–618.

Poplack, S. (1981). Syntactic structure and social function of code-switching. In R. Duran (ed.) *Latino Language and Communicative Behavior* (pp. 169–84). Norwood, NJ: Ablex.

Potter, B. (2012). Salma Hayek: "I'm Dyslexic, Short and Chubby." Retrieved February 7, 2013, from www.entertainmentwise.com/news/90155/Salma-Hayek-Im-Dyslexic-Short-And-Chubby.

Powell, B. B. (2009). *Writing: Theory and History of the Technology of Civilization*. Malden, MA: Wiley-Blackwell.

Powell, R. A., Digdon, N., Harris, B., & Smithson, C. (2014). Correcting the record on Watson, Raynor and Little Albert: Albert Barger as "Psychology's lost boy." *American Psychologist*, 69(6), 600–11.

Premack, D., & Premack, A. J. (1983). *The Mind of an Ape*. New York: Norton.

Premack, D., & Woodruff, G. (1978). Does the chimpanzee have a theory of mind? *Behavioral and Brain Sciences*, 1(4), 515–26.

Presnell, L. (1973). Hearing-impaired children's comprehension and production of syntax in oral language. *Journal of Speech and Hearing Research*, 16, 12–21.

Pressley, M., & Hilden, K. (2005). Teaching reading comprehension. In A. McKeough, L. M. Phillips, V. Timmons & J. L. Lupart (eds) *Understanding Literacy Development* (pp. 49–64). Mahwah, NJ: Erlbaum.

Price, I. K., Witzel, N., & Witzel, J. (2015). Orthographic and phonological form interference during silent reading. *Journal of Experimental Psychology: Learning, Memory, and Cognition*, 41(6), 1628–47.

Price, J. R., Roberts, J. E., Hennon, E. A., Berni, M. C., Anderson, K. L. et al. (2008). Syntactic complexity during conversation of boys with Fragile X syndrome and Down syndrome. *Journal of Speech, Language, and Hearing Research*, 51(1), 3–15.

Priddle, T. H., & Crow, T. J. (2013). The protocadherin 11X/Y (PCDH11X/Y) gene pair as determinant of cerebral asymmetry in modern Homo sapiens. *Annals of the New York Academy of Sciences*, 1288(1), 36–47.

Prins, D., Main, V., & Wampler, S. (1997). Lexicalization in adults who stutter. *Journal of Speech, Language, and Hearing Research*, 40, 373–84.

Prior, H., Schwarz, A., & Güntürkün, O. (2008). Mirror-induced behavior in the magpie (Pica pica): Evidence of self-recognition. *PLoS Biology*, 6(8), e202.

Profita, J., & Bidder, T. G. (1988). Perfect pitch. *American Journal of Medical Genetics*, 29, 763–71.

Pronko, N. H. (1946). Language and psycholinguistics: A review. *Psychological Bulletin*, 43, 189–239.

Prufer, K., Munch, K., Hellmann, I., Akagi, K., Miller, J. R. et al. (2012). The bonobo genome compared with the chimpanzee and human genomes. *Nature*, 486, 527–31.

Pujol, J., Deus, J., Losilla, J. M., & Capdevila, A. (1999). Cerebral lateralization of language in normal left handed people studied by functional MRI. *Neurology*, 52, 1038–43.

Pun, J. K., Chan, E. A., Murray, K. A., Slade, D., & Matthiessen, C. M. (2017). Complexities of emergency communication: Clinicians' perceptions of communication challenges in a trilingual emergency department. *Journal of Clinical Nursing*, 26(21/22), 3396–407.

Quarrington, B., Conway, J., & Siegel, N. (1962). An experimental study of some properties of stuttered words. *Journal of Speech and Hearing Research*, 5, 387–94.

Quigley, S., & King, C. (eds) (1982). *Reading Milestones: Level 5*. Beaverton, OR: Dormac.

Quine, W. V. ([1960] 2016). *Word and Object*. Cambridge, MA: MIT Press.

Raffaele, P. (2006). The smart and swinging bonobo. *Smithsonian*, 37(8), 66.

Rafferty, E. A. (1986). *Second Language Study and Basic Skills in Louisiana*. Baton Rouge: Louisiana Department of Education.

Ramachandran, V. S., & Blakeslee, S. (1998). *Phantoms in the Brain: Probing the Mysteries of the Human Mind*. New York: William Morrow.

Ramachandran, V. S., Rogers-Ramachandran, D. C., & Stewart, M. (1992). Perceptual correlates of massive cortical reorganization. *Science*, 258(5085), 1159–60.

Ramsey, S. R. (1987). *The Languages of China*. Princeton, NJ: Princeton University Press.

Ramus, F., & Fisher, S. E. (2009). Genetics of language. In M. S. Gazzaniga, E. Bizzi, L. M. Chalupa, S. T. Grafton, T. F. Heatherton et al. (eds) *The Cognitive Neurosciences*, 4th edn (pp. 855–71). Cambridge, MA: MIT.

Ratiu, P., & Talos, I. F. (2004). Images in clinical medicine: The tale of Phineas Gage, digitally remastered. *Journal of Neurotrauma*, 21, 637–43.

Rauscher, F. H., Krauss, R. M., & Chen, Y. (1996). Gesture, speech, and lexical access: The role of lexical movements in speech production. *Psychological Science*, 7(4), 226–31.

Rayner, K. (1975). Parafoveal identification during a fixation in reading. *Acta Psychologica*, 39, 271–82.

Rayner, K. (1978). Eye movement latencies for parafoveally presented words. *Bulletin of the Psychonomic Society*, 11(1), 13–16.

Rayner, K. (1986). Eye movements and the perceptual span in beginning and skilled readers. *Journal of Experimental Child Psychology*, 41, 211–36.

Rayner, K. (1998). Eye movements in reading and information processing: 20 years of research. *Psychological Bulletin*, 124, 372–422.

Rayner, K., & Duffy, S. A. (1986). Lexical complexity and fixation times in reading: Effects of word frequency, verb complexity, and lexical ambiguity. *Memory & Cognition*, 14, 191–201.

Rayner, K., Slattery, T. J., & Belanger, N. N. (2010). Eye movements, the perceptual span, and reading speed. *Psychonomic Bulletin & Review*, 17(6), 834–9.

Rayner, K., Pollatsek, A., Ashby, J., & Clifton, C. (2012). *The Psychology of Reading* (2nd edn). New York: Psychology Press.

Rayner, K., Foorman, B., Perfetti, C. A., Pesetsky, D., & Seidenberg, M. S. (2001). How psychological science informs the teaching of reading. *Psychological Science in the Public Interest*, 2(2), 31–74.

Rayner, K., Inhoff, A. W., Morrison, R. E., Slowiaczek, M. L., & Bertera, J. H. (1981). Masking of foveal and parafoveal vision during eye fixations in reading. *Journal of Experimental Psychology: Human Perception and Performance*, 7, 167–79.

Rayner, K., Sereno, S. C., Morris, R. K., Schmauder, A. R., & Clifton, C., Jr. (1989). Eye movements and on-line language comprehension processes. *Language and Cognitive Processes*, 4, SI21–49.

Raza, M. H., Mattera, R., Morell, R., Sainz, E., Rahn, R. et al. (2015). Association between rare variants in AP4E1, a component of intracellular trafficking, and persistent stuttering. *American Journal of Human Genetics*, 97(5), 715.

Reardon, S. F. (2011). The widening academic-achievement gap between the rich and the poor: New evidence and possible explanations. In G. Duncan and R. J. Murnane (eds) *Whither Opportunity: Rising Inequality, Schools, and Children's Life Chances*. New York: Russell Sage Foundation.

Reardon, S. F., & Bischoff, K. (2011). Income inequality and income segregation. *American Journal of Sociology*, 116(4), 1092–153.

Reardon, S. F., Valentino, R. A., & Shores, K. A. (2013). Patterns of literacy among U.S. students. *The Future of Children*, 23(2), 17–37.

Reder, S. M. (1973). On-line monitoring of eye position signals in contingent and noncontingent paradigms. *Behaviour Research Methods & Instrumentation*, 5, 218–28.

Rehm, H. L., Williamson, R. E., Kenna, M. A., Corey, D. P., & Korf, B. R. (2003). *Understanding the Genetics of Deafness: A Guide for Patients and Families*. Cambridge, MA: Harvard Medical School Center for Hereditary Deafness.

Reicher, G. M. (1969). Perceptual recognition as a function of meaningfulness of stimulus material. *Journal of Experimental Psychology*, 81(2), 275–80.

Reichle, E. D., Rayner, K., & Pollatsek, A. (2003). The EZ Reader model of eye-movement control in reading: Comparisons to other models. *Behavioral and Brain Sciences*, 26(4), 445–76.

Reiss, D., & Marino, L. (2001). Mirror self-recognition in the bottlenose dolphin: A case of cognitive convergence. *Proceedings of the National Academy of Sciences*, 98(10), 5937–42.

Rescorla, L., & Achenbach, T. (2002). Use of the Language Development Survey in a national probability sample of children from 18 to 35 months old. *Journal of Speech, Language, and Hearing Research*, 45, 733–43.

Reyes-Alami, C. (2003). Interview with a person who clutters. Retrieved August 25, 2017 from www.mnsu.edu/comdis/kuster/cluttering/camil.html.

Rialland, A. (2005). Phonological and phonetic aspects of whistled languages. *Phonology*, 22(2), 237–71.

Ricciardelli, L. A. (1992). Bilingualism and cognitive development: A review of past and recent findings. *Journal of Creative Behavior*, 26, 242–54.

Rice, M. L. (1997). Specific language impairments: In search of diagnostic markers and genetic contributions. *Mental Retardation and Developmental Disabilities Research Reviews*, 3, 350–7.

Richards, J. C., & Rodgers, T. S. (1987). Through the looking glass: Trends and directions in language teaching. *RELC Journal*, 18(2), 45–73.

Richards, J. C., & Rodgers, T. S. (2001). *Approaches and Methods in Language Teaching* (2nd edn). Cambridge: Cambridge University Press.

Richgels, D. (1995). Invented spelling ability and printed word learning in kindergarten. *Reading Research Quarterly*, 30, 96–109.

Ridley, M. (2003). *Nature via Nurture: Genes, Experience, and What Makes Us Human*. New York: HarperCollins.

Riley, J. R., Greggers, U., Smith, A. D., Reynolds, D. R., & Menzel, R. (2005). The flight paths of honeybees recruited by the waggle dance. *Nature*, 435(7039), 205–7.

Ring, M., & Clahsen, H. (2005). Distinct patterns of language impairment in Down's syndrome and Williams syndrome: The case of syntactic chains. *Journal of Neurolinguistics*, 18, 479–501.

Ripich, D., & Terrell, B. (1988). Patterns of discourse cohesion and coherence in Alzheimer's Disease. *Journal of Speech and Hearing Disorders*, 53, 8–15.

Rischel, J. ([1970] 2009). Consonant gradation: A problem in Danish phonology and morphology. In J. Rischel, *Sound Structure in Language* (pp. 26–43). Oxford: Oxford University Press.

Ritti, A. (1973). Social Junctions of Children's Speech. Doctoral dissertation, Columbia University, Teachers College.

Roach, P. (2000). *English Phonetics and Phonology: A Practical Course*. Cambridge: Cambridge University Press.

Roberti, J. W. (2004). A review of behavioral and biological correlates of sensation-seeking. *Journal of Research in Personality*, 38, 256–79.

Roberson, D., Davies, I. R., & Davidoff, J. (2000). Color categories are not universal: Replications & new evidence from a Stone-Age culture. *Journal of Experimental Psychology: General*, 129, 369–8.

Roberson, D., Davidoff, J., Davies, I. J., & Shapiro, L. R. (2005). Color categories: Evidence for the cultural relativity hypothesis. *Cognitive Psychology*, 50, 378–411.

Robinson, S. (2006). The phoneme inventory of the Aita dialect of Rotokas. *Oceanic Linguistics*, 45, 206–9.

Rockwell, P. A. (2006). *Sarcasm and Other Mixed Messages: The Ambiguous Ways People Use Language*. New York: Edwin Mellen Press.

Roelofs, A. (1997). The WEAVER model of word-form encoding in speech production. *Cognition*, 64, 249–84.

Roelofs, A., Ozdemir, R., & Levelt, W. J. (2007). Influences of spoken word planning on speech recognition. *Journal of Experimental Psychology: Learning, Memory, and Cognition*, 33(5), 900–13.

Rogalsky, C., & Hickok, G. (2011). The role of Broca's area in sentence comprehension. *Journal of Cognitive Neuroscience*, 23(7), 1664–80.

Rollins, P. (1980). *Benjamin Lee Whorf: Lost Generation Theories of Language, Mind, and Religion*. Ann Arbor, MI: University Microfilms International.

Romani, C., & Martin, R. (1999). A deficit in the short-term rention of lexical-semantic information: Forgetting words but remembering a story. *Journal of Experimental Psychology: General*, 128, 56–77.

Rosemann, S., Altenmüller, E., & Fahle, M. (2016). The art of sight-reading: Influence of practice, playing tempo, complexity and cognitive skills on the eye–hand span in pianists. *Psychology of Music*, 44(4), 658–73.

Ross, D. S., & Bever, T. G. (2004). The time course for language acquisition in biologically distinct populations: Evidence from deaf individuals. *Brain and Language,* 89(1), 115–21.

Ross, J., & Melinger, A. (2017). Bilingual advantage, bidialectal advantage or neither? Comparing performance across three tests of executive function in middle childhood. *Developmental Science*, 20, e12405.

Rothman, J. (2008). Why all counter-evidence to the critical period hypothesis in second language acquisition is not equal or problematic. *Language and Linguistics Compass*, 2, 1063–88.

Rouger, J., Fraysse, B., Deguine, O., & Barone, P. (2008). McGurk effects in cochlear-implanted deaf subjects. *Brain Research,* 1188, 87–99.

Rowe, M. L. (2012). A longitudinal investigation of the role of quantity and quality of child-directed speech in vocabulary development. *Child Development*, 83, 1762–74.

Rubin, D. C., Schrauf, R. W., Gulgoz, S., & Naka, M. (2007). On the cross-cultural variability of component processes in autobiographical remembering: Japan Turkey, and the U.S.A. *Memory*, 15(5), 536–47.

Rumelhart, D. E. (1975). Notes on a schema for stories. In D. G. Bobrow & A. M. Collins (eds) *Representation and Understanding: Studies in Cognitive Science.* New York: Academic Press.

Rumelhart, D. E. (1980). On evaluating story grammars. *Cognitive Science*, 4(3), 313–16.

Rumelhart, D. E., & Norman, D. A. (1982). Simulating a skilled typist: A study of skilled cognitive motor performance. *Cognitive Science*, 6, 1–36.

Rumelhart, D. E., McClelland, J. L., & the PDP Research Group (1986). *Parallel Distributed Processing: Explorations in the Microstructure of Cognition* (vol. 1). Cambridge, MA: MIT Press.

Rutter, M. (2000). Genetic studies of autism: From the 1970s into the millennium. *Journal of Abnormal Child Psychology*, 28(1), 3–14.

Ryalls, J., & Miller, N. (2015). *Foreign Accent Syndrome: The Stories People Have to Tell.* London: Psychology Press.

Rymer, R. (1994). *Genie: A Scientific Tragedy* (2nd edn). New York: Harper Perennial.

Sabbah, N., Authie, C. N., Sanda, N., Mohand-Said, S., Sahel, J. et al. (2016). Increased functional connectivity between language and visually deprived areas in late and partial blindness. *NeuroImage*, 136, 162–73.

Sachs, J. S. (1967). Recognition memory for syntactic and semantic aspects of connected discourse. *Perception & Psychophysics*, 2, 437–42.

Sachs, J. S. (1974). Memory in reading and listening to discourse. *Memory & Cognition*, 2, 95–100.

Saeed, J. I. (2008). *Semantics: Introducing Linguistics* (3rd edn). Oxford: Wiley-Blackwell.

Saffran, J. R. (2003). Statistical language learning: Mechanisms and constraints. *Current Directions in Psychological Science*, 12, 110–14.

Saffran, J. R., Aslin, R. N., & Newport, E. L. (1996). Statistical learning by 8-month-old infants. *Science*, 274, 1926–28.

Salvesen, K. Å. (2011). Ultrasound in pregnancy and non-right handedness: Meta-analysis of randomized trials. *Ultrasound in Obstetrics & Gynecology*, 38, 267–71.

Sambin, S., Teichmann, M., de Diego Balaguer, R., Giavazzi, M., Sportiche, D. et al. (2012). The role of the striatum in sentence processing: Disentangling syntax from working memory in Huntington's disease. *Neuropsychologia*, 50(11), 2625–35.

Sampson, G. (2005). *The Language Instinct Debate*. London: Continuum.

Sampson, T. R., Debelius, J. W., Thron, T., Janssen, S., Shastri, G. G. et al. (2016). Gut microbiota regulate motor deficits and neuroinflammation in a model of Parkinson's disease. *Cell*, 167(6), 1469–80.

Samuel, A. G. (1981a). The role of bottom-up confirmation in the phonemic restoration illusion. *Journal of Experimental Psychology: Human Perception and Performance*, 7(5), 1124–31.

Samuel, A. G. (1981b). Phonemic restoration: Insights from a new methodology. *Journal of Experimental Psychology: General*, 110(4), 474–94.

Samuel, A. G. (1987). Lexical uniqueness effects on phonemic restoration. *Journal of Memory and Language*, 26(1), 36–56.

Samuel, A. G. (1991). A further examination of attentional effects in the phonemic restoration illusion. *Quarterly Journal of Experimental Psychology A: Human Experimental Psychology*, 43A(3), 679–99.

Samuel, A. G. (1996). Does lexical information influence the perceptual restoration of phonemes? *Journal of Experimental Psychology: General*, 125(1), 28–51.

Samuel, A. G., & Ressler, W. H. (1986). Attention within auditory word perception: Insights from the phonemic restoration illusion. *Journal of Experimental Psychology: Human Perception and Performance*, 12(1), 70–9.

Sanford, A., Garrod, S., Lucas, A., & Henderson, R. (1983). Pronouns without explicit antecedents. *Journal of Semantics*, 2, 303–18.

Santesteban, M., Pickering, M. J., & Branigan, H. P. (2013). The effects of word order on subject-verb and object-verb agreement: Evidence from Basque. *Journal of Memory and Language*, 68(2), 160–79.

Santiago-Rivera, A. L., & Altarriba, J. (2002). The role of language in therapy with the Spanish-English bilingual client. *Professional Psychology: Research and Practice*, 33, 30–8.

Santiago-Rivera, A. L., Altarriba, J., Poll, N., Gonzalez-Miller, N., & Cargun, C. (2009). Therapists' views on counseling the bilingual English-Spanish client: A qualitative study. *Professional Psychology: Research and Practice*, 20, 436–43.

Sassenberg, U., & van der Meer, E. (2010). Do we really gesture more when it is more difficult? *Cognitive Science*, 34(4), 643.

Saunders, G. (1998). *Bilingual Children: Birth to Teens*. Philadelphia: Multilingual Matters.

Saussure, F. de ([1916] 1977). Cours de linguistique générale (trans. W. Baskin). Glasgow: Fontana/Collins.

Savage-Rumbaugh, S., & Lewin, R. (1994). *Kanzi: The Ape at the Brink of the Human Mind*. Hoboken, NJ: Wiley.

Savage-Rumbaugh, S., Shanker, S., & Taylor, T. (1998). *Ape, Language and the Human Mind*. New York: Oxford University Press.

Savage-Rumbaugh, E. S., Sevcik, R. A., Brakke, K. E., Rumbaugh, D. M., & Greenfield, P. M. (1990). Symbols: their communicative use, comprehension, and combination by bonobos. In C. Rovee-Collier and L. P. Lipsitt (eds) *Advances in Infancy Research* (pp. 221–78). Norwood, NJ: Ablex.

Savin, H. B. (1963). Word frequency effect and errors in the perception of speech. *Journal of the Acoustical Society of America*, 35(2), 200–6.

Sawyer, R. K. (2006). *The Cambridge Handbook of the Learning Sciences.* New York: Cambridge University Press.

Schacter, D. L., & Buckner, R. L. (1998). Priming and the brain. *Neuron*, 20, 185–95.

Schachter, S., Christenfeld, N., Ravina, B., & Bilous, F. (1991). Speech disfluency and the structure of knowledge. *Journal of Personality and Social Psychology*, 60, 362–7.

Scharinger, M., Monahan, P. J., & Idsardi, W. J. (2011). You had me at "Hello": Rapid extraction of dialect information from spoken words. *NeuroImage*, 56(4), 2329–38.

Schelvis, M. (1985). The collection, categorisation, storage and retrieval of spontaneous speech error material at the Institute of Phonetics. *PRIPU*, 10, 3–14.

Schick, A., & Melzi, G. (2010). The development of children's oral narratives across contexts. *Early Education and Development*, 21, 293–317.

Schmandt-Besserat, D. (1996). *How Writing Came About.* Austin, TX: University of Texas Press.

Schmelz, M., Call, J., & Tomasello, M. (2011). Chimpanzees know that others make inferences. *Proceedings of the National Academy of Sciences*, 108, 17284–9.

Schmid, M. S., & Jarvis, S. (2014) Lexical first language attrition. *Bilingualism: Language and Cognition*, 17(4), 729–48.

Schmidt, A. (1985). *Young People's Dyirbal: An Example of Language Death from Australia.* Cambridge: Cambridge University Press.

Schmidt, G. L., Kranjec, A., Cardillo, E. R., & Chatterjee, A. (2010). Beyond laterality: A critical assessment of research on the neural basis of metaphor. *Journal of the International Neuropsychological Society*, 16, 1–5.

Schnadt, M. J., & Corley, M. (2006). The influence of lexical, conceptual and planning based factors on disfluency production. Proceedings of the twenty-eighth meeting of the Cognitive Science Society.

Schneider, B. A., & Pichora-Fuller, M. K. (2001). Age-related changes in temporal processing: Implications for speech perception. *Seminars in Hearing*, 22, 227–39.

Schober, M. F., & Clark, H. H. (1989). Understanding by addressees and overhearers. *Cognitive Psychology*, 21, 211–32.

Schriefers, H., Meyer, A. S., & Levelt, W. J. (1990). Exploring the time course of lexical access in language production: Picture-word interference studies. *Journal of Memory and Language*, 29(1), 86–102.

Schulkind, M. D. (2004). Serial processing in melody identification and the organization of musical semantic memory. *Perception & Psychophysics*, 66(8), 1351–62.

Schulkind, M. D., & Davis, S. J. (2013). The cohort model of melody identification: Evaluating primacy and similarity. *Psychology of Music*, 41(4), 422–39.

Schumacher, J., Hoffmann, P., Schmäl, C., Schulte-Körne, G., & Nöthen, M. M. (2007). Genetics of dyslexia: The evolving landscape. *Journal of Medical Genetics*, 44(5), 289–97.

Schvaneveldt, R. W., & Meyer, D. E. (1973). Retrieval and comparison processes in semantic memory. In S. Kornblum (ed.) *Attention and Performance IV* (pp. 395–409). New York: Academic Press.

Schwanenflugel, P. (1991). Why are abstract concepts hard to understand? In P. Schwanenflugel (ed.) *The Psychology of Word Meanings* (pp. 223–50). Hillsdale, NJ: Erlbaum.

Schwartz, B. L., & Brown, A. S. (2014). *Tip-of-the-tongue States and Related Phenomena*. Cambridge: Cambridge University Press.

Schwartz, C. R., & Mare, R. D. (2005). Trends in educational assortative marriage from 1940 to 2003. *Demography*, 42(4), 621–46.

Schwartz, M. E., Saffran, E. M., Bloch, D. E., & Dell, G. S. (1994). Disordered speech production in aphasic and normal speakers. *Brain and Language*, 47, 52–88.

Schwarzschild, R. (1999). GIVENness, AvoidF, and other contraints on the placement of accent. *Natural Language Semantics*, 7, 141–77.

Schweizer, T. A., Ware, J., Fischer, C. E., Craik, F. I., & Bialystok, E. (2012). Bilingualism as a contributor to cognitive reserve: Evidence from brain atrophy in Alzheimer's disease. *Cortex*, 48(8), 991–6.

Scott, S. K., Lavan, N., Chen, S., & McGettigan, C. (2014). The social life of laughter. *Trends in Cognitive Sciences*, 18(12), 618–20.

Scovel, T. (1988). *A Time to Speak: A Psycholinguistic Inquiry into the Critical Period for Human Speech*. Rowley, MA: Newbury House.

Searle, J. (1975). Indirect speech acts. In P. Cole & J. L. Morgan (eds) *Syntax and Semantics*, vol. 3: *Speech Act* (pp. 59–82). New York: Academic Press.

Searchinger, G., Male, M., & Wright, M. (Writers) (2005). *Human Language Series* [DVD]. United States: Equinox Films/Ways of Knowing Inc.

Sebastian-Galles, N., & Bosch, L. (2009). Developmental shift in the discrimination of vowel contrasts in bilingual infants: Is the distributional account all there is to it? *Developmental Science*, 12(6), 874–87.

Sebba, M. (2009). Sociolinguistic approaches to writing systems research. *Writing Systems Research*, 1(1), 35–49.

Segal, P. (2004). *Fifty First Dates* [Motion Picture]. United States: Columbia Pictures.

Seidenberg, M. S. (1985). The time course of phonological code activation in two writing systems. *Cognition*, 19, 1–30.

Seidenberg, M. S., & McClelland, J. L. (1989). A distributed, developmental model of word recognition and naming. *Psychological Review*, 96, 523–68.

Seidenberg, M. S., Waters, G. S., Barnes, M. A., & Tanenhaus, M. K. (1984). When does irregular spelling or pronunciation influence word recognition? *Journal of Verbal Learning and Verbal Behavior*, 23, 383–404.

Selfridge, O. G. (1959). Pandemonium: A paradigm for learning. In D. V. Blake and A. M. Uttley (eds) *Proceedings of the Symposium on Mechanisation of Thought Processes* (pp. 511–29). London: HMSO.

Selkirk, E. O. (1984). *Phonology and Syntax: The Relation Between Sound and Structure*. Cambridge: MIT Press.

Senghas, A. (2005). Language emergence: Clues from a new Bedouin sign language. *Current Biology*, 15, 463–5.

Senghas, A., & Coppola M. (2001). Children creating language: How Nicaraguan sign language acquired a spatial grammar. *Psychological Science*, 12, 323–8.

Sereno, S. C., O'Donnell, P. J., & Rayner K. (2006). Eye movements and lexical ambiguity resolution: Investigating the subordinate bias effect. *Journal of Experimental Psychology: Human Perception and Performance*, 32(2), 335–50.

Seshadri, S., Beiser, A., Kelly-Hayes, M., Kase, C. S., Au, R. et al. (2006). The lifetime risk of stroke: Estimates from the Framingham Study. *Stroke*, 37(2), 345–50.

Severens, E., Kühn, S., Hartsuiker, R. J., & Brass, M. (2012). Functional mechanisms involved in the internal inhibition of taboo words. *Social Cognitive and Affective Neuroscience*, 7, 431–5.

Seyfarth, R. M., & Cheney, D. L. (1992). Meaning and mind in monkeys. *Scientific American*, 267, 122–9.

Seyfarth, R. M., Cheney, D. L., & Marler, P. (1980a). Monkey responses to three different alarm calls: Evidence of predator classification & semantic communication. *Science*, 210(4471), 801–3.

Seyfarth, R. M., Cheney, D. L., & Marler, P. (1980b). Vervet monkey alarm calls: Semantic communication in a free-ranging primate. *Animal Behavior*, 28(4), 1070–94.

Shammi, P., & Stuss, D. T. (1999). Humor appreciation: A role of the right frontal lobe. *Brain*, 122(4), 657–66.

Shankweiler, D., & Studdert-Kennedy, M. (1975). A continuum of lateralization of speech perception? *Brain and Language*, 2, 212–25.

Shao, Z., Janse, E., Visser, K., & Meyer, A. S. (2014). What do verbal fluency tasks measure? Predictors of verbal fluency performance in older adults. *Frontiers in Psychology*, 5, 772.

Shapiro, L. R., & Hudson, J. A. (1991). Tell me a make-believe story: Coherence and cohesion in young children's picture-elicited narratives. *Developmental Psychology*, 27, 960–74.

Shattuck-Hufnagel, S. (1979). Speech errors as evidence for a serial ordering mechanism in sentence production. In W. E. Cooper & E. C. Walker (eds) *Sentence Processing* (pp. 295–342). Hillsdale, NJ: Erlbaum.

Shattuck-Hufnagel, S. (1992). The role of word structure in segmental serial ordering. *Cognition*, 42, 213–59.

Shaywitz, S. E., & Shaywitz, B. A. (2004). Neurobiological basis for reading and reading disability. In P. McCardle & V. Chhabra (eds) *The Voice of Evidence in Reading Research* (pp. 417–42). Baltimore, MA: Brookes.

Shen, J. X. (1992). Examples and categorization of slips of the tongue in Chinese. *Chinese Language*, 4, 306–16.

Shermis, M. D., & Burstein, J. (eds) (2013). *Automated Essay Scoring: A Cross-disciplinary Perspective*. Mahwah, NJ: Lawrence Erlbaum.

Shibata, M., Terasawa, Y., & Umeda, S. (2014). Integration of cognitive and affective networks in humor comprehension. *Neuropsychologia*, 65, 137–45.

Shook, A., & Marian, V. (2012). Bimodal bilinguals co-activate both languages during spoken comprehension. *Cognition*, 24, 314–24.

Sidnell, J. (2010). *Conversation Analysis: An Introduction*. London: Wiley-Blackwell.

Silva, P. A., Hughes, P., Williams, S., & Faed, J. M. (1988). Blood lead, intelligence, reading attainment, and behavior in eleven year old children in Dunedin, New Zealand. *Journal of Child Psychology and Psychiatry*, 29(1), 43–52.

Simons, G. F., & Fennig, C. D. (2017). *Ethnologue: Languages of the World* (20th edn). Dallas, TX: SIL International.

Singh, J. A. (1926). The diary of the wolf-children of Midnapore. Retrieved July 17, 2017 from www.midnapore.in/wolf-children-of-midnapore/wolf-children-of-midnapore1.html.

Siok, W. T., & Fletcher, P. (2001). The role of phonological awareness and visual-orthographic skills iin Chinese reading acquisition. *Developmental Psychology*, 37, 886–99.

Sitnikova, T., Perrone, C., Goff, D., & Kuperberg, G. R. (2010). Neurocognitive mechanisms of conceptual processing in healthy adults and patients with schizophrenia. *International Journal of Psychophysiology*, 75(2), 86–99.

Skehan, P. (1998). *A Cognitive Approach to Language Learning*. Oxford: Oxford University Press.

Skinner, B. F. (1957). *Verbal Behavior*. Acton, MA: Copley.

Skuse, D. H., Mandy, W. P., & Scourfield, J. (2005). Measuring autistic traits: Heritability, reliability and validity of the Social and Communication Disorders Checklist. *British Journal of Psychiatry*, 187(6), 568–72.

Slattery, T. J., & Rayner, K. (2010). The influence of text legibility on eye movements during reading. *Applied Cognitive Psychology*, 24, 1129–48.

Slobin, D. I. (1985). *Crosslinguistics Studies in Language Acquisition*, vol 1. Mahwah, NJ: Erlbaum.

Sloboda, J. A. (1974). The eye-hand span: An approach to the study of sight reading. *Psychology of Music*, 2, 4–10.

Sloboda, J. A. (1977). Phrase units as determinants of visual processing in music reading. *British Journal of Psychology*, 68, 117–24.

Slobodchikoff, C. N. (2002) Cognition and communication in prairie dogs. In M. Bekoff, C. Allen and G. M. Burghardt (eds) *The Cognitive Animal* (pp. 257–64). Cambridge, MA: MIT Press.

Slobodchikoff, C. N., Paseka, A., & Verdolin, J. L. (2009a). Prairie dog alarm calls encode labels about predator colors. *Animal Cognition*, 12(3), 435–9.

Slobodchikoff, C. N., Perla, B.S., & Verdolin. J. L. (2009b). *Prairie Dogs: Communication and Community in an Animal Society*. Cambridge, MA: Harvard University Press.

Slobodchikoff, C. N., Kiriazis, J., Fischer, C., and Creef, E. (1991). Semantic information distinguishing individual predators in the alarm calls of Gunnison's prairie dogs. *Animal Behavior*, 42, 713–19.

Slowiaczek, M. L., & Clifton, C. (1980). Subvocalization and reading for meaning. *Journal of Verbal Learning and Verbal Behavior*, 19, 573–82.

Small, B. J., Herlitz, A., Fratiglioni, L., Almkvist, O., & Bäckman, L. (1997). Cognitive predictors of incident Alzheimer's disease: A prospective longitudinal study. *Neuropsychology*, 11(3), 413–20.

Smith, D. J. (1988). An investigation of the effects of varying temporal settings on eye movements while sight reading trumpet music and while reading language aloud. Doctoral dissertation, UMI 890066.

Smith, J. M., DeThorne, L. S., Logan, J. R., Channell, R. W., & Petrill, S. A. (2014). Impact of prematurity on language skills at school age. *Journal of Speech, Language, and Hearing Research*, 57(3), 901–16.

Smith, M., & Wheeldon, L. (1999). High level processing scope in spoken sentence production. *Cognition*, 73, 205–46.

Smith, R. A., & Davis, S. F. (2012). *Psychologist as Detective: An Introduction to Conducting Research in Psychology* (6th edn). New York: Pearson.

Smith, R. J., Shearer, A. E., Hildebrand, M. S., & van Camp, G. (1999). Deafness and hereditary hearing loss overview. In R. A. Pagon, M. P. Adam, H. H. Ardinger et al. (eds) GeneReviews®. Seattle: University of Washington, Available from: www.ncbi.nlm.nih.gov/books/NBK1434.

Snow, C. E. (1972). Mothers' speech to children learning language. *Child Development*, 43, 549–65.

Snow, C. E. (1977). The development of conversation between mothers and babies. *Journal of Child Language*, 4, 1–22.

Snow, C., Scarborough, H., & Burns, S. (1999). What speech-language pathologists need to know about early reading. *Topics in Language Disorders*, 20(1), 48–58.

Snowling, M., & Frith, U. (1986). Comprehension in "hyperlexic" readers. *Journal of Experimental Child Psychology*, 42, 392–415.

Sobel, C., & Li, P. (2013). *The Cognitive Sciences: An Interdisciplinary Approach*. Los Angeles, CA: Sage.

Sommer, I. E., Aleman, A., Somers, M., Boks, M. P., & Kahn, R. S. (2008). Sex differences in handedness, asymmetry of the planum temporale and functional language lateralization. *Brain Research*, 1206, 76–88.

Soriano-Mas, C., Pujol, J., Ortiz, H., Deus, J., López-Sala, A. et al. (2009). Age-related brain structural alterations in children with specific language impairment. *Human Brain Mapping*, 30, 1626–36.

Soskin, W. F., & John, V. P. (1963). The study of spontaneous talk. In R. Barker (ed.) *The Stream of Behavior*. New York: Appleton-Century-Crofts.

Souter, T. (2001). Eye movement and memory in the sight reading of keyboard music. Doctoral dissertation, University of Sydney.

Spalding, D. (1873). Instinct, with original observations on young animals. *MacMillan's Magazine*, 27, 282–93.

Spencer, P. E., & Marschark, M. (2003). Cochlear implants: Issues and implications. In P. E. Spencer & M. Marschark (eds) *Deaf Studies, Language and Education* (pp. 434–50). London: Oxford University Press.

Sperlich, A., Meixner, J., & Laubrock, J. (2016). Development of the perceptual span in reading: A longitudinal study. *Journal of Experimental Child Psychology*, 146, 181–201.

Sperling, G. (1960). Negative afterimage without prior positive image. *Science*, 131, 1613–14.

Sperry, R. W. (1964). The great cerebral commissure. *Scientific American*, 210, 42–52.

Spieler, D. H., & Griffin, Z. M. (2006). The influence of age on the time course of word preparation in multiword utterances. *Language and Cognitive Processes*, 21, 291–321.

Spitzer, M. (1993). The psychopathology, neuropsychology, and neurobiology of associative and working memory in schizophrenia. *European Archives of Psychiatry and Clinical Neuroscience*, 243, 57–70.

Spitzer, M., Weisker, I., Winter, M., Maier, S., Hermle, L. et al. (1994). Semantic and phonological priming in schizophrenia. *Journal of Abnormal Psychology*, 103, 485–94.

Stanovich, K. E. (1986). Matthew effects in reading: Some consequences of individual differences in the acquisition of literacy. *Reading Research Quarterly*, 21, 360–407.

Stanovich, K. E., & Cunningham, A. E. (1992). Studying the consequences of literacy within a literate society: The cognitive correlates of print exposure. *Memory & Cognition*, 20, 51–68.

Stanovich, K. E., & Cunningham, A. E. (1993). Where does knowledge come from? Specific associations between print exposure and information acquisition. *Journal of Educational Psychology*, 85, 211–29.

Stanovich, K. E., & West, R. F. (1989). Exposure to print and orthographic processing. *Reading and Research Quarterly*, 24, 402–29.

Sterne, A., & Goswami, U. (2000). Phonological awareness of syllables, rhymes, and phonemes in deaf children. *Journal of Child Psychology and Psychiatry*, 41, 609–25.

Stein, J. (2001). The magnocellular theory of developmental dyslexia. *Dyslexia*, 7(1), 12–36.

Stein, J., & Kapoula, Z. (2012). *Visual Aspects of Dyslexia*. New York: Oxford University Press.

Stein, N. L., & Glenn, C. G. (1979). An analysis of story comprehension in elementary school children. In R. Freedle (ed.) *New Directions in Discourse Processing*. Norwood, NJ: Ablex.

Stemberger, J. P. (1984). Lexical Bias in Errors in Language Production: Interactive Components, Editors, and Perceptual Biases. Carnegie-Mellon University. Unpublished manuscript.

Stemberger, J. P. (1985). An interactive activation model of language production. In A. Ellis (ed.) *Progress in the Psychology of Language* (vol. 1). London: Erlbaum.

Stemberger, J. P. (1989). Speech errors in early child language production. *Journal of Memory and Language*, 28, 164–88.

Stevens, G. (2004). Using census data to test the critical-period hypothesis for second-language acquisition. *Psychological Science*, 15, 215–16.

Stewner-Manzanares, G. (1988). The Bilingual Education Act: Twenty years later. *New Focus, Occasional Papers in Bilingual Education*, Number 6. Washington, DC: National Clearinghouse for Bilingual Education.

St. Louis, K. O., Myers, F. L., Bakker, K., & Raphael, L. J. (2007). Understanding and treating cluttering. In E. G. Conture & R. F. Curlee (eds) *Stuttering and Related Disorders of Fluency* (3rd edn) (pp. 297–325). New York: Thieme.

Stoel-Gammon, C. (1988). Prelinguistic vocalizations of hearing-impaired and normally hearing subjects: A comparison of consonantal inventories. *Journal of Speech and Hearing Disorders*, 53, 302–15.

Stokoe, W. C. (1960). Sign language structure: An outline of the visual communication systems of the American deaf. *Studies in Linguistics: Occasional Papers (No. 8)*. Buffalo, NY: Dept. of Anthropology and Linguistics, University of Buffalo.

Stokoe, W. C. (1978). *Sign Language Structure: The First Linguistic Analysis of American Sign Language*. Silver Spring, MD: Linstok Press.

Stokoe, W. C., Casterline, D. C., & Croneberg, C. G. (1965). *A Dictionary of American Sign Languages on Linguistic Principles*. Washington, D.C.: Gallaudet College Press.

Stone, A., Kartheiser, G., Hauser, P. C., Petitto, L., & Allen, T. E. (2015). Fingerspelling as a novel gateway into reading fluency in deaf bilinguals. *PLoS ONE*, 10(10), e0139610.

Strauss, K. P. (2006). *A New Civil Right: Telecommunications Equality for Deaf and Hard of Hearing Americans*. Washington, D.C.: Gallaudet University Press.

Ströckens, F., Güntürkün, O., & Ocklenburg, S. (2013). Limb preferences in non-human vertebrates. *Laterality: Asymmetries of Body, Brain and Cognition*, 18(5), 536–75.

Stroop, J. R. (1935). Studies of interference in serial verbal reactions. *Journal of Experimental Psychology*, 1(6), 643–62.

Stuart, M., Dixon, M., Masterson, J., & Gray, B. (2003). Children's early reading vocabulary: Description and word frequency lists. *British Journal of Educational Psychology*, 73(4), 585–98.

Studdert-Kennedy, M., Shankweiler, D., & Pisoni, D. (1972). Auditory and phonetic processes in speech perception: Evidence from a dichotic study. *Journal of Cognitive Psychology*, 2, 455–66.

Sturt, P. (2007). Semantic re-interpretation and garden path recovery. *Cognition*, 105(2), 477–88.

Sukumar, R. (2003). *The Living Elephants: Evolutionary Ecology, Behaviour, and Conservation*. Oxford: Oxford University Press.

Sun, B., & Kennison, S. M. (2015). Comprehending pronouns in Chinese: Evidence from online sentence processing. *Language Sciences*, 47A, 56–65.

Sundara, M., Polka, L., & Molnar, M. (2008). Development of coronal stop perception: Bilingual infants keep pace with their monolingual peers. *Cognition*, 108, 232–42.

Svensson, I., Nilsson, S., Wahlström, J., Jernås, M., Carlsson, L. et al. (2011). Familial dyslexia in a large Swedish family: A whole genome linkage scan. *Behavioral Genetics*, 41, 43–9.

Swanwick, R. (2016). Deaf children's bimodal bilingualism and education. *Language Teaching*, 49(1), 1–34.

Sweetland, J. (2002). Unexpected but authentic use of an ethnically-marked dialect. *Journal of Sociolinguistics*, 6, 514–36.

Taft, M. (1981). Prefix stripping revisited. *Journal of Verbal Learning and Verbal Behavior*, 20, 289–97.

Taft, M., & Hambly, G. (1986). Exploring the cohort model of spoken word recognition. *Cognition*, 22(3), 259–82.

Tai, Y. C., Sheedy, J., & Hayes, J. (2006). Effect of letter spacing on legibility, eye movements, and reading speed. *Journal of Vision*, 6(6), 994a.

Takeuchi, A. H., & Hulse, S. H. (1993). Absolute pitch. *Psychological Bulletin*, 113, 345–61.

Tan, P. K. (2005). The medium-of-instruction debate in Malaysia: English as a Malaysian language? *Problems & Language Planning*, 29(1), 47–66.

Tanenhaus, M. K., Carlson, G., & Trueswell, J. C. (1989). The role of thematic structures in interpretation and parsing. *Language and Cognitive Processes*, 4(3/4), 211–34.

Tanenhaus, M., Spivey-Knowlton, M. J., Eberhard, K. M., & Sedivy, J. C. (1995). Integration of visual and linguistic information in spoken language comprehension. *Science*, 268, 1632–4.

Tannen, D. (1992) How men and women use language differently in their lives and in the classroom. *Education Digest*, 57(6), 3–4.

Tannen, D. (2001). *You Just Don't Understand: Women and Men in Conversation*. New York: Quill.

Tannock, R. (2014). DSM-5 changes in diagnostic criteria for specific learning disabilities (SLD): What are the implications? Retrieved September 4, 2016 from dyslexiahelp.umich.edu/sites/default/files/IDA_DSM-5%20Changes.pdf.

Taraban, R., & McClelland, J. R. (1988). Constituent attachment and thematic role assignment in sentence processing: Influence of content-base expectations. *Journal of Memory and Language*, 27, 597–632.

Tardif, T., Gelman, S. A., & Xu, F. (1999). Putting the "noun bias" in context: A comparison of Mandarin and English. *Child Development*, 70(3), 620–35.

Tarnopol, L., & Tarnopol, M. (1981). *Comparative Reading and Learning Difficulties*. Lexington, MA: Lexington Books.

Tass, N. (Director) (2001). *The Miracle Worker* [Motion picture]. United States: Walt Disney Video.

Taylor, I., & Taylor, M. M. (1995). *Writing and Literacy in Chinese, Korean and Japanese*. Amsterdam: John Benjamins.

Teichmann, M., Darcy, I., Bachoud-Lévi, A., & Dupoux, E. (2009). The role of the striatum in phonological processing. Evidence from early stages of Huntington's disease. *Cortex*, 45(7), 839–49.

Teichmann, M., Dupoux, E., Cesaro, P., and Bachoud-Levi, A. C. (2008). The role of the striatum in sentence processing: Evidence from a priming study in early stages of Huntington's disease. *Neuropsychologia*, 46, 174–85.

Teichmann, M., Dupoux, E., Kouider, S., Brugieres, P., Boisse, M. F. et al. (2005). The role of the striatum in rule application: The model of Huntington's disease at early stage. *Brain*, 128, 1155–67.

Terrace, H. S. (1979). *Nim*. New York: Knopf.

Terrace, H. S., Petitto, L. A., Sanders, R. J., & Bever, T. G. (1979). Can an ape create a sentence? *Science*, 206, 891–902.

Tesak, J., & Code, C. (2008). *Milestones in the History of Aphasia: Theories and Protagonists*. Hove: Psychology Press.

Tetnowski, J. A., Richels, C., Shenker, R., Sisskin, V., & Wolk, L. (2012). When the diagnosis is dual. *The ASHA Leader*. Retrieved April 14, 2017 from http://leader.pubs.asha.org/article.aspx?articleid=2280140.

Theocharopoulou, F., Cocks, N., Pring, T., & Dipper, L. T. (2015). TOT phenomena: Gesture production in younger and older adults. *Psychology and Aging*, 30(2), 245–52.

Thermenos, H. W., Whitfield-Gabrieli, S., Seidman, L. J., Kuperberg, G., Juelich, R. J. et al. (2013). Altered language network activity in young people at familial high-risk for schizophrenia. *Schizophrenia Research*, 151(1/3), 229–37.

The Telegraph (2010). Oldest example of written English discovered in church. Retrieved August 7, 2015 from www.telegraph.co.uk/news/uknews/7345039/Oldest-example-of-written-English-discovered-in-church.html.

Thiessen, E. D., Hill, E., & Saffran, J. R. (2005). Infant-directed speech facilitates word segmentation. *Infancy*, 7, 53–71.

Thoma, P., & Daum I. (2006). Neurocognitive mechanisms of figurative language processing: evidence from clinical dysfunctions. *Neuroscience Biobehavorial Reviews*, 30, 1182–205.

Thompson, R., Emmorey, K., & Gollan, T. H. (2005). Tip of the fingers experiences by deaf signers: insights into the organization of a sign-based lexicon. *Psychological Science*, 16(11), 856–60.

Thornbury, S., & Slade, D. (2006). *Conversation: From Description to Pedagogy.* Cambridge: Cambridge University Press.

Thorndyke, P. W. (1977). Cognitive structures in comprehension and memory of narrative discourse. *Cognitive Psychology*, 9, 77–110.

Thornton, R., & Crain, S. (1994). Successful cyclic movement. In T. Hoekstra and B. D. Schwartz (eds) *Language Acquisition Studies in Generative Grammar* (pp. 215–52). Amsterdam: John Benjamins.

Thornton, R., & Light, L. L. (2006). Language comprehension and production in normal aging. In J. E. Birren and K. W. Schaie (eds) *Handbook of the Psychology of Aging* (pp. 262–87). Burlington, MA: Elsevier Academic Press.

Thorpe, D. (Director) (2014). *Do I Sound Gay?* [DVD] Sundance, Utah: Sundance Selects.

Thurston, A. (2014). The potential impact of undiagnosed vision impairment on reading development in the early years of school. *International Journal of Disability, Development & Education*, 61(2), 152–64.

Tierney, A., Dick, F., Deutsch, D., & Sereno, M. (2013). Speech versus song: Multiple pitch-sensitive areas revealed by a naturally occurring musical illusion. *Cerebral Cortex*, 23, 249–54.

Tilque, D. (2000). Borrowed English: Word ways. *Journal of Recreational English*, 33(2), 114–18.

Tisljár-szabó, E., Rossu, R., Varga, V., & Pléh, C. (2014). The effect of alcohol on speech production. *Journal of Psycholinguistic Research*, 43(6), 737–48.

Titze, I. R. (1994). *Principles of Voice Production.* New York: Prentice Hall.

Titze, I. R. (2008). The human instrument. *Scientific American*, 298(1), 94–101.

Toga, A., & Mazziotta, J. C. (2000). *Brain Mapping: The Methods.* New York: Academic Press.

Toglia, M. P., & Battig, W. F. (1978). *Handbook of Semantic Word Norms.* Hillsdale, NJ: Erlbaum.

Tomasello, M. (2000). Do young children have adult syntactic competence? *Cognition*, 74, 209–53.

Tomasello, M. (2003). *Constructing a Language: A Usage-based Theory of Language Acquisition.* Cambridge, MA: Harvard University Press.

Tomasello, M., & Call, I. (1997). *Primate Cognition.* Oxford: Oxford University Press.

Tomasello, M., Carpenter, M., & Liszkowski, U. (2007). A new look at infant pointing. *Child Development*, 78, 705–22.

Tomblin, J. B., Records, N., & Zhang, X. (1996) A system for the diagnosis of specific language impairment in kindergarten children. *Journal of Speech and Hearing Research*, 39, 1284–94.

Tomblin, J. B., Records, N. L., Buckwalter, P., Zhang, X., Smith, E. et al. (1997). Prevalence of specific language impairment in kindergarten children. *Journal of Speech & Hearing Research*, 40(6), 1245–60.

Tomlin, R. (1986). *Basic Word Order: Functional Principles*. London: Croom Helm.

Towers, T. (2016). Get naked at work! Hundreds post nude photos of themselves stripped off while working after Belarus president's slip of the tongue goes viral. *The Sun*. Retrieved July 31, 2016 from www.thesun.co.uk/news/1359183/hundreds-post-nude-photos-of-themselves-stripped-off-while-working-after-belarus-presidents-slip-of-the-tongue-goes-viral.

Townsend, D. J., Carrithers, C., & Bever, T. G. (2001). Familial handedness and access to words, meaning, and syntax during sentence comprehension. *Brain and Language*, 78(3), 308–31.

Transler, C., Gombert, J., & Leybaert, J. (2001). Phonological decoding in severely and profoundly deaf children: Similarity judgment between written pseudowords. *Applied Psycholinguistics*, 22(1), 61–82.

Transler, C., Leybaert, J., & Gombert, J. (1999). Do deaf children use phonological syllables as reading units? *Journal of Deaf Studies in Education*, 4, 124–43.

Traxler, M. J. (2012). *Introduction to Psycholinguistics: Understanding Language Science*. Chichester: Wiley-Blackwell.

Traxler, M. J. (2014). Trends in syntactic parsing: Anticipation, Bayesian estimation, and good-enough parsing. *Trends in Cognitive Sciences*, 18(11), 605–11.

Traxler, M. J., Pickering, M., & Clifton, C. (1998). Adjunct attachment is not a form of lexical ambiguity resolution. *Journal of Memory and Language*, 39, 558–92.

Traxler, M. J., Long, D. L., Tooley, K. M., Johns, C. L., Zirnstein, M. et al. (2012). Individual differences in eye-movements during reading: Working memory and speed-of-processing effects. *Journal of Eye Movement Research*, 5(1), 1–16.

Treffert, D. A. (2011). Hyperlexia: Reading precociousness or savant skill? Distinguishing autistic-like behaviors from autistic disorder. Wisconsin Medical Society. www.wisconsinmedicalsociety.org/professional/savant-syndrome/resources/articles/hyperlexia-reading-precociousness-or-savant-skill/.

Treiman, R., & Hirsh-Pasek, K. (1983). Silent reading: Insights from second-generation deaf readers. *Cognitive Psychology*, 15, 39–65.

Treisman, A. M. (1969). Strategies and models of selective attention. *Psychological Review*, 76(3), 282–99.

Tremblay, A., & Spinelli, E. (2013). Segmenting liaison-initial words: The role of predictive dependencies. *Language and Cognitive Processes*, 28(8), 1093–113.

Tremblay, A., & Spinelli, E. (2014). English listeners' use of distributional and acoustic- phonetic cues to liaison in French: Evidence from eye movements. *Language and Speech*, 57(3), 310–37.

Tremblay, K. L., Piskosz, M., & Souza, P. (2002). Aging alters the neural representation of speech cues. *NeuroReport*, 13, 1865–70.

Trueswell, J. C., Tanenhaus, M. K., & Kello, C. (1993). Verb-specific constraints in sentence processing: Separating effects of lexical preference from garden-paths. *Journal of Experimental Psychology: Learning, Memory, and Cognition*, 19, 528–53.

Trueswell, J. C., Sekerina, I., Hill, N. M., & Logrip, M. L. (1999). The kindergarten-path effect: Studying on-line sentence processing in young children. *Cognition*, 73, 89–134.

Truitt, F. E., Clifton, C., Pollatsek, A., & Rayner, K. (1997). The perceptual span and the eye–hand span in sight reading music. *Visual Cognition*, 4(2), 143–61.

Tsuji, H., & Doherty, M. J. (2014). Early development of metalinguistic awareness in Japanese: Evidence from pragmatic and phonological aspects of language. *First Language*, 34(3), 273–90.

Tsujimura, N. (ed.) (2005). *Japanese Linguistics: Critical Concepts in Linguistics*. Oxford: Routledge.

Turing, A. (1950). Computing machinery and intelligence. *Mind*, 59(236), 433–60.

Turner, A. C., McIntosh, D. N., & Moody, E. J. (2015). Don't listen with your mouth full: The role of facial motor action in visual speech perception. *Language and Speech*, 58(2), 267–78.

Tutunjian, D., & Boland, J. E. (2008). Do we need a distinction between arguments and adjuncts? Evidence from psycholinguistic studies of comprehension. *Language and Linguistics Compass*, 2(4), 631–46.

Tversky, B., Kugelmass, S., & Winter, A. (1991). Cross-cultural and developmental trends in graphic productions. *Cognitive Psychology*, 23, 515–57.

Tyler, K. L., & Tyler, H. R. (1982). A "Yankee invention": The celebrated American crowbar case. *Neurology*, 32, A191.

Tyler, L. K. (1984). The structure of the initial cohort: Evidence from gating. *Perception & Psychophysics*, 36(5), 417–27.

Tyler, M. D., & Cutler, A. (2009). Cross-language differences in cue use for speech segmentation. *Journal of the Acoustical Society of America*, 126, 367–76.

Tzeng, O. J., Chen, S., & Hung, D. L. (1991). The classifier problem in Chinese aphasia. *Brain and Language*, 41(2), 184–202.

Uchino, E., & Watanabe, S. (2014). Self-recognition in pigeons revisited. *Journal of the Experimental Analysis of Behavior*, 102(3), 327–34.

Ujhelyi, M., Merker, B., Buk, P., and Geissmann, T. (2000). Observations on the behavior of gibbons (Hylobates leucogenys, H. gabriellae, and H. lar) in the presence of mirrors. *Journal of Comparative Psychology*, 114(3), 253–62.

Ullman, M. T., Corkin, S., Coppola, M., Hickok, G., Growdon, J. H. et al. (1997). A neural dissociation within language: Evidence that the mental dictionary is part of declarative memory, and that grammatical rules are processed by the procedural system. *Journal of Cognitive Neuroscience*, 9, 266–76.

Ulmer, R. R., Sellnow, T. L., & Seeger, M. W. (2011). *Effective Crisis Communication: Moving from Crisis to Opportunity* (2nd edn). Thousand Oaks, CA: Sage.

UNESCO (2009). Whistled language of the island of La Gomera (Canary Islands), the Silbo Gomero. Retrieved June 17, 2017 from www.unesco.org/culture/ich/RL/00172.

UNESCO (2010). Literacy. Retrieved July 21, 2017 from www.uis.unesco.org/literacy/Pages/adult-youth-literacy-data-viz.aspx.

UNESCO (2017). Adult literacy rate, population 15+ years (both sexes, female, male). UIS Data Centre. Retrieved July 21, 2017 from http://data.uis.unesco.org/Index.aspx?DataSetCode=EDULIT_DS&popupcustomise=true&lang=en#.

University of Michigan (n.d.). Tom Cruise. Retrieved July 21, 2017 from http://dyslexiahelp.umich.edu/success-stories/tom-cruise.

Vaid, J. (2008). The bilingual brain: What is right and what is left? In J. Altarriba & R. Heredia (eds) *Introduction to Bilingualism*: *Principles and Processes* (pp. 129–44). New York: Lawrence Erlbaum.

Valli, C., & Lucas, C. (2000). *Linguistics of American Sign Language*. Washington, D.C.: Gallaudet University Press.

Van Berkel-van Hoof, L., Hermans, D., Knoors, H., & Verhoeven, L. (2016). Benefits of augmentative signs in word learning: Evidence from children who are deaf/hard of hearing and children with specific language impairment. *Research in Developmental Disabilities*, 59, 338–50.

Van Dijk, T. A., & Kintsch, W. (1983). *Strategies of Discourse Comprehension*. New York: Academic Press.

Van Galen, G. P. (1991). Handwriting: Issues for a psychomotor theory. *Human Movement Science*, 10, 165–91.

Van Gompel, R. P., & Liversedge, S. P. (2003). The influence of morphological information on cataphoric pronoun assignment. *Journal of Experimental Psychology: Learning, Memory, & Cognition*, 29, 128–9.

Van Gompel, R. P., Pickering, M., & Traxler, M. (2001). Reanalysis in sentence processing: Evidence against current constraint-based and two-stage models. *Journal of Memory and Language*, 45, 225–58.

Van Gompel, R. P., Pickering, M., Pearson, J., & Liversedge, S. P. (2005). Evidence against competition during syntactic ambiguity resolution. *Journal of Memory and Language*, 52, 284–307.

Van Horn, J. D., Irimia, A., Torgerson, C. M., Chambers, M. C., Kikinis, R. et al. (2012). Mapping connectivity damage in the case of Phineas Gage. *PLoS ONE*, 7, e37454.

Van Lancker, D. R., & Kempler, D. (1987). Comprehension of familiar phrases by left- but not by right-hemisphere damaged patients. *Brain and Language*, 32(2), 265–77.

Vanlancker-Sidtis, D. (2004). When only the right hemisphere is left: Studies in language and communication. *Brain and Language*, 91(2), 199–211.

Van Os, J., & Kapur, S. (2009). Schizophrenia. *Lancet*, 374(9690), 635–45.

Van Zaalen, Y., Wijnen, F., & Dejonckere, P. H. (2009). Differential diagnostics between cluttering and stuttering, part one. *Journal of Fluency Disorders*, 34(3), 137–54.

Vargha-Khadem, F., Gadian, D. G., Copp, A., & Mishkin, M. (2005). FOXP2 & the neuroanatomy of speech & language. *Nature Reviews Neuroscience*, 6(2), 131–7.

Veenstra, A., Acheson, D. J., Bock, K., & Meyer, A. S. (2014). Effects of semantic integration on subject-verb agreement: Evidence from Dutch. *Language Cognition and Neuroscience*, 29(3), 355–80.

Veldre, A., & Andrews, S. (2017). Parafoveal preview benefit in sentence reading: Independent effects of plausibility and orthographic relatedness. *Psychonomic Bulletin & Review*, 24(2), 519–28.

Verdolini, A. K., Rosen, C. A., Branski, R. C., Andrews, M. L., & American Speech-Language-Hearing Association (2006). *Classification Manual for Voice Disorders-I*. Mahwah, NJ: Lawrence Erlbaum.

Vigliocco, G., & Hartsuiker, R. J. (2002). The interplay of meaning, sound, and syntax in sentence production. *Psychological Bulletin*, 128(3), 442–72.

Vigliocco, G., Antonini, T., & Garrett, M. F. (1997). Grammatical gender is on the tip of Italian tongues. *Psychological Science*, 8, 314–17.

Vigliocco, G., Butterworth, B., & Garrett, M. F. (1996a) Subject-verb agreement in Spanish and English: Differences in the role of conceptual constraints. *Cognition*, 61(3), 261–98.

Vigliocco, G., Butterworth, B., & Semenza, C. (1995). Constructing subject-verb agreement in speech: The role of semantic and morphological factors. *Journal of Memory and Language*, 34, 186–215.

Vigliocco, G., Hartsuiker, R. J., Jarema, G., & Kolk, H. H. (1996b). One or more labels on the bottles? Notional concord in Dutch and French. *Language and Cognitive Processes*, 11, 407–42.

Vision Aid Oversees (n.d.). Key facts. Retrieved October 6, 2016 from www.visionaidoverseas.org/key-facts.

Vital-Durand, F., Atkinson, J., & Braddick, O. J. (eds) (1996). *Infant Vision*. New York: Oxford University Press.

Vitevitch, M. S. (2002). The influence of phonological similarity neighborhoods on speech production. *Journal of Experimental Psychology: Learning, Memory, and Cognition*, 28(4), 735–47.

Von Frisch, K. (1950). *Bees, Their Vision, Chemical Senses, and Language*. Ithaca, NY: Cornell University Press.

Von Frisch, K. (1967). *The Dance Language and Orientation of Bees*. Cambridge, MA: Belknap Press.

Von Frisch, K. (1974). Decoding the language of bees. *Science*, 185, 663–8.

Voyer, D. (2011). Sex differences in dichotic listening. *Brain and Cognition*, 76(2), 245–55.

Vrij, A. (2015). Deception detection. In B. L. Cutler & P. A. Zapf (eds) *APA Handbook of Forensic Psychology*, vol. 2: *Criminal Investigation, Adjudication, and Sentencing Outcomes* (pp. 225–44). Washington, D.C.: APA.

Vroomen, J., Tuomainen, J., and de Gelder, B. (1998). The roles of word stress and vowel harmony in speech segmentation. *Journal of Memory and Language*, 38, 133–49.

Vygotsky, L. S. (1978). *Mind in Society*. Cambridge, MA: Harvard University Press.

Vygotsky, L. S. ([1934] 1986). *Thought and Language* (ed. & trans. A. Kozulin). Cambridge, MA: MIT Press.

Vygotsky, L. S. (1987). Thinking and speech. In R. W. Rieber & A. S. Carton (eds) *The Collected Works of L. S. Vygotsky:* vol. 1. *Problems of General Psychology* (trans. N. Minick). New York: Plenum.

Waber, D. P., & McCormick, M. C. (1995). Late neuropsychological outcomes in preterm infants of normal IQ: Selective vulnerability of the visual system. *Journal of Pediatric Psychology*, 20(6), 721–35.

Wada, J. (1949). A new method for determination of the side of cerebral speech dominance: A preliminary report on the intracarotid injection of sodium amytal in man. *Igaku Seibutsugaku*, 4, 221–2.

Wada, J. (1997). Clinical experimental observations of carotid artery injections of sodium amytal. *Brain & Cognition*, 33, 11–13.

Wada, J., & Rasmussen, T. (1960). Intracarotid injection of sodium amytal for the lateralization of cerebral speech dominance: Experimental and clinical observations. *Journal of Neurosurgery*, 17, 266–82.

Wadsworth, S. J., Corley, R. P., Hewitt, J. K., Plomin, R., & DeFries, J. C. (2002). Parent-offspring resemblance for reading performance at 7, 12, and 16 years of age in the Colorado Adoption Project. *Journal of Child Psychology and Psychiatry*, 43(6), 769–74.

Walker, W., & Sarbaugh, J. (1993). The early history of the Cherokee syllabary. *Ethnohistory*, 40(1), 70–94.

Wallentin, M. (2009). Putative sex differences in verbal abilities and language cortex: A critical review. *Brain and Language*, 108(3), 175–83.

Walraven, V., van Elsacker, L., & Verheyen, R. (1995). Reactions of a group of pygmy chimpanzees (Pan paniscus) to their mirror images: Evidence of self-recognition. *Primates*, 36, 145–50.

Wan, I. (2006). Tone errors in normal and aphasic speech in Mandarin. *Tawainese Journal of Linguistics*, 4(2), 85–112.

Wan, I. (2007). The organization of Mandarin tone. *Lingua*, 117, 1715–38.

Wan, I., & Jaeger, J. (2003). The phonological representation of Taiwan Mandarin vowels: A psycholinguistic study. *Journal of East Asian Linguistics*, 12, 205–57.

Wang, Y., Harrington, M., & White, P. (2012). Detecting breakdowns in local coherence in the writing of Chinese English learners. *Journal of Computer Assisted Learning*, 28(4), 396–410.

Wanner, E., & Maratsos, M. (1978). An ATN approach to comprehension. In M. Halle, J. Bresnan & G. A. Miller (eds) *Linguistic Theory and Psychological Reality*. Cambridge, MA: MIT Press.

Ward, D. (2006). *Stuttering and Cluttering: Frameworks for Understanding Treatment*. Hove: Psychology Press.

Warner, J., & Glass, A. L. (1987). Context and distance-to-disambiguation effects in ambiguity resolution: Evidence from grammaticality judgment of garden path sentences. *Journal of Memory and Language*, 26, 714–38.

Warren, P., & Marslen-Wilson, W. (1987). Continuous uptake of acoustic cues in spoken word recognition. *Perception & Psychophysics*, 41(3), 262–75.

Warren, R. (1970). Restoration of missing speech sounds. *Science*, 167(3917), 392–3.

Warren, R., & Warren, R. (1970). Auditory illusions and confusions. *Scientific American*, 223(6), 30–6.

Warren, T., & Gibson, E. (2002). The influence of referential processing on sentence complexity. *Cognition*, 85, 79–112.

Warrington, E. K., & Shallice, T. (1984). Category specific semantic impairment. *Brain*, 107, 829–54.

Wartenburger, I., Heekeren, H. R., Abutalebi, J., Cappa, S. F., & Villringer, A. (2003). Early setting of grammatical processing in the bilingual brain. *Neuron*, 37, 159–70.

Waschbusch, D. A. (2002). A meta-analytic evaluation of comorbid hyperactive-impulsive-inattention problems and conduct problems. *Psychological Bulletin*, 128, 118–50.

Watkins, K. E., Dronkers, N. F., & Vargha-Khadem, F. (2002). Behavioural analysis of an inherited speech and language disorder: Comparison with acquired aphasia. *Brain*, 125(3), 452–64.

Watson, J. B. (1913). Psychology as the behaviorist views it. *Psychological Review*, 20, 158–77.

Watson, J. B. (1928). *The Psychological Care of the Infant and the Child*. New York: W.W. Norton & Co.

Watson, J. B. (1931). *Behaviourism*. London: Kegan Paul, Trench, Trubner and Co.

Watson, J. B., & Raynor, R. (1920). Conditioned emotional reactions. *Journal of Experimental Psychology*, 3(1), 1–14.

Waxman, S. R., & Lidz, J. L. (2006). Early word learning. In W. Damon & R. M. Lerner (series eds) & D. Kuhn & R. Siegler (eds) *Handbook of Child Psychology*, vol. 2 (6th edn, pp. 299–335). Hoboken, NJ: Wiley.

Weber, R., & Stolley, K. (2016). Transitional devices. Retrieved July 24, 2017 from https://owl.english.purdue.edu/owl/resource/574/02/.

Weber-Fox, C., & Neville, H. J. (1999). Functional neural subsystems are differentially affected by delays in second-language immersion: ERP and behavioral evidence in bilingual speakers. In D. Birdsong (ed.) *New Perspectives on the Critical Period for Second Language Acquisition*. Hillsdale, NJ: Erlbaum.

Weber-Fox, C., & Neville, H. J. (2001). Sensitive periods differentiate processing for open and closed class words: An ERP study in bilinguals. *Journal of Speech, Language, and Hearing Research*, 44, 1338–53.

Weekes, B. S. (1997). Differential effects of number of letters on word and nonword naming latency. *Quarterly Journal of Experimental Psychology Section A: Human Experimental Psychology*, 50(2), 439–56.

Wegner, D. M., Schneider, D. J., Carter, S. R., & White, T. L. (1987). Paradoxical effects of thought suppression. *Journal of Personality and Social Psychology*, 53(1), 5–13.

Weisbrod, M., Maier, S., Harig, S., Himmelsbach, U., & Spitzer, M. (1998). Lateralised semantic and indirect semantic priming effects in people with schizophrenia. *British Journal of Psychiatry*, 172, 142–6.

Weisleder, A., & Fernald, A. (2013). Talking to children matters: Early language experience strengthens processing and builds vocabulary. *Psychological Science*, 24(11), 2143–52.

Weisskopf, M. G., Kioumourtzoglou, M. A., & Roberts, A. L. (2015). Air pollution and autism spectrum disorders: Causal or confounded? *Current Environmental Health Reports*, 2(4), 430–9.

Wells, J. C. (2007). *English Intonation*. Cambridge: Cambridge University Press.

Wepman, J., & Jones, L. (1964). Five aphasias: A commentary on aphasia as a regressive linguistic phenomenon. *Research Publications of the Association for Research in Nervous and Mental Disease*, 42, 190–203.

Werker, J. F., & Tees, R. (1984). Cross-language speech perception: Evidence for perceptual reorganization during the first year of life. *Infant Behavior and Development*, 7, 49–63.

Werker, J. F., & Tees, R. C. (1999). Influences on infant speech processing: Toward a new synthesis. *Annual Review of Psychology*, 50, 509–35.

Werker, J. F., Polka, L., & Pegg, J. E. (1997). The conditioned head turn procedures as a method for assessing infant speech perception. *Early Development & Parenting*, 6(3/4), 171–8.

Wertenbaker, L. (1967). *The World of Picasso: 1881–1973*. New York: Time-Life Books.

Westergaard, G. C., & Hyatt, C. W. (1994). The responses of bonobos (Pan paniscus) to their mirror images: Evidence of self-recognition. *Human Evolution*, 9(4), 273–9.

Wetzel, P. J. (2004). *Keigo in Modern Japan: Polite Language from Meiji to the Present*. Honolulu, HI: University of Hawaii Press.

Whaley, C. P. (1978). Word-nonword classification time. *Journal of Verbal Learning and Verbal Behavior*, 17, 143–54.

Wheeldon, L. R., & Levelt, W. J. (1995). Monitoring the time course of phonological encoding. *Journal of Memory and Language*, 34, 311–34.

Wheeler, R., & Swords, R. (2006). *Code-switching: Teaching Standard English in Urban Classrooms*. Urbana, IL: National Council of Teachers of English.

White, B. V. (1984). *Stanley Cobb: A Builder of the Modern Neurosciences*. Charlottesville, VA: University Press of Virginia.

White, K. K., & Abrams, L. (2002). Does priming specific syllables during tip-of-the-tongue states facilitate word retrieval in older adults? *Psychology and Aging*, 17, 226–35.

White, L. (1982). *Grammatical Theory and Language Acquisition*. Dordrecht: Foris.

Whitehurst, G. J. (1997). Language processes in context: Language learning in children reared in poverty. In L. B. Adamson & M. A. Romski (eds) *Research on Communication and Language Disorders: Contribution to Theories of Language Development* (pp. 233–66). Baltimore: Brookes.

Whorf, B. L. (1956). *Language, Thought and Reality*. Cambridge, MA: MIT Press.

Wickens, A. P. (2015). *A History of the Brain: From Stone Age Surgery to Modern Neuroscience*. New York: Psychology Press.

Wickens, C. D. (2002). *Aviation Psychology*. Hove: Psychology Press.

Wickens, D. D. (1972). Characteristics of word encoding. In A. W. Melton & E. Martin (eds) *Coding Processes in Human Memory* (pp. 191–215). New York: John Wiley & Sons.

Wikipedia (2017). The Mosquito. Retrieved July 14, 2017 from https://en.wikipedia.org/wiki/The_Mosquito.

Wilbur, R. B. (2005). A reanalysis of reduplication in American Sign Language. In B. Hurch (ed.) *Studies on Reduplication* (pp. 595–623). Berlin: Mouton de Gruyter.

Wilbur, R. B., & Petersen, L. (1997). Backwards signing and ASL syllable structure. *Language and Speech*, 40, 63–90.

Wild, E. M., Teschler-Nicola, M., Kutschera, W., Steier, P., Trinkaus, E. et al. (2005). Direct dating of early Upper Palaeolithic human remains from Mladec. *Nature*, 435, 332–5.

Wiley, A., Rose, A., Burger, L., & Miller, P. (1998). Constructing autonomous selves through narrative practices: A comparative study of working-class and middle-class families. *Child Development*, 69, 833–47.

Wiley, E., Bialystok, E., & Hakuta, K. (2005). New approaches to using census data to test the critical period hypothesis for second language acquisition. *Psychological Science*, 16(1), 341–3.

Willems, R. M., van der Haegen, L., Fisher, S. E., & Francks, C. (2014) On the other hand: Including left-handers in cognitive neuroscience and neurogenetics. *Nature Reviews Neuroscience*, 15, 193–201.

Wilson, P. (2004). Visuospatial, kinesthetic, visuomotor integration, and visuoconstructional disorders: Implications for motor development. In D. Dewey & D. E. Tupper (eds) *Developmental Motor Disorders: A Neuropsychological Perspective* (pp. 291–312). New York: Guilford Press.

Wiltshire, C. E. (1998). Serial order in phonological encoding: An exploration of the "word onset effect" using laboratory-induced errors. *Cognition*, 68, 143–66.

Wimmer, H., & Perner, J. (1983). Beliefs about beliefs: Representation and constraining function of wrong beliefs in young children's understanding of deception. *Cognition*, 13(1), 103–28.

Winefield, R. (1987). *Never the Twain Shall Meet*. Washington, D.C.: Gallaudet University Press.

Winner, E., & Gardner, H. (1977). The comprehension of metaphor in brain-damaged patients. *Brain*, 100, 719–27.

Winxemer, J. (1981). A Lexical-expectation Model for Children's Comprehension of Wh-questions. Unpublished doctoral dissertation, CUNY Graduate Center, New York.

Witteman, J., van Ijzendoom, M. H., van de Veide, D., van Heuven, V. J., & Schiller, N. O. (2011). The nature of hemispheric specialization for linguistic and emotional prosodic perception: A meta-analysis of the lesion literature. *Neuropsychologia*, 49, 3722–38.

Wood, C. C. (1976). Discriminability, response bias, and phoneme categories in discrimination of voice onset time. *Journal of the Acoustic Society of America*, 60(6), 1381–9.

Wood, N., & Cowan, N. (1995). The cocktail party phenomenon revisited: How frequent are attention shifts to one's name in an irrelevant auditory channel? *Journal of Experimental Psychology*, 21(1), 255–60.

Woodhouse, L., Hickson, L., & Dodd, B. (2009). Review of visual speech perception by hearing and hearing-impaired people: clinical implications. *International Journal of Language and Communication Disorders*, 44(3), 253–70.

Wooten, J., Merkin, S., Hood, L., & Bloom, L. (1979). Wh-questions: Linguistic evidence to explain the sequence of acquisition. Paper presented at the biennial meeting of the Society for Research in Child Development.

World Health Organization (2017). Dementia fact sheet. Retrieved April 21, 2017 from www.who.int/mediacentre/factsheets/fs362/en/.

Wörmann, V., Holodynski, M., Kärtner, J., & Keller, H. (2012). A cross-cultural comparison of the development of the social smile: A longitudinal study of maternal and infant imitation in 6- and 12-week-old infants. *Infant Behavior & Development*, 35(3), 335–47.

Wörmann, V., Holodynski, M., Kärtner, J., & Keller, H. (2014). The emergence of social smiling: The interplay of maternal and infant imitation during the first three months in cross-cultural comparison. *Journal of Cross-Cultural Psychology*, 45(3), 339–61.

Wren, S., & Litke, B. (2006). *Reading Assessment Database for Grades pre k-3*. Austin, TX: SEDL.

Wright, M. T. (2012). *African Grey Parrots: A Complete Pet Owner's Manual*. New York: Barron's.

Wundt, W. ([1897] 1999). *Outlines of Psychology* (trans. C. H. Judd). Leipzig: Wilhelm Engelmann.

Wundt, W. (1912). *Apperception: An Introduction to Psychology*. New York: Macmillan.

Wurtzburg, S., & Campbell, L. (1995). North American Indian Sign Language: Evidence for its existence before European contact. *International Journal of American Linguistics*, 61(2), 153–67.

Xu, J., Gannon, P. J., Emmorey, K., Smith, J. F., & Braun, A. R. (2009). Symbolic gestures and spoken language are processed by a common neural system. *Proceeding of the National Academy of Science*, 106, 20664–9.

Yairi, E. (1993). Epidemiology and other considerations in treatment efficacy research with preschoolage children who stutter. *Journal of Fluency Disorders*, 18, 197–220.

Yale Center for Dyslexia & Creativity (n.d.). Whoopi Goldberg, Academy Award-winning actress. Retrieved September 16, 2016 from http://dyslexia.yale.edu/story/whoopi-goldberg/.

Yale Center for Dyslexia & Creativity (n.d.). Charles Schwab, founder of the Charles Schwab Corporation. Retrieved September 16, 2016 from http://dyslexia.yale.edu/story/charles-schwab.

Yan, S., & Nicoladis, E. (2009). Finding le mot juste: Differences between bilingual and monolingual children's lexical access in comprehension and production. *Bilingualism: Language and Cognition*, 12, 323–35.

Yan, M., Zhou, W., Shu, H., & Kliegl, R. (2012). Lexical and sublexical semantic preview benefits in Chinese reading. *Journal of Experimental Psychology: Learning, Memory, and Cognition*, 38(4), 1069–75.

Yeon, S. C. (2012). Acoustic communication in the domestic horse (equus caballus). *Journal of Veterinary Behavior: Clinical Applications and Research*, 7(3), 179–85.

Yip, J., & Martin, R. (2006). Sense of humor, emotional intelligence, and social competence. *Journal of Research in Personality*, 40(6), 1202–8.

Yip, M. (2002). *Tone*. Cambridge: Cambridge University Press.

Yin, R. (2014). *Case Study Research: Design and Methods* (5th edn). Thousand Oaks, CA: Sage.

Yiu, E. M., & Fok, A. Y. (1995). Lexical tone disruption in Cantonese aphasic speakers. *Clinical Linguistics and Phonetics*, 9(1), 79–92.

Yonan, C. A., & Sommers, M. S. (2000). The effects of talker familiarity on spoken word identification in younger and older listeners. *Psychology of Aging*, 15(1), 88–99.

Yu, V. Y., MacDonald, M. J., Oh, A., Hua, G. N., de Nil, L. F. et al. (2014). Age-related sex differences in language lateralization: A magnetoencephalography study in children. *Developmental Psychology*, 50(9), 2276–84.

Yuill, N., & Oakhill, J. (1991). *Children's Problems in Text Comprehension: An Experimental Investigation*. Cambridge: Cambridge University Press.

Zero to Three (2016). Learning to write and draw. Retrieved September 16, 2016 from www.zerotothree.org/resources/305-learning-to-write-and-draw.

Zhang, J., & McBride-Chang, C. (2014). Learning to read around the world. In A. J. Holliman (ed.) *The Routledge International Companion to Educational Psychology* (pp. 73–82). New York: Routledge/Taylor & Francis.

Zhang, N., Baker, H. W., Tufts, M., Raymond, R. E., Salihu, H. et al. (2013). Early childhood lead exposure and academic achievement: Evidence from Detroit public schools, 2008–2010. *American Journal of Public Health*, 113, e72–7.

Zhang, S. (2011). Speech-to-song illusion in MC: Acoustic parameter vs. perception. Poster presented at the biennial meeting of the Society for Music Perception and Cognition, Rochester, NY.

Zhang, S., & Perfetti, C. A. (1993). The tongue-twister effect in reading Chinese. *Journal of Experimental Psychology: Learning, Memory, and Cognition*, 19, 1082–93.

Zheng, M., & Goldin-Meadow, S. (2002). Thought before language: How deaf and hearing children express motion events across cultures. *Cognition*, 85, 145–75.

Zhou, B., & Krott, A. (2016). Data trimming procedure can eliminate bilingual cognitive advantage. *Psychonomic Bulletin & Review*, 23(4), 1221–30.

Ziegler, J. C., & Goswami, U. (2005). Reading acquisition, developmental dyslexia, and skilled reading across languages: A psycholinguistic grain size theory. *Psychological Bulletin*, 131(1), 3–29.

Ziegler, J. C., & Perry, C. (1998). No more problems in Coltheart's neighborhood: Resolving neighborhood conflicts in the lexical decision task. *Cognition*, 68(2), B53–62.

Zimbler, M., & Feldman, R. S. (2011). Liar, liar, hard drive on fire: How media context affects lying behavior. *Journal of Applied Social Psychology*, 41(10), 2492–507.

Zipes, J. (2002). *The Brothers Grimm: From Enchanted Forests to the Modern World* (2nd edn). New York: Routledge.

Zuckerman, M. (1984). Sensation seeking: A comparative approach to a human trait. *Behavioural and Brain Sciences*, 7, 413–71.

Zuckerman, M. (1985). Sensation seeking, mania, and monoamines. *Neuropsychobiology*, 13, 121–8.

Zürcher, E. J. (2004). *Turkey: A Modern History*. Oxford: I.B.Tauris.

Zwaan, R. A., & Radvansky, G. A. (1998), Situation models in language comprehension and memory. *Psychological Bulletin*, 123(2), 162–85.

Zwitserlood, P. (1989). The locus of effects of sentential-semantic context in spoken-word processing. *Cognition*, 32, 25–64.

SUBJECT INDEX

NAME INDEX

Engelborghs, S. 439, 477
Engle, R. W. 169, 471
Epstein, J.A. 438
Erard, M. 265, 283, 442
Ericsson, A. K. 184, 186, 442, 446
Ericsson, K. A. 438
Eriksen, C. 127, 129, 442
Eriksson, A. 486
Eriksson, P. S. 240, 485
Eriksson, K. I. 486
Ervin, R. A. 480
Escandell-Vidal, V. 453
Eskenazi, M. A. 309, 443
Estes, R. D. 39, 443
Estigarribia, B. 478
Estival, D. 5, 443
Estruch, S. B. 25, 380, 443
Evans, J. L. 380, 443
Everett, C. 274, 443
Everett, D.L. 26, 27, 146, 274, 443, 447, 485
Everling, S. 442
Eysenck, M. 420

Fadiga, L. 440, 449
Faed, J. M. 500
Fagard, J. 480
Fahle, M. 57, 443
Fairthorne, R. A. 178, 443
Falk, S. 83, 443
Fan, S. P. 272, 443
Farah, M. J. 485
Farmer, T. A. 156, 179, 443
Farris, C. 443
Fathman, A. 269, 443
Faurie, C. 330, 331, 443, 473
Faust, M. 292, 434, 444
Fay, D. A. 480
Fay, R. R. 60, 444
Fayol, M. 451, 465
Fecteau, S. 464
Federmeier, K. D. 334, 444
Fedorenko, E. 168, 180, 181, 444, 447
Feldman, H. M. 468, 471
Feldman, L. B. 133, 444
Feldman, R. S. 47, 48, 444, 516
Feng, G. 476
Fennig, C. D. 7, 28, 472, 501
Fenson, J. 430
Fenson, L. 211, 421, 430, 444
Ferderer, L. 437
Ferguson, C. 262, 444, 485
Fernald, A. 223, 224, 444, 461, 512
Fernandez, E. C. 466
Fernández, S. 271, 272, 489
Fernyhough, C. 103, 417, 438
Ferrari, P. F. 73, 446
Ferraro, V. 445
Ferreira, F. 148, 149, 151, 153, 155, 156,
    157, 160, 161, 309, 432, 433, 444,
    445, 458, 488
Ferreira, V. S. 106, 110, 115, 180, 256, 291,
    445, 453, 491
Fey, M. E. 441
Fiebach, C. J. 448
Fielding-Barnsley, R. 476
Fifer, W. P. 213, 437, 482
Filik, R. 103, 445
Filipovic´, L. 445, 275
Fillmore, C. J. 135, 159, 194, 231, 445
Finger, S. 319, 445

Fischer, A. L. 434
Fischer, C. E. 499, 501
Fischer, L. B. 48, 445
Fischer, S. 347, 445
Fisher, J. 359, 445
Fisher, J. M. 473
Fisher, S. E. 25, 379, 380, 443, 445, 447,
    493, 514
Fishman, J. 25, 262, 445
Fitch, W. T. 44, 51, 445, 457
Fitsiori, A. 318, 445
Fivaz, D. 35, 445
Fizet, J. 480
Flanagan, J. L. 58, 446
Flege, J. 269, 446
Fletcher, L. B. 477
Fletcher, P. 290, 380, 446, 501
Flett, S. 453
Flinker, A. 316, 446
Flor, H. 339, 446
Flores-Pajot, M. C. 382, 446
Flower, L. 114, 457, 458
Fodor, J. A. 22, 108, 112, 447
Fodor, J. D. 145, 447
Fogassi, L. 73, 440, 446, 449
Fok, A. Y. 335, 515
Folk, J. R. 309, 443
Foltz, P. W. 182, 446, 470
Foorman, B. 311, 493
Foote, W. E. 131, 457
Forbes, K. E. 385, 446
Foroays, D. G. 326, 481
Foroughi, C. K. 186, 438, 446
Forrest, J. A. 444
Forster, K. I. 116, 129, 139, 140, 141, 446,
    447
Foster, R. 463
Foundas, A. L. 468
Fouts, D. H. 447
Fouts, R. S. 32, 33, 447
Fowler, A. 314, 380, 382, 440
Fowler, C. A. 85, 449, 462
Fowler, L. N. 314
Fox Tree, J. E. 88, 95, 432, 447
Fox, E. 382, 447
Fox, M. 350, 447
Fozard J. L. 482
Franaszczuk, P. J. 446
Francis, W. N. 123, 447
Francis, W. S. 276, 277, 447
Francks, C. 514
Frank, M. 27, 447
Frank, R. 437
Franks, J. J. 427
Fratiglioni, L. 501
Frauenfelder, U. 456
Fraysse, B. 496
Frazier, L. 22, 145, 147, 148, 149, 150, 153,
    157, 419, 433, 439, 447, 450, 454
Fredrickson, B. L. 455
Freedle, R. O. 432, 503
Freedman, M. 104, 423, 435, 478
Freud, S. 89, 97, 100, 137, 448
Frewen, P. 234, 448
Frick, P. J. 391, 448
Frick-Horbury, D. 254, 448
Friederici, A. D. 332, 377, 448, 456, 469
Friedman, R. B. 452
Friel, B. M. 279, 448
Friesen, W. 223, 253, 442

Frijters, J. C. 299, 448
Frishberg, N. 348, 448
Frith, U. 288, 289, 421, 448, 502
Frömer, R. 304, 448
Fromkin, V. A. 90, 91, 93, 94, 97, 108, 109,
    113, 115, 420, 485, 486, 448
Fruensgaard, K. 424
Frye, R. E. 473
Fukuda, C. 238, 448
Fukuda, S. 280, 448
Fukuda, S. E. 448
Fukumine, E. 276, 277, 448
Furlonger, B. 365, 449
Furneax, S. 309, 449
Furstenberg, F. F. 421

Gabrieli, J. D. 439
Gadian, D. G. 509
Gaillard, W. D. 422
Galaburda, A. M. 301, 423, 437, 449, 451
Galambos, S. J. 273, 449
Galanter, E. 432
Galantucci, B. 73, 449
Gallaudet, E. M. 346, 351, 449
Gallese, V. 73, 440, 449
Gallup, G. G. 49, 449
Gandour, J. 92, 449
Gannon, P. J. 515
Ganong, W. F. 79, 82, 400, 449
García, A. M. 425
Garcia, M. 422, 459
García, Y. F. 419
Gardiner, A. H. 344, 449
Gardner, B. T. 32, 447, 449
Gardner, H. 336, 465, 514
Gardner, R. A. 32, 447, 449
Gardner, R. C. 270, 449
Gardner, R. I. 422
Gardner-Neblett, N. 228, 449
Garey, L. J. 321, 449
Garmon, L. 24, 25, 28, 450
Garnham, A. 188, 189, 190, 194, 196, 199,
    201, 255, 429, 435, 450, 462, 486
Garnsey, S. M. 155, 450
Garrard, P. 387, 450
Garrett, K. 423
Garrett, M. 146, 446
Garrett, M. F. 91, 109, 110, 112, 113, 436,
    446, 450, 510
Garrity, L. I. 166, 450
Garrod, S. 180, 189, 190, 200, 427, 450, 497
Gaskin, W. 193, 450
Gasser. T. 377, 450
Gathercole, S. E. 380, 419
Gauna, K. 490
Gaustad, M.G. 361, 468
Gazzaniga, M. S. 319, 326, 341, 451, 493
Gazzola, M. 266, 451
Geers, A. E. 353, 451
Geissmann, T. 508
Gelman, R. 453
Gelman, S. A. 505
Genesee, F. 271, 272, 451, 488
Gentner, D. 276, 461
Gernsbacher, M. A. 110, 111, 193, 196, 198,
    199, 200, 363, 425, 450, 451, 488
Geschwind, N. 316, 331, 449, 451
Geuze, R. H. 464, 474
Geyer, S. 321, 451
Giavazzi, M. 497

Pineda, D. 425
Pineda, J. 424, 430
Pinker, S. 23, 26, 205, 223, 233, 235, 241, 350, 491
Pirozzolo, F. 463
Piske, T. 446
Piskosz, M. 507
Pisoni, D. B. 59, 86, 452, 474, 491, 504
Pléh, C. 506
Plomin, R. 511
Plotnik, J. M. 50, 491
Pohl, M. E. 7, 118, 491
Poline, J.-B. 488
Polka, L. 504, 513
Polkey, C. 473
Poll, N. 497
Pollack, M. 442
Pollatsek, A. 122, 129, 132, 134, 142, 305, 308, 309, 310, 420, 461, 472, 491, 493, 494, 508
Pope, K. O. 491
Poplack, S. 281, 282, 492
Popper, A. N. 60, 444
Post, I. 424
Postma, A. 486
Potter, B. 302, 492
Poulin-Dubois, D. A. 424
Powell, B. B. 7, 492
Powell, R. A. 12, 492
Powelson, J. A. 424
Powis, J. 450
Prakash, R. S. 442
Premack, A. J. 33, 492
Premack, D. 33, 46, 492
Presnell, L. 363, 492
Pressley, M. 183, 492
Price, I. K. 167, 492
Price, J. R. 380, 492
Price, T. R. 459
Priddle, T. H. 390, 492
Prieto, P. 453
Prindle, J. 468
Pring, T. 505
Prins, D. 96, 460, 492
Prior, H. 50, 492
Proctor, R. W. 470
Profita, J. 83, 492
Pronko, N. H. 6, 492
Prufer, K. 34, 492
Psarakos, S. 50, 478
Puhlik-Doris, P. 478
Pujol, J. 329, 493, 502
Puls, B. 472
Pun, J. K. 5, 492
Putnick, D. L. 438

Quarrington, B. 96, 493
Quer, J. 421
Quigley, S. 363, 493
Quillian, M. R. 111, 199, 434
Quine, W. V. 218, 493

Rabbitt, P. 480
Radvansky, G. A. 196, 516
Raffaele, P. 34, 493
Rafferty, E. A. 273, 493
Ragheb, J. 481
Rahn, C. L. 491
Rahn, R. 491, 494
Ramachandran, V. S. 338, 430, 493

Ramírez-Esparza, N. 480
Ramon-Casas, M. 272, 426
Ramsey, S. R. 262, 493
Ramus, F. 380, 492
Raphael, L. J. 503
Rasmussen, T. 326, 339, 340, 401, 410, 427, 511
Ratcliff, R. 191, 476
Rathcke, T. 83, 443
Ratiu, P. 320, 493
Rauscher, F. H. 255, 493
Ravin, Y. 445
Ravina, B. 498
Raymond, M. 330, 331, 443, 473
Raymond, R. E. 516
Rayner, K. 78, 127, 128, 130, 133, 136, 139, 142, 147, 148, 149, 150, 153, 154, 166, 190, 200, 287, 292, 301, 303, 304, 305, 306, 308, 309, 310, 311, 419, 420, 425, 427, 433, 441, 447, 450, 461, 475, 491, 493, 494, 500, 501, 508
Raynor, R. 12, 512
Raza, M. H. 96, 494
Read, J. 481
Reardon, S. F. 298, 494
Records, N. 507
Records, N. L. 507
Reder, S. M. 304, 494
Rehm, H. L. 344, 494
Reich, P. A. 99, 438
Reicher, G. M. 129, 494
Reichle, E. D. 308, 309, 491, 494
Reid, A. K. 37, 219, 491
Reimann, K. 451
Reisberg, D. 463, 475
Reiss, D. 50, 491, 494
Relkin, N. R. 467
Remez, R. E. 81, 86, 488
Repka, R. J. 101, 103, 191, 438
Requin, J. 429
Rescorla, L. 272, 488, 494
Resnick, L. B. 432
Ressler, W. H. 80, 497
Reyes-Alami, C. 97, 494
Reynolds, D. R. 495
Reznick, J. S. 444
Reznick, S. 444
Rheingold, H. L. 214, 472
Rialland, A. 36, 494
Ricciardelli, L. A. 273, 494
Rice, M. L. 379, 494
Richards, D. G. 459
Richards, I. 476
Richards, J. C. 265, 494, 495
Richards, T. L. 477
Richels, C. 505
Richgels, D. 294, 495
Richter, E. M. 442
Rickards, F. W. 449
Ridley, M. 18, 23, 495
Riley, J. R. 41, 495
Ring, M. 382, 495
Ripich, D. 386, 495
Rischel, J. 217, 495
Risley, T. R. 224, 457
Ritti, A. 246, 495
Rivero, F. 430
Rizzi, G. L. 422
Rizzi, L. 456

Rizzolatti, G. 440, 449
Roach, P. 15, 495
Robbins, T. W. 460
Roberson, D. 275, 495
Roberti, J. W. 236, 495
Roberts, A. L. 512
Roberts, J. 478
Roberts, J. E. 492
Roberts, L. 321, 326, 489
Robe-Torres, K. 443
Robinson, S. 15, 495
Rockwell, P. A. 234, 495
Rodgers, T. S. 265, 494, 495
Rodier, P. M. 419
Rodman, R. 448
Rodrigues, C. 485
Roelofs, A. 104, 495
Roelstraete, B. 457
Roeper, T. 439
Rogalsky, C. 316, 495
Rogers, J. D. 273, 419
Rogers, T. T. 463, 470
Rogers-Ramachandran, D. C. 493
Rohwer, W. D. 19, 463
Rollins, P. 26, 495
Romani, C. 165, 495
Rommers, J. 460
Romski, M. A. 513
Rose, A. 514
Rose, M. 474
Rosemann, S. 308, 495
Rosen, C. A. 510
Rosen, G. D. 449
Rosengren, 422
Ross, D. S. 331, 496
Ross, J. 273, 496
Rosselló, J. 389, 459
Rosser, A. E. 460
Rossu, R. 506
Rothman, J. 269, 496
Rouger, J. 74, 496
Rovee-Collier, C. 497
Rowe, M. L. 224, 257, 496
Rowley, K. 479
Rubin, D. C. 282, 496
Rubin, J. 54
Ruddy, M. G. 480
Ruiz de Mendoza, F. 487
Rumbaugh, D. M. 454, 459, 497
Rumelhart, D. E. 114, 140, 155, 194, 475, 496
Rüschemeyer, S.-A. 488
Ruse, M. 475
Rushworth, M. F. 439
Russell, J. A. 253, 484
Russo, A. 274, 474
Rutter, M. 380, 496
Ryalls, J. 386, 496
Rymer, R. 269, 496

Saariluoma, P. 186, 487
Sabbah, N. 339, 496
Sachdev, S. 463
Sachs, J. S. 160, 496
Sadler, R. C. 456
Saeed, J. 158, 346, 356, 359, 471, 496
Sáfár, A. 330, 488
Saffran, E. M. 499
Saffran, J. R. 21, 206, 443, 496, 506
Sahakian, B. J. 460